HUDSON TAYLOR

&

CHINA'S OPEN CENTURY

Book Three: If I Had a Thousand Lives

HUDSON TAYLOR

&

CHINA'S OPEN CENTURY

BOOK THREE

If I Had a Thousand Lives

A J Broomhall

HODDER AND STOUGHTON
and
THE OVERSEAS MISSIONARY FELLOWSHIP

Chinese calligraphy by Michael Wang. Cover design by Melvyn Gill based on the insignia of a Qing (Ch'ing) dynasty viceroy or provincial governor (courtesy of the Victoria and Albert Museum, Crown copyright).

Subsequent volumes in this series will be in large format paperback. The publishers intend to reissue the first volume in this format, subject to demand.

British Library Cataloguing in Publication Data

Broomhall, A. J.
Hudson Taylor & China's open century.
Bk. 3: If I had a thousand lives
1. Taylor, Hudson 2. Missionaries—China—Biography
I. Title
266'.0092'4 BV3427.T3

ISBN 0 340 32392 2

 Printed in Great Britain for Hodder and Stoughton Limited, Mill Road, Dunton Green, Sevenoaks, Kent by Richard Clay (The Chaucer Press) Ltd, Bungay, Suffolk. Photoset by Rowland Phototypesetting Ltd, Bury St Edmunds, Suffolk.

Hodder and Stoughton Editorial Office: 47 Bedford Square, London WC1B 3DP.

Foreword to the Series

China appears to be re-opening its doors to the Western world. The future of Christianity in that vast country is known only to God. It is, however, important that we in the West should be alert to the present situation, and be enabled to see it in the perspective of the long history of missionary enterprise there. It is one of the merits of these six remarkable volumes that they provide us with just such a perspective.

These books are much more than just the story of the life and work of Hudson Taylor told in great detail. If they were that alone they would be a worthwhile enterprise, for, as the *Preface* reminds us, he has been called by no less a Church historian than Professor K S Latourette 'one of the greatest missionaries of all time'. He was a man of total devotion to Christ and to the missionary cause, a man of ecumenical spirit, a man of originality in initiating new attitudes to mission, a doctor, a translator, an evangelist, an heroic figure of the Church.

The historian – whether his interests be primarily military, missionary, or social – will find much to interest him here. The heinous opium traffic which led to two wars with China is described. The relationship of 'the man in the field' to the society which sent him is set before us in all its complexity and (often) painfulness. And the story of Biblical translation and dissemination will be full of interest to those experts who work under the banner of the United Bible Societies and to that great fellowship of men and women who support them across the length and breadth of the world.

Dr Broomhall is to be congratulated on writing a major work which, while being of interest *primarily* to students of mission, deserves a far wider readership. We owe our thanks to Messrs Hodder and Stoughton for their boldness in printing so large a series of volumes in days when all publishers have financial problems. I believe that author and publisher will be rewarded, for we have here a fascinating galaxy of men and women who faced the challenge of the evangelisation of China with daring and devotion, and none more so than the central figure of that galaxy, Hudson Taylor himself. The secret of his perseverance, of his achievement, and of his significance in missionary history is to be found in some words which he wrote to his favourite sister, Amelia:

'If I had a thousand pounds, China should have it. If I had a thousand lives, China should have them. No! not *China*, but *Christ*. Can we do too much for Him?'

Sissinghurst, Kent Donald Coggan

PREFACE

(See also the General Preface in Book One)

This book is the third in a series designed to bring to light from the unpublished papers of Hudson Taylor more material about the man and his times. Like the rest, it is written primarily for those who want the facts in full. It cannot stand alone, being the continuation of a narrative interrupted only for the convenience of handling.

In *Barbarians at the Gates* the unrelenting pressure of the West forced China to yield a foothold at five mainland ports to merchants, missionaries and their consuls. The history of that period and its missionary pioneers forms the essential background to the life and work of James Hudson Taylor. (A résumé forms Appendix 1 in Book Two.) A tapestry of secular events, Western trade and diplomacy, Catholic and Protestant missionary heroism and faults, and the part played by individuals, shows Hudson Taylor's indebtedness to others and the sources of his motivation.

In *Over the Treaty Wall* Hudson Taylor learned by painful experience how to live and work in the grim circumstances at Shanghai into which he plunged, alone, at the age of twenty-one. Effectively prevented by mandarins' accusations and consular summonses from carrying out his own and his Society's intention to break out of the treaty ports and live in the forbidden 'interior' of China, he went in the company of William Burns to Swatow (Shantou), only to find adamant resistance there as well. Hoping that a medical clinic would soften the prejudice, he had come back to Shanghai for drugs and equipment, and had gone aboard ship to return to Swatow, when he learned that Burns had been arrested. What should he do while he waited for Burns' release and for Swatow to become open again? Nǐngbo offered the best opportunities. Until the dust settled he could but rejoin his colleagues there – Dr William Parker and the ailing John Jones, tormented again and again by renal colic. Jones and Hudson Taylor reached Ningbo from Shanghai on October 20, 1856, three days before the bombardment of Canton by the British;[1] and the stage was set for the episodes of this third book.

If I Had a Thousand Lives picks up the threads and goes straight on, following the uniform pattern of the series – using archive material chronologically, in parallel with facts from secondary sources, to show Hudson Taylor in the perspective of history and of his notable contemporaries. As in the first book the monumental importance of the earliest missionaries was stressed, and in the second book the part played by the London Missionary Society (LMS) and Church Missionary Society (CMS) pioneers and by William Burns, so in this volume the importance of John and Mary Jones in shaping Hudson Taylor's future is newly emphasised.

AJB

ACKNOWLEDGMENTS

The encouragement and help received from my faithful advisers again deserve my sincerest thanks. That Bishop Stephen Neill, so deeply involved in his own massive undertakings, should once again have spared so much time and thought, puts me yet more in his debt – not least for intercepting another potential howler or two. To Jane Lenon, Drs H H Rowdon and F Roy Coad, and the Secretaries, archivists and librarians of the Baptist Missionary Society, the Bible Society, the Church Missionary Society, the Royal College of Surgeons and the London Hospital I am grateful for personal communications and for permission to quote at some length from official records. Efforts to trace relatives of the Rev F F Gough and Rt Rev W A Russell have been unsuccessful, so to any who may read this book I offer my sincerest apologies where they may be due. The consensus of advice has been that the story of Hudson Taylor's difficulties in Ningbo and London should be frankly related, as throwing valuable light on his and others' personalities. The approval of the Home Secretary of the CMS for this course is specially appreciated.

As in *Over the Treaty Wall*, the main source for this book has been the Hudson Taylor archives, but the notes (pp 472–488) detail others. In particular I acknowledge with thanks quotations from S C Neill's *A History of Christian Missions*, and my indebtedness again to the First New Haven National Bank, Yale University Divinity School and the Macmillan Company, New York, for material from *A History of Christian Missions in China* by K S Latourette; to Harper & Row, Publishers, Inc, *A History of the Expansion of Christianity* Vol 6 by K S Latourette; to Collins Publishers, *William Booth: The General Next to God* by Richard Collier; to Harvard University Press, *Trade and Diplomacy on the China Coast* by J K Fairbank; to Dr George Woodcock, *The British in the Far East* (Weidenfeld & Nicolson); to Constable & Company Limited, *The Last Great Empress of China* by Charlotte Haldane; and to Dr J Edwin Orr, *The Second Evangelical Awakening in Britain* (Marshall, Morgan & Scott). Hosea Ballou Morse's *The International Relations of the Chinese Empire* is again an indispensable source.

For the light relief of the sketch on page 403 I am indebted to the Baptist Missionary Society

Last, but far from least, many thanks again to Jane Lenon, Leslie Lyall, Pauline McIldowie and Howard Peskett for their valued advice, to Val Connolly for the artwork, to Mollie Robertson and my wife for endless typing, and to many critics and periodicals for generous reviews.

AJB

KEY TO ABBREVIATIONS

ABMU	= American Baptist Missionary Union
American Board (ABCFM)	= American Board of Commissioners for Foreign Missions
Bible Societies	= American Bible Society, B & FBS, National Bible Society of Scotland
Bible Society (B & FBS)	= British and Foreign Bible Society
BMS	= Baptist Missionary Society
Bridge Street	= Wugyiaodeo premises of CES in Ningbo
CES	= Chinese Evangelization Society
CIM	= China Inland Mission
CMS	= Church Missionary Society
EIC	= East India Company
E-VA	= Ever-Victorious Army
FES	= Foreign Evangelist Society
Gleaner, The	= *The Chinese Missionary Gleaner* of the CES
HTCOC	= Hudson Taylor & China's Open Century
JHT	= James Hudson Taylor
LMS	= London Missionary Society
MRCS	= Member of the Royal College of Surgeons
OMFA	= Overseas Missionary Fellowship Archives
P & O	= Peninsular and Oriental Steam Navigation Company
Paris Mission	= Société des Missions Étrangères de Paris
RBMU	= Regions Beyond Missionary Union
RCS	= Royal College of Surgeons
RTS	= Religious Tract Society
SPCK	= Society for Promoting Christian Knowledge
SPG (USPG)	= Society for the Propagation of the Gospel
The Society	= Chinese Evangelization Society
UMFC	= United Methodist Free Church
WMMS	= Wesleyan Methodist Missionary Society
YMCA	= Young Men's Christian Association

BOOK THREE: IF I HAD A THOUSAND LIVES

CONTENTS

MAPS

ILLUSTRATIONS

PART 1

BITTERSWEET

1856–58

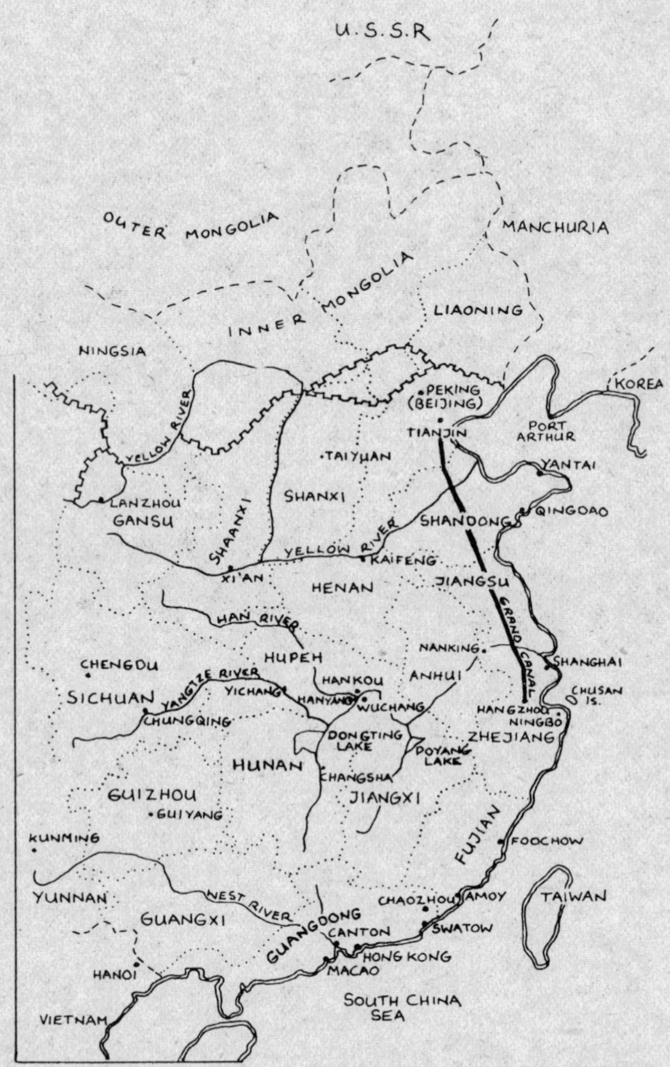

CHINA: MAIN CITIES

PROLOGUE

Castaway *October–November 1856*

The two men and a child who arrived at Ningbo on Sunday, October 20, 1856, created a stir in the foreign community. Hudson Taylor was not expected. He had left three weeks before to return to Swatow. John Jones[1] and his son Tom had gone with him as far as Shanghai, a sea and canal journey of some two hundred miles, 'for their health' and a little business, and should have been back in Ningbo ten days ago. They arrived ill and exhausted with a story of recurrent agonising attacks of renal colic and dysentery, of adventure and tragedy. Their Chinese companion, coming to join Dr Parker's hospital staff, had been drowned on the way, and only last night they themselves had narrowly escaped with their baggage from the wreckage of their boat.[2]

Mary Jones had been living with the Goughs[3] of the Church Missionary Society (CMS) while her husband was away, so they took John in and nursed him back to strength far short of health. Hudson Taylor crossed the river and surprised Dr and Mrs Parker[4] by turning up at the hospital in the old Chinese farmhouse among the ricefields when they thought he was far away in Swatow. By the evening everyone in the foreign community knew – and a few uncomprehending eyebrows were raised, that a Sunday had been spent, not wherever the travellers happened to be when the day dawned, but in travelling!

The next day, Parker took Hudson Taylor with him when he paid his weekly visit to Miss Aldersey at her boarding school in the Chinese city.[5] Over lunch with her and her assistants, the two Dyer girls, the whole story must have come out, but even so Mary Ann Aldersey was apparently not satisfied. Sabbath observance was a matter of strong principle.

The place of Burella and Maria Dyer, now twenty-one and nineteen, was unique in Ningbo as a focus of attention, for apart from the Cobbolds' schoolgirl daughter they were the only unmarried young women there. The kindly R H Cobbolds, the Goughs and Russells, were CMS missionaries.[6] The American Baptists were represented by Dr Macgowan, the E C Lords, the Knowltons and Josiah Goddard of Bangkok; and the Presbyterians by Dr McCar-

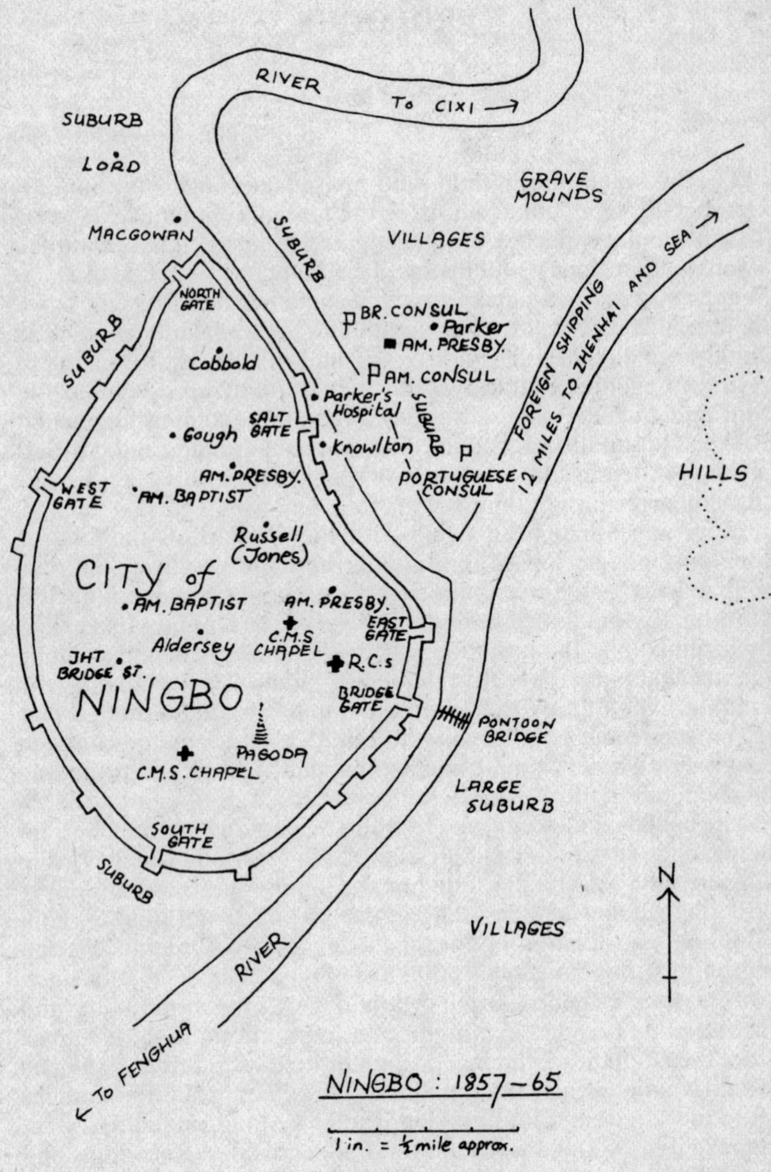

NINGBO: 1857–65

tee, the Ways, Rankins, Martin brothers and the Neviuses, John Quarterman, William Gamble and others. All the Presbyterians except the W A P Martins lived across the river near their boarding schools for Chinese scholars, and William Gamble's printing press, between the American and British consulates (map, p 22). The sameness of their otherwise restricted lives was varied by the presence of the consulate staffs, a few merchants and visiting ships' officers. Unmarried young men like John Quarterman and the British consulate interpreter Robert Hart, as well as Joseph Edkins, William Aitchison, the widowed John Burdon and others in Shanghai, could not but be interested in the Dyer girls.[7]

At the weekly 'concert of missionaries for prayer' all who could manage it met together, a friendly bunch of people among whom Hudson Taylor might have felt very much at home if he were not once again the jetsam of circumstances, thrown up on the Ningbo shore by tumultuous events in the south. The arrest of William Burns, his companion in Swatow, had barred the way to Hudson Taylor's return there, compelling him to wait until an all-clear came for him to set off again.[8]

Burns[9] had been travelling up-country with two Chinese colporteurs (Bible sellers) when they had been arrested and after long delays separated, the Chinese to be imprisoned wearing the cangue (*see* Book 2, p 369), and Burns to be conducted overland under escort to Canton and delivered to the British consul for reprimand and perhaps a fine. Only the news of the arrest had so far reached Shanghai and Ningbo, and it was to be some weeks before word came that Burns had been handed over to Harry Parkes, the consul, well and unharmed. He had reached Hong Kong intent on returning at once to Swatow to secure the release of his companions. But, just three days after Hudson Taylor and John Jones arrived in Ningbo, Admiral Sir Michael Seymour bombarded Canton and Viceroy Ye's palatial *yamen*,[10] and the British plenipotentiary in Hong Kong, Sir John Bowring, prohibited William Burns from leaving the island. Burns meanwhile was expecting to hear that Hudson Taylor, under no direct sanction, was back in Swatow, beyond the treaty bounds but tolerated by the mandarins. All news travelled slowly. Even news of the bombardment took two weeks to reach Ningbo and, when it came in mid-November, that alone was 'a sufficient reason' for Hudson Taylor not to return. But to be at a loose end, the odd man in a close-knit community, was unsettling.

The Goughs, the Joneses and Hudson Taylor, however, had a

great deal in common, in temperament, vocation and spirituality, and circumstances drew them together. While Hudson Taylor joined in Dr Parker's medical work, John Jones took to going with Frederick Gough from street to street, preaching in the open-fronted tea-shops, the Chinese equivalent of the English pub as a meeting place or clubhouse. Mary Gough took Mary Jones with her to visit Chinese women in their homes. And frequently Hudson Taylor joined one or other of the men, picking up more of the Ningbo dialect as he worked. By degrees John and Mary Jones were becoming more fluent too, and learning Chinese customs, the essentials for any rapport with the people.

Dr William Parker's 'shipping practice' with its contract for twelve hundred pounds or more a year, for being on call to merchant vessels, and the takings of his dispensary for Chinese, were making his dream come true. He had begun to lay the foundations of a new hospital on the riverbank site he had built up, walled and made secure outside the Salt Gate. After the hospital he planned to build a chapel and a home for his family on the same reclaimed site. But he also made time to supervise a little school in the city and to go out distributing tracts and Scripture with Hudson Taylor as they used to do in Shanghai.

As physician and surgeon to the community and its schools and congregations Parker was popular and indispensable. In the CMS *Intelligencer* W A Russell praised 'the very generous unsectarian spirit' of Parker's work, and appealed for five hundred pounds towards his hospital.[11] George Smith, the Bishop of Victoria, Hong Kong,[12] who was closely associated with Wilhelm Lobscheid and Gutzlaff's German and Swiss missionaries in Guangdong,[13] sent greetings to the 1857 Annual Meeting of the Chinese Evangelization Society (CES) paying tribute to 'the high character and efficiency of those of your missionaries with whom I have become acquainted'; and 'I hear the highest reports of your missionaries in the more northern ports' – of Shanghai and Ningbo.[14] Parker knew what he wanted to do and was doing it fast and effectively, in keeping with his personality. His reputation in the city and countryside brought him patients in their scores.

Hudson Taylor was impressed. He could see the value of Dr Parker's skill and friendliness in making the populace open and receptive to the evangelists, and wished he could start the medical work in Swatow he had been on his way to establish. 'I do most earnestly long to go back,' he wrote in long letters describing the harrowing experiences and disappointments of the past few weeks. He could not understand why he should be prevented. Apart from mere circumstances, he told himself, the spiritual lessons of such hindrances could only be that he needed to be 'disciplined', a depressing thought. Had the future been open to him he would have seen that the gates of his lifework were hinged upon this very setback. Not surprisingly, a reaction set in after all he had gone through, and he felt gloomy about where it was all leading. He had had his fill of killing time in Ningbo in the autumn, waiting for funds to buy drugs and equipment. Yet here he was again, rootless, and helpless to do anything about it. The one bright break in the clouds was that he found a hundred Tiejiu (Swatow) men in Ningbo,[15] pleased to have a foreigner preach to them in their own dialect. And by hobnobbing with some Fujian people he was picking up their dialect variations too.

Disregarding what the Parkers owed him for his help when they first reached Shanghai, he wrote, at two a m, to his parents, 'I am much in debt to Dr Parker (for his kindness)' and asked his father to send up-to-date drug and instrument price lists. For himself he included a shopping list of things to replace his own losses. And at eight a m he concluded, 'I am not certain what my course may be; perhaps I may be led to spend the winter here,' and enclosed the two letters from William Burns, dated July 18 and August 5, about the robbery before his arrest.[16]

CHAPTER ONE

LONG SHADOWS OF WAR
1856–57

All quiet? *November 1856*

The legacy of friendly relations between the people of Ningbo and the foreign residents, dating from the disciplined military occupation of the city in 1840–41 and Gutzlaff's administration of justice,[17] did not extend to the Cantonese or to every mandarin. Many mandarin officials were from distant provinces, ill-disposed towards foreigners in general and seeing little of them. Cantonese city merchants and Cantonese pirates operating within and from the Hangzhou estuary were hand in glove with each other, unloved by the local people but too rich and powerful to be resisted. So while the literati on the whole appreciated the good work of the hospital and mission schools, and the common people apart from the underworld were even cordial, the consuls always watched the mood of the city cautiously.

Foreign attitudes to Canton were prejudiced by years of experience and tales of 'factory' life in the ghetto there, ended only fifteen years ago, and little good was said or thought of the place or people. So when the first reports arrived about the boarding of the *lorcha Arrow*,[18] and then of the bombardment of the Canton forts and city, Hudson Taylor's comment was a conventional echo of current opinion.

> While it is sad that war should break out at all, . . . the number of executions of rebels daily performed in that City is such, that it would be a blessing if it was razed to the ground . . . [He saw] the goodness of God in removing dear Mr Burns *in time*, from Swatow; for if I may judge of the feelings of the Canton men there, by what I have seen today here, it would not go well with anyone in their hands just now.

When details of the October bombardment came to hand, however, it was a very different matter. Then he castigated the British for reputedly firing on 'thousands' of fleeing men, women and children in the crowded narrow streets.

A week later, John Jones in writing to the CES said that while war in the south (more rightly 'hostilities') hindered them from travelling in the country as planned, in Ningbo itself all was quiet. 'We go in and out among the people very freely.' But the prospects were not good.

> [Events] in the south may be expected . . . to close the door . . . it is a heavy trial just when we begin to feel at home among the people, to be threatened with a general war . . . I had hoped that Mr. Taylor would labour with us here but now this is by no means certain.

By then John Jones was out and about much more. When they rented a house from the American Presbyterians, 'in the heart of the city' near the East Gate and moved in on November 17, Hudson Taylor joined them for a few days. It was a big step for a couple with so little command of the language, but when Mary Jones called on her Chinese neighbours they welcomed her, and returned her call. Their nearest missionary neighbours were the Russells some streets to their north and Miss Aldersey's home and school the same distance to the west.

On their second evening Miss Aldersey invited the three of them to dinner. Hudson Taylor had noticed that a few Chinese had brown hair not very unlike his own,[19] and had stopped dyeing his. It had grown to full length and was plaited as a *bianzi* (a Chinese queue). Invariably he wore Chinese clothes – to Miss Aldersey most eccentric and absurd. When he wrote to his sister Amelia, he wished she were there with them. She would be in good company. But on second thoughts he would have to keep her 'in the interior', for it was not safe in the city, 'there is such a marrying spirit abroad just now'! Two ships' captains had recently had their weddings there, and

> my friend Mr. Burdon has been down from Shanghai, and has succeeded in making it up with the eldest of the Miss Dyers . . . and the other, despite the slightest cast of the eye, a good looking girl, had been desired by another of the Shanghai missionaries, but getting laughed at by her, he was too bashful to persevere. I don't know whether Mr. Burdon's success may encourage him to try again or not . . . Everybody seems to be successful in these matters, including you, while I alone have to wait in doubt . . . But I am thinking that if there were no Elizabeth, bachelors have the best of it after all . . .

He was back to wishful thinking about Elizabeth Sissons and watching the mails for another letter, after twice having a clear No to his proposal of marriage. 'Tho' I began to realize I have got a decided refusal for the present, still a ray of hope lingers,' he said doggedly.

If he was to be tied down in Ningbo he could not for ever foist himself upon his colleagues so he followed William Burns' example and hired a houseboat as a temporary home. As John Jones wrote, at this stage Hudson Taylor had no intention of staying any longer than necessary. This was clear. When conditions in the south improved and Burns was free to return, he would rejoin him in Swatow. Meanwhile with a boat he could live as a Chinese, use the local Ningbo waterways and preach to his heart's content. When moored near the city he could help to initiate John Jones into street preaching. At other times Frederick Gough, John Nevius, John Quarterman and others would be glad to lend Jones a hand. Each of them was preaching at Parker's dispensary in Bridge Street, and Nevius as the Presbyterian pastor was baptising those who responded.

John and Helen Nevius had their own anxieties. They were faced with parting for two years or so. She had contracted tuberculosis and had been strongly advised to go back to the States. When in W A P Martin's hearing John Nevius proposed to go with her, she replied, 'John! Sooner will I remain and die here than have you leave your work.' She travelled with the McCartees by fast tea-clipper and was back after eighteen months. Such was the calibre of Hudson Taylor's friends.

Eight Korean fishermen blown far south by 'a mad wind' were being entertained in Ningbo at the emperor's expense until they could return home, so Hudson Taylor and John Jones took to visiting them also. With a Korean vocabulary acquired from Dr Medhurst and the ability of one Korean to write some Chinese, it was possible to communicate.

Independence, living on his own in a boat again, made Hudson Taylor 'feel quite at home'. Wishing he could 'pop in and see you', he told his mother ' . . . do not . . . [think] of me as the Ghost of my former self, for I am through the goodness of God as well . . . as ever I [was] . . .' All the missionaries and their children, in fact, were well now that the summer heat had passed and it had turned wintry. Even the Parkers' emaciated child had recovered. Log fires and charcoal stoves were in use, but Hudson Taylor was snug in his wadded Chinese gown and laughed at his friends. Judging by 'the united testimony of the fire burners and wearers of the truly barbarian costume of western Europe', they were feeling the cold. Not he. But either because the cold increased or it was not safe enough from attack by Cantonese to be out on the river, before Christmas he took over Parker's schoolroom at Bridge Street[20] and adapted its attic as a home. The school used the ground floor, so with the children memorising aloud he had the sound of their piping voices at full pitch for hours every day. Not that he minded; this was Shanghai happiness over again.[21] When the children left, the hall was used as a preaching chapel.

Enter the city from the riverside, he said descriptively to his friends in England, go through the great city gate under the ancient castellated battlements, cross the first canal inside the city by a rough but substantial stone bridge, pass an immense Confucian temple and go straight on down the stone-flagged main street for half a mile. If you see a man beating a large bronze bell with a faggot, go up and you will hear him inviting everyone in to hear the gospel. Cross a well-flagged courtyard into the large guest hall and there you will see us about to start.

The *Retrospect* recorded his memories of the place.

> I have a distinct remembrance of tracing my initials on the snow which during the night had collected upon my coverlet in the large barn-like upper room . . . The tiling of an unceiled Chinese house may keep off the rain – if it happens to be sound – but [snow] will beat up through crannies and crevices . . . But . . . there I thankfully settled down, finding ample scope for service – morning, noon and night.

Fortunately it was a mild winter. He whitewashed the wooden walls and papered over the cracks where he could, to make it less draughty and more home-like, but in his present situation nothing could be 'home'.

A month in the desert *December 1856–January 1857*

As the days passed, Hudson Taylor's isolation began to weigh on him, and with a recurrence of dysentery his despondency returned. But that was incidental. Gradually it was dawning on him that even to that cordial company of missionaries it mattered that he was neither an ordained minister nor qualified as a doctor. Ordained visitors were asked to preach at English and Chinese church services, but so far he, like Christian consuls and ships' captains, was not, although fluent and well able to take his turn with the rest. Even among the missionaries he was the odd man out. And although Miss Aldersey and the Russells said nothing to him, to them he was only an eccentric. He sensed their coolness towards him. But deeper than these superficial hurts, to be spurned by Elizabeth after three years' courtship was most painful. He began to wonder whether after all, while Swatow was closed and war was in the air, he should go home to England, qualify as a doctor, marry and come back with the doubtful but apparently necessary asset of professional status. Brooding over it did him no good, but he tossed it to and fro until at his most dejected he contemplated giving up altogether – so he confessed to his mother. Elizabeth's father had said he would withdraw his objection to their marriage if Hudson Taylor were living in England. For a brief time this was a temptation, but he recognised it and reacted quickly. 'This has brought great spiritual dearth over me and I find I must not think even for her of leaving my work.' God's call was to China. Had he heard, perhaps, what Helen Nevius said of her husband's intention to take her home? 'When I think and talk of going home,' Hudson told Amelia, 'I always get into a bad state of mind and do not find blessing connected with it but otherwise . . .'

Christmas came and all the English missionaries, fifteen including Hudson Taylor and Joseph Edkins from Shanghai, celebrated with a party at the Goughs'. For a time his troubles were forgotten.

> We had a famous dinner – beef and plum pudding – and in the afternoon the Misses Dyer enlivened us playing some duets on Mr Gough's piano-forte, a very superior one, so with the party and my mail I had quite a treat. You see you have not *all* the good things at home . . .

Since the theft of his concertina Hudson Taylor had been realising how much he had been missing music, always so necessary to him. On December 26 he told his mother,

> The military proceedings in the south have prevented my returning to Swatow and so here I remain for the present . . . Miss Cobbold is going to lend me her concertina!!! . . . The American missionaries here all have harmoniums . . . very sweet instruments . . . I have had some thoughts of getting you to inquire for me, thro' Mr Faulding perhaps, if portable ones are made in England.

If one could be had for twelve or fifteen pounds would they please buy and send it to him.

But that was where cheerfulness ended. He had other worries, not least his Society's treatment of him. He went on to protest that the CES were disregarding his letters month after month – except once, 'as a complaint that I seemed to be thinking too much about money'. Since September 1855 he had received only twenty-five pounds from them. By living in Chinese style he could just make Mr Berger's donations meet his own and his work's expenses. And then, in an exposure of how far he had drifted from dependence on God to meet his needs,

> . . . is it right of me to allow my best years to pass over without some attempt to improve my position – which might leave me at any moment penniless on a foreign shore, without means to go home and without any trade or profession to turn to? . . . Neither a minister nor a doctor, to what Society can I look in case of my own failing me? If I were qualified, either the Church or the London [Mission] I am inclined to think would welcome me.[22]

In 'the desert of [his] loneliness' he was for once failing even to examine it all in a spiritual light, and had resorted to conventional thinking.

That same day, December 26, Maria Dyer went visiting Chinese homes with Mary Jones and 'took tea' with her on their return. Afterwards, to her secret pleasure, Hudson Taylor escorted her home, but his thoughts and 'lingering hope' were still far away. A few days later, indeed, another letter came from Elizabeth. As before she was trying to say No to China and to him as kindly as she could, but still he saw hope where there was none. Money, marriage, medicine, Swatow, Canton and his own spiritual state churned round and round in his mind when he was alone or writing to his faithful confidantes, Amelia and his mother. Another fifty pounds arrived from William Berger and he recognised it as coming from the Lord.

> He knows what is best for me; He will provide – but still there is not that certainty . . . I should like if I could choose. But I cannot so must try to be content and thankful that I am provided for and not left in want.

That was it. His confidence in God was more backward-than forward-looking, more 'He can, He does' than 'He will'. Tomorrow was still an anxiety. To his mother he went further on January 12,

1857, in a historic statement of John and Mary Jones' part in his odyssey of faith.[23]

> Last month Mr Bird sent me £25 instead of £70, 'hoping next mail to do more,' – but next mail nil. True Mr Berger has sent me £50 from Marseilles and the Tottenham people have sent me £5, so that the Lord provides for me . . . but this is not the way to have the mind at rest, or a position to get married in. . . . Then the political state of the whole world is extraordinary, and so is our relation to China. A few months *may* see China opened. A few days – nay hours . . . may see it closed entirely for the present. In the midst of this maze I sometimes think I must come home and try to get a degree and a wife – then I find my mind gets into a bad spiritual state . . . The Parkers think the best thing I can do is to go home and qualify. The Jones think of China and wonder I can think of leaving the field – and Mrs Jones thinks she knows what would make me settled, and recommends me to try and get married, promising me her influence in my favour with Miss Aldersey's assistant Miss M. Dyer, who is in the field, speaks Chinese best but one in Ningpo, etc – but who has a cast of her eye . . . and of whom I know nothing really but that she is an orphan – dedicated to mission work by her Father on his death bed, and very earnest and zealous I am told. This is all very well, I say but suppose there were no other objections . . . and all else were satisfactory – I am not in a position to marry and am not supplied with funds enough to keep me *alone* in European style. To this they reply that I am supplied by the Lord with what I now need and that if my need was greater my supplies would be so too . . .[24] When I think on these things I know not what to do – then I cast all my care on the Lord and feel my burden lightened. Then I take it again . . . with the same [result] . . . and am obliged to seek the same aid. Till I can no more wonder at the Israelites but only at the goodness of God in not getting tired of me and casting me off altogether . . . I think those who against their own voluntary promise and agreement have forced me into this position are much to blame – and so am I for allowing these outward things to disturb my peace of mind and lessen my usefulness. I have once more cast myself on the Lord with that helpless feeling one has in the water . . . He will make all right yet, I know – may He make *me* right for Jesus' sake . . . The present state of China is . . . very critical. Soon we may be obliged to move for safety, in event of general war . . . Yesterday I spoke in the Episcopal . . . church, in the absence of Mr. Cobbold . . . [an exception, for attitudes had not changed]. Pray burn this nonsense as soon as possible . . . I am trying to do a little, but do not get much done from one thing to another – chiefly hindrances which more zeal and settledness of mind would overcome, I am sorry to say.

At this crisis of discouragement a letter came from Miss Stacey, the Quaker lady of Tottenham, written after news of his expulsion from Chongming reached her. She made the observation that it was the experience of missionaries in every land that success and encouragement are followed by Satan's attacks, health breaks down or,

> some other obstacle arises to try the faith. I cannot understand why the subtle foe should be allowed to put forth so much power . . . [But remain] peaceful in the certainty that Jesus . . . cannot be defeated . . whatever trials be permitted to befall you, cleave to Jesus, and you will be made more than conqueror.

All too soon Hudson Taylor and John Jones were to find themselves faced by another serious turn of events. The Chinese Evangelization Society's being in debt came to their notice. The shock of learning this stung Hudson Taylor into a new understanding of what he had already believed in his days at Hull, though its implications were too far-reaching for his full comprehension. Words written in retrospect when everything was clear, expressed the crystallisation of his new thinking; in the event he was to take some time to come, with John and Mary Jones' help, to this calm conviction:

> To me it seemed that the teaching of God's Word was unmistakably clear: 'Owe no man anything.' To borrow money implied, to my mind, a contradiction of Scripture, – a confession that God had withheld some good thing, and a determination to get for ourselves what He had not given . . . I could not think that God was . . . short of resources, or unwilling to supply any want of whatever work was really His. It seemed to me that if there were any lack of funds . . . then to that degree, in that development, or at that time, it could not be the work of God.[25]

In all this turmoil John and Mary Jones stood by him faithfully, feeling for him and buttressing his faith with insight and understanding. How much Hudson Taylor confided in them is not recorded, nor how much Mary knew of Maria Dyer's hopes, but he patently needed a wife and they thought she suited him. To his prayer of 'many months' about this need, at last he added Mary Jones' suggestion, Maria, asking God to guide him. It was his first open admission that Elizabeth might all along have been his wilful choice and her love a fantasy, while God had been preparing someone else for him. Soon he became contritely certain of this. Blind obedience was so difficult. If only clear light could fall on his path.

Uncertainty about the political situation and William Burns' intentions added to his perplexity. He could not wait indefinitely. His Swatow 'excursion' had been experimental from the first. South China with its dialects was a separate field from the north and, like Chongming, had been closed against him. Burns was his dear friend, but his colleagues of his own Society were in Ningbo, and the pillar of cloud was standing still. On Christmas Day John Jones had written, 'Mr. Taylor has judged it well for the present to settle among us.'

And in the new year, 1857, Hudson Taylor decided more positively to stay at Ningbo. He wrote to tell William Burns. His letter apparently crossed one from Burns (back in Swatow) dated November 28, 1856, saying that orders had come from Canton for the release of the two Chinese Christians. The landlord's family were moving out and he would have the whole premises to himself and the colporteurs. 'Our position here does not seem to have been injured but I think rather improved by my being arrested and then so respectfully treated . . .' But he made no reference to the hostilities at Canton or to the prospects of all-out war. That came later.

Burns had found letters for Hudson Taylor waiting in Swatow, which he now enclosed, hoping they would not pass him on the way.

> You may think it safer to wait until you hear from me here and therefore I shall send them. May the Lord give you clearness of mind as to the path in which He would have you walk . . .

But Hudson Taylor's letter with his decision about Ningbo arrived soon afterwards and on January 23 Burns wrote again,

> Your not coming South was a great disappointment . . . You had not then received my letter . . . I only pray that the Lord may direct your path, and if He send you back to us here I shall rejoice, but if He keep you in the North and make you a blessing there I shall for this also seek to praise Him.

'Rich and poor, the rulers and the ruled' were well-disposed to him, Burns wrote to *The Gleaner*; the chief mandarin who had been healed was very friendly, and the commanding officer of the fort, happening to pass when Burns was preaching, stopped to listen, invited him round and discussed the Canton fighting and the gospel with him.

If Hudson Taylor had not already concluded that to stay at Ningbo was the right course for him, he might well have taken this news as the signal he had been waiting for. He might even have questioned his decision, had not Burns' letters arrived when Ningbo was on a knife edge, Hudson Taylor was needed, and Swatow could be assumed to be as unstable. To this we will return.

Meanwhile he had been drawn into as close a fellowship with John and Mary Jones as with William Burns – or closer, for all through the time with Burns, on the eventful Shanghai boat trips, in the immobile period at Swatow and even when country visits became possible, Burns had preferred to live separately, and often to work alone. Burns was a lone wolf by nature, till the end of his missionary career, and Hudson Taylor's greatest suffering at Swatow had been his own loneliness. At no time did he state this, but that it had counted with him in facing the future must be surmised. The missing piece in the jigsaw of this period could be his avoidance of this topic.

In contrast John and Mary Jones were 'like a brother and sister', and needed him too. William Burns had the two Chinese colporteurs working with him again and, always a pioneer, when other missions came to Swatow, and Tianjin and Peking became accessible, he himself moved to the far north, in 1863.

To W A P Martin, the academic in the American Presbyterian compound in Ningbo city, this young fellow Hudson Taylor in his Chinese clothes seemed just 'a mystic absorbed in religious dreams, waiting to have his work revealed – not idle but aimless.'[26] Little did he know with what determination Hudson Taylor had been pressing 'inland' for three years while he himself, the future Sinologue with imperial honours, pored over his books and taught his students in cloistered orderliness.

Miss Aldersey and the Dyer girls *1843–56*

To the perceptive, pungent American, W A P Martin, Mary Ann Aldersey was

> the most remarkable figure in the foreign community . . . Born with beauty and fortune, she escaped matrimony, not for want of temptation . . . [and] remained at home nursing her aged father until he no longer required her care.[27]

So she was no longer young when she took up Chinese again in Java (having studied under Robert Morrison in 1826) let alone in 1844 when she came to Ningbo. She acquired enough to be able to read and 'to speak it in a way to be understood by her pupils if not by strangers'. Self-disciplined and requiring the highest standards from everyone, she ran her girls' school as a model institution, Martin wrote in 1896,

> and I cherish a vivid impression of the energy displayed by that excellent woman [in spite of poor health] . . . The impression she made on the Chinese, whether Christian or pagan, was profound. The latter firmly believed that, as England was ruled by a woman, so Miss Aldersey had been delegated to be the ruler of the foreign community. The British consul, they said, always obeyed her commands. Several shocks of earthquake having alarmed the people, they imputed the disturbance to Miss Aldersey's magic power, alleging that they had seen her mount the city wall before the dawn of day and open a bottle in which she kept confined certain strong spirits, which proceeded to shake the pillars of the earth. No wonder they thought so. The wonder is that they did not burn or stone her for a witch . . . The year round she was accustomed to walk on the wall at five in the morning, and with such undeviating punctuality that in winter time she was preceded by a servant carrying a lantern. A bottle which she carried in her hand really contained 'strong spirits', the spirits of hartshorn, which she constantly used . . . as an antidote for ill odors.
>
> In the summer . . . she would climb to the ninth story of a lofty pagoda and sit there . . . sniffing the wind that came from the sea . . . always accompanied by some of her pupils (by whom she was greatly loved), so that work was not for a moment suspended . . . In the long list of devoted women who have labored for China, I know of no nobler name than that of Mary Ann Aldersey.[28]

K S Latourette did not hesitate to use the word 'domineering' of this little dynamo, for by sheer force of personality she came to receive, and expect, the deference of all alike. Chinese misconceptions of her role were excusable. By her schoolgirls, nevertheless, she was respected and loved as a strict grandmother, not a tyrant. And between the two Dyer girls and herself existed an affectionate relationship after only three years together. Perhaps her friendship with their parents in Malaysia (as Malaya, Borneo and what is now Indonesia were then called), and acquaintance with them as children, were the explanation.

Back in November 1843, when news had come to Singapore of their father Samuel Dyer's untimely death 'of a burning fever', after the first missionary conference at Hong Kong, everyone had rallied to help their mother, Maria Tarn Dyer, in her bereavement.[29] John and Alexander Stronach had buried him beside Robert Morrison in Macao and wrote about his last hours, telling her that he had said, 'Oh how delightful the thought of being soon with Christ'. His own affectionate thoughts for her he had himself written a few days earlier. Miss Buckland, the Dyers' colleague, was like a sister to Mrs Dyer.[30] And their friends Sir William Norris, the Chief Justice in the Straits, and Lady Norris, with great kindness had taken their ten-year-old boy to be with their own son of the same age, for two or more years, and when he was thirteen took him home to England. Miss Buckland informed the grandfather John Dyer, Chief Clerk to the Admiralty, who in turn wrote a wonderful letter to his widowed daughter-in-law in which he described Miss Buckland's tribute to Samuel as 'one of the most interesting and affectionate letters I have ever read'. Though Samuel was his son, his letter referred to him only by name or as 'your husband', and expressed no grief, only rejoicing over the 'crown' he had won.

Very shortly afterwards her baby boy's *ayah* (nurse) dropped him on some stone steps and he died. Still the young widow was unshaken. She informed the LMS that she wished to stay and continue Samuel's work at her own expense. She had private means, so all that Samuel left was donated to the mission. The Norrises invited her and the girls to stay with them and ten-year-old Samuel on Strawberry Hill, Penang Island, and always kept her informed about him. Surrounded by such a strong, affectionate and godly example, Burella and Maria Jane could not be sad. When about two years later their mother had married the missionary J G Bausum and come to live at Penang, he had been a good step-father to them.

But in October 1846 their mother herself had died, and the following February, at the ages of twelve and ten, the girls had been sent home to their uncle, William Tarn, a director of the Religious Tract Society, and his wife, who became their guardians. On the Dyer side they had their father's four brothers and three sisters and their families. With their uncles: two naval officers, a doctor, a minister, and the eldest who succeeded his father as Chief Clerk to the Admiralty, and their brother Samuel near by, life was interesting and happy for them during their school years. Burella and Maria were inseparable, so when Burella finished her schooling and went to college to train as a teacher, Maria went with her. They found themselves at Tottenham, among the people who also became Hudson Taylor's good friends.

When Miss Aldersey's companion in Ningbo became engaged to W A Russell, Miss Aldersey, herself linked with Tottenham since attending Morrison's Chinese classes at Hackney, wrote inviting Burella to come and take Mary Ann Leisk's place. Burella was a convinced Christian, preparing to fulfil her parents' wish by becoming a missionary to the Chinese. To Maria religion was still a matter of external observance, devoid of a conscious relationship with Christ, but for the same reason she too intended one day to return to East Asia. Burella accepted the invitation on condition Maria might go too. In September 1852, therefore, as Hudson Taylor moved to London, they joined the Cobbolds on the *Harriet Humble* and set sail for China, at their own expense, without dependence upon Miss Aldersey except as friend and chaperone.

Maria's motive in going, apart from respect for her parents' wish, was philanthropic, 'to help forward the moral renovation of China'.

> But as she prepared to embark on this enterprise, she was led deeply to feel that she lacked one all-important qualification for this service [Hudson Taylor later recounted]. A devout member of the Church of England with a sincere desire to serve God, nevertheless she felt she was not saved . . . She was not prepared for death . . . for eternity. And desiring this preparation, she had sought for it, but was stopped [by] . . . the mistaken idea she had of repentance . . . as if *it* were the door, whereas Christ says, I am the door.

She did not know precisely how or when the change took place, when her beliefs ceased to be second-hand and became her own, but only that during or soon after the voyage she came to feel 'that if *God* had accepted Christ for us, *she* could not do less than do so too, thus finding . . . the peace of soul she had so long desired'.

On the voyage Mr Cobbold taught them Chinese. As children they had spoken some, and Malay too, so that when the *Harriet Humble* reached Java and they were entertained by the Malay governor of Pulo Buro they recalled enough to chat with two girls of their own age, already mothers, and could understand the remarks bystanders were making.

And so on January 12, 1853, four days before Maria's sixteenth birthday, they arrived at Shanghai and went on to Ningbo, to find that they could already make themselves understood and start teaching. 'From constant . . . living among the girls in the school, and study with a [language] teacher, her knowledge of the vernacular of Ningpo became both extensive and idiomatic' – to the extent that she could read to the older girls from an English book, translating into Chinese as she went. There were not more than twenty Chinese Christians in Ningbo at the time.

After their father's death his good friend and colleague Evan Davies had written a small book about him with many quotations familiar to Burella and Maria.[31] They knew what kind of man he had been and how he had written to their mother, 'I cannot but sing "Oh China when I think of thee [I] sigh to be so far away, so distant from the land I love".'

And from Hong Kong before he died,

> From our window we look upon the lofty summit of the Chinese Hills . . . The sight is almost overwhelming. In my happiest moments just two thoughts seem to concentrate [my] every feeling . . . One is, that the name of Jesus may be glorified in China; – and the other, that you, and each one of our dear children . . . may live only to assist in bringing this about . . . Cease to serve the cause of Jesus . . . I never can while I have a head and hands to work . . . For the evangelization of that benighted land, come sorrow, come joy, – come grief, come delight, all, *all* shall be welcome for the love . . . I bear to him who bled on the mount of Calvary . . . Sometimes I think of the work to be done, and could almost wish to live a century, but at others I think 'The time is short'.

It was. Two weeks later he was writing of the death of one after another in the epidemic that soon took his own life.

This was the mental picture of a model missionary which Maria carried with her, yearning for the love of the mother and father whose memory she adored, though they had been dead nearly ten years. While Hudson Taylor found his feet in Shanghai, receiving his baptism of war, fire and sickness, and began to travel in the country, Burella and Maria were teaching girls of their own age and older, and sharing in the life and pioneer activities of the Ningbo missionaries. When the Jones family arrived at Ningbo with the blind Chinese, 'Agnes Gutzlaff', the Dyer girls took her into their small world and in spite of her handicap she taught with them.[32] The slightest 'cast' in Maria's eye was easily overlooked, for she was vivacious, witty and intelligent, a very attractive nineteen-year-old with her fine, warm, light-brown hair and slim figure. Inevitably she had her suitors.[33]

Maria's diary *October 1856–January 1857*

Maria kept, spasmodically, a pocket engagement diary in which she jotted down in pencil, with extreme economy of words, some indication of what transpired from day to day.[34] So circumscribed was the existence of that little alien community that the entries read like excerpts from Rose Macaulay's *Orphan Island*. Peppered through the notes of who called, dined, took tea, escorted them home or preached on Sunday are the titters and flutters of excitement as decorous matchmaking progressed. On October 7, 1856, it was a Chinese wedding and feast, and the Neviuses, Russells and Mr Quarterman 'dined with us'. On October 8 the prayer meeting was at Mrs McCartee's; on October 14 Mrs Bausum arrived with her children; and so on. After their mother had died in 1846, and Burella and Maria left Penang, their good step-father Mr Bausum had married again,[35] but the death toll continued and he himself died a few years later. His widow continued his work until Miss Aldersey, approaching sixty, invited her to come and take charge of her school in Ningbo. So here she was, and on October 18, 1856, Maria accompanied Mrs Bausum 'to call round' at the various missions.

On October 21, the day after Hudson Taylor arrived in Ningbo, her entry was simply 'Dr and Mrs Parker and Mr Taylor came to dinner', and on November 23, 'Mrs. Jones . . . proposed to me to go out together to Chinese houses'. At last Mary Jones had enough of the dialect to make visiting worthwhile, with a fluent companion to help her. Before Helen Nevius went home Maria had been doing the same with her, and running an infant school with Mary Gough.

Day by day the comings and goings followed one another. Then on Friday, December 12, 'Mr Edkins arrived in Ningpo . . . [and] Mr Q [Quarterman] walked home with me.' December 15, 'Mr Edkins called.' But in vain; a proposal from poor Edkins reduced her to giggles for he was about forty and she was praying that Hudson Taylor would notice her. The missionaries made frequent visits to each other, as on December 18 when she wrote, 'Dined at Mrs Cobbold's. Spent the night!' In what could have been a deadly monotony of very similar days, this custom of days and nights at each other's homes freely crossed national and denominational lines.

She was with Mary Jones one day when Hudson Taylor dropped

in, fresh from papering and whitewashing his Bridge Street attic. Writing to Amelia sixteen months later Maria told how Mrs Jones

> jokingly said to him, 'You'll soon be ready for a visitor.' I looked as grave as I could, as if I had no interest at all in him or in the subject which our friend was hinting at; for at that time I studiously kept my feelings . . . concealed . . . He as gravely . . . replied, 'Yes, I hope I shall have a good many visitors.'

On Christmas Eve Maria noted 'B's [Burella's] wished-for letter has arrived' – from John Burdon. And on Christmas Day after a children's party and Christmas tree at the Martins, dinner followed with the Goughs, Cobbolds, Russells, Parkers, four wifeless men, Nevius, Edkins, Hudson Taylor and H Z Kloekers of the Netherlands Chinese Evangelization Society – and of course Burella and 'Miss A.'. The following day Maria went out with Mary Jones and 'took tea' with her, and 'Mr Taylor walked home with me'. Nothing in the diary or contemporary letters suggests that this was any more than the required courtesy. Hudson Taylor's way home to Bridge Street was past Miss Aldersey's home and school, and by Chinese custom they would have walked suitably far apart, with a serving woman in attendance. But they were coming to know each other.

Maria's friendship with Mary Jones was deepening, and although Maria had not known Mrs Bausum before, they too were drawn to each other. She was motherly, and wise. On January 6, 1857, the diary records, they 'Had a long conversation'. Maria seems to have told her about Joseph Edkins' proposal, for Mrs Bausum was forthright with her. Maria confided to her brother that 'Mrs B' said,

> A lady ought not to expose a gentleman to ridicule because he loved her and was not loved in return, or to despise him for thinking highly of her . . . that a refusal ought not to be given hastily and without prayer any more than a consent.

Edkins after all had given years of his life to the kind of dangerous pioneering best done by an unmarried man. He deserved the companionship he wanted. When Maria answered that she could not think of accepting him, Mrs Bausum

> asked me if my affections were pre-engaged. I . . . explained to her my feelings towards Mr. Taylor. She said she had not seen anything which would lead her to think that he was interested in me . . .

– not surprisingly, for at that point Hudson Taylor was still unconvinced that his hopes of Elizabeth were a mirage.

Also around this time Maria had a proposal from Robert Hart, the interpreter at the British consulate. Sir John Bowring had appointed him to Ningbo and he was doing well. When a British general advised Sir Frederick Bruce, Lord Elgin's brother, to keep his eye on Hart because 'some day he will do something', Bruce replied, 'Oh, I have already had my attention called to him by the Foreign Office'. Robert Hart was promoted to Canton in 1858 after the hostilities ended, and eventually became Sir Robert, the 'Great I G', Inspector-General of the Imperial Maritime Customs.[36]

Maria's twentieth birthday on January 16 came and went, and her pocket diary gave little indication of what was happening at Canton or outside her immediate circle. 'Heard bad news about proceedings in the South' it said on the 12th, but otherwise it was *Orphan Island* as before. January 16, 'Spent the night at Mrs Jones.' 17th, 'Miss A called for me at Mrs Jones. Took a walk with her. Called in at Mrs Knowltons. Received a letter . . .' – Robert Hart's? Sunday, January 18, 'A M Mr Kloekers preached P M Mr Russell read a sermon' – Yet this was the day they had learned of a Cantonese plot to massacre the whole foreign community. On succeeding days her entries continued as before.

The prayer meeting massacre plot[37] *January 1857*

When Commissioner Ye vowed vengeance for the desecration of his palace and the city of Canton, and put a price on every barbarian head, foreigners were in mortal danger wherever the news reached the notoriously aggressive Cantonese. On January 14 four hundred people in Hong Kong fell desperately ill and two died. A master-baker named A-lum, supplying half the foreign community with bread, mixed in it so much arsenic, six grains per ounce, that it was detected or many more would have died. Forty-nine under-bakers were arrested but A-lum escaped by steamer. Englishmen gave chase in another, captured him and his family, and so deprived him of the head money he would have claimed for each dead foreigner. Excusably, the wags put it about that it was alum in the bread! An attempt was made to rescue all the culprits from prison – and the plotters joined them inside. From then on, only Parsee bakers were allowed to supply the foreign settlement.[38] But on January 30 Wilhelm Lobscheid wrote to George Pearse, while on night watch at two a m,

> which all foreigners must keep for the security of their lives and property. The abandoning of Canton by the admiral seems to have

> given new courage to the Chinese, who start the most terrifying reports of what they are going to do with the foreigners . . . everyone is convinced of the danger of fire and poison.

Anxiety was felt in other ports, but not at Amoy or Swatow. Amoy was again a remarkable exception because of the missionaries' and British navy's intervention after the Triad occupation three years previously. The people had not forgotten how Captain Fishbourne, RN, and William Burns, 'the man of the book', 'the only person who was allowed to pass unmolested through the streets', had come to their rescue.[39] So the events at Canton were forgiven. In any case no love was lost between the Amoy people and the Cantonese. Carstairs Douglas reported to the LMS, 'The people are as friendly as ever . . . The British and American consuls consider that there is no danger here at all.' When a British warship came to deal with a pirate fleet on the Amoy coast this popularity was enhanced. Captain Fishbourne sympathised with China, blaming the opium traffic, the coolie traffic scandal and the drunkenness and immorality of foreign sailors for the anti-foreign feeling.

At Swatow the return of William Burns and release of the Chinese colporteurs had had the effect of changing the attitude of this city also towards him. From the beginning his use of the Cantonese dialect had disposed the Canton merchants in his favour. Now the chief magistrate became openly friendly. Apart from the merchants and Burns' friend Dr de la Porte far out at Double Island, there were no other foreigners to demonstrate against.

The Shanghai community was well-protected and nothing was attempted against them on this occasion. But at Ningbo a gangster breed of Cantonese engaged in piracy and smuggling had to be reckoned with. Hudson Taylor explained,

> There were then a considerable number of Cantonese junks engaged in convoying native craft up and down the coast. Report gave them the credit of protecting those who employed them and pillaging those who did not. Not a few Portuguese and a few British-owned *lorchas* were also engaged in this convoying business, to the great annoyance of the Cantonese, who desired a monopoly of it.

On Christmas Day John Jones had written to Charles Bird, the CES secretary,

> The disturbances in the South do not appear to affect the people here in any evil way towards us, although there are rumours among them that the Emperor has ordered us to be expelled . . . now that

> such an event seems somewhat probable, we begin to realize what it would be to leave . . .

And on January 12, in his letter to his mother about Mary Jones' suggestion that he should consider Maria, Hudson Taylor had said, 'The present state of China is . . . very critical. Soon we may be obliged to move for safety.'

Suddenly on Sunday, January 18, all was alarm and excitement. A Chinese Christian learned of the plot to kill every foreigner. The story was borne out by events and troop movements which the community had attributed to the general war situation. At the end of December or in early January the headman of the Cantonese *lorcha* fleet had proposed to the *daotai*, the Prefect of Ningbo and other cities, a scheme to exterminate the foreigners while safeguarding his reputation. He answered, 'If you can, kill them,' so preparations were begun. Among his officers, however, was one who had a friend working for a missionary. He warned this friend to leave and told him why. The friend elicited the fact that an attack was to be made one Sunday evening when most foreign residents met for worship at the Russells' house near the Salt Gate. It was known they would be unarmed. Any who were not present would be simultaneously attacked at their homes and killed. Enquiries convinced the missionaries that the report was true.

On Monday, January 19, Hudson Taylor wrote to George Pearse and to his family, because '. . . in the present times, I feel it is desirable to avail myself of [the opportunity], for we may truly say we know not what a day nor an hour may bring forth.' He dealt with some minor business matters and went on,

> our stay among this people may be soon brought to a close – as far as I can see another month or two at the outside will see matters very much altered, if not China without missionaries. Our position in Ningpo is very critical. The other ports are provided with a man of war – there is none here. There are secret reports among the people, and secret talkings going on, which are stopped when we or a native Christian is seen approaching. From several sources we have been told however that there is to be a simultaneous attack and massacre of all foreigners, about the Chinese new year's day – a week today – some say it is to be attempted at all the ports. Some think this is a private attack by Canton men – others that it is on the part of the Government. The military force of the Chinese is daily being enlarged, and reviews are frequent – the streets of the city are also being filled with gates which are closed at night. These things should,

> and I hope in some measure do, stir us up to more prayer and zeal, for our time of labour seems to be shortening fast – soon we may be called upon to suffer . . . Oh! for grace to serve Him wherever, whenever and however He may direct . . . in our present position it is impossible to conjecture what may transpire in a short time. From day to day we are cast on the Lord, who will 'guide us according to *His* counsel and afterwards receive us to glory'. The difficulty is . . . to know what is duty – to stay or to go. If we had anything tangible, if we knew there *would be* a rising and consequently that if our lives were spared, we should be unable to work, our path might be more clear, – as it is we can only wait on the Lord. We [the missionaries] meet again this afternoon for special prayer for ourselves and the native Christians.

To Amelia he said,

> We may have to leave at a moment's notice . . . Thank God we have His peace . . . in our hearts – and we *may* be called to suffer . . . perhaps even to seal our testimony with our blood.

A letter forwarded from Swatow had just brought him fifty pounds, 'which is very good just now, as I may have to pay for a passage from China to some other place any day.'

On this day Maria simply entered in her diary, 'Mr Kloekers and Mr Taylor called. P M P. [prayer] meeting at Mr Knowlton's. Mr Taylor, Mr Nevius and Mr Hudson [an independent English Baptist missionary] engaged in prayer. Came over with Mrs Way. Miss A dismissed her school.' The prayer was for protection; 'came over' meant across the river to the relative safety of the Presbyterian compound between the American and British consulates.

Hudson Taylor's account of the occasion was less laconic. 'Realising the gravity of the situation, they determined to meet together . . . to seek the protection of the Most High, and to hide under the shadow of His wings.'

Having reached sixty Miss Aldersey was wanting to retire and hoping that the CMS would take over her school. When they were unable to do so she arranged for the American Presbyterians to administer it with their own schools, and Mrs Bausum, Burella and Maria, all contributing their services gratuitously to the Presbyterians, were to continue as before. The Cantonese plot precipitated this transfer. Miss Aldersey sent her schoolgirls home and retired, but stayed in the city at the Russells'.

Dr Parker wrote ten days later that the danger was so great that the merchants put their goods on board ship at single anchor and prepared for flight. They and some missionaries had their houses guarded by armed men. More missionaries in the city began to pack and move their families and valuables to the comparative safety of the Presbyterian compound, and made preparations for retreat to Shanghai. On January 24 Miss Aldersey proposed that Burella and Maria go to Shanghai with them, but as Mrs Bausum and Miss Aldersey had elected to stay, the two girls chose to stay too. That night F F Gough was alone at his house in the city and the indomitable Miss Aldersey alone at the Russells' house, they having moved across the river. She would not retreat. She had a coffin and bearers ready, and at the first sign of trouble would be carried in it to safety!

Referring to the way the mission homes were scattered about Ningbo, Hudson Taylor wrote,

> It was thought . . . best to move the ladies and children in time, as at this season, if trouble came and escape were possible, it might cost some of them their lives from exposure to cold, etc.

And Dr Parker added, 'seven other missionaries, including myself and Mr. Jones were led to send our wives and families to Shanghai.'

Maria's diary recorded an evening of singing at Mr Nevius' house, and the preparations for moving. 'Spent the day in the city packing things,' it read on January 24. On Sunday the usual morning service was held but none in the evening, the proposed occasion for the attack, and on the following day two ships sailed for Shanghai. Now Maria's diary became almost verbose: 'Went down to the *Japan* to see the party that were going to Shanghai . . . P M Two parties left Ningpo.'

On the *Japan* were the W A P Martins, John and Mary Jones and their children, Mrs Parker and hers, Mrs Gough and hers, and Hudson Taylor. With the least developed work and fewest church claims binding them to Ningbo, Jones and Hudson Taylor as the most free of all the men had been asked to escort the women and children. Two more American families were on the second ship, the *Foam*. Maria, writing to her brother Samuel in England, said 'Mr Taylor went up to Shanghai, against his own inclinations, at the request of a friend to take care of his friend's wife and family.' That friend was F F Gough. 'Before he left,' she continued, 'I had some little reason perhaps, to think that he might be interested in me, but I thought I had better not be too sanguine . . .' After Mary Jones' prompting Hudson Taylor could not but be interested. But what sharpened that interest at this time of danger was that Maria was staying at Ningbo, and the fateful Chinese New Year was only a day or two away.

The following day Maria scribbled, 'Made a purchase of a dress.' *Orphan Island* was back to normal. 'Took tea to Mrs R's.' Not for nothing were the Dyer and Tarn family mottoes, '*Deus providebit*' (the Lord will provide) and 'More than conquerors'. By the 29th Miss Aldersey had had enough of coffins in the city and made arrangements to join the others across the river. Parker's house was silent. 'I am left alone,' he wrote, 'and must confess I do not enjoy my solitude, although I am still going on with my work as usual.'

The story had a few more pages to run. The mandarin responsible to the *daotai* for matters affecting foreigners became alarmed when he heard of the plot, and remonstrated with him for permitting the Cantonese to hatch it. It would only bring vengeance from the foreign powers and the destruction of the city. Hudson Taylor gave this account of the interview,

> The Taotai replied that he had foreseen this, but that it was so arranged as to clear him of all complicity in it. A party of Cantonese were to seize the Salt Gate and drive the guard from it, and hold it, while others entering proceeded to the residences of the various foreigners in the City . . . in due time tidings would reach the Taotai. He would at once proceed to collect troops and retake the Gate from the Cantonese, and then send relieving parties to the [foreigners'] houses, which would arrive after the massacre and pillage were over. Similarly abortive efforts would then be made to rescue the foreigners outside the City; and the Cantonese themselves would only escape because the Taotai had no force able to cope with them. But, added the Taotai, this is not all. Should the foreigners come in force to avenge their countrymen, I will urge them to exterminate the Cantonese, and thus not only turn their anger away from the City, but also rid us of a complication almost as annoying as the foreigners themselves. The remonstrating Mandarin . . . finally said that he had reason to believe that the foreigners were both aware of the plot and of the Taotai's complicity in it, and were fully prepared for the expected attack. The Taotai at once became alarmed and thereupon sent a messenger to the Cantonese . . . forbidding the attack . . .

Dr Parker gave another insight.

> This alarmed most of us, and the American Consul requested a private interview with the officer for foreign affairs, who confessed

> that . . . a number of Cantonese . . . requested permission to destroy the Portuguese against whom and the English he said they were very much exasperated, because of the large number of their [piratical] vessels they have destroyed. It was again reported that our houses were to be set on fire. It is remarkable that on the same day and probably at the same hour in which the Taotai withdrew his consent, we were met for special prayer.

That final statement Hudson Taylor also made in the *Retrospect*, with the addition that this fact was not known to the missionaries until some weeks later.

Miss Aldersey was a woman of sagacity and strong opinions. She suspected that Maria's rejection of her suitors had an explanation and that Hudson Taylor was involved. If so she disapproved. From what she had heard, some of his views were unorthodox. Maria must make a good marriage as Burella was doing with John Burdon. Miss Aldersey seems not to have known that her own circle of friends at Tottenham and Hackney not only approved of but loved Hudson Taylor. But as Hudson Taylor had been thinking about Mary Jones' advice he had begun to realise that she could be right. And the more he saw of Maria the more attracted he became. While at least one good friend was ahead of him in seeking her hand and his own rejection by Elizabeth would not leave his mind, his only course had been to suppress the new thoughts about Maria. So, far from encouraging the friendship, he had done his best to show no hint of how his thoughts were moving.

> And in this I thought I had succeeded and that none knew of it, but . . . it was not quite unperceived by [Miss Aldersey], though one to whom she mentioned it, thinking it was not so, she thought she must be mistaken.

So he was troubled, pulled this way and that as he prayed 'for Divine light and guidance'. He hardly dared to think at all, after two futile courtships, lest yet another painful failure follow. His problem was to know how to distinguish his own infatuations and true – if mistaken – love from direction by God to the right partner in life. His whole life story bears out the impression that he had an unusual capacity for loving, whether it be children or colleagues, including the women, especially if in distress. Since Amelia's engagement his affectionate correspondence with her had had to change its tone. She was no longer a substitute and he needed an outlet for his strong emotions. But he thought Maria was too good for him. And she had given him no hint of her feelings. His one faint hope, he felt, might lie in that slight 'cast' in her eye. She might not spurn him. The request to escort the refugee families to Shanghai had come as a relief. And then Maria came down to the ship to see them off . . .

As the *Japan* was towed downriver to the bay and hoisted her sails, few of her passengers were not anxious. Their missionary and Chinese friends were in mortal danger, their city homes vulnerable to the mob. Mrs Gough and Mrs Parker had left their husbands alone. Hudson Taylor sat out on deck with the Gough baby on his lap, 'this darling babe' of three months, born shortly before he reached Ningbo. He looked after her 'most of the way', sunk in 'deep thoughts' – 'it helped me to conceal my feelings [on] leaving Maria in Ningpo'.

The journey with unfavourable winds could take ten days, but in six or seven they reached Shanghai, on January 31, and were taken in, as always, by their longsuffering colleagues. Mrs Gough went to the CMS and the Americans to Hongkou. Once again the LMS opened its arms to Hudson Taylor and the Jones and Parker families. An unoccupied house was put at their disposal and they began another makeshift existence with no idea how long it would last. 'I think we are on the eve of a general war with China,' Hudson Taylor wrote home as they caught up on world news. 'If that comes, Shanghai will probably be the only post held . . . If Mission work is stopped, however, we shall most likely leave China . . .'

Whether they would then go to the islands of South-East Asia where Chinese abounded, or to California or Australia where there were so many immigrants, or return home to England, he could not know. Even the writing of letters was difficult in these circumstances. What was certain was that this was not the end. He hoped his parents would buy him a copy of Morrison's massive Chinese dictionary, available very cheaply in England, he had heard. And as he was feeling well off he would like to pay for his sister Louisa to go to a finishing school 'if Father was willing'. He knew that she was kicking over the traces and had run away from home on one occasion. A cousin had already eloped.[40] He sympathised, and enclosed twenty pounds in his next letter home. 'I hope you will not disappoint me in this castle I have built, for I have plenty of disappointments as it is. Most of my fancies come to naught.'

About the harmonium he had asked them to buy him – it must have five or more octaves so that he could play duets with the wife he hoped one day to have. He had concluded at last that his infatuation with Elizabeth was 'a hopeless case' and he was grateful to God that the realisation had forced itself gradually on him – for he was about to learn that while corresponding with him she had been in and out of an engagement to someone else. A letter was on its way which when it arrived provoked this comment to Amelia, 'I am not surprised at the opinion you have formed . . . I have a letter from her, quite decided in tone, and really, if she is so changeable, as she had proved with me, and this gentleman [was] first accepted and then refused, I cannot but think that . . . the Lord has graciously dealt with me in so ordering it.' And to his mother, 'I have quite dismissed the matter . . . and shall henceforth feel myself as free as she evidently does. May God bless her and . . . give her a good husband, is my prayer.'

The shock of that revelation had not struck him yet but already Hudson Taylor was in a painful quandary about Maria.

Shanghai interlude *January–April 1857*

'On the eve of war with China' was the phrase on foreigners' lips in Shanghai in January 1857. Since the British had bombarded Canton and Commissioner Ye had put a price on every 'barbarian' head in the southern provinces under his jurisdiction, everyone was thinking, What next? But for the present only the threat existed, not war.

Shanghai was changing every day, turning into one unbroken mass of houses and streets from Hongkou (Hongkew) to the Chinese city and beyond (map, Book 2 p 120). The French had occupied the open areas between the *Yangkingpang* and the ancient walls. The old mud and cinder roads were being metalled with granite. 'St Catherine's' bridge spanned the Suzhou river beside the British consulate, and along the Bund a score of two- or three-storey business houses flew their company flags. The social milieu of an expanding foreign population had also changed considerably from what Hudson Taylor had first known. The concubinage practised by the unmarried merchant *taipans* and 'griffins' in Shanghai, as in Hong Kong, and the excesses of every breed of foreigner, had led to what Sir John Bowring complained was a

> large population of children of native mothers by foreigners of all classes [who] seemed wholly uncared for, beginning to ripen into a dangerous element out of the dunghill of neglect.[41]

The system of insistence by the merchant firms on five years' service without marriage was still to blame. European men outnumbered women in the foreign community by ten to one. Even at Ningbo a vice-consul had taken one of Miss Aldersey's schoolgirls as his mistress, until denounced by the Bishop of Victoria, Hong Kong. Missionaries and British women in all the ports raised such an outcry, to save the Chinese girls from exploitation, that by the 1860s the public shared their opinion, and British traders and officials could no longer keep Asian women without incurring a social stigma. The antagonism that developed between the business and missionary sections of the community lingered for decades. And yet at the time of Lord Elgin's mission to China in 1858 it was possible for a missionary, Hawks Pott, to write of

> people riding or gyrating daily on the racecourse. Those who prefer gossip to exercise frequent the Bund, a broad quay which extends the whole length of the Settlement . . . The harmony and hospitality of Shanghai make it infinitely the most agreeable place of residence to the Mission.[42]

In contrast, relations between the missionaries and Chinese were improving as they saw and appreciated more in each other. Griffith John's companion Alexander Williamson described 'the energy which pervades the masses'; boats scurrying to and fro on the Huangpu mirrored the vast resources of China in natural and human potential.

> Their minds have received a different kind of training [he wrote appreciatively] but were they to undergo the same process, I am convinced they would take a position not at all inferior to their Western brothers.[43]

Joseph Edkins of the LMS, John Burdon of the CMS and William Aitchison of the American Board were still travelling and preaching together, penetrating throughout the area of Jiangsu province south of the Yangzi and of Zhejiang north of Hangzhou in which Hudson Taylor had worked with them. Unhindered and even 'always cordially received' they distributed thousands of Scriptures at the imperial examinations in major cities. Even two years earlier such liberty had been unthinkable. In October 1856 they succeeded in renting a house in Pinghu, a city of one hundred thousand, in the centre of a densely populated plain. Prejudice was wearing away, but still all they could claim was, jealous authorities watch with a suspicious eye every movement of the foreign barbarians, and while human treaties exclude us from the perishing millions of the vast interior, we gladly take possession in Christ's name, of any spot outside the 'five ports'.[44]

This was the changed world of Shanghai to which Hudson Taylor had returned. To him there was nothing new in being uprooted and having to live simply in the empty LMS house with John and Mary Jones and their children. They occupied their time (when Jones was well enough to go with him, for he was often ill), preaching and disseminating Scripture in the Chinese city, at the CMS and LMS chapels, and in the countryside, as he had done so often in the past. No one could foretell when it would be possible to return to Ningbo, or whether they would soon be swept into a great exodus from China. But the fact that as they had sailed away from Ningbo Maria was staying in the place of danger had shocked him. He realised that he minded, acutely. But for the present he kept it to himself.

As the weeks passed, they heard that three new missionaries of the CES, a Mr and Mrs C J Hall and Miss Magrath, were on the way to join them. Whether or not conditions returned to normal, they would have to wait for them. But there was no knowing when they would arrive. How the Society would support them, when it was unable to provide what it had promised to its missionaries already in East Asia, they were not told. And sure enough, by the end of February the scare at Ningbo was over. Dr Parker came for his family and reported that patients and mandarins alike were polite and friendly. Most of the other refugees returned also, but Mrs Gough stayed as did the Joneses and Hudson Taylor, who wrote,

There is going to be a vessel of war stationed at Ningpo and all is quiet there I believe. But the Lord who brought us here has not taught us to go back and so we are still remaining, till the pillar move.

Although Parker was a member of their Society, his work in Ningbo was closely linked with his fellow Presbyterians, whereas no regular congregation had begun to take shape through Hudson Taylor's and John Jones' preaching. They could afford to delay their return.

There was more in it than that, however. A letter from William Burns dated February 2 arrived at about this time. All was serene in Swatow and the people still friendly, in spite of the hostilities round the corner at Canton. He hoped Hudson Taylor would be coming, but dared not urge him to do so. He must do what he believed to be

God's will for him. Hudson Taylor replied in the same key. Without clear guidance he dared not now put Swatow before Ningbo. Through circumstances not of his own making, his 'excursion' to Swatow had been brought to an end, strong links with the members of his own Society had been forged at Ningbo, and now Maria had been made to matter to him almost against his will. In terms of a permanent mission, Ningbo's claims seemed stronger. Years afterwards he recognised that this decision between Swatow and Ningbo was the turning point on which his creative lifework depended.

It was exactly three years, only three years, since he had first set foot on Chinese soil. It felt like a lifetime. But his contract with the Chinese Evangelization Society was for three years. If he chose to resign, and he had ample justification for it, he was entirely free to do so. In fact, the three years since he signed the agreement had expired in September 1856, but because the Society regarded his arrival in China as the operative date he did nothing. His personal friendship with George Pearse was ripening in spite of the way the Society had treated him. But this time there was a difference. He and John Jones were seriously considering resignation. That the CES should countenance going into debt was to them a fundamental issue, a departure from the Biblical principle, 'owe no man anything'.

At the beginning of March Hudson Taylor told his mother, 'I find more real companionship and sympathy in the Jones than I have done since I left home, only excepting Mr. Burns.' Mary Jones came from a 'very well circumstanced' family who had lost almost everything through a swindle, he said. Her sister in Bognor 'seems to love her with unbounded affection – and deservedly so'. Mary was like a sister to him. After two unsuccessful courtships he could not even bring himself to say more about Maria. For five or six years he had caused his mother and Amelia endless heartache and embarrassments, and it had all been of his own contriving. He could not involve them in another debacle. Nor could he bear to be another Edkins, the butt of drawing-room tittle-tattle after Maria rejected his proposal. But with John and Mary Jones it was another matter. He could open his heart to them. They had long conversations about their future. And needlessly he wrote again to sever the last of his links with Elizabeth Sissons, a postscript to a tale once told, but in April had not even posted it. As he explained to Amelia, 'while I love and esteem her as a friend, as a Christian, I do not feel as I once did . . . I send the note open, you can read it.'

During March the thought came to him that if he was to get in touch with Maria without anyone else knowing of it the best way would be through Mary Gough who was returning to Ningbo. He knew Maria had no parents, and thought she was already of age and free from obligation to Miss Aldersey, whom he assumed to have been her guardian. Encouraged, it would appear, by John and Mary Jones, when he sat down and wrote on March 21, 1857, he went farther than to open a correspondence. What he said can only be surmised from references to the letter in subsequent exchanges. He expressed his feelings and made some 'proposals', asking Maria to burn the note if she could not accept them. But Mary Gough had sailed to Ningbo without his letter. For two days he kept it and on the 23rd posted it, with one to Frederick Gough a few days later.

By then, on March 25, Mary Jones had gone down with smallpox. John committed the three small children – aged four, two and one – to Hudson Taylor's care and isolated himself with his wife. So now Hudson Taylor's hands were very full and he had scant time for thinking. While they slept he wrote on April 2 to Mary Jones' mother and sister and to his own. Mary had been dangerously ill, he reported.

> She is such a real *sister* to me, kind, sympathizing, *all* I could wish her to be, and her husband as dear a brother. I have not met many, if any, more advanced in the Christian life, more dead to the world, more anxious always to be about the Master's work. Mrs. Jones' illness has been a very heavy trial . . . [Now that it] has begun to decline, she seems somewhat cast down, she thought she was going home – I hope not now.

Four days later she was recovering fast.

Amelia's recent engagement drew from him a reflection of his own deepest thoughts. For two long pages he expatiated to her in the manner of his letters from Hull, on the love of God and the preciousness of Jesus. Then,

> have you read much of the 'Song of Solomon' – it is a rich garden to revel in, and so is Psalm 45 . . . the dearest and sweetest of earthly ties but faintly shadow forth the love of Jesus to his redeemed – to me – . . .?

And a few days later, sensing that Amelia's upbringing was giving her a foreboding in spite of her longing for marriage,

> These feelings are planted in the heart by God; and all the circumstances connected with them ordained and allowed by Him for our

> Highest Spiritual Good, as well as temporal happiness . . . They are used by the Holy Spirit to typify the love and relationship between God and His people, in nearly every, if not every book in the bible. And in an especial manner do they point us to 'the Bridegroom' to whom we have been 'espoused as chaste virgins to Christ'. With that love you love your husband . . . you are to love Jesus – nay more. Are you sad or lonely when he leaves you, so you should be while absent from Jesus. Do you long for the completion of your union – so you should for the return of Jesus to take you to Himself. [As for Benjamin, her fiancé,] He must love you as Christ loved the Church, and you must love, honor and obey him as the church ought to love, honor and obey Christ, or you will not get the blessing God intends you [to have] from it.

Knowing what he wanted, to please God in everything he did, and yet to be married and rid of tension and frustration, he was also painfully aware of how out of reach fulfilment was – unless Maria responded favourably. Then he would return to Ningbo and begin a new life. After another week he wrote to Amelia again. He was longing for a kiss and the familiar feeling of her arm round his neck, he said. But she was far away. 'I do so long for some one to have unrestricted communion with – for some one to love and confide in.'

April advanced, Mary Jones recovered, Jones and Hudson Taylor resumed their country evangelism, and still no sign of the Halls and Miss Magrath, and no news of their ship. They went to the Longhua pagoda at the temple festival (drawing, Book 2, p 206), to reach as many people as possible with the gospel. But 'the violence and rudeness of the mob' forced them to withdraw. Then as the month progressed and the Halls' arrival became more imminent, absence in the country was unwise and they took to caring for destitute people in Shanghai city. In John Jones' words,

> In Shanghai are many poor creatures, either beggars or strangers, daily dying by the roadside. Whenever we found such we procured what shelter we could for them and provided them with food; we visited them daily and endeavoured to point them to Jesus.

But they could see that their days in Shanghai were numbered. The LMS would need their house within a few weeks, and as soon as the Halls' ship came in they would all have to move on together.

News of the great Dr Medhurst's death in London at last reached China and Hudson Taylor told of how William Muirhead preached a memorial sermon extolling 'the last of China's first missionaries'.

Grief was compounded by the knowledge that he left a widow, widowed for the second time, two widowed daughters with children, a son with the same names as himself, now consul in Fuzhou and already a widower, and a sixteen-year-old daughter. An epoch had ended. Shanghai would never be the same again.

But there was more in their minds than that. All lived with death as a close reality and were thankful for each other, each day of life. The mortality rate in the West was high but to leave home and go to China was still as likely as not to be goodbye for ever. Dysentery was the great enemy in China. Amoebic dysentery dragged on and on, debilitating and painful until complications claimed the sufferer's life. But frequently acute attacks of another type resembling cholera struck suddenly and were severe. Often the strong would die while paradoxically the weak survived. No one knew why.

As for the threat of war, the sanguine watched events at Canton and saw the beginning not of the end, as some did, but of all China opening to foreigners. And they were right. In Ningbo Dr and Mrs Parker were out for a walk together when a mandarin came by and in a rare gesture stopped his sedan chair and retainers, got out and 'was extremely polite'. At last the CMS missionaries succeeded in buying land some miles outside Ningbo and established their first outstation – a historic development. And as Hudson Taylor and John Jones consulted together, bound more and more closely to one another through the intimacy of their experiences, a clear pattern began to form in their minds. It pointed to Ningbo again, but no longer as 'agents' of the CES.

Maria's predicament *April 1857*

The tangled story of 1857 could make light opera, a tragi-comedy of Victorian mores enacted in a Manchu world of missionary romance. Or it could be passed over in a few paragraphs, so losing a real-life situation full of insights into several personalities and the interplay of a diverse community. Under the restrictions of a treaty port in dangerous times, personal relationships came under stress. Because Hudson Taylor and Maria played leading roles, some detail from their papers may be justified.[45]

Hudson Taylor's letters reached the Goughs together on April 7. The first had taken over two weeks. The next morning Maria was busy in school (reopened when peace returned after the massacre plot), when Mrs Gough called to see her. She put into Maria's hands two letters in an unfamiliar handwriting, one addressed to Frederick Gough and one to Maria herself. Without reading them Maria went back to work, 'as if nothing had happened or was going to happen'.

As soon as she was free she went to her room and before opening the letters prayed over them. She hoped they were from Hudson Taylor but thought 'the other gentleman' might be trying again. Then she opened the one to Mr Gough. It said that the writer had twice asked for the Goughs' prayers and now believed that God's guidance had been given. And the signature was Hudson Taylor's. She was reading the second when she was interrupted and had no privacy to finish it until the next morning, but this she had managed to read,

> how he believed God had given him that love for me which he felt . . . I could hardly understand that it was a reality. It seemed that my prayers were indeed answered . . . He begged me not to send him a hasty refusal, which he intimated would cause him intense anguish.

Above all, she inferred, ridicule would be most painful.

Twice had words in Psalm 37, which she believed were God's assurance to her, been brought to her notice: 'Commit thy way unto the Lord, trust also in him, and he will bring it to pass'. She had done so from the very first and this was the result. Not imagining how the news would be received, she told Burella, who was delighted and congratulated her. But when she told Miss Aldersey, 'She remarked that she supposed I would not think of accepting him, and suggested that they should write to William Tarn, her uncle and true guardian in London, to ask him to find out more about Hudson Taylor.

This setback was disturbing. Maria asked Mr Gough's permission to show Hudson Taylor's covering letter to Miss Aldersey 'because I thought it evinced a most Christian spirit,' but 'She . . . said it did not change her mind at all; it was just such a letter as she should expect.' Accusing him of cant! Maria reeled. Was this all Miss A thought of him?

It was. Miss Aldersey saw Hudson Taylor as an unconnected nobody, an eccentric with a pigtail, a Plymouth Brother who regarded the Sabbath as no more sacred than any other day.[46] Had he not arrived at Ningbo on a Sunday? Even if after a robbery, drowning and shipwreck with a sick and exhausted John Jones and his child, it was a Sabbath-breaking. She wished far better for Maria and was sure her family would also. And she was offended at his not having asked her permission to write to Maria. So she 'urged my declining Mr T's proposals and wished me to request him never, at any time, to refer to the subject again, and to put the subject entirely from my mind'.

Now Maria was in a quandary. Her circumstances bound her to respect and even to obey Miss Aldersey although she was under no legal obligation to do so. But Miss Aldersey was adamant and Maria was shaken. *Did* Hudson Taylor hold unusual views? Would they be unable to agree? She needed to find out. So while Miss Aldersey wrote to the Tarns disparaging Hudson Taylor, Maria began a letter to them saying how she felt about him and asking for their approval.

In London William Tarn had been totally incapacitated for over a year with a spinal disease and lay in great pain on a specially constructed couch, but he was wholly alert and at once began impartial enquiries about Hudson Taylor.

A reply to the 'proposals' was more difficult for Maria. She wanted to encourage Hudson Taylor, but to Miss Aldersey's eyes it had to look like a rebuff. Could she make it say both – enough to satisfy Miss Aldersey and buy time? – 'for I thought that while some of the objections which Miss Aldersey urged *lasted*, I myself could not accept him'. And Mary Gough while sympathising warmly was urging her to obey Miss Aldersey. 'I feel that she stands in the place of a mother to you; and whatever your own feelings may be, you would not feel it right to follow a course to which she is so directly opposed.'

Maria took her advice. The letter she wrote to Hudson Taylor has survived, a faded copperplate model of propriety, kindliness and very carefully chosen words, with more between the lines than in them, the distillate of rough drafts partly in shorthand.[47]

> April 16/57
>
> My dear Sir,
>
> I have to acknowledge receipt of a letter from you dated March 21st, – which was put into my hands yesterday week, April 8th by Mrs Gough, – and to thank you for the kind Christian spirit which breathed throughout it.
>
> I have made the subject of your letter a matter of earnest prayer to God, and have desired I think sincerely only to know His will, and to act in accordance with it. And although it does indeed give me no pleasure to cause you pain, I must answer your letter as appears to me to be according to God's direction. And it certainly appears to be my duty to decline your proposals. But think not dear Sir that I do so carelessly, and without appreciating the kind feelings which you

> express towards me. And I have too great a respect for those feelings (although my duty requires me entirely to discourage them,) to expose you and the subject of your letter to ridicule. It was right that I should acquaint Miss Aldersey and my sister with the matter, and Mrs Bausum is the only other person besides the parties through whom your letter came, who knows anything about it, – as far as I am aware. And it is my desire that no one else except my own immediate relations, and those whom you have thought or may think proper to acquaint with the matter, – should ever know anything about it. Before I close this letter, I shall take an opportunity of burning yours as you desired me. I regard you dear Sir, as a Brother in Jesus, and hope ever to bear towards you those feelings which Disciples are commanded to bear one towards another. But ask me not for more. I request you not to refer to the subject again as I should be obliged to return you the same answer. You will perceive by the tone of my letter that I have not *lightly* sent you a refusal. I have written with less reserve to you than I should have done to one to whom I did not feel bound by ties of Christian fellowship. And now may Jesus himself bless you abundantly, and make you a blessing. And may you be the honored instrument of leading many souls to Jesus, and have many crowns of rejoicing in the day of Christ.
>
> I remain,
> Yours in Jesus,
> Maria Jane Dyer

Now, would that satisify Miss A *and* give Mr Taylor the right clues? Would Miss A take up the fact that she had omitted to tell Hudson Taylor 'never at any time' to raise the subject again? Would he weigh the solicitousness against the stark refusal? Would he see that disciples were told to love one another, that God's direction was only to do her duty towards Miss Aldersey? And that her pointed reference to the tone of her letter, in such a fulsome final paragraph was the key to her predicament? That she was putting him off for the present only, and asking, not forbidding him to try again? With Miss Aldersey's approval she gave her letter to Mrs Gough to send through Mary Jones in Shanghai.

> After I had sent the letter [Maria told herself] I felt that I could not wish one way or the other: I could only leave the matter in God's hands, praying him to do what he saw best.

As for Maria's letter to her uncle and aunt, before even a rough draft was completed, Miss Aldersey discovered what was in the wind and through Burella 'strongly urged' her not to write. Maria put the unfinished draft in her writing desk and there it was to lie for three months. Her conviction that God had heard her prayers and moved Hudson Taylor to love her was lost in doubt. 'For who was I that I should set myself up, as it were, against Miss Aldersey, an old established Christian?' There was nothing she could do but wait.

'The odd sparrow' *April–June 1857*

At the end of April or in early May Hudson Taylor received Maria's cryptic reply. Although it was 'kind' it was 'unfavourable' and he suffered 'agony'. As he read and reread it he saw that it could be taken in two ways, yet at face value it was not ambiguous. It clearly said 'No and please don't try again.' 'I felt I must leave it in the Lord's hands – and strongly suspected the hindrance lay with Miss Aldersey.' References in his letters to John and Mary Jones leave no room for doubt that he shared the news with them, but there was no more he could do.

> My dear Brother and Sister, Mr and Mrs Jones, are more than I could have hoped to have found them or any one else to be, but their kindness, love – and the happiness they enjoy and love they bear to each other, seem to make me long the more for the same blessing . . .

Life had to go on. His mother had sent him a box full of useful things, a pair of boots, books, drugs and small luxuries to replace his losses, so he packed up some more curios and gifts for them and friends, saying, 'I am preparing a few things to send you in your *old red box*. A famous traveller it has been, has it not?' It kept going to and fro in this way. He asked them to send 'a good violin' as a gift to John Jones who was helping him so much, and a good reference Bible for himself, to be divided into four and rebound with interleaved blank pages for his own notes – at any expense. In passing he mentioned that he had a severe headache and pain in his chest, something that was to recur in his letters during the next three years.

All through May he worked hard, going every day into the city to preach in the LMS chapel, morning and evening, and in tea-shops and temples. Suiting his Chinese to the dialects of the men he talked with, mandarin for those from the northern provinces, Hokkien (Fujian) with men from Taiwan, Amoy and Fuzhou, Tiejiu with Swatow sailors, and Shanghai for local people, he made the most of the adaptations that had been forced upon him. Master of none, he could talk freely with users of each. Some accepted his leaflets only to destroy them at once, a new trend. Others showed actual pleasure on receiving them. One said, 'You make man too cheap – too bad – there are many good people,' and some asked, 'Do you only get your *soul* saved, or do you get rice too?' Every comment led to an explanation. John Jones saw how useful fluency was and worked almost too hard at the language when he was not handing tracts to passers-by as Hudson Taylor preached.

Behind the temple of the tutelary god of the city was a flower garden with winding walks, rockeries and tea-stalls for the public, where they often went to preach. There they met a man ripe for the reaping.

> I was preaching in the temple of the guardian god of the city one afternoon, had been dwelling on the love of God, and the blessing of sonship given to believers, when a man came forward and said, 'When a man believes and wishes to join the church are there any ceremonies to be observed?' I told him of baptism . . . and explained it as typical of death to the world and regeneration, resurrection – a new creature . . . He said, 'I greatly believe in Jesus, I *do* believe in him and will come to be baptised.' He came . . . and said, 'When I heard you preach I found what I wanted. I was so overjoyed if you had said I must be immersed in fire instead of water I should have desired it with all my heart.'

He had despaired to the point of being ready to drown himself. Prayers to Buddha, a vegetarian diet, attempts to reform had all failed. When he said he was a maker of incense and Hudson Taylor pointed out that a livelihood from idolatry was incompatible with faith in Christ his instant reply was 'Then I must change it.'

The problem of how to help the destitute, the sick, dying and dead by the roadside in Shanghai was always with them. The *Overseas China Mail* of May 16 reported two thousand destitute refugees from Nanking alone. Major philanthropy which struck at the root causes was impossible. The Taiping rebellion and insurgency of other kinds were constantly swelling the numbers of the homeless. The government increased rather than eased their sufferings.

> We tried to rent a house, in which we might receive and care for the sick beggars, but our attempt was unsuccessful. In our search we came upon the ruin of a house . . . It afforded some little shelter from the weather, and had been taken possession of by the beggars, and in it we found a great number collected, some well and able to beg; others ill, some dying from hunger and disease. From this time we made a regular visit to these poor people and helped a little those who

> were unable to help themselves . . . Sometimes we were able to give a supper to 20–25 of the poor creatures . . . We found, as is always the case, how difficult it is to care for the body and the soul together.

One day one of these men begged them to adopt his son, a boy named Tianxi (T'ienhsi), Heaven's Delight.

> We found him with his father sick in the ruins . . . both would have perished of disease and hunger. Through God's blessing, however, both of them recovered. The father was a shoe mender . . . and we supplied him with a little leather, scissors, needles, thread, etc, to commence again . . . but he was too weakly to earn enough for himself and his son. He asked us to take his son and bring him up.

They did so, took him with them when they later went back to Ningbo, educated him and in time saw him become an active church member.

All this time Hudson Taylor and John Jones were facing together the prospect of resignation from the CES. There was still no word of the Halls' ship, but any day could see three more swelling their neglected team. Wilhelm Lobscheid had resigned in March and was about to sail from Hong Kong 'to settle everything personally' in London. The Society's moral failure to keep their promises was distressing. Knowledge of William Berger's gifts and, since March, of George Müller's also, did not absolve them from their obligations.

With the patronage of the Ningbo foreign community Dr Parker was in no way handicapped by the Society's failings. He simply protested against them, repeating Hudson Taylor's censure of their methods. While 'hundreds, nay thousands are convinced that the doctrines of Christianity are good', why was he being left to pay his own way? he asked.

> In addition to the hospital I have been supporting a school, a medical assistant and an evangelist, for . . . the Society has never given me anything for mission purposes, but is now a *hundred pounds* [underlined four times] in my debt, which I look for every month.

John Jones' letters to George Pearse were always cordial, even affectionate, and above mere business. He accounted for such sums as he had received and expressed his gratitude. But in answer to a request from the secretaries for an estimate of his future needs he replied, 'I hope to use that which God sends me and as He shall direct.' No complaints, no requests, just gratitude and confidence that by some means or other God would provide all he and his wife and children and work might ever need. He did not want more or believe he would receive less. His receipts were the measure of his need and he would cut his coat according to that cloth.

Hudson Taylor could not yet see things in the same light. Back in September 1856 he had written to George Pearse,

> You have mentioned the position of Mr Jones – You seem to like it, and so I believe does he – but to me it seems a bad one, and is one I would not voluntarily occupy, though as you say as I *am* it *practically* comes to the same thing. My position therefore is one which I do not like in this respect. If I am to look directly to God alone for my supplies, I had rather not have a Society between me and the Lord and His people – the Society being *supposed* by all to supply me with what is needed. This however I do not think *is* the best way, nor do I think it implies any want of trust in God, to wish to be connected with a Society to which I can look at stated intervals for a stated sum, any more than it argues want of faith in God to look for a salary at home, or seek by profession or business to provide for necessary wants. I think that every missionary ought to be provided regularly with a stated sum by the Society or Church he is sent out by, so that he may *depend* on it, and act accordingly. I think too he ought to be supplied with a little more than his absolute expenses . . . so that he may have somewhat of his own, that he forget not to sacrifice, to do good and to communicate to others or to the cause of God.
>
> As to receiving money from the heathen, as for instance for medicines or medical treatment, it seems to me much like Paul's laboring with his own hands, for his support; and to help others, in the same way if practicable, seems to be no more objectionable.[48]

Such were his feelings at a time when so much seemed against him. But he was thinking, praying about it and learning from John and Mary Jones.

At home in Hull and London Hudson Taylor had proved to his own satisfaction that God would supply his need in answer to prayer alone, influencing other people as his way of doing this. In Shanghai he had seen that under the stress of necessity the same thing happened, even when the CES was the agreed if ineffective channel for his supplies. Now, as he faced George Pearse's almost contrite recommendation that he cease to count on the Society as a source of income but still let it serve him as far as it was able and as John and Mary Jones were doing, he was loth to accept the change. He still favoured the policy he had adopted so deliberately when he joined the CES. Even the nominal backing of a society was a buttress to faith. No other current source of income held out more than a frail hope of future provision. To be bound by rules but not freed from worry was another matter; it was irrational.

He failed to recognise that John Jones and George Pearse had conceived a relationship between missionary and society full of potential benefits. It was no less than the very relationship Hudson Taylor was to adopt in a wider context a few years later. Pearse was for changing unwelcome rules into principles, and Jones was for representing a body of Christians in the homeland, a society of like-minded people whose principles he was putting into practice abroad, without counting on them for a regular income. Pearse shared this concept of faith in God apart from a guarantee of support by any organisation. He had been driven to it by the Society, of which he was a director, defaulting in its undertakings. But it was John and Mary Jones who had sailed away with their children to the other side of the world, banking on God alone.

Until this interlude in Shanghai Hudson Taylor had remained unconvinced by their reasoning, for he doubted, not whether God *could* do it but whether it was his intention to provide in that way. What money was sent by the Society was reaching them as old Spanish dollars, disfigured and giving the dull ring of debased metal. To change them into Shanghai dollars involved a thirty-five per cent loss by discount. Never mind, he commented confidently enough, 'I have been plentifully supplied through Mr. Berger's liberality, and the Lord, as a faithful Master, will not leave me destitute but will in His own good time open up my way before me.' The faith was there, if the reasoning was different, until it came home to him that in fact the Joneses and he were already living almost entirely on donations from individuals, not the CES, as God's channel of supply.

The example of George Müller (Appendix 1) appealed strongly to them from reading the *Narrative* of his life. Müller had married the sister of Anthony Norris Groves, the missionary to Baghdad and India, who lived by the principle of trusting in God to supply his material needs. Together the Müllers had chosen the same way of life, believing, as his biographer A T Pierson put it, that God would care for 'the odd sparrow'.[49] Matthew's Gospel spoke of two for a farthing and Luke's of five for two farthings. The one odd sparrow was no less to receive the heavenly Father's care! They determined never to contract a debt but to spend or give away only what they actually had in hand. A sum designated for one purpose they would not use for another – that would be borrowing.

As he established his homes for orphans in Bristol and his commitments grew, Müller adhered to these principles. Sometimes their need for money or goods became extreme and they lived from day to day or even hour to hour, turning only to God for help, careful not to betray the existence of their need to others, but gifts came to them from all over the world. So confidence in God became the characteristic of George Müller.

In 1839 he received some valuable jewellery. Before he sold it he engraved with a diamond ring on his window pane the words 'JEHOVAH JIREH' – 'the Lord will provide', and whenever he was faced with a need he would see this reminder intensified by the light shining through it. (Sixty years later, in 1898, his children's homes, caring for two thousand orphans, were still being provided for on the same principles. And in addition he had distributed sums of money to missionaries overseas totalling over £260,000.[50])

When in May 1857 Hudson Taylor and John Jones considered severing their formal links with their Society, Taylor was influenced by the important corollary that the sword of consular penalties for working outside a treaty port always hung over his head. As long as he represented the CES the responsibility rested ultimately on them. They could not bear a heavy fine, so he ought not to incur it. If he did, it would increase their debts. So he felt inhibited by them. If independent he could take greater risks.

Then, if he and Jones resigned how would they order their lives and their work? Itinerant evangelism unconnected with a local church seemed to Hudson Taylor increasingly ineffective after a certain point – the work done and the response evoked were not consolidated. He feared they were being lost. Both agreed with Gutzlaff's principle that the best evangelism would be done by Chinese Christians, but that was only possible if they were maturing spiritually and being well taught. John Jones was unfit to travel much, and had his family to care for. Hudson Taylor knew the limitations of itinerating alone. He could not count on having Chinese colleagues trained by other missions: nor upon doing better than before in starting settled work beyond the treaty limits.

They arrived at the conclusion that they would work together in a treaty port until a congregation of Chinese Christians was formed, a long-term policy. They would aim to develop the gifts in those Christians and encourage them to go out with the gospel to their own people. They would pool their resources, living as one family and sharing a common purse. Where, then, should they do it? They had made a start at Ningbo. They would return there and co-operate with Dr Parker and the other missions with whom they were already on such good terms, while establishing and training another congregation. A mere hop, skip and a jump? But as history was to show, this was the great leap forward. Nothing great or grandiose, no far-seeing vision or daring adventure, but a settled occupation in a treaty port, within the law, and shared with two of the best friends Hudson Taylor had known, was the right path for the foreseeable future. Chinese Christians, trained as colporteurs by his working and worshipping with them, would be companions when the time arrived to press farther into the interior again. That was enough for the present. Hostilities between China and Britain had broken out again and the immediate future was dark, but if and when peace returned there was the likelihood of wider liberty for missions to extend their operations.

On May 29, 1857, therefore, a week after his twenty-fifth birthday, Hudson Taylor sent George Pearse his letter of resignation: 'I wish to allude to my position with the Society.' He had given ample notice in earlier letters. Now he dealt with the practical implications step by step. One condition of service with the CES was that all surgical instruments and books belonged to them.

> In the event of my connection with the Society being dissolved . . . I wish you *either* to give me these things out and out . . . *or*, to inform me what you wish to be done with them . . .
>
> If I possess any legal right on the Society to draw, or sue for salary due, but not sent, I now wish to relinquish that right. You feel you owe me a fixed sum every quarter, which your funds do not enable you to send, and . . . monies sent to me . . . I do not feel free to use. For these reasons I relinquish my salary entirely. If the Lord blesses you, and leads you to send anything to me, either in the way of counsel, pecuniary aid, or otherwise, I hope to receive it as from *Him*, and with thankfulness to Him and you. If He see fit to supply my need in some other way the glory be ascribed to Him alone. It seems to me that after taking these steps there is no longer any advantage in a formal connection with the Society, while it is to some extent a tie to me, that if in excursions into the country I am seized and brought before the Consul, I may be subjected to a heavy fine, for which the Society is responsible. To avoid this, *I resign my connection with the Society entirely, from this time forth*. My doing so cannot, as far as I foresee, at all injure the Society, nothing is further from my desire than this . . . If therefore from any cause, such as violation of the treaty by excursions, etc, I should be summoned

before the authorities, I shall inform them I only am responsible for the consequences, my connection with the Society having been terminated. And now may the blessing of God rest on this step, which I have taken, I believe desiring His glory alone. May His blessing rest on you and on your labours, and on all the Committee and board . . . I do not resign from any disapproval of the Society or its principles, – but resign for the reasons above stated.

Believe me, in our Lord,
Yours aff^{ly}
Jas. H. Taylor.[51]

John Jones resigned a few days later. They were in this together. With a light heart Hudson Taylor commented to his mother by the next mail,

I . . . rejoice in the trustful way in which you express yourself with regard to me and my affairs. And . . . I feel assured the step I took . . . terminating my connection with the Ch. Ev. Socy. is one which will cause you neither anxiety nor grief. My soul has been much blessed in connection with the step . . . My position was anomalous. If asked if I had a fixed salary or not, I could neither say yes or no, without equivocation or more explanation than I could in propriety make; and monies sent out to me . . . I felt I could not conscientiously use for myself . . . their claim on me for instruments, books, etc, I determined to end, either by having the things given to me, *bona fide*, or by having nothing to do with them at all . . . I hope you will continue your subscriptions to the Ch. Ev. S. as before. They will very likely send me quite as much as before. [As for marriage] The Lord . . . will find me a partner, and means too, if that be a 'need', or a 'good thing' for me . . . But pray that He may never grant me the desire of my heart, and with it leanness of soul, as when He granted quails to Israel in the wilderness.

At a bound his fledgling faith was airborne – quickly to suffer from qualms. So far the setback from Maria was driving him closer to God. He was content to let him solve that problem. As he prepared to return to Ningbo he knew that he would have to tread warily, treating Maria as if nothing had passed between them. He did not yet know that Miss Aldersey was involved.

Reaction in London to the resignations was mixed. Hudson Taylor's *Retrospect* recalled with some forgetfulness the conclusions reached with John Jones that,

. . . we were both profoundly thankful that the separation took place without the least breach of friendly feeling on either side. Indeed, we

> had the joy of knowing that the step we took commended itself to several members of the Committee, although as a whole the Society could not come to our position. Depending on God alone for supplies, we were enabled to continue a measure of connection with our former supporters, sending home journals, etc, for publication as before, as long as the Society continued to exist.
>
> The step we had taken was not a little trying to faith. I was not at all sure what God would have me do, or whether He would so meet my need as to enable me to continue working as before. I had no friends whatever from whom I expected supplies. I did not know what means the Lord might use; but I was willing to give up all my time to the service of evangelisation among the heathen, if by any means He would supply the smallest amount on which I could live; and if He were not pleased to do this, I was prepared to undertake whatever work might be necessary to supply myself, giving all the time that could be spared from such a calling to more distinctly missionary efforts. But God blessed and prospered me; and how glad and thankful I felt when the separation was really effected! I could look right up into my Father's face with a satisfied heart, ready, by His grace, to do the next thing as He might teach me, and feeling very sure of His loving care.[52]

No funds he could bank on receiving, and an open mind on earning his living by secular employment if need be, were enough of a recipe to make him light-hearted. The proof of the pudding would be in the eating. He was not to wait very long for the testing. On Sunday, June 7, word came that the Halls' ship was at the Yangzi mouth after six months at sea. Both John and Mary Jones and Hudson Taylor went down to Wusong to welcome them and Miss Magrath, a well-educated woman in her thirties, bringing them back to their house in the LMS compound.

Hardly had they arrived than a furore, such as Shanghai seemed to love, broke over their heads. This time Hudson Taylor was not to blame, but again it was the CES in the thick of the trouble. The Halls had employed a Chinese woman as their servant on the journey. She had become pregnant by a man on board who asked the minister C J Hall to marry them. With the captain's approval Hall obliged. As soon as this was known to the merchant community there was uproar. In the view of many, Chinese women could be used but marriage to them was a crime! The missionaries rallied behind Hall. John Burdon as acting chaplain to the Settlement declared the marriage to be valid and proper, and himself became the butt of strong criticism.

Alexander Wylie showed his usual hospitality, conducting Hall round the LMS activities. They found Muirhead and Edkins each giving Bible-teaching to thirty Christians, and heard of others of two societies successfully living miles inland from Shanghai, who 'will stay till forced away by the authorities', Hall wrote.

> I think in connection with this [LMS] mission alone there is accommodation for from 1100 to 1200 people in their various chapels – a glorious thought that so many may hear the gospel. They have services every day . . .

William Aitchison wrote from Pinghu,

> We can travel scores of miles in every direction, without the fear of annoyance . . . Quite recently, in company with the Rev. Mr. Edkins, I visited the city of Hangchow, which has no superior in size and importance. We . . . lay anchored within half a mile of the wall [for three days] and we rambled about at will . . . a Manchu official called upon us, . . . but he made no objection to our stay.
>
> The Rev. Mr. Williamson *and wife*, of the LMS, have now been residing more than a month in their own hired house at Sungkiang [Songjiang, thirty miles from Shanghai] . . . Some little opposition . . . but our brother wisely disregards it.

The consuls were taking no action unless the Chinese officially complained to them. If Hudson Taylor felt any injustice in this, no hint remains.

After a week preparations were completed, Hendrick Kloekers took over the care of the destitute in the city, and the whole party set off for Ningbo – Hudson Taylor, the Jones family, the Halls and Miss Magrath.

To Hudson Taylor in after-years, the initiation of their independent mission to Ningbo represented the conception of the China Inland Mission. The birth was not until eight years later. But during that time the validity of the principles they had agreed upon was tried and found trustworthy.

Anarchy and Elgin — *1857*

On June 16, 1857, the day Hudson Taylor and the Jones family left Shanghai with the C J Halls and Miss Magrath to begin their 'Ningpo Mission', the CES in London addressed a petition to the Earl of Clarendon at the Foreign Office. Referring to their interview with him in 1856 they urged that Lord Elgin (son of the seventh earl, of Elgin marbles fame) be instructed as the Queen's envoy to Peking to give attention to the needs of Christians in China when negotiating with the imperial government. On June 22 this reply came from Lord Clarendon,

> the Earl of Elgin has been instructed to obtain for the members of all Christian communities security for the free exercise of their religious worship, and protection for the lives of missionaries and other peaceful travellers in the interior of China; and that . . . Her Majesty's Government would gladly see, in any treaty with China, a renunciation, on the part of the Chinese Government, of any interference with Chinese subjects who embrace Christianity.[53]

For all their administrative failures the Chinese Evangelization Society made two major contributions to the general, widespread evangelisation of the 'celestial empire'. They launched Hudson Taylor upon his career, and they helped to ensure that in the new treaties of Tientsin and Peking the omission of Christian interests from the Treaty of Nanking was made good. However, while diplomatic negotiations were one thing, aggression to obtain concessions was another matter. Impatient with obdurate attitudes, the imperial powers of the West were to plunge into more wickedness and to extort what they wanted from an unwilling China by unpardonable carnage and vandalism.

Anarchy reigned on the China seas. The growing traffic in coerced and kidnapped Chinese labourers for the gold-fields and plantations of the Americas and Australia, coastal piracy and the opium scandal, flourished almost unchecked.[54] All British ships were bound to report for inspection at Hong Kong and unwilling coolie 'passengers' were released – only to be picked up and transported in non-British ships. For fear of their guards, most were unwilling to say that they were held against their will. There in Hong Kong two hundred and thirty-two coolies were found locked up for three weeks waiting for a ship. Forty-two were in a sixteen-by-fifteen-foot room for twenty days. In February the coolies overpowered and killed the captain and officers of a French ship, the *Anais*, and ran her ashore on the China coast. Two hundred were burned or drowned when the *Carmen* caught fire. The Portuguese, last to renounce slavery in Africa and last to end their coolie trafficking in China, delivered their cargoes to Peru and Cuba. On April 15 the *Overseas China Mail* carried a report by the Cuba correspondent of the *New York Herald* that of six hundred coolies from Swatow in one ship, three hundred and five died of dysentery at sea. In most ships the hatches were battened down on the holds in which they were incarcerated and, escape impossible, some crazed victims chose to set the ship on fire and die rather than be slaves.

Many instances of courage in attempting to escape were reported to the Chief Justice of Hong Kong. When finally a Chinese coolie succeeded in leaping overboard from the *Maria Luz* at Yokohama and swam to a British man-of-war, the captain refused to give him up. The Japanese discovered what was happening, returned the whole consignment of wretches to China and the traffic soon ended. (Not for another five years, in 1863, was slavery in the United States to be ended. The world's conscience was very slow to awaken.)

Piracy was increasing and feuds between pirates and 'protection' gangs becoming more bitter. For years the Chinese fishing fleets and inter-port traffic had been under Portuguese 'protection'. But the Cantonese resented the strong-arm tactics and piracy of the Portuguese, armed their own junks and hired French escorts. Resentful in turn of what they considered an infringement of their monopoly, the Portuguese *lorcha* men attacked the French.

On April 11, 1857, the *Lady Mary Wood* heard heavy firing and on investigation saw eight very large pirate boats led by a heavily-armed *lorcha* with a hundred or so Chinese and foreigners attacking rice-junks from Formosa. She drove them off and towed the junks to Amoy. In May the Cantonese and French defeated the Portuguese. The *Overseas China Mail* complained, 'These fights have become a perfect nuisance to foreigners and Chinese.' Crossing Hangzhou Bay Hudson Taylor and the Jones–Hall party had a narrow escape from pirates. Since Walter Lowrie's death at pirate hands no one imagined they were immune. But the 'perfect nuisance' was to pursue the new missionaries to their very doorsteps a few days later.

The anarchy was not only at sea. Kashgar in far Xinjiang fell to the Muslim rebels. The Hakka rebels were pressing hard on Canton's landward gates. The same issue of the *Overseas China Mail* spoke of famine prices for rice even at the Huangbo anchorage below Canton, and in May concluded that higher up the river the horrors must be extreme, so many decapitated and mutilated bodies were to be seen in the waters of the estuary. It was the 'starving month' and 'bloody month' of 1855 over again.

But this time the British were deeply embroiled. Admiral Sir Michael Seymour was blockading the Canton river. On April 29,

CHINA: BORDERS, PROVINCES AND MAIN RIVERS

1857, four more warships arrived. Four days later a Chinese attempt to blow up HMS *Acorn* failed. During May and June British men-of-war attacked Chinese junks anchored in the Canton estuary and 'carnage' ensued. A correspondent of *The Times* wrote, 'Half an army of ten thousand men were in ten minutes destroyed by the sword or forced into the broad river.' Another writing to *The Friend of India* described the scene of blood and severed limbs littering the water as British boarding parties attacked the junks. Britain's shame was being compounded.

Lord Elgin was on the way to Hong Kong. When he arrived the whole matter between Britain and China was to be brought to a decisive conclusion. But on May 10 the Indian Mutiny erupted with murders at Meerut near Delhi. Lucknow and Delhi quickly fell. Massacres at Delhi and Cawnpore followed. When Elgin reached Hong Kong on July 2 in the most up-to-date screw-steam frigate *Shannon*, ostensibly to 'inspect' Chusan (Zhoushan), Taiwan and the northern ports – a sinister expression – a strong plea from Lord Canning in India was awaiting him. It was impossible to consult Whitehall in time. Would he proceed at once to Calcutta with all his troops to assist General Havelock? Elgin immediately responded. By the time he arrived, the first four and a half critical months of the mutiny had elapsed.

In August Charles Bird wrote that 'the India Crisis has completely put the Chinese Affair in the background', once again making Christians forget the need to provide for their missionaries. George Pearse told Hudson Taylor that a national day of prayer and fasting had been well observed. 'Many preachers referred to the sins of the Indian Government in reference to the Opium Trade.'

After September, when Delhi was recaptured and 'Havelock's Saints' relieved Lucknow, the situation improved enough for Elgin to return to China, but remained serious until March 1858, four months after he left. It flickered on until the end was declared on December 20, 1858. By then a Royal Proclamation had abolished the East India Company and placed India under the direct rule of the British Government. But before that time China was to suffer yet another thrust of Britain's armed diplomacy.

CHAPTER TWO

'THE COURSE OF TRUE LOVE . . .' 1857–58

Ningbo misnomer *June 1857*

If the responsibility of the city of Ningbo, Peace to the Waves, was to maintain security on the high seas, her task was impossible. On her very doorstep piracy and war between rival pirate gangs went on unchecked. The Manchu government was powerless. Containment of the Taiping, Hakka, Miao, Muslim and Nian-fei rebels tied down all available forces.[1] Policing of the sea by lumbering war junks was futile against the fast *lorcha* wolf-packs of the Portuguese, French and Cantonese. They were left to control each other – except when armed British or American merchantmen (for all had to be well-armed) or warships took a hand.

When Hudson Taylor, John and Mary Jones, the C J Halls, and Miss Magrath travelled from Shanghai in June 1857 the danger from pirates was present whichever route they took. By sea they faced storm and shipwreck as well as the most aggressive pirates. Overland, the way Hudson Taylor preferred for speed and greater economy, robbers on the provincial boundaries and pirate junks (relatively small fry, in the Hangzhou Bay) might be encountered. There is no hint which route they took or what happened next, 'On our way, our Father preserved us from pirates; and here we have been kept in peace, while a war of extermination has been going on . . .'

New excitements banished details of the journey even from Hudson Taylor's letter to his sister. They arrived at Ningbo on June 20 and split up, the Halls and Miss Magrath crowding into the Parkers' home in the fields beyond the foreign settlement, and the Jones family and Hudson Taylor taking over the Russells' old house inside the Chinese city, near the Salt Gate (map, p 22).

No thought of his future lifework as the pioneer leader of hundreds was in Hudson Taylor's mind as he returned to Ningbo, this time to stay. Qualms and confidence jostled uncomfortably for dominance as he contemplated the days ahead. He was content to live a day at a time. He had asked to be allowed to see more of Maria Dyer, to get to know her with a view to marriage, and had had a firm rebuff – and yet, he could not be sure that the careful wording of her refusal did not veil a hidden meaning.

He was not left in doubt for long. His arrival back in Ningbo seemed to trigger off two reactions. The first was not as trivial as it appeared. If he had been on the rack already, that was emotionally nothing in comparison with what he was to suffer now, for the formidable Miss Aldersey declared war on him. It was not that he defied her or that Maria gave her cause for alarm.

> I avoided in every possible way meeting Miss Dyer [he explained] and did not move in the matter at all. I felt the door was shut, and waited hoping the Lord would open it in His own good time. But though I did not move . . . Miss Aldersey did, and this in such a way as to show me where the difficulty lay . . .

And Maria wrote to her aunt, 'I avoided calling at Mrs Jones's and he had too much feeling to intrude himself upon me.'

No sooner had they settled in than Hudson Taylor and John Jones plunged into the work they believed themselves called to do. They planned a short journey into the countryside involving a night or two away and Mary Jones, wanting to take up her visiting of Chinese homes where she had left off, asked Maria to go out with her and to keep her company in the house while the men were away. Maria seems to have agreed and to have mentioned it at home, for in no time Miss Aldersey called on Mary Jones to say that she did not wish Maria to go with her. Moreover as Hudson Taylor put it, she 'informed her of her strong objections to my proposals, and sought a pledge from her, not to promote our meeting'. And Maria told her brother Samuel in a letter, 'It was I believe during this conversation that Mrs – learnt that my rejection of Mr T's proposals was not a voluntary act . . .'

Mary Jones told her husband and Hudson Taylor, who went to the Goughs for advice, only to learn that they were implicated too.

> Miss Aldersey got into a great stew when I came down, went to Mrs Gough's and made her promise not to promote our meetings or help the matter on. Then she came to Mrs. Jones and under fear of being prevented working with dear Maria got her to make a similar

> promise, and wanted her to promise not to tell me anything about it. This she would not do, and told me where the difficulty was.

But choppy water in the missionary teacup was of no account when five days after their return a fleet of Cantonese *lorchas* and armed junks arrived and anchored provocatively near the Portuguese settlement. Following the Portuguese attack on the French and Cantonese convoy-protection vessels in April and their counter-attack at the Chusan (Zhoushan) islands in May, the *daotai* of Ningbo had banned both sides from the Ningbo river for a month. But the Portuguese *lorchas* had encounted a superior force of Cantonese and been swept up the coast. Banking on security at Ningbo they had defied the ban and returned to base at the confluence of tributaries between which the city lay (map, p 22).

With the *daotai*'s connivance the Cantonese had then come up and anchored aggressively close to the Portuguese, the same Cantonese who had plotted the general massacre in January, now reinforced by twenty French, American and British mercenaries.

> Seeing a large number of vessels [John Jones wrote] Mr Taylor and I went on board most of them, giving tracts and speaking of Jesus. We were generally well received and listened to with attention. Our purpose to renew our visit was fearfully frustrated . . .

To allay fears of a general massacre the Cantonese notified the *daotai* and consuls of their intention to avenge the Portuguese killings in the previous fight and with that 'be satisfied', and at noon the next day, Friday, June 26, they attacked. Boarding the Portuguese *lorchas* they killed the crews and followed those who escaped ashore, attacking next the Portuguese settlement. Fleeing Portuguese sought sanctuary at the British and American consulates but were refused admission by T T Meadows, HBM vice-consul (the hero of Taiping reconnaissances) lest a general anti-foreign attack result. Parker and Hall were at a nearby American Presbyterian home when they saw armed Portuguese running across the open land towards their house and families, pursued by Cantonese. They hurried home in time to receive the wounded and to intercept about forty Portuguese calling for protection, but before they agreed the British and American consuls came up, explained their policy of neutrality and insisted that none of their nationals were to become involved. Nothing could be done except to turn the unwounded men away. They fled into the country where the Cantonese butchered half their number. A few reached Shanghai. Others were taken by the French and handed over as criminals to the Portuguese governor of Macao. Between sixty and seventy had died. This all went on outside the city walls while Hudson Taylor and the Jones family were inside.

Two immediate developments of the fracas were to affect the welfare of missions and churches in Ningbo. Dr Parker with Hall assisting him bravely went out among the Cantonese to attend their wounded, and was appalled by the flotsam of half-submerged bodies at the water's edge. And a Shanghai merchant named Winch who happened to be there, went about collecting wounded men and bringing them to Parker. When he later learned that Parker refused remuneration for what he did, Winch asked his consent to raise funds in Shanghai towards the completion of his new hospital on the riverside outside the Salt Gate, and collected over one thousand two hundred dollars.

To the alarm of the foreign residents, however, when the massacre was over and twenty Portuguese *lorchas* had been captured, the bloodthirsty Cantonese remained at Ningbo. They were not to be trusted. Then, fortuitously, on the 27th, a twenty-six-gun French frigate direct from South America happened to put in at Ningbo and forced the Cantonese farther upstream. 'Was ever an arrival more providential?' asked Sir Robert Hart's biographer. But as the Cantonese retreated to the din of gongs and gunfire they came nearer than ever to the city and foreign settlement.

After a few days calm returned, the French frigate left, and soon afterwards the British gunboat *Nimrod* arrived, steamed up past the Cantonese and anchored off the British consulate. If this restored some sense of security it was soon shaken, for a Portuguese force of one brig-of-war, twelve armed *lorchas* and two merchant vessels also arrived with the intention of striking back, retaking their captured *lorchas* and re-establishing their consulate and trade. The Cantonese manned the city wall and mounted guns, and the missions and consulates on the east bank were threatened with involvement in the hostilities. Again the British declared their neutrality. Then posters purporting to represent all the people of Ningbo appeared in various parts of the city calling upon the officials and merchants of Britain, America and France to drive both Portuguese and Cantonese away from where their fighting endangered everyone, to the open sea where they could do their worst. But what began as an appreciative but indignant manifesto ended ominously.

> We were expecting that the fearful work would again begin [John Jones wrote on August 22] and if it had we should have been in considerable danger . . . our houses, especially ours in the city, would have been riddled by the [cannon] balls, (the Cantonese in sport a few days after the massacre put two balls into one of the missionary's [*sic*] homes). The people had put up placards to the effect that they had nothing to do with the quarrel, that we could prevent them being killed . . . and that if we did not they would rise and slaughter us as well.
>
> The Portuguese raised their anchors, and everyone thought they were about to commence the attack, when they quietly dropped down the river . . . People say [they] have left to procure reinforcements, intending to come up 100 vessels strong. We endeavour to live a day by day life. The Cantonese junks lie here. They are as lawless a set as earth can boast. It is the general impression that while the English man-of-war is here, they will not attempt anything . . . But there is a stronger One for us, who can use that vessel or not . . .

The tension continued into October and beyond, for the city of Canton was in the throes of starvation from the British blockade and from assault by the Hakka rebels. Lord Elgin had arrived at Hong Kong with his expeditionary force, and to everyone's amazement departed again to India. Trouble was afoot. Nowhere was the mood of the Cantonese to be trusted.

This was the Ningbo in which Hudson Taylor and John Jones began their 'Ningpo Mission' and Miss Aldersey set out to protect Maria from the suitor of whom she strongly disapproved.

Two interviews[2] *July 1857*

As a type of the Establishment Miss Aldersey was impeccable. A devout Anglican, dedicated, self-sacrificing and ecumenical she gave herself and her independent means impartially to Chinese and fellow-missionaries. To be queen of the foreign community was her right by seniority and character. She had known Maria's father and mother thirty years before and was old enough to be her grandmother. Burella and Maria had been committed to her care and their aunt and uncle, the Tarns, considered her responsible to them for the girls' well-being. While she administered her school of sixty chosen girls, the two sisters did most of the teaching. Until she retired, early in 1857, committing school and Dyer girls to the care of the motherly Mrs Bausum, the three of them lived happily together on terms of loving respect.

Then this apparently feckless youth Taylor arrived. At first the sole representative of his Society, a peculiar trans-denominational innovation, he talked of the impossible, of living beyond the treaty ports, and drifted here and there preaching in the streets and temples. Unordained, unqualified and apparently penniless, he showed all the evidence of eccentricity in dressing and living like a Chinese. Coming and going for no reasons she could understand, he appeared unstable and indecisive into the bargain. Reports had it that he belonged to the new sect, the Plymouth Brethren, and held unorthodox if not unbiblical views on a variety of subjects, not least the ministry. When his colleague Dr Parker arrived and was so commendable from the start, this Mr Taylor continued his fickle ways.

Others in Ningbo shared her disapproval. W A P Martin was prepared to wait and see, but W A Russell, as good as a son-in-law to Miss Aldersey, agreed with her. When therefore she suspected that the impressionable Maria found Hudson Taylor interesting, Miss Aldersey was concerned; and when without more than superficial acquaintance over a few months he had the audacity to propose preliminaries to marriage she was indignant. But that he should return to Ningbo after Maria had had the sense to see wisdom and brush him off, infuriated her. No gentleman would behave like that. Forgetting that Joseph Edkins came and went as before and Robert Hart remained at the consulate, meeting her frequently, she thought Hudson Taylor should stay away. What did he intend? It was up to her to be a parent to the fatherless girl and protect her from this unscrupulous youth and her own vulnerability. She had no doubt what the Dyer parents would have wished her to do if they had been alive, or what Maria's guardians in London would think. She was mistaken.

The news that Mary Jones gave Hudson Taylor after Miss Aldersey's visit set him thinking. Her anxiety and her indignation spoke volumes. Her influence must have prompted Maria's cryptic letter, as he had guessed. Had he offended her by sending his proposal through the Goughs instead of her? He must grasp the nettle, call on her and put it right. He would ask what her objections were and answer them. The massacre was over, *Nimrod* was anchored just beyond the city wall from where he and the Joneses were living (map, p 22), but the Portuguese retaliation was threatening. It would be good if this matter with Miss Aldersey could be cleared up, and he could find the true state of Maria's feelings.

He consulted the Goughs and on July 7 called on the Russells, now in the Cobbolds' house near the North Gate, and asked to see Miss Aldersey who lived with them. She received him politely. No, it was not that the letter had gone through Mr Gough – it was that he had written direct to Maria, a minor, without her permission. Hudson Taylor was stunned. He had blundered badly. Then Miss Aldersey was Maria's guardian still? Not strictly so, she told him, but Maria 'was in *some* measure entrusted to her "charge", that she felt assured that our engagement would not meet with the approbation of Mr. and Mrs. Tarn . . . to whom she had referred the matter.' And because of this, 'she could not approve (or allow – I cannot remember the *word* used) of that for which you might reproach her,' he reported to the Tarns.

Miss Aldersey felt she had a difficult duty to perform and was doing her best. But she was not Maria's guardian after all, and never had been. And since January she had relinquished Maria to Mrs Bausum's protection. What then were the objections which made her intervene so strongly? In courtesy he should have consulted her first. But, he answered, that 'would not have been a proper step before I knew the feelings of the lady herself'. If Maria had been 'disposed to entertain the question' would not that have been the time to consult others? What other objections were there? Miss Aldersey did not think it necessary to tell him. Pressed, she mentioned that he was said to belong to the Plymouth Brethren, and that he disregarded and desecrated the Sabbath; that his 'religious views differed so much from' Maria's.

That was not difficult to answer. He had never belonged to the Plymouth Brethren. In Hull and Tottenham the congregations he joined had never been Plymouth Brethren (*see* Appendix 2). He was a Methodist until the disruption and had been independent as a student and a missionary ever since. As for the 'Sabbath', he preferred to call it the 'Lord's Day', '. . . the day and its duties and privileges I prize and love and respect'. He was aware that among the missionaries in Ningbo there were both strict Sabbatarians and lax – those who taught that rigid observance of a Christian Sabbath was too great a burden to lay upon young converts in a hand-to-mouth secular society. Her expressed objections had been 'founded on erroneous reports'.

What else had she against him? She would not say. Months later he told W A Russell,

> I felt the injustice of this, in that these objections were being sent home, while I was without the means of answering them – nevertheless I did not press for them *at all*, for I know One who *could* take, even as He *has* taken my part.

How then about Maria's letter, did it represent her own feelings? Once more Miss Aldersey 'gave herself away'. She said she had forbidden Maria to write to her guardians for their approval, and the request that Hudson Taylor should not refer to the subject again 'was the result of her dictation'.

That flung the whole question wide open again. Now he believed that Maria's 'No' did cover at least a wish to see more of him. Miss Aldersey was afraid Maria would say 'Yes'. For a week he prayed about what he should do next, and concluded 'that the Lord *had* opened the door for further steps' – first of all to call on Maria and ask her consent to his writing to the Tarns. Then he consulted his 'friends'. Whether the Joneses or Goughs or both is not stated. They agreed with the 'importance and desirability' of an interview with Maria. It was no use asking Miss Aldersey's permission to see Maria, lest the Tarns blame her. 'I therefore took the most open and only remaining step, and one which it seemed to me on account of its openness . . . was unimpeachable – the step of calling on Miss M D *at* (the Ladies House).'

Odd scraps of Maria's engagement diary[3] have been preserved, including jottings on July 13–19:

> July 13 Holidays commenced. Went to Miss A's [at the Russells].
> 14 Union meeting. Returned home. [This was the periodical meeting of all Christians in Ningbo, of all churches, Chinese and foreign.]
> July 15 Took the children on the wall before breakfast, took some to Mrs G's. At the door waiting we . . . received a note: declined the request. Mrs B received the visitor. Talked with Mr and Mrs G. On return home heard what had passed. Thought of writing home . . . Mr and Mrs G came to tea.
> 16 Wrote in the afternoon my letter
> 17 Took 10 children to Mr. Way's. After breakfast B [Burella] brought 10 more. Violent storm. Could not return . . .

Not a word of the Cantonese threat or the reason for taking the schoolgirls across the river to the relatively safe mission compound and school between the British and American consulates.

The interpretation of Maria's cryptic entries is clear from other records. On July 15 Hudson Taylor wrote a brief note to her and took it to the Ladies' House and school where she lived with Mrs Bausum and Burella. Permission to write to her true guardians was all he wanted. When he arrived at the front gate and was admitted to the courtyard, Mrs Bausum, Burella and Maria were about to leave for the Goughs'. The tactful servant showed him indecorously into an adjoining ironing-room while she took the note in, and Maria, hearing his voice, hurried out of the way. This was an all-female establishment. But she was also honour-bound to evade him. When the note was delivered to her with the remark that a foreign gentleman was waiting outside, she scarcely knew what to do. Hudson Taylor's pencilled draft of the note reads,

> My dear Miss Maria,
>
> Last week I had an interview with Miss Aldersey and learned from her that she had written to your guardians on the subject of my letter from Shanghai and that till an answer was received her objections (wh. she wd. not name) cd. not be rem. [removed] and from prayerful consid. [consideration] of that which then occurred, it has appeared to me that a further step might be desirable. Neither am I alone in this opinion, but before taking steps I of course wish to see you upon the subject and most earnestly beg you to grant me an interview of a few minutes – and I may add that the importance and desirability of this is fully agreed in by [those] who have fav[d] me with their prayer and counsel.

Intentionally he did not say what the interview was to be about. He did not know who might read it. Maria told the Tarns,

> I was in a state of great agitation . . . I allowed Mrs Bausum and Burella to read it, and I told Mrs Bausum she should decide . . . whether Mr Taylor and I should have the interview or not. Burella very strongly opposed it, thinking Miss Aldersey would not approve . . .

To Burella 'Miss A' was their 'mother'. So that was that. The two sisters went on to the Goughs while Mrs Bausum stayed to entertain Hudson Taylor.

She invited him to the living quarters upstairs and he found an ally. Mrs Bausum was an unusually fine woman. Uncowed by Miss

Aldersey, she steered a careful course through the next six months of tension, quietly supporting Maria and Hudson Taylor under stress. He told her about his interview with Miss Aldersey and his discovery that although she was not Maria's guardian she had written to the Tarns about him. Before he could write too he needed to know whether his affection for Maria was reciprocated. 'Mrs B. could not deny that it was.'

That confirmed his deductions from Miss A's remarks and Maria's letter of refusal. He was on safe ground at last. How could he obtain Maria's consent to his writing? They left it that Mrs Bausum would talk with Maria about it and ask Miss Aldersey if he might have an interview with Maria in her, Mrs Bausum's, presence. Nothing came of that.

Maria told the Goughs what had happened, but Mary Gough's hands were tied by her pledge to Miss Aldersey. They decided to play their part cautiously. Already Frederick Gough had assured Hudson Taylor, 'Your matter will be breathed to no one here. You have *our* sympathy, and our frequent prayers,' (for he himself had had a similar experience). F F Gough was 'an exemplary Christian, and one of those whom to know is to love and to be loved'.

The next day, July 16, Maria sat down and poured out the whole story to her aunt and uncle, how she had written in April but had not been allowed by Miss Aldersey to send the letter, how she did not know for certain till yesterday that Miss A had written, but 'in compliance with her earnest entreaties I wrote and declined [Mr Taylor's proposals]. This I did in direct opposition to my own feelings –'

She told of how she had been interested in him for nearly a year already. She had prayed that God would restrain her or influence him towards her, so that in his proposals 'I thought I saw the answer to my prayers'. She wished to appreciate Miss Aldersey's opposition but found it very difficult. 'But I think she is mistaken' (in her opinion of him). The opposition did not alter her belief that their friendship was the will of God.

> I think Mr. Taylor has acted in a Christian manner throughout the whole matter. And since his return to Ningpo, now nearly four weeks ago, we have not exchanged a word.
>
> May it not be that [God] is placing this obstacle in the way to try us whether we will trust the matter in His hands, for Him to work it out in His own way? . . . Though I sometimes feel that the greatest earthly pleasure that I desire is to be allowed to love [Mr Taylor] and to hold

> the closest and sweetest intercourse with him spiritually as well as temporally that two fellow mortals can hold, I desire that he may not hold the first place in my affections. I desire that Jesus may be to me the Chiefest among ten thousand, the altogether lovely. And whatever may be your opinion in this matter, will you pray for me that Jesus may be all in all to me.

On July 22 she continued her letter, making no mention of the dangers all round her, for by then there was much more to say. John Burdon had arrived in Ningbo again and Burella was with him. Maria was alone in her room when Mrs Bausum came in and they were able at last to talk freely about Hudson Taylor.

> I asked her to pray with me, which she did very appropriately and we afterwards read the 69th Psalm together [a prayer in distress: Save me, O God; for the waters are come in unto my soul] . . . I knew that Mr. Taylor wished to speak to me, and I wished to have an opportunity of speaking to him. So I prayed that if it was not wrong we might have an interview. [I could easily have arranged it, but] preferred that it should be of God's overruling and not my arranging.

That afternoon the Ladies' Prayer Meeting was held at the Joneses'. Burella was preoccupied so Maria went with Mrs Bausum. Hudson Taylor told the Tarns,

> I thought it undesirable that I should be at home that evening. I therefore expressed my intention to go down to a merchant's residence, some distance outside the city to see about some boxes of testaments just arrived for me from Shanghai. When the evening came on however it rained so heavily as to make the carrying about of books impracticable.

He took his writing materials to the top of the house, intending to stay there until the supper bell rang. But the thought came to his mind, May not this rain have been sent to bring about the meeting I so much need by preventing my going out . . .? It was the last opportunity before the outgoing monthly mail. With a delay of four months before a reply could be received from London, it was almost a case of now or never. So he prayed for an unmistakable indication from God if he 'was to leave the room before Maria went home.'

> Shortly before the meeting closed a British missionary called. I was called down to see him, his stay was short, and thus was brought about the desired interview –

Maria was still there. She told her guardians,

> I was lifting up my heart in prayer just as Mr Jones came into the room, and called me aside. I went with him out of the room, when he said, 'Mr. Taylor begs that you will allow him to have an interview with [you]'. I said, 'It is what I of all things wish . . . Is it to be private or may another person be in the room?' He said, 'It is to be as you wish.'

She asked for Mrs Bausum to be present and they were shown into John Jones' study. After a few moments Hudson Taylor came in. What they felt under the constraint of those circumstances can be imagined. Their accounts are objective. It was the first time they had spoken to each other since the *Japan* sailed in January. He apologised for having caused her so much distress and said his reason for wanting the interview was to ask her consent to write to the Tarns. 'I told him he had it, and that I had already written . . . and was writing again.' More than that, she confessed that when Miss Aldersey compelled her to reject his proposals she suffered 'agony'. There were no two interpretations of that. Maria suggested that they pray together and the three of them knelt while Hudson Taylor prayed.

Aftermath — *July–August 1857*

Although the tension between the Cantonese and the community continued, the letters to the Tarns now mattered most. The lift in Hudson Taylor's spirit is discernible, though the earliest a reply could come would be by the late November mail. Giving an account of all that led up to his return to Ningbo for medical supplies, he told how he met Maria and after Burns' arrest came back again until January, how his proposal was rejected and his suspicions aroused.

> And now, just in time to write for the mail, I know that my love is reciprocated, that her first declining my proposal was compulsory, and I have her full consent . . . to write. Gladly therefore do I commit the matter to Him who has the direction of all events in His hands, and pray that He may guide you to a right decision – and hope you may be led either to sanction our union, or to permit Miss M.D. to act for herself in the matter as the Lord may lead her . . .

Courteously he asked that their decision might be sent direct to Maria and himself as well as to Miss Aldersey, and gave the names of friends who could be consulted as his referees. The Chinese Evangelization Society needed no mention. John Hobson,[4] the

Shanghai chaplain, and Archdeacon R H Cobbold were on leave in England. John Whitworth of Barnsley knew his background. William Burns would be known to them, so he enclosed Burns' last intimate letter as an unpremeditated testimonial. As for his position and circumstances, 'Here I apprehend has been the real cause of objection, viz. that I am not connected with any of the older and more established societies . . .'

Hot on the scent, he had yet to discover the roots of Miss Aldersey's prejudice. He had indeed resigned from the CES, 'as I prefer to preach the Gospel to the heathen without a fixed salary . . .' He could not say more without disloyalty, so he set out his current financial position – enough to wreck his hopes unless the Tarns were very unusual Christians.

> The Lord, through those whose hearts he has inclined to assist me and the work with funds, has richly, – nay bountifully, supplied me with more than I could have desired. But it is not on this I lean – His promise assures me that all my need shall be supplied, and that no good thing will He withhold from me. Resting on this more sure guarantee than any human Society can give, – I *know* that not only temporal means will He supply, but if for our good and His glory, He will remove all the obstacles to my union with Miss M. D., and the promise to supply my need equally hold good as to hers, so there is no room for doubt on that score.

Forsaking the reservations he had named to George Pearse, he had set out the principles, this time going beyond the past and present to profess confidence for the future. Orthodox evangelicals could acknowledge the theological soundness of them and still legitimately hold that God intended them to be fulfilled through conventional means – that to cut yourself off from your organised supporters was hare-brained. In fact, during that July the Joneses' receipts were very low and Hudson Taylor's little better. And news had come that William Berger, his most constant channel of supply, was dangerously ill (with typhus or typhoid)[5]. He does not seem to have been troubled. After the anxiety and distress, his reaction was euphoric. Maria's new happiness justified a long letter and the Tarns' response he could leave with God.

> Her anxious tried look and paleness have pained me exceedingly, but I hope and trust that since the Lord has graciously given us to meet, and know each other's feelings, and together to commit the matter to Him in prayer, that a burden has been taken off her mind, as it has off mine . . .

Love and Miss Aldersey were strong undercurrents, but the tide of life and work flowed on. He was renting the Bridge Street house again as a preaching point and with Jones had his hands full with a tight routine of meetings. A taste of relief work for the destitute in Shanghai had opened their eyes to the needs of the poor in Ningbo, and, appalled by the physical and moral degradation he saw on every hand, Hudson Taylor began helping opium addicts to break their addiction. At last he found that three-foot model pagoda Charles Bird wanted, and purchased it. That he had left the CES made no difference. It could help to arouse interest in China. John Jones baptised the children's *amah* whom they believed to be a sincere Christian, and they were looking for a house in the country where they could establish an outstation.

The Halls had found one room in the Parkers' home too cramped for their needs and were now living with the E C Lords, American Baptists of sterling quality. Miss Magrath, who had never known a day of real illness, was finding the tropical heat and frequent ailments distressing. She removed to the Jones household but before long withdrew to Hong Kong, a casualty.

Parker's dispensary and hospital were never large enough. Each bed had several patients waiting to enter it, and urgent cases were admitted to mattresses on the floor. Hudson Taylor, John Nevius, Frederick Gough and Chinese Christians preached to the patients. Steadily the congregations served by each mission were growing. But Hudson Taylor and John Jones had nothing to show for all their effort.

He finished his letter to the Tarns, and sent it through his mother by expensive express mail via Trieste, to inform her belatedly of what was going on. A copy he sent round to Maria with a leaflet about Jesus walking on the water to the disciples in a storm. 'It is I; be not afraid', and with new liberty his covering note began 'Monday morning. Dearest Maria,' – at last.

After their interview at the Joneses', Maria wrote a second letter to her aunt and uncle, filling in the story now that she knew a little of Hudson Taylor's side from him and Mrs Bausum. And on July 27 and 29, before the mail left, she added the latest developments. Miss Aldersey was up in arms. Another screed had to be written to her brother. He was the only one to whom she could pour it all out. Samuel had said in his latest letter, after hearing of Burella's engagement to John Burdon, 'I suppose at some future period, we shall have an account of how Miss M.J.D. and a certain Mr Blank met and loved and – all the rest of it?' Maria wrote,

> When your letter arrived I was in the midst of writing to Aunt and Uncle about my love affairs . . . Last Autumn I met a gentleman, and, I cannot say I loved him at once but . . . I could not forget him . . . he was very unobtrusive and never made any advances. I took the matter from the very first to my God . . .

and away she went, leaving little unsaid about her woes and hopes.

But such letters took days to write, and nothing stood still in Ningbo. From a note by Mary Gough to Maria on 'Saturday mor[g] 25th', it appears that Maria told the Goughs about her interview with Hudson Taylor and their intention not to tell Miss Aldersey or Burella what had happened, for Mary wrote,

> In thinking over the matter of which we spoke last evening, I am more and more convinced, that *concealment* is undesirable; and I would suggest that you consult with Mrs Bausum whether it would not be best for you to tell both Miss Aldersey and your sister the present state of affairs, both as regards your unpremeditated interview, and the fact of your having written home. You know dearest we never really lose by straightforwardness and I think to keep them in ignorance of the steps you have taken will only add to the difficulty by and bye. I am strengthened in my opinion by the circumstances of your sister expressing to me last evening her surprise at the *first* interview being attempted. Fearful, lest she should allude to anything since, I turned the conversation . . . and so avoided saying one word to arouse her suspicions. I will indeed pray for you that light may be given . . .

Whether Maria told Burella as messenger to Miss Aldersey or word reached them another way, Maria was in trouble. She had to go and explain. Concerned to save her from a serious mistake, Miss Aldersey could see only false motives in Hudson Taylor and her. Innocently Maria told her that she had been praying for a chance to talk with him – and was in fact praying about it when Mr Jones asked for a word with her. Miss Aldersey saw red. That was 'cant learned from my new friends'. Since making these friendships she was estranged, Miss Aldersey protested, from those closest to her. Maria was distressed. 'How could she be in the wrong and I in the right?' she asked Samuel. That was how it appeared. And yet 'I must allow no one's judgement to come between me and my God.'

The heat of the summer and hot tempers are traditionally related. It was on July 26 that the emperor came into the open backing Commissioner Ye's militant stance. On July 27 Miss Aldersey wrote bluntly to Hudson Taylor. The harmony characteristic of missionary relations in Ningbo was to be rudely shattered for a few months.

> Sir, when you favoured me with a call you remarked . . . that you were not aware . . . that [Miss M D] was a minor . . . however you might be at a loss to know the right course of action through want of information as to the proprieties which obtain at home, but now Sir you have placed yourself in a very different position with respect to my estimate of your character as a *man* and still more as a *Christian* for, when you *did* know from me that Miss M.D. was a minor, you went to [the Ladies' House] determining if possible to take advantage of her youth to induce her to trample on the prohibition which had been laid upon her . . . The interview . . . prevented, you have subsequently had recourse to an expedient which I can regard in no other light than as *disgraceful*. In the absence of myself or of the elder sister you have availed yourself of a meeting concerned exclusively for religious exercises . . . to obtrude upon Miss M.D. the forbidden subject. While I am astonished at the offensive indecorum of this last step, it (with all other like acts) makes my path of duty more clear with reference to your proposals; and I now beg to say that if you persist in continuing your addresses, not awaiting the permission of Miss M.D.'s aunt I shall be constrained to take steps of a more formidable character than you are prepared to meet. . . . I think I may without hesitation say that no mere worldling *if a gentleman* would have wronged Miss M.D. and myself in the character of her protectress as you have done. . . . It was surely a bad thing that a person calling himself a missionary should be found industrious as you Sir are in endeavouring to lead the daughter of deceased missionaries to take a step which all who know them must know would be displeasing to them! I am Sir yours faithfully . . .[6]

Piqued that he should have proposed without asking her permission, despising him for what she thought he was, now she thought he had cornered Maria on her own, and was implying that it was immoral of him to do so. If she did not apply to the consul for an injunction to restrain him, she would remove Maria from the school and keep her under observation, incommunicado. That would be a public scandal and disgrace him as he deserved.

W A Russell took the note to Hudson Taylor and championed her cause. It was *immodest* of Maria to give him an 'interview', he said. But Mrs Bausum was present! Taylor protested. Then Mrs Bausum was guilty of impropriety in permitting it.

Afterwards he showed Miss Aldersey's note to John and Mary Jones.

> . . . it so pained dear Mrs Jones to see *me* so spoken of, and treated [Hudson Taylor commented] and to see the unkind and unchristian spirit manifested by Miss A. that she looked quite ill and soon had a return of haemorrhage from the lungs, rather violent . . . It is consumption.

He also passed the note to Maria, so that she might be prepared for strong action.[7]

Maria was fond of Miss Aldersey and knew how hard she found it to accept opposition. But such a tirade was too much.

> I think Miss Aldersey has acted without proper information [she told the Tarns. She seems] to think I should be 'throwing myself away' by marrying Mr T. I desire his character and principles to be sifted. And if they can bear an unprejudiced scrutiny – has Miss Aldersey, or Burella, or have I any right to trifle with his feelings and my own?

Mrs Bausum also found herself in a difficult position, unable to act for or against either side until better informed. So she called on Hudson Taylor and asked him to explain his beliefs, opinions and actions. He did so to her satisfaction. In Maria's words to the Tarns, from him she went to F F Gough,

> a Church Missionary, beloved and respected by all who know him, and most beloved and most respected by those who know him most intimately – and obtained a most satisfactory account of Mr Taylor's Christian life and principles. . . . While she was gone out I prayed that she might find out the truth with regard to Mr. Taylor . . . I will ask you not to act either for or against Mr. Taylor until . . . you have examined his character as a Christian and a gentleman and his principles.

There were however some other factors John Burdon said she should consider – as Maria put it,

> I was informed that [Mr Russell] said to Mr. Taylor that if he would go home to England and take a medical degree, or be ordained *they would all take him by the hand.*

Hudson Taylor himself gave William Berger at his request this statement,

> It was said to me that if I would go to England and get a Medical title, or take a Clerical one, all opposition would cease and every aid be afforded me, – even pecuniary aid was offered if needed.

John Burdon wrote,

> But does my sister [Maria] think it right that a man should ask her hand in marriage before he has an acknowledged position either in one way or another, or with one who has so little decision of character as to be unable to join himself with any single body of Christians? I would waive every other point but this.

That it could take greater strength of character to reserve judgment on the denominations, to deviate from convention and to be wholly ecumenical he appeared not to consider. In his hearing Hudson Taylor had remarked on the discrimination he faced in Shanghai through not being ordained or medically qualified and at the time was considering going home to 'remove his anomalous position'.

> *Now,* [Burdon went on] I think his affection for you is another call to him to pursue this course and if he is unwilling for your sake to do it, I would think him unworthy of your heart and hand. Both of you are young yet . . . If Mr. Taylor did this I would respect him as a man of decision and steadiness of purpose, as I now love him as a Christian Brother.

So position, title and income would make the difference where suitability on other grounds was conceded. And an interval of two or three years and eighteen thousand miles might give time for clearer thinking. Maria's reaction was on a different plane. If Hudson Taylor were to go home for a diploma or the title of Reverend to increase his usefulness, she hoped she would have the grace and strength to give him up for a time.

> But if he is to leave his missionary work and spend time and money that ought to be given to his Master, in order to gain a *name* for the sake of marrying me, I do say that I do not want him to love me more than Jesus. . . . if he were to leave the Lord's work for the *world's* honor, I would have nothing further to do with him.

If she were to marry an unordained missionary, Maria went on, she would not be acting differently from her own mother,

> and if I may have an unordained missionary as a *brother*, why may I not as a husband? [Her brother Samuel was in training at the time.]

> Mr Taylor was set apart by a body of Christian ministers, but he requested that it might not be called an 'ordination' but a 'recognition' service . . . he had seen ordination so much abused.

– he was set apart, ordained by God, that is, apart from any human ceremony or title. Miss A had said, 'I do not think that Mr. T. without education and without position as he is . . .' was a worthy suitor. Now Maria replied,

> Mr. Taylor had a medical education of five years and wanted only six months more when he might have taken his diploma. But the Society thought that the call to China was of more importance . . . Our own Father had he completed one more term might have obtained a Scholarship, but his view of the importance of missionary work led him to renounce his legal studies . . . It has seemed to me that Mr. T. is just such a person as my dear Father were he living would approve for me. The very fact of his being esteemed and loved by Mr. Gough . . . is in itself a recommendation . . .

Hudson Taylor's own comment was similar.

> Of course my own reply was that God had sent me and was blessing me in my work, and I could not and would not leave it till *He* taught me to do so.

Miss Aldersey might hear from the Tarns in August. Maria's letter to her guardians might bring her an answer at the end of October. Hudson Taylor could not hope for anything before mid-November and more likely December. But Maria would come of age on January 16, 1858. Nothing would make much difference, except an immediate approval of marriage, and of meeting enough to know each other better before then. But ironically, on the day Miss Aldersey penned her tirade against Hudson Taylor, Mrs Tarn, still in ignorance of it all, was writing to Burella and Maria protesting that Miss Aldersey had passed them on to the care of Mrs Bausum without consulting her; that Miss Aldersey in fact was responsible until released, but no longer had authority over Maria.

Hot summer — *August–October 1857*

The summer heat made cool tempers all the harder to preserve but Hudson Taylor was finding this summer in Ningbo easier to endure than the previous two for a hypothetical reason – 'this I partly attribute to my regularly using a little pale ale'. But each day's very full routine of work at the Bridge Street preaching hall involved him personally, for John Jones was still unable to speak Chinese fluently enough. So again Hudson Taylor had to admit, 'After all is over – I am spent.'

He listed his day's activities for his mother: One hour, private devotions; 7.45 family prayers in English; 8.00 breakfast; 8.30 Chinese prayers – open to neighbours passing by; read and expound 20–30 verses of Scripture; 12.00 lunch and preparation for going out; 1.30 preach in street chapel; 4.00 dinner; 5–7.30 English meetings 5 days a week; 8.00 tea; 8.30–9.30 Chinese meeting with preaching to 30–50; after this perhaps a family hymn, private devotions. So by then he was too tired to write. To Mr Berger he added,

> Our public services, three times a day are generally attended by some who are interested . . . passers by come in and go out . . . ask questions and offer objections . . . We trust to *see* fruit, and believe that the day of Christ will reveal many cases where the good seed has borne fruit to the glory of God . . .

They were still hoping to open a preaching place in the country and sometimes went out prospecting together. From a hill behind a large temple, 'an excellent place for mission work', they saw two large and fertile valleys full of villages within a convenient distance. Pilgrims on their knees, knocking their heads on the ground at every third step, moved them to pity. 'When I learn the price they are willing to give in order to lay up for themselves treasure in heaven, I am ashamed,' Jones wrote.

The Shanghai cobbler's boy Tianxi was still wholly dependent on them and they were helping destitute people, but their practice was to preserve the dignity of the recipients by finding some kind of work for which to pay them. A country teacher who could not pay his way home after an illness they took into their own home while he wrote Scripture posters in large characters. When not working he read avidly and amazed them with his perception. On the flyleaf of the New Testament they gave him he wrote, 'The most precious and complete record of the saving of the world, and of the words spoken from heaven by the LORD CHRIST JESUS, THE SON OF GOD', with a confession of his own faith. Of the death of Jesus, 'Jesus is dead! Then my heart has peace . . .' At last they were seeing results from their spiritual work. It was a spiritual war that they were engaged in and Hudson Taylor saw the trouble over Maria as part of it.

His August home-letter threw more light on his circumstances. Since Mary Jones's smallpox his mother had been corresponding with Mary's sister, Miss Young, and this delighted him,

> because we here all love one another so. We feel we are the Lord's and all we have and are is His too, and so we do not consider this mine and that yours, but hold all things in common . . . God has greatly blessed me with peace and means since leaving the Society. Last mail brought me £50 from Mr Berger, this £40 from Geo. Müller . . . dear Mr. Berger has been at the point of death from typhus fever . . . and his recovery . . . was by no means confidently expected when I heard last.

To William Berger himself Hudson Taylor wrote with that touch of sincerity, affection and spiritual fellowship which made his friends feel at home with him. Of the fifty pounds he said,

> It came at a very opportune time, and we received it as an answer to prayer, and a proof of the watchful care of our heavenly Father, who both knows *what* we need and *when* we need . . . He sent the supply a short time before it was needed, but the discounting of the bill occupying a few days, the *money* came to hand just in time, so in it we saw *His* wisdom and foresight and love, as well as your Christian affection . . . these little things . . . will interest you and show you how in a time of great trial (arising through entirely different circumstances) the Lord has been showing us His love, and strengthening our faith in Himself.

They had the words EBENEZER – 'Hitherto hath the Lord helped us' – and JEHOVAH JIREH – 'the Lord will provide' – written out in Chinese and hung in their preaching hall to temper their own faith and testify to all who saw them and enquired the meaning. The reality of their faith was not lost on the Chinese who so closely observed their daily lives. Hudson Taylor wrote again of one and another Chinese showing considerable interest in the gospel, and of his going downstairs after all the household had retired to bed and finding one of the servants on his knees praying.

Towards the end of August the long-continued heat was wearing them all down. John Jones, never well, told George Pearse, 'We have learned to consider it a great blessing to be no worse than usual.' Dr Parker wrote of being exhausted, and of having paroxysms of intermittent fever, fortunately at night so that his hospital work by day was not interrupted. Greatly increased numbers of patients were keeping him at full stretch. And (to read between the lines) he was anxious for all the foreigners after what he had seen of the Cantonese butchery. Britain's blockade of Canton could have serious repercussions.

Hudson Taylor succumbed at last with prickly heat so extensive and infected that Parker ordered him to stop work and stay on his bed. In such heat there was no such thing as 'in' bed. He obeyed spasmodically, but Jones was not fit enough to carry the load. Both he and Mary had acquired a skin disease which was to deprive them of sleep and comfort for more than a year. And their youngest child nearly died of dysentery. So Hudson Taylor carried on in spite of being 'confined to the house', (taking meetings, running a dispensary at the Bridge Street house, visiting patients in their homes, sometimes four or five times in a day and out in the country), although through September and into October, while Miss Aldersey and Russell intensified their opposition, his whole body was 'more or less covered with an eruption' of 'eczema' and boils. The whole community suffered in one way or another. Maria's illness was brief. But October was to become the month of extreme suffering and deaths.

The long wait — *August–October 1857*

External tensions and discomforts could be taken as they came; as the summer progressed Miss Aldersey's sense of duty remained strong. Through W A Russell she asked of Hudson Taylor a pledge that he would not meet or speak with Maria until her guardian's permission was received. And to Maria she wrote a letter (not preserved) which plunged her into tears, and by repeated rebukes increased her misery. Hudson Taylor learned from her what was happening.

> I was not a little tried [he wrote] by the strange and groundless accusations brought against me, in order to alienate the affection of Miss Dyer from me. Want of position – medical or clerical, disease – moral, physical and mental and I know not how many other things were said against me.

But Maria herself was not spared. He told his mother,

> Dear Maria is charged with also being a maniac, being fanatical, being indecent, weak-minded, too easily swayed; too obstinate, and everything else bad for preferring the counsel of the Lord and seeking to do His will, and being willing to throw herself away on one

> who is neither ordained nor a fully qualified medical practitioner. One day we are so much alike in our views and feelings that we are not fit to be united – the next so very diverse our union could not be happy.

Maria told her brother enigmatically,

> my Christian character has been impeached and my trust in God has been spoke of as 'fervors' for which perhaps others were praising me . . . Mr. Taylor is short – wears the Chinese dress and has been connected with a missionary who holds some strange and peculiar views – which views he is supposed entirely to concur with. [Only Gutzlaff fills the bill.] But the mind's the stature of the man and his intellectual capacities are by no means of an inferior nature.

Hudson Taylor was at the Goughs when Russell told him that the pledge Miss Aldersey was expecting in writing was 'neither to communicate with Miss M.D. personally in writing or thro' a friend . . .' He promised to consider doing so but gave no undertaking, and Frederick Gough said he in the same situation would be very careful as to what pledges he gave, in view of Miss Aldersey's expressed intention 'to leave no stone unturned to hinder or oppose our union'.

In spite of everything, Hudson Taylor was trying to understand Miss Aldersey's situation. If she felt responsible to the Tarns and disapproved of him, it was a heavy load for her to bear. There was a good deal to be said, he told his parents, in excuse for an old lady of sixty with a failing memory, who had always ruled supreme over a large establishment and been spoiled by the deference and flattery shown to her. She could brook no contradiction, so her chagrin over resistance by Maria and himself was understandable. And her religious background was very different. She could not understand their belief in prayer and trust in God over everyday affairs. Her yardstick was that of the Establishment and his the product of his pietist family and friends. That the Goughs, the Joneses and Mrs Bausum were among the latter puzzled and displeased her.

Gough and Jones were, as Hudson Taylor put it in his voluble home-letter in August, the 'only two Englishmen here who are Gentlemen . . . by birth and manners'. Gough, the double honours graduate of Cambridge and scholar of St John's, was a saint with a pastoral gift. 'I feel he has been like a brother to me,' Maria told Samuel. Twice he had knelt with her and Mrs Bausum to pray over these problems they brought to him.

'Satan is opposing, the world is despising, the worldly-minded among the Lord's redeemed people are alas too much in the same mind,' Hudson Taylor wrote cryptically to George Pearse. And to his mother, 'we shall have to be very cautious to avoid a disturbance.' They were not cautious enough.

While John Jones and C J Hall were writing at length about the comings and goings of murderous pirates and ships-of-war, Hudson Taylor was giving them scarcely a thought. And Maria, continuing her little diary, from August 16 for a few weeks, was as silent. She had a new chapter to record in her stormy love story. With the help of the other records, her entries tell their own tale. Failing to obtain a pledge from Hudson Taylor, Miss Aldersey turned to Maria.

August 16	. . . Miss A wanted to walk home with me. I stayed there to tea instead. Painful conversation. Miss A required the promise of me.
17	Breakfasted at Mrs Gough's. Told my errand . . . Mr G called upon Miss A. Result did not speak to Mr. T. I began a letter to U & A [uncle and aunt].
18	Received a note from Mrs Gough. Went there with the [Bausum] children. Heard particulars of Mr G's visit . . .
20	Miss A. watched me again. At dinner time Mr. E [Edkins] called and brought me some Chinese books. . . . Miss A. called.
21	Burella and the [Bausum] children and school children left city. [The school had now completely moved across the river to the American compound.]
22	Afternoon Mr. Edkins called and walked with us to the Pr. M. [Prayer Meeting] . . . Stayed to tea at Mrs G's. Mr. E came to tea and walked home with us.
Sunday 23	. . . An evening of Consolation. Mrs. G walked home with me after Miss A's request.
25	. . . heard that the landlord would take possession today. Hastened our moving . . . Slept at Mrs G's. Mrs. J sent us some dinner.
26	. . . After dinner found it necessary to go to Mrs G's. Cld. not go to Pr. M. Wrote my letter. Slept at Mrs G's. [One of the most tearful occasions.]
27	. . . Left the city as a residence.
31	Began school again. [Now living and teaching at the American school on the north bank,]
Sun. Sept. 20	After morning service . . . I handed Miss A my note . . .

. . . Borrowed . . . book on Solomon's Song . . .

21 . . . Evening company [with two lieutenants from *Hornet*].

28 'If God be for us who can be against us?' Letter from Samuel, also from Miss A.

It appears that Maria had returned home without giving the required pledge of silence, but after talking with the Goughs agreed to comply, and Mr Gough went to inform Miss Aldersey. Weeks of mental suffering and increasing tension then tortured Hudson and Maria. With Miss Aldersey watching her and sending notes of rebuke, Maria felt persecuted by what he called 'cruel and tyrannical treatment'. Years afterwards Mary Bausum, one of the children, recalled her impression that Maria was constantly unhappy and often in tears.

The Goughs did all they could to comfort Hudson and Maria. But so soon after declaring their love and without ever having been alone for a moment together, inevitably the strain was telling on them. They avoided even seeing each other for a month and both found comfort in the fervid 'Song of Songs'. Maria apologised to Miss Aldersey for allowing herself to become estranged from her but it was more than she could stand. To kiss her when they met smacked of hypocrisy but when she shook hands another storm broke over her.

The unfairness of this battering added insult to injury, but Maria tried again and October 3 declared her intention to restrain her natural feelings.

> I hope and pray that the time may yet come when your heart and mine may be united in intenser affection than ever they were, – when I may again enjoy your esteem as well as your love. I shall rejoice when my motives and my conduct are explained . . .

But her letter was returned with another from Miss Aldersey.

> I require of you . . . the following apology,
>
> 'Miss Aldersey I have erred in my conduct towards you, *and* I am sorry for it' or 'I ask your forgiveness'.

For full measure Maria combined the confession, apology and plea for forgiveness after 'My dear Miss Aldersey' – and it was accepted. Probably no one knew that Mrs Bausum wrote to Mrs Tarn in Maria's favour, a letter that confirmed her aunt's deductions, but it did not reach her until the Tarns had made their own enquiries and written to Miss Aldersey and to Maria.

Death of John Quarterman *October 1857*

During the first week of October John Quarterman, still unmarried, was ill with 'intermittent fever' and on the 8th Dr Parker diagnosed confluent smallpox, a particularly virulent form. Quarterman's sister, Mrs Way, had to think of her children and could not care for him. Her husband was away from Ningbo. So John Nevius, a fellow-American Presbyterian, stepped in and nursed him for a few days. When Hudson Taylor heard of it he offered to take over, pleading the protection of his vaccination. Recalling the time, Helen Nevius, still away on sick leave, described how Hudson Taylor 'the strong, gentle, quiet young man', 'headlong' in love with 'my dear friend Maria Dyer', took John Nevius' place.

> No words can express my gratitude to him for his kindness in relieving my husband from his disagreeable and also very dangerous task. How well it illustrated his beautiful unselfishness!

And one of the children, Georgia Way, remembered how Hudson Taylor, who was often in their home, came to the rescue in this 'very alarming' situation. He 'cut himself off from everyone and devoted himself to the care of' the patient in isolation. There was no hope of John Quarterman's recovery and Hudson Taylor could only ease his suffering and help him to face death by anticipation of 'the joy that was set before him'. So,

> before his death, Mr. Taylor would repeat from 1 Corinthians 15.53 'For this corruptible must put on incorruption' – Mr. Q would add, 'this mortal must put on immortality' – and so to the end.

After four days John Quarterman died, to Dr Parker's grief, for he was 'one of [the Lord's] most diligent and devoted servants . . . regular and zealous in his work'. Almost daily he had preached to the dispensary patients and spent hours in the wards. After dinner he would go into the city for two or three more hours 'sitting in his chapel pleading with sinners to turn from their sin'. Hudson wrote to Amelia, 'He has been taken home to Jesus and sweet was his end and great my privilege in being permitted to minister to Jesus in his person and see the *power* of grace exemplified' – as if Jesus were the patient. But William Parker's love for John Quarterman did not stop there. He cared for the bereaved Way family so affectionately that another sister writing from the States thanked him specially for this, as much as for jeopardising his own life for her brother, before Nevius and then Hudson Taylor took over.

Maria noted his death in her diary, starting again on October 13 to make the entry, without a mention of Hudson Taylor. A meeting of all the Chinese and foreign Christians was called at once and addressed by John Nevius. The next day Maria simply wrote, 'Followed Mr Q's remains.' The memorial service was on October 16. But two days later Maria's distress found expression in one of her longest entries, apparently completed later,

> Oct. 18 '*Let my prayer come before thee.*' Supplicating prayer on behalf of G B [George Bausum] L J [Louisa Jones, the youngest] and another individual. The first two were sick and I feared the latter might be so or might be taken sick shortly. My fears were not groundless . . . [he] was sick at the time. All three prayers were answered . . .
>
> 20 Heard of –'s sickness . . . Miss A called.

When John Quarterman died and Hudson Taylor had finished preparing his body for burial and cleared up, all the clothes he himself was using had also to be burned. But at that time his cash in hand had sunk very low and he could not replace them.

> . . . prayer was the only resource. The Lord answered it by the unexpected arrival of a long-lost box of clothing from Swatow . . . [it] brought a sweet sense of the Father's own providing.

But hardly had the shock of John Quarterman's death been accepted by the community than Hudson Taylor himself went down with a high fever.

> . . . When all was over I was very exhausted . . . and I had absorbed a good deal of the poison . . . and tho' I believe I have not been delirious I have been very much excited from the fever [he wrote for Amelia in pencil on flimsy Chinese grass-paper on October 20.] This morning at 3 am I heard a voice which awoke me and caused me to get up very much alarmed – you will judge of the state of my nervous system when I tell you I could not bear the sound of my watch lying at the other end of the room and had to have it wrapped up.

He could not get to sleep so he read his Bible for a while and then lay down again,

> but [with] my heart fluttering like a frightened bird, and my mind too excited to sleep. All at once I became conscious of the presence of Dear Maria. She came in noiselessly as a breath of air and I felt such a tranquillity steal over me – I knew she must be there. I felt spellbound for a short time, but at length without opening my eyes I put out my hand, and she took it so tenderly and with such a soft warm grasp, that I could not refrain from a look of gratitude. She motioned to me not to speak and put her other hand on my forehead and I felt the headache which was distracting and the fever retire before it and sink as thro' the pillow. She whispered softly to me not to fear nor be uneasy, she was my Maria and I her dear Hudson, but to keep tranquil and try to sleep, and so I did and awoke in the morning at 8 pm [*sic*] well of the fever, but very weak. It was a sweet dream, (I would call it, but I was as wide awake then as I am now, and saw and felt her plainly as I do pencil and paper), and all my fear in the fever had been that our love would be in vain and not come to anything so you may guess how it soothed me. It would have been a severe case of smallpox, had not God, through the protection of my previous vaccination preserved me . . . Dr. Parker has been very attentive and kind and the dear Jones, and more than ever endeared themselves to me by their love and care. Mr. Burdon is here. He is to marry Miss Dyer Nov 10th (D V) I wish it was over and they returned, as she is very much opposed to her sister's union with me . . . Pray that He who guides all affairs, from those of an animalcule to those of a system of stars, may remove all obstacles and give us a speedy and happy union, and bless it greatly.[8]

After such feverish excitability a quiet convalescence would have been appropriate, but irrepressibly Hudson Taylor tried to return to normal life. On October 22 Maria's diary read, 'To my surprise saw – after service.' But he was at the end of his tether. That night he poured out his woes to his mother.

> My own dear, precious Mother,
>
> . . . Would that this night I could intermingle my tears with yours . . . You will . . . perhaps think me foolish when you learn that the cause of my trouble is Dear Maria's being about to proceed to Shanghai for a month with her sister . . . But I know they *hope* to keep her longer and that thus the affair may be kept in abeyance or broken off . . . it is not *safe* travelling between Ningpo and Shanghai from pirates and once there, it may be months ere there is an opportunity of returning, for a single lady cannot travel about on boats with only one or two Englishmen whose lives are worse than beasts. If I could but have an interview with her – but how I know not – she is watched like I know not what. God can give me one however, if it is His will. May He do so, if not contrary to His mind.

He had to return to bed. But the baptism of the first male convert had been arranged. Ni Yong-fa was the leader of a reformed Buddhist sect which shunned idolatry and was searching for truth. One evening when Hudson Taylor was preaching 'the glad tidings of salvation through the finished work of Christ' this middle-aged man stood up and addressed the audience.

> I have long sought for the truth – as my father did before me [he declared]. I have travelled far, but I have not found it. I found no rest in Confucianism, Buddhism, Taoism, but I do find rest in what I have heard tonight. Henceforth I believe in Jesus.

Soon Ni took Hudson Taylor along to a meeting of the sect and told them about the peace he had found, with the result that another member too was converted and baptised. How long, Ni asked, had the gospel been known in England? For hundreds of years, Taylor answered.

> What! [Ni exclaimed] and [you] have only now come to preach [it] to us? My father sought after the truth for more than twenty years and died without finding it. Why did you not come sooner?

So for this man's baptism Hudson Taylor left his sick-bed and on the 25th preached for one hour. 'I was so exhausted that I could do nothing till Thursday.'

Chance meeting[9] *October–November 1857*

He was distraught. He lay thinking about Maria. The scheme to take her to Shanghai was proceeding. He had to consult Mrs Bausum about it. Maria must be warned not to go. It was an opportune time to visit Mrs Bausum at the American compound because Maria was at the Russells' keeping Burella company until her wedding. He knew that she would be there until mid-November. But his plan miscarried.

On Friday, October 30, Miss Aldersey escorted Maria to Mrs Bausum's and returned home. So when Hudson Taylor presented himself at the door and said that he supposed he could call without fear of doing the wrong thing, to his surprise Mrs Bausum replied, 'No you cannot for Miss Maria is now in the house.' But she invited him in, showed him into the sitting room and asked him to wait while she warned Maria not to come downstairs.

This looked too much like the heaven-sent opportunity that he had been praying for. He begged to be allowed to see her, but 'for fear of a row' Mrs Bausum was adamant and left the room. 'Scarcely had she gone when by another door dear Maria entered and so I got my interview.' Maria's diary simply said in her laconic style, 'Miss A went with me to Mrs B's. Going through the Sitting room to the Dining room most unexpectedly saw a visitor. Mrs B went to Miss A's.'

The inevitable repercussions followed and Hudson Taylor's statement refuting an accusation of deliberate deception ran, 'At that moment by another door Miss Maria entered the room and was no less surprised to see me seated there, than I was to see her.'

They were scarcely over their surprise and greeting when Mrs Bausum returned and recognised the fortuitous nature of their meeting. In her presence Hudson Taylor told Maria of the plan to take her away, and she said she knew and was determined not to go. They talked briefly together and Mrs Bausum then 'thought it might be well to prevent annoyance, to acquaint Miss A, with the circumstances of the call, an opinion with which I entirely concurred'. Mrs Bausum gave her own reason for telling Miss Aldersey as being to 'prevent any distorted accounts reaching her ears and to show her that the interview was entirely unpremeditated'. So for the moment that was that. 'It has helped me, you don't know how much better I feel for it,' he told Amelia. The Parkers invited him to their home for a few days of convalescence and then he was back with John and Mary Jones in the thick of their work.

For Maria it was more difficult. During the next few days she was having 'conversations' with John Burdon, Burella, Miss Aldersey, Mrs Bausum and Mrs Gough. Determined to get her out of Ningbo the opposition wanted her to go first to the CMS outstation in the country until she left with John and Burella for Shanghai after their honeymoon. She refused, but made preparations in case it should be forced upon her, underlining in her diary the printed words, 'Trust in Him at all times', and 'In Me is thine help'.

But they were also hoping William Aitchison would court her. He and John Burdon had succeeded in occupying Pinghu, just across the bay, and could often come over to Ningbo. Hudson Taylor wrote, 'I was told by several persons that another Gentleman was much smitten . . . one whom I looked on with great respect and love in the Lord . . .' If he had been allowed to have open dealings with Maria, he said to himself, poor Aitchison would not have come 'to cherish feelings which I knew must be disappointed'. Aitchison was staying with the Ways, so Hudson Taylor called on Mr Way 'and found he had been misled and given to understand we were not and not likely to be engaged . . .' So he explained that they were waiting for a reply from Maria's guardians and considered themselves conditionally betrothed already.

About this time a Dutchman named Gaillard came down to Ningbo, and Hudson Taylor welcomed him to stay at the Bridge Street house with him. To his amazement this gentleman confided that he had written to two ladies in Holland and Germany proposing marriage, but the charms of Miss M Dyer so attracted him that he would in preference try to win her. 'Inwardly furious', as he put it, Hudson Taylor simply asked the Dutchman, 'What would you do if all three accepted?' In fact they all declined.

It was an increasingly unsatisfactory situation to be in. Gruesome news from the mutiny in India and disturbing news of growing antagonism to foreign interference in China made the future more than uncertain. Some expected all missionaries to be forced to leave the country. If the worst came to the worst, for Hudson Taylor and Maria not even to have their relationship recognised – let alone to be formally engaged – would create new problems. Within the month the Tarns' reply to Maria's first letter could be expected. But Hudson Taylor was worried about Aitchison. 'I had no doubt of dear Maria's constancy', but the enforced secrecy was not fair on Aitchison or anyone. So he took the matter into his own hands. He contemplated a legal engagement formally announced, and that without delay. But how to discuss it with Maria he could not see.

Elgin's stained credentials[10] *July 1857–Spring 1858*

At Canton the British blockade, begun early in 1857 against all shipping, continued. But China was growing desperate. Conditions in Canton were intolerable. With the rebels holding the countryside the blockaded river approach remained her only hope of supply. Daring junks broke through. Some were gun-running. In September the *North China Herald* reported the interception of fourteen merchant junks and eleven salt junks. And, up-river, two hundred war junks were under construction.

Sir John Bowring and Sir Michael Seymour still imagined that Commissioner Ye at Canton was keeping the Peking Court in the dark and acting alone, because of silence for nine months from Peking about the south. He had been degraded in rank 'for not controlling the Cantonese' but left in office. It was a mere rap on the knuckles. Suddenly to their great surprise the *Peking Gazette* broke silence. On July 26 the emperor openly backed Ye, restoring his high honours, approving his strong action, urging preparations for war, and authorising him to appropriate 600,000 taels from Customs and Salt revenue. But the Court was making a fatal mistake. In spite of the 1840–42 war it continued to treat the affair as locally confined to Cantonese waters. Peace reigned in other ports but trade was stagnating, the *Overseas China Mail* declared.

In Peking the Xian Feng (Hsien Feng) emperor, the dissolute young weakling, had at his side an innocuous empress but also a dynamic concubine, known by her Manchu name, Yehonala. At twenty-one Yehonala was already the most influential person in the empire, and destined to become the notorious Empress Dowager Cixi (Ts'u Hsi).[11] Back in 1850 when the Dao Guang emperor had died, a legendary tale of court intrigue with all the high drama of fiction had begun to be enacted in real life and history. The heir to the dragon throne, Xian Feng, had needed a consort and from among hundreds of potential wives and concubines, the daughters of Manchu nobility throughout the empire, sixteen or seventeen were chosen. Of these, two received the 'yellow invitation' to meet the young emperor and his mother. Yellow, the imperial colour, spoke of the golden sun, the golden throne, all the magnificence of imperial wealth and power. One of the favoured two was a sister of Xian Feng's dead wife. The other, then only sixteen,[12] was Yehonala – the dream princess with a voice of velvet, a high intelligence and the ability to cast a spell of fascination upon everyone she met. Her aesthetic taste was highly developed. She painted expertly and her calligraphy was admired. All the complicated subtleties of correct decorum she had mastered. She was irresistible. But she was in love with her cousin, also of the Yehonala clan, an imperial bannerman, an officer in the Imperial Brigade of Guards, named Yong Lu. They were all but betrothed.

Xian Feng took both girls, making his first wife's sister Empress Consort. But she bore him only daughters while Yehonala's first child was a son. All through Yehonala's life strong doubts remained as to who was the child's father. Even when officially in disgrace for public indiscretion, Yong Lu could speak much as he liked to Yehonala, and when there was no greater power in the kingdom than she, his influence over her was strong.

As mother of the heir apparent, Yehonala, the Imperial Concubine Yi, was a woman of consequence; but within five years her strength of personality and quiet intrigues had made her the dominant force behind the throne. Sixty years later she was unrivalled in this position. Coincidentally, almost all that happened in Yehonala's life-span happened in Hudson Taylor's, for she was just three years younger than he. Yehonala's world was the world of her ancestors. She knew little of the fire-boats and fire-power of the red-haired barbarians from the West. Her attitude was that of the young emperor and his advisers who replied to Queen Victoria's congratulations on his accession with the message,

> Foreigners are under obligation to be grateful for our generosity; but their recent proceedings in forwarding despatches direct to ministers of state can be looked on only as contumacious and insulting.

It was this climate which the allies hoped to see altered, but the Court had no such intention. A show of vigour, and settlement with the barbarians from a position of strength, was necessary. The intention was noble, for insurrections, locusts and famine were bleeding the empire white. Even in Peking the poor were hungry. Russia offered to end the Taiping rebellion in exchange for three provinces on the Manchurian coast but misjudged the emperor. At the same time as Japan was about to open her ports to all nations, a yacht was being fitted out at Hong Kong as Queen Victoria's gift to the Emperor of Japan. Foreigners were hobnobbing with Thai royalty in Bangkok. China was tragically obscurantist and the West had long since tired of attempting moderation.

Coastal mandarins now took note and a proclamation by the *daotai* of Shanghai warned in October of tightening regulations. This time it was merchants, not missionaries, who were taken to task. A contemporary translation ran:

> With respect to foreign merchants purchasing and transporting [silk] cocoons out of the country . . . Should any evil-disposed Chinese league themselves with barbarians, and together dare to proceed into the interior, no matter whether they have caused a disturbance or not they will be immediately arrested and punished with the utmost rigorousness [*sic*], while the barbarians will be taken into custody and handed over to their consuls, to be kept under rigorous control, and be punished as laid down by the Treaties . . . foreign merchants are not permitted to secretly proceed into the interior . . . No indulgence will be shown. Do not disobey! . . .

This was the climate referred to in Ningbo letters, letters by Hall and Jones at least, for it was new to them. To Hudson Taylor and the old-timers 'all is quiet at present' marked the contrast with what they had known. C J Hall reported, 'The state of uncertainty continues.' Great anxiety was felt over the Indian mutiny and its possible effects in China if it gained strength. Optimists saw the powers forcing China more widely open; others doubted their ability to hold on. Parker deferred the completion of his hospital. The talk among Ningbo missionaries was of their numbers being reduced, either by evacuation or deployment inland. Hudson Taylor even admitted the possibility of Swatow coming into the picture again, for he believed it would be possible to continue somewhere. He asked for good large blankets, feather pillows and English cutlery to be sent out at once. He could be Chinese to the Chinese and at the same time English to his English bride. And he fully expected to be married before the things could reach them. After January 15 they would sink or swim together, 'for better or for worse'.[13] For the present they had Miss Aldersey and Russell and matchmakers and Dutchmen to contend with. But the Tarns' reply was already on its way.

In the Shanghai area the experience of William Muirhead and Griffith John only encouraged optimism. Back from a long journey John wrote on October 6, 'The people of Shanghai take no more interest in the Canton war than they do in the Indian . . . The people here are as well disposed as ever.' They had spoken to thousands in the interior and never once been asked about Canton. During the year he had been with Joseph Edkins into the city of Suzhou (Suchow), with a population of one and a half million. No foreigner had previously visited the city undisguised. To them the prospects were good.

In December Lord Elgin came back to Hong Kong with fresh troops at his disposal. A French force under Baron Gros joined him. August Chapdelaine, victim of judicial murder, was to be avenged.[14] But coming from Calcutta Elgin's ship foundered. The CMS *Intelligencer*, never silent about Britain's high-handed policy in China, seized on the news.

> It is said that Lord Elgin's credentials as Plenipotentiary to China, are literally stained with opium. They went down with the *Ava* when she foundered . . . and when recovered by the divers, it was found that they were damaged by the drug which formed part of the cargo.[15]

The French joined at once in blockading Canton. And Lord Elgin lost no more time. His first aim was to teach a lesson and settle old scores. On December 28 the attack began. James Legge was in the city of Canton at the time. As the London *Times* correspondent stated, 'The unarmed, defenceless city of Canton with a population of a million, was bombarded for twenty-seven hours, on December 28, 1857.' The *Chinese Missionary Recorder* gave it as thirty-eight hours. A matter of degree? But on the 29th the allies entered the city. Hudson Taylor wrote, not naming his sources, 'Guns were trained up the narrow, crowded streets of Canton and innocent civilians, (women and children) were mowed down by the thousand.'

The flags of Britain and France flew from the five-storey pagoda near the north gate as the forts overlooking the city from the hills were assaulted and taken. The old city, two-thirds of the whole and occupied by Manchus, and the new city, the southern third, were

'NARROW CROWDED STREETS'

both captured. The entire circuit of the two was ten miles, with six miles of ancient wall, twenty feet thick and twenty-five to forty feet high. This time there was no 'retreat' by the conquerors. Commissioner Ye went into hiding and his chief mandarin was appointed governor and viceroy by the allies in his place, a puppet with two allied commissioners flanking him. The year ended and the search for Commissioner Ye continued. On January 5, 1858, he was caught, disguised as a coolie. Obese and with hands uncalloused he could not play the part. They shipped him to Calcutta where he languished and died in the state prison. The Tartar general, commander of the Manchu garrison at Canton, also fell into their hands.

That done, Lord Elgin and Baron Gros turned their attention to the matter of a new treaty with China. Attempts to negotiate a revision of the 1842–44 treaties had been rebuffed for twelve years. They demanded an audience but were crying for the moon. 'To wake [the emperor] from his dream of supremacy the Allies resolved to transfer the scene to the north' wrote W A P Martin of Ningbo.[16] All pretence of a *diplomatic* mission to Peking was dropped; instead it was to be diplomacy at gunpoint. When America and Russia saw what was in the air, they too determined to revise their treaties. The Sinologues Martin and the dispossessed Wells Williams[17] of Canton were called to serve as American interpreter-negotiators. By the spring of 1858 the four powers were clamouring insistently at Tianjin (Tientsin), the gateway to the capital, Peking. By then Hudson Taylor's affairs had long since come to a head.

'Do come quickly' *November 1857*

To the conventional, Hudson Taylor and John Jones appeared very eccentric. They experimented to the limits of their faith. Following George Müller's principles of never using cash they did not have in hand but always putting to use what they did, they were forever generous and, to foreign eyes, forever looked poor. Daily as the weather became wintry a crowd of sixty to eighty 'poor, lame, blind and destitute' people came to their door first thing in the morning for a bowl of hot rice gruel. Costs mounted up. Because their funds in hand fell too low they tried to sell off some possessions but no Chinese would buy. A fellow-missionary bought a dictionary and some soap on condition they would buy them back when their next remittance arrived! He knew he could not 'lend' to them. But this small sum was soon reduced to less than one dollar, after three dollars had been set aside for the rent.

Saturday, November 4 dawned and they had not told the poor not to come. The mail was not due for another week. Over their mantelpiece they had text scrolls like those at Bridge Street, 'Ebenezer' – 'Hitherto hath the Lord helped us' and 'Jehovah Jireh' – 'the Lord will provide.'

> He kept us from doubting for a moment. . . . Not that faith never feels weak and doubt never arises [Hudson Taylor explained to George Pearse]. I must confess . . . as our little stock of money got lower and lower . . . the question did often arise, are we called on in these circumstances to continue this help to them? . . . My dear Bro. and Sister Jones had no doubt at all . . . I believe – they are older pilgrims, and had more faith and light than I had.

But Sunday was coming. A dead man from the hospital lay in the house waiting to be buried and they could not afford the costs. The same good friend bought more of their odds and ends, and saw to the burial. Still there was no lamp oil for the evening meeting and the poor would be back for breakfast on Monday. But then a letter from William Berger to John Jones with a credit note for $214 was delivered – a week before time – and the poor had their breakfast as usual. Reviewing the situation they eventually decided that they must be going beyond the will of God or he would provide more adequately, and they reduced their benevolence. Brinkmanship was not part of their spiritual charter.

In gratitude for Hudson Taylor's care of John Quarterman, his relatives the Ways made a fine gesture, offering him their harmonium – a precious thing to them. He understood and was grateful but suggested a book instead, afraid that some people might misinterpret the gift as 'a sort of payment',

> and this of course I guard against, as I would not have *any* to think I wish for payment for services to the Lord's people . . . more especially as many think I am very poor. This certainly is true enough in one sense, but thank God it is 'poor and making many rich, having nothing, yet possessing all things'. . . . I would not be otherwise than I am, dependent on the Lord and used as a means of helping others.

When Mr Berger's gift arrived,

> We thanked God and took courage . . . Oh! it is sweet thus to live *directly* dependent on the Lord who *never fails us* . . . We could not

> help our eyes filling with tears of gratitude when we saw not only ourselves supplied, but the widows and orphans, . . . the friendless and destitute through the liberality of dear Mr Berger . . . 'O taste and see, that the Lord is good, blessed is the man that trusteth in *Him*' . . . 'The young lions *do* lack and suffer hunger, but they that seek the Lord . . . shall not lack *any good thing*.' And if *not* good, why want anything?

That week everything suddenly happened in a rush. Harassed though both Hudson Taylor and Maria were by ploys to separate them by distance and in affection, they intended to wait as patiently as possible for the Tarns' decision. On October 31 Hudson had written to his mother, 'Today the child of one of the missionaries whom I much love has died [of dysentery]. What a mercy dear Louisa Jones [the baby] is spared to us!' And on November 18 he went on, alluding to the attempt to interest William Aitchison in Maria, and to the discovery that the first Christian they had baptised, the Jones children's *amah*, was pregnant by their cook and planning to kill herself and the child, 'I was tried almost beyond measure, above strength.'

Increasingly he felt he must talk with Maria about letting all the community know where they stood. Reports reached him that Maria was after all going to Shanghai with Burella and that yet another missionary was hoping 'to gain her hand'. It was high time it all came out into the open. If only the Tarns' reply would come. With the Goughs and Joneses and good Mrs Bausum who 'has taken my part' under constraint not to give active support, consultation with Maria seemed all the more vital. 'But how to get an interview I could not see.' When all the dust had settled he told his mother,

> I think had I not been enabled to see her and get a decided promise on Nov. 14th I could not have borne much more. I was so ill . . . from constant anxiety and mental anguish that I seriously believe a protraction of this trouble would have caused mental derangement . . . But the Lord did not require more than I could bear.

On Saturday morning, November 14, he called on his friends the Knowltons, the parents of the dead child. Their American Baptist mission just outside the Salt Gate lay opposite the Presbyterian school on the far bank where Maria now lived, and a ferry plied regularly at that point. The Knowltons were leaving Ningbo for Shanghai in a day or two. And they too had heard that Maria was going to Shanghai. Together they agreed to invite her to come over and talk. A formal betrothal was what Hudson Taylor wanted. But Mrs Knowlton sent this note over to Maria.

> My *dear* Miss Maria, I understand you are talking of going to Shanghai and we are intending to start on Monday, and may I ask you if you will kindly come over here a little while, as I would like to speak to you of a little matter – if quite convenient will you come at once –
>
> *Very* affly. yours, L.A. Knowlton
>
> PS If . . . engaged, please mention when you can call.

Such subterfuge could not escape rebuke when the final reckoning was made. Unsuspectingly, Maria came. Hudson Taylor told his mother,

> tho' frightened at first (for Miss Aldersey is so violent) I succeeded in getting a *private* interview – my first – and I was not a little astonished when we parted to find it had only been of six hours' duration! . . . the result was that we were engaged whether the guardian's answer was favourable or otherwise. She is a dear, noble, disinterested, devoted girl, and now I know *all* she has passed through, I love her more and admire her more than ever . . . When they told her, if I would go home and either be ordained, or gain a medical diploma, their opposition should cease, and they would in every way help our union, she told them, she would be much mistaken and disappointed in me if I would; and if for the sake of a worldly honor or her hand, I would leave the work God had called me to, she would be ashamed of me, and have nothing more to do with me. Noble girl, I *am* proud of her!

Fifty years later he told his son, 'We sat side by side on the sofa with my arm round her waist.' He did not attempt to say in his home-letters all they had talked about. But he did confess (with a slip as to the timing) that he had sent for a harmonium for her.

> She gave me a sweet kiss that would have alone paid for a dozen . . . this has done me more good than half a dozen bottles of Quinine, Port Wine, or any other strengthening medicine could have done – in fact I never felt in better health or spirits in my life . . .

To Amelia he was more specific,

> I was not long engaged without trying to make up for the number of kisses I *ought* to have had the last few months . . . Scarcely have I had a thought by day or night in which dear Maria has not been mixed in one way or another . . .

John Burdon and Burella were to be married on the 16th, and 'the pain of parting' would be increased if Burella knew of this new stage in Maria's defiance of Miss Aldersey. So they decided to keep it a secret until after the honeymoon. But Hudson Taylor went straight to Aitchison, 'and told him how grieved I was that the silence I had been obliged to observe should have left an open door for so painful a disappointment . . .' To his joy Aitchison assured him that 'the report was utterly unfounded'. He had known all along 'and of course had not allowed such a thought to have a place in his mind'. He thanked Hudson Taylor for his frankness and their esteem for each other was increased. So that complication at least was resolved.

The Burdons' wedding went off in style, and ten days later they returned to Ningbo. A love-letter from Hudson Taylor of as late as November 24 has survived, in which he strongly advised Maria not to go to Shanghai with the Burdons.

> I feel sure you will regret the step should you be induced to take it, and I trust you may not be surprised into consent at the last moment . . . the giddy gayity [*sic*] of Shanghai would try you more than you are aware of, and the journey . . . is neither pleasant nor safe, owing to pirates. These are not worth a thought if duty calls, and the finger of God points the way, but otherwise they are.

Now was the time to face the music. At the weekend he called at the school, sent in his card to Maria and was shown in by Mrs Bausum to whom they divulged their secret. Together they discussed how, as a token of respect for Miss Aldersey's seniority they should inform her first and make the news of their betrothal least painful to her. On Monday evening, November 30, Hudson Taylor called on Miss Aldersey and frankly told her what had happened.

> She said little – she evidently did not trust herself – but this morning [Dec 1] . . . I found [Maria] had received a note from Miss A requiring her to call on her as her guardian . . . without delay. To this Maria replied that she could not look on her, (and believed she had never done so) as her guardian, but that as a respected friend she would gladly call on her at any time . . . Maria will not go alone.

There was no knowing what Miss Aldersey might attempt in her zeal to save her from youthful folly. When the Tarns' reply to her warning letters arrived she would be on firmer ground, but until then, she was convinced, it was her duty to be adamant, with W A Russell's help.

Russell arrived home the next day from a country journey. Nothing if not loyal to Miss Aldersey and staunchly upright, he at once went round to confront Hudson Taylor, spoke his mind, and a few days later banned him from entering his house, where Miss Aldersey also lived.[18] Once again F F Gough moved in as peacemaker, urging Hudson Taylor to give as little ground for criticism as he could. And after consulting Maria, he wrote accepting his advice. Without admission of fault, but 'simply with the desire to promote the unity of the body of Christ, and at the sacrifice of our personal feelings . . .' they agreed, with certain reservations, neither to meet nor to correspond until Maria came of age on January 16 or the Tarns' approval arrived. Should the Tarns oppose their wishes they would also be bound by the same decision, until January 15. The reservations were these: in the event of serious illness or political changes making it probably necessary to leave Ningbo, or other unforeseen circumstances of sufficient importance, they would not be bound. Nor if Maria were to be subjected to 'annoyance' or interference.

It was anguish wasted. The very next day, December 11, Maria received a letter from her aunt, Mrs Tarn. At the same time came a strong note from Miss Aldersey, still determined to save Maria.

> Once again I come to you dear Maria as your faithful monitor warning you against the mad step to which a strange infatuation characterized by and endorsed by religious romance appears to be hastening you . . . I have now to inform you . . . that Mr Russell said he was so impressed by your undutiful and unbecoming conduct [that he will refuse communion if you present yourself for it, and] can in no way recognize [Hudson Taylor] as a Christian brother. [All the missionary brethren with whom Mr. R. had spoken were indignant with Mr. T's conduct, she continued] and are pretty well agreed in the opinion expressed to Mr T. by the mild and temperate Mr Russell that a man acting as Mr Taylor 'ought to be horsewhipped' . . . Now my dear Maria retrace your step – believe me it is *not too late*. A promise made to one who has so dishonourably drawn it from you by trampling on my expressed restrictions, is verily null and void. . . . Reflect dearest Maria is there any prospect of *happiness* not to speak of *usefulness* if you unite yourself to one who can treat the aged as Mr T. is wont to do, and who can disregard the truth as he has done? My dear Maria . . . I now as your Guardian *require not request* you to come and stay with us here . . . until we hear from your Uncle and Aunt.

But Maria wrote at once to Hudson saying,

My own dear –
I have received a letter from my Aunt, and she tells me that she and my Uncle certainly have not heard anything to induce them 'to oppose my wishes'.
Do come quickly.

Your own loving
Maria

After that they announced their engagement and spent every evening together. Miss Aldersey was silent. The Tarns wished Maria not to marry until after she came of age, so they deferred making any arrangements.

Christmas came, and with it all the usual parties. Helen Nevius had not yet returned from the States, but John Nevius, 'the most genial of companions', reported to her all that was going on. In her *Recollections* she wrote,

> [Hudson Taylor's] fiancée with her strong emotional nature was in this respect not unlike him. My husband was rather an intimate friend of both, and he sometimes indulged his propensity for good-natured teasing at their expense . . . One evening the young people sat around a table playing a game which required their hands to be hidden beneath it. To his surprise Mr. Nevius received an unexpected squeeze. Guessing at once that it was a case of 'mistaken identity' and enjoying the joke he returned the pressure with interest. In a moment Maria his next neighbour discovered the mistake, but when she would have withdrawn her hand it was tightly held . . . Not until the flushed cheeks and half-tearful eyes warned him that the joke had gone far enough did he release her. Those were the days when to laugh was easy . . . Also sitting at that 'round table' [was] he who is now Sir Robert Hart . . . a frequent visitor at our house.

The Tarns' replies to Maria's second and Hudson Taylor's July letters were by then overdue, and Miss Aldersey had given no indication of having heard from them. But this bitterest of all years was coming to an end and Hudson Taylor felt he could not let it do so without first trying to become reconciled with his critics. On the 27th he wrote on his own and Maria's behalf to Russell. It was the Lord's Day evening and he was pained by the state of affairs between them, he said. They had worked and worshipped and prayed together but were not even on speaking terms. Loved, redeemed, sanctified, members of his body and wanting to glorify him, sent to show the heathen how disciples of Jesus love one another – even if there was cause for coolness it was their duty to forgive.

> Shall we not from this time be reconciled, and thus fulfil the law of Christ? . . . I pray God that we may be bound *more* closely than ever in the bonds of brotherly love . . .

Two days later he received Russell's reply and there was more to follow. But Maria's little diary closed the year on a cheerful note,

> —came to dinner. Pr.M. [at] Mrs Way. —not there. Shortly after arriving home heard his knock. My hope is in thee. Bless the Lord O my soul and *forget not* all his benefits.

Peace with honour *January 1858*

The murderous bombardment of Canton began on December 28. It was the spirit of the age. W A Russell, reflecting Miss Aldersey's views, set out on twelve foolscap sheets their indictment of Hudson Taylor and his conduct. A long recital of the history of events as they saw them led on to their deductions and a demand that he atone for his faults. He must, in spite of the Tarns' approval,

> Consent to appear before all the parties reasonably connected with this affair and in their presence retract or apologize . . . and at the same time to agree to discontinue your present connection with Miss Dyer for . . . say three months, you and she in the mean time to be considered unbound by the engagement . . . which I and others hold to be null and void in the sight of God . . .

Otherwise he could see no other course than 'a continued manifestation of our strong disapprobation of your conduct'.

Hudson Taylor answered the statements point by point, to establish the facts and to correct misconceptions. He could not see how he would act differently if in the same circumstances again. And he was ready to forgive wrongs done to him, without apology or reparation. By then the Tarns' letters to each of them had arrived and he quoted their words – to Maria – we '*fully approve of your choice*', and to himself, we '*entirely approve* of the *proposed union*'. There could be no thought of breaking the engagement or delaying their marriage.

He sent his letter off to Russell and a note to Maria:

> . . . he has it ere now. Now my dearest one, accept this note as a promissory note for as many kisses as you wish, and it shall be

payable at sight. May Blessing from the God of all grace rest on you . . . Your own Hudson.

Mr and Mrs Tarn had received Miss Aldersey's first letter in September and made their own enquiries. They had turned to George Pearse whom they knew personally and had at once been reassured. He found Miss Aldersey's opposition hard to understand. Did she perhaps not want to lose Maria from her school? To Hudson Taylor he generously wrote, bearing no ill-will for his resignation from the Society:

> But she does not know as I do the value which very many in England put upon you, and . . . *our* anxieties would naturally be for you, that you should have a lady who would not be a hindrance to your work but rather the contrary. But this I feel satisfied is the case . . . You need not suppose that anything but the most kind and friendly feeling will exist on the part of the Committee towards you and yours.

He also sent his greetings to Maria. She would probably not remember his meeting her at the Tarns' home in Brunswick Square just before she sailed to China, when she was fifteen. 'May you be enabled to *live down* all opposition by quietly and meekly bearing for your Master's name and in His spirit what you have to meet with.'

To Hudson Taylor's parents George Pearse had more to add,

> I have given *no qualified* opinion of him. I think they are quite satisfied. I have expressed my anxiety that he should find *one suitable* to himself, and I have no fear for any lady whom he may take . . . All accounts of your son are most satisfactory.

On October 9 (when Hudson Taylor was nursing John Quarterman) Mrs Tarn had written at length to Maria, a letter almost devoid of normal punctuation. She and her husband, still on his back and in pain, were glad of her 'long and candid' letter, she said.

> . . . We certainly have not heard anything to induce us to oppose your wishes, . . . It certainly would have been more satisfactory if you attached yourself to one who was connected with the same body of Christians as your self, one who shifts about from one body to another appears unstable, what signifies the baptism by water it is only emblematical the baptism of the Holy Spirit is all . . . I trust he is and you are assured of it, that he is baptized by that blessed Spirit as a man of God . . . It is impossible for us to judge the suitability of Mr. Taylor to be your husband . . . and therefore can only leave you in the

> Lord's hands . . . guiding you to do what is right and preserving you from what is wrong.

She then turned to financial matters. They hoped Mr Taylor would not renounce his salary from the Society. (Little did they know the dismal facts.)

> [For] even in the times of the Apostles societies were formed to promote the work of the Lord . . . there are circumstances when we must look entirely upwards for a supply of our wants –

but fixed salaries were desirable for missionaries to spare them anxiety. As for Maria's private property, they advised her to settle it 'not only on yourself but upon those who come after you'. And 'state to Mr. Taylor that it is our request'. In addition, she must be let into a secret. A legacy in favour of Maria's mother had been judged by the lawyers to belong to Mrs Bausum. But Mrs Bausum, although a widow with children unprovided for, had given instructions that it should go to Samuel, Burella and Maria. Would it not be right to acknowledge such nobility of character by directing the executor to divide the legacy into four, the fourth part going to Mrs Bausum's own children?

> You understand that we do not oppose your uniting yourself to Mr. Taylor though we see some objections. I have written to Miss Aldersey [and] Burella stating that we cannot oppose what you feel to be for your happiness.

That was as far as they could then go. But a fortnight later William Tarn, director of the Religious Tract Society, himself wrote a few lines in a different key. 'Since your aunt wrote you from Brighton I have received very satisfactory letters from Archdeacon Cobbold and [Chaplain] Hobson . . . so that we fully approve your choice'.

To Hudson Taylor he was expansive. His and Maria's letters being so full and candid were very satisfactory. He had been in touch with the referees Hudson Taylor had named, and with the Chinese Evangelization Society, and

> the testimonies of all these gentlemen are as favourable as we could wish and such as to lead us to approve of the proposed union. [But his resignation from the CES especially in prospect of marriage] we cannot at all approve of – our minds have however been relieved on this point, in some measure, by the information . . . that they intend to send you supplies as heretofore – and we trust you will not hesitate to accept what they send. In some cases, it may be allowable to act on

> faith, as Mr. Müller of Bristol for his Orphan School, but I think in regard to a wife and family, it is not justifiable . . . I must urge on you and Maria the importance of having the whole of her property settled upon her children – This proposal has been agreed to by Mr. Burdon and Burella . . .

Maria's assets were set out by her cousin, another William Tarn, on a scrap of paper, undated, showing a total of £1,550.17.5. It would provide an income of not more than forty to fifty pounds a year, 'very inadequate for the support of a family'.

A very different letter was soon on the way to Hudson Taylor from George Müller himself, from 21 St Paul St, Kingsdown, Bristol, dated December 9, 1857.

> My dear Brother,
>
> It affords me much joy in the Lord, to have it in my power to send you the enclosed Forty Pounds, which I have obtained from the Lord simply in answer to prayer. Let this be a further encouragement to yourself, as to the readiness of the Lord to hear your prayers, when, in your need, you call upon Him.
>
> I was glad to find that you had resolved to trust in the Lord alone, for the supply of all necessities. I have myself proved Him thus faithful for more than 27 years, during which time I have to Him alone made known my wants . . . I would gladly write more, but I have thousands of correspondents, besides all my other work.
>
> I remain, dear Brother,
> Yours affect. in our Lord,
> George Müller.[19]

Nothing now stood in the way of marriage except the date of Maria's coming of age, preparations for the chosen day, Wednesday, January 20 – and whatever Mr Russell might yet decide he should do. If he and Miss Aldersey, and the Tarns in London, had known what was happening at the Salt Gate house, they might well have redoubled their efforts to prevent this apparently 'harebrained match' (in Latourette's words) from taking place.

Maria was coming to tea at the Joneses' on January 6. But although they were no longer feeding the destitute, their common purse was empty. When Hudson Taylor thought of crossing the river to defer Maria's visit and balanced what they had in hand against the rent and wages due to be paid, he found he had not even enough to pay the ferryman. Between them they had only two cash, one eighth of a penny. The cook would gladly have lent a few cash, but they were firm about going into debt. There was no way out but to sell something. With John Jones he decided on an old iron stove fit for scrap, and they set out for the pontoon bridge on the other side of the city to cross over to the foundry, only to find that the pontoons were being repaired. A ferry had replaced the bridge. Again they were baulked. Tired, hungry and faint they trudged home, made two cups of cocoa for their dinner and prayed together, 'Give us *this day* our daily bread'.

Mary Jones was out and there was enough food in the house for the children, but soon Maria would be coming to tea. There was a knock at the door. It was the postman. In the mail he delivered was a letter from Mr Berger containing forty pounds.

> Oh! dear Brother [Hudson Taylor replied] you do not know how tears of joy filled our eyes at the sight. We thanked God, borrowed a few cash and got something to eat, then went and got the bill cashed – and thus God fed us.

To his son in 1904 he commented, 'No such trial ever came to us again in later life.' The lesson had been learned and it was not necessary to repeat it.[20]

Far from being the mature men of faith they were to become, they were experimenting fearlessly and up to the hilt. But prayer, not panic, was the answer to testing. Bank draft in hand, they felt free to accept the fifty cash from the cook to buy some food and take the draft to Davidson the merchant. Accepting it he said he would have the silver in a few days' time. Their hearts sank. Then, as they were leaving he added as an afterthought – Would sixty or seventy dollars be welcome to get on with?

'I not only had the pleasure,' Hudson told Amelia, 'of having tea with [Maria], but of telling her what great things the Lord had done for us.' And to Maria he had said, 'You see how difficult our life may be at times,' offering to let her withdraw her promise, but she had not wavered. Instead she had answered, 'I have been left an orphan and God has been my Father all these years. Do you think I shall be afraid of trusting Him now?'

By the time the rent and wages had been paid and other expenses defrayed, however, very little of Mr Berger's gift was left. As January 20 came nearer, 'God . . . gave her faith to trust Him for the future.' Because her trust in God himself was already deep, putting this kind of faith into practice, though new to her, was no problem.

In a letter of thanks on the 27th, writing candidly at William

Berger's specific request, Hudson Taylor said, 'Brother Jones had no remittance and has had none since, but as he shared his with me when I had none, so mine was shared with him.'

So as the wedding day approached he had too little money to provide the new clothes convention required, or even a wedding cake. With only thirteen dollars left he had consular fees and honeymoon costs to meet. Then gifts began to come in from friends. 'One gave cards and another printed them.' Some gave ingredients and others cooked them. To Amelia he went on,

> We married in faith; I had not money to support us a fortnight, but we had the bank of faith to draw on and it has hitherto, and ever will, prove amply sufficient. [And to his mother] The day we were married I had not more than $7 in hand – she knew it, but knew too that the Lord would withhold no good thing – so she had no fear . . . no one but God, ourselves and the Jones' knew how much we were in need. But He supplied *all* our need.

Maria wanted him to wear English clothes for the wedding and he was growing the hair on the shaven front half of his head and preparing to sacrifice his natural *bianzi* (queue),

> but it would not grow long enough in time, [Maria told Amelia] and this and other considerations made me waive my objections to his appearing as a [Chinese] that day. Now I think I should hardly like to see him in the English dress.

January 12, 1858, was the day for making the final preparations. After breakfast and their family prayers Hudson Taylor visited a patient and went on to ask Frederick Gough to marry them, 'the Consul's not having (thro' an accident) the power'. Then to the vice-consul in charge, T T Meadows, at the consulate across the river, to give notice of intention to marry.

'A week from this day (D.V.) I am to go and get the licence,' he reported, and the wedding was to be the next morning. Then home again and a letter to his mother.

> I can scarcely realize that . . . after all the agony and suspense we have suffered we are not only at liberty to meet and be much with each other, but are likely within a few days to be united. God *has* been good to us, he has answered our prayers . . . I wish you knew my precious Maria, she is a treasure, she is all I desire . . . May God give us His own rich blessing, and keep us from making idols of each other.

That same day Russell sent Hudson Taylor a strong note rejecting his explanations of ten days before and reiterating his own demands.

> I . . . retain unaltered the views I presented to you . . . It is plain however that further controversy between us . . . would only tend to embroil matters more and more. I would therefore suggest our leaving the matter to the arbitration of the *three* senior missionaries of the three mission bodies at Ningbo, . . . and to abide by their decision whatever it may be.[21]

R Q Way was the senior Presbyterian, F F Gough the Anglican, and T H Hudson the Baptist.

When Hudson Taylor had considered this blow and no doubt consulted Maria and his friends, he replied,

> Your note of Jan 12th both grieved and surprised me . . . The questions of *my present relation to Miss Dyer, my intended union with her and the period when that shall take place* are not matters I can submit to arbitration, they having been settled by reference to Mr. and Mrs. Tarn. But as to whether I have given sufficent cause of offence to justify you in still withholding from me the hand of fellowship, I shall be glad to submit *that* to arbitration if that is the only way . . . though I have serious doubts as to the desirability of the step.

More notes passed between them that same day, January 14, and finally Hudson Taylor yielded to Russell's demands. 'All I want is *your* misapprehensions to be removed and you to be satisfied,' he wrote. But on no account would he allow his present or future relations with Maria to be debated. '. . . nor . . . could any parties be found at Ningpo who would enter on that question were I willing to submit it'.

Maria was left out of these proceedings and kept busy with wedding preparations. Soon it would all be over and they would be together as man and wife whatever was said. Consulting Hudson Taylor about making John Jones a trustee of her personal property, she addressed the note that Saturday morning to 'Revd. J.H. Taylor, Gt. Russell St, Ningpo.' Naughty girl!

Russell and Taylor signed under eight agreed points for arbitration, showing yet more accommodation by Hudson Taylor, and either on the 16th or 18th the hearing took place. A scrap of paper with his pencilled notes as he listened are the only record of proceedings apart from the decisions of the arbitrators. A strong case was made for Miss Aldersey's responsibility as *de facto* guardian of the Dyer girls in Ningbo; that the consul and community assumed it and anyone doubting it should have challenged it openly; and that missionaries' children and Chinese, including Mr Russell's servant who had eavesdropped, were shocked by Maria's resistance to Miss Aldersey.

At last the arbitrators' conclusions were handed over: Miss Aldersey had been Maria's protectress, even though not her guardian, so Hudson Taylor had in some instances not paid the respect due to her. The interview at the Knowltons' had been highly injudicious and improper in the circumstances, but the engagement was valid, and his intentions in telling Miss Aldersey of it had been good. As for Mr Russell's part, he had used expressions calculated to wound Mr Taylor's feelings and 'mutual forgiveness and courtesies' would be a suitable end to it all.

Whether the arbitrators intended to be as inoffensive as possible or saw the issue as one of hurt pride rather than offences to be disciplined, Miss Aldersey and Mr Russell were placated at last. Hudson Taylor refrained from claiming that persecution beyond endurance had driven him and Maria to their 'injudicious and improper' meeting, and they kept the Tarns' consoling opinions to themselves.

After one more blow the opposition ended. Two years before his death, when Hudson Taylor's son and daughter-in-law were preparing one day to write his biography and were questioning him, he told them that Russell and Consul Meadows went on a shooting trip of some days in the week of the wedding. But Meadows had signed the marriage certificate before he left and was represented by his assistant – Robert Hart, the disappointed but magnanimous suitor.

Six months later Hudson Taylor told his mother,

> the Russells and Miss Aldersey are now *Friendly* tho' not very familiar. Till lately Mrs. Burdon [Burella] (who was influenced by Miss A) did not write Maria, but she has now commenced to do so, and in an affectionate manner. I think now we may thank God and say we are at peace with all.

About mid-January Mrs Bausum had received a warm letter from Mrs Tarn, who in November had been concerned for Maria that she had 'no one to counsel her as a mother'. All their enquiries in England, she said, had produced 'very favourable accounts' of Hudson Taylor and nothing in Miss Aldersey's letter justified them in opposing Maria's wishes, in fact it in my opinion condemned her whole manner of proceeding. I have by return of mail told her so and condemned her want of judgement. Your letter has tended to confirm this opinion, and in all that now concerns Maria we trust you will act a Mother's part . . . I should be very sorry that any reproach should fall on the mission by any unwarrantable conduct by Miss Aldersey – and after having resigned them to your care it would be unjustifiable to place [Maria] anywhere else or place a restraint over [her] actions.

What, dear Mrs Bausum, can be the cause of Miss A's strong objection and prejudice against Mr. T – it is so weak to be influenced by his personal appearance and as to his Medical Qualification the Society that sent him out as well as himself was anxious that there should be no delay to his engaging in the work, therefore he did not wait to pass his examination.

To look ahead, when Mrs Tarn in August 1858 received the marriage settlement and other papers from Maria, she made a final comment,

I wrote to Miss A. and stated that not having heard anything respecting Mr. T., but what was to his advantage we could not withhold consent . . . that letter was received by her and I was in hopes that it would have satisfied her . . .but [I have been] dissatisfied with the course Miss A. has pursued.

For Miss Aldersey had transferred the girls to Mrs Bausum's care without first obtaining their guardians' approval. Moreover she had written that they were still to regard her, Miss A, 'as a friend', which the Tarns had understood to be an unwarranted relinquishment of responsibility. At the same time the Tarns were glad, for as a wife and mother Mrs Bausum

was far better qualified to protect and watch over you, and . . . it was to be expected that you would transfer your confidence to her. I have a high opinion of Mrs. Bausum and you may remember I referred you to her [in the Straits] . . . should anything occur to oblige you to leave Ningpo . . .

But Mrs Tarn was fair as well as frank.

As you may in after life be called to be a guide to others [she continued faithfully] I would point out from your own statements wherein I think you have acted with impropriety, or rather Mr Taylor has and though much, I doubt not in prayer, yet there appears a mistrust in the Divine guidance, he took the matter into his own hands, remember the heart is never to be trusted, it is *always*

> *deceitful*, more or less; and your reasoning dear Maria is not sound when you draw your conclusion that your way is right, and that God is guiding you, because some things happen as you could wish! So Jonah thought when he was fleeing from the Almighty and found unexpectedly a ship ready to carry him away . . . I consider Mrs Knowlton was very wrong (and Mr. Taylor wrong also in doing it and she in complying) to send for you to urge you to an immediate engagement: this was very sad, why could he not trust the Lord that He would bring it to pass . . . and you do not appear to have consulted Mrs Bausum. You have now both cooled down, and can look [at] the circumstances calmly and as in the sight of a heart-searching God, . . . and in discovering what was wrong in yourselves, you may be led to feel the more for those who have erred also.[22]

Wise old aunt, they knew she was right. She also asked, 'Why do you not say anything about Burella . . .?', adding that Burella had not mentioned Maria. She needed no reply. But that was in letters before May, when Burella began writing affectionately again.

So ended the unhappy experience, so human and self-revealing, which ten years later was to prove invaluable to Hudson Taylor as a leader of men under criticism and opposition no less daunting.

CHAPTER THREE

'THE HAPPIEST YEAR . . .' 1858

Honeymoon and home[1] *January–April 1858*

If 1858 was to be the happiest year of Hudson Taylor's life so far, it was not for lack of difficulties. In spite of so little real knowledge of each other he and Maria were blissful, discovering that they were perfectly matched and of one mind on everything. The tragi-farce of arbitration and placated pride had intruded brutally upon their preparations for marriage but once over was banished from their thinking. Dark though the shadow of that memory might be, the happiness ahead shone too brightly to be dimmed. They put the past behind them and made the most of their limitations.

The community rose gallantly to the occasion. Close to Maria's new home with Mrs Bausum at the Presbyterian school lived the R Q Ways. Glad to show their gratitude to Hudson Taylor and love for Maria, they insisted on the wedding being held at their house. So 'in our parlour', Georgia Way recalled, F F Gough conducted the marriage service, exhorting Hudson and Maria from the text they had already appropriated, 'keep yourselves from idols'. He saw as they had done the danger of their idolising each other. The slim young bride *en règle* in grey silk dress and bridal veil took Ningbo's nobody in Chinese gown and *bianzi* 'for better or for worse'. The American consul put his elaborate sedan chair at her disposal. The civil ceremony at the British consulate, in what had been a Chinese temple nearby, took place in the presence of twenty-four friends, including the officers of the British ship-of-war. And the consular assistant, Robert Hart, had a consoling kiss from the bride. 'The sun shone brightly and all our friends seemed pleased to see us happily united' as they trooped back to the Ways' for the wedding breakfast at their expense.

When Hudson proffered his fee for consular services Consul Meadows would not hear of it. How often, he asked, had Taylor interpreted for him without accepting payment? Treasured among Maria's possessions and now with her letters is one in romanised Chinese from two of her schoolgirls,

> We have just heard you are leaving us and our hearts are very sad. How you loved us, how thoughtful of us you were, comforting us. We had no idea you would leave us so soon . . . But we want you to be very happy . . .

The only sadness was that Mary Jones had news of her mother's death and could not be at the wedding – and neither Miss Aldersey nor the Russells were there.

Thirteen miles from Ningbo, and reached after a canal journey and some miles by sedan chair into the hills, the Nie Wang monastery had guest rooms for visitors, often used by city people escaping the heat of summer. In January it was secluded and peaceful. There they went for three weeks' honeymoon. It is not difficult to imagine how the hardened traveller Hudson Taylor felt on this very different kind of journey. Exultant with his bride at last, each in a sedan chair, and followed by their cook, a general servant and coolies jogging along with bedding bundles and the paraphernalia of semi-European living on their carrying poles, his heart was singing.

Maria had never worn Chinese clothes and did not do so as long as they stayed in Ningbo. Nor was Hudson in a hurry to convert her to his Chinese way of living. Home with her became an oasis of peace and comfort in an increasingly demanding life among the people. So

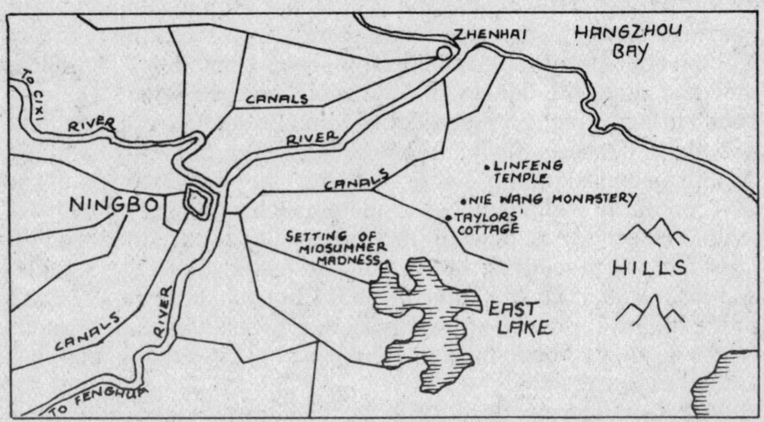

NINGBO COUNTRYSIDE: EAST LAKE

at the monastery they were comfortable. Yet it was a working honeymoon. They wanted to spend the time telling the gospel to everyone in the neighbourhood. John Jones was not well enough to carry the load of weekend services, so after only two days they returned to the city to help, walking the first seven or eight miles and telling people along the way about Jesus. To have a wife alongside him to speak to the women and girls was to Hudson Taylor an old dream come true. He was anxious about John and Mary, for that chronic skin disease was depriving them of sleep – 'it has almost worn them out . . . I fear the result.'[2]

They stayed in Ningbo over Monday to meet the Methodist George Piercy,[3] driven out of Canton, and for a few more days were back again at the monastery, mulling over Piercy's news and advice, and writing long letters home when rain prevented them getting out. 'God has turned our sorrow into joy and given us a garment of praise for a spirit of heaviness,' Maria chortled as she wrote the words, 'My dear Mother!' For eleven years, she said, since she was ten, she had been unable to write that. But now how different things were. And to be able to write about 'my Husband'! Every morning before getting up they were studying a chapter of the Greek New Testament together! And she memorised a verse while dressing.

Piercy had made that Monday evening one of Hudson Taylor's happiest for many months. When the Wesleyans had been unable to send him to China Piercy was still so sure that God was telling him to go that he went alone. Hudson Taylor had followed his story in the CES *Gleaner* for five years. The Wesleyans adopted Piercy when they saw how effective he was, but meanwhile he had formed some ideas of the greatest interest to Hudson Taylor, especially since his recent experience of funds dwindling to nothing. If his *only object* was to spread the knowledge of the truth, George Piercy suggested, the effect on the Chinese of the missionary working to provide his own livelihood like the tent-making Apostle Paul could only be good. 'There is *such* a tendency', Hudson Taylor told William Berger from Nie Wang, for converts to leave their old occupations and to depend on foreign funds for support as teachers and evangelists. To be able to pay your way and to be seen to be doing it would have so much to commend it. So he was wondering 'whether . . . the finger of providence might not be teaching or leading to a different course of action'. Might God be saying, not 'trust Me when you are moneyless' but 'trust Me to provide for you as I will do for your converts'?

At the same time he answered Mr Berger's question as to how he could contribute directly to the work, by saying that although the subject was 'replete with difficulty', if only from the lack of suitable Christian workers to support, he was 'inclined to think the support of a native Evangelist would be as good as, or better than any other plan'. It would cost thirty pounds a year. But who could be so employed? The Christians in other churches were trained and directed by their own missionaries. John Jones and he had under training only one baptised believer, with four preparing for baptism and several interested. So involvement by Mr Berger in that way would have to wait. Another possibility lay in their hope of renting premises in the country – already thwarted on several occasions. He and Maria on their walks to and from the monastery were making enquiries.

Another common bond with Piercy was that both he and Hudson Taylor had been Methodist local preachers and liked the pastoral system of class and class-leader as well as any. To his father he wrote that George Piercy agreed, 'the local preacher is the glory of Methodism . . . We seemed to have similar views on almost every point we conversed on.' Piercy had been having problems over not being an ordained minister. 'The people who make most of it here have least to be proud of,' Hudson Taylor remarked. But Piercy had a story fresh from Hong Kong. A certain bishop was looking for a missionary to superintend the cutting of Chinese printing blocks and someone suggested Piercy because of his knowledge of Chinese characters. The bishop protested, 'But he is not ordained!' Hudson Taylor gave it five exclamation marks. His Quaker friend Miss Stacey was as irreverent. When the criticisms against Hudson Taylor reached her she wrote to his mother,

> As people there think so much of Ordination, and dear J.H.T. is wholly given to the work of the Gospel; I quite think if I were in his place, I should allow myself to be styled *Rev.* by a few brethren clapping their hands on my head.

But she was not the purist he was.

During the last weekend of January he and Maria planned an at-home for all their friends at the end of their honeymoon, and the beginning of a new phase of their life together. At a village near the East Lake, nine miles from Ningbo, they found and rented a Chinese cottage and prepared to work there during each week and in Ningbo at the weekends. But hardly had they begun than Maria fell dangerously ill with typhoid fever and he was faced with losing his precious bride.

He had her carried to Ningbo and nursed her with Mary Jones' help, but she showed no sign of improvement. All the fears and heartaches of his lonely years began to sweep over him. He told Amelia how the last six months 'of heart-breaking suspense and anguish' had been followed by such joy, only to be threatened again. After some weeks she turned the corner, but then Hudson Taylor fell ill as well and they were moved to the Parkers. It was April before they were both well enough to convalesce at Mrs Bausum's. Her peaceful home and rose garden were what they needed.

Meanwhile a new CMS couple, Rev and Mrs George E Moule[4] were expected, and John and Mary Jones had to move out of the Salt Gate house to Chinese premises in 'one of the lowest quarters' of the city and began again to befriend their neighbours and preach the gospel to them.

> The people have been allowed to come freely to our house, some for medicines, others simply to look about. . . . In doing this we have braved their . . . skin diseases and insects . . . but sunken as they are in physical abominations – and of this you can form no idea, it is not to be compared with their moral uncleanness, which cannot be named.

Punch at that time carried jokes about bedbugs and fleas in seaside lodging houses and the poor in Britain were not so very different, but life at close quarters with such degradation was difficult for people of John and Mary Jones' refinement.

In mid-April Hudson Taylor announced to his mother that she could expect 'a Christmas Box – that will transform you into a Grandmother'.

> I want your prayers for my precious Maria – that she may be preserved from all the dangers . . . and for me that I may be spared sorrow upon sorrow . . . I cannot tell you how much I love my precious wife. I am fully satisfied in her . . . perfection is nearer come to in her than I ever expected . . . There is great danger of not, in happiness, finding our delight in the Lord, as in sorrow and trial.

And Maria was enjoying belonging to a family again. 'I do like hearing him talk about his Mother and Sister, and to see his tender love for them,' she told Amelia.

Then on April 26 they took over the old attic above the school and street chapel in Bridge Street where he had lived as a bachelor. They had it divided into smaller rooms and re-floored to make it less draughty, and Maria recalled Mary Jones' teasing about Hudson papering the walls a year before to receive a visitor. Now they had a real home of their own, however simple, and the cottage near the East Lake to work from whenever they could, 'until we can secure a suitable house in the country'. Between them they owned very little for setting up a home and entertaining fellow-missionaries in the way they expected. So home-letters began to include requests for tablecloths, cutlery, tumblers and wine glasses, to be charged against the account he kept with his parents. Maria and he were meeting mid-way in their life-style. He opened up his dispensary and again began treating opium addicts, not that medical cures lasted long, but to give him the opportunity to bring the addicts to faith in Christ, the only lasting cure he knew. In gratitude for Maria's gratuitous teaching in their school, the American Presbyterians gave her a beautiful clock and twin oil lamps. They drew a groan from Hudson. Costs were high and income low just then. A gift of 'bread and cheese would have made me a happy man'. But he knew the Ways and Neviuses could not be content with less. Helen Nevius arrived back in Ningbo and old friendships were renewed. When the bill of lading for the harmonium from England arrived, Hudson presented it triumphantly to Maria and they tried to wait patiently for its music to fill their preaching hall.

Church planters — *May–June 1858*

Private life with all its complications had to be fitted in with work. The CES had accepted the Joneses' and Hudson Taylor's resignation graciously and, responding to his suggestion, made him a gift of all the medical books and instruments they had provided. But losing such well-loved missionaries and their best correspondents was harder to accept. The Board asked them to retain 'a nominal connection' with the Society and were less than candid about telling their supporters of the resignations. The editor of *The Gleaner* wrote, 'Although Mr. J. Hudson Taylor and Mr. Jones are not entirely supported by the funds of the Society, yet we desire to cherish the same interest in them as though they were . . .'[5]

Hudson Taylor asked to be referred to more accurately as a missionary 'aided' by them, and when he read *The Gleaner*'s misleading statement, protested that readers would judge that he and Jones were receiving considerable support from the Society, a grossly unreal state of affairs for many months already. In fact the remaining CES missionaries, the Parkers and Halls, were currently suffering the neglect Hudson Taylor had always known. Through all this George Pearse and the Tottenham friends, the Howard family in particular, gave generously and did their best to influence the administration. Then Charles Bird, the querulous salaried secretary and Achilles heel of the Society, on the verge of a nervous breakdown, was hurled from an express train in a derailment and thrown forty feet down the embankment. He never returned to his work, and the burden of replacing him fell on George Pearse, the already overworked stockbroker. But by then the confidence of the public had been lost and after a year of struggle to restore its fortunes, the CES limped sadly downhill to its dissolution.

May was a good month for all the missions in Ningbo. The carnage at Canton was still having no effect on the friendly Ningbo people. Their own experience of the Cantonese was of trouble-makers. And the passage of Lord Elgin up the coast to Dagu (Taku) with the allied force of nineteen vessels caused no alarm. In April Griffith John had carried six thousand New Testaments to the previously resistant city of Hangzhou and succeeded in distributing them all. In itself this was no small achievement but Griffith John saw it only as a step towards the aim he had announced a month earlier, 'I intend, as soon as possible, to proceed to Hangchow, the Athens of China [to establish an institution for] the education of Christian men who have given proof of piety and zeal.'

He had already shown that he could live and work with his wife and child at Pinghu without trouble from mandarins or consul, and with Muirhead had established several outstations for the LMS in the country round Shanghai. Lockhart, Williamson and Edkins had all returned to Britain. Muirhead was preaching to two or three hundred daily in Shanghai, with his sights set on establishing Christian communities in many places with Chinese pastors in charge, helped by the missionary. City people come and go, he pointed out. Country people are stable. So for permanence go to the country. Wylie too had penetrated farther north beyond the Yangzi than any previously. Travelling for three weeks to seven cities and many large towns he had been received without evidence of disapproval. William Burns was still in the same house at Swatow, but until he left he had no success to report. Writing to congratulate Hudson Taylor on his marriage he asked for prayer that his own faith might not fail under this long testing. Carstairs Douglas wrote that Burns was visiting Zhangzhou (Changchow), the place where several Christians had been executed. Change was in the air.

Without the intervention of the Western powers China was beginning to accept the foreign missionary for his own worth. Hangzhou was the seat of the viceroy and provincial governor, the Ningbo *daotai*'s superior. So Ningbo was doubly open to the gospel. But then the Taipings came southward on the rampage again. In early May they were only twenty-five miles from Hangzhou and consternation reigned, for Ningbo was the next big city after Hangzhou. A report reached Shanghai that the rebels had reached Ningbo and foreigners had taken refuge on HMS *Surprise*, but it was false. At critical times people were more ready to listen to a message of hope, and this tended to make them more open towards the Christians.

Dr Parker was engrossed in his work, almost single-handedly seeing fourteen thousand patients a year and having every accident case of any severity brought to him from many miles around. His reputation brought him contacts with people of all kinds. High-ranking mandarins invited him to their homes. Leading Chinese merchants even consulted him about which ships' captains were reliable. 'One of the first questions asked was "Is he a Christian? If so we will employ him at once."' His new hospital on the riverbank outside the Salt Gate was nearing completion, with six wards, to be opened in August, and on May 6 Hudson Taylor helped him to move his dispensary into the new premises, so much nearer to the city and on the same side of the river that they were able to do more together from then on. A home for himself alongside the hospital was Parker's last objective. As his fees came in, from attending the merchant community and visiting ships, he continued to build. A handbill issued by him reads,

> Ningpo Hospital and Dispensary
> In-patients Taels 1–2 per day
> Ships attended for twenty taels a month
> or 5 taels a visit.
> W Parker MD, Surgeon[6]

He also made time to enter into the non-medical activities of his colleagues of all missions. With five hundred pounds from the Glasgow Bible Society he supervised the printing of hundreds of

Gutzlaff Bibles, using the blocks Lobscheid had had cut. People sang his praises on every hand. Only the CES, his own Society, failed to appreciate him, to send him the support they promised or to understand why he did not send long letters which they could publish in *The Gleaner*. With typically dour brevity he referred them to the Halls for news, saying, 'I may venture to go on noiselessly with the more important duties of my mission work.'

Hall was still trying to make himself understood in the language, while visiting country villages with the American Baptist E C Lord four afternoons each week. Neither Parker nor Hall was able to join in the work the Taylors and Joneses were building up, though meeting with them for prayer and the Lord's Supper week by week. So the burden of evangelistic and pastoral responsibility rested on Hudson Taylor.

It was heavy going. John Jones was a sick man and Mary Jones' tuberculosis was worse. Disconsolately he wrote on May 5, with a brave cry of faith,

> The people listen to the gospel message with the utmost indifference, without any sign of feeling; they acknowledge the truth of it, and yet are unaffected by it. We are ploughing the ground all around us, and casting in the seed. We expect a crop.

He was not making sufficient allowance for the inscrutability of the Chinese. Behind those expressionless faces were some very thoughtful people. But he had also met opposition from Chinese who spoke of the Taiping rebels as Christians. 'The rebels being in this province, the general mind is very unsettled, and it is feared that they may soon take the city.' Some people had made a great mistake in thinking that the Church of God

> could be built up with the help of that unholy movement . . . I have been met with objection that the rebels destroy temples and idols, and worship the one God; and yet, in addition to their being rebels, and thus worthy of death, they commit every excess . . . Such a movement can never recommend anything good . . .

He and Mary often went out together and would sit down among the village people and gossip the gospel as they sipped the tea brought to them as a welcome. Often a hundred women would gather round and then John would preach to them.

Hudson Taylor's impression of the meetings in Ningbo was more cheerful. Attendance and attention were good, he told William

Berger. But he too remarked that some listeners treated the gospel as empty or amusing or nothing to do with them. He found it humbling to realise that there was nothing in what they preached or how they preached it that would convert a Chinese unless the Holy Spirit of God supplied the missing factor. With the help of a girl whom she had taught for four years and trained for one year as a teacher, Maria opened a school for nine or ten girls at their Bridge Street house. The children of neighbours, they would normally be sewing at home to earn their own food, so the only way they could be set free to attend was by Maria compensating them with a pint of rice every four days.

Apart from the deceitful *amah* they now had three baptised Chinese worshipping and working with them, and more 'enquirers' to instruct. Each Sunday these believers and the four families of missionaries met together at the Joneses' quieter place, the nucleus of what was slowly growing into an established church. And by June a hundred were attending the daily morning preaching at Bridge Street. Seating for eighty was provided but sometimes a hundred and fifty crowded in. They came and went at will, puffing at their pipes and looking around unless riveted for a while by the speaker. Most were simply curious passers-by who never came again. But some came often and these the missionaries concentrated upon. Hudson Taylor also ran a night school for men, teaching them to read the Scripture in Martin's romanised Ningbo vernacular. After six months it proved the last straw on his overladen back, for the days and nights were hot and airless, and as the summer wore on John Jones suffered more pain and fever and could do less and less of the work.

On the night of May 13 Hudson Taylor was separated from Maria for the first time since their marriage. The Goughs' baby, not yet two years old, had died of dysentery, and he was guarding her little body against the rats until the funeral in the morning. In a wistful pencilled note to his mother he exposed the tenderness of his own heart as he recalled sitting on deck with the child in his arms as the *Japan* took them to Shanghai after the prayer meeting massacre plot. '. . . I nursed this darling babe most of the way [he mused]; it helped me to conceal my feelings [on] leaving Maria in Ningpo and knowing nothing of her love towards me . . .' He was reminded of the Goughs' great kindness to them through the time of opposition, and their godly wisdom.

> Sometimes when I think of my happiness I feel bewildered. That *I* – who have so long been lonely and despised . . . – been tried and wronged and persecuted, almost to despair should now be able to clasp to my bosom, *my own*, my precious, my tenderly affectionate wife . . . I sometimes feel as if it must be a dream . . .

Since their marriage, funds had come to them in adequate but not large amounts. Maria's private income met her own needs of food and clothing but not more. Hudson Taylor found it interesting that the few dollars he had left for the honeymoon, supplemented by the consular fee he did not have to pay, lasted until their illness. Then they ate and did so little that expenses were minimal. And when normal life was resumed, remittances came again. But on May 5 they were at the end of all they had and on their way to bed. As they knelt together and prayed for their needs the next day to be supplied, a consular messenger knocked loudly at the front door. The Taipings and the Canton war were in everyone's thoughts.

> We had not before been visited at so late an hour, and at first I thought it must be a notice of some political change of importance, in connection with the war, but the packet proved to be two letters [he told Mr Berger], yours and one from Mr. Pearse. You may imagine our joy. The man who brought the letters must have been enjoying himself with some of his friends, or the letters would have reached me sooner.

Now they were rich, with seventy-one pounds in hand. It had come in less than two months, a week or two sooner than usual.

In the same letter he revealed that cruelly soon after Mrs Bausum's move with Miss Aldersey's school to the Presbyterian premises, she had been dismissed and left without support, in part the price of loyalty to Maria and Hudson Taylor. With her children dependent on her she had no alternative but to return to England. 'She is a true missionary,' he wrote. If Miss Stacey's Ladies' Association at Tottenham would support her even to the tune of one hundred and sixty pounds per annum she could manage. Mrs Bausum was warmly received when she reached home, and before long returned to Ningbo.

War in the north — *April–June 1858*

After the capture of Canton foreigners tried to return to the city to build up what had been destroyed. Not surprisingly the people resisted them and attacks on individuals forced them to withdraw again. Even missionary doctors and the well-known George Piercy and Josiah Cox found the resentment too strong. During the occupation Lobscheid was employed to investigate the inmates of the Chinese jails and established that five per cent had been imprisoned as traitors simply for their association with the barbarians. Records in the viceroy's archives were studied and among them a report to the throne by Qi Ying (Ch'i Ying) in 1844 during the 'diplomatic honeymoon'.[7]

On his way north to force his demands upon the Manchus, Lord Elgin called in at Swatow and Shanghai, sounding the opinions of merchants and missionaries. On March 13 William Burns wrote to Hudson Taylor,

> . . . a week ago . . . I was asked to meet him at Breakfast on board ship. I had a full opportunity of speaking with him on . . . opium, the coolie trade, etc. Let us pray that the negociations [*sic*] in which he and others will soon be engaged may be overruled for, if not directed to the good of this people and the establishment of God's Kingdom among them.[8]

At Shanghai Elgin was presented with memorials from both sections of the British community. He responded sympathetically to the missionaries without referring to his instructions from Lord Clarendon. To their request for treaty clauses ensuring toleration for Christians entirely distinct from that granted to Frenchmen and Roman Catholics (for why should they be tarred with that brush?) and for freedom to travel and preach, he replied that foreign protection for Chinese converts would invite hypocritical professions of conversion. And he was right. Then he went on to the Beihe (Peiho) and Tianjin (Tientsin) to fulfil his instructions. To the merchants he said pointedly,

> Christian civilisation will have to win its way among a sceptical and ingenious people, by making it manifest that a faith which reaches to heaven furnishes better guarantees for public and private morality than one which does not rise above earth.[9]

– not that he regarded the merchants as missionaries or naively hoped they would change their ways. He was saying they could not have all they demanded.

By now Britain was alive to the evils of the opium traffic as she had not been a generation earlier, but the problem of extrication from the toils of her wickedness defied the best-intentioned politicians. With the Indian Mutiny still active, though its back was broken, and the assumption by London of direct government in India, immense revenues were needed. It was no time for cutting off the staple source, opium, and shouldering the burden by taxation at home. In February Lord Palmerston was temporarily replaced as Prime Minister by Lord Derby, and Gladstone as Chancellor had to cover the costs of the adventure in China. Lord Elgin had no illusions about the evils of the opium traffic but his instructions were to facilitate it as an open trade. While the Chinese were saying to Ningbo's W A Russell, 'Why offer us life with one hand and death with the other?', Britain's aim was to force China open to her 'civilising influences' while shamefully (and not without a sense of shame) extending the opium trade.[10]

The Dao Guang emperor's impassioned protest before he died eight years previously, was still at least nominally the policy of the Chinese government.

> It is true I cannot prevent the introduction of the flowing poison. Gain-seeking and corrupt men will, for profit and sensuality, defeat my wishes. But nothing will induce me to derive a revenue from the vice and misery of my people.

But since April 1857 the mandarins, with or without imperial sanctions, had been levying a tax of twelve taels per chest (of 133 pounds weight).[11] The hypocritical attitude of Britain, glad of a sop to her conscience, was in 1858 what it had been when Sir Henry Pottinger said to the Chinese commissioners,

> Your people must become more virtuous, your officers incorruptible and then you can stop the opium coming . . . other people will bring it to you, if we should stop [its] cultivation . . . You cannot do better than legalize it.

The voice of the Society for Suppressing Opium Smuggling[12] from its office next door to the CES (respectively 13 and 15 Bedford Row, Holborn) was loudly and consistently raised. Its president, the Rt Hon the Earl of Shaftesbury, and other parliamentary vice-presidents and its committee, strongly representative of all the leading missions and the Bible Society, with Henry Venn,[13] Hudson Taylor's close friend J E Howard, others of the CES, and Captain Fishbourne RN, gave the government no rest. But Parliament then and for fifty more years was to be deaf to plea and protest, so far as effective action went.

Lord Elgin did not share the official sentiments or mention opium in his negotiations. But this was incontrovertibly the second Opium War as much as it was a Western insistence on being recognized as China's equal . . . That

> wretched question of the *Arrow* is a scandalous one [he protested]. Nothing could be more contemptible than the origin of our existing quarrel. I thought bitterly of those who for the most selfish objects are trampling under foot this ancient civilization.

But the incident of the boarding of the *lorcha Arrow* and its use as a *casus belli* was largely forgotten. Realistic reasons for war were now prominent. At last China must accept foreign trade. The reluctant earl's instructions were plain, and all too soon Lord Elgin was to out-Herod the worst culprits, by the sack of the Summer Palace in 1860.

On April 20 the four envoys' fleet of nineteen warships arrived off Dagu (Taku), the fortified mouth of the Beihe, Tianjin's river (map, p 216). With Elgin were the French Baron Gros and the American plenipotentiary, W B Reed. The Russian envoy, as became the nation worsted in the Crimea, held aloof and acted independently when he could. A demand for the treaties of 1842–44 to be revised was sent ashore, but Peking temporised. While the allies were demanding greater concessions, China held that the earlier treaties had conceded too much. Queen Victoria addressed the Xian Feng emperor as 'most high, most mighty and most glorious prince', and the American President hailed him as his 'great and good friend' but identical replies came back to the envoys not from the Court but from the Viceroy of Zhili (Chihli). And the name of each country was provocatively written a space lower than that of China.[14]

All but the Russian envoy returned the messages as unacceptable. The Russian, however, obtained an audience of the viceroy and was with him when word came that six allied gunboats had crossed the Dagu bar and were steaming towards the batteries. The viceroy was for annihilating them but the Russian envoy warned him solemnly of the consequences and the warships were allowed to anchor within easy range of the Chinese guns. Painful negotiations followed, with Samuel Wells Williams and W A P Martin, assisted by Liang A-fa's son A-de, at the heart of them as interpreter–negotiators, responsible for detecting flaws and subterfuges.

The viceroy was obdurate, speaking of the American President as *Guo wang*, insinuating 'vassal prince'. When Ambassador the Hon W B Reed insisted on his using either the word President or the emperor's own title, the viceroy derisively said, not 'the illustrious monarch of your honourable country' as courtesy demanded, but 'your chief king'. The allied envoys then insisted on negotiating with plenipotentiaries, for the failure of Peking to ratify the 1842–44 treaties had led to protracted bickering. The Court would not agree. The negotiations about protocol therefore failed.[15]

On May 20 the British and French bombarded and stormed the Dagu forts, losing twelve dead and seventy-four wounded when a Chinese mine was sprung. They then prepared to advance up the

A PEKING CITADEL AND WALLS

Beihe to Tianjin. Consternation reigned. For fear of the threat to the capital, the government's attitude changed. Imperial representatives were at last appointed and Lord Elgin slowly steamed up the Beihe with the French, American and Russian envoys to reap the spoils. Along the riverbanks the awed populace *ketou*-ed as the 'fire dragons' passed. Palatial quarters were put at the envoys' disposal. Elgin and Gros occupied 'two light and airy pavilions' in a former imperial residence quickly refurbished and repapered, overlooking the junction of the Grand Canal with the Beihe. Their staffs were housed in temples with the idols, all set within spacious enclosed gardens. British and French sentries stood guard at the entrances, the national flags floated over the palace and gunboats were moored within twenty yards of the windows.

The Chinese plenipotentiaries of the highest imperial rank arrived on June 2, resplendent with a cavalcade of carriages and baggage carts, and on the 4th began exchanges with the foreign envoys. Once again Qi Ying, now an old man, was saddled with this hopeless task. Cruelly his reports of 1844, unearthed at Canton, were used 'to laugh the aged diplomat into his grave'.[16]

Within nine days, on June 13, the Russians agreed on their treaty. The next day Wells Williams and Martin obtained a copy of the terms and on the 15th the Chinese agreed to the inclusion in the American treaty of all it contained, only to renege and renegotiate until on the 18th the American treaty was concluded.[17] The British and French took their time and not until a week later, building on the American and Russian texts, declared themselves satisfied. Lord Elgin signed on the 26th and Baron Gros on the 27th.

With minor variations the treaties were alike. To China's chagrin and humiliation ten more ports were to be thrown open to foreign trade and residence. Newchang (now Yingkou) in Manchuria took the barbarians to the far northern shore of the Yellow Sea. Because Elgin and Reed did not wish Tianjin to be a nest of intrigue or afford European powers a position from which they could overawe the capital, and to avoid an impasse with China, no insistence on the inclusion of Tianjin was made. But Yantai (Chefoo) on the north coast of the Shandong peninsula was substituted.[18] Two ports in Taiwan and one on Hainan Island in the far south, together with Swatow, opened up the southern trade extensively. The whole Yangzi river was thrown open, with Nanjing (after the Taipings were defeated) and Hankou, eight hundred miles inland, as the main ports and Zhenjiang (Chinkiang) and Jiujiang (Kiukiang) as additional 'ports of entry and discharge'. Diplomatic representatives of the treaty powers were to take up residence in Peking, foreigners were to travel and live in peace outside the treaty ports, indemnities were exacted and toleration of Christianity was guaranteed. Missionaries *and* Chinese Christians were promised protection in the exercise of their faith. Opium was not mentioned though opium was in everyone's mind.

A misconception subsequently arose through a remark of the American envoy that toleration of Christianity was 'brought forward and encouraged by the Chinese Commissioners themselves'. The mistaken inference was that missionaries were in China 'at the invitation and under the authority and sanction of the Empire of China'. Samuel Wells Williams was at pains to present the facts in the *Chinese Recorder* twenty years later.[19] The erroneous impression arose, he maintained, from a reported conversation between the Chinese Commissioners and the Russian envoy. The Commissioners expressed a willingness for foreign missionaries to go into the interior but not for merchants to do so. They had in mind the 'quiet, gentlemanly, learned members' of the Orthodox Church with the Russian trade mission already in Peking, who had no evangelistic aims. So the Russian treaty contained permission for missionaries to travel in the interior and practise their faith. By the 'most favoured nation' precedent this concession could therefore be claimed by other nations.

When Wells Williams and Martin discussed these terms with the Chinese they found them strongly opposed to other missionaries travelling inland. But on June 15 the Russian terms were conceded, only to be withdrawn at 9 pm 'in the most decided terms', with the insistence that American missionaries be confined to the treaty ports. Toleration for Chinese Christians was granted but the words *nei di* (*nui ti*, inland) were struck out. Early on the morning of the 16th, before Ambassador Reed and the Commissioners met to sign the treaty, Wells Williams and Martin submitted a new draft incorporating toleration of Christianity with freedom to worship and distribute Christian literature. The last phrase was rejected, but the protection of Chinese Christians went through. The Commissioners also offered to allow a limited number of missionaries with passports but without families to travel anywhere in China and preach, but this was seen to be restrictive and the Americans rejected it. With the concessions gained it was found that in practice everything required was practicable, for the text provided that missionaries and converts were 'in no case to be interfered with or molested in teaching or practising the principles of Christianity'.[20]

Lord Elgin saw the American form of words and used an abbreviated version in the British treaty. Economy of wording could achieve more, by allowing broader interpretation.[21] Sufficient detail made the meaning incontrovertibly plain, however, as Hudson Taylor and others were to prove by painful experience in 1868 and subsequently. The *North China Herald* published the fifty-six articles of the Treaty of Tientsin (Tianjin) in full. Article 9 conceded travel and residence in the interior under a moderate passport system, and Article 29 read,

> . . . Hereafter those who quietly teach and profess these doctrines (Protestant and Roman Catholic) shall not be harassed or persecuted on account of their faith [and] . . . shall be in no way interfered with or molested . . .

The whole treaty was due to be ratified in Peking within a year. The London *Times* of September 16 commented,

> The next article strengthens all the facilities for spreading our faith among the Chinese; for it permits all British subjects – merchants, missionaries or travellers – to pass up and down, throughout the length and breadth of China. This decisive concession opens up the whole country.[22]

It remained a moot point whether or not the inclusion of such terms side by side with those governing marketing and tariffs was beneficial or degrading.

The CES *Gleaner* echoed the general jubilation of the missionary world with the words,

> Thanks be to God! unfeigned, fervent thanks! All China is open! the prayers of half a century are receiving their fulfilment! . . . A new era dawns upon the work of Missions in China – new territories present themselves, provinces as large, and some of them more populous, than European kingdoms . . .[23]

The American Minister had weightier comments to make when his work was done,

> I consider the missionary element in China a great conservative and protective principle. It is the only barrier between the unhesitating advance of commercial adventure, and the not incongruous element of Chinese imbecile corruption. The missionary, according to my

> observation, is contented to live under the treaty and the law it creates; or if, in his zeal, he *chooses* to go beyond it, he is content to take the risk without troubling the Government to protect him . . . [Missionaries] are essential to the interests of our country. Without them . . . I could not have [discharged] my duties here . . . The Chinese plenipotentiaries promptly acceded to the article as it now stands.[24]

The French came last and the treaty they concluded on June 27 went further than the others. It spelled out in detail the meaning of toleration:

> . . . the members of all Christian bodies [communions] shall enjoy full security for their persons, their property, and the free exercise of their religious worship; and entire protection shall be given to missionaries who peacefully enter the country, furnished with passports . . . No obstacle [shall be raised] . . . to the recognized right of any person in China to embrace Christianity.

But then followed the sinister addition which was to lead to untold harm and bloodshed,

> Whatever has been heretofore written, proclaimed, or published in China, by order of the Government, against the Christian faith, is wholly abrogated and nullified in all provinces of the empire.[25]

The Roman Church was acutely conscious of history, and by this stroke attempted to wipe the slate clean of any and all appeals to the past which might again be used against her. But to Protestant commentators it was at once apparent, as it seems was not until too late realised by the Chinese, that decrees confiscating Catholic property were also abrogated. This threw the door wide open for Rome to claim valuable sites and buildings in use by influential Chinese for generations since confiscation. The cathedral sites in Peking were among them.

In 1861 Monsignor Mouly, Vicar-Apostolic of Peking, on a visit to France, told how his Christians expected violent persecution when war broke out. Already in 1858 in the one province of Guizhou (Kweichow) they lived in constant danger, hiding in caves to elude their tormentors. The past fifty years had seen forty persecutions. Two hundred Chinese Christians had been banished, twenty had died and five had been executed. But now all were surprised by the turn in events. Prince Kong, brother of the emperor, called for Mouly to mediate between the Chinese and French. The bishop was conveyed with great honour to Peking, but arrived after Prince Kong had accepted the treaty conditions. The old cathedral grounds were restored to the Church and liberty granted to erect a cross on the new building. As elsewhere in the world France was setting herself up as protector of papal interests.[26] John Burdon saw it as 'a powerful French ecclesiastico-political organization in favour of Romish missions in China' inadvertently abetted by Britain's joint intervention in Eastern affairs. But it was a *fait accompli*. At long last liberty to be a Christian openly and without fear was at least in sight. For a time, however, it was dangerously elusive.

To anticipate subsequent events – although the Chinese negotiators had plenipotentiary credentials, the Court not surprisingly disowned their sweeping concessions. Instead of the gates of China being flung open and peaceful relations at last being established, confusion, insults and provocations followed, until Lord Elgin and Baron Gros, at home again in Europe, were sent back to the Beihe two years later. Then the merchants' demand for Tianjin to be an open port was met. But the first reason for Peking's failure to honour the agreement was the barbarians' own ineptitude: as soon as the treaties were signed and the last bows exchanged, they sailed away bag and baggage from the Beihe, as if escaping. At once the *Peking Gazette*, mouthpiece of the emperor observed, 'The barbarians had come headlong with their ships to Tientsin. Moved by the imperial commands . . . they now weighed anchor and stood out to sea.'[27]

Harry Parkes, H B M Consul at Canton and a future Minister at Peking saw that 'by that step they [the foreign envoys] undid all they had previously done'. To register the imperial disapproval of his own envoys' conceding what any negotiator would have had to concede, the emperor graciously sent the chief commissioner 'the silken cord of self-despatch as a mark of the Throne's benevolent leniency'. Suicide was the honourable and preferable alternative to capital punishment.[28] And Rutherford Alcock warned the Foreign Office that privileges so indiscriminate as to include residence in the interior were bound to lead to international incidents. When he himself returned to China with a knighthood as British Minister in Peking, this was the hot issue he had continually to handle. Missionaries were as deeply involved as any, and his Shanghai acquaintance Hudson Taylor was involuntarily to have the consuls, minister, Foreign Office and House of Lords in heated altercation about the rights and wrongs of the situation. But that was a decade later.

'The seals have been broken' *June–October 1858*

Only a month after the signing of the Treaty of Tientsin, Griffith John remarked on the change in attitude of the Chinese he encountered. And two weeks later a marked change in the demeanour of officials prompted him to write,

> The seals have been broken, and a wide door has been flung open to the Christian Church. May God be pleased to raise up men of burning zeal, intense devotion, and deep piety for this land! I am anxious to get far into the interior as soon as possible.[29]

A few weeks later he made his first attempt. William Muirhead remembered Valignano's prayer and wrote: 'The rock is opened and the prayer answered.'[30]

In August proclamations began to appear in the streets of Chinese cities announcing peace and agreement between the nations, and missionaries were able to return even to Canton. The ageing and disconsolate Bishop of Victoria, George Smith, wrote home of the great opportunity unfolding but, to judge by the response of the Church in Britain so far, the small likelihood of her rising to the occasion. In fourteen years he had seen little inclination to respond to repeated pleas on China's behalf. With barely enough reinforcements to replace losses by disease and death, he could point only to Ningbo as a place where appreciable results were to be seen. To him this indicated a need for greater effort, not a shrug of ecclesiastical shoulders. 'Once more I appeal to British Christians that while India [is receiving abundant help] China may not be overlooked . . . I know by experience the mental sickness of hope long deferred . . .'[31] But the CMS never took up China to the same degree as Africa and India.[32]

Appeals of one kind and another multiplied. Dr E Wentworth of Fuzhou (Foochow) addressed an open letter to all churches and missions. In the light of the new treaties he proposed what Charles Gutzlaff had proposed prematurely, a conference to agree on a division of the whole of China into areas of responsibility. It was the Church's golden opportunity to co-operate, intelligently and so avoid overlapping and discord. His initiative drew little response while, piecemeal, missionaries of all kinds prepared for dispersion into the interior.[33]

Carstairs Douglas wrote from Amoy to Donald Matheson, (the former partner of Jardine, Matheson and Company who resigned in protest against the opium traffic and gave himself to missions), pointing out that Hokkien, the dialect of Amoy, was also the language of Taiwan. The English Presbyterian Mission should send men there. This was taken up the following year and the Church of today in Taiwan stems from his initiative.[34]

The *Gleaner* published two letters from Hudson Taylor dated October 30 and November 15, 1858, appealing for prayer 'that many labourers may be raised up, both here and in other lands, to preach Christ and him crucified to the untold millions of this now opened land.' He himself was anchored by responsibilities he could not shelve, but his concept of the expansion of the Church was clear,

> We are likely to lose some of the Ningpo missionaries who will go to new ports or inland. And oh! will not the Church at home awake herself, and send out many to publish the glad tidings . . . Many of us long (oh! how we long!) to go, but there are duties, and cares, and ties that bind us, which none but the Lord can unloose. May He give his gifts to many of the native Christians, qualify them to be pastors, evangelists, etc, so that they may be able to take the care of the Churches already formed, carry the word to the regions beyond, and set us at liberty for this work.[35]

The *Missionary Reporter* quoted another letter from him,

> Rome is prepared to push her advantages. Merchants and others in trade will use the extension of their privileges. May those who seek the salvation of this people, by the truth as it is in Jesus, put forth renewed and mighty efforts for their salvation . . .

The Wesleyan Josiah Cox reported to his board from the house he bravely rented in Canton city that buildings were rising again and shops reopening. 'Surely plain masonry is lovely where desolation reigned before.' Chinese merchants were trading again with foreigners.

> We are all ready for work; we never felt so attached to our glorious calling as we do now . . . Who that has ever felt the kindling of a missionary zeal, would not envy our present prospects in Canton? Yet the missionary students shrink from joining the China Mission because of its difficulties? No, it cannot be! Depend upon it, we are envied, and the best men you have got would hail your orders to come out here. Try them; give the call, and, moved by the Holy Ghost, chosen men will be at your service; for our work is of God . . .[36]

At the same time his colleague John Preston was exhorting their directors from Macao. He had just heard of one new missionary to be sent,

> As I think now of 'one to be sent' *some time* . . . as the recorded resolution of an eminently Missionary portion of Christ's church . . . I feel some righteous indignation . . . If ever God by His providence opened doors of access to a people, and pointed them out to the church to enter in, He is doing so in China; and if ever a people would repay earnest missionary toil, that people are the Chinese; and yet we read of 'one to be sent' some day in the course of time. Has the promise of God the Father to His eternal Son, 'I will give the Heathen for thine inheritance', been lost sight of by the church of Christ? . . . The honour of God, jealousy for Christ's glory, the welfare of souls, the nearness of eternity call upon all, 'Do something, do it, do it.'[37]

In a population of four hundred million and more there were only ninety Protestant missionaries (Latourette said eighty-one of twenty societies, some were on furlough), and fifty Chinese Christian preachers. In comparison Britain's thirty million shared thirty thousand ministers and as many lay workers. Surely the Church could afford to look farther afield? Moreover, of the missionaries in China two in every three were American.[38]

Those eighty or ninety lost no time in putting their new advantages to the test. The British and Foreign Bible Society rose to the occasion as always. Its work in Canton and Hong Kong disrupted by hostilities and subversion and in other areas by colporteurs being mistaken for Taiping rebels, the Society still had massive stocks of Scriptures to distribute. There were too few Chinese Christians to draw upon. At Shanghai William Muirhead was secretary of the Bible Society committee in succession to Walter Medhurst. Knowing that Alexander Wylie had pointed out the folly of indiscriminate printing for rats, termites and fire to devour, while an accumulation of forty thousand Old and New Testaments awaited use, he proposed to the LMS that Wylie be released to promote distribution.

It was an appointment after Wylie's own heart and what he was in fact requesting. As Travelling Agent he began to organise a distribution network and prepared 'for an extensive circulation throughout the empire'. In October Lord Elgin after concluding his treaty with Japan, 'with characteristic promptitude' made his way with a steam squadron far up the Yangzi to Hankou and Wuchang, now Wuhan, 'that great central mart of China'. Wylie went with him, distributing Scripture. Elgin's purpose was to test China's sincerity and to inaugurate British trade at the river ports. Wylie then began a series of intrepid journeys north, south, west and east. It was also at this time that he joined the veteran E C Bridgman in forming and contributing to the new North China Branch of the Royal Asiatic Society, with an erudite article on the *Coins of the Ch'ing Dynasty*. This cabinet-maker-turned-printer was well on the way to becoming one of the greatest Sinologues.[39]

History was also made by the retired Miss Aldersey. Still concerned for if not administering the blind school in Ningbo, taught by 'Agnes Gutzlaff', she began training the pupils to be teachers of the blind, and requested the Bible Society to publish the Gospel of Luke in embossed romanised Ningbo vernacular Chinese for the blind among the thirty to fifty million using the dialect.

Euphoria is wholly understandable and pardonable in the climate of the Treaty of Tientsin. Ignoring the extent of upheaval by the various rebellions, the Bible Society hailed the terms of the treaty as if they were about to be translated into action everywhere in the land. The annual report said, 'Not only is peace restored to India, but China, with all her barriers withdrawn, is accessible to the Gospel. "This is the Lord's doing, and it is marvellous in our eyes." '[40] Funds were made available, Samuel Dyer's movable fount was put to use again, and millions more Scriptures printed, and all societies increased their efforts to send them in the hands of travellers to every part of the empire. But George Pearse sadly confessed that the CES was 'so driven into a corner for funds' that they could do nothing.

In 1858 August Hanspach of the Berlin Mission began the extensive travels in the interior which went on for eleven years. Renowned for the speed and extent of his journeys he went in danger of his life and more than once was severely wounded. He was a truly apostolic figure who made a deep impression on the Chinese.

Now also began a series of ambitious travels by Muirhead, Griffith John, Edkins, Aitchison, Nevius, Burdon and others such as Hudson Taylor would have joined before his adoption of the new policy with John Jones. Instead he was to have his own adventures at Ningbo. Muirhead reported to the LMS that all missions found Chinese Christians, with notable exceptions, still to be reluctant preachers but good in personal evangelism. The weight of pioneering would continue to rest on the foreigner while Chinese evangelists were being trained. While some missionaries travelled, others must settle and build up instructed congregations. In Ningbo success was rewarding this phase of the work.

In the early summer of 1858, while the allied envoys were negotiating at Tianjin, Edkins and Aitchison ventured as far as Hangzhou and traversed the West Lake, most flourishing seat of Buddhism in China. Learned priests held conversations with them and they were visited at their boat by Manchus from the ten-thousand-strong garrison. But their reception could have been very different. Aitchison and Burdon had gone on living quietly at Pinghu until John Burdon's remarriage, and after that in Shanghai.[41]

As soon as the terms of the Treaty of Tientsin became known, the CMS *Intelligencer* carried an article by Burdon saying 'it became a point of great interest to ascertain how far its stipulations would be recognized by the mandarins'. With William Aitchison he had set out to test them.

> The authorities, at all the cities and towns visited during this tour, acknowledged that the missionaries were at liberty to proceed if they so decided. Thus the disturbed state of the country (due to the Taipings) alone prevented them from advancing beyond the Yang-tzekiang [Yangzi river].

For in October he found that in some regions the treaty could not be enforced, when with Griffith John, Aitchison and others he attempted to travel north as far as the Yellow River.[42]

Pressing westwards from Shanghai at first to join the Grand Canal, they penetrated beyond Suzhou to Changzhou, Marco Polo's great and noble city, where the governor-general had his residence (map, p 202). At various points they were stopped and questioned but always permitted to proceed. 'What would have been impossible two years ago was accomplished with the most perfect ease.'

There was consternation when they spoke of crossing the Yangzi and going to the north. All was commotion over there with large cities in hourly danger of falling to Nian-fei, rebels and bandits. Officials treated them on terms of absolute equality and they were free to preach and worship as they wished. The common people were quiet and inoffensive, innocently saying to each other in the hearing of the missionaries, 'He's a devil, a real devil,' the only term they knew for 'a foreigner, a real foreigner'. So far inland, beyond where the gospel had before been preached by Protestant Christians, 'The soil seemed more sacred and the heavens more divine . . .

an hour, this, never to be forgotten.' Affable mandarins with their retinues visited them and exchanged gifts, military mandarins came aboard their boats and approved of their object 'to exhort people to turn from the bad and follow the good', but made it obvious that travel on the north shore of the Yangzi would be foolhardy. They visited Zhenjiang (Chinkiang) at the junction of the Grand Canal and Yangzi, and found it desolate, occupied only by troops and the merchants who served them. The city was still too close to the Taipings to be worth restoring.

So they abandoned their plan and turned southward to Hangzhou down the Grand Canal again via Suzhou. In June 1859, however, Muirhead and Griffith John were to succeed in reaching the old bed of the Yellow River at Qingjiang (Tsingkiang), three hundred miles from Shanghai, and returned only just in time to avoid being caught by a reversal of China's attitude towards foreigners. Back in 1856, Burdon and Edkins had been turned away from the gates of Suzhou and only managed to enter clandestinely. Now the population of two million were as open to them as anywhere near Shanghai. At Hangzhou too, where a missionary had recently been sent back to Shanghai under escort and Muirhead had been questioned by the chief magistrate, no one in authority asked why they came or where they were going. For four days they preached without hindrance.

So now John Burdon joined his appeal to the rest, speaking from experience,

> There is hardly an important city that we visited at which a judicious man, by kindness, and patience, and prayer, might not be able to establish himself, and, by living amongst the people, far from all foreign influence, gain a permanent footing, first for himself, and then for the Gospel . . . Are we to have the men to occupy these cities, and to take possession of this empire in the name of the Lord? For many years we have been praying for the result which has now been brought about, and how are we prepared to meet it? Our own Mission here consists of two men, and one of us [W H Collins] is necessarily . . . tied to Shanghai by a missionary school . . . I have confidence in the zeal and love of Christians at home that they will not leave us long without assistance, or suffer us to fight single-handed against Satan in his very seat.[43]

Alas, his confidence was unjustified.

In 1859 Burdon was to make an attempt to settle in Hangzhou, at about the same time as John and Helen Nevius. These three were the first (George Moule followed five years later.) Twenty-four years had elapsed since Gutzlaff advised the CMS to make Shanghai and Hangzhou their goals, and eight years since Lobscheid had drawn attention to Gutzlaff's advice. A much used cliché describing the prerequisites of a successful pioneer missionary – 'grace, grit and gumption' – originated at this time from young Griffith John. None of these men lacked any one of these qualities.[44]

But in October 1858 the Taipings, pent up like a volcano before eruption, burst out of Nanjing yet again. Their territory extending at this time from Jiujiang (Kiukiang) in the west to near Zhenjiang (Chinkiang) in the east gave room for manoeuvre. With the four regional 'Kings' or princes of the North, South, East and West dead, of the early hierarchy only Hong Xiu-quan (Hung Hsiu-ch'üan), the Taiping Wang, and Hong Ren, the Shield King, survived. Both had become high-handed, violent men. On October 23 the *North China Herald* carried the chilling news of the breakout by 'the long-haired men' and the fall of towns in Anhui province and the cities of Yizheng (Iching) and Yangzhou in Jiangsu. Both were near the Grand Canal and Zhenjiang (map, p 202). Other rebels, unconnected with the Taipings, took a town which had long resisted them, and massacred every man, woman and child. From Shanghai to Ningbo fear gripped the hearts of everyone. It was not until eighteen months later that their area was invaded, but at Ningbo there was carnage before the Taipings came.

Midsummer madness[45] *July–August 1858*

July 1858 began well for Hudson Taylor and Maria. With Miss Aldersey and the Russells friendly again and Burella writing affectionately from Shanghai where she and John Burdon were making a home for William Aitchison, life was as peaceful as the work would allow. Maria's harmonium had arrived, so damp and damaged that it was unusable, until Hudson Taylor restored it. More important were the surgical instruments and drugs to replace his losses. Photographs adorned the walls and table and Maria was beginning to feel a part of the family she had never met. With Amelia's marriage approaching Hudson wrote brotherly letters full of the advice of an established family man!

But the summer heat was extreme. The roof tiles became so hot and their attic so oven-like that he had large mats secured over the roof to bring the temperature inside down to 85 degrees Fahrenheit sometimes, from the ninety-eight degrees it was otherwise. Dr

Parker wrote home that all foreigners in Ningbo were suffering from the heat and his own son William was 'reduced to a skeleton'. He and his family were still in the house among the rice-fields and suffering from ague. Hudson Taylor had a painful boil and John and Mary Jones were still losing sleep from their intractable skin disease. Foreigners were slow to understand tropical hygiene. Earlier in the year F F Gough, in a note accompanying a gift of half a dozen flannel vests from his home in England, commended them to Hudson Taylor as 'very comfortable under a Chinese dress this hot weather'. Flannel 'cholera belts' were in use as recently as 1940, so slowly did misconceptions die. In 1858 convention still forbade light clothing – except when wearing Chinese clothes.

Whatever the temperature, they could not sit and do nothing. All carried on with doctoring, routine meetings, and visits to the country. Daily teaching of the baptised believers and preparation of others for baptism demanded considerable effort, and Hudson Taylor found preaching and teaching in the presence of fellow-missionaries on Sundays an added strain. They expected formality. It was easier to relax and be a Chinese among the Chinese. Promulgation of the terms of the Tientsin treaties ensured freedom from attack for the present, and John Jones took to spending most of every day out in the villages preaching.

In early August Mrs Bausum and her three children left for England. Ningbo was not the same to Maria and Hudson Taylor without them. 'She is almost my mother-in-law,' he wrote home. 'She has taken my part in the difficulties I have had . . . her kindness will be a claim to your love.' A whole year later he was still writing to commend them to his parents' care,

> You know how kind she was to me, and that too when others were afraid to aid me, however much they felt with me . . . her losing her position in the school there was probably owing in part to her kindness to me . . .

But the hot season is the riot season when tempers boil over. The promontory to the east of Ningbo around and beyond the East Lake (map, p 128) was too hilly to allow of enough rice fields to support all its population. So the villagers supplemented their farming income by fishing and selling their catches to a Ningbo strong-man named Li, a salt merchant, in exchange for cash vouchers nominally a thousand brass cash in value. With the passage of time Li, 'odious for injustice and oppression', took more and more commission when the people redeemed their vouchers, until they were getting only five hundred cash. In mid-July they came to the conclusion that justice could only come by the chief magistrate's intervention. Unarmed and intending only a peaceful demonstration, the village elders assembled on a drill ground outside the city near the bridge of boats and requested an interview. The *daotai* and district magistrate went out to meet them, but weighing Li's influence against the villagers' they brushed aside the complaints. A rabble of city people then seized the opportunity to make trouble, broke up the mandarins' sedan chairs and abused the magistrates.

Aghast at the turn in events, the villagers determined to put things right. Disowning the rabble they apologised for their own part and sent five hundred elders and old people in small groups to another conference with the magistrates on the drill ground. This time trouble-makers posted a notice in the city alleging threats by the countrymen to destroy the house and family of strong-man Li. Five hundred hired men with Li's son at their head confronted the deputation and fired on them, killing ten and wounding many villagers and bystanders.

Now the country-folk vowed reprisals and the alarm raised in the city was enough to make wealthy people send their families and valuables away to safety, trade to be suspended and the poor to be

'VILLAGE NEAR THE LAKE'

thrown out of work. Hudson Taylor and John Jones went to the aid of the wounded in the suburbs and out in the villages near the lake where they were known. Discovering that Chinese 'doctors' were charging the wounded seventy dollars for unskilled treatment, they set to work. In thanking his parents for the surgical instruments, Hudson Taylor wrote on August 11,

> they have established my fame in the . . . [market] town where most of those who were wounded resided. As I cut out shot after shot, the poor ignorant people looked on with wonder and admiration exclaiming 'is he not one of the gods or genie!' Should I not make a good trumpeter, eh?

The people wanted to prepare a feast for them and to pay for the hire of their boat, urging them to come and live there and offering a house for rent or to sell land for them to build. Frequent visits were necessary to care for the wounded, so Maria went with him and talked with the women.

On the night of the 11th they reached home at 9.30 p m. At midnight seven hundred of Li's men set out in three companies to attack the peasants from different directions at daylight. But the villagers were expecting trouble, destroyed the bridges behind the attackers, decimated one company with mattocks and farming implements and trapped two hundred more. A hundred and twenty were killed in the fighting and thirty prisoners put to death. Strongman Li's son was killed and quartered on the field. Two of the severely injured came to Hudson Taylor in Ningbo for treatment. On August 30 he could say, '. . . My medical work here has been very heavy, early and late, and often without time or opportunity for eating.' A month after the battle he was still treating the wounded. But his main responsibility was for preaching, a lot of it to the same Chinese audience every Sunday, so that much hard work in preparation was involved.

On the same day a short note from John Burdon reached Maria. Her sister Burella, his bride, was dead. She had suddenly gone down with cholera. John wrote, 'I really feel unable to write. Please accept this as a token of unabated affection and with love to Mr. Taylor . . .' It was only nine months since the wedding. At thirty-two he had twice been bereaved of a wife, once of a child, and was solitary again. He returned to his evangelistic travels with Aitchison, as intrepid as ever, but months later he was still tearful when he spoke of Burella. More than ever the uncertainty of life came home to everyone. Burella had only just commented on the unexpected death of two ladies in the merchant community, wondering who would be next. From now on Hudson was everything in life to Maria, for her brother Samuel was unpredictable and soon emigrated to New Zealand.

'Settled' work[46] *September–December 1858*

With the coming of September a nostalgic note crept into Hudson Taylor's letters as had happened before. The four years since the traumatic parting from his father at the Liverpool station in September 1854 when 'the engine soon dragged the train out of sight', seemed twice as long. The same nagging question came to mind. 'Will I see them again in this life? or will it be when beautiful and glorified? . . . I sometimes feel half-inclined to envy the old red box' – which still travelled to and fro carrying gifts, curios and equipment. The sense of separation was being increased by the failure of the postal service to and from Ningbo. He might go two or three months without any letter, and had to explain that he was writing as regularly since his marriage as before. The failure of those responsible 'twice out of three times' to catch the European mail ship at Shanghai always added a fortnight or a month to the time lag before a reply could come. Since John Burdon took to travelling again after Burella's death there was no one in Shanghai to give the personal attention to mails that made all the difference. But never mind all that,

> I think the happiness of one week of married life exceeds that of a year of single life [far exceeding even his expectations]. . . . loving her (such a darling) so tenderly, does not make me love you less dearly, but rather the opposite . . .

His capacity for affection was inexhaustible.

All the money they needed was coming to them now, and George Pearse assured them that even if the CES could not send any, he and his close friends would do what they could. The Society was out of debt at last – but talking again of sending more new missionaries while Dr Parker waited for the arrears in his salary to be made up. But while many thought Hudson Taylor poor he was enjoying being able to share what he considered abundance with others he knew to be in need, even thirty pounds to his parents who had suffered financial losses, and twenty to his grandmother.

William Parker's hospital on the riverside was in full use and they were now building his own home, to the great admiration of W A P Martin.[47] Nothing deterred this man. Working to the limit of his strength he could still add building after building to his mission station with 'characteristic energy and perseverance'. Hudson Taylor was helping him medically, and both he and John Jones took a day's duty, preaching and talking with patients in the wards. The brief phase Taylor had at Swatow of feeling that medical work wasted his time was well over. The *Lancet* was coming by each mail and he was reading up his medicine and surgery with a view to completing his course and qualifying whenever he might go back to London. To this end also he worked systematically as Parker's formal assistant. Whether or not his work was in mind, Moorfields Hospital at this time issued a special report on diseases of the eye most prevalent in the East and offered to train missionaries in their treatment, saying that 'in China missionaries thus educated have effected a great deal of good'.[48]

Parker had thousands of handbills and placards printed with the heading 'FREE MEDICAL HOSPITAL' to say that patients were now seen at the new hospital every day except Sundays, the dates of which he supplied, but emergencies at any time. Wrapping papers for medicines carried the same information. But the river was a busy thoroughfare between the city and country, and the nearby ferry carried thousands. Everyone watched the hospital going up and valued it. Patients were learning to read in romanised Chinese while in hospital, and went out with the Scriptures to amaze their friends at home. Martin remarked that people 'from the country becoming Christians form the nucleus of daughter churches'. Every church in Ningbo was benefiting. The Bishop of Victoria, visiting Ningbo, was impressed. Yet with all his other work William Parker found strength to enjoy a change and go preaching in the country on Sunday afternoons with John Jones.

More and more Hudson Taylor's letters showed the pressure upon him, as he switched from topic to topic. 'I am *very* hard-worked,' he wrote on September 25. 'I have not finished my work before 12 p.m. for the last five nights.' His own dispensary at Bridge Street looked impressive with new bottles adorned by yellow labels from home. But his daily round of preaching and teaching kept him most busy, while Maria ran her school by day and when free from that ran a sewing co-operative of neighbourhood women while she read and taught them from the Bible. She herself collected orders and supervised the work to provide a livelihood for them. From England with Miss Stacey's help she also ordered a small printing press, and before long was employing a woman full time, printing leaflets in romanised *t'u wo* (*tu hua*) a patois more basic than the Ningbo dialect of educated people. This activity continued until and after her death more than a decade later.

For years there had been a flourishing American Press at Ningbo, but in October 1858 a new manager arrived who was to revolutionise its work and to become a good friend of the Taylors. William Gamble was an admirer of Samuel Dyer, Maria's father, and repeated Dyer's early research in order to update it.[49] Collecting all the books used by Christians in China and the Straits, he analysed the Chinese characters in use, in order of frequency, calculating the number of each needed, and produced the smallest possible typeface. Then he reorganised the arrangement of his founts, enabling his compositors to do three times the work in the same time as before. In 1859 he printed 7,400,000 pages, and in 1860 he moved the press to Shanghai to enjoy decades of immense achievement.

The year 1858 had begun with only one Chinese Christian as the fruit of all Hudson Taylor's and the Joneses' effort and prayer, the repentant *amah* who had to be disciplined. The second, the reformed Buddhist Ni, being a cotton-worker with seasonal employment, was free to go out preaching with John Jones. He could hold an audience of his own people. Another young teacher named Tsiu, who became the third to be baptised, soon brought his mother to share his faith in Christ, and Ni, exhorting the other members of his Buddhist sect, persuaded one, a basket-maker named Feng Nenggui to follow his example.[50] A deaf old neighbour of the Joneses, brought in to hear the gospel by the young man's mother, was the sixth, baptised in August.

This motley group, so outwardly unpromising and so often disappointing as their pagan attitudes changed slowly, was the church on which Hudson Taylor, Maria, John and Mary Jones spent many hours in individual and group instruction. But it was the training school which only a few years later was to provide the evangelists and pastors of the fledgling China Inland Mission. 'In watching over them', John Jones wrote, 'I see much to grieve me, as I do in my own heart . . . Our hearts are often made heavy by discovering things far different from the fruits we expected to find.' Dishonesty was the common failing. One of them protested in self-defence that it was the universal custom in Ningbo. It was, and not only in Ningbo. They had to learn to substitute Christian standards.

Sunday worship all together was held morning and afternoon, with the Lord's Supper, and an hour of individual instruction for each member, a day's work in itself. But evangelistic meetings for the public followed each session, so that the morning's activities ran from 9–10.30 and 10.45–12 noon, and the afternoon meetings from 2–3.30 and 3.45–5. On Monday evening they all met again to pray, and once a month concentrated their prayer on the world at large. The church of which this handful was the nucleus had a missionary heart from its inception. Whenever the able-bodied were free they accompanied the missionaries on their preaching trips into the country. It had to be an expanding church, adding to its numbers by true conversions through their own testimony, or it would wilt instead of growing, and die before maturing. This was in Hudson Taylor's mind when he told George Pearse apropos of the opening of all China to the gospel, 'Many of us are bound by ties which we cannot release ourselves from, to this place and neighbourhood. The work keeps us here, may it increase more and more.'

All this painstaking effort was against the background of ill health and political unrest. On September 25 Charles Hall, in a chatty letter about his own work with the E C Lords, said almost as an afterthought, 'We are expecting attacks from the countrymen daily. We are, however, as safe here in our Father's keeping as in happy England.' The others made no mention of it at the time. In November Hudson Taylor, in reassuring his mother about the Taipings, whom false reports had taken as far as Ningbo even before their October breakout, filled in the story.

> Tho' we have had some local troubles and riots near Ningpo, *the* Rebels have not been anywhere near us. One city, Nyinghai, was actually taken, and the Mandarin, who was very oppressive, was killed by a party of villagers headed by a lad of 16 . . . (In a dream he saw the imperial dragon coming down out of heaven to him, which was interpreted to mean that he should become Emperor.)

But that was forty miles from Ningbo and the uprising was put down by local citizens who killed and scattered the bemused villagers. A month later beheadings in reprisal were still being meted out.

October was a difficult month. Someone was ill in every missionary home in Ningbo, and at times more than one. Parker, the doctor, and Mrs Hall were racked by malarial paroxysms.

Halfway through a pregnancy, she lost her child. At about the same time Maria's babe was born prematurely at seven months and died. Intensive care was unknown in those days. To Hudson's mother she wrote, referring to home-letters written since hearing of her pregnancy,

> I had never before realised what a Mother I had in you. For more than half my life I have been motherless, and it was a new and strange pleasure to me to feel that there was one who loved and cared for me . . . We did again and again dedicate the little unborn infant to God and He . . . surely accepted the intention of our hearts.

She and Hudson, John and Mary Jones and one of their children were at one point all ill together.

Concurrently, Hudson Taylor was involved with the British consul over the lawlessness of British ships' crews.

> Last Wednesday 6th, as I was going through the city, I saw an immense crowd near one of the American Presbyterian chapels and inquiring the cause, was shown three English sailors bound in a boat, with another man wounded and unbound. They had been in the country robbing and – worse. Ten went, four were seized, six tried to swim away, half succeeded, half drowned. I took them to the Consulate. Thursday – we went to [the] village – Consul, Naval officers and several boats of men: I was interpreter. Got some information. Next day had a trial which had to be adjourned for want of evidence – the Chinese being afraid to come forward as witnesses, for fear of further trouble. Yesterday we were examining into it again, and today again I have to go and see about it . . . We must do our best to protect the poor Chinese from these rascals.

One sick woman was so alarmed by the sailors taking things off the bed on which she was lying that she died. As an assessor in the consular court Hudson Taylor's work was to cross-question witnesses in Chinese and advise the consul, who as foreign magistrate passed judgment.

It was all part of missionary life as week followed week and the heat of summer changed to cold and windy winter. In November the novelty of the preaching wore off and attendance by townsfolk dropped. An announcement that Hudson Taylor would display picture posters and expound them filled the hall again, but while Maria and Mary Jones were unable to attend, Chinese women stayed away. John Jones cheerfully noted that in the country 'the knowledge of God and His Son' was gaining ground, and the handful of Christians and enquirers in the city was steadily advancing, enjoying fellowship and reading the Bible together. The ups and downs had to be taken as they came.

In what was probably cerebral malaria Mrs Hall became feverishly excited and at times delirious. It was impossible for her husband to do any work. He took her and their infant son to Shanghai. They had hardly learned enough Chinese yet to get a footing in Ningbo, and had suffered so much from sickness and the heat that the opening of north China offered strong attractions to them. 'Little is known at present of the province,' *The Gleaner* commented, for few facts had been learned of it since the visit by Medhurst in the *Huron* twenty-three years earlier. In that invigorating climate, where 'the blue air sparkled like champagne' so much more could be achieved, Hall thought.[51] 'I should be glad to hear that the English Baptists were able to establish a mission in the north of China.' But after a few weeks in Alexander Wylie's house, while he was away with Lord Elgin's Yangzi squadron, Mrs Hall's condition improved enough for them to return to Ningbo and their strong inclination to head straight for Shandong in the north was set aside for the present. Even though the people of Shanghai and Ningbo gave Hall the impression of having heard and rejected the gospel, it would be impossible to take his wife as the only foreign woman into an area unexplored since Medhurst's voyage in the *Huron* in 1836.

In the ship going back to Ningbo the Halls' baby was fretful. Before they realised what was happening he was dead. They had thought he was only teething. So their first act on reaching Ningbo, their furnace of afflictions, was to bury him. Reporting their movements to George Pearse, Charles Hall confided,

> You at home can form little idea of the influence of this climate upon the mind and the fearful depression commonly caused by severe trial. Instances abound on every hand – all are more or less affected by it. I do not think there is a foreigner in China who is not more *irritable* and uneven in temper than he would naturally be at home.

'To take her mind off her loss' he helped his wife to become engrossed in school teaching and country preaching trips. But the deciding factor which soon drove the Halls to leave Ningbo and resign from the CES was the old story of neglect. When February 1859 came round it was the second anniversary of their first child's birth and burial at sea on the way to China. They felt 'lonely and alone in this sense' with three babes dead in infancy. But what distressed them more was that the CES claimed that they had come out to China on

> the faith principle as some term it . . . I had not adopted that principle . . . You offered (Bro. Taylor) £75 per Quarter as a single man, the same amount which you said you would *endeavour* to make up to me, at that time a married man with one child!! . . . £300 per an. coming irregularly . . . is not enough to provide for our wants and for our work.

If they could not meet his requirements, would they please send on to the Baptist Missionary Society the application for membership which he enclosed,

> And if my inconveniences and troubles should eventuate in that portion of the Church to which I belong taking up a portion of the work here I am more than content . . . You say have faith in God – I trust I have it –

But he also believed in adequate support by the body that sends out a missionary.

> I shall not leave China till I am *forced* to do so, and . . . I am ready to go to any part of the interior or coast provided that the expenses are *promised* to be borne by friends at home . . . [He wanted to know] if you think it better to put forth new efforts rather than to support those already in existence, or if you think it best to give up one missionary in order to send out another. Until I can make some arrangement . . . I shall be obliged for anything you may be able to send . . .

He was dismally echoing the complaints of every 'agent' the Society had sent out. By then the CES itself was tottering towards collapse. The BMS did take up the Halls and they later went to Shandong.

In the aftermath of the Treaty of Tientsin missionaries in every port were restless to launch out to newly-opened areas. John and Helen Nevius had their eyes on Hangzhou, key city to two provinces, seat of the viceroy and of learning, home of intellectuals and gem of art and history. After being in Tianjin and parleying with the highest in the land from Peking itself, W A P Martin would be content with no less than returning there. Alexander Williamson visited Shandong, (the first since W H Medhurst in the *Huron*). Before the year was out the Southern Baptist J L Holmes and his wife were living on a sailing ship in the harbour at Yantai (Chefoo), on the north coast of Shandong, and going ashore to work.[52] For several months it was their home. Only after ratification of the treaties were they able to rent a house and welcome other missionaries to join them.

Griffith John and his wife had been living in Pinghu and were to be there for some more months while he travelled round the whole area so freely that Suzhou, Wuxing (Huchow), Songjiang and even Hangzhou 'were as familiar to me as Shanghai itself'. He opened outstations in several of these cities and towns, including the first-ever preaching hall in Suzhou. But all were later broken up by the Taipings. From Songjiang, Hudson Taylor's early stamping ground and the home of the teacher Tsien with whom he used to travel, Griffith John wrote, as published in *The Gleaner*, that there were ten believers, some of whom said their wives were believing too. Of 'the infant church in the house of Tsien' he said, 'My heart glows when I think that this may be the commencement of Christ's speedy triumph in this city.' One sowed and another reaped. No happy comment on this by Hudson Taylor appears to have been preserved. Perhaps it was a different Tsien. When the upper reaches of the navigable Yangzi and the teeming cities of Hankou and Wuchang and the vast provinces to their north, west and south became better known to Griffith John, the call for him to go there became insistent. Wuhan was to become the sphere of his great lifework.

In Ningbo Hudson Taylor's blood ran fast as news of Lord Elgin's October penetration as far as Hankou arrived. The Taipings at Nanking shelled the squadron on its way up-river and 'had to learn a very severe lesson'. Wuchang, larger than Canton, was still as desolate as when the Taipings destroyed the city. Officers of the squadron put up pheasants in its empty streets. Hankou in contrast had largely been rebuilt since it had been evacuated and scorched some eighteen months before. An immense commerce like that of Shanghai and Canton was seen to be flourishing, with the rivers alive with craft and half a million inhabitants in the city. The Han River at its confluence with the Yangzi was two hundred yards in width, and the Yangzi itself more than half a mile wide, eight hundred miles inland from its mouth. Just a year previously the fleet of junks had burned for four days. Now new ones filled the rivers as far as the eye could see. This was a prize for merchant and missionary, if only they were free to move. On the way back, Elgin was met by apologetic Taipings and presented with a manifesto of religious and political ideas 'for the jewel glance of His Excellency Earl Lai' (Elgin). It was filled with 'a tissue of blasphemous absurdities'.

> Our Elder Brother by the same mother is Jesus. Our younger brother is the Eastern King. In the 3rd moon of 1848 God descended and commissioned the King of the East to become a mortal. In the 9th moon the Redeemer descended and commissioned the King of the West to manifest divine powers. The Father and Elder Brother [Jesus] led us to sit on the throne of the Heavenly Kingdom.

So it went on. (The Eastern King later claimed to be the third person of the Trinity.)

In a letter to his mother Hudson Taylor opened his heart after writing of the fever of movement,

> Our way is not open to move . . . But if the Lord should increase the number of our . . . believers, and qualify some of them for the various offices, and give them the gifts needed, for the well-being of the Church, then perhaps our way might be made plain to enter into the fields beyond. But will not British Christians care for these millions? Will none from the Churches, so favoured and so gifted, at home, come and spread forth the standard of the Cross, in the sight of the heathen? Papists *will* come, whether Protestants will or not. It depends under God, mainly on the exertions of British and American Christians, whether the opening of China is a blessing or a curse to the people. May God stir up *his* people to activity and zeal in labour and prayer for this mighty nation.[53]

An established indigenous church, setting its missionary founders free to start again elsewhere – did he sense that this was the kindling flame of the fire within him that was to burn with ever more heat until he discovered God's full purpose for his life? For the present the little congregation and the pagan Chinese of Ningbo were enough to fill his thoughts – except for one other well-digested and defined topic, home leave in England.

> It may be that I may yet see you again . . . – my opinions on this point, as on many others, have undergone a considerable change. Not that for the pleasure of seeing even you would I leave my work, and now I could not leave it if I would. But if the Lord should at some future time open my way, I do not know whether [and here he stated lasting principles] for the encouragement and help of communion with Christians in England, for the spiritual blessing and stimulus, and for the improvement in health and therefore in ability to labour for the Lord, I might be led to come to England for a short time.[54]

A sixth baptism was due to take place on the next Lord's Day. His joy was deep as he went on with not a word unproved by experience.

> With faith strong, Jesus before our eyes, and heaven in prospect, we may always rejoice, – in sorrow and trial, in loss and reproach, as in prosperity . . . But let our spiritual vision be clouded and faith be flagging, and we may always mourn; for this world cannot satisfy even those who enjoy most of it.[55]

Christmas came and all the Christians, Chinese and foreign, celebrated together with fun and games, hymns and talks by Hudson Taylor and John Jones and, joy upon joy, by one of the church members 'now a local preacher'. Five members had been added since last Christmas. Taylor's mind worked characteristically as he wrote, 'We must labour and pray that at least thirty may be added during next year, to keep up the *ratio* of increase.' It was symptomatic of the spirit of all the Ningbo missionaries as 1858 came to an end. With 'a great desire for a revival of the Lord's work here, by missionaries of all denominations', special meetings of all Christians in the city were being held. And the Bridge Street church added three more meetings each week for prayer and preaching. This spirit could not but affect those Chinese most closely connected with such people; Maria heard her serving woman praying in her room. As for Hudson Taylor, he could say without question, 'This has been the happiest year of my life.'

PART 2

DE PROFUNDIS

1859–60

CHAPTER FOUR

SUCCESS AT A PRICE 1859–60

Progress *January–June 1859*

The New Year dawned with optimism high in the foreign community in China. Though the Tientsin Treaty was not due to be ratified until June, merchants and mandarins, Church and consuls assumed the way to be clear and began to move to the new treaty ports. Far ahead of the Protestants, the Roman Catholics were in a position to advance where their rivals were tied down by obligation to emerging congregations and static institutions. Always ready and planning to exploit new opportunities, merchant shipping visited the ten new ports to establish land bases. The colony of Hong Kong ceased to control British trade. Consuls were appointed for each port, with the consulate-general at Shanghai. The Continental European missionaries returned to their mainland stations in Guangdong made safe by joint British and mandarin excursions to reassure the previously hostile populace, and one who was given an official escort had no need of it, so friendly were all the people. They lived in Chinese homes at close quarters with Christians under training as catechists, and anti-foreign agitation was a thing of the past.

Not only in China was a new spirit in evidence. For two centuries Japan under the Shoguns had banned Christians from landing, but in 1859 both Protestant and Roman missionaries were admitted. Christianity for Japanese was still proscribed however, and a decade later Christians refusing to recant were exiled and suppressed. But a beginning had been made.

Taking advantage of the new climate, John Nevius, accompanied by Dr Bradley, the U S consul at Ningbo, and W A Russell, visited illustrious Hangzhou with its one million inhabitants, and in February rented rooms on the outskirts. In April when Helen Nevius joined him and they became the first to begin what they intended as settled residential missionary work there, John Burdon was lodging for a time inside the city.[1] They joined ranks and visited from temple to temple together. Finding rooms attached to an old Taoist temple, the Neviuses moved into the city, and began calling from *yamen* to *yamen* (official residences) paying their respects to the mandarins. They were well received and exchanged gifts. 'We met with only respectful treatment from all quarters . . . and felt more than ever its desirableness as a mission station.' So welcome were they made that when a brief visit to Ningbo became necessary, only a hundred and twenty miles away, they were seen off by two to three hundred people and left their possessions in safe keeping at the temple. W A P Martin had only praise for John Nevius, saying,

> To him, under God, I am indebted for dissuading me from a half-formed purpose to quit China at that early stage. His inborn dignity compelled respect from the highest. A strong body, a vigorous and well-trained intellect, a sound judgement and a firm will – these were the corner-stones of [his] character . . . Serious but not morose; at times mirthful but never frivolous, he was the most genial of companions.[2]

A strong friendship sprang up between the Neviuses and Taylors, so alike in age, temperament and pioneering zeal.

John Burdon was ploughing his lonely furrow. Late in January when he arrived in Ningbo from Shanghai, his first return since his wedding and honeymoon less than fifteen months before, there were tears in his eyes while he talked with Hudson and Maria before going on to Hangzhou. The freedom to begin work there was too valuable to be disregarded, although at Ningbo the missions, all meeting with the new wave of success, would have been glad of his services. Hudson Taylor wrote home, 'In four villages where about two months ago the truth was unknown, there are several tens of inquirers, some of them seeking with tears the pardon of their sins.'[3]

Each Church had new baptisms to report. To George Pearse he reported 'monthly concerts of prayer' at which Chinese and foreign Christians of all Churches met to pray for God's blessing on Ningbo, in addition to their own frequent prayer meetings and 'bi-monthly meeting for discussing our work'.

> The work here is most cheering at present. Our Baptist friends here have 7 most interesting young men candidates for baptism. Our Presbyterian friends admitted no less than 12 (six of each sex) into the Church last Lord's Day but one . . . and the Lord's day previous to that 4 or 5 [were received] into the Episcopal Church.

THE ANGLICAN CHURCH, NINGBO
(by courtesy of Mrs Cave-Browne, née Cobbold)

John Jones called it 'quite an awakening here'. The Presbyterian congregation now numbered a hundred and the Baptists thirty. The Bridge Street church had grown to eight in addition to missionary members, and with thirty as their goal for 1859 their eyes were set on a hundred as soon as possible. Why was it, George Pearse had asked, with the partial comprehension of a distant observer, that with China opening up Taylor and John Jones stayed at the coast in Ningbo? And what were they doing to train Chinese preachers? Patiently and at length Hudson Taylor explained,

> We all feel as desirous as . . . the friends in England do, with regard to . . . Labour in the interior, and Native Agency . . . We came out to China with this hope . . . and *could* we do so . . . our own desires are still that way. There is at present however no way open for such a step . . . The little church the Lord is gathering around us, needs much care and ministry, and is not at all in a fit state to be left. Pray that the Lord will . . . give gifts to the members of it, for its edification and increase . . . They need dealing with, with so much gentleness and persistence and love . . . on the most simple points of morality even – as honesty, industry, truth, for instance . . . They *are* babes in Christ, both in knowledge and in grace. Very few of them have *much* acquaintance with [Scripture]. They are inexperienced and weak . . . The *result* of our sending those whom the Lord had not called or qualified, would of course be failure, and injury to themselves . . . We look [for] signs of fitness . . .[4]

But George Pearse had reported 'an extraordinary paragraph' in a leaflet by a missionary from China accusing the CES missionaries of divisiveness, 'sheep-stealing', by which he meant enrolling other men's converts, and the obtrusion of their own views upon Christians of other Churches.[5] He had questioned the statement and quoted to Hudson Taylor the reply he received. Now Hudson Taylor went on writing until one a m to deny the charges and answer 'the father of lies' and 'accuser of the brethren', Satan. The close co-operation he and Dr Parker and John Jones enjoyed with the other missions in Shanghai and Ningbo was the plainest answer. In Shanghai they had only worked to feed believers into the existing Presbyterian and CMS Churches, preaching and doctoring at their chapels and at their request.

> Here at Ningpo, those who have been converted through the truth heard while in Dr. Parker's hospital, have been left to join the churches they preferred, and while some have joined both the Episcopal and the Presbyterian Churches, some have joined our

> church. All the numbers God has given us, have been converted from the world, either through God's blessing on our labours, or thro' those of our own members. While therefore most distinctly informing you that no attempt has ever been made, or thought of, of the kind, to my knowledge, or such an idea suggested by anyone as having been made, I thought it necessary to do more than this . . .

He showed George Pearse's letter to the minister of each Church, John Nevius, the Presbyterian, Frederick Gough of the CMS, and Miles J Knowlton of the Baptist Church. 'With sentiments of affection and high esteem' each replied denying any knowledge of the activities alleged 'in connection with my own mission or any other' (to quote Knowlton) and testifying on the contrary to harmonious co-operation. The rumour died a natural death and another lesson in forbearance had been learnt.[6]

But Hudson Taylor was thinking still about the nagging question of status. Perhaps ordination or medical qualification or both were necessary to satisfy people who thought in those terms? In February he asked his mother to find or obtain evidence of his appointment as a local preacher in the Methodist Church. That would be a beginning. The local preacher's certificate

> would be very useful to me here, and might help to neutralize the harm done to me by . . . some . . . who *did* wish to represent me as one totally worthless, called by no one, connected with no one, and recognized by no one as a Minister of the Gospel. Now something of this sort would show that my call [from God] to preach the Gospel has been recognized by the Church. The parties who then tried to injure me are *now* friendly enough, but the effect of some things they have said and done is by no means removed. God will cause it too, to be for His glory . . . something of [that] nature may help to convince them and others of their mistake . . . The title Rev^{d} I do not wish for – but the title Minister of the gospel I do claim, for this is the work God has called me to and is graciously helping and blessing me in.

He took up dissecting again and asked his mother to send out some little china 'cutty pipes such as I used to smoke' to counteract the stench. 'I am obliged to smoke, tho' I do not at other times.' Herbal incense coils such as the Chinese used to drive away mosquitoes or to mitigate bad odours were not strong enough.

Home-letters were on the whole light-hearted. Through January both Hudson Taylor and Maria were well and happy, happier in fact than ever. Her cooking had improved, thanks to a book on 'domestic economy' from his mother. He enclosed two gutta percha photographs, peeled off the glass, 'invaluable for sending them in letters', and was having a study-darkroom built. But time was the problem. Enclosing some successful exposures on glass he wrote in March that 'should I find such a mare's-nest as a leisure day' he would take and develop some more. Amelia's marriage in February and his younger sister Louisa were never far from his thoughts. Always a tease, he wrote the first page of a letter to Amelia in Ningbo romanised. Maria set out to make a translation of it – until she found how 'naughty' it was. For the rest, they had had snow for the first time and he had lost sleep over an opium-poisoning case. Louisa had confessed to him that she could not sincerely 'repent and be saved' because she did not feel like a sinner. So he wrote,

> Do not wait till you feel sorry for sin . . . I never did, till some time after conversion. [She could still turn to Christ and apart from any feelings ask for his forgiveness.] Oh, Louisa, turn to the Lord. There is no time to lose.

Then suddenly in early February Maria was desperately ill again, vomiting incessantly and twice thought to be dying. Dr Parker did all he could and had nothing more to suggest.

> Life seemed fast ebbing away . . . When I spoke to her of her serious state, and asked what message I should send her dear brother, if she was taken, she was quite unmoved, for she was resting on the Rock of Ages.

The only hope seemed to be that God might revive her in answer to prayer. Hudson Taylor sent an urgent request to his fellow-missionaries, and as he told George Pearse afterwards, 'unitedly and earnestly as well as privately [they] prayed for us . . .' He could not be at the prayer meeting himself, but as he watched Maria a new idea came to him, a remedy that had not been tried. Before he could use it he felt he ought to consult Parker. But that meant leaving the dying Maria. 'It was a moment of anguish. The hollow temples, sunken eyes, and pinched features, denoted the near approach of death.'

It was nearly two miles to Parker's house and as he hurried there crying to God for her, 'every moment appeared long'. The words 'Call upon Me in the day of trouble; I will deliver thee, and thou shalt glorify Me' came to him as in previous emergencies and, as he later wrote, '[I] was enabled to plead them in faith, and the result was deep, deep, unspeakable peace and joy . . .'

Dr Parker approved of the treatment proposed, but when Hudson Taylor reached home again he 'saw at a glance that the desired change had already taken place, in the absence of this or any other remedy'.[7]

From that time she made an uninterrupted recovery, but so slowly that for another week he was afraid she might relapse. On February 16 he wrote asking his mother to send a 'Patent Pneumatic bed', six feet by four, in all probability a comment on the hard bed of wooden or bamboo slats they normally used.

> Today I ventured to make her bed . . . I trust she will be spared to me, and to the Lord's service, tho' I cannot yet say she is out of danger. Oh! my dear Mother. I cannot tell you what I felt when I thought that dear form was soon . . . to be lifeless and still. But the Lord has been better to me than all my fears.

They moved over to the Parkers, now in their new home beside the hospital, and by the end of March knew that the likely explanation of her illness was toxaemia of pregnancy. In April he was writing about 'the dear little immortal who will soon (D.V.) be given us . . .' But apprehension about the dangers of pregnancy and confinement stayed with him. In June he wrote of being before long, 'a happy papa – or – oh! so desolate . . . sometimes I have to cry, Lord, I believe, help thou my unbelief'.

But the demands of personal and family life had to fit in with the incessant pressure of responsibility for the growing church and with outside calls for help. John Jones was never well and often 'suffering very acutely' from kidney stones and their effects. Mary's hands were full caring for him and their children. But John continued working and the two families fondly clung together in their distress. Hudson Taylor asked his mother to send story books, especially *Robinson Crusoe* for the Jones children, and enlisted Amelia's husband Benjamin to buy and send a microscope as a gift to John. Not once since the dramatic incident after their honeymoon had they been without ample funds. George Müller faithfully sent what he could and others also.

In a March letter Hudson Taylor told of another attack on the market towns and villages by the lake, when the greater part of three towns was burned to the ground. On a visit to them he found the people too poor to rebuild their homes. Most were living in thatched shelters.

> The people recognized us, and begged us to go and live there, but I cannot see how we can do this, – I wish we could. The work here is

> becoming more important from day to day, as God is adding to our numbers, and the distance is too great to enable us to do very much both there and here.

The Bridge Street church had received two more members and another two were preparing for baptism. It was to his mother, not for publication, that he went on,

> May the work go on, and the multitude of China yet [see] a glorious day, when the heralds of the cross shall in every part of this populous empire proclaim the tidings of free salvation . . .

A few days later he was writing that after thirteen years of work the American Baptists, good hard-working and devoted missionaries, had no more than twenty in their Ningbo congregation and ten on Zhoushan (Chusan) Island. In Siam the Congregational missionaries were withdrawing after eighteen years without baptising even one Siamese, and the Presbyterians who stayed on did not baptise their first, Nai Chune, until 1859.[8] So 'God has highly favoured us.' But, 'We have many cares and many anxieties on their [the Christians'] behalf.'

John Jones wrote more specifically. One believer asking for baptism explained,

> there is a piece of land which passes in rotation to every family of [my] clan. The clan numbers 120 families. The land has been in possession of my family for three generations . . . The present year, the term of our holding it expires, and before I hand it over to my successors, I am required to call the clan together to a feast, and sacrifice to our ancestors. Omitting this there is a penalty; my house would be torn down, and my name would be eternally disgraced . . . I do not believe in sacrifices to ancestors [but] I cannot, on account of the consequences, disobey this requirement of custom.

The church was 'praying daily for this poor man' and telling him that as a Christian he could not serve two masters.

> One of the members, perhaps the most useful one . . . is a soldier and has been chosen with three or four hundred others to go to a neighbouring district to . . . put down a rising of the people. These conflicts are fearfully cruel, and when parties are neighbours, it seems to render them more horrible. We long for your prayers in these and many other difficulties.

Missionaries and new Christians were learning together, searching the Word of God for guidance in these quandaries. One old member was tempted to take his own life because his heathen sons would not allow him to observe the Lord's Day. Another, the basket-maker, Feng Neng-gui, had 'a zealous heart and a fast tongue', the cause of repeated friction. In a revealing sentence John Jones said, 'One member of Mr. Taylor's family and one of ours, servants, were baptized on Lord's day last.' And Hudson Taylor's unrelated remark to Amelia after her marriage carried the same sense, 'Try and feel as if you engaged your servants and assistants less for their services than that you might *serve them*, by bringing them under [the gospel].'

But it was not an obsessive slaving at work without relief. At the end of April the Parkers and Taylors took a six-day holiday together and visited two waterfalls of six and seven hundred feet.

> [The] bewildering grandeur and sublimity [of the scenery was] something we shall never forget, should we live to be a hundred years old . . . To get there we had to go a long way on rafts (of bamboo bent upwards in front) up the mountain streams.

It was their last such holiday together.

A wave of suicides by opium and drowning was plaguing Ningbo, and Hudson Taylor's time was sometimes largely taken up with struggling to save these people. On Sunday, May 8, he had a full day, preaching twice and conducting a baptism and the communion service. So he was already tired when a man was brought in, determined to die from the overdose of opium he had just taken. Several times the patient broke away from the people who held him while Hudson Taylor tried to administer an emetic, and ran like a man mad to escape from being cured. Soon after two a m he considered him safe to leave and went to bed. The next day he wrote, 'He has been in this morning to thank me for saving his life.'

The man baptised that day was Wang Lae-djün, one of China's great, if unsung, Christians. A painter and interior decorator by trade, he was up a ladder working when he overheard a conversation between the lady of the house and the basket-maker brought in for instructions. To his surprise Feng Neng-gui was saying he could not make incense containers for her as he was now a Christian. Wang's interest soon led to his conversion and after Pastor Hsi (Xi) Sheng-mo of Shansi[9] he was perhaps the most notable Chinese connected with the early China Inland Mission. With F F Gough, Hudson Taylor and Maria he was to revise the romanised Ningbo vernacular New Testament for the Bible Society, and later to serve for decades as pastor of a church in Hangzhou. But for the present he was a beginner being given personal tuition by Hudson Taylor and John Jones, like every other member of the embryo congregation of six men and four women.[10]

The tone of Hudson Taylor's correspondence with George Pearse shows a marked change from the tensions and protests of the days before he resigned from the CES. The Society itself was on its last legs, but in sending a gift of money George Pearse asked how he was getting on financially and in training Christian workers for the Church. He replied,

> Through various channels our Heavenly Father supplies our need as He sees best, and it is sweet to feel that the proofs of the love and care of all our friends, sweet in themselves, are also tokens of the ceaseless care and love of God our Father.
>
> The only one of our members who has manifested a gift in speaking is under training, and that of the best nature, from the fact that he is unaware of it [Wang Lae-djün] . . . Two of the others are promising men, one young, the other old, but both have families and have only been members of Christ a short time [Tsiu and Ni or Feng] . . .
>
> Coming out as I did rather prejudiced against [boarding schools as a missionary activity], and having those prejudices rather confirmed by some schools I saw and heard of, I must say that from longer experience [and, should he have added, Maria's influence?] those prejudices have been removed, and that I have a growing opinion of their value and importance . . . not only many of the scholars, but also teachers and servants connected with the [Ningbo] schools have been converted and from them have come persons with a greater amount of scriptural knowledge and otherwise better fitted for the work of the Lord, than most of those who have not enjoyed similar privileges.

The training of catechists was the current priority of the CES.[11] They instructed Dr Parker to consult with Jones and Taylor before replying. In the event all three wrote, each revealing his own personality and gifts. Parker as always was terse and practical. Jones revealed his pastoral heart and evangelistic zeal. Hudson Taylor dwelt on the wider principles and strategy, applying them in the practical situation. A training school for Chinese Christians was needed, Parker held, but only when a missionary was available to run it without distraction by other responsibilities. Other missions trained and employed their own converts.

John Jones agreed with Parker but pointed out that there was only one in their little congregation with the gifts and character necessary, and he was already working with them and soaking up the Scriptures while reading the Bible as Jones' language teacher. Feng Neng-gui was potentially suitable, 'but he does not appear to have that meek and humble spirit without which we fear to see him in any permanent position . . . The Lord will certainly fit some of them for His work, and in His time show the ones He has selected' – meanwhile the missionaries had been made pastors responsible for protecting them from premature advancement. 'The people are very accessible wherever we go,' he added, '. . . there is not a village that will not furnish a congregation.'

Hudson Taylor was at pains to check the Society's ardour, writing,

> . . . there is more danger of our bringing young Christians forward too soon, than of the opposite error . . . *Perhaps* something might be done [if it was a matter of teaching all the Christians] leaving it to be seen whether the Lord would call and qualify them for evangelists, colporteurs, teachers . . . or have them remain private members of the church.

He judged that the difficulties were perhaps more numerous than the Committee at a distance could imagine. These believers were only now emerging from paganism and five out of six already had families dependent on them. A formal training school was not the most appropriate answer to their needs. It was difficult for committee-room strategists to understand.

Living at close quarters with heathen neighbours and with their homes to a large extent open to their coming and going, the Joneses and Taylors were constantly exposed to the unashamed expression of pagan thoughts and daily lives. In February John Jones had written, 'Four days since, we were talking together, my wife almost weeping over the depravity of the people as bearing upon the little ones.' And in July Hudson Taylor told his mother,

> You can have no idea of the impurity of this people. You cannot sit at home without hearing expressions so bad, that no English expressions I have heard (and I have heard some of the worst in London and elsewhere) would translate them. And the language is only the expression of what exists in fact. Bad diseases are more common and virulent here than in France even, and we Westerns think it is the worst place in the world . . . vice is open and unheeded. Pray for our [unborn] little one, that God may keep it from the dangers around.

It happened that Dr James Legge was in London on leave from Hong Kong and addressed the Annual Meeting of the CES. After twenty years as an educational missionary he was disillusioned by the failure of the Anglo-Chinese College, devoted to developing Christian preachers from raw Chinese youths.[12] 'I have done with education,' he declared. 'Let education grow out of the Christian Church, and don't let us expect that we shall gather a church out of our schools.'

And *The Gleaner* reported,

> he felt that his duty was to obey the command of the Lord, and to preach the gospel to the heathen . . . they could only carry on [the work] efficiently as they were from day to day in the Spirit of the Lord, and gave themselves to the Word of God and to prayer. He would rather . . . go . . . from village to village and town to town . . . to speak to the people that they might be saved . . .

The LMS wanted as many missionaries in China as all societies together had at present, Legge went on. Every society should set out at least to double its number of missionaries. All the indications were that if only the gospel were preached in China the whole land would 'be illumined by [its] light' – prophetic words. In later years, from the eminence of his chair as Oxford's first professor of Chinese (1876–97) he saw his dream come true.

The more Hudson Taylor saw of the effectiveness of the gospel in changing the lives of those who believed, the more the fires of longing burned in his own soul. Having ten Christians to worship with and to train provoked the heart-cry,

> May God soon give us ninety more living monuments of His grace and mercy . . . Ask for us and for our native brethren more steady, constant earnestness, for the conversion of souls to Jesus and building up of ourselves in Him. And oh! join us in prayer to the Lord of the harvest that labourers, many and speedily, may be sent into this vast empire, to assail the kingdom of Satan, and preach the gospel of salvation to his bondmen.

The germination of the huge enterprise he was so soon to initiate had begun – an innovation further from his thoughts in 1859 than the growing suspicion that his days as a missionary might be numbered.

The emperor's change of mind[13] 1859

In Europe Louis Napoleon, the third emperor, was infected with Bonaparte belligerence and at war with Austria. His aggressive attitude and undisguised hatred of Britain prompted the formation of a home guard, the Volunteer Movement, an endless inspiration for *Punch* in the 'Dad's Army' image it presented. But France's adventures in Indo-China were leading him into difficulties.

Britain, so recently allied with France in the Crimea and at Tianjin, was uncomfortably obliged to join hands again with both France and Russia, as well as the United States, to force the Xian Feng emperor's ratification of the Treaty of Tientsin. Lord Elgin's brother, Sir Frederick Bruce, returning to China with the Treaty ratified by Queen Victoria, to receive the emperor's ratification and take up his office as British Minister Plenipotentiary in Peking, hardly expected the surprise awaiting him. Arriving at the Beihe in June, (map, p 216) he and the other envoys were faced with a Chinese demand for modification of the treaties and when the allied ships under Vice-Admiral Sir James Hope tried to force a way in towards Tianjin they were resisted.

W A P Martin was there again at the invitation of the Honourable John E Ward, the new American Minister, and described events. When the emperor's change of mind became apparent, the strong-arm methods of the previous year were assumed to be the way to teach him a lesson in international relations. A chain barrier had been stretched across the mouth of the river, but on June 24 a single shell from the fleet severed it and thirteen gunboats steamed in and opened fire on the Dagu forts. Unfortunately the Chinese batteries had been rebuilt and equipped with 'guns of a formidable type'. A cannonade from the forts until nightfall fell on the concourse of ships, and the admiral himself and the French commander were wounded. In the morning a storming party of five hundred landed, wallowed through estuary mud and found themselves separated from their objective by a moat too broad and deep to cross without pontoons. Its existence had not been detected. Half the force were killed or wounded by musket fire within the first few minutes. The rest floundered back to their boats and the desperately bungled operation ended with four hundred and sixty killed or wounded and six gunboats out of action.

While cries of 'Chinese perfidy!' and vows to avenge their injured pride and enforce the treaties mollified the allies, Martin drily commented that open aggression had met its match. The Americans in fact had not taken part and sent a message ashore to that effect, hoping their treaty would be ratified. They were disappointed. The worsted envoys could do nothing but report to their governments – who began preparations for another campaign.

Confucius taught that an oath made under duress was void, the ancestral spirits did not recognise it as valid. So from the Chinese point of view there was no need to honour such undertakings, which anyway could not be enforced. This was not perfidy. The emperor, and Yehonala in the wings, were true to their lights. Allied 'retreat' in 1858 and repulse in 1859 left him absolved from obligation. But experience of barbarian bellicosity moved the Court to prepare for trouble.

Imperial forces pinning down the Taipings in the Yangzi valley were dangerously reduced to meet the new situation.

Before the news reached England, even before the debacle took place, Lord Derby's government had fallen and the seventy-five year-old Palmerston had become Prime Minister again. He was to hold office until October 1865 when he died at eighty-one with a half-finished despatch on his desk. Obliged to include Gladstone and other opponents in his cabinet, with Lord John Russell willing to accept no other ministry than the Foreign Office, thereby excluding Lord Clarendon, Palmerston remained in sufficient control to make a militant solution of the China problem a foregone conclusion. The Treaty of Tientsin was dead, until the shock treatment of a *coup de main* brought it to life again.

Repercussions *1859*

During June 1859, while diplomatic exchanges at Dagu were building up to the clash of arms, William Muirhead and Griffith John were making their epic preaching journey to Qingjiang (Tsingkiang) on the old bed of the Yellow River, three hundred miles north of the Yangzi. On the way there they met with no Nian-fei rebels, or hostility from officials or the people. But at that place attitudes changed and the suspicions they encountered decided them to be content with what they had achieved. On their safe return to Shanghai the *North China Herald* carried their report in full and they learned of the repulse at Dagu. They had turned back none too soon. As the news of the hostilities spread quickly through China, anti-foreign feeling began at once to be expressed. 'An edict of persecution put out by Peking was put into effect' in Zhejiang, Fujian and Jiangxi, and in 1860 in Hunan.[14] Missionaries and converts were attacked. As Griffith John put it, where before people had been friendly and respectful, now they were 'bold as lions and often intolerably impudent'.

John and Helen Nevius had left Hangzhou temporarily with the goodwill of the populace.[15] On June 27, two days after the battle at Dagu, they returned. But news of the diplomatic confrontation had preceded them and their landlord was threatened with decapitation if he did not send them away. Then rumours of British gunboats being destroyed were confirmed from Ningbo. The friendly magistrate in Hangzhou sent a message saying he hoped they would soon be allowed to stay but urged them to leave at once for safety's sake. The weather was dangerously hot for travel and they feared that by going they might prejudice their chances of returning, so they declined his advice. And when *yamen* underlings extorted money from their landlord he still asked them not to go.

But inflammatory rumours were circulating and true reports of foreign excesses in the coolie traffic were common knowledge. In an earlier letter to Louisa, Hudson Taylor had written,

> I hope some check will be put on the coolie trade, which to use Mr Burns' words . . . 'is rapidly assuming all the features of the African Slave Trade!!!' The poor men are stolen and kidnapped, bought and sold just like cattle, packed in the hold, not indeed as slaves used to be, but in such numbers that a fearful amount die from disease . . . many of them are in a condition compared with which negro slaves are happy and free . . . They are called 'Emigrants', and are engaged for eight years' service. The money paid for them is only an *advance* of *wages* to help them to outfit; and when they are sold, it is only the employer paying back the advance and their passage money!!! Most of the masters find it convenient to work them to death . . . Then what avails of the promise of $4 a month for the eight years? and afterwards liberty to do business on their own account . . .

A French ship loading coolies at Wusong for shipment to Havana was accused of kidnapping and of firing on some of its cargo trying to escape. The stories linked the traffic with Christianity so Christians had to bear the blame for its iniquity. John Nevius learned that people were being warned against being caught and taken overseas by them to be killed and made into opium. An army was said to be stationed in the hills to protect him and his wife; that was why they were not afraid to stay! Even so their meetings were well attended by educated people and several showed signs of true faith. Only the advice of their consul on the intervention of the provincial governor made them withdraw in August, once again leaving their possessions as a pledge of their intention to be away for as short a time as possible.

The sequel may be told here. Not long afterwards the Taipings broke through the imperialist cordon at Nanjing and in March 1860 captured Hangzhou, 'with scenes of atrocity and cruelty as we never could have endured to witness. Nearly all our acquaintances fled from the city or were killed or captured.' Two hundred thousand inhabitants were massacred or committed suicide. The temple was burned but the Neviuses' quarters were occupied by the rebel commander until they too were destroyed with 'considerable loss of the Neviuses'' goods. Appointed *pro tem* to Japan by their mission board, and later to Shandong, they were never able (though they tried) to continue the work so promisingly begun in Hangzhou.

On Sunday morning, July 31, the temperature in Ningbo was 104 degrees Fahrenheit in the shade and John Jones was conducting the worship service alone when Maria, with Hudson and Mary Jones to help, was safely delivered of her babe. 'I had longed to have a little miniature of my precious Maria,' he told his parents in announcing their first grandchild, so he was pleased that it was a girl, Grace Dyer Taylor. A week later the lowest the thermometer had fallen was 88 degrees at one a m during a thunderstorm, and the baby was suffering from prickly heat. Adults found it hard to lie on a bed and no easier to find the strength for any movement. But anti-foreign feeling was running so high that most other missionaries had moved out of the city. It was classic riot weather. Tempers were frayed. Hudson Taylor and Maria chose to stay, content to borrow a small boat from a friendly neighbour and keep it moored on the canal behind their house. A rope from an upstairs window would get them down to it if a street mob attacked from the front (see p 310).

Three days later Maria was writing as her husband's amanuensis because he had epidemic conjunctivitis,

> Owing to the kidnapping villainies of those slavers engaged in the coolie trade, – forcibly seizing villagers and carrying them in sacks to their vessels, public excitement has reached a very high pitch. Rumours have been circulated that these persons have been seized at the instance of the defeated British who wish to reinforce their numbers and again attack Tientsin. Violent incendiary papers have been posted up, all our lives and property have been in imminent

> danger, and our own house has been somewhat mobbed. The excitement is . . . decreasing now, and we hope the worst is past; as the people know that measures are being taken by some of the missionaries in conjunction with the Foreign Authorities to search to the bottom of this abominable affair.

But hardly was that written than the Parkers urged them to come out of the city to the quieter, safer hospital compound between the river and the city wall. A scribbled note from Maria reads,

> My own precious dearest love,
> Dr and Mrs Parker have kindly received your fugitive wife . . . The people did not seem excited as I came along, but the Salt Gate was shut. Just before I arrived at the Gate I met Mr Jones who kindly turned back and saw the two gates opened for me. No objection was made . . . When shall I kiss you again and feel your loving arms around me. God bless you my own precious Hudson, my Husband, and keep you from all harm . . .

Such a note would have been taken to him by a messenger, who probably waited while Hudson Taylor wrote his reply. By then it was two-thirty p m.

> If you wish to come to the city and arrange anything there is no reason to prevent it that I know of – all is for the present peaceful. But as we have accepted Dr Parker's kind hospitality we had better stay there a day or two and see how matters terminate . . .

But if she decided to come it must be in a curtained sedan chair – hidden from view. The next day they added a postscript to the letter home. They were together at the Parkers'. A letter by John Jones on the same day, August 12, gives colour to his friends' calm statements.

> We are living only from night to day and from day to night. The people here are thirsting for our blood. Satan has filled the multitude with lies . . . The people say that these kidnapped [men] are put in front of the fight against their own emperor . . . They mix up together missionaries, traders and the government. There was one man who raised a mob at Bro. Taylor's, but no damage was done . . . They have placarded the streets calling for our blood; one of the most forward in this is the man who supplies the officers with buckets to contain the heads of the decapitated, a fearfully large trade here . . . Our wives and little ones are in the same danger, but we are resting on Him who says to them, 'thus far shalt thou go, and *no farther*' . . . When they told [an enquirer] that we . . . were fighting his emperor and taking his

NINGBO'S SALT GATE
(from *The Story of the Cheh-Kiang Mission*, by courtesy of the CMS)

> fellow-townsmen to fight against their own sovereign, he said, 'There must be a mistake somewhere. Satan has blinded your eyes; for those with whom I am joining . . . only preach Christ; they have nothing to do with fighting.'

Some furniture was broken at the Presbyterian chapel, but otherwise in Ningbo no harm was done. In Shanghai it was a different story. Placards were posted denouncing the religion of Jesus. One foreigner was killed and two others injured near the Settlement. On August 6 a hundred to a hundred and fifty men broke into the LMS chapel and smashed everything. But the *daotai* posted guards at all other chapels and compensated the LMS for their losses.

At Suzhou a proclamation was posted in the streets alleging that the Shanghai magistrates had warned against foreigners purporting to be preachers – a subtle evasion of the terms of the Tientsin Treaty already observed for a year. A translation of it ran,

> Of a truth all natives professing their doctrines are devils, are demons. Now, lest the simple people in their greed . . . be beguiled in this way, let the people of the towns and villages [unite to] set upon and kill every foreigner . . . that the kidnapping of our men may be put a stop to.

For a year the tension persisted and missionary movement outside the treaty ports was restricted. Threats and anger failed to erupt into more violence, until in March 1860 Griffith John could write that peace and quiet had been restored. But his inveterate optimism was unrealistic. Not until late in that year would it be so. In the ports, however, work went on. Ningbo settled down. Stresses of a different nature stretched the missionaries to breaking point.

'Always facing death'[16] — *August–December 1859*

In the afternoon of August 25 Mrs Parker was feverish, but 'ague' was nothing new to her. The family were always struggling against it. At four a m however 'she was taken very ill'. For half an hour she tried not to disturb her overworked husband but had to wake him. By then 'the serious nature of the case was too evident'. She had cholera, and 'suffered severely the greater part of the day'. All day long Dr Parker worked to relieve her suffering and save her life. Hudson Taylor took charge of the hospital and out-patient clinic to leave him free. But about midnight she died.

Parker was shattered and unable to resume work. With his five motherless children, the youngest not yet one year old, he nursed his grief, and with one semi-trained assistant Hudson Taylor kept the medical work going. John Jones could not carry the responsibilities of the church alone, so much of that came on him also.

To Dr Parker it was the end of everything. He would have to take the children home to their grandparents in Scotland. And that meant the end of the private medical practice by which he earned the funds for running the hospital. Hudson Taylor, he knew, would not be consulted by the merchant and shipping community as he was. So the hospital would have to close. He only hoped he would keep on the out-patients. Hudson Taylor's view was different. A brand new hospital in running order should not lie empty for no stronger reason than that. If it was God's will that he should keep it open, God would provide the means.

By mid-September he had made up his mind and taken over from Parker.[17] Greatly increased pressure of work prevented him from writing home, and from now on fewer letters and less news reached his family. Maria wrote for him. Her first, on August 30, to his mother, and another to George Pearse, had said that he was well but over-fatigued. Thank God, they were spared to each other while 'others have been cut down around us'. She had begun telling about Mrs Parker's sudden illness and death, when her writing petered out. Hudson Taylor added two lines to end the sentence. Over a century later that moment of emotion may be felt. How easily Maria herself could have died in February, or her infant with her at her confinement. But Parker and his children were desolated and Hudson had been spared the same grief.

On September 30 Maria wrote again. By then Hudson Taylor's face was 'long and thin'.

> He comes upstairs, perhaps between 10 and 11 P.M. tired out and poorly, and after sitting or lying down a little while, goes down again to see some of his hospital patients and to make up some medicine for them . . . A few months ago . . . Mrs McCartee said to me, 'I prophesy . . . in a few years Dr. Parker will be taking his family home and . . . Mr Taylor will take Dr P's practice . . .'

Maria had laughed at the thought. It had come true in months, not years.

Parker was preparing to leave Ningbo within a few days. His baby was not expected to survive the journey to Shanghai, and when

Hudson Taylor wrote on October 15, the news he had received was that the child was dying. The Taylors moved into the Parkers' house beside the hospital. 'I am not likely to be much troubled with ennui . . .' he wrote. 'For funds to carry on this expensive work I must look to the Lord.'

For the first few weeks attendance at the hospital dropped, until Hudson Taylor, relatively unknown as a 'doctor' until then, established his own reputation. But in October, with no more funds in sight and hospital employees' wages to be met, he called the staff together and explained the situation. He was unwilling to go into debt and they had their families to provide for. They must feel free to find employment elsewhere. If they stayed it could only be without any claim upon him. The staff then talked it over together and most of them reluctantly chose to retire. Hudson Taylor turned to the Christians of the Bridge Street church and prayed with them about this quandary. Then he offered them the terms on which he himself worked – nothing promised but a share of whatever the Lord provided. One of those who offered his services was Wang Lae-djün. A colporteur named Miao Shi-fu (S-vu) and Hudson Taylor's friend of Shanghai and Chongming days, Gui-hua, now his cook, also stayed on.

Later in the month Gui-hua announced that he had opened the last bag of rice. This was the signal. The hospital would have to close if funds did not arrive very soon. Hudson Taylor said, 'Then the Lord's time must surely be near, to meet our need.'

The arrival of a letter from W T Berger dramatically changed the picture. A legacy from his father had reached him, he said, but he would not be changing his own standard of living. The enclosed fifty pounds was to be used at Hudson Taylor's discretion. And would he kindly indicate how more could be used? Praising God together, Hudson Taylor and Maria translated the letter to their young Christian assistants. The usually undemonstrative Chinese broke into hallelujahs and went into the wards to tell the patients what had happened.

On October 31 Hudson Taylor told his mother,

> I had no expectation of help (save the belief that God would provide funds for His own work) but $100 has been given me for it, and $170 from my liberal-hearted brother Mr. Berger . . . to be disposed of as I see fit, if not wanted for my personal need. I shall probably devote most of this to the hospital.

The current exchange rate of $3.40 to the pound was less than half of what it had been, but the hundred-dollar gift in Ningbo had brought it (he said philosophically) to the equivalent of $5.40. But all things considered, the strain on him was great. To George Pearse he had written on the 16th,

> The events of the last month or two appear like a dream. The confinement of my dear wife – the disturbances after our repulse from the Pei-ho [Beihe] – the death of Mrs Parker – the departure of our bereaved brother – our removal to his house and taking charge of the hospital – together with the duties connected with our own little church, and daily affairs, have been crowded into a few weeks and we have not yet got settled, nor have we recovered from the state of confusion in which we have been thrown . . . I have the assistance of a very worthy and efficient native Christian, Miao S-vu, for whose support I shall be glad to have your aid.

Mr Pearse had asked for word of any Chinese Christians whose training he might sponsor.

Then on November 1 Hudson Taylor greeted another month with words reflecting the uncertainty of life, 'another month; if we are spared to finish it, may it be spent in His service . . .' And on December 1 Maria reported that he was 'far from well'. Two weeks later his own letter spoke volumes.

> God is blessing the hospital. Among the inpatients there are *four* men candidates for baptism . . . How good it will be to *rest* from our labors – in heaven, to see that it has not been in vain . . . I am not *very* well, but as I have not been so for a long time, that is nothing unusual. I suspect that there is mischief at work in my chest . . . Mr. Jones' eldest, Tom, I fear commenced an attack of hydrocephalus. [Today he would no doubt say meningitis.] . . . I fear the worst . . . This is a sad, weary world, a wilderness indeed. But it is thro' the goodness of God so filled with love and mercies that we are too apt to cleave to it.

He was still longing for Louisa's conversion, and as the nearness of death weighed upon him he thought and prayed increasingly for her. But in Ningbo the spiritual momentum continued. The woman employed by Maria as a typesetter responded to a tract she was setting up, and was baptised. Now they were halfway to Hudson Taylor's goal of thirty. Four more patients were preparing for baptism and to his joy the very first Chinese he had pointed to Christ, Gui-hua, and the destitute cobbler's son, Tianxi, whom he and John Jones adopted for five years, were showing signs of fitness for baptism too.

Over this stressful scene hung another cloud. The ill-fated CES, so well-meaning, formed and supported by such godly men, but crippled from the start by ignorance of China and the incompetence of the chief secretary they employed (so George Pearse revealed in later years), decided its own usefulness had ended. The last regular *Gleaner* appeared in October. But already a strong letter had come from London to Dr Parker. An individual at odds with him had accused him of profiting personally from his medical work, in violation of his terms of engagement with the Society. Hudson Taylor had tried to warn the Society against this person, but the accusation was believed and lamentably their rebuke and demand for an explanation had arrived in Ningbo at the time of Mrs Parker's sudden death.

Hudson Taylor and John Jones had risen to Parker's defence, taking responsibility for advising him to return home with his children without delay. Sheer overwork and the shock of losing his wife had been too much for him, but his children too were debilitated and in need of more care than could be given them in China. These 'forcible' reasons were enough, but the arrival of such a letter was the last straw, they protested.

> You will be sorry when you learn this, that you should, at such a time, add to the suffering of our brother. But you will be even more sorry when you learn that the things communicated to you are just a slanderous fabrication. The amounts reported by your correspondent as received by Dr P. for attendance upon various bodies here are very incorrect; the receipts from the Chinese exist only in the mind of your inventive correspondent.

It had been well known to the Society all along that Dr Parker practised for remuneration, they went on. He had said so openly, they had both referred to the fact in letters, and the Society had even approved of it in a letter to Dr Parker. How else could he build and operate a hospital and his other work? Why had they not checked the allegations with others in Ningbo before acting on them? His Ningbo colleagues would all testify to his uprightness, as letters of sympathy showed. So the Society would be well advised to give the subject 'as favourable a turn' as possible.

It was too late. Parker, the last missionary of the CES in China, resigned after arrival in Britain. One other, Dr Pruen of Penang, died on his voyage home. In May 1860 the CES presented its last annual report and accounts and in the autumn ceased to exist. In the last year or two they had sent Hudson Taylor not more than thirty pounds altogether, an accumulation of small gifts from subscribers.

The 'Awakening'[18] *1859–60*

As for Ningbo at the end of 1859, the missionary and Chinese Christian community were being drawn even closer together. Ripples of the Evangelical Revival in North America and Ireland were lapping against the shores of China.

After ten years of spiritual doldrums in the United States, associated with civil unrest over slavery, there followed a great turning to God. From five hundred thousand to one million people experienced evangelical conversion and swelled the Churches during 1857–58. Business was at times almost at a standstill in Boston, New York and elsewhere as businessmen flocked to meetings for evangelism and prayer.

In Ireland revival of the same nature began in connection with a group of Christians meeting regularly at Kells, near Ballymena, to beseech God to do the same for Ireland. Brownlow North, the 'dissolute roué-turned-gentleman evangelist' (son of the bishop, successively of Lichfield, Worcester and Winchester, and nephew of George III's prime minister Lord North) moved thousands. Henry Grattan Guinness of Dublin drew the greatest crowds in Ulster, preaching from the roof of a cab to fifteen thousand in an open space in August 1859, and, as J Edwin Orr wrote, won 'multiplied thousands of converts'. The Hon and Revd Baptist Noel, previously a distinguished Anglican clergyman and a member of the CES Committee, preached to twenty thousand in a field at Armagh. His estimate of one hundred thousand conversions in Ulster was called an understatement by *The Nonconformist*.

Scotland had known revival through William Burns and others. Now crowds of twenty thousand gathered in Glasgow and thousands in other places to hear Brownlow North and Reginald Radcliffe, the solicitor–evangelist, preach until they had no strength to continue.

England was slower to respond. The established Churches on the whole stood indifferently by, and strong prejudices led to determined opposition to revival as it spread. *The Times* and *The Lancet*, which Hudson Taylor was taking, shamelessly used distortions and intemperance to vilify what was taking place; it was 'a moral epidemic and a contagious hysteria', filling the streets of Belfast with prostitutes and drunken revellers – in one way the truth, for unrepentant antagonists were convicted in the courts in greater numbers than ever. But a Dr J Edward Cranage, a loyal Anglican who had witnessed revival in Ulster, began an interdenominational meeting for prayer in Wellington, Shropshire, attended by forty-five thousand in two years and marked by up to twelve conversions nightly. Five years before William and Catherine Booth began the work which led to the founding of the Salvation Army (in 1878) they travelled widely as evangelists, and saw the beginnings of the 1860–65 movement towards God.

This spiritual awakening, as historic as that of Wesley and Whitefield in the eighteenth century, was to continue for a full fifty years,[19] contributing immensely to the missionary movement Hudson Taylor was already unconsciously initiating. Grattan Guinness and Reginald Radcliffe were to become his intimate friends and colleagues, and Geraldine Guinness, a daughter, his own daughter-in-law. Timothy Richard, a convert of the Welsh revival in 1859, offered his services to Hudson Taylor who referred him to the BMS, and he became one of China's greatest missionaries.[20]

From Ludhiana, in India, came a call to colleagues in China to devote a whole week 'to fasting, humiliation, prayer and praise' in supplication for the Holy Spirit to turn many Chinese to God, and preparations were made to observe this in January 1860. The old year ended on a high note of expectancy.

'If I had £1000'[21] *January–June 1860*

Of the two hundred and fourteen men missionaries in China since the arrival of Morrison in 1807, forty-four had lost their lives, and the wives of fifty-one had died.[22] The average life expectancy of a missionary was still a mere seven years, made as high as that by the survival of a few veterans like W H Medhurst, E C Bridgman, Samuel Wells Williams and Miss Aldersey. Death had struck again and again among the few in Ningbo and no one knew who would go next. But as John Jones declared, 'If we had to choose again, we would choose just this work in this place.' All lived in awareness of the threat, and the shock was no less when it came, but the joy of the angels over one sinner repenting was the joy of each missionary over every Chinese brought to Christ. Rejoicing over his newborn child,

Hudson Taylor could say, '. . . a soul born again . . . still better news' than the birth of a firstborn. But as Christmas passed and the old year died, his own condition had steadily deteriorated.

The new year, 1860, began with one of the Bridge Street Christians, a sixty-three year-old man named Dzing, ill with pneumonia. Hudson Taylor took him into his own home and cared for him until he died. Sitting beside him he read John 17, focusing the old man's mind on the words 'Father, I want those you have given me to be with me where I am, and to see my glory' . . . 'with Christ which is far better'. It was the first death in the little church and the Christians showed their love to Dzing's old widow by largely supporting her from then on. But the peaceful unity of the church was shaken when Feng Neng-gui the basket-maker had to be disciplined by the others, a measure which in time brought him back contrite and matured.

Then came the second week of January and daily meetings held in English and Chinese to pray for spiritual awakening. When Hudson Taylor conducted and preached at one of these in the American Baptist chapel, most missionaries and two hundred Chinese Christians were present, a thrilling, monumental figure for Ningbo. In Shanghai revival broke out among the missionaries themselves, Eugene Stock recorded.[23] The movement was becoming worldwide. Pearse wrote to Hudson Taylor, 'Although the Society terminates I still trust to think and pray and labour for you . . . The revival has reached London and hundreds are being converted.' A pool of potential missionaries was being formed, men and women upon whom the societies were to draw after 1860. On January 25 the frail Mrs Berger wrote to Maria,

> Stirring meetings have been held . . . all over London and in many parts of England, arising out of an invitation from Christians in India . . . Oh how I wished to be in the very heart of these mighty workings! But . . . one has to learn to deal with the Lord alone.

The 'love and unity . . . and some new zeal' apparent in Ningbo made Hudson Taylor tell George Pearse, 'I believe we are on the eve of some great blessing – and this poor people *does need it.*' He was not mistaken. In John Jones' words,

> While some of our outposts, probably all, have been driven in, we have yet been able till now to preach Christ freely in the city of Ningpo and its neighbourhood, with scarcely a day's exception.

Anti-foreign feeling was making country preaching difficult. But instead of attempting it Taylor and Jones rented a house in a village and in February the young teacher, Tsiu, and his mother opened a school there, to break down prejudice.

Soon one mission and another began to report responses to the gospel and by March 1 Jones could report, 'the Lord is visiting us with a harvest here'. As a direct result of his dangerous illness, a thing of the past, young Tom Jones joined those preparing for baptism, and on March 5 five additions brought the church members to eleven men and six women. One had been rescued from opium suicide by John Jones only to fall ill with typhoid and be admitted to hospital close to death. Continuous nursing by the Christians, and feeding with sips of wine, brought him through and won his heart.

During February the climate of opinion had changed and in March they could say 'no hindrances now'. Three or four times a week they were preaching and distributing books in the villages as before. Now there were twenty-one members in the Bridge Street church and two had been appointed Class Leaders on the Wesleyan pattern, helping to teach the rest.

Gough of the CMS, Knowlton the American Baptist and the Presbyterians Rankin, Martin and Nevius were regularly helping Hudson Taylor by conducting services in the hospital chapel for waiting patients. As usual, some who believed through their preaching chose to join other churches. It made no difference. All rejoiced together. To be 'in Christ' was all that mattered. Hospital attendance was increasing too. 'My work already exceeds my time and strength,' Hudson Taylor confessed. He planned to take a week's holiday at the Chinese New Year, closed the dispensary and reduced the number of in-patients to twenty whom John Jones would care for,

> but just at that time a number of persons shot or wounded by pirates were brought to the hospital . . . One of these, a boy of about eighteen, who was shot through the neck, and whose life was almost despaired of . . .

recovered and became a believer. Another's wounds after Hudson Taylor performed a double amputation of his legs, were fully healed in a fortnight.

He was also earning a reputation for breaking opium addiction, with thirteen addicts freed before the end of January. Applicants for treatment became too many and to relieve the pressure from mid-February to mid-May F F Gough opened his own premises to opium addicts and admitted a hundred and thirty-three in three months.[24] The development of this work had a historic sequel, no less than the founding of the CMS hospital at Hangzhou made notable by Dr Duncan Main. An Inspector of Opium Manufacture in the Indian Government who became conscience-smitten when the effects of the opium trade came home to him, and resigned, was later to send £3,000 to the CMS for the relief of opium victims in China, and the CMS offered it to Hudson Taylor for that purpose.[25]

The more he saw of opportunities and response to the gospel in China, the more he thought in terms of more missionaries to make the most of them. But no longer was this a personal hope. Together he, Maria and John and Mary Jones had agreed to make it an objective of their prayers. The openings at Ningbo demanded it, and none of them was fit enough to cope. Only reinforcements could meet the needs. The germination of the future China Inland Mission was assuming a new form.

In January he asked his parents if they knew of any devoted young men who would give even five years of their life to China, 'much in the Wesleyan manner . . . Oh! for four or five such helpers!' But on February 1 he enlarged on the idea to George Pearse in growing rhetoric, as if hoping for publication and addressing the Church at large. Wholly forgetting Miss Aldersey's and W A Russell's views, and breaking away from conventional concepts of missionary qualifications to form his own judgments from personal experience among the common people of city, town and village, he put into words a principle on which he was to act when he returned to Britain.

> The language is of the simplest nature, the talent needed does not exceed the power to read and write, and anyone qualified to labor amongst the poorest and most ignorant rustics of England, needs only God's blessing to make him as useful, or more so, here. I do not either think, or mean to say, that this is the only class needed here – far from it. But we do need, and much need, many laborers of this class. Persons who from the way they have been accustomed to live, are *able* to endure labor and hardship. I do believe there are many such in England who would rejoice to devote five years of their lives to this work, and ask no reward on earth for it. Oh! that we had some of them here. (They would be able to render three years and six months of effective work out of the five.) But I have no doubt love for

> the work, the people, and for the converts God would have given to them, would induce many to labor for a longer period, or to devote their lives to the service of God in this part of His vineyard . . . Christian Brethren! Will you not come over and help us? Can you turn a deaf ear to the wail of the millions – the perishing millions of China? Is it *taking up* your cross and *following Jesus*, to sit quietly at home and let them perish? Or to think that a subscription can fulfil the Saviour's – *your Saviour's command* 'Go *ye* into all the world and *preach the Gospel* to every creature?' – It was not in this way our *redemption* was effected . . .
>
> Mr Lord, an American Baptist missionary, was left a widower last week, with five children, the youngest 8 days old. Life is short here, the work is great, the summons is often very sudden. We all need to be busy, and ready, that our work finished, we may gladly enter into our promised rest . . . The enemy is numerous. The enemy is strong. But they that are with us are more than those in hostile array against us. We doubt not the issue. Every sheep shall hear *His* voice. And hearing shall *live*, live for ever. Satan may rage, will rage, does rage. But he rages in vain. Foes within and without – in number innumerable – in power, to the unaided arm of flesh, irresistible – may oppose – but all, but all must fall before . . . Jesus our Captain. . . .[26]

His own awareness of a tenuous hold on life gleams between his lines. If John Jones, dying by slow degrees, and he himself were to depart, someone must take their place in Ningbo. It is these appeals to his parents and Mr Pearse, and through them to the Church, that have been called 'the germ of the China Inland Mission', but they were more than that, the breaking through of the sturdy shoot that grew into a tree. For this was the clarion call to enlarge the scope of their 'Ningpo Mission' which led directly to the enlistment of James Meadows, the first member of the China Inland Mission.

On February 14 Hudson Taylor took up the long-standing offer by the CES of funds to support Chinese workers, and claimed help for five. On that day twelve more candidates were considered for baptism. At last the fitful Gui-hua and Tianxi were among them. The old Christians were maturing well. Parker's premises were extensive and the chapel met their need as numbers grew.

> You will see from [this] that a great change has taken place in our circumstances since you wrote to us on the subject of native assistants, training, etc. The number of our members has more than doubled, and the position I am now in gives me advantages and facilities I did not then possess.

But already a letter of January 9 from Pearse was on its way, telling Hudson Taylor of a new friend, 'W.R.' from whom he enclosed a hundred pounds each for him and Jones, fifty each to support a Chinese worker and the rest for personal needs.

Hudson Taylor also wrote urging his father to influence the Wesleyan Reformed Church to support five Chinese, for one hundred pounds a year, or to send out their own missionary. 'We are wearing down and must have help. You have given your son, give your influence too.' And to Amelia he repeated the appeal in a long, urgent letter of the same date, February 14,

> Oh! there is such a boundless sphere of usefulness opening up before us. But the laborers are few, and weak, and worn, and weary. They need help and rest. Oh! that the Church of God were alive to its duty, to its privileges. Then many would come and labour for Christ here.

Young men giving five years' service would use six months at sea learning Chinese, four years at work and the last six months returning home. They would work with a Chinese local preacher, living in Chinese style in the country at minimal cost. But that was not all.

> I have not yet given up hope of seeing you and your dear husband here. I believe you will come yet. I believe you will be sent here by God. And I assure you the work *is* a happy one. We have none but God to look to for *means*, for health, for encouragement. And we need none other. He gives us all we need, and He knows best what we need . . . If I had a thousand pounds, China should have it. If I had a thousand lives, China should have them. No! not *China* but *Christ*. Can we do too much for Him? . . .[27]

As 1860 progressed the pressures on him continued to increase.

> I find the labor of it heavy, and feel that I must try to get a few days' relaxation soon, or I may require a greater rest, as I feel the weakness of my chest increasing, and recent attacks of ague have affected me much.

A week later he closed the out-patient dispensary again for two weeks and 'went into the country'. The change did him good and he 'seemed very much invigorated' on his return, Maria noted. But still he was too unwell to reopen even the dispensary and they moved over to the Joneses' in the city. There at least he was not on call day and night. On March 25, 1860, he wrote at length to his mother, explaining that to save them anxiety he had said little about his health, but now

> perhaps it is due to you that I should inform you that for some time past it has been failing, and that I have felt more and more unequal to my work. It is a very difficult thing to be one's own physician and there are many sources of error into which one may fall . . . so that my conclusions may be received with some . . . reservations. I think, however, . . . that my chest is affected with tubercular disease . . . it may not be present at all . . . attacks of ague caused by going about at night to see [seriously ill patients] . . . have more or less injured my liver and spleen . . . Here, at any rate, at present is my position; and I trust . . . I shall not leave it before, or remain in it after, such is His will. . . . It may be that . . . I may be able to continue the work . . . Or it may be that I may be sent home for a season . . . Dearly as I should love to see you . . . may I never, never be permitted to turn back from the Gospel plough . . .

His medical language is almost meaningless today, and his guesses at a diagnosis of his illness carry little weight. Not only his own but all medical knowledge was rudimentary in 1860. Nothing in his subsequent history supports his use of the term 'tubercular'. Today a conjecture that infective or amoebic hepatitis and enteritis were his trouble is more likely to be near the mark. Soon he confirmed this. It could account for his chest pain.

On April 2 and again on May 10 he wrote that Maria had not been well either, with 'ague'. But on April 24 he had more serious news for his father.

> I do not feel well enough to write much . . . I am just now quite laid aside from hepatitis and jaundice . . . I feel that my health is so thoroughly breaking down that I may suffer much if spared to reach or pass through another summer.

His reason for writing was in case his father should need to amend his will,

> as I feel I am not to be counted on. . . . Thanks be to God, I know He will not leave me . . . to grope in darkness. And He *will* be a Father to my babe and a husband to my tenderly affectionate wife; and I know, too, that you will love them for my sake, should I be removed . . . *He* has been very gracious . . . and has blessed us in every respect, leaving little to be desired save more holiness, more likeness to Jesus.

In his May 10 letter he said,

> I suppose I must say something about myself too . . . [The] attack of jaundice . . . passed off but has returned . . . and the summer is before us. Were this *all* that is the matter with me, I should think less of it, but it is a very serious complication of the disease in my chest . . . I have thought seriously of a voyage to England. What I desire to know is, how I may best serve China. If I am too unwell to labour here and by a voyage home might either re-establish my health (if but for a time), or if I might rouse others to go and take up the work I am unable to continue, I think I ought to do so . . .

He thought they would probably go over to Zhoushan (Chusan) Island for a medical opinion (by a ship's surgeon). Then he went on to say that they were expecting four more baptisms on the next Lord's Day, which would bring the church membership to thirty 'including ourselves' – meaning John and Mary Jones, Maria and himself. 'We have just had a fast-day to pray for God's blessing and have published a new hymn-book containing twenty hymns translated by Maria and myself.'

They had put out their appeal none too soon. At some point between mid-May and June Hudson Taylor received an independent medical opinion that it was high time he left China. He would probably never return. By June 11 the decision had been taken.

CHAPTER FIVE

OUTRAGE AND AFTERMATH 1860

Taiping holocaust[1] *March–June 1860*

The debacle at Dagu in June 1859 was more than 'perfidious Albion' and her allies could stomach. Whatever the rights and wrongs, whatever the Confucian concepts of morality, they were of one mind that 'Chinese perfidy' must meet with vengeance due. Through that autumn and winter preparations for a formidable expedition were in motion. Lord Elgin and Baron Gros were reappointed and a force of ten thousand British and six thousand French under Sir Hope Grant as commander-in-chief embarked for China. A thousand British cavalry and the first battery of Armstrong guns to be used on active service showed Palmerston's determination to achieve his aims. This time the emperor would be left in no doubt of allied superiority and, willy-nilly, foreign ministers would take up residence in Peking.

On March 8 an Anglo-French ultimatum was delivered. Success the previous year and inability to grasp the seriousness of the situation led the Court to choose resistance. Troops were withdrawn from the Yangzi front. The military containment of Nanjing was fatally weakened, and the Taipings responded immediately with a massive breakout. In a determined thrust southward by Zhong Wang, the Loyal King, they advanced rapidly on Hangzhou (map, p 202), stormed and sacked the outer city on March 19, and after 'three days' pillage and bloodshed – a time of unspeakable horror when sixty thousand died, they evacuated the city, wheeled round, bypassed the imperial forces 'limping heavily in pursuit' and reached Nanjing again. There they swept away the besieging government forts and encampments and annihilated the imperial power from the vicinity for the time being. True to type, seventy thousand imperial soldiers changed sides, joining the rebellion.

In spite of this, on April 5 the emperor rejected the allied

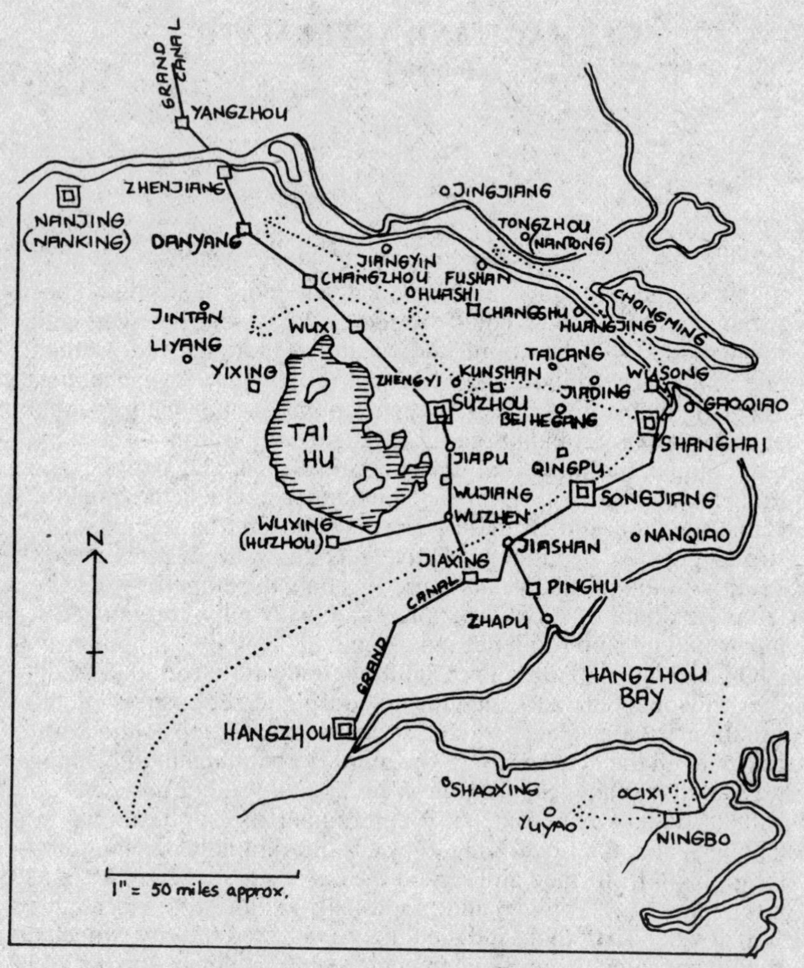

TAIPING INCURSIONS: 1860–64

ultimatum. Now only factors of distance, time and co-ordination between the allies delayed their attack. America and Russia prepared to join in, and for the next three months North China waited for the barbarians.

In February Joseph Edkins and Griffith John had been refused admission to Suzhou and Hangzhou, but in March they travelled freely and new members were admitted to the churches in Songjiang and Suzhou. Griffith John was always on the move. His Welsh exuberance could not be content with routine duties in the city of Shanghai. But he himself admitted thirty years later that in those early days he 'knew more about how things should be done than all his seniors'. Their lack of success, he held, was due to lack of insight. So he was appointed to country itineration to absorb his energy. In April he found Suzhou untouched by the rebels, but on May 3 the Taipings repeated their eruption from Nanjing, this time routing the imperialists, retaking Zhenjiang (Chinkiang) and permeating the Jiangnan territory, all between the Yangzi and Hangzhou Bay. On June 2 they occupied Suzhou. The viceroy was disgraced and Zeng Guo-fan (Tseng Kuo-fan)[2] appointed to replace him. Consternation reigned in Shanghai and immediate preparations were begun to resist the Taipings if they threatened the city or Settlements. The *daotai* formally requested the allies to defend the Chinese city and knowing of the carnage at Hangzhou they complied. When three American missionaries visited Suzhou during that month they found the beautiful city wrecked. 'Above is heaven; below, Hangzhou and Suzhou.' But no longer.

On May 19 Wylie and Griffith John left Shanghai and followed Hudson Taylor's painful route through Songjiang, Jiashan and Shimen, going on to Hangzhou. The city gate was opened to let them in and they found some of the fairest parts of this heavenly jewel of China in charred ruins, and the whole of the west suburb. A mass grave holding a thousand bodies was only a drop in the ocean of misery. The ponds and wells in the city's walled courtyards were filled with women and girls who had drowned themselves as their only way of escape. The mosque was standing in a welter of wreckage, a hundred families in the Muslim colony had perished although they were not idolaters, and Taipings extorting money had killed the mullah with the sword. The faith of Hangzhou in their gods had been shaken. One man said, 'They have no power over the affairs of the world, it is limited to Hades.' On the last day of May Wylie and John were back in Shanghai.

After what they had seen and heard, a strong bias against the Taipings would have been understandable. But in Shanghai reports and opinions differed widely. To some they were demons, to others saints. Griffith John determined to visit the Taipings if he could to mature his own impressions. He was by no means the only one with this hope. In July Edkins and he, with Macgowan and Hall, spent a week in rebel territory. (Whether C J Hall, now in Shanghai under the BMS, most probably, or W N Hall, newly arrived for the Methodist New Connexion, he did not say.)

It was the most eventful week in Griffith John's life so far. Passing through no-man's-land between free and rebel territory brought them under fire from both sides. On the fourth night their canal boat had to push for two hundred yards through log jams of decomposing corpses, suicides and victims of Taiping savagery. Rather than fall into rebel hands, men, women and children of the upper, moneyed classes took their own lives. When the party joined a body of a hundred horse and foot, they found them friendly. From them they learned that Hong Ren, the one-time evangelist and cousin of the Taiping Wang, Hong Xiu-quan, was now second-in-command with the title Gan Wang, Shield King. Finally they reached the rebel leaders at Suzhou, secure among thirty thousand insurgents – and were favourably impressed.

On their return to Shanghai a starry-eyed report by Edkins on their findings was published in the *North China Herald*, with a note by Griffith John on the Taipings' beliefs and practices and his views on the British policy of neutrality towards them. The quasi-Christian use of Old and New Testaments and of prayer and worship had influenced the missionaries. Their reception as honoured guests completed the conquest. The red and yellow banners of the Taiping nobility, with yellow robes and turbans, were surpassed by the magnificence of the Zhong Wang's court. Yellow was traditionally the Chinese symbol of royalty. The visitors were escorted up a 'long and gorgeous vista' formed by an avenue of a hundred lantern-bearing men in robes and caps of red and yellow silk, on carpets of red. Deafening music and gongs and a salute of six shots heralded their arrival. Only the Zhong Wang in his rich yellow robes and gold-embroidered head-dress remained seated while he questioned them on their doctrines and accepted gifts of Bibles and other books. Finally they were escorted on horseback to their boats. Later the Zhong Wang and Hong Ren exchanged letters with them and invited them back to Suzhou. So began a dramatic development in foreign relations with the Taipings, at first all that they could wish for, but with an unexpected ending.

'Our duty to come'[3] *June–July 1860*

Incredibly, in Hudson Taylor's and Maria's surviving correspondence no mention is made of these volcanic upheavals, not even the terrifying sack of Hangzhou, when refugees flooding to Ningbo brought panic to Ningbo's populace in turn. Their days and their hearts were too full. Intense concentration on living and working for their patients and Chinese fellow-Christians determined what they wrote. In any case they habitually refrained from sending alarming news. Other missionaries, even those they were closest to and meeting frequently, the Goughs and E C Lord, and even Mary Jones, are passed over. It was as much as they could do to keep the wheels turning in church and hospital. All the more Christians needed to be taught the foundation truths. Only prayer and personal persuasion involving time with addicts in the pangs of withdrawal crises could make the medical measures worthwhile. Only a new heart, from spiritual conversion, would make the cures permanent. Experience had shown year after year that potential danger to Ningbo often evaporated. Not until its spectre loomed up large and close need it interrupt activities. So the Taipings came and went at Hangzhou, Miss Aldersey departed in April to Australia, the good news came of Mrs Bausum on her way back to Ningbo, and only a passing reference or none at all interrupted accounts of the Christians' progress, the baby's development, their own health and the need for reinforcements.

On June 11 Hudson Taylor wrote his last letter from Ningbo to his mother, 'a few hasty lines to inform you that we have come to the conclusion that it is our duty to come to England for the benefit of my health'. He spoke of bringing a Chinese Christian with him, who could help anyone returning with them to learn the language on the way, 'and in the hope of spiritual benefit to the one we bring, whom we hope to be training for the Master's service the while'. The best training was individual, such as Timothy received from the apostle Paul. But Hudson Taylor was also worried about the sorrow his 'removal' would give his parents and 'my dear, dear, so dear' wife.

> I myself am much better than I was, so far as the liver is concerned; I cannot say so, however of my chest. I hope, if it be the will of God,

> the voyage may benefit that, that I may labor for China, – if not, all is well. I am *very* happy in Jesus. Never felt Him to be so *precious* a Saviour, Lover, Friend. Sometimes I think I shall not be spared to see you – sometimes I hope to labor long and more earnestly than ever for China – all is known to Him . . .

To William Berger he also wrote, 'I often doubt whether I shall be spared to see you.' But nowhere did he give more medical details by which his attempts at self-diagnosis may be assessed. The hepatitis alone was enough to reduce him to the state of weakness he mentions, and to cause persistent chest pain, while intestinal symptoms were customarily attributed to the liver. As quoted, he himself doubted the presence of pulmonary tuberculosis and never mentioned a cough. An amoebic abscess of the liver is a possible alternative. A chronic colitis afflicted him for years to come. The fresh-complexioned youth of the best-known portrait had long since changed to the mature young man with the 'long, thin face' of Maria's description.

The work they were called to do had barely begun. To stay longer, however, would clearly have been folly. Having reached a decision they lost no time in handing over their responsibilities and looking for a ship to Shanghai. The overland route through north Zhejiang and south Jiangsu was swarming with rebels in the process of destroying city after city.

During the nine months that Hudson Taylor was in sole charge of the hospital, sixteen patients had been baptised and thirty others 'became candidates for admission into one or other of the various mission churches in Ningbo'. In the first three or four months he had treated six hundred and sixty out-patients and sixty in-patients, before numbers increased, but no further figures have survived. He summarised the period with the words, 'Many lives were spared; persons apparently in hopeless stages of disease were restored; and success was given in cases of serious and dangerous operations.' In his baggage he carried surgical specimens to demonstrate at the Royal College of Surgeons. But of their nature no record has been found.

The Christian they were preparing to take with them was the painter, Wang Lae-djün. Hudson Taylor described him to W T Berger as consistent and industrious, with a love of the Scriptures. He had learned to write the romanised Ningbo colloquial and was teaching other Christians and enquirers in a school connected with the hospital, 'while he is himself training, I trust, for an evangelist among his own countrymen'. But they had a strategic purpose in taking him with them. They planned while in England to translate hymns and books into the vernacular, and to reprint the romanised vernacular Ningbo New Testament, at long last nearly completed by a changing team of missionaries.

Hudson Taylor handed over Dr Parker's premises to the chronically ill John and Mary Jones on whom the full burden of the church work was to fall. Of the more than thirty members some were able to share in teaching basic doctrine to beginners and enquirers. And with great satisfaction he was able to leave more funds for carrying on the work than he had possessed when he took over from Dr Parker. Without a doubt he had been able to 'trust in the Lord and do good', had 'dwelt in the land' and been fed. The opium-breaking work was to continue under F F Gough, but until Dr Parker returned, other medical work would have to be in abeyance. By selling books and surgical instruments he provided for five adopted orphan boys until now unmentioned in his letters, and on June 18, it appears, he and Maria said their final goodbyes.

When he wrote to his parents from Shanghai on June 28 he and Maria were staying with John Burdon. He had already booked passages on the only home-bound ship available, the *Jubilee*, 'a fine, strong vessel of more than 700 tons'. In fact she was a sleek new tea-clipper of 760 tons, a true 'ship', square-rigged on three masts. Passengers were expected to fend very largely for themselves, though they dined with the captain. So, feeling 'very unfit for any place but bed' in spite of some improvement since leaving Ningbo, he was busy laying in stores and buying two goats to provide milk for the baby. The captain looked irritable 'and may I fear, make us uncomfortable at times, but we look to God . . .' How fully his forebodings were to be justified, he fortunately did not know. It was the typhoon season, and this too prompted the words 'if we are spared to see you'. Shipwreck was still all too common. A box of supplies on the way to him had gone down in one ship, and a recent home mail with fifteen pounds for him in another. Submissively, with confidence in God he quoted,

> The worst that *can* come
> But shortens the journey and hastens us home.

Enclosing a credit note for thirty pounds, surplus to all his expenses including the passage-money for Wang Lae-djün, he gave instructions that if they did not reach England it should be sent to John Jones or used to send someone to take his place in China. So many before him had died on the voyage home.

They were to sail on July 13. A mail ship came in and on the 12th the postmaster obligingly opened the Ningbo mailbox and found two letters for Hudson Taylor. One was from Louisa, dated May 18. True to type it teased him about his spelling, wished him well for his birthday in three days' time and rambled on about her own twentieth birthday coming soon, while saving up her real news to the end.

> And now dearest brother what would be the very best news that this letter could bring you? Would it be . . . if I told you I was converted? If it would make you happy be happy for it is true and your many prayers are at last answered.

At about three a m Hudson Taylor was too hot to sleep and rose to comment briefly by lamplight to his mother, 'I felt like Simeon of old – "Now lettest Thou Thy servant depart in peace" . . . and Maria was so overjoyed. Praise God for His goodness. He was feeling 'very unwell" but managed to 'scratch a line' to Louisa too.

> In view of my own ill-health and the probability of my removal there has been a load on my mind, now, thank God, removed. Cleave to the Lord, my doubly dear sister (now doubly my sister) with true purpose of heart and you will find your joy to be full. My lamp is going out, so I must go to bed again. God bless you. Goodbye.

But the *Jubilee*'s Shanghai pilot 'brought us into collision with the HMS *Furious*, breaking our jib-boom and her bowsprit'. (The jib-boom is the spar rigged out beyond the bowsprit). Captain Jones refused to proceed, and anchored at Wusong until the damage was repaired, while Hudson Taylor took his little family back to the comfort of John Burdon's house. The next day he despatched a letter to William Berger. A gift of a hundred and twenty dollars forwarded from Ningbo had arrived in time to allow him to provide more adequately for the voyage and leave enough in hand to replace the surgical instruments he had sold. Thanking Mr Berger he went on to say how he feared for his life. The opinion he had received from the doctor at Zhoushan (Chusan) had been very outspoken, and 'I cannot but feel how very desolate my departure would leave my dear wife.'

At last on July 18 they dropped down the Yangzi to anchor near the lightship at the mouth, ready to make sail in the morning, and the pilot took a 10.30 p m note to post for him, 'My two pets are asleep, and I am nearly so . . .' Two seasoned campaigners were about to take their first leave, Hudson Taylor after six years, Maria after seven and a half, he at the age of only twenty-eight and she at twenty-three. Little more than ten years had passed since he had surrendered himself to do whatever God required of him. On the ebb tide at daybreak on July 19 the *Jubilee* put out into the China Sea and their ordeal began.

Hudson Taylor had his friends and those who recognised his worth. But others who knew him less well were ignorant of what lay beneath the surface. Even W A P Martin, his associate in Ningbo, wrote in old age, knowing little of Hudson Taylor's love story and tribulations,

> When I first met him he was a mystic absorbed in religious dreams, waiting to have his work revealed – not idle but aimless. When he had money he spent it on charity to needy Chinese, and then was reduced to sore straits himself. When the vocation found him, it made him a new man, with iron will and untiring energy.[4]

If Martin was blind to these traits in Ningbo, and earlier, while Hudson Taylor exchanged the relative safety of the foreign settlements for penetration beyond the 'treaty wall', he was not the only one. K S Latourette in assessing Hudson Taylor's part in *A History of the Expansion of Christianity* recorded these impressions in words which appear to enjoy the irony, 'Then ill health forced him home to England, in 1860, and it looked as if his apparently mad venture in China had ended . . . Not so to the faith of Taylor.'[5]

Hong Ren[6] — *July 1860–1861*

To break down in health and be forced to forsake China at such a time as this was a trying but not unexpected experience for Hudson Taylor. The ratification of the Tientsin Treaty with all its concessions and guarantees was about to be enforced. The Allied fleet was on its way north. Within a fortnight China would be flung open or hostilities would begin. Primarily to force China open for trade, these measures would coincidentally make preaching possible in every province of the empire. The restrictions and uneasy peace of the past months were to be removed, and missionaries of several societies were poised to penetrate deeply into the interior. Given the reinforcements for the Ningbo mission for which they had appealed, he and Maria could within a year or two have been free to press inland themselves. Granted a quick return to health their stay in England would be short and they could hope to be back again within two years. But short of a miracle recovery they would be delayed far longer than that, in which case with all the hindrances removed it would be tantalising, galling to his ardent spirit to be prevented from returning – if he recovered.

Planning to take Shanghai as a port, the Taipings were biding their time through June and July – while Hudson Taylor and Maria were there. But already Shanghai was echoing with the favourable reports brought back from Suzhou by Joseph Edkins and Griffith John. For all the savagery of their troops, the spiritual leaders of the Taipings appeared to favour missionaries of the gospel. Vistas of hope had appeared, that untaught, misguided rebels open to the pure gospel and exposition of the Scripture would yet be the means whereby the whole of China could be reached. Foreign aid could tip the scales and end the civil war. A new dynasty favourable to Christianity and dedicated to the ending of idolatry would create a spiritual vacuum for the truth to fill. Hong Ren himself, known personally to Hudson Taylor and intimately to LMS missionaries as a true Christian intent on the evangelisation of China, had invited them back to Suzhou and was coming from Nanjing to meet them (map, p 202).

John Burdon joined Edkins, Griffith John and two others on the second journey. They arrived in Suzhou on August 2, the day after the Allies landed to attack Dagu in the north. With the same pageantry as before the five men were ushered into the presence of the Gan Wang, Hong Ren. Seated in his rich robes and the gold-embroidered head-dress of a Ming dynasty prince when they arrived, he stood up and shook hands. Then he enquired after old friends and the progress of the gospel in the treaty ports. After a while he dismissed his officers, put off his robes and chatted freely as in the days when he was with the LMS. Grateful to James Legge and Edkins, and to Theodore Hamberg in Hong Kong for kindnesses in the past, he only wanted to renew the fellowship and stay on spiritual topics. Before they left he chose a hymn and himself led them in singing it, and Edkins prayed. So genuine did Hong Ren appear to be in numerous dealings with missionaries that Latourette entertained the hypothesis that he hoped by association with his cousin Hong Xiu-quan to elevate the faith and tenets of the Taipings in the cause of China's conversion.

The next day they returned to Hong Ren, but found him agitated. A Shanghai merchant was with him. Hong Ren had put out friendly feelers to the foreign powers at Shanghai and his letters had not even been opened. Worse still, the British and French were taking up military positions to defend the Chinese city. Not only had they insulted him but had broken the neutrality. The warm relations he had hoped to establish had failed at the outset. After Sir Frederick Bruce's repulse by the Manchus at Dagu in 1859, the foreign powers had been tempted to side with the Taipings and end the Qing (Ch'ing) dynasty. If Shanghai and Ningbo had been yielded to the Taipings and used to supply arms and ammunition, or if later on Charles Gordon and his force had fought for the Taipings instead of against them, the dynasty might well have been overthrown. This potentiality, since called 'the Great IF' of the period, became the topic of heated debate among merchants and missionaries.

After the merchant left, Hong Ren calmed down, chatted with the missionaries, sang a hymn and himself prayed that all idols might perish, all temples be converted into houses of God and pure Christianity become the religion of China. Then he sent them on their way with gifts and they reached Shanghai on August 5. Edkins and Griffith John were still impressed, but to John Burdon the gross errors in the Taiping creed excluded co-operation and hope of reform. Arthur E Moule, the brother of George Moule, arrived in China in 1861 in time to witness the alarms and atrocities of the Taiping invasion of Ningbo. Yet in lecturing on the insurrection he commented,

> One cannot refuse to recognise the conspicuous courage of the Taiping leaders; on the one hand daring to link a popular political movement with the profession of the religion of the unpopular foreigners; and on the other hand, daring to be consistent, and while earnestly desiring the friendship of the foreigner, openly avowing their intention to annihilate the trade in opium . . .[7]

With the Taiping occupation of Suzhou on June 2 and the threat it posed to Shanghai, the Volunteer Corps of residents was re-formed and Chinese merchants formed their own Patriotic Association. To add some more professional ability to the amateur force of clerks and merchants, some of the wealthy business houses under the guidance of Viceroy Zeng Guo-fan (Tseng Kuo-fan) employed two

American adventurers to raise a body of mercenaries, mostly deserters and 'Manila men' (Filipinos). Frederick Townsend Ward was first officer on ships in the China trade from 1851–57, a seaman with 'military instincts . . . great personal bravery, and his character commanded respect'. As officer of an armed Chinese steamer he offered to capture the city of Songjiang for a prize of thirty thousand taels, and so entered Chinese employ on a large scale. His companion Henry Andrea Burgevine, aged twenty-four, was 'a more unscrupulous soldier of fortune'. Supplementing his mercenaries with Chinese whom he disciplined and trained into an efficient fighting force, Ward fought so well when the clash came that they earned the name 'Ever-Victorious Army'. On July 17 Ward and his force took Songjiang by assault.

The rebuff to Hong Ren's peaceful overtures played into the hands of the belligerent Zhong Wang, the Loyal King. His army advanced on Shanghai and on August 18 he sent the foreign consuls an ultimatum. He intended to take the Chinese city but to leave the Settlements unharmed. Foreign lives and property were safe if neutrality was observed. But he seized 'Siccawei' (Xu Jia Wei/Hui) the Jesuit headquarters, and made it his own. From there he advanced to within a mile of the city, his coming heralded by the billowing smoke of burning villages. The excitement in city and Settlement reached its highest pitch. Manned barricades were set up in every street. The population was swollen by fifteen thousand refugees before the advancing long-haired rebels.

In a message the Zhong Wang declared he had come only to open communication with the foreign powers. This was the turning point. British and French regular troops manned the Chinese city's walls with flags flying and refused to confer with him. Their only reply to any further advance would be 'by shot and shell'. Hearing of this Griffith John was indignant. To him and others the best hope for China was being dissipated without adequate consideration. But they were few among the seventy missionaries then in the Settlement waiting for the outcome of Lord Elgin's action in the north.

The Taipings approached the South Gate of the city and met fire from British rifles and ships' guns. A sharp engagement took place, but they tried again at the racecourse. This time although fired on they did not return the fire and withdrew. They then seized the wealthy suburb of Nantao, pillaging and massacring until the French came and cleared the area, burning the suburb to the ground. In a situation worthy of Lewis Carroll, missionaries caught between the Taipings and the defenders shouted for the British to hold their fire until they were past and, each time, to the rebels whom they kept meeting in the otherwise empty streets, they called 'We worship God', to which the 'long-hairs' replied 'We also worship God' and let them pass.

On August 20 the Taipings advanced again on the West Gate and Settlement but after two hours of shelling from the river withdrew again towards Siccawei. The young British interpreter R J Forrest bravely rode out with a declaration to the Zhong Wang that the Chinese city was under the protection of the British and French and went again the next day to receive his reply. He found the outposts manned only by straw dummies. The Taipings had gone.

In spite of this, and of subsequent hostilities in which the Taipings suffered repeated setbacks, Hong Ren invited more missionaries to visit and to live and preach in their capital, Nanjing. He asked Joseph Edkins to return and 'instruct him more perfectly in the way of Salvation'. Edkins did so and obtained permission to bring his wife and settle there. But for a variety of reasons the plan never materialised. Josiah Cox, the Wesleyan from Canton, the native place of the Hong cousins and many Taipings, visited Nanjing but was refused permission to preach and returned thoroughly disillusioned. Issacher J Roberts, Hong Xiu-quan's old instructor, (and the instigator of Hudson Taylor's early departure from Britain without qualifying as a doctor), who failed in 1854 to reach Nanjing, was now made welcome and stayed for fifteen months. But he too left, utterly opposed to the Taipings and convinced that Hong Xiu-quan was insane. Griffith John and the Dutchman Hendrick Kloekers, by then in the Baptist Missionary Society, spent a month visiting the Taipings, however, and obtained an Edict of Toleration from them, granting full permission for missionaries to work in Taiping territory and ordering that they be treated well. One proclamation read,

> Foreigners are never to be called by opprobrious names; missionaries are to travel, to live, to preach everywhere. Railroads, steam-boats, fire and life insurance companies and newspapers are to be freely introduced for the good of China.'[8]

In his report to the LMS Griffith John said he felt that the rebellion had

> created a vacuum not only in the temples but also in the hearts of the people which remains to be filled. This is the missionary's work – a

> work which might be done immediately were it not for the unaccountable policy of the representatives of foreign powers at this port [of Shanghai] . . . I fully believe that God is uprooting idolatry in this land through the insurgents and that he will . . . plant Christianity in its stead.[9]

For once his optimism outstripped events. He planned to move to Nanjing but was advised to defer going. To do so would cut him off from other missionaries and sources of support, make him dependent on the Taipings and so compromise his own position. He waited, and on visiting Nanjing again the following April found a change for the worse in the character of the leaders and in the conduct of their followers. Also in 1861 William Muirhead stayed for a month in Nanjing preaching freely around the palace of the Tian Wang. Yet he reported his conclusion that the rebellion was destructive, not constructive.

By then the Western governments had made their peace with Peking and were considering active support in the imperial campaign against the Taipings. Foreigners who previously had been hopeful now disowned the rebels as fanatical and savage. Gone were the days when Dr W H Medhurst wrote of a Taiping publication,

> The reasoning is correct, the prayers are good, and the statement of the doctrine of human depravity, redemption by the blood of Jesus, and renewal of the heart by the influence of the Holy Spirit are sufficient to direct any honest enquirer on the way to Heaven.

All that had changed and blasphemous fantasies increasingly took its place. Pro-Western attitudes veered from neutrality to antagonism, and foreign governments ordered armed intervention to protect their nationals.

The Peking outrages[10] *August–October 1860*

Travelling together, Lord Elgin and Baron Gros arrived at Hong Kong on June 21, 1860, (after the shipwreck en route) and lost no time in taking action. In reply to the emperor's rejection of their March ultimatum, on the 26th they declared a state of war and proceeded north to Shanghai, with Admiral Sir James Hope in command of the fleet. Elgin summoned Consul Harry S Parkes and Lieutenant Thomas F Wade, both men of marked ability, to be his interpreters, and Baron Gros appointed the Baron de Méritens and the Abbé Delamarre as his.

When the Allied warships arrived off Dagu they found the chain barrier restored and the forts strengthened. Convinced that the miles of marshland almost surrounding the town and forts would protect them as they had before, the Manchu and Chinese officials looked on complacently, waiting for the barbarians to repeat their mistakes of the previous year. But General Sir Hope Grant, commanding the land forces, this time was prepared for innovations, with eighteen thousand men in the Anglo–French force and a labour corps of two and a half thousand anti-Manchu Cantonese.

Eight miles north of the winding Beihe, the river between Dagu and Tianjin, another river reached the sea at the town of Beitang from which it was named. Between the two lay nothing but great tidal salt flats and swamps. But near the mouth of the Beitang some desolate ground dotted with grave mounds gave on to a raised causeway a mile from the shore and a good cart track sweeping inland to a fine open plain, excellent cavalry country. The causeway was defended by infantry and an élite regiment of Tartar cavalry was strategically encamped near Xinhe (Sinho) south of the plain, well inland from the Dagu forts. Raised causeways also crossed the swamps between Dagu and the camp. Without doubt Grant's thousand cavalry held the key to success.[11]

On August 1 the Allies began to land at Beitang and advanced along the causeway. Resistance was determined. Then on the 12th their cavalry made a wide flanking attack and defeated the Tartars at Xinhe. Tanggu fell on the 14th, and on the 21st (the day the Taipings were repulsed at Shanghai) the North Dagu forts were assaulted in one of the epic actions of military history.[12] On August 25 the Allies occupied Tianjin, thirty miles inland, without a blow. It was a classic outflanking operation, a miniature of the Alamein type. But unfortunately the Manchu rules of honourable warfare demanded frontal attack and this stab in the back infuriated Peking. An imperial edict of September 6, 1860, exposed the naivety of Xian Feng, Yehonala and the Court's thinking. Their insularity still left them ignorant of the barbarians' power. Blind and deaf to such information as reached them, though Chinese scholars had been visiting Europe and America for almost half a century, the obscurants pronounced that it was scandalous for Lord Elgin to want to be received on equal terms, decreeing,

> When the British and French repent of their evil ways and return to their former allegiance, we shall be pleased to permit them to trade again . . . [if not] our armies must mightily smite them . . .[13]

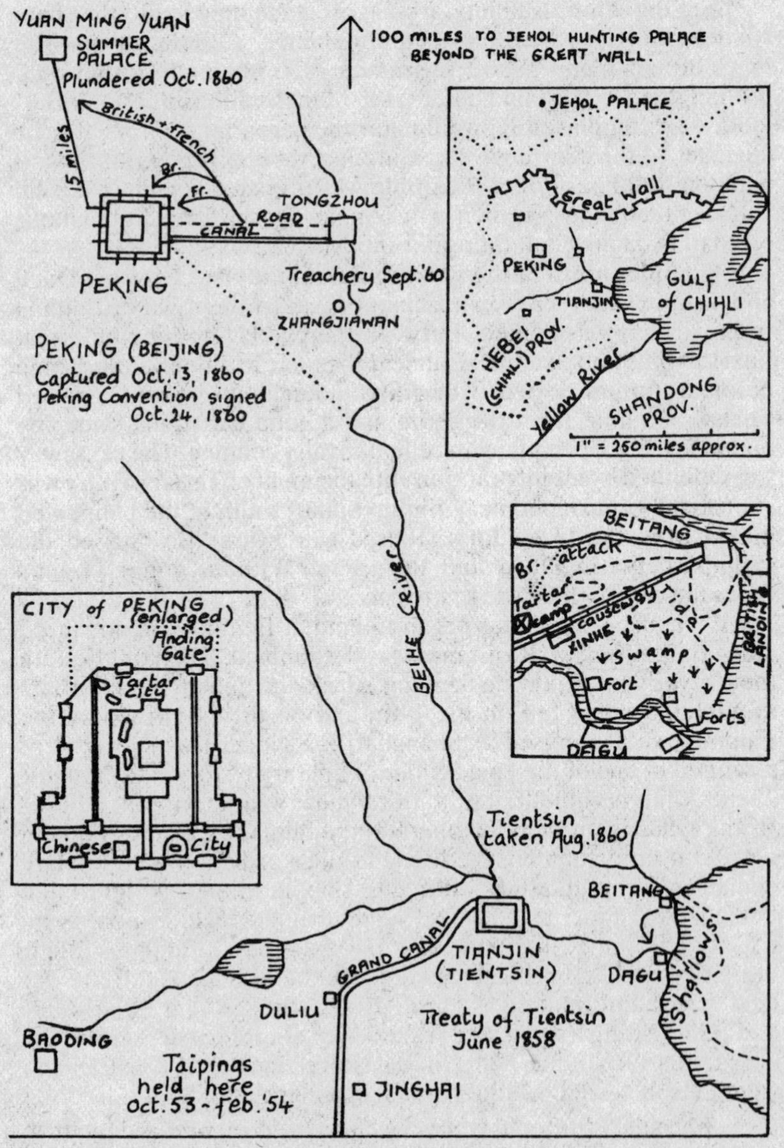

ALLIED INVASIONS: DAGU, PEKING, 1858–60

Imperial High Commissioners were appointed, but Lord Elgin and Baron Gros were in no mood for diplomacy at Tianjin. This time it was ratification of the treaties within the walls of Peking or capture of the capital. Consul Harry Parkes with a score of officers and men accompanied by a French delegation, a *Times* correspondent and interpreters, in all thirty-eight men, went up to Tongzhou, now Tong Xian, twelve miles east of Peking, under a flag of truce, and preliminary negotiations appeared to proceed hopefully. Parkes had been at the forefront of every dangerous action. A basis of agreement was reached and they started back to report.

Now barbarian perfidy was to be answered with Chinese perfidy. Parkes had sensed trouble and, recognising an ambush laid for the Allied force, succeeded in alerting his superiors. But on September 18 all his truce party was seized at Zhangjiawan (Changchiawan), trussed up like pigs for market, cruelly tortured and most of them massacred and mutilated. The rest were imprisoned as hostages. Held in the Manchus' power, Parkes resolutely refused to intervene in negotiations or even to communicate with Lord Elgin lest his plight should affect Elgin's judgment, for Lord Elgin still believed the truce party to be safe and well treated. When the truth was known, his despatch to Whitehall ran,

> Mr Parkes' consistent refusal to purchase his own safety by making any pledge or even by addressing to me any representations which might have embarrassed me in the discharge of my duty, is a rare example of courage and devotion to the public interest . . . leaving my hands free . . .

Sir Hope Grant confirmed that his forces were being hemmed in, and at once attacked. Only military command of Peking and signed treaties on Allied terms would now satisfy the plenipotentiaries. Twice the massed imperial armies made a stand and twice they were routed by greatly inferior numbers.

W A P Martin of Ningbo was there again as an interpreter in the American delegation.[14] On a wall in Tianjin he read a reflection on the Chinese attitude to the ruling Manchus in the person of the Tartar general, translating it,

> When he fights and runs away,
> Is it war or is it play?

At that point also a young captain of the Royal Engineers joined Grant's force. After serving in the Crimea he had been retained to map the Russo–Turkish border in Armenia and was then posted to Lord Elgin's expedition. Charles Gordon was to have no great part in this campaign but, paradoxically, before he left China he was decorated by the emperor with the highest honours as a brigadier of the imperial army. In Europe 'Chinese Gordon' and years later 'Gordon of Khartoum' were the titles by which everyone came to know him.

With the advance of the Allied army towards the Yuan Ming Yuan, the imperial Summer Palace fifteen miles north of Peking (map, p 216), the Xian Feng emperor panicked. Yehonala, the Concubine Yi, persuaded two Grand Secretaries to dissuade him from fleeing but her rivals overcame her advice and in the words of a Chinese diarist, the emperor 'attended by all his concubines, the Princes, Ministers and Dukes, and all the officers of the household, left . . . in a desperate rout and disorder unspeakable'.[15]

Officially the court had gone 'on a tour of inspection' beyond the Great Wall far to the north. Yehonala's son was four now, and Yong Lu, perhaps his father, commanded a strong detachment of troops in the imperial bodyguard. As soon as they reached safety the emperor ordered his brother Prince Kong to continue the war, and to put all prisoners to death.

Left behind in the Summer Palace were twelve prisoners, survivors of the Zhangjiawan treachery. Harry Parkes was one, and with him a friend, the future Sir Henry Lock, historian of the event and later Governor of the Cape (1889–95), at the time private secretary to Lord Elgin. Together they and the ten others had been marched to the Summer Palace and incarcerated, bound hand and foot. The Allied force found them all, the dead and the living, 'with appalling wounds and mutilations', and vowed vengeance. Of twenty-six British half were killed. Of thirteen French only five lived. Under General de Montauban the French proceeded to occupy and plunder the palace from October 6 onward. British troops joined in later.

First they secured the surrender of Peking. They reached the city the same day, and on October 7 while an attack on the Anding Gate was being mounted, delivered an ultimatum requiring the gate to be opened to Lord Elgin by noon on the 13th. As an engineer Charles Gordon was busy mining the gate. Just before midnight on the 12th however, one of the Commissioners, Heng Qi, at one time in the Customs at Canton, and now a minister at Peking, persuaded the military mandarins to open the gates, and the Allies took posses-

ONE OF THE GATES OF PEKING

sion. Later it transpired that it was Heng Qi who had thwarted the imperial order to kill all the prisoners, so saving the lives of Parkes and Lock.[16] Seeing the flags of Europe flying on Peking walls and filled with tales of Taiping atrocities and the imperial troops' even greater excesses, the people of Peking prepared to jump into their wells or hang themselves – until word spread that the invaders had halted and were harming no one.

Lord Elgin then faced two problems. With the Court in full flight with whom was he to negotiate? And how was he to punish the emperor and his advisers for their treachery? The two answers were to remain as major factors in international relations for the next forty years. The future of China hung in the balance. The Allied ambassadors were seriously considering negotiation with the Taipings at Nanjing, when appeared 'a slender thread on which history dangles',[17] to change their minds. A young man of twenty-seven came forward with credentials empowering him to represent the emperor. Prince Kong, the younger brother of the decrepit opium addict Xian Feng, without the backing of any apparent power, won the admiration of the British by behaving with great dignity and composure in a very embarrassing situation. Betraying no sense of weakness he did his best to obtain the most favourable terms possible.

The Allied envoys' answer to the second problem reflected mid-nineteenth century European imperialism at its worst. In order to punish the emperor rather than the people, Elgin and General de Montauban had decided to sack the Summer Palace. Now British troops joined in the desecration. The palace was a great imperial complex of two hundred beautiful buildings spread among exquisite gardens and lakes over an area ten miles by eight in extent. Temples, pagodas, lodges and residences, none were spared. Captain Gordon wrote of that day, October 18,

> . . . after pillaging it [we] burned the whole place, destroying in a vandal-like manner most valuable property . . . it made one's heart sore . . . Quantities of gold ornaments were burned, considered as brass . . . Everyone was wild for plunder . . . You would scarcely conceive the magnificence of this residence, or the tremendous devastation the French (and we) have committed. The throne and room were lined with ebony, carved in a marvellous way. There were huge mirrors of all shapes and kinds . . . magnificent china of every description, heaps and heaps of silks of all colours . . . large amounts of treasure. The French have smashed everything in a most wanton way . . .

The accumulated tribute of vassal states, clocks presented by Ricci and others, filled the palaces and fell under the vandals' blows. But while he deplored it all, young Gordon was a party to it, writing, '. . . although I have not had as much as many, I have done well'. For twenty-four hours clouds of smoke 'hung like a vast pall' over the scene.

Prince Kong submitted absolutely to all the Allies' demands and on October 24 ratified the Treaty of Tientsin and signed the Convention of Peking in a scene of great pomp in the Hall of

Ceremonies. 'British bayonets bristled in the very heart of the Imperial City' at the signing, but from the time they knew the fate of the truce party, the troops were so vicious they had to be kept in camp under strict control lest they exact revenge on the Chinese. So not even company commanders could be present at the ceremony. Full ratification followed on the 28th.

The terms of the Peking Convention, confirmed by an imperial edict, were unquestionably harsh.[18] But with the Taiping rebellion also threatening the Qing dynasty neither Prince Kong nor the emperor had room for manoeuvre. Thwarted conquerors could be expected to ally themselves to Hong Xiu-quan. Besides the concessions of the Tientsin Treaty and heavy indemnities, the Manchu court and European powers were at long last to exchange diplomatic representatives on terms of equality, ministers were to reside in the capital, Tianjin and Tongzhou, (between Tianjin and Peking) were opened to foreign residence, Yangzi ports were opened to foreign ships – and Britain was given the right to organise and appoint the head of the Imperial Maritime Customs! Already, since 1854 and the Triads' seizure of Shanghai, customs collection had been in the hands of the Settlement authorities. Duty on imports was agreed and a clause tantamount to legalising the opium traffic read, 'The restrictions affecting trade in opium are relaxed . . . opium shall henceforth pay 30 taels per picul import duty'.[19] By a fixed tariff the importing of vast quantities of the drug was protected from lethal impositions of duty.

This was the knell. China was helpless to resist the exploitation. Griffith John had written a year before that ten to fifteen years ago no one dared to smoke publicly, but always in a locked room or in the dark, from shame as much as fear. Addicts were still regarded as undutiful self-murderers. After 1860, as the measure of Britain's 'commercial' success, opium dens were open all and every day, and people smoked in broad daylight – until the mid-twentieth century. With the Xian Feng emperor – like Dao Guang before him, an addict – the mandarins were smoking perhaps more than any other class in the community. Soon after the Peking Convention was signed, the opium depot hulks at Wusong moved up to Shanghai and to Britain's disgrace opium imports from India continued uninterrupted for over fifty more years despite strenuous efforts by the anti-opium lobby. Other concessions of the Peking Convention were that the Jiulong (Kowloon) peninsula, on the mainland opposite Hong Kong, was ceded in perpetuity to the British, the right of foreigners to live and work in the interior of China was confirmed, and Chinese Christians were to be protected. Indemnities were increased, beyond the terms of the Treaty of Tientsin, 1858, to eight million taels to each of the Allied forces. Another 'unequal treaty' had joined its predecessors. That winter Prince Kong as Chancellor of the Empire and Chief Minister of Foreign Affairs founded the Tsungli (Zong Li) Yamen or Foreign Office, and a new era in international relations began.

The purpose of the expedition fully achieved, as Lord Elgin thought, he withdrew from Peking, leaving not even a token force. And once more the Court reviewed the situation and felt consoled. The barbarians had occupied only one gate, not the capital, had hurried away again, a sign of weakness if not of fear, and as Consul W H Medhurst Jr pointed out, had left undetermined the crucial question in the eyes of China, that of access to the emperor – the sticking point since Lord Macartney in 1793. Twelve years later Medhurst was still surmising that relations between the Manchus and foreign nations would never become stable without 'the expenditure of still more blood and treasure'. How right he was had to be proved from time to time, culminating in the tragic Boxer Rising of 1900 – for the highly cultured and intelligent Yehonala would never forget the outrage upon her beloved Summer Palace. The Forbidden City enclosed within the Imperial City in the heart of greater Peking was soulless and claustrophobic. 'It is so cold . . . it has no heart,' she said. At the garden pleasance of Yuan Ming Yuan her spirit had been free. She was prepared to bide her time until she could exact revenge.

Old era and new *1860–1900*

The Peking Convention of 1860 marked the end of 'the Opium Wars' begun in 1840 – seeing opium could now be imported legally – but not of Western aggression. A taste of success went to the heads of imperialist Russia, France and Britain, and soon of Prussia and other nations. Russia consolidated her occupation of territory along the Amur River in Manchuria (map, p 73), and the next phase of China's dismemberment, known as 'Slicing the Melon', had begun. Mgr Mouly secured the return of the ancient cemetery in which Matteo Ricci and Adam Schall von Bell were buried, and the remains of four churches. The reopening of one, the

Nan Tang, was celebrated by a *Te Deum* in honour of Napoleon III and the French army![20]

But in that the opium wars were primarily the reaction of the West to decades of insult and obstruction to legitimate commercial ambition, beyond the endurance of nineteenth-century pride, the Convention marked a great change of relationship, whatever underlying attitudes remained. The clash of cultures had produced at the least an unhappy agreement to co-operate. The Chinese view of an all-powerful emperor ruling by arbitrary edict was forced to recognise and abide by the Roman alternative of law and evidence. And the Chinese low view of the merchant and his occupation had to concede the facts of economic and political power wielded by foreign traders. The drain on silver alone was touching the government's pocket and teaching its own lesson.

With the end of the emperor's having the upper hand, the Western powers, and before long Japan as well, were to wring from a weakening dynasty more and more concessions. But before that movement gathered momentum, a phase of overt co-operation began. China welcomed British help not only in her Imperial Maritime Customs but in her armed forces, in policing the Yangzi River with gunboats and soon in her postal services, railways and salt gabelle (tax) system.

Sovereignty over her main internal waterways had been surrendered. This profound subjection to semi-colonial status represented China's entry into what H B Morse termed the Period of Submission (1860–93). Her descent from the glory of dynastic domination to inferiority and dependence was heartbreaking to all in China whose intellect and insight recognised the transformation for what it was. So great a people could never bow interminably to such injustice. While the obscurants in the Peking Court vowed old-fashioned revenge, true statesmen like Prince Kong, Zeng Guo-fan and Li Hong-zhang, began working towards recovery. But far-seeing foreigners no less regretted what had happened, while they availed themselves of its advantages. W A Russell voiced the feelings of the missionaries when he wrote,

> [China] has been forced by Christian England, at the very point of the bayonet, to throw open her gates to the free and unrestricted introduction of opium, and to the reception of it on the part of her people . . . Christian England, her rulers and people generally, have really forced open the gates of Peking, and burned down the imperial

> palace, in order to secure legal access to all parts of China, as well for the merchant with his opium as for the missionary . . .

And the CMS was criticised for the ceaseless protests in the CM *Intelligencer* against Britain's high-handed policy in China, piling up 'evidence of the iniquity of the trade and of the misery it was bringing upon China'. One such protest was a statement signed by twenty-five distinguished medical men, including no less than fourteen Fellows of the Royal Society.[21] In Shanghai Bishop William Boone lamented what he called American aggression, for although the United States took only a small part militarily she was firmly on the bandwagon in the person of her plenipotentiary the Hon John E Ward at Peking.

Difficulties between China and the West soon multiplied. Wresting satisfaction for old grievances only bred increasingly complicated relations in which each new treaty port became a potential storm centre. In the long run nobody came out well. An unwilling, offended China continued sullenly resentful of the conditions imposed by the treaties. Although a new era of co-operation replaced the old era of confrontation, new tensions mirrored those that had led to war. One of the worst sprang from the covert action of one man. His bad faith was not long in coming to light.

After the Chinese Government's capitulation at Peking, Baron Gros took his time in completing the French treaty, the French language version of which was defined as authoritative. But his interpreter, the Abbé Delamarre, a priest of the Paris Mission (Société des Missions Étrangères), in translating the treaty into Chinese took it upon himself to interpolate four clauses without the Baron's knowledge. His deceit was later welcomed as useful and was therefore excused. In the French version the toleration clause resembled the American and British, but Delamarre's insertions authorised the punishment of those who persecuted Christians, and gave Catholic priests the right to rent land and buy or build houses anywhere in the empire. This, with the demand for the return of confiscated property, or compensation where restitution was impossible, was the germ of far-reaching effects. 'The French Government took full advantage of this pious fraud' and a French protectorate over Roman Catholics in China quickly developed.[22]

> From 1860 to 1888 all Roman Catholic missionaries carried a passport, delivered to them by the consular agents of France, and written in both French and Chinese. The Chinese text stated that the bearer was French, whatever his nationality may in reality have been.[23]

So Stephen Neill summarised the practice. Delamarre himself left Peking in December 1860 with twenty-seven passports for his society's missionaries in Sichuan, Yunnan and Guizhou. When the Chinese discovered the discrepancy between their version and the French they rightly pleaded that as the ruling French version lacked Delamarre's clauses they were void. In answer the French only pressed for a rescript which not only retained them but in addition protected Catholics from demands for contributions to idolatrous practices.

By the 'most favoured nation' principle, what was granted to France was equally applicable to other nations, but Britain and America wanted nothing to do with it. Until the American commercial treaty of 1903 which secured for all missionaries the right 'to rent or lease in perpetuity buildings or lands in all parts of the empire', no Protestant mission based any claim on the French clause, H B Morse records. 'The Catholic missions were alone in holding the land in the interior as freehold property.' In practice, however, when foreign individuals later bought or rented property with official Chinese authorisation and were molested in any way, British and American consuls supported them in the name of justice.

In theory China was now open to foreigners to travel and reside wherever they wished. But it was 1876 before either travelling or living in the interior had the genuine protection of the Chinese authorities, and then only after fresh negotiations following the murder of a British consul.

Domination by the Western powers was bad enough, but Prince Kong recognised that for the present they were satisfied. The threat to the Qing dynasty still posed by the Taipings, Nian-fei and other rebellions was an even more serious matter. On widely scattered fronts the major Manchu forces seemed helpless to defeat them. As in 1853 when the northern army of Taipings knocked at the gates of Tianjin and were repulsed from Duliu by Zeng Guo-fan, so as the Anglo-French force advanced on Peking the same man brought brief comfort to his masters by halting a Taiping advance in Anhui. But to press the victory home was beyond him.

Serious as the foreign invasion and exactions were, young Prince Kong knew that insurrection among his own people was more dangerous. The barbarians, he declared, were 'an affliction of the limbs', but the Taipings were 'a disease of the vitals'. (Eighty years later Chiang Kai-shek was to quote this saying in reference to the

Japanese invasion and to Mao Tse-tung's communists entrenched at Yan'an (Yenan).

So the policy Kong adopted was to placate the West while trying to quell the rebellions and eradicate the Taipings. Tactical concessions to the superior powers would be justified if they would in turn train China's armies and build up a navy to restore internal peace and stability. In time those very forces could back her demands for sovereign rights to be restored. The Tsungli Yamen (the Foreign Office) which he established to treat with foreign envoys at Peking, was also to promote Western scientific education and a college of interpreters, and to control the Inspector-General's office of the new Imperial Maritime Customs.

Prince Kong was not mistaken. Britain's grievances and policy of co-operation with the imperial government settled to her own satisfaction, she forsook the stance of neutrality towards the Taipings. Things had moved a long, long way from the relationship Robert Morrison had known at the Canton of 1810, or for that matter from the Canton of 1839 when William Lockhart witnessed the garrotting of a Chinese as an act of provocation in the 'Factory' grounds. Now, only twenty-one years later coastal and river ports were open from the far south to the far north and from the seaboard to remote western provinces in the interior. For fifteen or more years individual travellers were to find conditions hazardous once they penetrated beyond the consular centres, and even in them, but these were teething troubles in a China at last thrown open to merchants and missionaries alike.

While Hudson Taylor and Maria sailed painfully home to London, uncertain even of survival to return to Ningbo, the changes they had anticipated were taking place. And while they recuperated, wrestling with difficulties they could not foresee, the old order changed in the China they had known. When at length they returned a great deal was different. And so were they.

PART 3

AN INVALID IN LONDON!

1860–65

CHAPTER SIX

A YEAR TO RECUPERATE 1860–61

The voyage of the 'Jubilee'[1] *July-November 1860*

Early on July 19 Captain Jones made sail and on the ebb tide put out from the Yangzi estuary into the China Sea. Beating southward against the monsoon winds the *Jubilee*'s motion quickly reduced Wang Lae-djün, Hudson Taylor and the child to seasickness. For the present Maria held out and could care for them. But Grace was cutting her teeth and inconsolable. Before long the captain gave them the first taste of his temper. In his pencilled log Hudson Taylor wrote, 'Captain very cross, told me . . . he could not allow [the baby] to cry in that way.' But on Sunday, 22nd, he went on, 'Asked Capt. with great trepidation to allow me to conduct divine service among the men. He consented . . . In the afternoon I found 2nd. Mate was a Christian . . . was much cheered by this discovery.'

His sermon notes for Sunday after Sunday through the long voyage show careful preparation and a determination to make the gospel as plain as he could to all the men, from every angle. 'Thou God seest *me*' he expounded on this day. A week later he chose 'Come, let us reason together – though your sins be as scarlet – double-dyed . . .' For thirteen weeks without a break and then for another month he put his heart into that missionary purpose. But by the time he had found his own sea-legs Maria was helplessly sick with dysentery, and had to leave the baby and the goats, her milk supply, to Lae-djün's care most of each day.

Hudson Taylor's own recovery was short-lived. Dysentery became prevalent in the ship, and as they tossed and rolled, 'Generally beating about . . . close to Formosa' and then Amoy, all of them were 'sick and miserable again'. But Maria did not pick up when the others did, and on August 8 Hudson noted, 'Maria very ill . . . Gastroenteritis – unable to keep anything, food or medicine.'

She was worse the next day, when the ship's motion was very

great in heavy seas. And four weeks after leaving Shanghai, although improving, she was unable to go out on deck. He carried her out two days later, but when they passed Bangka Island near Sumatra she was 'still very sick at times'. Now they knew that she was pregnant again and going through the extreme evidences of toxaemia which she had experienced the last time. It did not help matters that Captain Jones, having 'scarcely had a good sleep' since Shanghai, was more short-tempered than ever. He did not trust his crew, and in the dangerous Gaspar Strait between Bangka and Billiton islands, was justified in his suspicions. 'In spite of a wreck, and in the midst of shoals we had scarcely come down to dinner when the man at the wheel was steering a point and a half [17°] from her course.'

But Hudson Taylor and Maria could not sleep for other reasons. Their cabin was infested with bedbugs. He kept a tally of kills. 'Day by day we kill 20 or 30 or 60, and yet after all we cannot sleep for them. They have got into our boxes and drawers and clothes.' Any complaint or request for help to deal with them was out of the question. Years later a friend jotted down what Hudson Taylor told her about the journey.

> The captain was an extraordinary man . . . subject to fits of awful passion, above all delighting in cruelty. His cruelty to both his poor

'HEAVY SEAS'

> wife . . . and to a poor insane woman (sometimes maniacal) . . . were shocking. The poor woman was kept chained up, sometimes on deck. He used to beat them both with a dog whip unmercifully; and his wife was in terror of him.

Even friendliness to her was misconstrued.

But their problems had barely started. On Sunday, August 26, they were off Anjer, the provisioning point in the strait between Java and Sumatra, and Captain Jones began buying fowls, yam and fruit, a monkey and a parrot, from boats that came out from the shore. Hudson Taylor was preaching as usual to the crew and passengers in the large, airy saloon. In his recollections, (though not in his journal), he said,

> I incurred his hatred by refusing to translate and bargain for him with the natives. This made him furiously angry. I did it from conscientious motives and explained to him as well as I could why I felt it wrong . . . and that I . . . would far rather do without . . . than break the Lord's Day . . . For the next three or four months he did everything in his power to render my life miserable.

The trouble was that Hudson Taylor was still ill himself and anxious about Maria. In a letter he posted at Anjer to his parents he had said,

> I am decidedly better than when we left Ningpo [but until a few days back] my chest was only relieved when a diarrhoea almost incessant was on; and when it was more than checked, my chest suffered.

And he had a distressing neuralgia. But when the sea was rough Maria's condition was alarming. After two months he scribbled in his journal,

> Sometimes I hope she is gaining ground, and sometimes fear she is losing. I do not know what to do . . . ought I to ask Captain Jones to put us ashore [at the Cape] . . . Our Father can care for us as well at the Cape as in England . . . He *will*, I *know* it, direct me aright.

The captain 'rudely refused' a suitable diet for her and insisted that Maria should eat what others did. He forbade the cook to do anything else for her, and banned any kind of lamp or cooking device in the cabin. Desperate, Hudson Taylor took a risk.

> Fortunately I had a large pile of old magazines with me, and by tearing out page after page, twisting them tightly, and lighting them one by one, I was enabled to cook in a small tin cup a few teaspoon-

> fuls of arrowroot at a time, which was the only means I had of keeping her alive.

In his recollections he recounted, '[I] implored the Captain to land us at the Cape . . . His spite however prevailed, and he refused.' But his journal omits any reference to that episode, and towards the end of September as they beat down the coast of Africa her condition improved and her appetite began to return.

When he could, he was spending time with Lae-djün, sometimes having a communion service in Chinese with him and Maria in the cabin. Throughout the journey they were praying together for those five new missionaries to be sent to replace them at Ningbo. The need felt more urgent the farther away they sailed. He was also reading the Bible with the ship's cook and teaching the carpenter and other members of the crew.

He made an inventory of the books he had considered worth bringing with him – one hundred and fifty-seven volumes including six of Matthew Henry's commentary, Robert Morrison's dictionary in six volumes, eight of 'classics', eight of surgery, three of anatomy, and a long list of others – a Latin–Chinese dictionary, books on chemistry, botany and geology, Wesley's sermons, a biography of General Havelock, hero of Lucknow, travel books and so on. Another list detailed their baggage, including 'Large Medical Chest' and a 'Black seaman's chest'. But today the 'Upper and lower Drawers' are of interest, for they now adorn the United Kingdom office of the mission he founded – two large brass-bound oak chests, each with tiers of drawers and designed to stand one upon the other – useful furniture in a floating home for what could be a six-month journey. During the voyage he translated hymns into the Ningbo dialect, and began working out how to revise the romanised vernacular New Testament.

On September 26 Maria was so much better that there was no longer any need to think of landing at the Cape. They passed it three days later and turning north into the Atlantic ran into a gale. At last, on October 10 Maria was well enough to come out on deck, the first time for many weeks. 'May I be truly thankful and she be fully restored,' he sighed.

Then Sunday, November 18, their eighteenth on board, saw them entering the English Channel. At four next morning they passed the Isle of Wight; and Beachy Head at nine. His last entries convey his excitement and relief. They spent the day packing up their cabin possessions. The ordeal was over. Waking on Tuesday, November 20, they saw they were at anchor off Gravesend, and lost no time in getting ashore. Incredibly, it had been a fast voyage of only four months and three days instead of the six months they might well have taken in an older ship. A voyage or two later Captain Jones died of cholera. But the *Jubilee* lived on to the ripe old age of eighty-seven, to be broken up in 1944.

Crinolines and swansdown *November–December 1860*

To Wang Lae-djün everything was as new as the Huangpu River and Shanghai had been to Hudson Taylor six years before. He had never seen a railway, let alone travelled on a train. With only the essentials of hand luggage they disembarked at dawn and took the train to London, crossed the city and at 'about breakfast time' arrived at Westbourne Grove, Bayswater. In this respectable residential area on the fringe of London, when Notting Hill was virgin parkland, conveniently close to his business in New Bond Street, Benjamin Broomhall's neighbours saw coming down the road a sight to bring them to their windows. A well-built Chinese, 'a fine man, physically', in Chinese clothes, carrying a child of sixteen months 'in English dress, her white drawers down almost to her ancles' [*sic*] in the fashion of a decade back, was flanked by an English woman in equally outmoded clothes, (for bonnets were no longer worn 'off the head' and big crinolines were in vogue, to reach their maximum in 1864). She surely was his wife, they heard onlookers remark. And with them came another in Chinese clothes, 'short and unimportant in appearance'. This was Hudson Taylor – considerate of Lae-djün's feelings or conscious of his own old English clothes being unfit for wear.[2]

Amelia had married Benjamin in February 1859, still willing and even hoping to join her brother in China. But Benjamin had no sense of vocation there. A zealous Christian, his interests were largely in the novel Young Men's Christian Association started by his friend George Williams. For the present his mind was open and Hudson Taylor's great hope was to bring him to a decision, to be the first, perhaps, of the five reinforcements they had been praying for.

Hudson Taylor's letters from Ningbo painting pictures of his failing health had alarmed his family. Their urgent protests that he should come home before it was too late reached China after he had sailed, and also William Berger's letter underwriting the fare. But his notes from Anjer had reached England by the overland route and the travellers were expected sooner or later. Meanwhile Dr Parker had visited Barnsley and reassured them with the opinion that Hudson Taylor was inclined to be more alarmed by ill health than he need be.

So the doors of 63 Westbourne Grove (soon renumbered 35) were flung open and the little family made welcome. Joy upon joy, Louisa was there too. 'I dressed Maria up in a black silk skirt of mine,' Amelia wrote, '. . . then a tailor made a jacket . . . We quickly got them rigged out in suitable apparel.' For Maria that meant a full crinoline. And as soon as possible Hudson Taylor dashed off a few lines to his parents. 'I am considerably better for the voyage. The ship . . . will soon be in dock and then in a few days I hope we shall be clear of the Customs.' Business in London must delay them briefly so he could not say when, but they would come up to Barnsley at the first opportunity. Packing up, travelling to London and all the excitement led him to add, 'I am very weary, and I have not time to tell you how much love we send you –'

While 'Lae-djün whom we soon learned to love and respect' (in Amelia's words) took note of everything and continued caring for Grace, Hudson Taylor plunged into the affairs he had determined to set in motion before going on to Yorkshire. He called on a doctor and to his delight was given a favourable report.

> We hope, D.V. to be able to return to China in about a year [he told William Berger some days later]. My medical adviser gives me great hope of such a restoration as may enable me to do much for [China].

With this reassurance he undertook too much and by the second week was worn out. Steering the baggage through Customs and transporting it to the West End was a big undertaking in itself. His mother was sewing shirts and swansdown waistcoats for him, she wrote, but shopping to outfit himself was urgent. He had important interviews to fit in before he could relax at home for Christmas, so he must be dressed respectably.

In the summer of 1859 Mrs Bausum had been staying with Maria's aunt and uncle, the William Tarns, and Maria's first duty would have been to call on them with her husband. No record has come to light, but references to meeting their son, Joseph, and another cousin suggest that both William and his wife had died. Another Dyer cousin in 1864 lamented hearing no 'tidings of "little Maria" since the death of your dear Aunt Tarn'. William Tarn had been a director of the Religious Tract Society, but now on December 1 Hudson Taylor addressed a formal letter to a stranger.

> Permit me to lay before you the claims of the Romanized Colloquial, as used in Ningpo, and to solicit your aid in bringing out *in England*, some new translations of that system – the books to be *sold* in Ningpo, to the native converts and missionaries at reduced prices.[3]

Proceeding to define and explain what was meant by the term 'Romanized Colloquial', which uneducated Chinese with the intelligence of artisans were learning to master in evening classes within two to three months, he listed the available books and presented the need for more durable paper and binding than were available in China. Various parts of the New Testament translated into the vernacular by Cobbold, Russell, Gough, Rankin, Way and W A P Martin would be for the Bible Society to consider. But *Pilgrim's Progress* and *Line upon Line*, translated by R H Cobbold, now the rector of Broseley in Staffordshire, sermons by Russell, hymns by Rankin, books on geography, history and arithmetic by Martin, booklets by J L Nevius, a catechism by Mrs Knowlton, and other material, deserved to be made more widely available. A Book of Common Prayer was also in preparation. Baptists, Presbyterians and Anglicans were sharing in the work and using each other's products.

The difficulty in using a higher style of Chinese ideograms instead of the romanised colloquial, he explained, was that it was intended for visual reading, the characters conveying the meaning. When read aloud, the hearers were left guessing what was meant. And in another dialect area extempore translation sentence by sentence was imperative. The process was so long and tedious that the meaning was commonly lost. If in England the word for 'hair' had to be used to represent 'air', or 'his' to stand for 'is', the same kind of confusion would arise, he explained.

> In our own church, out of thirty-three native members not more than three could read an epistle intelligently in the character, and not one of them could understand a psalm in the Version published by the Bible Society.

The romanised colloquial enabled them to read for themselves and to others.

Hudson Taylor's emphasis on selling the books he asked for was the mature fruit of experience. Literature received gratis was seldom valued, and too often fell into the hands of illiterates, only to be made into shoe soles. A few years later an inter–mission conference of Ningbo missionaries unanimously adopted the principle of selling instead of giving away Christian literature.

He ended his letter by saying that he was 'induced to apply for aid immediately upon my arrival in England by the hope that if the work be soon commenced I should be able to render some assistance in correcting the proofs for the press before return to China.' In the draft copies preserved, 'before my return to China' was crossed out by Maria, less sanguine than he about his health.

He planned also to open negotiations with the Bible Society and main missionary societies, and notes by his biographer F Howard Taylor say that he did within a few days have preliminary interviews with leaders of some of the main missions. But memoranda or reports of such meetings have not yet been traced.

In Westbourne Grove was a Baptist Church, conveniently close for Hudson Taylor and Maria to attend. They felt sufficiently at home there to enrol as members during their five months with Amelia in Bayswater, and to strike up a friendship with W G Lewis, the pastor. As the secretary of a committee of the Baptist Missionary Society (BMS) and editor of their magazine, he was a useful link with the society. The BMS were taking on C J Hall of Ningbo and Hendrick Kloekers as their missionaries. So Hudson Taylor pressed upon them the need to send as many missionaries to China as they could.

By December 5 when he wrote to his father he still hoped to do more. He had begun the letter a week before but every day was too weary to finish it, he said. It was tantalising to be kept away from home so long. 'I have hardly patience to get through my missionary work, and really cannot delay many days. I have done more than I had strength for . . .' In spite of that, business with the Tract and Bible Societies or with the BMS might detain him longer. But only three days later, on December 8, with Maria, Grace, Wang Laedjün and Louisa he left London and at last was reunited with his parents in his childhood home.

The untimely end of the CES *1859–60*

While they had been at sea the Chinese Evangelization Society had finally been dissolved. In July 1859 *The Gleaner* had rehearsed the aims of the Society and bravely claimed that under other existing missions each one was being carried out, so that there remained no need for a separate organisation like theirs. The CES had no denominational Church behind it, voluntary donations had been inadequate, appeals to individuals had not been welcome, members of the Committee had too often put their hands into their own pockets to meet deficiencies, and costs and difficulties had far exceeded what was anticipated. So the Society was to be dissolved unless 'a general expression were given by our supporters in favour of a continuance'. It was not forthcoming.

Final accounts and reports were presented, and after a long interval the last issue of *The Gleaner* appeared in September 1860. News of Hudson Taylor's illness and sailing had been received. *The Gleaner* reported that he was 'quite incapacitated . . . for labour . . . We trust his valuable life may yet be spared for China.' On the other hand good news from the German missionaries[4] made a fitting climax. Ferdinand Genähr was evangelising freely on the mainland where no foreigners had been before. Winnes was back in Pukak, scene of the riot, and living undisturbed. In Canton the missionaries had an 'open field' with more baptisms in the past year than in all the decades before. The Paris Missionary Society, another of Charles Gutzlaff's progeny, and the Methodist New Connexion had each sent two young men to Shanghai, and six had gone out under the LMS, some for the interior. *The Gleaner*, 1850–60, is today a useful source of information.

The demise of the CES had long been expected. From the beginning Hudson Taylor had questioned their financial methods, and in the coming years gave the subject a great deal of thought. But the failure of the Society was all the more unfortunate because it occurred on the very eve of the Peking Convention which made possible the fulfilment of its far-seeing principles. Ill-starred from the first, the CES for all its notable General Committee and Board of Management proved to be a vapour.

While it lasted its influence was strong. Dr William Moseley,[5] instrumental in sending Robert Morrison to China, was an early member of the Board of Management. Robert Bickersteth, Bishop of Ripon, the Archbishop of Dublin, the Earl of Cavan, Dr Arthur Tidman – an LMS Secretary – prominent bankers and merchants as members of the General Committee shared responsibility with the 'Foreign Secretary' and editor. Its magazine *The Chinese Missionary Gleaner* carried influential reports and editorials. But from the first setback when Charles Gutzlaff's Chinese Union failed, the

Christian public seemed slow to transfer its confidence to the Society in its own right. Subscriptions and donations lagged painfully behind the Committee's hopes – and commitments. Without sufficient information they budgeted with fatal inaccuracy. Assuring their missionaries of regular salaries they apologised for failure to provide even the basic sums promised and urged them to trust in God, while the Society undertook new projects. News and hopes expressed in letters from China were publicised with unwarranted hyperbole, and edited without understanding, to the dismay of the missionaries and ridicule by others in China. Injudicious rebukes and criticisms of their 'agents' Arthur Taylor, William Parker and Wilhelm Lobscheid alienated them and undermined Hudson Taylor's confidence in the Society's fitness to direct him from so far away. Their adoption of new commitments in Malaya while defaulting on their responsibilities in China proper was the last straw.

George Pearse,[6] stretched to the limit by financial crises in the City of London, due to the Crimean and other wars and the Indian Mutiny and by the failure of Charles Bird, the only salaried administrator, gave himself unstintingly as the Foreign Secretary. Responsible for the overseas application of the Society's policies, he won Hudson Taylor's respect, admiration and affection as a saintly man. His shortcomings could be forgiven on the ground of ignorance and remoteness. He himself lamented after it was all over, 'We were all novices.' Indeed, few men knew enough of Asian people and conditions. CES blunders paled into insignificance beside mercantile and diplomatic mistakes. High motives and emotional publicity were not enough. And yet the story could have been very different if the Christian public had responded to the lead they were given. Adequate funds at the disposal of the Committee would have allowed adequate support of the missionaries, only nine all told. But in spite of the generosity of a few individuals who dug into their pockets again and again, the total receipts of the Society in ten years amounted to no more than about fifteen thousand pounds[7]. Christians in Britain were only slowly discovering the rich dividends derived from open-handed stewardship, that 'He who is kind to the poor lends to the Lord, and he will repay him' (Prov. 19:17 RSV) is brother to the promise, 'seek first his kingdom and his righteousness, and all these things shall be yours as well' (Matth. 6:33 RSV) – a discovery which support for Hudson Taylor's mission in later years did much to demonstrate.

So the tenth Annual Report of the Society, in *The Gleaner* for

September 1860, following its last issue in October 1859, began, 'The Chinese Evangelization Society having been dissolved, it remains now only to give to the Subscribers and friends, the statement of accounts for the year 1859–60.' It then announced the resignation of Dr William Parker on his return to the United Kingdom. And not having heard of Hudson Taylor's departure, it said that he and John Jones 'two esteemed missionary brethren, who originally went to China more or less in connection with the Society' were still working successfully in Ningbo. Their wives, as the custom was in most missions, were not mentioned. A wife's function was to be 'a comfort and companion' to the man who did the work. In his initial recruiting Hudson Taylor himself retained this attitude until he saw its injustice and in 1865 began enlisting and assessing the suitability of women for his own mission.

Of Taylor and Jones, *The Gleaner* again declared disingenuously,

> although they were not entirely supported by the Chinese Evangelization Society, they were assisted by funds sent occasionally by the Society. Now that it is dissolved, it is desirable that they should be kept in view . . . (Mr George Müller of Bristol and Mr George Pearse, Stock Exchange, London E.C. would willingly remit sums to them.)[8]

Of John Jones the phrase 'more or less in connection with the Society' appears to be true, for in the earliest reference so far found, Hudson Taylor had written rejecting Jones' arrangement with the CES. He was working with them and welcoming any remittances coming from them, but desired no fixed salary and was peacefully more than content to receive whatever else he might need from God himself through any channel he might choose to employ. In George Pearse's list of missionaries and the amounts they were due and permitted to draw, until the system was changed, Charles Hall is included but John Jones omitted.

This was certainly not Hudson Taylor's position in 1853 when he left England or until he resigned from the CES in the summer of 1857. He went to China as a salaried 'agent'. And when the CES, unable to meet its commitments, changed its policy to one of sending what it could, instead of what it had promised, none of the missionaries accepted the change. To Hudson Taylor the Society was defaulting on its promises. To Parker it was in his debt and he named the sum owing to him. To George Pearse it constituted a radical change to a spiritual principle familiar to George Müller but not so far to those on whom it was being imposed. His jotted criticism reads, 'Our giving up the principle of the missionary drawing on us – and we sending out what we receive – leaves us with the principle of dependence and our missionaries too.' Dependence on God, that is. His brief attempts to commend this to the missionaries as a reliable way of living were too disjointed. John Jones understood it and Hudson Taylor came to accept it – without CES control – but the Society as a whole seems to have lacked understanding of anything other than appeals for donations, from supporters still unable to provide enough. As for the statement that Hudson Taylor went out, like John Jones, 'more or less in connection with the Society', this could have been simply a slip by Robert Fowler, a new Treasurer, not associated with the CES when Hudson Taylor sailed. History may, however, highlight a far more serious error by the boardroom statesmen than the failure to trust and support their missionaries – their sally into international politics.

'The Missionary Question' *1859–1903*

The Society's memorandum and deputation to Lord Clarendon on behalf of missions to China led directly to Lord Elgin being instructed to include toleration clauses in the treaties he negotiated.[9] This firmly, if incidentally, linked the penetration of China by messengers of the gospel with concessions gained by force of arms, with the legalisation of opium trading, and with consular protection of British missionaries whether they wanted it or not. Lord Elgin was going with a powerful force and in collusion with France, at the instigation of the British Government. As in 1842 the treaties might have included no reference to Christian missions, apart from the initiative of the CES. Elgin himself foresaw the incentive to hypocrisy by Chinese claiming to be converts for what they could gain from protection by the foreigner. The spiritual health of the Church was at stake. That initiative by the CES certainly did no more to instigate the second opium war than the representation to Lord Elgin made by the missionary community in Shanghai when he passed through on the way north. But the inclusion of religious as well as commercial and political clauses did result in the legal penetration and occupation of China by foreign missionaries, and sparked a controversy whose loud echoes and clichés are still heard today. 'The Missionary Question' reached its climax ten or fifteen years later, but began to be voiced as soon as the Peking Convention was signed.

The argument ran roughly like this: diplomats relied largely on missionaries for information and communications with the authorities in China, and missionaries benefited from treaties made under duress. The diplomats were in some cases committed Christians, and naval officers and others in the armed forces distributed Scripture wherever they went. So-called Christian nations forced their will upon China, and missionaries as a result could go wherever they wished and preach at will, under the protection of their consuls and gunboats. The Chinese could be forgiven for regarding them as spies and collaborators, and their proselytes as traitors. If missionaries were not the cause of war they undoubtedly rode high on the vehicle of armed intervention. Protests in the national press in Britain and the States were fully justified, the critics claimed.

Such arguments contained the truth but could not bear impartial examination. The history of foreign relations with China, the pressure of growing manufacturing and mercantile power, the insatiable demand for more and better ports, for unrestricted opium trading, for liberty to penetrate the mainland and sell to the great consumer market of four hundred million Chinese, the intransigence of the Manchus – these and other factors were well known to be the cause of the wars, of the terms of the treaties and of the resentment aroused. The first treaty, of Nanjing, had catered for some British citizens and omitted to provide for the needs and rights of others, the missionaries, arguably as deserving as anyone. The fact that they were loyal citizens called upon to assist their country's representatives could be expected to elicit the same response as if merchants or adventurers were given the same summons. If governments made war and treaties, were missionaries to refuse to allow their cause to benefit? Should the apostles and other early messengers of the gospel have refused the help of *Pax Romana*? For lack of protection by their own government, were aliens *and* those Chinese who were associated with them to be defenceless? Was the Canton Factory ghetto system to be perpetuated? Were massacres as in Japan and Madagascar to be tolerated without attempts to secure the recognition of international rights? The counter-arguments at least balanced the criticisms.

Indignation over 'the Opium Question' was voiced often and clearly, but in neither Church nor missions did the Christian conscience doubt the rightness of acting on concessions granted in the wake of war. According to Eugene Stock, only one Church of England periodical denounced the war itself, but as Latourette wrote, 'No one of influence in the Church seems to have questioned seriously the consistency of entering the Empire in the wake of armed forces and under the protection of treaties.'[10] Some deplored the fact that missions and the opium traffic benefited by one and the same treaty, but in both China, Europe and America mission circles welcomed action to throw China open. In the nineteenth century force in 'a righteous cause' was considered permissible, if not laudable. With hindsight definitions of such causes may be different. The CMS deplored the use of any instrument to throw China open to the gospel *and* to opium. And the LMS while deploring the war hoped the opium traffic would be stopped and missions be safeguarded. Most missions, seeing the hand of God working through the nations, welcomed the benefits derived from the means they deprecated. And this was true of Hudson Taylor and his Ningbo colleagues. In 1863 the Bible Society report lamented the restrictions against Protestants' residence in Peking while Catholic priests lived there unhindered. 'Is the influence of England unable, or reluctant, to obtain a like concession?' the editorial asked.

In the last analysis governments, missions and individuals were carried along by forces beyond their control, and the work of missionaries was to be dogged for decades by accusations, not that they profited from opium wars but that they and their guilty governments were inseparably to blame. Culpability apart, the *fait accompli* remained that the Treaty of Tientsin and the Peking Convention provided a legal basis for the advance of missions throughout China.

An imperial rescript of 1862 established Delamarre's fraudulent clauses as law, and extended protection to Catholic converts when they resisted compulsion to contribute to idolatrous practices or suffered persecution.[11] But what constituted persecution? In any lawsuit persecution could be pleaded. Foreigners could intervene in disputes between Chinese. Converts were to some extent under the aegis of foreign powers. Adherence for false motives soon adulterated the Churches. Quality suffered in the process of growth. Communities grew up partially removed from the jurisdiction of the Chinese government. Some, especially French priests, exercised a measure of civil authority over their converts. The 'French Protectorate' became a racket, with other nationals applying for French passports to travel safely in China.

own faith in Christ. It had been a ban on this practice – as well as doctrinal changes in the main Methodist body – that had driven the reformers to secede.

Naturally James Taylor shared his son's letter with his friend, and Henry Bell knew that one of his young men was just the type needed. James Meadows was a Norfolk man converted at Perth a few years previously. Recalling years later what then happened he wrote,

> I knew of no other men in Barnsley of like-spirit with Mr Bell and [James Taylor]. Their hearts were intensely set on saving souls, and their sympathies went out to the heathen world everywhere . . . Mr Bell came to me and said half-seriously, 'James, I have got a job for you to do. Will you do it?' I asked him, 'What job?' He answered 'Go to China.' I said, 'I will go,' but asked for time to pray about it. So I fasted and went into my little workshop and knelt down one dinner-time . . . and asked the Lord 'Shall I go?' The answer that I got there and then was, 'Go, and the Lord be with you . . .' Mr Bell . . . was one of the right kind of old Methodists, who feared God, lived Holy lives, and honoured their King and Saviour Jesus Christ. Would that we had *now* a whole stock of such robust earnest men and women . . .[14]

James Meadows certainly was the cut of man Hudson Taylor was praying for, a missionary before he left Britain. When he and another named Whiteley came to see him, Maria told the Bergers that Hudson was 'very pleased' with him. Meadows knew that God had called him. Whiteley was sizing up the situation and after a few months withdrew.

Christmas was a family reunion. Amelia and Benjamin came up from London and Hudson Taylor's favourite aunt Hannah Hardey, the portrait painter, and her husband Richard joined them from Hull. Eight years had passed since they were all together like this, and now Maria, Grace and Lae-djün were with them too.

But as Hudson Taylor's strength returned he was impatient to get on with his printing. Soon after the New Year they travelled first to Hull, visiting his grandparents, the Hudsons, and interviewing another potential recruit, and from there to London. Apparently this was by sea (the least expensive way), for the journey took three days, from January 11 to Monday, 14th. Still Louisa stayed with them, inseparable from the brother who had prayed and urged her out of scepticism into faith.

His relapse in December drove him on his return to London to consult Dr Andrew Clarke, his former teacher at the London

Hospital. And this time the verdict was different. He must give up all thought of going abroad, for several years if not permanently. To do otherwise would be to throw away his life. His liver, digestion and nervous sytem were seriously impaired, Clarke told him. Vague as this terminology is today, the clinical judgment of so eminent a physician was unlikely to be at fault. No mention of pulmonary disease was made. His condition was so far from normal as to need years of a favourable climate and diet to recover. Latourette's unprofessional comment that he was 'so threatened with tuberculosis' was unjustified.[15] Hepatitis and colitis, perhaps amoebic, would again appear to be more likely. Be that as it may, hopes of escorting Meadows, Benjamin and Amelia and others back to Ningbo after a few more months had to be abandoned.

Making the most of it — *February–March 1861*

The consultant's verdict put a totally new complexion on things. What now was the right way to face the future? Maria's baby was due in April and Amelia welcomed them to stay with her until it was born. Dealings with the Religious Tract Society would take some weeks before printers' proofs could be ready for attention, and then Hudson Taylor must expect many errors to correct, for the compositors would be working with hand-written romanised Chinese, completely new to them. If the Bible Society agreed to reprint the Ningbo New Testament, this would give him more weeks or months of work. Better still, the delay would permit more thorough revision. If five recruits for China came to him for assessment, training and preliminary language lessons he would have more than enough on his hands. 'Taylor was undiscouraged,' Latourette observed. He was too busy to mope.

Meanwhile his first concern remained to prevail on the existing societies to send more missionaries to China. In his old age his son and daughter-in-law, Howard and Geraldine, spent weeks with Hudson Taylor persuading him to reminisce, and making verbatim notes as he talked. On this period, 1861, they stated in two separate memoranda,

> We know from Mr. Taylor himself that one of his most earnest desires during this first furlough, was to encourage the great Missionary Boards to undertake work in Inland China. He had interviews or correspondence with the Secretaries of most if not all the principal English Societies.[16]

TAO-KAO.

"Tao-kao z-'eo ng-lah væn-pah sô gyiu-go, tsih iao siang-sing, ziu we teh-djôh." Mt. xxi. 22.

"Ng-lah cong-nyiang ziah yiu liang-go nying læ di-'ô 'eh-k'eo-zi-dong iao gyiu ze-bin soh-go z-ken, Ngô t'in-zông-go Ah-tia pih-ding teng gyi-lah tso-dzing. Ing-we feh-leng soh-go u-sen, ziah yiu liang-sæn-go nying we-leh Ngô-go ming-deo jü-long-kæn, Ngô læ keh-deo dô-kô læ-kæn." Mt. xviii. 19, 20.

"Hao gyiu, ziu we teh-djôh, s-teh ng-lah-go hwun-hyi we mun-tsoh." I'e. xvi. 24.

Ts. xxiv. (6) Mt. vi.

THE NINGBO VERNACULAR, ROMANISED

During the Evangelical Revival of 1859, the number of places of worship in Britain had been greatly increased to cope with additions to the Church. Yet during the first stages of this great movement a decadence of concern in the nation for the world-wide mission of the Church had set in. The men of vision pleaded in vain that the work of taking the gospel to all the world had barely begun. The Societies still owed their existence to the voluntary commitment of individuals, and the Churches had yet to awaken to their corporate responsibility.

The denominational societies still sent unordained men such as printers for practical appointments, and put men with limited education through training courses before ordaining them, but looked to the universities and clergy for their principal reinforcements.[17] But since 1835 an outstanding example of another attitude had been proving its value at their doorsteps. The London City Mission, like its inspiration, the Glasgow Mission, primarily drew its men from the artisan class, with striking success. These 'Scripture Readers' of petty-officer type, carried the gospel to the man in the street and fed converts into the Churches. But Church leaders were slow to see the immense potential in this 'untapped reservoir' for service overseas.

As Hudson Taylor (and later F F Gough with him) met the secretaries of the missionary societies and urged them to send men in greater numbers to China, he received sympathy but the same sort of answer from one after another. Their funds were not equal to existing demands, let alone expanded commitments. It was better to wait until in God's providence China was widely open to the gospel. The Wesleyan Methodists were discouraged by the long-sustained resistance to the preaching of their missionaries, George Piercy and Josiah Cox at Canton. They judged that, rather than lose more valuable men in unproductive areas new missionaries would be better employed elsewhere.[18]

Among his old friends at Tottenham and Hackney Hudson Taylor met with a very different attitude. Their interest was as alive as ever, and their concern for China and friendliness to him personally were undiminished. George Pearse's confidence in him was increasing, and William Berger's no less.

It was the Baptist Missionary Society who actively took him up. W G Lewis recommended him to allow people to call him 'Reverend', and this time he agreed. (Because he remained on the members' roll of Westbourne Grove Chapel for several years, he has been called a Baptist, but his views were not those of the denomination. His spiritual allegiance was no less to all true Christians and remained so all his life.) After one more spell of illness which confined him to bed for a while, and a short convalescence, he began speaking about China at meetings in Tottenham for his Brethren friends, at Bryanston Hall, a Congregational chapel at Portman Square, and at Lewis's chapel.

At the end of January Dr William Parker spent a day with them in Bayswater. They had plenty to tell him about Ningbo, and fresh news of the events at Peking and Shanghai was coming in by every mail. Past, present and future concerned each of them intimately. Parker was preparing to marry again and return to Ningbo, and Hudson Taylor hoped to find more missionaries to go with them.

A disconsolate letter from John Jones gave food for thought and discussion. Carrying the care of the Bridge Street church in Ningbo alone, his health was deteriorating fast. His good friend F F Gough of the CMS had also left China with his seriously ill wife, and with only E C Lord to consult Jones was trying to cope with 'disorderly' church members. Bickering, dishonesty and non-attendance were sapping the vitality of the congregation. Daily life was being lived against the background of war, outrage and their aftermath in the north, and the Taiping rampages in Jiangsu and Zhejiang, following their repulse by the foreign allies at Shanghai. A gentle man, facing death from renal failure, John Jones was apprehensive about his responsibilities, longing to hear that Hudson Taylor would soon be on his way back. Only nine or ten missionaries were left in Ningbo, three of them young men new to the job and the language – the only provision for a province of twenty or thirty millions.

After Dr Parker left, Hudson Taylor wrote to his mother telling her the news.

> You know what it is to have a sick child at a distance; and we feel what it is to have children in the Lord Jesus morally sick; but what can we do? We can scarcely go back at once. I know how we are needed; but the object sought in our coming home does not seem gained yet.

Health and reinforcements, apart from James Meadows, were scarcely in sight.

Ten days later the Goughs arrived in London. But it was not the happy homecoming the Taylors had had. Mary Gough lived only four more days and it was her dead body that Gough took home to her family for burial at Alderley Edge. She was only thirty-four. From her home Gough wrote to the Taylors,

> And now let me assure you my dear brother and sister, that He who has smitten me, (*you* know how sorely) has shown his tender mercy, first in the *bright* end of *her* conversation . . . and now again in not suffering me to sorrow as others who have no hope, but drawing nearer to me at times than I ever felt before. But oh *pray* for me, I *need* it much . . .

By mid-March Hudson Taylor reported progress to his parents. The RTS responded to his application; the Ningbo hymn-book had gone to press and soon other books followed. He completed his application to the Bible Society on March 15 asking them to sponsor the reprinting (only) of the Ningbo 'Colloquial' New Testament in romanised script. And in a birthday letter to his father he announced a major decision. He was going to take up medicine again. The problems were the time needed, the expense, and the competition with all his other work. But already his plans to move near to the London Hospital in the East End were well advanced. He had consulted the surgeons he had known in 1853 and had been recommended to take the diploma of the Royal College of Surgeons. Having seen how much the title alone mattered to some people, and knowing from experience how much more his skills would be trusted if he was formally qualified, he wanted to get it all finished and behind him. But what a price to pay for the label! he remarked. At best it would take more than a year. At the worst he could have it hanging over him for three years.

A letter from William Burns added fuel to the growing fire in his bones. At long last three believers had been baptised at Swatow. Another English Presbyterian had joined him there, and two American Baptists from Hong Kong. But there was scope for many more.

> Four married missionaries for each station [in Swatow] are urgently needed [Hudson told his mother on March 27]. But the Church is asleep; and armchairs, and sofas, and English comforts possess more attractions than perishing souls . . .

As Tolstoy said on his only visit to affluent London, in this same year, 1861, when he was thirty-three, 'This kind of civilisation repels me. I feel a positive nausea', so (like many a missionary since) Hudson Taylor was appalled by the apathy of comfortable Christians, even at a time of spiritual 'awakening'.

Of the three young men he had interviewed in Barnsley and Hull two were wavering. Whiteley was now thinking of joining the Wesleyan ministry. Hudson Taylor was disappointed, but two weeks later he wrote that he was hopeful of James Meadows going as he said, to China 'with us . . . I think *he* is in earnest.' Medical caveats seem to have escaped him at that point.

He was in close touch with the BMS. On March 14 their China Sub-committee resolved to invite him to address their Annual Meeting.[19] on March 27 he told his mother, 'The Baptists are going to send out six more missionaries to China! I speak at their meeting . . . DV on the 17th. prox.'[20] And on April 9 he confirmed that he had 'a speech to prepare for the Annual Meeting of the China Branch of the Baptist Missionary Society' on Wednesday, April 17. After that their association became closer. A Minute of the General Committee of the BMS on July 10, 1861, marked a new proposition,

> A recommendation of the China Sub-committee was read viz. – That the Committee be recommended to have an interview with the Rev. J.H. Taylor of Ningpo, with the view of determining whether he shall be invited to devote himself to mission work in China in connexion with the Society. It was resolved – That this recommendation be adopted.[21]

The interview apparently took place, though no contemporary record of it has been traced. In his old age he told his son Howard that he 'became connected with the Baptist Missionary Society' and did 'a good deal' of deputation speaking for them. They had responded to the opening up of China, had adopted the C J Halls and Hendrick Kloekers, and now had these six recruits to join them. Hudson Taylor felt the disadvantage of being unconnected with any body of missionaries, and was open to new ideas. As the secretaries, Dr E B Underhill and F Trestrail came to know him better, they asked him to go out as leader of their team, and he agreed. But on each side there were problems.

Hudson Taylor had strong reservations. He thought it 'unsuitable' that an ordinance like baptism, and at that a mode of baptism, 'should be the centre of union'. In fact, although he had enrolled in a Baptist congregation, at heart he was too ecumenical, too unsectarian for the differences at issue to determine his own actions. In this he was far from alone. At the Conference on Missions convened at Liverpool in 1860,[22] Dr Arthur Tidman, Foreign Secretary of the LMS and still a member of the CES Committee cried, 'Let all differences be forgotten; let them not remember that they were Churchmen or Dissenters, Baptists or Wesleyans, Presbyterians or Episcopalians.'

For their part the BMS secretaries were facing a drop in financial support. To avoid going into debt they reduced the number of recruits to be sent with him to two. He had moved a long way since rebuking the CES for adding liabilities when income was inadequate to support their 'agents' already in China. Personal dependence on the Giver of all good things had proved very satisfactory. So he could not accept that the availability of funds should decide BMS policy and action where he personally was concerned. To withdraw from the position already adopted, with six new missionaries called by God and accepted as suitable, was to him a mistake. If God called, he would provide. On this principle he was himself trying to find more men to send.

He tried to stir up the BMS to greater undertakings, to an even wider movement, with a special fund for the work in China, distinct from that for India and Africa. No, they could not consider that. He then proposed to the Committee that he and his family should not be chargeable to BMS funds. He would look to God and his faithful servants independently if the BMS would use his share to send two or more of the missionaries instead. Still the cautious wisdom of conventional attitudes governed their reply. What if his optimistic method did not work – if his own faith failed? He would become chargeable to the BMS after all. They would have to step in and support him. After that they parted amicably, and Hudson Taylor returned to looking independently for reinforcements for Ningbo.

With the Bible Society he encountered a new problem. The General Committee met on April 1, 1861, and 'Read a letter from the Rev. J.H. Taylor' – his March 15 proposition. Copied into their foolscap 'Editorial Correspondence' manifold it took up eight pages.[23]

He proposed that the Bible Society should print one thousand or fifteen hundred copies of the New Testament in the romanised Ningbo vernacular with marginal references. So that readers would appreciate the book more highly, all should be for sale. Then he explained at length that this translation had been in preparation for ten years by three missionaries of the CMS and three of the American Presbyterian Mission. As a vernacular version it was needed because the Delegates' Version was unintelligible to the man in the street. (It happened that Joseph Edkins was pressing at the same time for a similar mandarin version.[24]) And finally Hudson Taylor listed two dozen or so other existing publications in the same romanised vernacular, named F F Gough, one of the translators, as being available in the United Kingdom, and enclosed a letter from another, Archdeacon R H Cobbold, also of the CMS, commending the proposition and saying, 'I do hope the Bible Society will take the matter up.' Hudson Taylor simply offered to prepare the marginal references and to correct the proof sheets.

In the next few years many developments hinged upon this matter, so some detail is justified. The Committee were in a quandary. Hudson Taylor was not representing a society. They resolved that he should be asked to forward his application through the BMS, with which they thought he was connected. But when they next met, their problem was unresolved. Another letter from Taylor, dated April 9, explained his difficulty in complying through the BMS – he was not in fact formally connected with them.

What was he to do? He wrote to Frederick Gough who rose to the occasion and consulted the Rev J Mee, one of the Bible Society secretaries.[25] The need for revision of the translation had been generally agreed, for the text as it stood contained many errors and inconsistencies. But for the present a reprinted small edition of unrevised text would be enough to tide them over in Ningbo. Here too lay a difficulty, Gough replied,

> Mr. Mee told me, that they would scarcely print less than 10,000 copies – now I think your application for 1000 or 1500 is enough or nearly so, considering that the version will all be *revised*, I hope, soon . . . – yet any such proposed revision does not make this [limited edition] undesirable – for the need for some time past has been very great.

Gough had left the draft of his work on Revelation, the last book to be translated, for Rankin to complete when he and Mary left Ningbo.

> and I hope we may get it soon, but, if needed, I might do something with Lae-djün, or rather *we* might, finish it altogether, with his help – it would be delightful to work with *you*.

This proposition, originating from one of the translators, led on to Hudson Taylor's profound involvement in not only proof-reading and the provision of cross-references, but in actual revision, for the presence of a native of Ningbo, Lae-djün, in his home made a vital difference.

Soon another note from Gough brought the good news that Hudson Taylor's application to the Bible Society was on the way to Henry Venn, the influential Secretary of the CMS, with a covering letter from Gough asking the CMS Committee to endorse it. They adopted Gough's compromise and asked the Bible Society for two thousand complete New Testaments and a thousand extra copies of the Gospels and Acts. Within a week Gough and Taylor were on to the technicalities of expressing Biblical names in the Ningbo dialect, revising the New Testament to give uniformity to the translation, with Wang Lae-djün as the indispensable 'informant'.

For the Bible Society it became plain sailing. The CMS forwarded F F Gough's letter in which he concurred with Hudson Taylor's views and was prepared to complete the first translation of Revelation himself. The Editorial Committee of the Bible Society wrote to William Muirhead in Shanghai for an independent opinion and on July 17, 1861, with his recommendation before them, passed one resolution stating that the Society should comply with the application by the CMS, and another

> that the Secretary communicate with Mr. Taylor in reference to his undertaking the Editorship of the work with such general assistance from the Rev. Mr. Gough as may be found necessary.[26]

Hudson Taylor had not let the grass grow under his feet.

No 1 Beaumont Street *April–July 1861*

A great deal had happened since March. Lae-djün had been taken to the Prince Consort's second Great International Exhibition at the Crystal Palace; on April 3 'consternation' had reigned at 63 Westbourne Grove over the 'sudden arrival' of Maria's first son, Herbert Hudson; Hudson Taylor himself was editing the Ningbo dialect hymn-book and had one hundred and eighty hymns in print by May; at the same time he had begun work on the New Testament, and was writing articles on China for magazines. Shortly after April 9 he had taken Maria, Lae-djün and the children and set up a home of the simplest kind at 1 Beaumont Street, Mile End Road, a few blocks from the London Hospital. The BMS annual meeting and other speaking engagements followed. On May 6 he had started a course of practical chemistry, familiar ground, at the Medical College, to fulfil examination requirements, and on the 21st the full hospital curriculum. Ill health faded from the records.

The one new missionary now being sent to China by the CMS was

Arthur E Moule, a brother of George, already in Ningbo, and of Handley Moule the future Principal of Ridley Hall and Bishop of Durham. As a Cambridge don, F F Gough had been tutor in Greek to George Moule, and whether at his suggestion or by more direct links, Hudson Taylor compiled and posted a Ningbo *t'u-wo* (colloquial) vocabulary for Arthur to work on during his voyage. It came too late. He had just sailed. But his father, the Rev Henry Moule, on June 7 wrote warmly to thank him. He had been wanting to get in touch with Hudson Taylor and Wang Lae-djün.

> . . . the interest I feel in this T'u-wo I cannot express [he wrote]. I feel certain that the reducing of it to writing and the printing of the Scriptures and other religious books in it will have an effect, (D.V.) on that part of China corresponding with that of the writing and printing of German and English works at the Reformation.

But Arthur Moule's departure had another significance, in that to a small extent it forged another friendly link between Hudson Taylor and the CMS. In 1860 another CMS missionary, T Fleming, had reached Ningbo to join John Burdon. And in 1864 as Fleming was invalided home, J D Valentine arrived. Hudson Taylor and Maria were to spend many hours writing out vocabularies for them to memorise on their journeys to China. A decade earlier W A Russell had written, 'Twenty men could well be employed by the CMS in and around Ningpo.' But the claims of India and Africa were as great as ever, and the response to appeals for reinforcements was never enough to allow of China receiving more than a token force.[27] In his *Story of the Cheh-kiang Mission*, Arthur Moule was to lament in 1878 that 'during the twenty-eight years of the "Cheh-kiang Mission", only fifteen clergy of the Church of England ever served there.'[28]

With the coming of summer and the long vacation for hospital students, Hudson Taylor tackled the New Testament again. He was still waiting for the Bible Society to hear from William Muirhead and to reach their decision. But with a verbal assurance through George Pearse he felt free to start. With Lae-djün and Maria fluent in the Ningbo dialect, on hand to be consulted, and Gough contributing by post from Gorsebrook House, his family home at Wolverhampton, where he was finishing the translation of Revelation, Hudson Taylor made good progress in revising the text of Matthew's Gospel. After hearing from the Bible Society he took it in sections to Spottiswoode's the printers, and corrected the proof-sheets as they came back. When the Gospel was all in print he despatched copies to Ningbo for comment and in September started on Mark. It would be months before a reply could be expected.

On July 25, the day after receiving the Bible Society's decisions, he wrote to give Mr Berger the news. They would start printing 'as soon as I have sufficient "copy" ready for the Printer to begin with'. About two-thirds of the hymn-book was now in print. It was nearly four months since Herbert's birth, yet it was in this letter that they told the Bergers of Maria's safe delivery.

> I have not been able to do much more with reference to the plan of sending out helpers for the Mission work, from the class that Missionary Societies usually think beneath their notice. Most of those I have had correspondence with, have proved to be under matrimonial engagements . . . I should like to have further conference with you, on this subject.[29]

Enquiry as to what lay between the lines could start from several clues. A 'plan' was known to Berger. Was he a party to it? Had they discussed financial factors? Was Mr Berger offering to pay for some passages to China, as he later did? How did the fiancées affect him and the plan, apart from doubling the passage money needed and increasing the cost of their support on arrival? Before he left Ningbo Hudson Taylor had written in terms of single men giving five years' service. Was this still in their minds? The expression 'sending helpers' marked an advance or at least a distinction from his pressure on the Societies to send more to China. This was strictly a plan to provide help for the Bridge Street church, for what was soon to be in his thinking the 'Ningpo Mission'.

In the verbatim records of Hudson Taylor's recollections is a note that Berger knew all about his dealings with the BMS and said nothing to influence him. But when they ended and Hudson Taylor reverted to personal efforts to find missionaries for Ningbo, Berger's interest deepened. When James Meadows moved to London to live with and learn from the Taylors and Wang Lae-djün, the Bergers became more directly involved.

A product of the Methodist revival with two of his brothers, William Berger had been converted through the testimony of a Christian girl at a party. Responding at once to Christ, he had gone behind a door to hide his emotion of gratitude. But when he and his brothers told their clergyman what had happened he scolded them roundly and sent them packing. From that time Berger's own zeal for the spread of the gospel never diminished. Until his death in 1899 he was to be Hudson Taylor's faithful colleague in all that followed.

The Jehol plot[30] *1860–61*

On September 22, 1860, while the *Jubilee* was 'beating along the coast of Africa' towards the Cape, Yehonala, the Concubine Yi, was in mortal danger. Remotely separate as she and Hudson Taylor were, though much of the same age, events and influences touching the lives of one and the other ran in curiously parallel ways until the climax forty years after the Summer Palace went up in flames.

With the flight of the Xian Feng emperor on that September day, after Yehonala's advice to stay and face the barbarians was overruled, it was plain to her that she had powerful enemies to contend with. She knew who they were – the three courtiers, the Prince of Cheng, a Manchu noble, Cai (Ts'ai) Yuan, Prince of Yi, of the imperial blood, and Su Shun, a multi-millionaire extortionist of the same clan, who had schemed his way into the position of a Grand Secretary. And she rightly guessed that her own life was at stake.

Her four-year-old son, heir to the Dragon Throne, was travelling with the Empress Consort as the panic flight to the safety of the far northern province of Jehol took shape and became euphemistically a 'tour of inspection'. It was common knowledge that opium addiction and disease had brought the emperor close to the end of his young life. The three conspirators aimed high – to seize control of Xian Feng's successor, to accuse Prince Kong, the emperor's brother, of conspiring with the Western powers, and to rule the empire themselves. Knowing Yehonala's astuteness, Su Shun was for killing her at the first opportunity on the hundred-mile journey. But they had a major difficulty to contend with. In command of the armed escort to the cortège rode Yong Lu, the imperial bannerman to whom she had once been betrothed. So the others were for greater subtlety.

On arrival at the Jehol hunting palaces beyond the Great Wall (map, p 216) on October 2, Yehonala's fears were confirmed. She was relegated to seclusion in the Cold Palace, an inferior residence reserved for concubines, out of reach of the now very sick emperor. But her son passed into the care of Cai Yuan's wife. Yehonala took note and acted quickly. The conspiracy, to make Cai Yuan and Prince Cheng co-regents, involved prevailing upon the emperor to

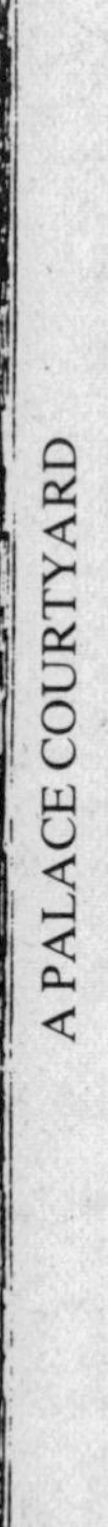

A PALACE COURTYARD

promulgate an edict sealed with the dynastic seal inscribed 'lawfully transmitted authority'. As the months passed and he sank lower and lower, however, they searched in vain for the seal, supposing that it had been mislaid in the confusion of flight. Young Yehonala had been wise enough to be on good terms with the Chief Eunuch, in the classic milieu of an Oriental court. As soon as she sensed her own danger and the likelihood of a conspiracy, she turned to him, and through his trusted assistant, attending the emperor, had secretly secured possession of the seal.

Undeterred, the conspirators obtained the emperor's signature to a decree in their own favour, counting on its validity being conceded in the unusual circumstances of the Court's sudden exile. As soon as he died, on August 22, 1861, they proclaimed the child believed to be his son as Emperor, themselves and others as Regents and the two young women, the Empress Consort and Yehonala his mother as Empresses Dowager, with the titles Ci An (Tz'u An), the Eastern Empress, and Ci Xi (Tz'u Hsi), the Western Empress, after the palaces they occupied at Peking. As Ci Xi, an Empress Dowager, Yehonala was in no less danger than before. Titles and preferment were commonly the prelude to disgrace and execution. But she was equal to this situation also. Through the eunuchs she had informed Yong Lu and Prince Kong of the plot ten days before, and was calmly acting as if ignorant of what was going on. For fear of them her enemies were still playing their cards carefully.

Prince Kong's diplomacy, and Western tardiness in understanding the Chinese, had long since led to the Allies withdrawing from Peking. So now the deceased emperor's body was carried in an ornate catafalque draped with yellow silk embroidered with gold thread, back to the capital, a hundred and fifteen miles distant. Custom demanded that the entire Court remain in attendance until the journey began, but once on its way, the two widowed empresses were sent ahead under escort by Cai Yuan's bodyguard to welcome its arrival with full observance of the appropriate rites. Yong Lu and his imperial guard were ordered to escort the slow-moving catafalque at the rear. In the last mountain pass before the capital, both empresses were to be assassinated.

Even in this tense situation Yehonala and Yong Lu kept their heads. When he judged the moment right, Yong Lu gave his troops the signal, forsook the cortège and conspirators, galloped ahead and surrounded Yehonala in the midst of Cai Yuan's men. From that moment the fate of the three schemers was sealed. As soon as they knew what had happened, their only hope was to bluff their way through.

Centuries of dynastic precedent could not be set aside. Impeccably the solemn protocol was followed. At the city gates the child emperor, the two empresses and Prince Kong with his guard of honour welcomed the cortège. The 'co-regents' formally reported their mission of escorting the coffin accomplished, and Yehonala thanked them. Then she declared them discharged from their function as regents. Desperately playing their only remaining card, Cai Yuan and Prince Cheng produced the edict bearing the Xian Feng emperor's signature. In answer Prince Kong drew out another edict sealed with the dynastic seal in the name of Yehonala's son, the child emperor, Tong Zhi (T'ung Chih). It charged Cai Yuan and his collaborators with responsibility for the 1860 war, with the treacherous seizure of Harry Parkes and his truce party, and of causing Xian Feng's death by trying to undermine Prince Kong's settlement with the Western Allies. And it appointed the two empresses, Ci An and Ci Xi – Yehonala – as regents. At a signal from Prince Kong his men arrested the conspirators. Su Shun, who had advocated killing Yehonala on the way to Jehol, rounded on the others and said, 'If you had listened to me this would not have happened!' But it was too late. They were led away to be stripped of rank, titles and wealth. Then the two princes were strangled and Su Shun decapitated.

The Court was back in the capital, the power was in the hands of young Yehonala – Ci Xi, 'Motherly and Auspicious', the name by which she became best known – and her advisers. The placid Empress Ci An was no threat to them, and for ten years at least the child emperor would have little influence. The dynastic title Tong Zhi (T'ung Chih), 'All-Pervading Tranquillity' was chosen for him (or equally, according to H B Morse, 'Peace with Honour'). And Ci Xi in her wisdom abandoned her anti-foreign stance, whatever dark thoughts lurked in her soul, and supported Prince Kong's statesmanlike policy.

It was unfortunate that young Tong Zhi showed a preference for the 'Motherly and Restful' Ci An, but the dashing Yong Lu, appointed a Councillor of State, became his instructor in horsemanship and archery. An interested observer at Court noted in his diary that Yong Lu could not have been more attached to Tong Zhi had he been his own son. Prince Kong became the equivalent of

Prime Minister, retaining control of foreign affairs, and the Manchu dynasty was stable again – stable, that is, but for the resurgence of Taiping power, and of near-anarchy in almost every inland province.

'The year of truce' *1861*

Those months of August, September and October 1860 when the Allies landed at the Beitang above Dagu, took Tianjin and forced the Peking Court to flee, were as full of action in the Yangzi region. After the Taiping failure to take the Chinese city at Shanghai and to reach an accommodation with the foreign powers for the sake of having a coastal port, they turned south. Ningbo was the nearest alternative port (map, p 202). Twice, in March and May, they had broken the imperial cordon at Nanjing and pleased themselves as to where they went. The Hangzhou holocaust in March was followed by the violation of beautiful Suzhou in June. There they stayed for two months, extending their hold to a large part of Jiangsu, while Hudson Taylor and Maria went to Shanghai and boarded the *Jubilee*. This was when Edkins, Griffith John and two others spent a gruesome week behind the rebel lines. Then the loss of Songjiang to Townsend Ward's mercenaries and the reverse at Shanghai resulted on September 8 in the Taipings' capture of Zhapu on the Hangzhou Bay, the Manchu garrison city so familiar to Hudson Taylor, lying opposite Ningbo. But when they turned west again to retake Hangzhou, at the head of the bay, they failed. Wherever they went corpses multiplied. An estimated ten million lives had been lost since the hostilities began twelve years previously in 1849.[31]

With peace on the Peking front and the treaties signed, the Allies returned to the south, and with the end of the winter began testing the sincerity of the imperial government. A British adventurer named Captain Blakiston succeeded in travelling westwards as far as Tibet, but was turned back at the border. By now the sympathies of most foreign powers were firmly on the side of Peking against the rebels. The only foreigners supporting them were mercenaries.

The neutrality of the Allies might have continued if the Taipings had stayed clear of the treaty ports, but under threat, however blundering the Taiping attack on the Chinese city of Shanghai had been, once the Allies had taken up arms their course was set. Free use of the great Yangzi River as an artery of trade, however, involved reaching an agreement with Hong Xiu-quan, the Taiping

Wang. So in March 1861 Vice-Admiral Sir James Hope with Consul Harry Parkes and five warships steamed up to Nanjing and in spite of the clashes at Shanghai negotiated a 'year of truce' during which shipping on the Yangzi would not be molested and Shanghai would be left in peace.[32] From there they continued for six hundred miles up the Yangzi to Hankou, Wuchang and beyond. Everywhere they found that Peking's directives had been received and at Hankou, a treaty port under the Peking Convention, were given a good reception.

The navigation of the Yangzi above Nanjing was absolutely unknown to foreign shipping before Admiral Hope 'formally opened the great river' in 1861. And 'scarcely a rag of sail was to be seen' for everyone was lying low for fear of both Taipings and imperialists. But then trade

> burst upon the desolate scene like the blossoms of spring [and] within three months the surface of the river was alive with Chinese craft of all sorts and sizes. The interior of China had been dammed up like a reservoir by the Taipings, so that when once tapped, the stream of commerce gushed out . . .[33]

With the admiral travelled a number of diplomats and missionaries as guests or assistants to the various national delegations. William Muirhead was one, hot on the scent of new fields for LMS expansion in the west. Representing Bishop William Boone was another American Episcopal missionary, his outstanding young assistant, Samuel Isaac Joseph Schereschewsky, 'Sherry' to his friends.[34] The British had been training interpreters and no longer depended on the help of missionaries as they once had. Harry Parkes and most British consuls were expert linguists. But the American envoys still called upon the linguistic and cultural expertise in which some missionaries excelled. Schereschewsky was one of these. A well-educated young American rabbi of Russian–Lithuanian–Jewish origins, converted to the Christian faith, he was preparing to translate the Bible into easy *wen-li*, a literary form of mandarin Chinese.

At Nanjing Schereschewsky formed a 'decidedly bad opinion of the Taiping insurgents'. 'The spurious Christianity which they pretend to profess', he urged, was 'utterly unworthy of any Christian sympathy.' By then Muirhead and even Griffith John were regretfully beginning to share the same opinion from their own observations. What might in its early days have conceivably been shaped for China's good, as Hong Ren hoped, had degenerated beyond recall.

From Yueyang (Yochow) on the great Dongting Lake in Hunan, the admiral returned to Shanghai, but some of his party including Schereschewsky went on for hundreds of miles up the Yangzi gorges into Sichuan, as far beyond Chongqing (Chungking) as Pengshan on the tributary Min River (map, pp 20, 73). Below Chongqing they came upon a Catholic Christian village, and were guests of a priest in Chongqing itself. The day of unfettered travel and presentation of the gospel seemed to have truly come.

But in the same year, 1861, civil war erupted in America, absorbing the thoughts and energies of Christians in the States, so that the flow of reinforcements and supplies to missions in China all but dried up. For one society at least it was fifteen years before it began again. Instead of North American missionaries in China outnumbering European by two to one, the relative proportions were reversed.

When word of Sir James Hope's projected expedition reached the missionary community in Shanghai, Griffith John was away in the country. On his return the disappointment that he had missed an opportunity to go so far inland did not impede him. In April he revisited Nanjing – and this was when he found a change for the worse in both leaders and followers. But a greater anxiety troubled him more deeply, the well-justified fear that British guns would now force opium on to Yangzi markets where Taiping bans had for so long debarred its sale or use.

William Muirhead returned from Hankou greatly impressed by the strategic potential of the three cities at the confluence of the Han River with the Yangzi – Hankou, Wuchang and Hanyang, now combined in one, Wuhan. North, south, west and east the rivers and roads of central China brought merchandise from provinces as large as European countries and American states, and carried more back. It was the strategic crossroads for an outpost of the gospel. Shanghai was his own field. The irrepressible and intrepid Welshman Griffith John was the man to go. The CMS were intending to occupy Hangzhou. The American Presbyterians were already in Suzhou. Nanjing was out of the question still. Hankou was open and unoccupied by Protestant Christians.

On June 9, 1861, Griffith John and another LMS missionary, Robert Wilson, boarded a merchant steamer for Hankou. On the same boat were three Roman Catholic priests on their way to join twelve foreign colleagues and thirteen ordained Chinese in the one province of Hubei. Their bishop, a papal legate, had his headquarters at Hankou. An old edict of persecution had been acted on in Hubei, Jiangxi, Zhejiang and Fujian during 1859–60, but now and for the next forty years the tenacity of centuries was to be rewarded by considerable numerical growth of the Catholic Church in China.

Hankou had been in Taiping hands four times. Much was a desolate waste. But Griffith John was as impressed as Muirhead had been with its potential.

> I could hardly believe that I was standing in the very centre of that China that had been closed till then against the outer barbarian [he wrote on June 21]. I thought of Medhurst, and remembered the last prayer I heard him offer up at Shanghai, '*O God, open China, and scatter Thy servants*.'[35]

He returned to Shanghai on a Chinese junk in August, and by mid-September was back in Hankou with his wife and children. They set up their home in the most densely populated part of the Chinese city and began preaching the gospel. Soon he discovered that his audience contained people from twelve or more provinces. Mandarins and even the lieutenant-governor called on them in a friendly spirit and posted a proclamation at their door for their protection. Within six months twenty-two foreign firms had opened business houses in Hankou and begun to transform the wasteland designated for a foreign settlement into the city's most progressive quarter. Until a settlement chaplain came, Griffith John conducted worship for the foreign community. At his invitation Josiah Cox, the Wesleyan Methodist, joined him from Canton in 1862, and the evangelisation of central China had begun. Forty-five years later Griffith John was still there at Hankou, the patriarchal figure of a widespread, thriving Church.

The CMS pioneer of Hangzhou was John Burdon. John Nevius and his wife Helen, who had shared with him the first period of residence in the city in 1858, intending permanent occupation, were casualties of ill health as well as political upheaval. On medical advice, when Helen's health again deteriorated and work in their part of China was virtually at a standstill through the insurgents' unpredictability, the American Presbyterian Mission in June 1860 sent them to Japan. Commodore Perry's treaty made in 1853 had been ratified in 1858 and foreigners had begun residence there. But in Japan their lives were still at risk. In January 1861 an interpreter to the US Minister was assassinated, and civil war in the States meant added insecurity. The Neviuses were advised to leave while the going was good, and returned to Shanghai in February. They tried Ningbo again, but Hangzhou was still under threat and the future of Ningbo lay in the balance. So in May they set out yet again, this time to join the early pioneers at Yantai (Chefoo) in Shandong, where John Nevius' particular missionary genius was to be revealed.

In October 1859 John Burdon and two Chinese catechists had succeeded in staying at Hangzhou for a month, only to be forced out in November. He withdrew to Ningbo and from there shared in the evangelism which resulted in a score or more people turning to Christ in Yuyao, midway between the two cities (map, p 202). There in the winter of 1860–61, immediately after the Peking Convention, he armed himself with one of the new passports and with his novice colleague T Fleming tried again to establish himself in Hangzhou. It was a theatre of war and not surprisingly closed to him. So as the next best thing he rented a house in the city of Shaoxing, between Yuyao and Hangzhou. Even there the officials were suspicious of his motives, for many foreign mercenaries still served the rebels. By November 1861 when the Taipings, thwarted at Hangzhou yet again, were almost at the gates of Shaoxing he was forced back, first to Yuyao and then to Ningbo, taking the Chinese Christians with him. He truly was the apostle of this part of Zhejiang, in which George and Arthur Moule were later to play a part, and where the China Inland Mission put down its roots.[36]

On the Yangzi and within a radius of about thirty miles from Shanghai the truce held, but everywhere else the Taipings rampaged and where they could the imperialists made war on them. In 1853 after Zeng Guo-fan and Li Hong-zhang with their own militia turned the tide at Duliu, near Tianjin, Zeng was sent to Hubei to outflank the Taipings, with Li Hong-Zhang as his chief of staff. Victorious in that province in 1854–55 he was then sent to Jiangxi, in 1856 (map, p 73). After three years and many reverses he succeeded in pushing the rebels back into Hunan, Guangxi and Guizhou, and after the successive rebel eruptions from Nanjing was rewarded by appointment as titular viceroy of Nanjing with jurisdiction over the provinces south of the Yangzi known collectively as Jiangnan, including Zhejiang and part of Anhui.

While the emperor was on his deathbed and the *Peking Gazette*, the Court circular, recorded battles against rebels in the provinces of Shandong, Henan, Jiangsu, Anhui, Hubei, Sichuan, Yunnan,

Guizhou and Jiangxi, Zeng Guo-fan brought comfort in July 1861 to the anxious Prince Kong and Ci Xi (Yehonala), the real strength of the dynasty, by capturing Anqing, halfway between Nanjing and Hankou, after months of siege. He it was who then brought in F Townsend Ward to raise an irregular force for use against the Taipings. A scholar-statesman as much as general, Zeng still had a great future before him – and Hudson Taylor was to suffer bitterly at his hands.

The southward drive of Taiping forces was in large measure due to this pressure upon them from the north and west. In November of 1861 Ningbo's defences were inadequate and panic gripped the city.

'The London' *1861*

The East End of London to which Hudson Taylor had taken his family was the East End he had known eight years before. If in summer the stench at Westminster from the sewage on the banks of the Thames was so intolerable that members of Parliament could

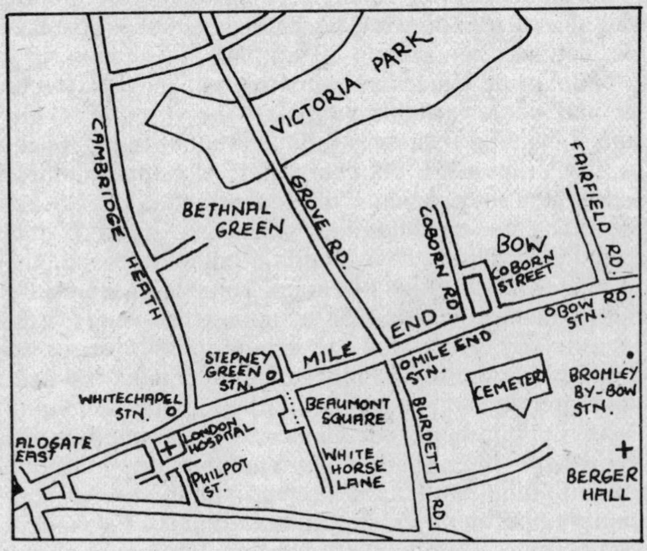

HUDSON TAYLOR'S 'EAST END'

not use their library, Mile End and Whitechapel were far worse. Cattle hides, stable dung, stagnant pools, alcohol, sweat, every imaginable smell hung over the streets and alleys. Barrow boys, reeling drunkards, scarlet women, ragged children and all the bustling crowds of ordinary working people jostled each other, dodging the endless stream of carts, wagons, cabs and carriages churning the slush of unswept streets. Drifting in from the country to find work in the East End's 'manufacturies', the population was growing uncontrollably.[37] An account of the London Hospital described its setting as,

> that toiling, noisy, crowded Whitechapel with its look of sitting up all night, and where even the children never seem to go to bed, doing its business diligently at midnight as at noonday . . . where the gin-palaces are in full force, and . . . the whole population is astir.[38]

It was the East End that was soon to capture the heart of Hudson Taylor's recruit, Tom Barnardo, when the boy he befriended led him to the roof-top where a dozen others huddled together, destitute. This was the London of unlit streets with link-boys ready for a coin to carry a flaming torch ahead of pedestrians, the London of footpads and garotters, inspiration of sick humour in the *Punch* of the time – a London little different from the Chinese cities Hudson Taylor knew so well.

No 1 Beaumont Street was one of three, taken for a weekly rent, unfurnished but respectable. In the last few years the local railway had been opened and the toll-gates at the deteriorating villages of Bethnal Green and Hackney removed, so access to Tottenham, and to the wooded countryside of Finsbury, Stamford Hill and Walthamstow had become quick and easy, for the price of a ticket.

Four or five minutes' walk down the road were the great London Hospital and its new Medical College building, inaugurated as the Crimean War began, after Hudson Taylor had gone abroad. Not greatly changed from what he had known and, in spite of the colonnades and long airy wards, the hospital practices were still as primitive. Three surgeons, three physicians, twelve assistants of various kinds, two house surgeons and two 'resident pupils' (students) on duty a week at a time, formed the staff. The old immoral hussies still attended the patients, but a Lady Superior and a few vocational nurses were beginning to introduce skilled care. Nursing schools were introduced from 1860 in some hospitals, but not at The London until 1870. The nurses were employees. In 1865 they petitioned the hospital governor for one week of holiday per annum. In admiration of her work at Scutari the governing body appointed Florence Nightingale an honorary life governor, and the lot and quality of nurses slowly improved.

So in the hospital Hudson Taylor began to attend again, conditions were still crude. A characteristic of the age was the high proportion of child-patients, victims of accidents and violence as much as of disease, so prevalent. Only the enlightened attitudes of the surgeons and physicians, and devoted visiting by their wives and members of the Flower Mission, who brought posies and tracts to the patients, relieved the atmosphere. The students' reputation for rowdyism, gambling and drunkenness was unchanged.

In total ignorance of the bacterial causes of disease, wholesale infection went unchecked.[39] Epidemics that swept through the crowded refugees in Shanghai also swept through London. Even Prince Albert died of 'typhus', still undistinguished from typhoid, that same December. In London as in China dysentery and cholera claimed multitudes of lives. In 1866 tens of thousands died of cholera in London. Operations were still being performed in frock coats, and the horrors that drove Charles Darwin to forsake a medical career thirty years ago still had not driven the profession to adopt James Simpson's chloroform or Morton's ether to prevent pain. There was no anaesthetist on the hospital staff. All such progress lay in the future. Prejudice was strong and change slow to come. The world of science was preoccupied with Charles Darwin's bombshell, *The Origin of Species*, published in 1859.

Hudson Taylor was older and far more experienced than most students at the time, and his former teachers welcomed him back with unusual warmth.[40] On July 27 he paid his last instalment of forty-two guineas and was free from more expense until his examinations. He was dividing his time equally between revision of the Ningbo New Testament and his medical work, working to complete the requirements for certificates of attendance. Because of his dissection septicaemia in 1852 and sailing on the *Dumfries* in September 1853, he still had courses of lectures to make up, and attendance at a recognised hospital during three winter and two summer sessions (October to March and May to July). Much would depend on the generosity of the hospital staff and the officials of the Royal College of Surgeons (RCS) if he was not to be tied to this routine for two or three years. Even to hope for leniency could be folly, let alone to suggest it.

On October 9 he registered his name at the Royal College. This was the first hurdle, for he should have registered as a student in 1852, nine years previously. When he told the Secretary of the RCS the reasons for not registering then, 'he said they would not refuse certificates on that account under the circumstances'. The first miracle had happened.

First of the five[41] *1861*

From April to October, 1861, apart from speaking at meetings Hudson Taylor worked steadily at his two main preoccupations. He was revising Mark's Gospel while Spottiswoode's were printing Matthew, and proof-reading as they progressed. Then in October Frederick Gough paid him a visit, and James Meadows came down from Yorkshire to join the family, to see if he had the aptitude to learn Chinese, and to reach his final decision about going to China after learning all he could from them. At the same time they would assess the genuineness of his vocation and his ability to fulfil it. Together they would pray for China and that they might discern the will of God for James and Martha, his betrothed, and the Ningbo church. That was how they saw it; certainly not as Hudson Taylor selecting a candidate.

Martha did not come, probably because they were not yet married, but possibly because the need to be as sure of the wife as of the 'missionary' had not yet come home to missions of any type. At twenty-six James was only three years younger than Hudson Taylor and two older than Maria, but still a youth in experience. His memories of arriving and becoming a member of the household, recalled forty-seven years later (with demonstrable errors), include vivid impressions of the uprooted, otherworldly pioneers of missions.

> The first thing that struck me about Mr. Taylor was, his utter indifference about his uncomfortable and poverty-stricken surroundings. His cook, who was the family washerman as well, was a Chinaman [Wang Lae-djün], who knew more about varnishing floors and painting small articles used in Chinese idolatrous worship than cooking an English meal or washing white linen garments . . . everything about the rooms, beds and bed-linen looked . . . 'seedy'. Scarcely a dozen hot coals in the firegrate and it was bitterly cold too. The crockery was all odds and ends and the cutlery at sixes and sevens!

> But none of these things moved our dear brother Mr. Taylor. Even his personal appearance struck me as being very untidy for a man in his position, the bottoms of his trousers were bespattered with mud . . . in this 'dishabille' he and the Rev. Mr. Gough . . . were intensely absorbed all day long . . . I had to patiently wait for hours before Mr. Taylor could attend to me . . . The next thing I was struck with was the gentle earnest piety of Mr Taylor and dear Mr Gough . . . I found that the good man was in poverty himself and had no means nor money to send me out to China! I had come all the way from Yorkshire to London and had left my weekly earnings which enabled me to live in greater comfort than that in which I found dear Mr. and Mrs. Taylor were living! But now, the very essence – so to speak – of Mr Taylor's life, work and success forced itself upon me. I could discern no anxiety in the good man's eye, nor in his speech and conversation. His strong yet quiet faith in the promises of Scripture, his implicit confidence in God, this it was which compelled submission on my part to whatever he proposed for me.
>
> He had a dear affectionate friend in the person of Mr. Wm. Thos. Berger – a wealthy man, but of whom and to whom he never referred when in want of means, he feared to spoil his prayer of faith, and never encouraged me to hope in any man.[42]

The Berger–Taylor partnership was taking shape, though in retrospect Meadows was in the last sentence anticipating events.

When Hudson Taylor and Maria first moved to Beaumont Street from Bayswater, his sister Louisa went with them. And when she left they employed a girl as nursemaid to the children, to free Maria to work on the New Testament. In early October F F Gough came down on a visit from Wolverhampton and stayed with them in Mile End. Hudson Taylor and he went for the weekend of October 5–7 to the Bergers at Saint Hill, their country home two miles outside East Grinstead.

> They were very pleased to see us and liked him very much [Hudson Taylor wrote] . . . Dear Mr Berger feels so interested in the plan of getting more helpers from the working classes. He feels deeply the state of the poor Chinese.

After their return Gough joined them at Beaumont Street for a fortnight and Hudson Taylor told his mother, 'Mr Gough has been helping me a little with Mark. He had finished the translation of the Revelation, but means to revise the whole book before printing it.'

At last after eighteen years of work the basic translation of the whole New Testament in the Ningbo dialect was finished and Gough was free to join in the Taylor's work. They had been intimate friends when Mary Gough was still living – a strength to Maria in her months of distress. When Hudson Taylor escorted Mary Gough and her children to Shanghai, and when he sat through the night guarding the body of the babe who had died, they had been drawn even closer together. Now conversation must have been about those days and Gough's dead loved ones. Only one daughter, little Ellen, remained to him, and she was with relatives. On October 24, after he went home, in writing about the translation work and James Meadows' coming, he ended with words which account for their ability to work together through the next three years. '*Much* love to you both . . . From your much indebted and affectionate Fredk. F. Gough.'

His loneliness and the difficulties of those three years were to try that friendship severely, yet without spoiling it. He must have gone to collect his necessities, for within a few days he was back again, on November 1 or 2, and 'likely to stay'. Hudson Taylor in writing to Louisa on the 6th said, 'He is helping me much with the Testament.' Naturally a good knowledge of Greek helped greatly, but Gough had also used the Ningbo dialect since 1848.

James Meadows was getting on 'very well', Hudson Taylor continued, still with the rest of them in No 1. But as soon as he was more at home they found lodgings for him outside for the next seven weeks. Apparently Louisa was finding it difficult to lead the Christian life in her new circumstances, for in the same letter her brother's advice to her was,

> Do not suffer any little or great annoyance you may meet with, to lead you to neglect your soul. It is never from Jesus that hindrances come, and though you will often meet with them from His followers, it is not because they are His followers; but rather because they are not perfectly like Him. Take your sorrows to Jesus, and your wants to Him also. You will not go in vain.

He himself was facing a 'sorrow'. His long-standing hope that Benjamin and Amelia would go to China was finally dashed by Benjamin's decision that it was not God's will for him. His place was at home. 'BB has decided *not* to go out.' Hudson Taylor's words were too terse to hide his disappointment.

By the end of November the first proof sheets of Matthew's Gospel had been sent to the Bible Society and received their approval, and to Ningbo for comment. Then on December 4 while waiting to attend a midwifery case Hudson Taylor told his mother that James was giving them 'unmixed satisfaction' and he was thinking that there was no need to delay his departure to China. In that event, could his parents collect anything towards his expenses? While relying solely on God to meet his own needs, he saw no inconsistency in collecting funds for others. Even though his agreement with Meadows was to be in terms of James and Martha depending on their heavenly Father without the promise of any salary from him or anyone else, only of prayer and such help as they could give, Hudson Taylor carried a sense of responsibility for them. He need not have troubled, for in his accounts of James' and Martha's expenses to the day of their sailing, three credits from William Berger to the tune of a hundred and sixty pounds more than covered everything.

James Meadows went home for Christmas to be married. The latest news from Ningbo was of the Jones family's illnesses and need of help. To ease the congestion in No 1 Beaumont Street and give more peace and quiet for work, little Grace was taken from time to time to stay with the grandparents in Barnsley, but now she was back with her parents and very disturbed and difficult. Henry Martyn's aphorism 'The power of gentleness is great' was tested to the hilt. Maria had a 'troublesome' cough and Lae-djün was ill with 'muscular rheumatism'. So they rented a room in the house next door but one, as a day nursery for Grace and were looking for a nurse 'with sufficient self-command to calm her down with judicious treatment'.

Then suddenly on New Year's eve Hudson Taylor heard of a fast first-class ship, the *Challenger*, in port and preparing to sail. He knew her and her captain and immediately got in touch. It would appear that Mr Berger had asked for word from him when a ship was found, for a gift of a hundred pounds came from him to pay for the Meadowses' tickets. In hand already was enough for their outfits and cabin equipment. The passages were booked at a discount of '£26 to £36' less than passengers usually paid, and Hudson Taylor hurried off to Barnsley to give James and Martha the news.

They had two days to make ready and say goodbye, left Barnsley together on Friday, January 3, had Saturday and Monday to complete their outfitting in London, and went on board at Gravesend on the afternoon of Tuesday, 7th. James had fitted in a hurried farewell to his father in Norwich as well. On board ship at Gravesend that evening he wrote a few lines to Hudson Taylor, saying he and his bride were in the hands of a Father God, so good, wise and loving. They were content with whatever he might allow. And on the morning tide they sailed out to the unknown. Dr Parker and his bride had sailed from Glasgow four days earlier. Not until late January did Hudson Taylor hear that as far back as November Ningbo had been threatened by the Taipings, business had been suspended, the city largely deserted, and the missionaries in peril.

The fall of Ningbo[43] *November–December 1861*

With his propensity for being in the hot spots, or because his superiors foresaw events, Harry Parkes was HBM consul at Ningbo, fully recovered from his injuries at Peking. In October reports arrived of two Taiping armies numbering forty thousand converging on Zhejiang from Suzhou to the north and from Jiangxi in the south-west (map, p 202). Because of its position between the rivers and near the bay, within encircling ramparts of the hills, a fifty- to one-hundred-yard moat and massive city walls, Ningbo stood as good a chance of holding off an enemy as any place in China – given troops with a will to resist. But the bloodbath at Hangzhou in 1859 and tales of the long-hairs' savagery everywhere had reduced the will of troops and people to impotence. Panic seized the city. The population of four hundred thousand quickly fell to twenty thousand as all who could took ship or junk to Shanghai or melted into the surrounding countryside with all their valuables. Hoping the rebels would not follow, most of them only fell prey to robbers on land and pirates around the Zhoushan (Chusan) islands. Those who fled to the countryside met the worse fate. In Ningbo the suspense built up to frenzy.

An October letter from John Jones in Ningbo to Hudson Taylor in London brought the sad news that all the Jones family were ill and the baby John had died. Little Louisa's lower limbs had become paralysed and before long she too died. He was afraid he and Mary might altogether break down or die, for the accumulation of distresses was too great. Then on November 3 just before the panic he wrote again, bravely bearing up against all odds with his faith as strong as ever.

> . . . the [three] little ones, who are left to us here, were very delighted with their [presents] . . . After their parents you are second to none . . . You are the only ones who have spoken of my dear John by name lately . . . sweet babe! Not a babe now perhaps.

Heaven was very real to them. John Burdon, he said, was not yet in from Shaoxing, although nearly a week ago he had stopped sleeping in that city lest it 'be inconvenient', and 'Yuyao is reported taken today'. After that Burdon arrived. Miles Knowlton, the American Baptist, out in the country met a merchant with five armed guards who told him it would be useless to go on. Then he saw villages fired by the rebels. 'Since he returned all has been uncertainty here . . . The hearts of the people are failing them for fear.' Four days later, on November 7, the rebels were within sight of Ningbo itself.

Arthur Moule and his wife had arrived in August. His eye-witness accounts were restrained. But he wrote, 'It was an unspeakably fearful sight to meet the crowds of refugees, reeling through the dripping streets, with despair on their faces.' Those who had elected to stay while they could protect their homes asked anxiously, 'Are they coming? Need we fly?' The answer came from the smoke of burning villages. Soon the rich suburbs with their magnificent temples were in flames, and a vast pall of smoke hung over the doomed city.

Suddenly on December 9 the Taipings stormed the West Gate. Some of those missionaries who had not moved over the river to the relative safety of the foreign Settlement escaped with difficulty. Like Saul of Tarsus, Henry Rankin was let down from the city wall in a basket. Others stayed. But the long-hairs ran through the streets with drawn swords shouting, 'Don't fear. We only fight against the imperialists and idols. You people need not be alarmed.' The Russells and John Burdon stayed to protect the CMS girls' school if they could. And George and Arthur Moule stood by the boys. When the Taipings tied boys together by their despised queues to drag them away they intervened and succeeded in getting them released. The Moules remained in the city for two weeks, until the rank and file of the rebels were seen to be so little under control that Consul Parkes ordered the missionaries over to the Settlement behind the protection of British gunboats. Years later a Taoist priest said how impressed he had been at the time. He said, 'If one of your people is missing, you don't rest till he is recovered.'

John Jones' next letter to Hudson Taylor read,

> Many whose lives a month ago appeared to be at least as secure as mine have now passed on . . . dying cruel and bloody deaths . . . By the mercy of God no Christian has suffered death as far as I can learn although many have been captured. The great majority . . . have also

> been released . . . Those who are taken by them have to work but are *well* fed.

Neng-gui, the Christian basket-maker called up to be a soldier, was among the prisoners whose lives were spared. Another on his way to Ningbo from the country had visited Wang Lae-Djün's wife and brought a letter asking John Jones to urge his immediate return, though their village was still untouched. The Joneses' own home was full of refugees.

It soon transpired that one of the rebel leaders had been a Triad chief of the Red Turbans in the Shanghai siege, and John Jones thought Hudson Taylor would remember him. The 'two leaders here . . . are very anxious to be all right with the foreigners and . . . have been very civil.' They assured Consul Parkes that foreigners' houses would be respected, and issued a proclamation against looting. Many of their soldiers were executed for disobedience, but still it went on. 'Poor Ningpo has been sadly pulled about . . . The rebels have made sad work with your [Bridge Street] house; they have stolen all the furniture and broken up the place considerably.'

Although sleeping in the Settlement, foreigners with passes were allowed in and out of the city. The preaching chapels were all closed but John Burdon, the only one who could make himself understood by the insurgents, was preaching to them. At great risk he and George Moule were even going into the country, but so far the rebels were showing them courtesy. John Jones was visiting the Christians in the city every day, and wrote, 'My heart bleeds when I go through it day by day . . . this is a bad time for property.' For this reason he had sold Hudson Taylor's encyclopaedia for fifty dollars before it was too late.

> These times have stirred up a world of evil and appear to have broken down many barriers . . . whether for good or for evil the idols seem to be completely forgotten . . . they have weighed them and found them wanting . . . Yesterday I gave the rebel leader . . . a tract which he read and pronounced to contain truth believed in by them.

The bulk of the rebels, however, were 'simply image-breakers' and knew little beyond a Taiping doxology. Russell in fact considered them worse than the heathen in that the bulk of them were left with no religion.

'You speak from time to time of rejoining us,' John Jones lamented, 'but the time seems long, very long.' He knew Hudson Taylor well, and the pace he lived at, but he himself was ill and under strain. Yet, always frank and capable of humour in unusual circumstances, whatever his mood, he prodded him with, 'To tell you the truth, your little shabby notes do not deserve such long letters and so many of them as I give in return.' And followed it with a very affectionate ending to his letter.

Expansion[44] *1860–63*

Only at Ningbo and in the other battle zones was freedom of movement for foreigners restricted. In theory at least that was the situation. In practice ravaging rebels and bandits of all hues, and resentful mandarins, frequently posed problems. But the little log-jam of Protestant missionaries pent up in Shanghai and Ningbo at last broke. At first only Griffith John moved up the Yangzi. Several headed for the enticing north, enticing because of its closure to the gospel until now. Peking, Tianjin and the magnificent people of the northern provinces drew like magnets, and the bracing climate offered hope for those like Dr McCartee and the Halls whose health failed in the humid south. Merchants in far greater numbers were on the move.

At this strategic moment for missions the sending Churches were caught napping without the reinforcements needed, but worse still without the experienced Chinese-speaking men to seize the opportunity. The unadventurous spirit which Hudson Taylor found blanketing the Church and many mission leaders in Britain was found also in the States. The Civil War immobilised them in the southern States and absorbed their attention in the north. When Mrs Bausum, back in Ningbo and married to E C Lord, the American Baptist, took his two children and her own to school in their respective homelands and tried to raise money in America to open an orphanage school like Miss Aldersey's, she received little.

The German Rhenish Mission on the contrary, when forced out of Borneo, chose in 1861 the challenging alternative of Sumatra with its so far impregnable Batak enclave, and in 1862 sent Ludwig Ingwer Nommensen, one of the great heroes of the faith. (By 1866 there were fifty-two Batak Christians and six years later five trained Batak evangelists. Within fifty years the Batak people's movement was sweeping tens of thousands into the Church.[45]) But the wheels of the China missions were deep in sand. Even five years later little response was in evidence. Other continents were still taking precedence. Hudson Taylor's experience in recruiting for Ningbo was no exception until 1864. But the stalwarts already in China could not be held back.

Rutherford Alcock, knighted and appointed HBM Minister at the new Peking Legation, asked William Lockhart to accompany him as surgeon to his staff. So after twenty years as a missionary, and with the honour of election to a Fellowship *emeritus* of the Royal College of Surgeons, Lockhart returned to China to become the first Protestant missionary to reside in the capital.[46] Debarred from proselytising, he opened a hospital like those he had started at Hong Kong and Shanghai. John Burdon was the next to be invited, and as quasi-chaplain to the legation stayed as an active missionary in Peking for eleven years. Consul Harry Parkes on leave in England did his best to persuade the CMS to take up North China as an area for expansion but without success.[47] W A P Martin was the first American missionary to reach Peking, but not to work there until 1863. Joseph Edkins, married at last, went to Yantai (Chefoo) in 1860, to Tianjin in 1861 and from there to Peking in 1863, free from diplomatic restrictions. The honour of baptising the first three Protestant Christians in Peking – unthinkable until only two years previously – very deservedly fell to him. After fifteen years in China (1848–63) he had thirty more ahead of him at Peking.

After his spree up the Yangzi Schereschewsky returned to Shanghai. St John's College (later to become St John's University) remained as a monument to his ability when the American Minister Anson Burlingame took 'Sherry' to Peking as his secretary–interpreter in 1861. There he continued his translation of the Old Testament from Hebrew into 'easy *wen-li*', until Bishop Boone withdrew the Episcopal Mission from the north and concentrated on the lower Yangzi valley. Burlingame, himself a zealous American Methodist, came to China from New York to become a legend in the history of missions, of diplomats and of China. Replacing Minister Ward who left Peking to resign in 1860, exasperated and complaining of the futility of trying to negotiate with the Manchus, Burlingame loved China from the first and was loved in return.

Shandong drew several. Here the Nian-fei rebels and marauding bands of brigands, flotsam of defeated armies, made life hazardous. But these pioneering missionaries were not looking for security. After months of living on his boat in Yantai (Chefoo) harbour, J L Holmes the American Southern Baptist managed to rent a house and was joined by John and Helen Nevius, the Presbyterians. Yantai was only their base. Holmes went up to Tianjin and returned alone on horseback, passing through villages not littered but 'crowded with the dead bodies of people and animals'. Wherever missionaries travelled in the empire they groaned for the sufferings of the people under the curse of so much evil. Nevius travelled by mule-litter to Dengzhou (Tengchow, now Penglai) where another Southern Baptist was finding a foothold, pressing the outreach of the gospel through the province. But in October 1861 when marauders with a reputation for atrocious tortures came within twenty miles of the city they were all forced to withdraw. When Dengzhou was peaceful again Calvin W Mateer, a young man with a great future, reoccupied it.

With the Russian occupation of the Amur region of Manchuria, Stephen Neill tells us, a new field fell to the care of the great missionary-hearted Orthodox archbishop John (Innokenty) Veniaminov, pioneer of the Aleutian Islands, the Kuriles and far north of Siberia. From the age of sixty to sixty-eight he gave himself to Amur province, Manchuria and Japan (in 1860) before retiring at seventy, only to be called back to serve as Metropolitan of Moscow for eleven more years. At seventy-three he founded the Orthodox Missionary Society. His aim, Neill wrote, was 'to expound the truth that missionary witness is a duty which is incumbent on the Church as a whole and on every member of it'. So even the Russian annexation of China's Manchurian seaboard had, in non-political terms, this redeeming feature.[48]

Although vast areas of China were now accessible and a Baptist and Presbyterian were already there, in 1861 Bishop Boone sent two new Episcopalian missionaries to Yantai. Comity agreements on areas of influence for the various denominations had at least twice been mooted to avoid such overlapping and contradictory teaching on Church order, but the wisdom of doing so had not yet been recognised. All were still Biblically evangelical in the essentials and co-operated amicably. When the insurgents came on to Yantai, one of Boone's men, H M Parker, courageously went out with Holmes to parley with them. Both were set upon and 'cut to pieces'. John Jones enlarged in a letter to Hudson Taylor on hearsay accounts of the tragedy. 'The French recovered the bodies.' He was writing on the day Yuyao fell to the Taipings and Ningbo came under threat, and his fears are discernible. Scarcely less tragic was the news soon to be received that Charles J Hall of the BMS so recently a CES colleague in Ningbo, had died of cholera shortly after preaching his first sermon at Yantai. The story of the Baptist

Missionary Society in China was to continue in this strain. Of the seven missionaries sent out in the fifteen years after the Peking Convention of 1860, only one was alive at the end of that period – Timothy Richard. Hendrick Kloekers survived in Shandong only from 1862–65 when he was invalided home.

The other Hall, W N Hall of the Methodist New Connexion, and a colleague named John Innocent, reached Tianjin in April 1861 and in the next two years penetrated far afield to Taiyuan in Shanxi and to Mongolia.[49] Following an unusual sense of God's leading in 1866 they went to Liaoling in Shandong, found a whole village ready to turn to Christ, baptised forty-five and so started a Church which spread like a bush fire to other towns. This kind of action by the Holy Spirit was what all missionaries prayed for and longed to see.

For the Bible Society 1860 was what the annual report called 'a night of toil'. So disrupted by political events was the work of distribution of Scriptures that a total dispersal of thirty thousand items of all kinds indicated the state of unrest existing. The following year things looked up. Even at Canton two colporteurs were free to work, and on Chongming Island, scene of Burdon's and Hudson Taylor's mobbing and expulsion in 1855, William Muirhead now received a tumultuous welcome. But while hopes rose in China, the destruction of Bibles and stoning of Protestant colporteurs by rioting mobs occurred in Holland.[50] Only one year later the wind changed again and the Bible Society reported the torture and death of a catechist in South China, 'cut down with a sword' because he would not renounce his faith. As if to counterbalance this news the Bible Society report made much of the 'Romanised Ningpo Colloquial',

> now in the course of being printed in London under the editorial supervision of the Rev. J.H. Taylor . . . any intelligent person can learn to read it in a few months, and to the women especially, the edition will prove an inestimable boon, . . . The Committee need scarcely say how gladly they have adopted Mr. Taylor's proposal, recommended as it was by the Committee of the Church Missionary Society.[51]

In Latourette's phrase 'the period of penetration' of China had begun. Extensive pioneering was to continue almost unchecked (certainly not unchallenged) for forty-five years, until 1895–96. Since Robert Morrison arrived at Canton fifty-two years had passed. In that time, at the end of 1860, Protestant missions could count only fourteen centres of work, with thirty-five separate 'stations' established. Between the 1842 Treaty of Nanking and the 1860 Peking Convention seventeen new Societies had joined the eight already in China, twenty-five in all. Five ceased to exist during the lifetime of Hudson Taylor. Of the one hundred and sixty new missionaries to arrive during those eighteen years, 1842–60, seventy had died or retired before 1895. So the period of penetration began with a sadly low muster, so thinly deployed that Hudson Taylor felt challenged and driven to pray and to recruit replacements even while fully employed with his medical course and New Testament revision.

CHAPTER SEVEN

UPHILL ALL THE WAY 1862–63

LM and MRCS Eng.[1] *1862*

When James and Martha Meadows, the first of the five reinforcements Hudson Taylor was praying for, had gone, he sat down to report to William Berger, the donor of all funds used to send them. Only James counted as a missionary, and only his letters give any impression of what Martha was like. Sheets of paper already used to jot down their expenses bear the rough draft of Hudson Taylor's letter to Berger. For James they had bought a cap, a carpet-bag, an overcoat, a suit of black cloth and one of light material, a dozen collars, two dozen shirts, drawers, hose, umbrellas, etc. For Martha, stockings, gloves, nightcaps, shawl and scarf, stays, bonnet, etc., etc. The cabin furnishing included bedding, sheeting, towelling, chair, washstand, looking glass and toilet set, lamps, candlestick and matches, hammer, nails and screws. Mr Berger had asked for an account of the early days of the Bridge Street church in Ningbo and Hudson Taylor wrote at length about how he and John Jones began, and how one by one believers joined them – the army officer who fell away, Ni the Buddhist leader, Neng-gui the basket-maker, the young teacher Tsiu and his mother, and of course Wang Lae-djün the painter, whom Mr Berger had met in London – a colourful catalogue for the Bergers' prayers to build upon.

Towards the end of January John Jones' November letter arrived, the mournful one. The Taipings were coming and John Burdon was not in from Shaoxing yet, though Yuyao, closer still, was reported taken. Hudson, Maria and Gough thought anxiously of their Chinese and missionary friends and prayed. At about this time, if not while James Meadows was still with them, an hour or more was given to prayer together for China every Saturday evening. The inviolable custom remained in practice for a hundred and ten years in London and continues at other times today.

John Jones thanked Hudson Taylor for a gift of money 'when you needed it yourselves'. He knew how they lived. Then his next letter brought news of the fall of Ningbo and of Lae-djün's wife pleading for him to return. This was more disturbing than ever. But Jones also wrote that W A Russell, Miss Aldersey's tireless henchman, was waiting for a ship to return home to England. To Hudson Taylor this was an ominous cloud on the horizon. He was not mistaken.[2] On January 31 John Burdon, in Ningbo, wrote thanking them for the 'latter part of Alford'.[3]

> Part of Vol. IV was destroyed along with a good many other books and things of mine by the Rebels when they took Shaohsing. [This timely gift would complete the set with what survived.] The first three are a very precious memento of my brother Aitchison, the last two will be the same of yourselves.

The intensity of missionary experience bound friends together so strongly. But the present state of affairs 'is a very sad one and a very dark one' he went on. There were nearly two feet of snow on the ground. 'The poor Chinese must be suffering intensely.'

Then in April he wrote again. The books had arrived, but he was en route to Peking 'with the Bishop of Victoria on a kind of exploratory tour'.

> The future looks dark and dreary so far as mission work is concerned. I feel for myself that perhaps it is not so much the aspect of the work that is discouraging as my own unfitness for such a work. I want more prayer, more faith, more self-denial, more of everything that is required for a missionary.
>
> Where I am going or what I am to do after returning from Peking, if I ever return, is very uncertain . . .
>
> Ever yours affectionately . . .[4]

He had been in China under war conditions for nine years, had been widowed twice and needed a change. His invitation to be chaplain to the embassy in Peking was not long delayed. He had the qualities – a bishop in the making.

Gough and Taylor were steadily translating together, but as Hudson Taylor had his medical course running concurrently, Gough took up anatomy at the hospital too and began dissecting. Working as hard as he could, Hudson Taylor could not complete his work in time for the examination in May, the 'Primary Examination' for membership of the Royal College of Surgeons. He told his mother that he was glad to have escaped dissection wounds, but, 'That my heart has borne the strain is another reason for gratitude . . . May we be drawn closer to our Father by His goodness, and not need the rod to drive us to Him.'

Maria was away, staying with Mary Jones' sister, Miss Young, on the south coast. In a note to her, Hudson Taylor said he had registered for the exam, 'But there has been such a rush of students that I shall not go up probably, till May 10. Perhaps the Lord knew if I went up sooner I should not be prepared.'

She was still away the following weekend when he told her of a missionary candidate and his fiancée from the Twig Folly Mission, where he sometimes preached, whom he was to interview that evening. It was their longest separation since marriage. But Hudson Taylor was tiring, and his friendly surgeon Jonathan Hutchinson advised him to take a week's holiday as the best preparation for the examination. He went up to his parents at Barnsley, taking the two children with him. It was only a change of scene. His mother told Maria in a note that he felt he could not afford time for anything except reading medicine. The next Sunday he managed a note himself, with a passage in Greek, and two days later was back in London bringing Louisa and praying, 'If it please God, may He prosper me in my examination, that I may . . . get on with the New Testament.' Saturday May 10 came and he told his parents that if successful in both paper and orals,

> I shall then lack nothing but hospital practice to go up for my second and final examination. [Hospital practice] will take up so little time that I shall be able again to give my strength to the New Testament. I long to be at it again, and to see it getting forward.

Examinations were held on Saturday evenings. For such an occasion Hudson Taylor and Maria probably took the horse bus all the way to Soho, where the College of Surgeons was still located. Maria sat in a restaurant while he signed in, and when he returned they sat together for the two hours before the papers began. Nervously he read up the larynx in his anatomy book, and left Maria in the restaurant praying for him while he went up to the examination hall. One question was on the larynx. The *viva voce* was on the following Wednesday. Back at home after it he wrote to his parents, 'God has helped me and I passed my primary examination easily.'

A few days later he said he was settling down to New Testament revision, but already he was looking ahead to his finals. An exciting possibility had come to his knowledge. He could not sit for surgery and pathology 'according to present laws, until after next winter session', but a hope of doing it sooner had arisen. By appealing to the Council of the Royal College the usual requirements might be waived. It had to be shortly before the final examination took place, in either three or six months' time. The sooner this distraction was disposed of the better, so he arranged for an interview at the College again on July 2 and explained his circumstances, applying for a waiver to allow him to take the diploma finals the same month. On getting back to Beaumont Street, however, he checked the answers he had given to their questions and discovered a discrepancy. At once he sat down to put it right.

> July 2, 1862
>
> My dear Sir,
>
> On looking over some memoranda, I regret to find that my memory failed me this morning on one point, with regard to the Hospital Practice at Ningpo. One month of the time, that I had included in the nine months during which I had charge of the Hospital, was before Dr. Parker left Ningpo, and is included in the six months for which I have his certificate . . . I had, however, the advantage of consultation with him, and of carrying out his plans.
>
> There were, therefore only 8 months – not nine as I incorrectly stated this morning, – *after* his return, when I had sole charge of the Hospital, giving a total of fourteen, not fifteen months' practice at Ningpo . . .
>
> I was with Dr. Lockhart from March 1 to September 1, '54. Assisted Dr. Parker from April 18th. to September 18th. '59. Had sole charge of the Hospital . . . till June 16th. or 18th. '60.[5]

The crux of the matter was that those eight months were not under supervision as was required.

On July 10 the Quarterly Meeting of the Council took place with 'Mr. Adams' present – probably the London Hospital surgeon. The Minute reads,

> Read a letter from Rev. J.H. Taylor requesting that under the circumstances, stated by him he may be admitted to the pass examination on the 26th. Inst. wanting one winter session of Surgical Hospital practice and Clinical Lectures on Surgery. Resolved: That Mr. Taylor's request be complied with.[6]

The name of William Lockhart, so recently honoured by the Council with a Fellowship *emeritus*, was in itself a recommendation. If this Mr Adams was his chief at the London Hospital he had a friend at court. So six months with Lockhart, six with Parker and eight running a hospital of forty beds alone, were accepted in lieu of the two academic years he might have been required to fulfil between his Primary and Final examinations. But the Council correctly expressed their waiver in terms of one long winter session under instruction 'wanting', while crediting him with the competence. He could now prove it by examination.

Apparently he took Maria and the children to Barnsley, and returned to London on Saturday, July 19, in time to put in some work at hospital before deciding what cramming he needed to do. As he went through the material he was shocked. He decided to read through as much of a book on surgery as he could before taking the papers in a week's time.

> May the Lord help me: unless *He* does, I shall surely break down [he wrote to Maria]. Then I thought of our work – the New Testament – the numerous friends we cannot see – Lae-djün so long away from home – Louisa – our own need for money, and guidance, and I need not say I felt we had work enough. What should, what could, we do, if we had not our precious Saviour to go to? I read till a few minutes from 12 p.m. and then read a little in my Greek Testament, concluding with Acts 12.5 (Peter in prison and the iron gates opening of their own accord) . . . That chapter was such a comfort to me when driven out of Tsungming, when the Consul threatened to punish me . . . And again when our own troubles were at the worst at Ningpo. And it does so now. No perplexity can be too great for God our Saviour. Indeed we must not mistrust Him. He will provide, and He will guide, in all our way . . . Dear love, we could not forget each other, could we? Nor could we be unmindful of each other's need. Well, so the Lord Jesus loves – not so but far more – each one of us. And if for His glory, or for the strengthening of our faith He sees it needful to try it, let us ask Him not to suffer *it* to fail, nor *us* to be ashamed . . . Yesterday I had to change a £5 note . . . I have only one more left. But He who feeds the Ravens, will give *His Children* bread, temporal and spiritual.

The iron gates had swung open of their own accord on other occasions and here in London Hudson Taylor was waiting for them to do so again.[7] Only occasional references to money matters occur in his letters and journals of this period (those preserved), but few to show where their funds came from, and usually they mark the crises.

On Friday, July 25, both Maria and he sent notes to each other. They expected to meet the next day but knew they could count on the post. She and the children were due at Kings Cross between four and five p m and home by six.

> My precious Hudson, . . . I do hope you may be prospered tomorrow. I will endeavour to pray for you, but let your trust be in God *alone* . . .
>
> And can He have taught us to trust in His name,
> And thus far have brought us to put us to shame?'

And Hudson Taylor wrote in pencil from the hospital,

> I have got my certificates signed ready for tomorrow. May God be gracious to me and assist me then. I have got cold and have a bad headache to-day again; but I hope it will pass off.

On Saturday night after the written examination papers the family had not arrived when he reached home. They did not arrive until late evening. So he wrote to his parents.

> I have to record the goodness of God in helping me . . . We have difficulties before us of which I cannot attempt to write. I do not see my way at all before me. But it is enough to know that He does, and will guide, and supply all our need . . . We must press forward, counting *everything*, and that includes a great many things, loss, that we may win Christ and be found in Him.

The oral followed on the Tuesday evening. At nearly midnight he dashed off another note to Barnsley – at last he was a fully qualified member of the Royal College of Surgeons, 'MRCS, England', in contemporary parlance a 'Surgeon'.[8] What he wrote was, 'The good hand of our covenant God being with me, your prayers have been answered, and I have successfully passed the examinations.' And would they please pass the news on to Martha Meadows' mother and sister that she and James had reached China safely.

Amelia threw light on Hudson Taylor's 'difficulties' when she wrote to her mother on July 31.

> We feel very thankful [about his examination results] as he will now be able to give more undivided attention to the Revision; and will feel more at liberty to take a little recreation. Bless him, the Lord seems to prosper all he takes in hand! . . .
>
> Mr and Mrs — have just arrived from Ningpo: and I think from what Maria says they are rather afraid he will throw some difficulties in their way with regard to the revision . . . The work however is the Lord's . . .

The Russells had arrived.

A week after the examinations the President of the Royal College staged an innovation, the first *Conversazione* open to Fellows and Members to demonstrate surgical specimens and answer questions. According to the Minutes of Council this one on August 5, 1862, was a great success, with new gas lamps from the ceiling giving a festive air, and many surgeons present and enjoying the novelty. Now that 'Large Medical Chest' in the *Jubilee* baggage inventory takes on some meaning. Hudson Taylor demonstrated three surgical specimens, duly listed in the *Conversazione* catalogue. But what they were remains a mystery – the RCS has no copy among its archives and the one Hudson Taylor sent home was lost.

William Berger was the owner of a rice-starch factory in Bromley-by-Bow and lived at Saint Hill near East Grinstead. At each place he built a chapel in which to have the gospel preached, and before long took to inviting Hudson Taylor to preach when he visited Saint Hill. At Mrs Berger's invitation the family enjoyed a week's holiday there after the *Conversazione*. Maria took the children on the 5th, and the next morning Hudson left home at five to reach Saint Hill for breakfast. It was the first of many such visits as the friendship between them deepened and William Berger's appreciation of the Taylors grew. And Mr Berger's sound business sense appealed to them as the right complement to his spirituality.

In 1861 Hudson Taylor had attended the Barnet Conference – three days of meetings held in July for Christians of all denominations, at Christ Church, Barnet, by the vicar William Pennefather, author of the much-used hymn 'Jesus, stand among us in Thy risen power'. For the past five years these meetings had been intended primarily for the deepening of spiritual life, but Hudson Taylor commented, 'best of all many souls were saved'. Dr Horatius Bonar, the hymn writer, Miss Stacey, George Pearse and others known to Hudson Taylor were there to hear Pennefather's exposition of Scripture.

Now in 1862 Hudson Taylor and Maria went again. In the letter telling his parents of this, he said that he proposed taking another diploma of the College of Surgeons in October, its Licentiate in Midwifery. 'You must not think because the Lord has answered prayer before, that my success has been of myself, and that there is less need for prayer now.'

A week before the examination he was in two minds about taking it. 'I am so busy that I feel undecided whether to go or not. I must decide by Saturday. If I go, may God help me. If I had better not, may He teach me so. Pray for me.' His days were full and became fuller, but on October 29 he took the examination and again passed, adding LM (RCS) to his Membership. At ten-thirty p m he was still at the Royal College writing to catch the post to his mother, carefully attributing his success to God, in keeping with the Scripture, 'In all thy ways acknowledge him, and he shall direct thy path.' He was so busy because at last the leaders of the United Methodist Free Church were interested in sending missionaries to China and involving him fully in their deliberations.

Recruits[9] *June–December 1862*

Back in June, after Hudson Taylor's first examination, the Foreign Missionary Secretary of the United Methodist Free Church (UMFC) had invited him to meet with him and the Treasurer. But in July came a notice of the secretary's funeral, and not until October did another, Charles Cheetham, get in touch with Hudson Taylor again. The Church meant business. They had carefully assessed the implications of a mission to China and were aware of the hazards. News of cholera at Shanghai, Ningbo and Yantai (Chefoo) taking missionaries' lives, including C J Hall's, and of the exacerbation of Taiping activities had not prevented the formation of a fund. And the Annual Assembly had passed a resolution to go ahead with plans in spite of objections that great expense and unproductive work made China an unsuitable field. They were already involved in Africa. Would Hudson Taylor kindly furnish information and advice? 'Are there any Methodists at Amoy? Do you still think Ningbo most desirable for us to occupy if any are sent?' Cheetham would be sorry to urge any steps on the Committee which it might later regret. Would Mr Taylor be able to spare time to come north and meet the Committee?

'Yes,' he replied, and immediately after his session with them at Rochdale on October 17, the Committee resolved unanimously to begin at Ningbo. 'It is left with the officers of our Connexion to seek out two suitable men – to receive instruction at your hands.'

That was the beginning. A week before his obstetrics examination a new Missionary Secretary, Samuel Barton, wrote asking him to teach a new recruit for East Africa the use of 'some of the simplest forms of medicine'. Three days later the arrangements were completed. In November Barton wrote that two young men had offered to go to China. If they were to be accepted, could he take them under his charge at once, to train them? Again it was Yes. In January 1863 a well-recommended local preacher in Rotherhithe named William R Fuller was before the Committee. Would Mr Taylor interview him and report his impressions, and discuss with him the study of the language and medicine? Fuller was ready to start at once. Could Hudson Taylor ascertain whether the London Hospital would admit him for brief medical training? Another recruit should be ready in two or three weeks' time. 'I am almost ashamed to give you so much trouble, but your kindness has made us bold.'

To Hudson Taylor it was all the vibrant answer to his prayers. But the BMS was about to send a Mr R F Laughton to Yantai to replace C J Hall, and would Hudson Taylor advise about elementary Chinese books? Then a note from Laughton in the hectic rush of preparing to sail and being unable to make time to call on him – could Mr Taylor possibly look in at the BMS, 33 Moorgate Street, if he was passing around midday?

That was not all. George Pearse had several times proposed that Hudson Taylor should publish his letters and journals in a connected form, to arouse interest in China. Now he was yielding, as he told his mother, 'I have always dismissed the proposition as untenable for want of time. But so many seem to think they would be useful and interesting . . . that perhaps I may be led to attempt it.' And he began collecting letters and past numbers of *The Gleaner* and *Missionary Reporter*, (edited by Mrs Berger's brother-in-law, James van Sommer) from his parents and friends. On November 12 he reported to the Bible Society that he and F F Gough were steadily at work on the Ningbo vernacular New Testament – 'While making slow progress we have been most laboriously engaged.'

In August the first sheet of sixteen pages of Matthew's Gospel, with marginal references, approved in Ningbo, had been through the ultimate process of typesetting, proof-reading, amendment and final printing. And in October the second sheet was printed. But it was January before the whole of Matthew was in print and they were on to printing Mark, for a new complication began rearing its head. The relationship between the godly Frederick Gough and Hudson Taylor was coming under strain. That they both coped with the difficulty so well as to deepen their friendship and initiate new measures for the evangelisation of China, during this period, speaks well for both men. To keep the cost as low as possible, once the type was set, delay of any kind had to be cut to a minimum, even if it meant working at night. While the medical examinations were looming, they had had to take priority. But at last Hudson Taylor was free to concentrate on New Testament revision and proof-reading – as free as family life and his other commitments permitted – only to find that Gough could not work under the same kind of pressure.

Family life included the birth on November 25 of Frederick Howard Taylor, named after Frederick Foster Gough and after the Howard brothers, John Eliot and Robert, who were so faithful as friends to Hudson Taylor. This meant broken nights. And Gough was still living in the Taylors' spartan little home. It was a relief to all when Hudson Taylor took Maria and the three children to Barnsley on December 18. But they were scarcely able to do so. They were almost out of cash again and praying for twenty-five pounds. As Hudson Taylor noted in the first of twelve penny pocket-notebooks which he used as a journal for two years, 'Feeling that we needed the change and that it was due to our parents, so looked to God to provide the means. On Xmas day Father gave me £5 . . .' He preached at a number of meetings and received a pound or two. Then on their return home to Beaumont Street on January 5, 1863, they remarked on how good it was to be reminded by the sight of the old 'JEHOVAH JIREH' scroll in Chinese to trust the Lord. And then, 'At 8 p.m. received a kind note from Mr Berger enclosing £20.0.0 for us. Praise the Lord.' Immediately they plunged back into New Testament revision and prepared for William Fuller to come for training. Neither he nor they were shaken by the turn of events in China.

The end of neutrality[10] *1862*

All through 1862 the news from Shanghai and Ningbo was alarming, and it looked as though James and Martha Meadows were sailing into serious trouble. With HongXiu-quan's authority waning and increasing hordes of his followers set on plunder and destruction, little sympathy for the Taipings remained. Even the hopeful missionaries saw that his early errors had become hardened blasphemies. His claim that he had received greater revelations from God than were ever given to Western Christianity justified to him all his excesses. But his armies were composed now of deserters from the imperial forces, outlaws and opium addicts, defying discipline.

Li Hong-zhang, appointed Governor of Jiangsu and Superintendent of Foreign Commerce in July, at the age of thirty-nine, was equally impotent, unable to move about his province or that of Zhejiang because most of this area was in Taiping hands.[11] Hangzhou was occupied by them from January 1862 until April 1864, and Shanghai was threatened from Suzhou (map, p 202). But Li Hong-zhang was never a slave to dynastic convention. He welcomed the fact that China's Western conquerors, content with their treaties, were ready to become her allies. To put down the Taipings and restore peace in which to trade was to their own advantage. But it was the Taipings themselves who precipitated the growing alliance.

When Admiral Sir James Hope's 'year of truce' with the Taiping Wang ran out and the Zhong Wang, the 'Loyal Prince', advanced from Suzhou in early 1862 proclaiming 'We must take Shanghai to complete our dominions', and heralded his coming with the smoke of burning villages, Sir Charles Staveley in command of British land forces took steps to protect the foreign Settlements of Shanghai, so aligning himself with Li Hong-zhang against the Taipings.

Frederick Townsend Ward, the filibuster, after his initial success at Songjiang had been unable to dominate the Taipings with his foreign mercenaries and ten thousand Chinese soldiers – the 'False Foreign Devils' in Western uniforms whom he was training. Hundreds more mercenaries were fighting for the Taipings, and unscrupulous merchants in Shanghai were supplying them with arms. For a year Ward had no more victories, and at Qingpu (where Medhurst, Lockhart and Muirhead were mobbed in 1846) he failed twice; Colonel Forrester his second-in-command was taken prisoner and Ward himself was wounded.

On January 11, 1862, a doubly dangerous situation developed.[12] Two Taiping armies began advancing on Shanghai. Having taken Ningbo in December the southern army advanced from Hangzhou through Songjiang again. And from the Yangzi region near Wusong the Zhong Wang struck directly towards the foreign Settlement, lying between them and the Chinese city of Shanghai. Townsend Ward met the southern army and defeated them at Guangfuling, just north of Songjiang, on January 15. But three feet of snow checked the Taiping advance from Wusong and it was February 25 before a combined force of British, French and American troops under the British admiral, with seven hundred of Ward's men, defeated the Taipings on their eastern flank at Gaoqiao (Kaokiao). The era of neutrality was finally over.

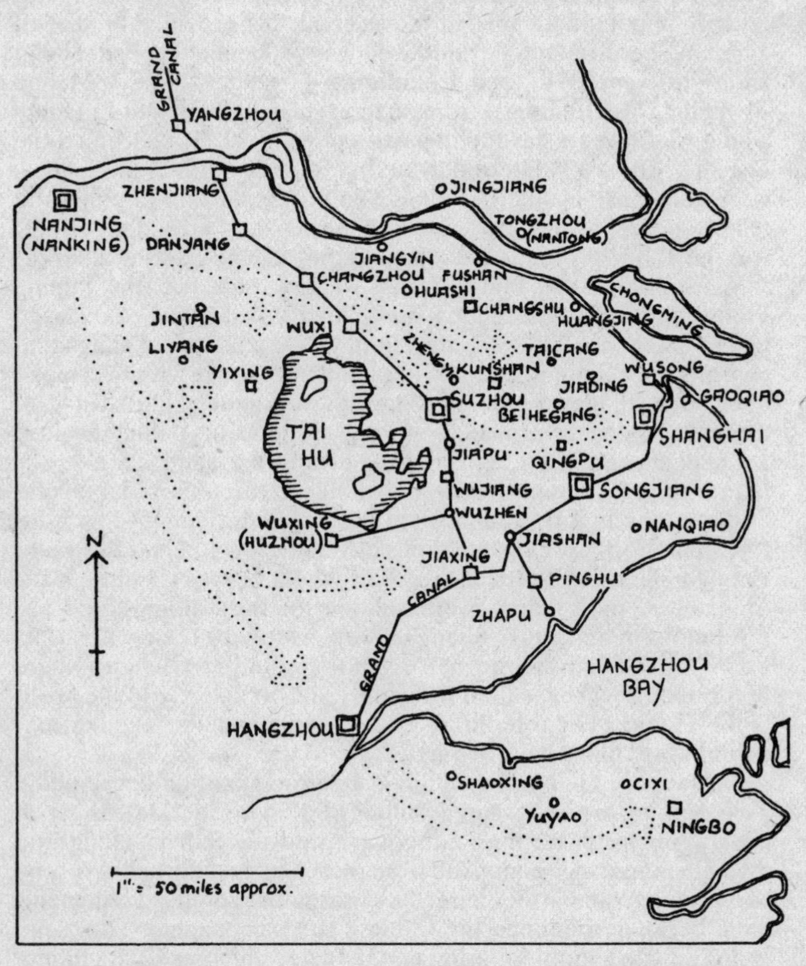

EVER-VICTORIOUS ARMY: FIELD OF CAMPAIGN

A week later Ward went on to trounce them at Nanqiao, south of Shanghai. For this action he was promoted to brigadier-general of the imperial army and his force was honoured with the title 'Ever-Victorious Army'. Sir Charles Staveley then set out to maintain a liberated territory with a radius of thirty miles from Shanghai clear of Taipings. A body of twenty young volunteers from the Settlement community formed the Volunteer Mounted Rangers and reconnoitred the country reporting on the movements of the enemy, while a mixed force defended the area.

The peculiar difficulties of operating in terrain so broken up by canals, irrigation channels and dykes led in May to Captain Charles Gordon, Royal Engineers, still at Tianjin, being summoned to Shanghai. A man of action with nothing to do in the north, he and a friend had explored the Great Wall of China from Kalgan (Zhangjiakou) to near Taiyuan, in a journey taking two months. Now as Commanding Engineer in Jiangsu, while the action switched to Ningbo again, he played a prominent part in the defence of Shanghai. As soon as he could move about in the zone, he personally visited and studied, as he claimed, 'every town and village in the thirty mile radius'.[13] He thought the worst was over and had no notion that before the end of the Taiping movement it would reveal 'so venomous a sting in its tail'. (During this lull first the Parkers and then Meadows arrived at Shanghai.) Exasperated by his defeats the Zhong Wang tried again.

The Ningbo front[14] *1862*

The winter following the fall of Ningbo to the Taipings was exceptionally cold with deep snow after a great storm. If it increased the hardships of the tens of thousands of refugees, it limited the forays of the rebels into deep country and so spared the lives of some civilians. But many more refugees even in the hills were hounded down, and everywhere the people were taxed exorbitantly. Those who did not pay up lost either their head or their house. Resentment boiled over and at one point in the West Pass the people took up arms, in February, and defeated a marauding force. Savage reprisals inevitably followed and the rebels utterly destroyed one town of ten thousand inhabitants.

With the coming of spring the Taipings in Ningbo became more unruly. Some even crossed the river to the foreign Settlement, flouting orders to return. Daily acts of violence in the city showed what could be expected. Knowing of the end of neutrality and the setback suffered by their armies in Jiangsu, in April the Ningbo rebels became menacing towards the foreign community. Consul Harry Parkes decided that the time had come to act. Security depended on clearing the rebels from the Chinese city. John Burdon left on April 14 to go to Peking with Bishop George Smith and from Shanghai wrote to Hudson Taylor on April 29 saying,

> At Ningpo things are looking very black. The villages present a fine field for labour, but unfortunately the interference of the English and French with the Rebels at Ningpo is expected very soon, and this gives us all a feeling of insecurity in going into the country . . .[15]

But already the Taipings had precipitated trouble. On April 23 a rebel chief arrived from Nanking and saluted the Settlement by putting ball-shot through the rigging of British and French ships. On the 26th six Allied warships arrived in the river, Captain Roderick Dew RN commanding three British frigates with two French gunboats in support.[16]

Parkes offered terms to the Taipings. They rejected them with scorn, putting a price of a hundred dollars on every foreigner's head. From May 1 a night attack on the Settlement was expected and the missionaries joined in night watches. The frigates moved upriver to lie between the Salt Gate and the Settlement (map. p 22). Dr Parker's hospital and house on the river bank below the city walls lay empty in no-man's-land. On their arrival in Shanghai he and his new wife had been advised to wait there for better conditions before going on to Ningbo.

About a hundred Allied fighting men faced thousands of Taipings,[17] and only by taking the initiative and dictating the course of action did they stand a chance of success. On the evening of May 10 Captain Dew reported to 'Vice Admiral Sir James Hope, Commander in Chief, East India and China', in a choice example of Victorian sang-froid,

> Sir, – I found it necessary to capture the city of Ningpo and drive the rebels out . . . This morning at ten o'clock the Kestrel and the French vessels *Etoile* and *Confucius* were fired on . . .

His own ship *Encounter* cleared for action and 'a volley of musketry was fired on us from the bastion abreast' – the city wall. *Encounter*, *Ringdove*, *Kestrel* and *Hardy* then shelled the walls, batteries and Salt Gate at point blank range,

> which was replied to with much spirit from guns and small arms . . . [By noon] having silenced the guns and knocked down the battlements, exposing the top of the wall . . . where I intended to scale, I ceased firing and went to dinner.

At two p m he installed a party of marines under a midshipman in a house commanding the walls – the Parkers' house – and readied scaling ladders. Joined by the senior French naval officer, a lieutenant, and his marines, and covered only by a gunner helped by cooks and stewards on *Encounter*, 'I scaled the walls, meeting with a most determined resistance.' The French lieutenant, one of the first on the wall, was dangerously wounded, but they took the Salt Gate.

NINGBO'S WEST GATE, A WATER GATE
(The view seen on p 310 was from the wall above this gate)

Hardy, *Kestrel* and *Confucius* were ordered to cut away 'the bridge of boats' near the East Gate and the junction of rivers, and to shell the South and West Gates. At four p m this was done 'under a galling fire'. Acting-Lieutenant E C Tinling and a boatswain landed on the bridge and spiked the defending guns while an assistant engineer cut the chains letting the pontoons drift apart, and so opened the bridge. While the Taipings were trying to retake the Salt

Gate, Captain Dew moved upstream and the city walls were scaled near the North Gate and the gate itself taken.

At five p m the Taipings, alarmed by these flank attacks, called off all opposition and fled.

> From the masthead the rebels were seen to leave the city, so I returned to the Salt Gate, placed the *Taotai* and Imperial soldiers, who now landed from their junks, in charge of the city, and re-embarked our own . . . people.

Captain Dew then detailed the prowess of his men. It was 'a narrow river with a spring tide running' yet 'the manner they worked their vessels and . . . guns (under fire from the walls) is beyond all praise'. But three of his men were killed and twenty-three wounded, ten severely. Mentioned in despatches and promoted to full lieutenant was E C Tinling. Captain Dew continued,

> Considering the vermin nature of these rebels, I felt that if one blow was not followed by another, most serious consequences might result to the foreign settlement and . . . our very safety rested on the capture of the city . . . The delight displayed by the Chinese at the fall of the city . . . was something extraordinary; throughout the day the bank of the river opposite the city was one sea of heads, and though round shot and bullets flew plentifully among them they never moved.

The admiral's despatch to the Admiralty on May 17 reported that,

> Two hundred of Colonel Ward's Chinese troops detached for the protection of the foreign settlement arrived the day after the action, and 500 more have since been despatched, which will constitute a garrison sufficient to ensure the safety of the city.

By then he had a low view of the Taipings as soldiers but he was not mistaken.

Among Hudson Taylor's papers is an incomplete copy of a letter dated May 12, 1862, probably from Mrs E C Lord, formerly Mrs Bausum.

> The city was taken at about three o'clock by about a hundred men, and the rebels have fled by thousands out of the West Gate. The city is now in the hands of the former rulers who, I fear, will be as little able to govern it as the Rebels and have the good of the people as little at heart. – We think we do already see a difference in the people. Since the rebels came they are more attentive to the Gospel when it is spoken to them and many are seriously beginning to think of their salvation.

Tuesday. Fresh alarm. The Rebels have made a strong hold of Tzeki [Cixi], a walled city about ten miles from Ningpo, the people are running thence for their lives. Perhaps they will try to make an attack on the North bank [the Settlement], and they might come down in a night, but our trust is in God. But having been driven out of Ningpo by foreigners the rebels are doubtless greatly enraged against them. Mr. Lord has more than two hundred refugee rebels to take care of, whom he has rescued from the cruel hands of the revengers, [the imperial troops]. They are most of them new rebels . . . compelled to become rebels by their captors. Every man must have his head shaved now, or he would not carry it on his shoulders for an hour. A week ago it was death to shave the head. What it will be a week hence who can tell? How suitable the 91st. Psalm for such times as these!

Thursday morning. All yesterday there was a dreadful excitement among the people. The Rebels took Tzeki and seem to have burned it and killed all the people they found there, even little children. There was no escape but by running and the multitudes that fled to Ningpo spread the alarm so that every countenance seemed to gather blackness. Last night and this morning it seems quiet . . .

On May 26 missionaries began working in the city again and Arthur Moule moved back into his home, but the tension persisted. The Taipings were firmly established in Yuyao and Fenghua as well as Cixi, with the city of Shaoxing, between them and Hangzhou, as their headquarters. There they stayed until August, while Ningbo trembled. Seventy-thousand refugees – fleeing from their own government troops as well as the Taipings – somehow packed into the international Settlement.[18]

With the more hopeful turn in events at Ningbo, first Dr and Mrs Parker and then James and Martha Meadows arrived from Shanghai. A steam-packet company with ten or a dozen steamers had started to ply between all ports from Canton to Tianjin and Japan. It was June 15 when they reached Ningbo and were plunged into the tensions and horror stories of the rebel occupation and expulsion. Only a week later James Meadows poured out his heart to Mr Bell, his Methodist class leader and confidant at Barnsley.

I have just got up from my knees. I have been weeping at the feet of Jesus because I cannot learn the dialect quick enough. Tens of thousands of souls are perishing all around me, and I cannot tell them about the Saviour. . . . I have found no one yet with whom I could [talk] as I could with you; but I know Jesus to speak to.

Hardly had they arrived in Ningbo than Martha Meadows was taken dangerously ill. When he wrote she was recovering, but both were homesick and suffering from the strangeness of everything. As they did the rounds of the missionaries, at his own request he was introduced as a Scripture Reader. His relative lack of education put him at a disadvantage and this description acknowledged that he was different from the rest of them. Martha wrote on June 30 to Hudson Taylor's mother,

> It is well for me that Mrs Jones is homely[19] and condescends to persons of low estate, else I should be most miserable, not being able to enter into the conversation of the ladies at Ningpo . . . (But I have been received everywhere with kindness.)

And James approved of the way the missionary community met to pray – 'They do not pray long and they pray very simply.' The hard realities of life purged them of stilted rhetoric.

On August 11 Captain Roderick Dew mounted an attack with a mixed force on Yuyao, forty miles west of Ningbo and took it, with the loss in action of Lieutenant Tinling, driving the rebels farther away and denying Cixi to them. Following the Shanghai pattern, Whitehall in its remoteness ordered that a thirty-mile free zone be established around Ningbo also. But how, with a handful of marines and sailors, could it be done? During July a Franco–Chinese contingent had been formed and took part in the Yuyao action. But on August 26 Shanghai was again under threat and further reinforcements could not be expected.

Uninhibited by all this, Mr and Mrs Lord were going ahead with preparations to build their new orphanage and school, so greatly needed. Estimates and plans preoccupied Mr Lord in a letter of August 28, but his wife's postscript on September 1 was closer to the scene and full of woes. 'The cholera has been making great ravages in the North,' she said – C J Hall buried in a common grave with two others; another missionary and his child, and the veteran Dr Culbertson dead from cholera in Shanghai. Though this refrain was so familiar, it always tugged at their hearts. Probably Martha Meadows' illness was of the same nature. Since little Louisa Jones died, both John and the new baby had been very unwell, but John managed to write to Hudson Taylor asking again why he did not return. He himself could not keep going, he could not care for the church members as a pastor should, and James Meadows was very much a novice.

On September 15 James wrote to Hudson Taylor. He was slowly getting the language. He was going to read a few remarks at the Ningbo octagonal pagoda (*ba-go-ta*) that evening. But John Jones' health was so impaired that he and his family had gone out to Tindong in the country on the safe side of Ningbo for a change of air, and James was trying to conduct daily morning and evening prayers and Sunday worship. He was reading the romanised Scriptures and prayers but not preaching. It was all a painful experience but profitable. He and Martha had settled in at the patched up Bridge Street house in mid-August. Alas, she was making only slow progress, picking up a little Chinese from her serving woman.

> This is a great trial because I am so desirous that we should as man and wife glorify God as we ought to do. [He was not content for her not to be a working missionary too] . . . she has no desire for studying and yet she longs for the language . . . she cannot buckle to and give herself to it . . . You (and Maria and Wang Lae-djün) are continually mentioned in the prayers of these Chinese converts.

But the respite was over. Three days later, on September 18 the rebels took Cixi again and were also marching on Ningbo from the south. The next day a large market town five miles away and many more villages were in flames. As they came they slaughtered, and a tidal wave of refugees fled before them. The same day a message from Ningbo reached John and Mary Jones at Tindong to warn them of the danger. But it was the 22nd before they were in Ningbo. A fortnight previously Mrs Parker had given birth to her first child, a son, but as it was too risky for the Joneses to be in the Chinese city she took them in, her home being outside the Salt Gate where they could easily cross the river to the Settlement. James and Martha stayed at Bridge Street. On the 20th one hundred thousand rebels were reported advancing from the southern pass. Country Christians who hid in water among reeds for three days reported that the tramp of rebels past them (presumably single file on those trails) continued unbroken for sixteen hours.

In Ningbo anxiety and hope together tore at people's emotions, for Townsend Ward himself had arrived on September 18 to lead his detachment of seven hundred men of the Ever-Victorious Army. With Captain Dew's small force he lost no time in moving against the rebels at Cixi and on the 21st took the town by assault. But 'during the escalade' Ward was 'mortally wounded'.[20] Brought back to Parker's hospital he soon died. The imperial forces are strangely absent from accounts of those days, but it is likely that they reoccupied Cixi. The threat to Ningbo city then became extreme and Captain Dew set up his command at the most vulnerable point, the West Gate, while the imperial garrison manned the walls elsewhere.

James Meadows' letters were often reminiscent of Marco Polo's journal, 'Now what I am going to tell you is the truth . . . I must mention the mosquitoes . . . there are lots of snakes and rats where we live.'

On September 22 he had plenty of time to write to Mr Bell,

> We are surrounded by the Rebels . . . There being only one gate permitted to be open, it was sad work for the gate-keepers. You could see the people fleeing from the country to the City, and from the city to the country . . . nearly every woman you meet is really a cripple [with bound feet] and walks just like a little boy . . . on stilts.
>
> Martha feels rather scared; I myself have felt a little anxious at night; but as soon as I look to the Lord, He gives me grace to surmount the fears and doubts; and sometimes I have felt as though I would die like a martyr shouting out 'Glory to God' . . . The people with their beds and household affairs were crushing through the gate . . . I did so long to speak to them . . .
>
> Today is the 23rd and the rebels have not hurt us yet, bless the Lord . . . I saw today on the opposite bank . . . of the river, ten or twelve persons with . . . what they were able to carry . . . all huddled together . . . the shelter they were under being scarcely sufficient to prevent the rain beating in their faces. As I passed them I felt I could shoot every rebel in the kingdom. I believe since foreign power has driven them out of Ningpo that they will show no quarter to any European whether missionaries or others . . . Captain Dew, Commander, by the bye is a very nice gentlemen, and favourable to missionaries.[21]

The next day the rebels were at the South Gate and James confessed he was feeling anxious. Writing to Hudson Taylor that day he doubted whether John Jones would live to see England again. After the scare was all over he lamented his own irritability and uselessness. 'I am such a poor help to him at present that I feel sometimes quite annoyed and grieved with myself and everyone else . . .'

The same day, September 24, Mrs Lord wrote to Maria. After so long and such intimacy, in the Victorian manner it was still 'My dear Mrs. Taylor'. There was no hope of the Jones family travelling home in the winter but by the spring John would be given medical advice to go 'should he live so long'. Mrs Lord had been out to Tindong to see them and on her way back,

> the canals were everywhere filled with boats crowded with *Man ming* [Manchus] and it was told us that the Rebels were within ten *li* [three and a half miles] of Ningpo city, and when I got home I found a bad state of excitement tho' the Panic had somewhat subsided as all the war steamers in the river had gone up [to Cixi]. The enemy was expelled that city and the Steamers returned to their former position, bringing back with them the famous General Ward mortally wounded – he was carried to Dr. Parker's but died on the same or following day. The Rebels are now threatening the city of Ningpo, and there has been a continual stream of wretched people passing our house . . . ever since nine o'clock last night . . . The rain was falling in torrents and the wind blew so hard . . . it was a pitiful sight to see these crowds . . . of every age . . . fleeing for their lives . . . '*Dza-kyih-lah ni*?' [Where is there to go?] is the continual question, and indeed this seems to be the beginning of the end . . . Oh, how much better it would have been for this poor people if the foreign powers had let the rebels alone, or cultivated friendly relations with them. They might have taught them how to govern, and the people might have prospered under their rule,but there is a diversity of opinion here on the subject, but one thing they must all allow that our prospects are worse than they have been – foreign and Chinese alike in danger now, as to missionary work you may guess as to how that goes on – I got a class of seven women yesterday but I suppose that today I could not get two to listen to anything but '*Dzang Mao*' [long-hairs].

A BRIDGE AT CIXI
(by courtesy of CMS op. cit.)

> Yesterday I kept their attention and interest pretty well by choosing that passage 'Fear not them that kill the body, etc' . . . Part of the South and West Suburbs have again been burned or otherwise destroyed by order of the imperialists.

On the 25th she went on,

> The people are still in a fearful state of excitement, and there is no doubt that the rebels are very near tho' nothing seems to be certainly known. The storm has been increasing all day, yet the people have been fleeing with all their portables . . . and all faces seem to gather paleness . . . by believing too little of Chinese reports we may be surprised by the rebels . . . but I do not indulge in fears . . .[22]

In fact the storm may have saved the city, for the rebels' hatred of fighting in the rain was notorious.

James Meadows noted on that day, 'Captain Dew placed some of his men on the wall last night for the first time.' Martha was ill again and fainted, the rebels were close, there was no doctor in the city, it was raining, and

> all these things I say rushing upon my mind rather frightened me . . . I prayed to the [Lord] while I stood, Martha came round, I washed her head in cold water . . . and we got to bed, enjoyed a good night's rest . . . have lived throughout the day up to the present moment – safe and sound.

It was strange to the Chinese, he went on, that Captain Dew should leave the safety of his man-of-war and large roaring cannon and sleep in the city. Then more of Ward's troops arrived, so the anxiety was over! The odds had become a thousand, plus the imperial garrison, against a hundred thousand.

> [George Moule] has been to our house twice, offering us if we feel isolated or anxious, apartments at their house. I can assure you it dropped like butter and honey on our souls, although we respectfully declined it. He and his dear wife have already enough to be anxious about.

Mrs Lord continued her letter to Maria on the 30th.

> The panic seems to have subsided in some measure, it is reported that the rebels have retired to a distance . . . Yesterday I had a great number of these Man ming [Manchu] women in our little chapel brought by the neighbours expressly to hear the gospel. [Then on October 3] Orders have been brought from England, to keep the Rebels from the ports of China *thirty miles*. Query, where is the

> force? However if they do so I may yet be able to build a school house.

Irrepressibly she bought a stock of rice very cheaply to provide for the orphaned schoolgirls. And her faith was rewarded. James Meadows on the same day added a postscript for Hudson Taylor, 'We are safe from the Rebels when this letter was posted.'

All through October the Taipings invested Ningbo, but showed no stomach for assaulting the city or Settlement. So the Ever-Victorious Army contingent returned to Shanghai and Captain Dew was not sorry, 'for Ward's men robbed and "squeezed" with great industry'.

Charles Gordon's biographer, Archibald Forbes, observed,

> Ward had gained a strange ascendancy over Europeans, as well as Chinese, by his cool and daring courage . . . but his ambition was boundless; and perhaps it was well for the Imperial Government of China that he was removed at this stage of the Rebellion.

But Hosea Ballou Morse took pains to show that the accusation of schemes for personal aggrandisement was unproved.[23]

Throughout the countryside instead, the Taipings' 'reign of terror' as foreigners called it, dragged on with massacre and mutilation, seemingly never enough to sate the rebels. Dr Parker had no respite.

> My hospital has been constantly full since my return. It is now full of wounded people from the surrounding country . . . without distinction of age or sex . . . wounded in a most horrid manner.

His Christian male nurses gave up their own beds to accommodate more victims, and slept on the floor.

The death of Townsend Ward was a blow to the Manchu government. They were under no illusions as to how much they owed to him. An imperial decree said the emperor was 'filled with admiration and grief' over it. The Peking Court ordered that altars be erected to his memory at Songjiang and Ningbo. At Songjiang, where Ward was buried, the edict was obeyed and Confucian rites with the burning of incense were continued as long as the dynasty lasted, for his capture of Songjiang marked the turning point in the campaign against the Taipings. But at Ningbo, not because his victory at Cixi was unimportant but because the American chargé d'affaires, a missionary, intervened, such veneration was avoided.

Robert Hart in Peking advised the Privy Council that a memorial tablet would be enough.[24]

At long last successes against the Taipings on the Jiangsu front drew substantial numbers of them away from Ningbo. But Hangzhou remained in their hands until April 1864, eighteen anxious months away. They directed their devastating attentions southward to Fujian instead, while for the present Shaoxing, too close for comfort, continued as their springboard.[25]

Gordon and the Ever-Victorious Army[26] *1862–63*

Shanghai in the summer of 1862 was enjoying a precarious peace, precarious in four senses. A narrow rebel-free zone remained more or less inviolate so long as the Zhong Wang considered the odds weighted against him, but no one could tell when he would move again. He did so on August 26 and penetrated to within two miles of the Settlements, at that time still separated into French, British and American sections. Driven off, his armies remained menacingly along the zonal periphery.

Inside the Settlements nearly a quarter of a million Chinese, not all of them refugees and therefore potentially dangerous, outnumbered the sixteen hundred Europeans. Yet this imbalance enjoyed a durability based on mutual dependence. The Chinese welcomed the presence of an enclave where they were safer than under the shifting imperial or Taiping control, even if paradoxically their legal status was that of aliens tolerated under extraterritorial rights.[27]

At the back of people's minds lay the third threat, the presence of Russian imperialism in the China sea. The Tsar's Far Eastern fleet roved freely between Vladivostok and South China. The ugly Crimean War was a recent memory, and the annexations in Manchuria showed how Russia's thinking lay. Within a few months in 1863 when the end of the rebellion was in sight, Russia offered Li Hong-zhang ten thousand troops to complete the work.[28] He saw that they could be more difficult to handle than the rebels, especially after victory, and declined.

A fourth enemy at Shanghai lay in an outbreak of disease among the refugees and residents. Smallpox, cholera and typhus carried off many Chinese and Europeans, among them missionaries. British troops and seamen fared badly in the summer, through their traditionally unsuitable clothing, housing and food. Serge was the uniform, so serge had to be worn whatever the debilitating cost in health. E C Bridgman (1863) and Bishop Boone (1864) were buried in the old cemetery, but by 1863 a new cemetery had had to be opened. The Shanghai of Hudson Taylor's 1854–55 experiences was submerged in new developments. Suburbs and extensions of the Settlement boundaries lay well beyond what used to be the racecourse. In 1863 the Americans and British amalgamated their sectors under joint authority, sharing the defence which tended to fall haphazardly to whichever concession might be attacked. But in 1862 when Captain Charles George Gordon arrived from Tianjin anything could still happen overnight.

At first as a subordinate of Sir Charles Staveley, he was faced with the task of clearing the waterways and walled cities of Taiping rebels. The campaign to keep a rebel-free zone with a thirty-mile radius had met with serious reverses, but with young Gordon in command, first Qingpu to the south-west, (where Ward had been wounded and Forrester captured), and then in October Jiading to the north-west (which Staveley had abandoned) were stormed and taken. When he began, the common people were dying of starvation. After these victories he could write, over-optimistically, '. . . the people have now settled down . . . and I do not anticipate the rebels will ever come back; they are rapidly on the decline . . .'

When Townsend Ward died in September and his second-in-command, Colonel Forrester, declined to succeed him in command of the Ever-Victorious Army, Li Hong-zhang seized his opportunity to bring Ward's boisterous and unruly force under his own control. In October he replaced Ward with his lieutenant, the even more unscrupulous soldier of fortune, Henry Andrea Burgevine, whose father had served as an officer under Napoleon. But Burgevine was soon at loggerheads with 'Governor Li' and after routing the Taipings at Beihegang (Paihokang) (map, p 292) he became intolerable. In January 1863 Li dismissed him and begged Sir Charles Staveley to appoint a regular army officer to the command of the irregular force of desperadoes. Staveley had to refer the matter to London, strongly recommending Gordon, now a major, but put his own chief of staff in temporary command. This Captain Holland attacked Taicang, beyond Jiading, and was disastrously defeated with the loss of officers, men and guns.

So when Gordon, just turned thirty, took over at Songjiang on March 25, 1863, it was a dispirited, rebellious force to tame and lead. With a buoyant temperament and the ability to find humour in serious situations he also possessed an intuitive dominance of personality over other men, and a temper with a low flash point.

> . . . if I had not accepted the command [he wrote home] the force would have broken up . . . anyone who contributes to putting down this rebellion fulfils a humane task, and . . . tends a great deal to open China to civilization.

Li Hong-zhang was impressed, as his diary revealed:

> I hate all these foreigners, but it would not be wise to let them know. It is not the men personally that I dislike, it is their air of wonderful superiority. Each and every one sings the same song, 'I will do this and I will do that . . . you must let me have my own way and not interfere.' [But he was prepared to make an exception in favour of Gordon.] It is a direct blessing from heaven, I believe, the coming of the British Gordon. He is superior in manner and bearing to any of the foreigners I have come into contact with and does not show outwardly that conceit which makes most of them repugnant in my sight. Besides, while he is possessed of a splendid military bearing, he is direct and business-like.

The Ever-Victorious Army under Gordon's control consisted at different times of three thousand to five thousand Chinese under one hundred and fifty foreign 'officers'. Seeing the poor physique of many, he began to recruit picked men from Taipings whom he captured – not a difficult feat as he paid his men well. And he dealt firmly with the insubordination and in-fighting among both men and officers, many of whom wanted Burgevine, until Gordon proved his superiority. Never sparing himself personal exposure in dangerous situations, his example inspired the force. For instead of carrying arms, like Ward he substituted a cane and personally led the assaults. His 'magic wand of victory' and apparently charmed life spurred his men to courage and energy which the rebels could not match. Appointed brigadier-general in the imperial army, he always signed himself 'Major, RE' and refused to be addressed as 'General' or to accept emoluments.

A week after taking command he daringly set the pace and raised the siege of Changshu, thirty miles farther to the north-west, by attacking Fushan from two steamers on the Yangzi. A month later Taicang, defended by ten thousand men, fell to his assault with fewer than three thousand. Between the strikes he energetically trained his men for the next, and brought in volunteers from the British regular army to add reliability among his officers. Maintaining his momentum and displaying the ingenuity for which he became renowned, he swept on, capturing the rebels' arsenal at Kunshan and threatening Suzhou itself. There Burgevine, in the service of the Taipings this time, failed to outwit him, and Gordon secured the surrender of the local rebel leaders (*see* Appendix 3).

Then occurred 'an act that sent a thrill of indignation through civilization'.[29] Gordon had stipulated that the eight Taiping leaders' lives be spared and the Chinese general assured him that Li Hong-zhang had declared an amnesty. Gordon rode into the city to see personally that they were all right. He found them about to mount their horses to ride out to Governor Li. They too assured him that all was well. Shortly afterwards he came upon their terribly butchered bodies on the canal bank and 'was enraged beyond bounds'. In his steamer *Hyson*, and on foot, revolver in hand he hunted for Li Hong-zhang, by then Governor-General of the two Jiang provinces and titular Viceroy of Nanjing, to avenge his own honour and the lives of the rebel princes. Governor Li evaded him. So, thwarted, Gordon in fury withdrew all his men to Kunshan and held them there until January 1864, to guarantee the security of Suzhou and Shanghai. Later Li Hong-zhang took full responsibility for the assassinations, pleading that Peking would have demanded his own head in lieu of the Taipings'. And he told Robert Hart to 'tell Gordon that this is China, not Europe'.

Li Hong-zhang was rewarded with one of the highest military ranks in the empire, Junior Guardian of the Heir Apparent, and its accompanying Yellow Jacket. But he praised Gordon's prowess and the Court – meaning Prince Kong, Yong Lu, Ci Xi (Yehonala) and others representing the child emperor – ordered that a new imperial decoration be struck and a gift of ten thousand taels of silver (about three and a half thousand pounds in 1863) be bestowed on him. He thus became the first recipient of the Order of the Imperial Dragon, forty years later restyled the Order of the Double Dragon, equivalent to the British CB, Companion of the Bath.[30] 'As for the honours,' Gordon wrote home, 'I do not value them at all, and never did.' And to the emperor he replied in righteous indignation but respectful address, '. . . that, owing to the circumstances which occurred since the capture of Suchow, he is unable to receive any mark of His Majesty the Emperor's recognition . . .'

Inactivity inevitably bred discontent in the hot-blooded Ever-Victorious Army. And seeing their chief opponent immobile, the Taiping movement began to recover hope. More foreign mercenaries joined their ranks and the imperialist armies were barely holding their own. Robert Hart, appointed in November as Inspector-General of the Imperial Maritime Customs after the dismissal of Horatio Lay, tried personally to prevail upon Gordon to reconsider his attitude for the sake of the threatened people of China, without success.[31] But the year 1863 ended with new hope of a change of mind in this man to whom all were looking.

The very stuff of saints *1862–63*

Against the glamorous backdrop of the Ever-Victorious Army's Jiangsu campaign and the brooding menace of the rebels at Hangzhou and Shaoxing, life in Ningbo slowly returned to normal. Impressed by the failure of the idols to keep their own heads on their shoulders – for images and the deities they represented were seldom distinguished from each other in the people's minds – and by the action of the foreigners in the crisis, the populace was open as never before to the gospel. Dr Parker told how the distress of the people called forth such sympathy from the foreign community, especially the missionaries, that a response of gratitude rebounded on them. He was expecting his brother to join him in Ningbo, in private medical practice,[32] but this was the moment for speaking to the wounded hearts of China's millions. Where were the men and women to do it? The depleted missionary staff did what they could to seize the opportunities, but like the Meadows several of them were newcomers without the language.

John Jones was too ill to do much more than advise the Bridge Street Christians, and James Meadows was left to his own devices. He was learning the hard way but in such a manner that, like Hudson Taylor, he was to know China and the Chinese from personal experience. He loved their astuteness. What he was about to go through contributed directly to the birth of the China Inland Mission.

Meadows had found ten boys for his personal language teacher to teach while he himself was otherwise employed. But his own financial position was worrying him. He thought he was looking to God alone for all he needed, but

> when I went . . . to see Mr. Jones, he told me that you had sent him word [and . . . money] to give me 36 dollars a month. Well I was sorry, grieved, annoyed and yet thankful and pleased rather, because you

> never said anything of that nature to me at home, nor in any of your letters . . .[33]

John Jones had inadvertently leaked a confidential arrangement, for while Hudson Taylor could give no promises he fully intended to do all he could for his new colleague, remembering his own hardships. He too was learning the interrelationship of faith and faithful stewardship as he read what Meadows went on to say,

> You asked me . . . if I could trust in the Lord and not put my trust in an arm of flesh. I said yes . . . therefore I told [my relatives and friends] that I was to receive no stipulated salary but what the Lord sent me from any quarter . . . I believe some of them feel rather uneasy about me . . . so don't you see Sir what I mean. If I had known what I know now I should have told them that I was to have a sufficient sum of money every month to live upon . . .

Would Mr Taylor please tell Mr Bell and the family how things stood. It was a letter that hardly mentioned the rebel situation. But a fortnight later he wrote at length to his brother and sister, largely on domestic matters. Pork was twopence a pound, goat-meat eightpence, beef like leather fourpence, but venison very cheap. Life was difficult and dangerous but, 'I am here and here I mean to stick as long as the Lord deem fit.' To Hudson Taylor he wrote again asking him to send two pounds to Martha's mother, to be deducted from his next remittance. 'I would not ask you, sir, I can assure you, were it not that you have given me so much every month to live upon . . .'

But he also had sad news to convey. Dr Parker's infant son had died the day before, December 17, of encephalitis. His wife was being comforted from the Scriptures *by Chinese Christians*, Parker wrote home emphatically with a note of joy. And John Jones was very ill indeed, unfit to wait for the spring before sailing for home. In January when Meadows wrote again he said how distressed Mary Jones was over her husband's condition. John himself, expecting to die, was peacefully unconcerned except for her. But now Meadows himself was ill with fever and jaundice – Hudson Taylor's incapacitating disease.[34]

On Saturday afternoon, January 31, 1863, Dr Parker[35] rode over to the Chinese Military Hospital. His way back lay across a narrow canal between steep stone walls, one of many intersecting the city. To allow for boats passing beneath the bridges they were mostly arched works of art in ancient stone, paved with great slabs of

TYPICAL CITY CANAL AND BRIDGES, NINGBO
(by courtesy of CMS op. cit.)

granite. As he crossed on his horse, one of these slabs, 'shattered probably by cannon-shot' but to all appearances not unsound, gave way beneath his weight. Parker was thrown violently and fell into the icy water, imprisoned in great pain between the steep 'kerb-walls'. Before the passers-by bestirred themselves to pull him out he was cold through and through and in great pain.

As soon as he reached home he told his wife he believed he had received fatal injuries and at five p m when George Moule saw him he was 'in so much anguish from difficulty of breathing which quite prevented his speaking to me'. On account of his thick winter clothing there were few traces of an impact with the bridge parapet when he was thrown, but the 'mysteriously painful accident' was consistent with broken ribs penetrating his pleural cavity. Added to that was his long exposure and inhalation of the cold, foul water. In spite of this the assistant surgeons of HMS *Encounter* thought a few days would see him well again and recognised no danger until the Sunday night.

The Jones family were due to sail for England the following Saturday and staying with the Parkers, John now very ill indeed. At midnight on Sunday Mary Jones went to summon George Moule to Parker's bedside. He arrived to find him 'eyes closed, gasping for breath, his hand still locked in [his wife's] until he died at two a m'.

Parker was 'one whom we all regarded as the most indispensable man among us, so healthy, so cheerful as he was an hour before the accident . . . the last man we would have thought of dying so soon'. The only other qualified doctor in Ningbo was *Encounter*'s naval surgeon, apparently not on hand. But it was Parker's young widow whose baby had died only six weeks before, who amazed her friends by 'her marvellous self-forgetfulness in the midst of her deep, deep grief' as she thought of *their* needs.

Captain Dew placed two of *Encounter*'s boats at the missionaries' disposal to carry the coffin and mourners across the river from the hospital to the Settlement. And the officers, consuls and wealthy Chinese from the city attended the funeral on February 4. Two days later the Jones family sailed away, bravely 'expecting a pleasant voyage', followed soon by T Fleming of the CMS who was also dangerously ill. Another, the American Presbyterian Henry Rankin, was talking of going but went instead to Yantai and died there, 'the dear man'. Just when more missionaries were needed their ranks were being drastically reduced. Dr William Lockhart in his book, *The Medical Missionary in China* published in England in

1861, had already paid this tribute to Parker: 'He went out to China with the matured judgment of a man who had practised his profession for some time . . . [which was] one cause of his success as a medical missionary.'

Without John and Mary Jones for company in her loneliness, Mrs Parker chose to invite James and Martha Meadows to come and live with her at the hospital. They saw through to her motives, for Martha, six months pregnant and now without the doctor who had been so kind to her was finding the crude and draughty Bridge Street garret a hardship. Having arrived at Ningbo almost at the same time, barely nine months previously, the three of them had much in common – not least the fact that Mrs Parker was a spiritually-minded Christian.

> I have not heard a murmur [from her, Meadows told Hudson Taylor. She says] 'the Lord gave and the Lord hath taken away, blessed be the name of the Lord' . . . You should hear her letters read which she has sent home to the Doctor's children . . . I don't know how she choosed two such worms as us to go and live at her house, to be a sort of comfort to her in her loneliness.

But she was not the only one being kind to Martha. Several times James said, 'Mrs George Moule is like a mother to my wife . . . that kindness slays me it knocks me in the head before God . . .' They hardly needed to buy anything in preparation for their baby's arrival, 'the Lord and His people are so kind'. The two Moule brothers and their wives were

> the most brotherly and sisterly that I have met with as strangers. They don't say, Were you an influential person before you left home? have you had a classical education? but with them [it] is this, Do you belong to Jesus? – then we are your brother and sister.

He was reminded of Hudson Taylor's kindness to his father, who had just died, and to Martha's mother, sister and brother-in-law, newly-converted, thanking him for 'such self-denial for me and my father'.

But before they moved over to join Mrs Parker, James and Martha had a narrow escape. At two p m on the day after the Jones family sailed, fire broke out in Bridge Street. With a strong wind blowing towards their home they watched forty to fifty houses going up in flames one after the other, and quickly moved most of their possessions to safety. It was almost time for the Sunday afternoon meeting and many of the Christians had come.

> The wind blew strong flames right over towards our house, and you know how soon Chinese [wooden] houses will burn down and the fire run from one place to another . . . We prayed that the wind might change around, and also that a stop be put to the fire . . . The wind when the fire was at the canal's edge veered round a little . . .

so that sparks did not ignite their own house.

This was not the only experience that thrust the Meadows and the Chinese Christians closely into each other's company. While John Jones was in Ningbo he was the pastor of the Bridge Street church, though able to do little for them. When he left he prevailed upon E C Lord to take his place. Lord wrote to Hudson Taylor,

> He has left the care of his church and congregation with me. I told him I could not do *much* for them . . . my own work needed all my time and energies . . . If *you* cannot come you must try and send someone else.

Both Jones and Lord seemed to discount James Meadows. The period of linguistic ineptitude had reduced another good man to humbling impotence. To be overlooked by his colleagues was even more galling.

> This reminds me [Lord continued] that you have already a missionary or missionary assistant here. Bro. Jones has put me in the place in which you put him . . . [but] the position is a very delicate one . . .

It was 'delicate' in that as an outsider he could exert little discipline and make no changes. James and Martha Meadows as Methodists had been baptised as infants, [not as believers or by immersion] so even they were excluded from taking communion at Lord's Baptist church. Now Lord felt uncomfortable about their continuing to take communion at Bridge Street but took no action.

John Jones had been so ill and preoccupied with preparing for his journey that he had not written to the Taylors about the church and his arrangements for it. At that distance in thousands of miles and months in mail times it was out of the question for Hudson Taylor to know or advise about the situation in Ningbo.

The answer lay all the time in the undervalued James Meadows. His story is typical of the experiences of most of the young men and women Hudson Taylor sent or brought to China in the succeeding years. On March 4, 1863, he reported that he was speaking Chinese more freely – but cheered to think that it was simple enough not to be 'with enticing words' but 'by My Spirit' that the real work would be done. Apart from overseeing his little school he was working through his end of the city with tracts and Scripture, and every morning visiting the homes of the Christians with the ex-Buddhist leader whom he knew as 'Nyi-hyüong', Brother Ni. This showed them 'that they are thought of, and I am quite sure it is one way of uniting my heart with theirs and theirs with mine'.

At each home the neighbours crowded in and were impressed by seeing how respectfully the Christians treated each other. It was encouraging them to attend the chapel with the Christians. He was planning also to present well-bound New Testaments to the local mandarins. As an evangelist and pastor he was winning his right to recognition without help or supervision.

Before the end of March William Parker's brother, Dr John Parker, arrived, and the Meadows returned to Bridge Street. Much as they admired Mrs Parker, 'gracious living' was not for them. A few weeks of European conventions in her roomy foreign house made James value less than ever 'the comfortable dwelling places of other missionaries', he told Hudson Taylor.

> I would not have the trouble of so many things so long as I was a preacher of the gospel, no not for £10 a week, but mind you dear brother I feel very thankful to God that these things do not affect me . . . I long for you to be coming out here – make haste and do not tarry – If those gentlemen [the Methodist Free Church missionaries] come out, please do not send them to my place, because I have only one bed . . . and cannot accommodate them . . . not many missionaries like this house [but] the Lord has placed me here and I'll stay till I think God says shift . . .

A week later he wrote again. As he corresponded with Hudson Taylor his confidence and freedom to open his heart to him grew.

> The more I know or the more God gives me to know of the language the more love He gives me to his own dear cause and precious souls . . . I am tried with the inconsistencies of these Chinese who profess to love Jesus . . . really I would not like to be a pastor, I should break my heart: now sometimes rivers of water run down my cheeks because they so rebel against my blessed Lord . . . notwithstanding I believe some of them are as complete in Christ as I myself am.

He was thinking of renting a room in a village for preaching. He wanted to learn some medicine 'for I have a thirst for knowledge'. He bought 'a vegetable' to eat and was so 'struck with admiration' and filled with 'burning admiration at my Father's wisdom and skill', that he longed to read 'Natural History or Botany'. Back in London Hudson Taylor delighted in his progress and the Saturday prayer meeting supported him and the church with their prayers.

Then on April 20 Meadows cut short his letter saying he was ill and in pain. On May 4 he wrote again. Dr John Parker had diagnosed smallpox and taken Martha, in her eighth month of pregnancy, with him to the care of Mrs William Parker. Arthur Moule promised to come and stay with James if he became more ill. And Mr Lord was visiting him every day.

The effect on James was typical. Well enough to read in bed, he gained 'a greater devotion and love for the Word of God'. 'I see such an ocean in the Word of God to be explored that I am lost with delight sometimes, and I often think of Dear Brother Burger's advice "Attend to the Word of God."' He usually wrote 'Burgess'.

But the doctor was mistaken. He had to admit that it was chickenpox after all.

So they were soon back to normal. Since a rebuff in January, the joint Franco–Chinese force had captured Shaoxing in March and pushed the rebels right back to Hangzhou, so travel in the country-side was possible again. But the Bridge Street church seemed to Meadows to be falling to pieces, with a few cheering exceptions. The foreign mercenaries attached to the imperial army used such blasphemy and oaths that the Chinese in Ningbo were picking them up; wickedness was rife in the city. But 'That Mrs Tsiu, she is a manhunter Mr. Lord says' – a soul-seeker always on the go to bring people to Jesus. 'I am always glad to see that woman . . . she loves Christ.' Apart from E C Lord's Sunday visit Meadows himself was leading the daily services, morning and night, with the Christians' help. His grasp of the dialect was improving daily.

By then it was June and he could say, 'The gracious Lord has given my wife a safe delivery of a man-child.' He was wholly absorbed in his work, visiting wealthy Chinese in their homes and official quarters, and always courteously received. He took to discussing individual Christians' problems with Hudson Taylor, as much for his prayers as for advice. One was in partnership with an ungodly man, buying and selling pillaged furniture. Others had gone back to working on the Lord's Day and could not attend services. Hudson Taylor's good Wesleyan annotation beside this was 'Discipline needed'.

But although Meadows' Chinese was improving, only a faithful three or four would come to his Bible classes in July, and by August none at all. In the great heat all were prostrated. The canal behind the Bridge Street house was dry and stinking. James, Martha and the babe had to move into a part of Mr Lord's house. Mrs Lord was away, taking their children home to the States and Europe. The Moules and others were ill. Among the 'rowdies', the mercenaries especially, disease and death were rampant. News had come of John Jones' death at sea and James was not surprised. Missionary ranks were getting thinner and thinner when the gates were wide open for more and more to come in. E C Lord wrote in August to Hudson Taylor, 'You speak of coming back with a goodly company, but you say not *when*. You can hardly wonder that I feel a little anxious on this point.' His concern was probably to have accommodation ready for them. How many were 'a goodly company' anyway? But Hudson Taylor was not yet far enough on to be specific. Numerous offers to go to China, or even many fit to go, did not always mean that they would do so.

Then rain fell again and there was water at Bridge Street. James and Martha Meadows went home with their babe on Tuesday, September 1. On Friday Martha was dead, of 'Ningpo cholera'.[36] She was ill with an intestinal upset when they moved back on Tuesday but no one had suspected her of being in danger. Medicine from Dr Parker soothed her and the next day she was better. 'On Thursday she was very weak and seemed to be stupid and wandering in her talk a little, but I ascribed that to the medicine as it contained opium.' She was throwing herself about and James had difficulty in getting the baby breast-fed. Once in the night she called 'James', but at five a m he found her arms and face covered with cold perspiration.

> I was frightened something was wrong and ran immediately for the doctor, with all my might. The doctor came with me immediately, but, oh, my dear Brother, my beloved wife was dead before we reached her . . .
>
> The Lord has turned my Eden into a wilderness place. And has made me desolate. . . . She is gone, the living one is gone . . . She has entered into peace, she is at rest in her bed, and because, Lord, thou hast done it, I will be silent, Thou shalt find no murmurings in my heart at Thy ways . . . I want Thee to tell me why, so that I may know how to improve her death as Thou, my loving God wouldst have me.

Then he realised that he was writing a letter, not his journal, and apologised, 'for my heart is full, and I can always talk to my Father best at such seasons'.

The same night he wrote to Martha's mother and sister.

> The doctor was like a brother and cried aloud with tears running down his cheeks, and embracing me like a brother . . . my dear wife is in her coffin to be buried tomorrow, God willing. All is still around me, I am alone . . . God alone is with me . . . Today I wanted to go with her, and the devil suggested, 'poison yourself, God is merciful, He will overlook your murder and forgive your sin'. Now that would be just the way not to get to her in heaven . . . No, I shall see her again . . . therefore get thee behind me Satan.[37]

On and on he wrote, comforting *them* from the Scriptures, saying in Yorkshire Methodist parlance, in another note to her mother, 'An early death has been an early crown! Thou hast a child in heaven!'

Lessons in dependence[38] *1862–63*

Kindness surrounded James Meadows in his grief. Mrs George Moule took his child and cared for him, until Mrs Parker took over, to her own comfort. Her own child had died at exactly the same age. Arthur Moule undertook all Martha's funeral arrangements and sympathy flowed from Chinese friends. Martha had been slow to pick up enough language to feel at home among them but was beginning to find her feet when she died. Despondent about her at first, James had been looking forward to their sharing the work together. And now that 'very amiable and excellent woman' was no more and he was alone.

The funeral and the hire of a wet-nurse cost far more than he could afford. Suddenly he was penniless, and for two months could not pay the postage to write to the Taylors. On November 3 when he did so he explained his plight:

> all the riches in the world combined I would not esteem too much to be paid for her burial, but I am talking . . . of business matters [as man to man] . . . but the Lord who is faithful, and to whom I looked for daily food sent me daily bread from a quarter I least expected, namely my old servant woman, for she seeing that I had nothing to eat and no money to buy oil for the lamp . . . every day provided me with food. I never asked her, I rather discouraged her from doing so.

It was the latest episode in a running correspondence between them from which Hudson Taylor was learning as much as James

Meadows in Ningbo. Both believed implicitly that God as their heavenly Father would provide enough for subsistence, not more than they needed, while sometimes letting them say with the apostle Paul, 'I know both how to be abased, and I know how to abound: everywhere and in all things . . . both to be full and to be hungry, both to abound and to suffer need.' (*Phil. 4:1*). Meadows knew from life at Beaumont Street that Taylor had nothing to spare and could only send to him when funds came in. So he was wholly committed to dependence on God alone. In fact, that same November 17 Hudson Taylor wrote in his journal,

> We have now but a few shillings in hand, but God is faithful. [And four days later] Received in answer to many prayers, from Mr. Müller, £20, some of it needed for today's use.

But when John Jones had told James Meadows of the funds entrusted to him, to be passed on in monthly sums, James found it difficult to reconcile his faith with provision already made.

> My dear brother [he wrote early in 1863] I hope you will not be offended . . . but . . . owing to the manner I receive my money at present, I have been living from hand to mouth' [far more frugally than other missionaries. It was not that he wanted more, only] I should like my money in larger quantities at a time, so as to be able to buy in bulk supplies of firewood, flour, rice, oil, etc . . . [as an economy]. I should not have mentioned this to you but that you have given me a stated salary . . . I should have looked straight to God to do this for me . . .

Then he was anxious lest Hudson Taylor put a wrong interpretation on his requests, and wrote again to sort things out.

But Hudson Taylor understood, and was hearing from E C Lord too, that while Meadows had said nothing he, Lord, considered the supposed 'salary' rather small. The cost of living had nearly doubled since the Taylors were in Ningbo. But by then it was clear to Hudson Taylor that James Meadows had adapted well to China and was able to manage his own affairs; so to E C Lord's relief he began remitting whatever donations he received direct to Meadows. And he wrote a careful explanation of their real relationship. His comment was that Meadows

> seemed distressed by receiving it [the money] so regularly and sufficiently as if it was not compatible with leaning upon God alone. I explained to him in my reply that this was not the case, and that as

> neither he nor I had any promise of another farthing from anyone, we needed to look to the Lord to supply us as He saw fit.

Meadows was delighted. It was all as he had thought.[39] He asked Hudson Taylor to write and tell Mr Bell who would explain to James' and Martha's relatives, all poor people,

> because it will make him and all who know it pray more earnestly for me and my wife [still living when he wrote]. You know that if we are conscious of a man being provided for . . . our prayers are apt to become cold, but if they know that no man or men undertake to provide for a man then are they led out towards God . . .

He could hardly have put the principle more simply. The influence of James Meadows' strong faith in God as a father providing for his children, and his preference for this relationship rather than a 'salary' must be given full credit in the development of the principles of the mission of which he became the first member after John and Mary Jones and the Taylors.[40].

Meadows had been praying for five pounds to send to his family at home, who ironically in their poverty were critical of his moving into missionary circles like 'a perfect gentleman', not realising that he and Martha had felt ill at ease, unable to enter into their colleagues' life-style or conversations, for all their brotherliness. He himself was wanting to show concern for his relatives, to change their attitude. 'I would rather suffer myself than have the cause of Jesus evil spoken of.' Now two gifts of five pounds came from Hudson Taylor and Maria. James was grateful, but even more so for his saying, 'write to me in the confidence of Christian love'. He replied, 'May the Lord bless you for that word.' He had only a few days to wait for the opportunity to put such confidence to the test.

When he had recovered from his hepatitis and had asked Dr William Parker for his bill, he had answered, 'Oh, we'll send it in some day.' Without telling James Meadows he had then asked John Jones to send it to Hudson Taylor, whose 'agent' he supposed James to be. John Jones had reluctantly agreed but in his sickness told no one. After Martha's confinement and death James took the matter up again, but by then William Parker had died, and the total sum involved, he learned, was forty dollars, a large amount to him.

> I asked Mrs. Parker to give me the bill and that I would take it to my Father, adding that I believe my God was as willing to pay my doctor's bills as any society ever was to pay their missionaries' bills

> . . . Now the Lord has not disappointed me. He has sent me the money and I have paid it.

Apart from what Hudson Taylor had sent, he had received an anonymous gift of twenty dollars in Ningbo.

Going on to say how living and moving about among the Chinese and teaching the schoolboys was helping him considerably to acquire the language, he confided,

> I very seldom go to any foreigner's house . . . I cannot imagine how missionaries can think of laying up money. I hope as long as I have a heart . . . that I may never have such a desire. Oh my dear Sir, to see these poor creatures here with . . . their corrupt [ulcerated] legs, bodies all over sores and moreover half starved, is enough to make any man cast away the idea of ever laying up treasure on earth.

In August a gift of clothes arrived from the Taylors, and in November he learned that they had repeated their occasional gifts to his relatives, this time to his step-mother. He was effusive in his thanks 'for your unspeakable kindness'. But if Meadows could be generous out of his own penury, his friends' motives were the same. In July his gratitude was for relief in the prostrating summer heat.

> I esteem all God's mercies special, the day before yesterday I felt as grateful to God for the nice breeze and shower of rain that He kindly sent us in answer to prayer as ever I felt for any supply of money, but some will say 'Bosh' at that. It does not matter to me what others say. We pray and we get, we ask and we have.

And on New Year's Day, 1864, as he looked back over that sad eventful old year he acted on Hudson Taylor's invitation to be frank and speak his mind.

> If I were to say that I have not lacked I should tell lies, but I have lacked such things by God's good providence since my wife's death that would be esteemed by some folks indispensably necessary to their comfort and almost their existence. But before I was converted to God, I knew what it was to be full and also to suffer want, so such things as I have not had since my wife's death I could look upon with indifference.

Not to sound as if in need or to make Hudson Taylor uneasy about him, but 'being fully persuaded that "the Lord will provide"', he outlined his current expenses, the barest minimum,

> for as far as I can judge of you, you are a man that feels the wants of one whom you respect and love very keenly. And I also believe that out of pure desire to please God that you are afraid of cutting my bread either too thick or too thin. Well my God will guide you.

During January he sold Martha's possessions and used the proceeds until only two or three hundred cash remained. At that point another remittance arrived, for a hundred and four dollars. In telling Hudson Taylor of this, and thanking him and the others at Beaumont Street for their letters of sympathy, James answered his own question, Why did God have to take Martha? His spiritual buoyancy was far ahead of Hudson Taylor's in his comparable loneliness in Shanghai ten years earlier.

> I know why God afflicted me, 'That I might be a partaker of His holiness' . . . I feel very lonely sometimes and very much cast down about the [church] members . . . The Lord had upheld me I can assure you dear brother. The prayers at home and your prayers have not been in vain. Many times have I had these pages applied to my heart . . . 'Fear not, for thou art Mine; I have called thee by thy name', – 'When thou passest through the waters I will be with thee, and through the rivers, they shall not overflow thee . . .', 'For I am the Lord thy God . . . thy Saviour,' 'Fear not, for I will not fail thee, nor forsake thee.' Oh what joy, and strength, and sweetness there is in God's blessed Book. Ever since Mr Burger [*sic*] strongly recommended me to adhere to the book I have thought of it more . . . That Word, I wish it to dwell in me in all wisdom . . .

Reading these letters from the first missionary he sent out to China, Hudson Taylor took heart. Here was proof of the sterling value of the type of person he was looking for, proof that while accepting his leadership they could leave full responsibility for their livelihood and contentment with God.

Revision against odds[41] *January–April 1863*

In following the parallel course of events in China and as they affected Hudson Taylor, the story returns to Beaumont Street, London in January 1863, and a striking profile of his personality when under social pressures. With medical studies a thing of the past and his surgeons' confidence in him fully justified, he seems to have had the freedom of the hospital and medical college in which to teach F F Gough and the young men coming to him for training, from the denominational societies. Family life had to proceed amid all the coming and going. And predominant in its claim on time and energy because of his obligation to the Bible Society as well as his urge to provide Ningbo with the finished work, the revision of the Ningbo vernacular New Testament with Gough was intensified.

In the little journal he began keeping at this time Hudson Taylor recorded day after day the hours he and Gough spent on fresh revision and the chores of meticulous proof-reading as sheets came from Spottiswoode's. Six to eight hours a day was their norm, during which everything that could wait had to do so, as Meadows had found on his first visit. And then in the evenings they attended meetings for prayer or for preaching the gospel, entertained guests or wrote their letters. Interruptions of work frequently tried their patience, and to their mutual distress Taylor and Gough found it difficult to work together and then to pray together. Hudson Taylor recorded no explanation.

> Fri. 9th (Jan) Only 1½ at NT. Visit of 3 Bausums and Mr Fuller. [These were relatives, for Mrs. Lord (Bausum) was in Ningbo until March.] Saty 17th £10 from Mr. Müller – another answer to prayer for supplies of money and faith. Were also helped to get through some of the sheets of Mk. without unpleasantness [the first reference to friction]. [Monday 19th Revision] till 1 a.m. when I posted the corrected 1st Mk to printers. Revision 9 hours.

The next day was the fifth anniversary of their wedding in Ningbo. But 'Revision 8 hours' is recorded with his regrets that he had not made more of 'fellowship in the Lord' with Maria. On Sundays they attended worship at a Congregational church in Stepney under a Mr Kennedy or visited other churches, and taught Wang Lae-djün systematically from the Bible. 'Sunday 18th . . . With Lae-djün in the evening on reward by grace *according to* works from Mt XXV et al.'

In 1855 the Earl of Shaftesbury had sponsored the Religious Worship Act in an attempt to remove legal impediments to services in unconsecrated buildings, and at the beginning of the Evangelical Revival public meetings in leading London theatres, including Sadler's Wells and the Garrick, drew large crowds, as well as in the Exeter Hall, St Paul's Cathedral and Westminster Abbey.[42] The 'gentleman evangelist' Reginald Radcliffe had led the way, starting at the Victoria Theatre, Lambeth. In January 1861 he called a business meeting in the Sussex Hall, Leadenhall Street, to discuss the special needs of the East End under the aegis of the East London Special Services Committee. But strong opposition against the whole movement as a 'travesty of religious worship', 'subversive of the ancient order', led to a debate in the Lords during which Shaftesbury enthralled the House for three hours with descriptions of London's poor and irreligious condition, a world unknown to them. On 16 July 1863 *The Revival* reported the climax of the continuing opposition by some clergy, and the passing of the Archbishop of Canterbury's compromise Bill which finally overcame high Church objections and 'legalized special services in unconsecrated buildings'.

Not surprisingly Hudson Taylor had to be in on such missionary-hearted efforts, so akin to preaching in the temple courtyards of China. So in January 1863 he recorded an evening spent at the Effingham Theatre where he rejoiced to see 'souls seeking Jesus', and was often taking part at the Twig Folly Mission and East End churches.

Mr and Mrs W R Fuller were accepted by the Board of the United Methodist Free Church and called at Beaumont Street to arrange for training by Hudson Taylor. He lent Fuller *Gray's Anatomy* and eleven bones, listed in his journal; went to arrange with Mr Adams at the London Hospital for Fuller to be admitted gratis to college lectures; began Chinese lessons with him; and from time to time examined him on anatomy. On January 30 he called to see Alexander Wylie, preparing to return to China with the Bible Society, but he was out. Then he met a 'Professor Summers and vindicated the Nestorian Tablet'[43] before calling at Spottiswoode's 'about the Heading of Mk.', and so home to do seven and a half hours' revision and to write letters, one of them enclosing a 'specimen of Photo-zincography'. The following day was Saturday, but with a visit to hospital about Fuller's lectures and nine and a half hours' revision he got the first fifteen pages of Luke's Gospel off to the printers.

This was the pattern of life, and February continued true to form. He interpreted for Wang Lae-djün when he spoke at Hackney 'after breaking of bread', introduced Fuller to Adams, lanced an abscess in Amelia's baby's neck, dissected with Fuller to get him started, entertained Carstairs Douglas of Amoy for one day and Summers again the next day, and yet did 8 hours' revision, 7½, 8½, 7, and on Saturday, February 7 after that kind of week, 11 hours' revision.

Gough was going through the tribulations of bereavement, and Hudson Taylor spent the next afternoon with him praying about their work together, Gough's hospital work, whether they should find a bigger house, whether Gough should marry again, or bring his little Ellen to live with him. Not everybody could tolerate the ruggedness of the conditions the Taylors accepted.

The pressure from Ningbo to return was unsettling. He knew how badly he was needed and that if a good vernacular New Testament was to be available to the Ningbo Churches it would take many more months to complete. Besides, he was under obligation to the Bible Society to do what he himself had asked them to sponsor. Strategically it took priority – it and the recruiting of missionaries. He needed godly advice. 'Also conversed with Maria about our movements and prayed about them: may the Lord teach us whether to consult the Bible Society or Mr. Müller, or Mr. Berger.' The time Wang Lae-djün had promised to stay would be completed in another six weeks and his wife was pressing for his return but he was needed in London as a linguistic informant. What were they to do? Would Lae-djün agree to stay? Maria was a wise person, but prayer was the first answer, together with others' help. Hudson Taylor's journal read: 'The letters I sent yesterday, home and to Bayswater, have doubtless been received and acted on. (I requested prayer for Lae-djün and self, relative to speaking about his return.)' What he wrote home was,

> . . . remember us and Lae-djün in prayer, that God who knows all the requirements of His work, all the circumstances of Lae-djün and his wife and child – may so guide *me* in speaking to him, and *him* in coming to the right conclusion that the result may be to His glory, and for the mutual good of all concerned.

Hudson Taylor and Maria had great hopes for Lae-djün. Not only was he useful now, but with steady teaching he could become a missionary to his own people. Some knowledge of medicine would help him, so, added to everything else, Hudson Taylor began teaching him anatomy too. 'Sat. 14th Lae-djün began dissecting today. May God bless him in it. Lord increase our faith in Thee.' Evening Bible study with him on Sunday was followed by an early start on Monday, before the day's work. 'Rose at 7 a.m. dissected with Lae-djün before breakfast. Then went to hospital: gave Mr. Fuller a lesson in anatomy . . .' And on that day Mr Berger offered to bear the whole or part of the cost of Lae-djün's returning to China. 'Thanks be to God for this proof of care.'

But a new disruption of work on the New Testament had arisen.

> In the night, while I was in the bath, was summoned to the London Hospital to see a stabbed [Cantonese]. Sent for Lae-djün, who was unable to understand him. Mr. Gough also came. Neither of them were able to stay long looking at [him], most of whose intestines were exterior to his abdomen. I was able to converse a little with him in the Swatow dialect . . . Spoke to him of Jesus . . . he frequently cried . . . Save me, – from pain doubtless. *May* God save him! Administered chloroforme to him during the latter part of the operation, wh. he bore remarkably well.

– so anaesthetics were mercifully in use at last.

The next day Hudson Taylor had to interpret on oath a statement by the victim accusing his assailant, and on succeeding days visited both of them, in hospital and Clerkenwell Prison. The patient was pleased and sat up with clasped hands when Taylor prayed for him. But the prisoner 'was very wretched and shed tears'. Both Lae-djün and Carstairs Douglas[44] went with him at times. Lae-djün thought their conversation was in English, so different were the dialects they were using from his native Ningbo colloquial. Even then the journal reads on the 17th, 'Evening revision – total 9 hours', and on the 18th, 'again at night – total 5 hours'.

But the victim died, calling on Jesus, and Hudson Taylor after attending the indictment of the assailant, wrote, 'Fear his story is made up'. He visited him again in Newgate Prison with Professor Summers and spent all of another day at his murder trial. He was acquitted of murder for lack of evidence and committed for retrial for stabbing. Hudson Taylor refused to accept the fee brought to him by a policeman, until the poor constable pleaded that it could cost him his job not to do as he was instructed.

For Hudson Taylor ever penny and hour mattered, but so did Lae-djün. After he decided to stay on for another year, Taylor set out to train him even more thoroughly as a Christian worker, by a basic knowledge of theology and medicine and a wider experience of life, not all too serious. He began writing out simple anatomy for him which could only mean doing it in Chinese. He took him to a variety of churches and public meetings. And they went to see the procession on the arrival of Princess Alexandra of Denmark to marry Edward, Prince of Wales, and again to see the illuminations after the wedding. He had mellowed since his censure of the pageantry at the Duke of Wellington's funeral in 1852.

Still the revision went on – eight and a half hours on the day he went with Summers, three and a half after the murder trial, seven hours after the procession. Actual revision had reached 1st Corinthians but printing lagged well behind. Probably proof-reading had to be repeated at more stages than usual because of the compositors' unfamiliarity with romanised Chinese. To his mother he confided,

> Pray that we may make good progress this month, . . . we are expecting the first sheet of Romans from the printers every day. Then according to agreement it will have to be sent to Mr. Russell. Pray that this may be overruled for good; and that the work may not be hindered.

So his fears had come true. Russell had a hand in it. But the unhappiness with Frederick Gough was returning from time to time. 'Lost very much time this morning owing to Mr. G not wanting to work together.' Gough's advanced academic training made him want to delve more deeply than Taylor thought the Bible Society intended. Gough had business with the CMS, attended the Islington Clerical Conference, and had personal matters to attend to. But the depression of inconsolable grief may have been at the heart of his difficulty. Helen Nevius' retrospective remark about Hudson Taylor being dogmatic in his youth is the nearest hint of a possible explanation on his side.

Maria and Lae-djün worked with them whenever required. But if this pressure was more than Gough could take, Hudson Taylor himself began suffering from headaches and 'tic', the term then used for neuralgia. He was teaching Lae-djün systematically through the Epistle to the Hebrews, and the Chinese prisoner from the Gospel of John.

Hudson Taylor's confidence in prayer about everything is reflected in his journal. Whether the children were ill or a decision had to be made, or cash was running low, there is a record of their praying about it – or of failing to pray. On March 24 he went to Newgate Prison but failed to see the prisoner. Previously the governor had allowed him in, even out of hours. Today they were coaling, but even so Hudson Taylor wrote contritely, 'I had not specifically asked for this in prayer!' So his failure to get in had wasted valuable time. But after entering the fact that he bought A H Francke's *Life*,[45] the man whose living by faith in God had inspired George Müller, he went on, 'Joined with Maria in prayer for guidance about leaving the house, for supplies, for guidance about sending to Barnsley for money, for the dear children's health, etc.' They used his father's Building Society as a bank, drew cash for rent the next day, and giving notice to the landlord were granted the option to go or stay. So the days went by.

News reached them of Dr Parker's death and the Joneses' departure from Ningbo, and a new urgency entered their lives. Did this alter everything? Ningbo without a missionary doctor meant even more suffering and death. James Meadows and the Bridge Street Christians without help was a situation to be avoided if at all possible. Ought they to leave the New Testament revision to Gough, Cobbold and Russell, all in England? Hudson Taylor let it be known that he might have to leave Britain at short notice, 'perhaps suddenly'.

Frederick Gough went home for ten days, and Hudson Taylor paid a quick visit to his parents at the beginning of April, to mark his father's retirement as a chemist, so as to give all his time to the Building Society he had founded. To Maria, Gough opened his heart a little to say he had found his 'darling' daughter (Ellen) well, and 'Tomorrow is *our* wedding day.' After being so deeply in love himself, living with lovers like Maria and Hudson Taylor could not have been easy.

The work on the New Testament was then more urgent than ever, and the hours given to it speak volumes: Saturday 11th – 9 hours; 13th – 9 hours; 14th – 9 hours; 15th – 10½ hours; 16th – 8 hours; 17th – 11½ hours; 18th – 11 hours; as well as the other affairs of life. That same day, April 18, Hudson Taylor met Mr Berger at his factory in Bromley-by-Bow and discussed his problems – their own return, James Meadows, Mrs Lord's orphan school, the Meadows bill from Dr Parker and the Joneses' plight. 'Received several answers to prayer today' could mean that William Berger had been generous, but there was far more to it than that. 'Guidance' mattered more than 'means' if they were to uproot themselves and go against Dr Andrew Clarke's advice to recover fully in Britain.

Miss Stacey was ill, so the next day, Sunday, after lunch Hudson Taylor walked the four or five miles to Tottenham to enquire after her, had tea with John Eliot Howard and heard him preach, asked Miss Howard to pray that the work of revision might be done *well* and quickly – and walked home again. That week he drove himself remorselessly. Twelve hours on Monday, 11, 10, 12, 9½, 13½ on Saturday and twenty-four more pages of Luke were off to the printers.

At the turn of the month the double joy of twenty pounds from George Müller and twenty-five from Mr Berger supplied their needs for the next few weeks. Maria, Lae-djün and Hudson Taylor prayed together (in Chinese) for good progress through John's Gospel and seemed pleased with results – until the difficulties so far experienced suddenly seemed like plain sailing in comparison with what transpired. Even the prospect of Lae-djün returning to China when the Gospels were finished was a small additional burden.

'Indefatigable opponents'[46] *May–December 1863*

The 'cloud' on the horizon when news came that W A Russell was on his way home grew no larger after he arrived, except when tentative revisions were submitted to him as one of the original translators for comment. At first this only involved delay. On May 6 Russell came to tea at Beaumont Street and stayed for the evening. It was after that that Frederick Gough tried to be more punctual. And Hudson Taylor, after going over Hebrews 11 with Lae-djün, writing to James Meadows and a new recruit in Yorkshire named Richard Truelove, and praying with Maria about everything including the revision problem, wrote in his notebook journal, 'Ah, to be more like the meek, forbearing, loving Jesus. Lord! make me more like Thee!' He might well have been thinking of Frederick Gough, for Gough was Christlike in so many ways, if otherworldly.

They had a good week and on two evenings Hudson Taylor found time to go 'through operations on the arm with Mr. Fuller and Lae-djün until 11 p.m.' Then on the 14th Russell and 'Mr. Moule' came for several hours. From correspondence with the Bible Society it may be taken that this was Henry Moule, the father of George, Arthur and Handley. And the first signs of Russell's intervention in the New Testament revision appear. 'Thank God for answering prayer and avoiding *keh-teh*,' Hudson Taylor wrote, meaning that friction between host and guests would have been regrettable. But a week later, on the eve of his thirty-first birthday, the trouble that had been brewing came to the surface and his journal reads,

> Mr. G at breakfast said that unless Mr. Russell were asked to prepare a *ti-ta* [draft] of the Gal[atians] he would feel it his duty to bring before the Bible Society the question of not reprinting the epistles. O Lord! make bare Thy arm and help us, for Jesus' sake. Lae-djün also

told me this morning that he wishes to return [to Ningbo] after the completion of the Gospels. Thy will be done, O Lord!

Gough's was an echo of Russell's view. Russell was lobbying for a less colloquial style, forgetting the object of the exercise. With so many other issues demanding Taylor's time and attention it could have been easy to yield and allow the Ningbo New Testament to become what Russell wanted. But Hudson Taylor's conviction and tenacity would not let him take the path of least resistance. Two days later Gough came up with a compromise draft of a letter to Russell asking him to revise Galatians 3–6 *in the same style* as the other epistles, and 'this request I endorsed' – although admitting Russell to the revision team boded ill for progress.

For a week they were away with Lae-djün as guests of George Müller and other friends in Bristol and Clevedon, and addressing his congregation at Bethesda Chapel and the orphans in their Homes. When they returned Hudson Taylor could write, 'Through the kindness of dear friends, many of whom never heard of our names before, all expenses have been covered and we have returned richer than when we went.'

But he found that matters had advanced significantly. He became involved in much letter-writing and then was so unwell that he had to lie down all day. He returned to the New Testament still feeling unfit, and put in a hard week's work with thirteen hours of it on Saturday. But he had a lecture on China to prepare for the CMS Quarterly Meeting at St Stephen's, Bow. Then on June 23 news came that Mary Jones and her three remaining children had arrived at Liverpool, and that John Jones had died at sea on May 4 and been buried at St Helena. At once he sat down to break the news by letter to John's mother, to Miss Stacey, the Bergers and other intimate friends.

On Monday, June 29, he grasped the Revision nettle.

> After much prayer went to City . . . to Bible Society . . . asked for Mr Bergne . . . He told me that he thought the work must end with Acts. I replied I hoped not. He said there was much opposition to the work – enquired of Lae-djün's status, and said the work must go before the Editorial Committee. I requested either to be allowed to see the Committee or to have the opportunity of seeing himself or Mr. Jackson. He replied that I (and at my request, Mr. Gough) might see the Committee on the 15th. Ult. at 1 p.m.[47]

Lae-djün was not a scholar but an artisan. That was of the essence. That very fact equipped him better to be the source of good colloquial Ningbo than a classical education would have done. If the critics could not appreciate this, the Bible Society did. But socially they were in a difficult position.

On the way home Hudson Taylor bought Josephus in Latin and Greek, Fox's *Book of Martyrs*, Medhurst's *China*, and other books. Ill again with dysentery for several days, he only managed a few hours' work each day, but was up for an interview with Mr S B Bergne and F F Gough on July 9. Then on the 15th they met the Editorial Sub-committee together and afterwards could say, 'We were assuredly prospered in answer to prayer.'

The sub-committee's Minutes are full and informative. A letter from W A Russell to the Society was read in which he proposed that the printing of their revision should stop with the completion of the Gospel of John, the Acts should be printed without revision, and 'the rest of the New Testament be left for the present until the Revision can be undertaken under more favourable circumstances'.

Gough and Hudson Taylor were then introduced. They explained that they were

> introducing uniformity between the several parts of the work in the preparation of which various Missionaries had laboured independently one of the other, [and read a letter from H V Rankin] one of the principal Translators of the work and Senior Missionary of the American Presbyterian Mission in Ningpo . . . [acknowledging] receipt of the . . . first eight chapters of St. Matthew, and stating that he had been charmed with its appearance, and that the native Christians were in raptures with it . . .
>
> Mr. Gough informed the sub-Committee that Mr. Russell's wish was to produce the work in a higher style of language which would in fact render it unsuitable for the Classes of the population of Ningpo and its neighbourhood for whom it was intended, in which higher style, moreover the Missionaries had not hitherto deemed it desirable to issue anything in print . . . [Mr. Gough] was now decidedly of opinion that it would be for the advantage of the Missionary Cause in Ningpo to complete the work as originally sanctioned by the Committee.

Hudson Taylor then testified that the services of Wang Lae-djün were 'precisely of the kind required by the Editors' – that is, himself with Gough's assistance – and after they had retired, the Committee resolved that the Secretary should correspond with Mr

Russell, 'it being understood that the printing of the work . . . shall in the meantime be continued'.[48]

The record of laborious hours spent on the New Testament continued through August and September, interspersed with notes of a full social life. Mary Jones and the children joined the family at Beaumont Street. They all went to Hackney for a day with George Pearse – Gough, Lae-djün, Taylors and Joneses – and then he came for an evening with them. Another day it was to Tottenham and the John Eliot Howards. And on September 6 he delivered Mrs Fuller of 'a fine boy'. All through this time he was interviewing recruits for China, finding accommodation with a City Missionary for Richard Truelove, buying furniture for him, and speaking at meetings – without any mention of the Bible Society or opposition.

Then on September 17 a letter came to Frederick Gough from Henry Venn, General Secretary of the CMS, and two days later one from the Bible Society to Hudson Taylor, 'asking who had authorised the revision of the New Testament'. This was serious. Hudson Taylor went out to Hackney and 'asked the prayers of several about our difficulties with the Bible Socy.' There he met 'Mr. Chapman of Barnstaple',[49] soon to become a loyal friend, at lunch with George Pearse, and in the evening he wrote to his mother,

> The indefatigable opponents of our colloquial Testament having been baffled at the Bible Socy., have set on us in another way. The Church Missionary Society endorsed my application in the first place, and they have tried through them to stop it . . . God will *surely* make all these things tend to the *furtherance* of the work and to His own glory – even if we now see not how . . . We are too busy to go teasing Secretaries and Members of Committees about it – but may we not the more confidently look to the Lord to work for us, if we are working for Him? . . . Remember the Test. [Testament] especially on Monday and Tuesday and Wednesday, as I hope it may be settled on one or other of these days. . . . Do not make this matter one of conversation. It is strange that there should be such jealousy amongst the people of God – There will be no strife *there*.[50]

On Monday, September 21, 'We all spent the morning in fasting and prayer about the Bible Socy. Then Mr Gough went to see Mr Venn and I began a letter to the Secy. of the Bible Society.' So much hung upon that letter that its drafting continued each day until the 24th. If they had known that a move was also on foot to get Gough sent back to China they might have been more disturbed. But the spiritual issues impressed them equally, as Hudson Taylor indicated on October 4. 'Determined by God's help to live nearer to Him and thus to ensure His help and blessing in this work'.

An informal note from George Pearse, again in possession of the facts though not on the committee, brought some consolation. 'There is no intention of taking it out of your hands. They are evidently satisfied with what you are doing, and the way you are doing it.'[51] Then on October 5 Hudson Taylor noted in his pencilled penny journal, 'Our money nearly spent. Paid in faith, however, what we were owing to tradesmen and servants . . . Mr Gough received a note from Mr. Venn about Mr. Russell's letter on the subject of the Revision.' Two days later, the 7th, 'Mr. Gough received a letter from Mr. Russell, very angrily speaking of him, of the Revision, and of me. Look, O Lord, upon this opposition and help and prosper us.'

Such a situation was most distasteful for the conciliatory Gough, so Hudson Taylor wrote off at once to his mother and Mary Jones, asking them to pray:

> It is assuming a very painful aspect, as some of the opponents are making it a personal matter. Poor Mr. Gough is getting quite disheartened about it, and it is not improbable, may throw up his share in it. The Church Missionary Society, who endorsed my application at the first, will have the matter brought before it on their meeting (on the 20th). I have of course, no business there, and Mr. Gough who cannot bear up against a rough and personal opposition, is I fear giving way; so that, humanly speaking, there is little hope of the continued aid of either CMS or of the B&F Bible Society. For *this* I care but little, as the Lord can very easily provide the *funds* we need; But the help of Mr. Gough in the remainder of the work is very desirable . . . I would look for special prayer then, –
> I. That the CMS and B&F Bible S. may be brought to that conclusion which will be most to the Glory of God and the *real* (if not apparent) good of the work.
> II. That if, as is almost certain, they throw up the work, and if it be most for the good of the dear converts of Ningpo Mr. Gough may be induced notwithstanding this, to continue . . .
> III. That if *he* should not do this, we may be guided aright as to *our* path; – whether simply to reprint the Epistles and Revelation; or in some measure revise them, correcting where we can, any glaring errors we may find; or whether to give up the work altogether.
>
> My present full conviction with regard to this work, – not a little confirmed and strengthened by the low ground taken in opposition to

> it, – and confirmed by the tidings which have just reached us of the removal of dear Mr. Rankin to his heavenly rest, – is that it is of the Lord. And that *He* is saying to us, 'Be strong and of a good courage and do it; fear not, nor be dismayed; for the LORD God will be with thee, until thou hast *finished* all the work for the service of the house of the Lord.' If this is *really* His will, by *His help*, I *will* go forward; may He teach me if it is not so.[52]

Hudson Taylor had already given two and a half years of hard work to this revision and believed it should be completed. The outcome of this opposition involved far more than simply the accuracy and intelligibility of this version of the Scriptures. It was a supreme test of Hudson Taylor's personality, of his spiritual attitudes, of his fitness for leadership, his confidence in prayer as a form of direct co-operation with God, and his ability to stand unshaken, without arrogance, against great odds. At the very time this setback tested his mettle, several applications for service in China were reaching him from men of good missionary potential.

When Gough called on Henry Venn on the 8th he 'was prospered in the interview'. While he was out Hudson Taylor took Lae-djün and a Baptist Mission recruit named Edwin Kingdon round to the hospital to dissect 'the front of a leg' – a demonstration perhaps of where a bold incision into the outer side of the thigh for the huge intramuscular abscesses common in China could do no harm.

He had introduced Mrs Lord and Mary Jones to George Müller and they were visiting Bristol. Mary came back on the 9th with a broken arm. But Hudson Taylor already had another problem.

> Our money all but spent. O Lord! our help is in Thee. Went with Mrs. Jones to see Mr. [Jonathan] Hutchinson, who very kindly refused to take any fee. Only 2/5½ left with the greatest management. 'I must have all things and abound, while God is God to me.'

October 11 was Sunday. After Bible study with Lae-djün, still undecided about returning to China, 'We gave 2/- today at the collection, in faith and as due to God.' Now things were really tight. On Monday Hudson Taylor spent six hours looking through the old translations of Galatians.

> It would never do to reprint it in its present state. The Lord guide and direct us. Lae-djün decided to stay and help us and dissect; I promised to get him entrance to dissection, either gratuitously or by paying the fee. Maria found 2d. in one pocket, and Mrs. Jones bought 1/- stamp of me.

Tuesday, 13th, was a cheering day, 'in answer to prayer received permission for Lae-djün to dissect. . . . Miss Young came to see Mrs. Jones and brought 1 goose, 1 duck, 1 fowl, etc.' And then came a substantial sum in dividends from the legacy in trust for Maria.

Hudson Taylor called on Henry Venn and left a copy of his letter to the Bible Society for him, and at a farewell meeting for twelve outgoing missionaries had a brief interview with him. The trouble over the New Testament was putting Taylor under strain. 'Felt very tired. May our Faithful and Covenant God undertake for us,' he told his journal. He found time, however, to write several pages of technical reasoning to the editor of a religious periodical defending the inclusion of Cainan, son of Arphaxed, in the Luke genealogy.[53] He also wrote to his mother and Amelia again asking them to pray, and spent Sunday afternoon praying mostly about it. Then on Monday, October 19,

> Went after prayer to see Mr. Venn about the Revision. Mr. Gough told Mr. Venn he was not prepared to join in a partial revision of the whole. I suggested revision of certain parts but that was not taken up. [So compromise was not to be the solution.] Mr. Venn said as 2 out of 3 of their [Ningbo] missionaries desired the discontinuance of the work, the majority must decide, and so we must stop at Acts. This unexpected and yet not unexpected decision made me quite poorly . . .
>
> [20th] Mr. Gough went to the Committee of the C.M.S. I with Mrs. Jones went to see Mr. Hutchinson about her arm. I gave chloroforme for him to a little girl while he operated on both eyes for double strabismus [squint] . . .
>
> Mr. Gough came home with tidings of an unanimous vote in favour of continuing the work. Not so thankful as I should be.

If Hudson Taylor had known that two representatives of the Bible Society had attended the CMS Committee meeting and advised the continuation of the revision to the end of the New Testament, he might have been less sick at heart, for that is what had happened, 'on the understanding that no further revision should take place than the correction of palpable errors'.[54] That in itself would curb academic zeal. And on the following day the Committee of the Bible Society also met and after reading letters from Russell and Moule heard Mr. Jackson's report on the CMS meeting he had attended. They then resolved to 'concur in the views of the C.M.S.'[55]

> That it appears to this [CMS] Committee desirable that the Bible Society should continue the reprinting of the New Testament in the Ningpo Vernacular Version under the Editorship of the Rev. Messrs. Gough and Taylor . . . [with the same provisos].[56]

That should have been the end of the matter, as Hudson Taylor told his parents,

> We have, I trust, seen the end of our difficulties with the Bible Society. God has indeed heard our prayers on this account, and answered them; to Him be the praise. We have still to deal with the difficulties of the *work* itself; – but these, by His help, and by patient perseverance will gradually lessen. But we need your prayers. Our expenses of late have been *very* heavy. Ask the Lord to continue to supply us with funds.

If only they could work more systematically, he went on euphemistically, work might proceed more steadily. And then, about Maria and himself, 'We both made a great mistake in not going to the seaside.' Neither of them was well. But instead of a return to systematic work, the old pattern of irregularity recurred.

On Monday night, December 7, after eight hours on the New Testament, Hudson Taylor's entry in his journal was, 'Maria writing vocabulary all day for Mr. Valentine; I helped her from 10.30 p.m. till 4.30 a.m. as they leave at 9.00 a.m.' The next day's work suffered, with Gough away all day, probably seeing Valentine, the new CMS missionary, off at Gravesend, but Hudson Taylor helped Lae-djün at the hospital and 'Left Dr. Legge's 1st. Vol. of Confucian Classics at the Baptist Mission House [in Moorgate] for Mr. Underhill.'

Whatever else happened he forced himself on to get the revision finished, seeing how many more months of work would be involved. His pace through December equalled anything he had managed before – including eight and a half hours on Christmas Eve, four on Christmas Day in the evening, and ten and a half on Boxing Day. During the week of December 7–12 he averaged three hours' work each night after ten p m.

For a few months Hudson Taylor made no more reference to W A Russell, while the record of hours at work ground on at its previous pace into the summer of 1864, in spite of growing commitments outside. They at least were worthwhile. Then, at some point Russell appeared again and began commenting on their work on the Epistles, and new difficulties arose.

All this time they were one at heart in their motives. Impressed with the vast need of China and the towering possibilities before the Christian Church, Russell proposed that the CMS should adopt as its slogan for China the words 'Onward and Inward'. Eugene Stock, historian of the CMS, lamented that the Church in the West neglected its opportunities, and later in his history referred to the China Inland Mission as the 'onward and inward Mission'.[57] In point of fact, precisely while the differences existed between Russell, Taylor and Gough, and Hudson Taylor was working on the revision of the Acts of the Apostles, in August and September 1863, the claims of all China, not only of Ningbo and Zhejiang, were being forced upon them. On the wall of his study hung a large map of the Chinese empire and as Gough and he worked and talked and prayed, its implications came forcibly home to them. Reminiscing in his old age he said,

> Mr. Gough, – a holy man – went through much of the same spiritual exercise. Often we could not go on working. We would stop, and call Maria and Wang Lae-djün into the room and together unite in prayer that God would send the Gospel all over China – before we could go on.

Those four people in Mile End praying together in Chinese, knelt at the threshold of undreamed-of advance.

Ningbo in Mile End[58] *1863*

All through that long year of 1863 No 1 Beaumont Street was the scene of activity over and above what went on in the study. W R Fuller came and went as he began to learn Chinese from the Taylors and Lae-djün. Encouraged by Hudson Taylor's willingness, his United Methodist Free Church (UMFC) friends, the BMS and other societies continued to consult him. After Fuller's intended companion withdrew and no substitute appeared for several months, the Mission leaders learned all they could by questioning Hudson Taylor about Ningbo and missionary conditions, and what books to put into the hands of young men bound for China.

One of the distinguished missionaries of later years, the direct fruit of Hudson Taylor's efforts at this time, was W E Soothill, Fuller's colleague at Ningbo, who after a time at Wenzhou (Wenchow) became a distinguished educator, Sinologue, translator, author and professor of Chinese at Oxford, in James Legge's Chair.

Soothill's *Chinese Dictionary* was the *vade-mecum* of generations of missionaries, merchants and diplomats.[59]

Dr Kesson of the Wesleyan Missionary Society came to arrange for one of their men, a Mr Parker, to join in at Beaumont Street, and he too needed coaching. Others came for interviews at the request of one society or another. And diversions like the case of the stabbed Chinese occurred from time to time. In February an old friend, Mr Faulding the manufacturer of piano frames and 'frets', invited Hudson Taylor to meet the minister of his church, William Landels of Regent's Park Chapel, and so began another life-long friendship. Illness in the family and among neighbours involved Hudson Taylor as a doctor. And all the petty affairs of life claimed his attention, as on February 19 when his journal entry ran,

> Saw Maria and baby into an omnibus; then met M.A. Doll, a French Canadian . . . and an Evangelist – gave him 10/- for Christ's sake. Got my hair cut and spoke to the barber about Jesus. On the way home got a manuscript book for Lae-djün . . . called at the photographers. After tea translated a certificate for a Norwegian sailor . . .

His contacts with Carstairs Douglas went beyond helping the Cantonese prisoner, for Douglas, an outstanding personality, was also recruiting missionaries for China. His best-known find was a young surgeon named James L Maxwell, FRCS Eng., whom he introduced into Taiwan in 1865 following their arrival back in China (1863). Under the English Presbyterian Mission Maxwell pioneered (with G L Mackay of the Canadian Presbyterian Mission after 1871) the now extensive Church in that island, and in 1878 founded the Medical Missionary Association (London), still very active.[60] He too was destined to be closely linked with Hudson Taylor and especially with Benjamin and Amelia Broomhall in their active old age.

When the desolate Mary Jones had arrived home without John and wanted to hand over all Ningbo affairs to Hudson Taylor, he went for a week to John's mother's home in Wendover to meet Mary. One of Mary's children had died before she went to China, another was buried on their arrival at Hong Kong, two more at Ningbo and now John at St Helena. Only Tom and two others remained to her. Together they went over the accounts and records of the Ningbo church. Of fifty-eight Christians twelve had died, but ten who were suspended as a disciplinary measure and the remaining thirty-six were under the pastoral care of E C Lord and James

Meadows. Then, as John's mother was elderly (and died soon afterwards) and Mary had nowhere to go, Maria and Hudson Taylor, like brother and sister to her, invited her to join them at Beaumont Street. It was always possible to expand into nearby houses. By the end of August she and the children were with them. By October Mary had rented a house of her own and in November took Frederick Gough's daughter Ellen in as one of her own family. Gough later became her lodger.[61]

Mary Jones had also brought a first-hand account of Dr Parker's death, of the Taiping menace and of how James and Martha Meadows were at the time she left. When Mrs Lord reached the United States from Ningbo and had arranged for her husband's children to be educated among relatives, she travelled on to England with her own three, Mary Bausum, now twelve, and the two boys. So on arrival in England it was natural for her too to gravitate to where Maria and the others were.

It happened to be September 21, the day of prayer and fasting and critical dealings with Henry Venn and the Bible Society. But they were all hardened travellers, so when she arrived in the evening it was natural that she should be welcomed in, and presumably the children with her.

As Mrs Bausum she was well-known at Tottenham, for her late husband had been 'a particular friend of A.N. Groves',[62] and the Ladies' Association had supported her since her previous visit home. John and Mary Jones had from the beginning been supported by gifts from Tottenham and George Müller, so it was natural for them to visit these friends together, coming and going at will.

No one knew how the Taylors stood financially, for life went on much the same from day to day. From time to time one or another would contribute to the cost of the communal living, but only when they were able or remembered. Hudson Taylor noted the fact gratefully whenever Gough paid in five pounds or 'Mrs. Howard and son sent £10 on account of Mrs. Jones being here'. But on the day Mrs Lord and Mrs Jones and her baby turned up from Bristol, Mary Jones with a broken arm, it was October 9, the day of the heart cry, 'Our money all but spent. O Lord! our hope is in Thee.' It was also the day that Theodore Howard, another of that good family, wrote to Hudson Taylor on hearing that Maria was ill, encouraging him to 'take it on trust a little while', knowing he would understand in God's own time why he allowed such things. Little did Mary Jones know how welcome her shilling for a stamp or her sister Miss

Young's goose, duck and fowl were to the household, or how glad Hudson Taylor was when she bought four copies of Moule's *Chinese Physician* from him *and* paid cash.

Sometimes twelve-year-old Mary Bausum was away with her mother, but she felt at home with Maria and the rest and often stayed: they were all one big family. The occasions when the Taylors were on their own together deserved to be recorded, as on November 1, 'Afternoon alone with Maria and the children'. Perhaps it was after Mary Jones' visit to Jonathan Hutchinson, when Hudson Taylor helped him operate on a child's eyes, that someone dared to suggest that Maria should have her 'slightest cast' corrected.

> I was indignant [Hudson recalled]. I loved her and I loved it. I loved her just as she was, and everything about her. I would not have had it changed on any account [or] anything she was or did.[63]

It was not long before the dividends which brought relief on October 15 were exhausted and again they had 'but a few shillings in hand'. The annual total in dividends was only seventy-six pounds. So when Mrs Lord this time arrived and stayed at Mrs Jones' new home a few streets away, he felt the relief. Then came twenty pounds from George Müller.

The bond between all these Ningbo friends was strong. Arriving back from Barnsley one Saturday night, worn out, Mrs Lord went to bed and before anyone else was up the next morning set off, walking the five miles to Bayswater to be on hand for Amelia's second confinement. Hudson and Maria were on their way there later in the day when he felt anxious about one of their own children who had been out of sorts, and returned to once, to find him very ill and needing attention through the night.

They were all together at Mile End when the news arrived of Martha Meadows' sudden death. Letter after letter from E C Lord and James Meadows had made the Taylors realise how much they were needed there. Now on top of all the other distresses reported from China this news made Hudson Taylor long more than ever to go back. Hope long deferred was making their hearts grow sick, he wrote, especially perhaps as they had hoped to travel with Lae-djün, and then with Mrs Lord on her return.[64] But it was time for her to go and neither the New Testament nor the minimal five new missionaries for Ningbo had yet materialised. With the winter coming on it was now or next spring, but now was out of the question. Next spring it would have to be, given the progress necessary. When Meadows wrote, in his letter about Martha, 'Oh pray I beseech you for this sink of iniquity, namely Ningpo', he also comforted himself with the brave thought: 'no silver without dross, no wheat without chaff, no rose without a thorn'. If he had to delay his own departure, Hudson Taylor had every reason to have confidence in Meadows to hold the fort till he came.

One direct outcome of the price James Meadows had to pay in losing Martha lay in an unexpected quarter. On hearing the news, William Berger was deeply moved and driven to reconsider his own consecration. 'I have determined, the Lord helping me [he wrote] to lay aside every weight, for communion with our Blessed Lord ought to come first.' Already generous beyond most, he was to become not only the self-denying friend and supporter of missions to China in particular, but co-founder with Hudson Taylor of the China Inland Mission.

After a farewell meeting at Hackney, with George Pearse, Frederick Gough and Hudson Taylor speaking, on December 3 Mrs Lord left for Liverpool, leaving her daughter Mary Bausum at school and Hudson Taylor again in charge as Mrs Lord's 'agent'. That at least meant one more missionary back in Ningbo. But not being ready to go himself did not mean having no prospect of going. When he wrote of returning with 'a goodly number' of new missionaries it was not wishful thinking. Of all his activities apart from the New Testament revision, what he most enjoyed was his dealings with the recruits. W R Fuller of the United Methodist Free Church, E F Kingdon of the Baptists, J D Valentine of the CMS (to some extent), Richard Truelove of Staincross and others under his own wing were well advanced in training.

To Truelove, relatively immature, Hudson Taylor was giving hours of precious time over the months when the New Testament work claimed so much. Pencilled into the back of his penny journal is his rough draft of the letter he had written to Richard on May 17, 1863, before he came to live with them in London. In view of what happened the following year, this letter repays attention, as expressing Hudson Taylor's view of the relationship between them:

> My dr. Br[other] in the L[ord],
>
> Accept my thanks (etc) . . . I have not felt able to write an answer to you sooner . . . This is a solemn matter . . . none of us can foresee the results of it – may they be entirely to the glory of God, and in accordance with His will. I trust that your desire to engage in this

> glorious work is from Him; if so, He will remove all difficulties, and make your way very plain. There are no difficulties with Him. They all lie in us. More faith, more simple childlike waiting on God, will remove them all . . . Nothing will give me greater pleasure than doing what I can to assist you. As to the matter of education, an humble, *teachable* mind, and a single eye to God's glory, will have God's blessings, either here or in China. What I would recommend you to do is to *study God's word*, and to try to improve yourself in writing, and English grammar . . .
>
> If you would wish me to try and assist you to go to China; and think you would like to assist me in the blessed work there; I shall be glad to learn from you your age, whether married or single, and if the latter, whether you are engaged to be married, or intend to marry before going to China, if the Lord open your way to go. I shall also be glad to learn how your health usually is, and what dangerous *illnesses* you have experienced in and since your childhood.
>
> And now my dear Brother I commend you to God and to the word of His grace. Live near to Him. Learn ever to be in the spirit of prayer, to live as seeing Him who is invisible. Do all that you can for souls around you now. Commit your way to the Lord and He will bring it to pass. J.H.T.[65]

This left Richard Truelove in no doubt that he himself must take the initiative as an independent person and Hudson Taylor would help him to go to China but not enlist or employ him. By a preliminary interview, however, he would judge how to advise him. It is a pattern of his dealings with others.

Another draft letter in Maria's hand from Hudson Taylor's dictation is dated June 13, on their arrival home from visiting George Müller in Bristol. No indication is given of whom he was addressing, possibly George Crombie:

> Is your trade of such a nature that if you were to leave it for a month or two you could return to it easily? Because if so and if the Lord should make the way plain, perhaps a month or two's study of the language might help both you and me to judge of your suitability for the Lord's work in China . . . I. if you were unable to make such progress in the language as seemed to promise future success in acquiring it, it would be a satisfaction to your own mind to have [settled] the matter early. II. If you were able to make a good beginning, you might return to your ordinary occupation able to improve your leisure time in the study of the language until the time for making immediate preparations for your departure should arrive.[66]

On October 2 William Fuller, the local preacher, under Hudson Taylor's instruction, took charge of his first midwifery case, good preparation for a life where such skills were few and far between. And soon afterwards it was decided that if the Taylors were not ready to sail in the spring, the Fullers would go without them.

Hudson Taylor's sympathy for them was stirred, for their baby had been very ill and might be endangered by the voyage. Already their departure had been deferred for this reason. Lae-djün decided to go with the Fullers, and in Hudson Taylor's journal, in 1864, entries about him multiplied – 'morning with Lae-djün', 'evening with Lae-djün', 'helping Lae-djün with anatomy', 'with Lae-djün on Romans 8', 'with Lae-djün, on repentance, with Truelove on Calvinism', 'with Lae-djün on Justification', with Fuller, Kingdon and Lae-djün 'went over ligaturing arteries of the arm and amputation of the fingers'.

Then Thomas Marshall, the minister of Bryanston Hall, Portman Square, sent a gift to Hudson Taylor by the hand of a German member of his congregation, Stephan Paul Barchet, who before long wished to learn Chinese. In December Stephan became one of the growing Beaumont Street household. A letter arrived from George Crombie, of Ellon, Aberdeen, the fiancé of Annie Skinner, a Scottish girl living with Mary Jones. Annie was a choice person and George her match. They were planning to marry and go to China in the spring. Hudson Taylor told him he was not able to make even tentative arrangements for them all to travel together. He himself did not now expect to be free to go for 'at least six or eight months'. For all his hard work the New Testament revision was dragging. Then on November 15 Mr Faulding and his daughter Jane came to see them – and left a donation of five pounds when they went. Hudson Taylor's story-telling friendship with nine-year-old Jennie ten years ago was beginning to bear fruit. At nineteen she was more than ever interested in China.

If Christmas could not interrupt Hudson Taylor's work on the New Testament, it was not allowed to prevent Stephan Barchet from having his four-hour Chinese lesson on Christmas Eve. He did not know that the Taylors were at the end of their cash again and drawing their last fifteen pounds from the Building Society. But that was how the year ended and how 1864 began, with the journal entry, 'that being the last of our own money, The Lord remember us for good'.

To look ahead, as spring came and went and the time for the

Kingdons', Fullers', and Lae-djün's departure came nearer, Hudson Taylor did more and more for them, buying outfits and drugs and furnishing their cabins. He presented Lae-djün one day with a set of surgical instruments, and on another day with a surgical dressing case. W G Lewis, the Westbourne Grove pastor, gave Lae-djün a magic lantern and slides of *Pilgrim's Progress*, and George Müller paid for his passage and initial support. Then on June 2, 1864, Hudson Taylor escorted them to Gravesend and took Lae-djün on board. Wang Lae-djün never failed him, living to old age as the revered pastor of a strong church in Hangzhou.

PART 4

A NEW TREND IN WORLD MISSION

1864–65

CHAPTER EIGHT

THE END IS THE BEGINNING 1864–65

The end of the Taipings[1] *1864–65*

In January 1864 Charles Gordon's protest against the brocaded perfidy of Li Hong-zhang ended, thanks to the renewed activity of the Taipings, the increasing accession of foreign mercenaries to their ranks, and to the successful proposal of a *modus vivendi* by Robert Hart.[2] Always 'able and clear-headed', and a man who not only admired but liked and therefore felt for the Chinese, Hart foresaw the undoing of all the hard-won gains if they were not pressed to the ultimate conclusion, the capture of Nanjing. And Burgevine was contemplating another alliance with the rebels.

Gordon was well aware of all that was happening, and believed that he could end the rebellion in six months, whereas it would fester on for another six years if he did not take a hand. He 'so far stifled his resentment as to have a personal interview with the Governor' Li Hong-zhang, and when Li agreed to issue a proclamation acknowledging that the massacre of the Taiping chiefs was in spite of a promise that their lives would be spared, Gordon mobilised his Ever-Victorious Army at Kunshan again, on January 30. It was no longer the unit it had been. Many of his best officers had been killed or had left and many men had never yet fought under him. Writing to Sir Frederick Bruce, the British Minister in Peking, to say that he personally assumed full responsibility for his actions, Gordon took the initiative of attacking again, on February 19. Bruce obtained a promise from the Chinese government that after the capitulation of the Taipings nothing would be done to prisoners without Gordon's concurrence. But how hollow this promise also was could only be seen after the event.

In the dead of winter, bitterly cold and snowy, Gordon struck westwards from Suzhou. He proposed to cut 'through the heart of the rebellion' by taking a line of cities between Suzhou and the rebel capital, Nanjing, driving between the Yangzi on the northern flank and the southern lakes (map, p 292). On March 1 he took Yixing (Ihing), west of the Great Lake, Tai Hu, and then Liyang – appalled to find the populace so starved as to have resorted to cannibalism while food was stockpiled in Liyang to feed the rebel forces. Immediately he opened the granaries and distributed the grain.

Jintan (Kintan) was the next objective, but in his rear the imperial forces failed to maintain the pressure. The Zong Wang, the Taipings' Loyal Prince, retook towns which should have been consolidated against them. Far in the rear Fushan and Changshu (where Hudson Taylor on his Yangzi reconnaissance had first slept rough and 'went Chinese'), thirty miles north of Kunshan, fell into the Zhong Wang's hands. So Gordon did not receive the support expected. Beaten back from Jintan on March 20 and himself wounded by a shot through the leg, his defeat encouraged the rebels to announce a new march on Shanghai. But Gordon, on a canal boat because unable to stand, penetrated with a few hundred men into the Taiping territory, attacked the city of Huaishu and after initial failure took it on April 11. By this northward push towards the Yangzi he cut off the Zhong Wang's forces from their Nanjing base.

South of the lakes the imperialist general Cheng took Jiaxing on the Grand Canal, so threatening Hangzhou, which yielded on March 31 before a combined Chinese and French advance. After nearly twelve months in occupation the rebels forsook the city in the night. At last this twin of Suzhou, with a death toll of between fifty and seventy thousand, as much from suicide as the sword, could begin to recover. From there General Cheng turned towards Nanjing, intending with Li Hong-zhang to achieve the final victory without Gordon's help.

Meanwhile, joining up with Li Hong-zhang's army and fighting together, the Ever-Victorious Army shared on May 11 in the capture of Changzhou from a garrison of twenty thousand rebels. With only the ancient Ming capital, Nanjing, less than a hundred miles away, remaining to be subdued, Gordon marched his men back to their base at Kunshan. There he found that the Order in Council permitting British officers to serve the Chinese government had been rescinded. He paid off all his men with a month's wages and travelling expenses to their homes, and by June 1 the Ever-Victorious Army no longer existed. It had fought a hundred battles and lost only three or four, capturing over fifty walled cities.[3]

Attributing the success of the campaign to General Cheng who was killed towards its close, Li Hong-zhang, incredibly to Western minds, omitted to mention Gordon in his reports. Ancient attitudes were accountable more than personal feelings. He knew that the Court were well aware of the facts. They marked the end of Gordon's service generously. Declining again a reward of ten thousand taels, from the emperor, Gordon wrote home that he was returning, in time for Christmas he hoped, 'as poor as when I entered [China]'.[4] But the *Peking Gazette* of June 16 announced that the emperor had promoted him to major-general and conferred on him the highest military honour of 'Commander-in-Chief with Yellow Jacket and short Peacock's Feather', Li Hong-zhang's own rank. Prince Kong asked the British Minister to bring Colonel Gordon's merits to the notice of Queen Victoria, and beyond the expectations of his friends he was made a Commander of the Order of the Bath. For all that the cynics said about a sinecure, he was also given the honour of improving the defences of the Thames and of the capital of the empire. To an admiring public, fed on his exploits, he was 'Chinese Gordon'.

Of real if incidental relevance to this history is the fact that hearing of Hudson Taylor's intended return to China with a party of young missionaries, Gordon became a donor to his enterprise and offered him 'an electro-magnetic machine' with which to make friends among the Chinese. For he was a dedicated Christian, inseparable from his Bible whatever the circumstances. Three or four years later, hearing of a young officer of the Ever-Victorious Army who since the end of the war against the Taipings had been converted through James Meadows and returned as a missionary in Suzhou, Gordon wrote, 'I was not so much surprised [to hear of his conversion] as I have been constantly and instantly praying for my old comrades, and I believe this is in answer to my prayers.' He himself was to return briefly to China sixteen years later.

No sooner was the Ever-Victorious Army out of the way than the dauntless Burgevine rejoined the Taipings. He had been deported by the American consul to Japan, but returned to Ningbo only to be taken prisoner in May the following year and, it was commonly believed, done to death. The official story that a ferry capsized and he lost his life accidentally sounded implausible in the circumstances.

On June 30, surrounded and unable to hold out against Zeng Guo-fan's armies, Hong Xiu-quan, the Tian Wang, committed suicide. And on July 19, 1864, Nanjing fell to the emperor's insatiably bloodthirsty troops. Least appalling was the destruction of this imperial capital of the Ming dynasty, built early in the fourteenth century. Its summer palace, imperial tombs, historic libraries and famous nine-storey octagonal porcelain pagoda were destroyed as if to crush for ever the possibility of another Ming uprising. But the carnage was indescribable. Colonel W C Howard of the 4th Chinese Regiment with Li Hong-zhang's army witnessed it. All promises were forgotten as ten thousand prisoners were taken. Four thousand old men and boys were stripped naked and turned loose to perish or survive if they could. Six thousand were herded together and butchered in cold blood. 'It was an awful sight to see Li Hung-chang's men hacking at them,' Colonel Howard wrote.

The Zhong Wang, the Loyal Prince, strategist and hero of all the Taiping successes in recent years, remained loyal to the end. Unable to capitalise on his brief counter-attack at Changshu, he made his way back to Nanjing. When the city fell, he mounted Hong Xiuquan's son on his own good horse, taking an inferior one for himself, to flee to safety. When he was captured, he was given eight days to write his memoirs, and then beheaded without torture. Griffith John's biographer, Wardlaw Thompson, wrote that Hong Ren, the evangelist turned Shield King or Prince, was with the son when they were caught, and that the boy was beheaded on the spot and Hong Ren later. Scattered to the four winds the remnants of the Taipings shaved their heads and mingled with the terrified populace. But the emperor's men showed no mercy, hounding them down and sweeping away the innocent with the guilty.

This rebellion was over. After sixteen years the *Tai Ping Tian Guo*, the Heavenly Kingdom of Peace, this 'tragic caricature of Christianity' that had never known anything but battle and blood, was no more – except that escaped rebels held Zhangzhou, near Amoy, until May 1865, and it was there that Burgevine was captured.[5] The Nian-fei rebellion in Shandong, Henan, Anhui and Jiangsu had four more years to run. In Yunnan and Gansu Muslim rebellions smouldered and flared for a decade, erupting in 1866 in far away Ili in Chinese Turkestan. And the Miao rebellion festered on in the Guizhou mountains.[6] By the assessment of many observers in China, accepted by critical historians, by K S Latourette and *The Times*, some twenty million people had perished in the Taiping rebellion alone, from fighting, reprisals, brigandage, famine and disease.

The whole of the civic structure of vast areas in eleven provinces had been disrupted for long periods. For years no State examinations had been held in several provinces and as reconstruction was undertaken a great dearth of qualified officials delayed the return to order. An immensely difficult task of resettlement faced government and displaced people. Records had been destroyed and the impossibility of establishing ownership of land and surviving property meant endless injustice and strife. Whole populations were on the move within a very short time, returning to their old homes. In Shanghai, streets of new houses in the Chinese city were left empty and property values in the Settlement plummeted. From a combined total of one and a half million at Shanghai the occupants dropped within a few months to two hundred and twenty thousand. Of these three thousand were foreign naval and military personnel and nearly three thousand other Westerners. With the end of hostilities these too were soon reduced and self-defence returned largely to the Volunteers. Travel between the ports in Jardine's and other companies' ships was by the beginning of 1865, 'as safe and convenient as in any part of England or the United States' with first-class steamers running daily, Mr Lord told Hudson Taylor.

The Chinese government re-introduced the *bao-jia* (*pao chia*) system by which each family unit was represented by a headman, each ten headmen by one of their number, each ten of those by one elected representative – and so on until the appointees of Peking had direct contact with the peak of a human pyramid responsible to them and the channel of their commands.

Potentially democratic, in reverse it was actually as well suited to oppression. So fundamentally sound and successful was the system, first used by the Zhou (Chou) dynasty a thousand years before Christ, that in the Communist take-over of 1948–50 *bao-jia* government was the first to be imposed upon the people. Any misdemeanour by any individual, and his district, village, group of families and immediate senior would be held accountable. The pressure of opinion and the instinct of self-preservation was quickly effective.[7]

Through the *bao-jia* network Zeng Guo-fan and Li Hong-zhang distributed seed and tools and resettled the land. Mutual recognition of relatives and neighbours established personal rights. Among the literati and scholar–generals of whom Zeng and Li were the most elevated, a close bond of loyalty was imperative. The restoration of stability mattered as much as food. And stability to them meant the Confucian order. Enough of innovations. So what is known as the Tong Zhi (T'ung Chih) Restoration took place, named after the child emperor. Unfortunately it was Confucian bureaucracy they had in mind and not the Confucian principle: 'In a political state the people matter most, institutions next and the monarch is least of all.'

Inevitably in so vast and fragmented a country, in which the horse was the fastest mode of travel and each province had a population like that of individual Western nations, the viceroys and governors tended to form power bases with officials under their own patronage, and literati, often retired grandees, hand in glove with them – as Hudson, Maria and their new colleagues were shortly to discover at the risk of their lives and the price of physical injury.

If Charles Gordon was honoured with the distinctions so far held by Zeng Guo-fan and Li Hong-zhang, they in turn were elevated to the heights of imperial favour. To Ci Xi (Yehonala), Prince Kong and the rest of the Court the relief of freedom from the claims of a rival dynasty, so-called, was immeasurable. While it lasted there had always been the possibility of fickle foreign alignment with the Taipings. So Zeng became a marquis of the first rank with a Double-eyed Peacock's Feather and the office of Senior Guardian of the Throne and Heir Apparent. Beneath the imperial family no one was now more exalted, while the imperial pleasure lasted. Li Hong-zhang received an earldom with appropriate emoluments, and was left to continue the good work of rehabilitation in the provinces known as the Two Jiangs and Anhui under Zeng as viceroy at Nanjing.[8]

A glance into the future is justifiable here. Together they set up an arsenal at Shanghai. To counter their power a naval dockyard was built at Fuzhou by Zuo Zong-tang (Tso Tsung-t'ang), the general who was soon to be sent against the Muslim rebels in the north-west. And at Nanjing Li was in 1867 to create so strong a force with its own arsenal that the Western powers became suspicious of his intentions.[9] Li had full justification for his action, for France had taken her opportunity while helping in the suppression of the Taipings to bring most of Indo-China under her own control and in 1867 began frank annexation. And in Manchuria the Russian possession of the maritime province and development of the great naval base at Vladivostok not only half encircled Chinese Manchuria but posed a threat to all her coasts. Britain had shown her hand so often that the memory of opium wars and treaties under duress was an open wound, while the personal attachment and justice of certain individuals continued to be appreciated.

Robert Hart, a man of outstanding financial acumen, strong will and Christian faith, utterly incorruptible, was allowed in 1865 to set up his headquarters as the Inspector General of the Imperial Maritime Customs, for long the highest Chinese rank held by any alien. The meteoric rise of Maria's disappointed suitor, just thirty on February 20, 1865, placed him where the Court and legations sought his advice for the next forty years. With a staff of two hundred and revenues of eight million taels when he began, Sir Robert 'the Great I.G.' by 1901 controlled 5,134 men and 27 million taels. A very different era, from that of the East India Company and Robert Morrison, had begun.[10]

The great IF[11] *1864–65*

Long before the end of the Taiping rebellion was firmly in sight Westerners were debating alternatives. For decades more, to the end of the century and to the present day, historians and missions have allowed themselves the indulgence of speculation. What if the Taipings had won?

No peoples are permanently content to be dominated by an alien race, and the Manchus were aliens. In language, manner and segregation into Manchu quarters in the great cities they showed their own colonial mentality, however much they acquired indigenous culture and customs. Secret societies kept the flame of Han China nationalism alive. And Ming pretenders waited for the wave on which to surf-ride to reinstatement. Manchu degeneracy and misrule, corruption, injustice and oppression, incited protest and rebellion.

The stage had been set when the ineffective rural dreamer Hong Xiu-quan and his Worshippers of Shangdi were taken up by the Ming partisan Zhu Jiu-dao (Chu Chiu-tao) and changed from a provincial faction at odds with the local government into a revolutionary movement with imperial aims. As an expression of general feeling it had drawn thousands to its ranks. Already an apathy about idols and temple worship existed, however warmly they might be associated with festivity, superstition and relief from the tyranny of life. The transition to iconoclasm gave expression to pent-up feelings. And regimentation to a new religious system, strange in the extreme, cost little in exchange for security, food and clothes.

IMPERIAL TROOPS WITH MITRAILLEUSE
(after an engraving in *The Graphic*)

Success on the first great march northward had seemed to augur well for a quick end to the alien dynasty. Nanjing had been the Ming capital until 1421 and, once occupied, felt to the Taiping movement's leaders like the attainment of their objective. The reduction of Peking and the Manchus was secondary. The first real setback at Duliu should have made the Taiping Wangs take stock. Any great leaders would by then have had a strategic view of their goals, their needs and how they could gain them. But here they failed.

Hong Xiu-quan appeared to think only in terms of his vision and its religious fulfilment. 'Only a complete misunderstanding of the message of the New Testament could have led to so great a travesty on the doctrines of Christ as that which existed at Nanking,' Latourette concluded. As younger brother of the Trinity, a quasi-sibling of Jesus, Hong was preoccupied with promoting the extravagances of protocol and religious observance. The thinkers among his companion leaders were each as limited as he in education and outlook. While they lived there was hope, for the Taiping moral code was high, their administration orderly and their vague intentions beneficent. But they showed no capacity for capitalising on their conquests or harnessing existing civil government to their purposes. From the strongholds they manned they made strong forays to destroy temples, idols and Manchus, but were seemingly incapable of ruling. When unscrupulous power-seekers began to hold the reins things changed for the worse. Hong Xiu-quan, always nominally supreme, became a gaudy cipher. As the years passed and more and more sided with the Taipings through greed, fear or force, the religious element all but vanished and latterly even political motivation was lost in the fight to survive no matter what the cost in human misery. They antagonised the masses and were anathema to the literati on whom they would be compelled to depend if ever a government were to be set up.

So the Taiping movement ended in a shuddering groan of grief and regrets. But foreign speculation as to what might have been continued. The early hopes of missionaries and Chinese like Hong Ren that this was a Christian movement open to improvement, evaporated upon closer acquaintance. Every missionary who visited Nanjing returned disillusioned. The optimism of Muirhead and Griffith John received rude rebuffs. But what if Hong Xiu-quan had been a saner, wiser, stronger man? He could not be altered. So what if his thinkers, like Hong Ren, had survived? That too was beyond control. What if through wisdom or mistrust those Hakkas, as most early Taipings were, had moved to bring the whole Hakka population on to their side – if instead of leaving them to be exploited by Triads and brigand factions with little motive beyond plunder around Canton, they had secured the South with Canton as their port? What if they had responded to the Triad overtures from the Shanghai siege in 1854–55 and supported their seizure of Amoy, instead of arrogantly going their own way in the certainty of success without complicating compromises with the secret societies? And not only forged an alliance with them but with the Nian-fei in 1853 and other minority people in the empire outraged by discrimination and oppression – the aboriginal tribes uncomprehendingly grouped together as 'Miao', in 1854, promising them autonomy, and the Muslims in 1862, guaranteeing religious liberty? They too banned idols, alcohol and opium. If their eyes had been open to the West's grievances, (for several of the Taiping leaders had had direct contacts with missionaries if not merchants), and if they had spoken early of friendly relations and open commerce under their dynasty – if as soon as they controlled the Yangzi river in 1853 they had welcomed foreign shipping and trade, what might not have followed? So ran the argument.

As for the Western powers, if instead of opting for neutrality and then antagonism they had espoused the Taiping cause, toppled the Qing (Ch'ing) dynasty and influenced or controlled the new dynasty, might not the opening of China to trade and Western influence have been advanced by several years? The imperialists were weakened by the 1840 war and heavy indemnities, so that their troops were poorly paid, rapacious plunderers, so alienating the common people.

After the 1860 war this was even more true. Imperialist outposts would fling their swords across to Taiping patrols in exchange for silver. But when in 1858 Sir Frederick Bruce arrived at the Beihe to ratify the treaty of 1856 and was ignominiously rebuffed, or in 1859 when the Allied ships were badly mauled in the abortive attack on the Dagu forts – if then the Western powers had cried Enough! and sided with the anti-Manchu forces, how different history would have looked. If they had simply contented themselves with giving arms and military advice they could have exchanged Manchu obduracy for future uncertainty. If instead of concluding the Peking Convention and opting to support the imperialists who had been fighting them in the North, they had supplied officers and men to the Taipings – if Charles Gordon had led his army against Li Hong-zhang after seeing the flight of the Peking Court into exile – the Allies could have dictated terms at will. Or if in 1854 or subsequently by positive diplomacy they had negotiated terms and guarantees with the Taipings, as Admiral Sir James Hope did in 1861 for the year of truce, might they not have avoided the costly conflict of 1860 and four more years of horrific suffering for millions? To some, an opportunity in a thousand had been lost by default. As William Lockhart observed, had Bruce decisively informed the Taipings of Allied intentions, and reasons for holding the city of Shanghai, their attack in 1862 would probably not have taken place or rebel ill feeling towards the foreigners been aroused.

'Vanity of vanities, all is vanity.' Daydreams could not reverse history. Sir John Bowring, British plenipotentiary, believed that British trade with China depended on the continuation of Manchu government. Sir George Bonham, his successor, after visiting the bizarre regime at Nanjing at the peak of its success, advocated caution by strict neutrality. The American Commissioner Marshall not surprisingly favoured the continuation of the Qing dynasty, after his arrogant welcome to Nanjing in 1854 by the illustrious Tian Wang:

> If you do indeed respect heaven and recognize the Sovereign, then our celestial court seeing all under Heaven as one family and uniting all nations as one body, will most assuredly . . . permit you year by year to bring tribute and annually to pay court . . .[12]

Little choice existed between old and new. Marshall's interpreter, the missionary Samuel Wells Williams, looking back in 1864 when the whole edifice had collapsed, wrote, 'I had no faith in this rebellion from the first as likely to prove a means of promoting the truth.'

By then it was a far cry from the rosy days of 1860 and Griffith John's optimistic report to the LMS, after receiving invitations to live and preach in Taiping territory:

> I fully believe that God is uprooting idolatry in this land through the insurgents and that He will by means of them, in connexion with the foreign missionary, plant Christianity in its stead.

But predictions right or wrong were not at issue in the debate called 'IF'. A merchant named Scarth in *Twelve Years in China, 1847–59*, expressed the opinion that if the British government had not been un-neutral while professing neutrality (for open intervention was delayed until 1862), the rebellion would have given China an opportunity to become Christian. He too was writing before 'Taiping' meant terror and little else. But W A P Martin of Ningbo in Hudson Taylor's day and at Peking after 1863, remained unrepentantly favourable to the Taipings when he wrote his *Cycle of Cathay* in 1896. By then he was President of the Imperial Tungwen College, an honoured servant of the emperor.[13]

The Roman Catholics on the other hand, after suffering greatly at the hands of the Taipings and imperialists, were more critical than any Protestant. Fifty years after the end of the rebellion, the leading Baptist, Timothy Richard, believed that Christianity in China was still suffering from the legacy of ill will generated by the Taipings' claims to be Christian. The deep and bitter prejudice in Hunan province against Christians and foreigners until decades later was attributable to their ravages. This also can only be surmise. In the final analysis the Christian overtones were accidental and unfortunate. The Taiping movement, after Zhu Jiu-dao (Chu Chiu-tao) linked up with the Worshippers of Shangdi, was firstly political, owing much in its trappings to contact with Christianity at Canton. As Latourette summed it up, it was,

> one in a long succession of movements in China which combined economic and social unrest with religious features and political aspirations, but unlike its predecessors this contained Christian elements.[14]

Yet this is not the last word, for out of the aftermath of the rebellion and the flight of rebels to find sanctuary wherever they could, came the son of a farmer born in 1866 between Canton and Macao and educated in Honolulu, who returned with a Bible, studied medicine at Hong Kong and met a Chinese Christian named Soong with the same secretly revolutionary views. Devoting all his energies to promoting revolution against the Manchu dynasty, with Soong as the financial head of the movement, Sun Yat-sen became the father of the successful Republican Revolution of 1911–12 and is honoured as grandfather of the present regime of the People's Republic of China. One of Soong's beautiful daughters married Sun Yat-sen and is today a member of the Politburo in Peking. Another is Madame Chiang Kai-shek. According to the biographer of Bishop William Boone Sr, Sun Yat-sen in his youth had close contact with groups of exiles of Taiping origin.

Empty speculation in the 1860s could lead nowhere. But as

history unfolded, the Christian Church had freedom under the Manchus to preach the gospel throughout the empire, and under the Republic until about 1950. During most of that near-century missionaries were largely free to do as they wished, often amidst the turmoil of civil unrest. Even Ci Xi failed to stop them. If the Western powers had backed the Taipings, would conditions have been more favourable?

Caught on the wrong foot *1864–65*

Rid of the Taipings, the imperialist government of China was too war-weary and too overstretched in dealing with the other rebellions to try its strength again with the Western nations. For them only the prospect of expansion into the vast hinterland remained. Merchants and explorers were on the move. By 1864 there were sixty foreigners resident in Peking itself, inviolable before 1860. Promotions had elevated Sir Rutherford Alcock to be HBM Minister to Japan and Harry Parkes as consul-general to a free-breathing Shanghai. Sportsmen sallied out from Shanghai to shoot duck from their houseboats where Gordon's fire-breathing gunboats had so recently ploughed the waterways among corpses. And Shanghai boasted gas-lighting in the streets of the Settlement, its first fire-engine, and a new newspaper, the *North China Daily News*. A railway linking Shanghai and Wusong was projected – but not completed until 1878.

Twenty-three years had passed since the Treaty of Nanking, six since the Treaty of Tientsin and four since the Peking Convention. The Church and missions were in terms of time well launched into 'the open century' and it was high time to forge ahead. But such expansion as had taken place in the last four years was only token in nature. Even so it left existing work in the treaty ports handicapped and struggling. Attenuation, not advance had taken place. With nearly a quarter-century's notice and six years' urgent reminder, the Church was still unready. Even four years gave time to find, train, send and teach the essentials of the language to the young men who should now be running with the veterans, preparing to take the baton from them. But a bare handful had come. Two years' training had produced in James Meadows a very worthwhile missionary. But death was depleting the ranks of experienced men as ruthlessly as ever. Ferdinand Genähr, pioneer of the Rhenish Mission died with his two sons when he befriended a destitute Chinese woman with cholera.

In the West war still disrupted life in America and Europe, but Britain was at peace. President Lincoln proclaimed the abolition of slavery on January 1, 1863. The Civil War began to go in his favour during the year, at the battles of Gettysburg and Chattanooga. General Lee surrendered to Grant on April 9, 1865, and Abraham Lincoln was assassinated on the 14th. The Civil War ended on May 10 and its wounds began to heal. But the Church took time to recover and American missions still suffered, some extremely, from neglect.

In Europe the sun was setting on the second Napoleonic empire but the German invasion of Schleswig-Holstein followed an ultimatum in January 1864 and hostilities continued until October. In England the rich waxed fatter, while the poor resented their flamboyant affluence and were powerless to do anything. Queen Victoria in her mid-forties was the grandmother of seven though married herself only twenty-four years earlier. And her multi-racial empire went on expanding. India and Africa, yielding to her control and colonisation were the natural field of missionary expansion. The glamour of the South Sea cannibal islands captured much of the missionary interest remaining in the Churches. But China's unpopularity inhibited the Christian public and church leaders alike. China struck them as being a troublesome, dangerous, unproductive place. Japan was vicious; Korea, the Spanish Philippines and Indo-China were as hermetically sealed against Protestants as ever. Buddhist Siam and Burma were open but adamantine, and Muslim Malaysia no less so. East Asia won little sympathy, although in India these were great days of expansion. In the established Churches of Britain the missionary spirit had diminished, and the awakened Churches of the revivals lacked information and enlightenment. Here however lay China's hope.

The Roman Catholic Church, although losing missionaries by violent death to the very end, benefited from its organisation and discipline. Men were sent out to swell its ranks, and absorbed without difficulty into the existing system. Protestant missions working piecemeal and haphazardly had not yet been given the recognition and support they assuredly deserved. In 1864 two CMS stations were destroyed in Fujian and two years later an English Presbyterian chapel was dismantled and the first Protestant Chinese martyr in Fuzhou gave his life.

But this sporadic trouble was in contrast to the general calm. The CMS, already in Hong Kong, Fuzhou, Ningbo, Shanghai and Peking, had the opportunity to expand into ravaged Hangzhou. After the Taiping withdrawal from Hangzhou, the provincial capital, in April 1864 two Chinese evangelists came to George Moule strongly urging him to strike while the iron was hot. 'This may be God's opportunity,' they said, 'don't let it slip.'[15] Years before, Gutzlaff had named Hangzhou as the key city for the CMS to occupy. In 1858 the CMS Conference at Ningbo had set its sights on the city. John Burdon and the Presbyterian Neviuses had lived there for months in 1859. So George Moule went there in the autumn of 1864. Finding it safe and being offered a house by a Ningbo neighbour, he took his family in with him a year later. By then the American Presbyterians had moved in too. Already they were established in Suzhou and Nanjing in the wake of the Taiping dynasty, as well as in Shanghai, Ningbo and Canton. And in 1866 Carl Kreyer, an American Baptist, followed. But before the end of 1865 the first baptisms took place in Hangzhou and the Church began to put down its roots. In 1866 Hudson Taylor and the China Inland Mission were also to make the great city their base.

At Hankou Griffith John extended his work across the river into much-ravaged Wuchang. And the Wesleyan, Josiah Cox, whom he had invited from Canton in 1862, made the first Protestant itineraries into rabid Hunan province, meeting opposition. They were joined by a Methodist doctor and in 1865 by the saintly David Hill, also a Methodist. A man of private means, David Hill lived very simply, like the Chinese people around him, using his money to relieve the destitute, the aged and the blind.

The Bible Society lost no time in carrying the Bible far and wide into inland China. Many cities were first visited by these intrepid men, no less than the LMS's Alexander Wylie for the British and Foreign Bible Society, and Griffith John's contemporary, Alexander Williamson, for the National Bible Society of Scotland formed in 1860.[16] Wylie travelled to every port where missions were established and to twelve of the eighteen provinces, setting up depots and committees in the ports to promote, at last, the widespread distribution of Scripture, in the way it had been done so intensively around Shanghai a decade earlier. Everywhere he himself engaged in colportage with foreign and Chinese Christians to teach them the art. Williamson, who had been invalided home in 1859, now made his base at Yantai (Chefoo) and covered North China, Manchuria and Mongolia. The LMS's R J Thomas literally risked his neck by taking Scriptures to Korea in 1865 for the Bible Society of Scotland and distributing them along the coast for two and a half months. When he tried again a year later, the ship ran aground in a river and was attacked and burned. Thomas and all aboard perished.

Following up their survey from Amoy into Taiwan and the Pescadore Islands, the English Presbyterians turned to other Amoy migrants in Singapore and the Straits as the natural development within the same dialect communities. The man who introduced them to Amoy and then moved on to pioneer Swatow (Shantou), William Burns, travelled to Peking in 1863. And there he published his inimitable translation of *Pilgrim's Progress*, so popular with the Chinese that it was still in demand in the mid-twentieth century.[17]

Magnificent as these achievements were, they were only a few drops in the bucket that was China. And while these stalwarts spread far afield, three veterans were lost to China altogether. George Smith resigned as Bishop of Victoria, Hong Kong, in 1864, succeeded by C R Alford. William Dean returned from Hong Kong to Bangkok where he founded six Chinese churches and a school. And Bishop William Boone Sr died in Shanghai. But they were not all. John and Helen Nevius after their return from Japan spent two years at Yantai and Dengzhou (now Penglai) before returning to Ningbo in 1864. Recalling those days Helen Nevius wrote years later, 'I doubt if anyone can now realise how experimental all kinds of missionary work were' in the '50s and '60s. But already John Nevius' strategic thinking was taking shape. To his American Presbyterian Board of Foreign Missions he expounded at this time principles which he was formulating, principles which he applied in Shandong and which in time directly resulted in the continuing great Church movement in Korea. Echoing Morrison and Gutzlaff, they gave rise to 'indigenous' policies in China: 'I believe it is generally admitted that the main work of preaching the gospel in China must eventually be performed by the [Chinese].'[18] The foreigner was too handicapped. His chief role should be to train Chinese. So Nevius advocated the institution of a theological school of not too high an academic standard to train country pastors. Such a school would be a strong bond of union between the missionary societies. But it would need 'uninterrupted continuity of effort'. He favoured Hangzhou as its venue.

But Helen's pulmonary tuberculosis recurred with serious symptoms. After a voyage up the Yangzi during the siege of Nanjing in

1864, they sailed for Britain to find treatment for her, and so linked up with Hudson Taylor and Maria again – whereby hangs a tale.

In 1842 only six Protestant Chinese Christians were known in China. In 1853 the total had reached three hundred and fifty. And that figure had increased to two thousand by 1865.[19] But half a century had passed and that was all that could be shown for so much labour and suffering. Without doubt it was slow and hard going. But where there had been a hundred and fifteen missionaries in 1860, only ninety or ninety-one were left in 1865. And they were in seven of the provinces, leaving eleven with none.

It was in this grim situation that the missionaries in China and missionaries invalided out appealed in vain for the Churches to wake up and act. The general decadence of missionary zeal – experienced from time to time in the past – seemed unshakable.[20] Now was the acceptable time, now the day of salvation. When missionaries began to flow into China at long last, they found the temples rebuilt and gaudy idols on the pedestals again, enslaving the hearts of the people.

Knowing all this and finding response from the United Methodist Free Church, a small denomination, but little elsewhere, Hudson Taylor's tenacity forced him to think: If the LMS and denominational Churches and missions cannot or will not rise to this great occasion, who will do so? Who is there to do so? And how can anything be done to take the gospel to those eleven unevangelised provinces? When will the Church wake from its preoccupations and look seriously at China? How long will China's hundreds of millions have to wait?

With William Berger and Frederick Gough he shared a deep concern. In Gough it found expression by prayer and actively joining Hudson Taylor in lobbying the missionary societies. In Berger the businessman, it touched his pocket and stirred his mind to thrash over the subject with Hudson Taylor. In the background, humbled by the fate of the CES but unable to lose his zeal, George Pearse gave them his moral backing, prayers and ideas long since set out in *The Gleaner*. But on Hudson Taylor with youth to his advantage it all weighed as a personal responsibility, one he must discharge by all means in his power.

He exerted a strong, continuing influence on the United Methodist Free Church; and according to his daughter-in-law's verbatim notes while he reminisced:

> [As in early 1861] Mr. Taylor and Mr. Gough made repeated efforts to induce the larger Missionary Societies to undertake a forward movement. Separately or together they called upon the Rev. Henry Venn of the C.M.S., William Arthur of the Wesleyan Methodists, Trestrail and Underhill of the Baptist Mission, Eckett of the Methodist Free Church and representatives of other Societies urging that some other effort should be made . . .

His own journal for May 7, 1864 reads, 'Mr Cockerton called this morning to say he had seen Mr. Prout of the London Miss. Society, who were not in want of any more Medical missionaries.'

There are records of Hudson Taylor's dealings with Robert Eckett, who died in July 1862, and then mainly with Charles Cheetham and Samuel Barton, but few memoranda or letters about the other interviews. Even his own journal recorded less of his daily activities as he became more pressed for time in 1864. The hours spent in revising the Ningbo New Testament became shorter, but how his time was occupied is often omitted, and letters by himself during that year have not been preserved. What is clear from his *Retrospect* and booklet *China: Its Spiritual Need and Claims* is that strenuous efforts to work through existing organisations were disappointed.

> Months of earnest prayer and not a few abortive efforts had resulted in a deep conviction that *a special agency was essential* for the evangelization of Inland China . . . The grave difficulty of possibly interfering with existing missionary operations at home was foreseen . . .[21]

So that was the direction of their thinking. China must have the missionaries. Existing societies could not do more than they were doing. Something new was needed, a channel to carry men and women to China, an approach to the Churches which would make the need known and tap resources of men and support without deflecting them from the existing channels. Hudson Taylor could see how deeply embroiled he himself could become, and shrank from it as 1864 progressed. At the same time letters from James Meadows and about him confirmed that men of his type possessed most promising potential. He was coping well with the Bridge Street church. Hudson Taylor could let his thoughts travel farther afield than Ningbo, to embrace the whole of China.

One thing after another[22] *1864*

Because so much happened in 1864 and so many incidentals competed with the Taylors' main preoccupations, the only coherent way to picture their life is to follow through the same period of time in a series of parallel accounts covering one aspect after the other. From the beginning of the year while in China the Taiping nightmare reached its climax and in the Ningbo Church life began to look up, the tempo of life at Beaumont Street increased. Still more people became involved and this meant more being done for them while New Testament revision proceeded at the old pace. The many strands in the household's existence competed for attention. Illness claimed more of Hudson Taylor's time and an empty purse tested him to the limits of his faith. The impending departure of Wang Lae-djün with the Fullers and Kingdons meant hours and complete days devoted to their final preparations. The Fullers at least were heading for Ningbo, but the BMS were sending the Edwin Kingdons to Shandong and all the Taylors did for them was for Christ's sake and for China.

Gratitude to Wang Lae-djün for staying away from his wife and children to work on the New Testament for so long, forced Hudson Taylor to go far out of his way to make his last few months in England memorable. Apart from giving him more personal coaching in basic theology and medicine, he took him to Guy's Hospital museum, the Royal Geographical Society, the Houses of Parliament, and to a service at Westminster Abbey. Wang Lae-djün could not have doubted the love and interest of Hudson Taylor and Maria in his welfare. Yet through it all there were new missionary candidates to interview and train, and patients to see and treat for Mary Jones, who could not live in East London without being a missionary.

Shortly after Mrs Lord and her boys left to return to the States and China, Hudson Taylor invited the young German Stephan Barchet and the Scotsman George Crombie to join him in Mile End, and his training of Barchet began. Annie Skinner, the Aberdeen lass engaged to Crombie, came to stay with them for a week, and Jennie Faulding dropped in from time to time. At nineteen she was still too young to talk of going herself to China, but liked lending a hand in all the bustle of activity.

'Tye-kim', a Chinese Christian connected with the Society for the Propagation of the Gospel (SPG) was in touch with them in March, and Hudson Taylor introduced him to the Christian circles in Hackney and Bromley-by-Bow, walking with Lae-djün and Tye-kim to Hackney and back on the Sunday morning and to Bromley in the afternoon. On Friday he also went out to East Grinstead to talk with William Berger about Tye-kim. A fortnight later he was still working on Tye-kim's affairs and on June 4 recorded in his journal that Tye-kim had sailed, as a missionary to 'Demerara in British Guinea', Guyana, South America.

When the Methodist Fuller found a ship bound for Shanghai and was given an option on a berth for Lae-djün at a discount, there was much coming and going, especially when the Baptist Edwin Kingdon and his bride arranged to sail at the same time, apparently on the same ship. Drugs, instruments, books, clothes, furniture, all the paraphernalia of a missionary in those days had to be bought, inventoried, packed and conveyed to the docks. Because of the damage to clothes by the salt air and ship's tar Maria advised the young bride to travel in old outer garments, with a bonnet, bonnet shapes and a hat for the voyage and to take enough drapery, hosiery and haberdashery for two years.

Then followed the farewell meetings when Lae-djün spoke at the chapels and assemblies he had attended – and finally the journey in a big group to Gravesend, the prayer together in the Fullers' cabin and the parting. Jennie Faulding was there, and F F Gough, for Hudson Taylor wrote contritely in his journal, 'Forgot Mr Gough's bag. He returned for it.' The words could mean anything, but it was important to avoid every potential cause of disharmony. The meticulous Hudson Taylor could be absent-minded. On another occasion he left his own silk umbrella and 'case' in the train. He was tired and unwell, having had headaches and short bouts of illness that kept him in bed for a few days, without hint of anything serious.

From time to time donations were coming in from friends, from George Müller and William Berger, as so often, and when Hudson Taylor visited Clevedon and other places to preach, the friends he met contributed to one activity or another. John Eliot and Robert Howard and Miss Stacey never failed him. But never was this income regular in either timing or amount, or to be counted on in such a way as to make the Taylors look to them and not to God to meet their needs. There is no evidence of collusion between them to ensure that he had an adequate income, or that he was provided for when they specified how any sum was to be used. When forty pounds arrived from Mr Müller on May 30, Hudson Taylor allocated fifteen to Lae-djün's passage, ten to Ningbo expenses and the evangelist Ni's support, keeping fifteen for his own purposes at Beaumont Street. This was how he managed all the time, never knowing, apart from Maria's small dividends, where the next provision would come from.

On June 6 he took Maria with their children and their nurse for a holiday in Yorkshire. The new baby was expected at the end of the month. They visited the grandparents, went on to York and at Scarborough played on the sands and fished, in a rare week of relaxation. On Sunday Hudson Taylor preached the gospel in a theatre service, and at different times put in several hours on the New Testament proofs and in writing letters to recruits. A new one was in touch with him, John W Stevenson, the twenty-year-old grandson of the Laird of Thriepwood, Renfrewshire. But Hudson Taylor's thoughts were concentrated on some magazine articles he had read and on three meetings he had attended in London towards the end of May. So he also wrote to George Pearse a letter laden with the seeds of destiny, soon to find itself in print. Then on June 15 they went back to Barnsley.

Maria was near her confinement and very weary, but on the 20th they all set off for London, only to miss their connection because of delays due to the Royal Review at Doncaster. So back to Barnsley they had to traipse. For the next four days Maria was ill and in pain, and on June 24 her third son, Samuel Dyer Taylor, was born. In February one of Maria's aunts had sent her the Dyer family tree and her own father, Samuel Dyer, was very much in her mind. At first both did well. Then five days later she was 'very feverish' again, an alarming sign in those days of little treatment for puerperal sepsis. 'I felt very anxious and cried to the Lord and by evening she was decidedly better,' Hudson Taylor wrote.

That meant staying where they were. He and his mother worked together on his China journals, preparing them for publication, and corresponded with Frederick Gough. Unpunctuality and differences of opinion were negligible problems compared with the latest development. Gough had written enclosing part of another letter from W A Russell, as ominous a portent as first impressions suggested. (We will return to this.) Hudson Taylor visited Richard Truelove and his parents at Staincross and gave Richard a lesson. But Maria could not travel and he himself must return to London, so on Monday, July 4, he left her with his parents and took Grace and Howard back with him.

The rent on No 1 Beaumont Street was due and the landlord was to come in the morning to collect it. Before going away Hudson Taylor had set it aside as usual, but when he checked the amount on reaching home he found it was a sovereign short. And he had no cash left to make it up. As a matter of principle, of integrity as a Christian and of faith that God would supply all his needs without his going into debt, it mattered greatly to him that he should not have to beg the landlord's indulgence. The morning came and no money arrived in the post, but neither did the landlord turn up. This was a relief, but he felt his predicament intensely; '. . . forty years afterwards he felt it still and told his [biographers] that it was one of the worst times he ever had of *personal* financial trial.' But when the landlord came on the 6th Hudson Taylor had the full sum for him. 'Paid my rent. Felt very happy in the Lord' was his comment.

Maria and the children returned from Yorkshire late on July 18, but all was not well. 'Maria felt acute pain, then was sick and very poorly. Afterwards she was feverish . . . O Lord! bless my dear wife and spare her . . .' When writing to Meadows he thought she had cholera, but the next day called it enteritis. By the 20th she was better but still very ill. And he himself was ill and 'feeling very much prostrated'. After another week Maria was able to dress and come downstairs. Giving thanks for 'the Lord's goodness to us', he wrote, 'How many husbands, wives, children, have been removed from the Missionary Circle, while we have been spared.'

So far so good, but all through this time their community life and revision work had to continue, at half pressure – 4½ hours, 3½, 2, 5, 3, 5 . . . and admitting in his journal 'Have but a few shillings left', Hudson Taylor walked from Mile End to Oxford Street to preach at Bryanston Hall on August 7. But on the 12th he was caught out. 'The Tax-gatherer called and I was obliged to defer him. Help us O Lord, for Thy name's sake.'

It was a family matter. He did not share such things with Gough or Mary Jones, now that they were living elsewhere. In January Miss Stacey had told him to let her know if Mary Jones or he and Maria were in need of funds, saying, 'We want such guidance in the fulfilment of stewardship.' But she had not said 'ever in need', and at the time they had had all they needed. Gough still came in to work at No 1 and the very simple lunch, or something, must have betrayed their secret. Hudson Taylor's penny journal reads,

> Told Nurse our position; she wished to lend me some money. Sought to realize that it is in weakness and need that the Strength of Jesus is perfected. At night after leaving, Mr Gough returned and put into my hand £7.0.0. begging me to accept it. Εὐλογητος ὁ Θέος [Blessed be God].

Mary Jones sent five pounds the next day. The emergency was over. And on the 20th another windfall of twenty pounds from George Müller and twenty from Berger, half of it for Richard Truelove, allowed Hudson Taylor to give their nurse ten shillings towards a loss by theft. Better still, on August 25 William Berger made them a major offer, 'to bear the expenses of Truelove, Crombie, Wilson and Stevenson, and ourselves to China. Τῷ Θεῷ χάρις [To God be thanks]'. James Wilson was the latest, short-lived recruit.[23]

Lessons in tolerance *June–November 1864*

The trouble over the New Testament revision began again in June 1864, just before the Scarborough holiday. Ever since the CMS and Bible Society had settled W A Russell's objections in October 1863, Gough and Hudson Taylor had done him the courtesy of sending proof sheets for him to see. All was well until the proofs of the Gospels and Acts were finished and they started on the Epistles. In actual revision they were well ahead and had finished Galatians in May. On June 2, Russell wrote to Gough 'about the sheet of Romans', making a new proposition. He offered his help. True to his generous nature and in spite of their previous problems,

> Mr G. proposed to write to Mr. Russell suggesting our working at Gorsebrook [Gough's home in the Midlands] with Mr. R. on the Epistles. To this I dissented. He was grieved. We much cast on the Lord. In answer to united prayer he gave it up at night very kindly and gave me £4.0.0.

If peace at a price was Gough's preference, Hudson Taylor's fear was again of losing a truly colloquial idiom as the price of Russell's co-operation. It would be at the cost of either a change of style or friction all along the way. So this was the time to settle the matter, before it went further. Then he and his family had to set off for their holiday.

Gough was feeling very unsettled about continuing. Prayer was Hudson Taylor's only recourse. 'Once more I cast it upon Thee, O

Lord. Undertake for us.' But from the nine- and ten-hour stints in early July even his time on revision dropped to half as much daily while Maria was ill. Then John Burdon arrived home in Britain and on August 8 Frederick Gough went to see him. Hudson Taylor felt uneasy. If another CMS colleague shared Russell's views, despite the Bible Society's decision supported by Henry Venn, the whole subject could open up again. Long months of very hard work still lay ahead, progress was slow and the claims of greater things were becoming stronger. So easily the way out of trouble would have been to turn the matter over to the Bible Society to be settled without him. But while doggedness was one of Hudson Taylor's qualities, the need in Ningbo where he expected soon to be at work again was for a truly vernacular version of the Scriptures, and the sooner the better. Only his pace would get it done. If he looked stubborn and unco-operative, his wide circle of friends and confidants and his daily living as 'a man for others' gave a different impression of his nature.

On October 17 who should turn up at the door but their old friend John Nevius, with Helen dangerously ill again. This affected them in two ways. Helping the Neviuses to unload from their ship and make arrangements in London took many hours. Helen wrote,

> Strangers in a strange land, we needed friends and advice, . . . for my health was then at the very lowest ebb, and my recovery seemed doubtful. We found in Mr Hudson Taylor just the friend we needed. There was nothing which he was not ready to do for us. We also found – what we had not realized before, – that Mr Taylor was a wise and judicious medical man . . .[24]

They consulted him as a doctor and he prescribed for her until he could take her to see Dr Andrew Clarke at the London Hospital, and again until she was admitted to a sanatorium at Sudbrook Park, near Richmond. Nevius had business with the Religious Tract Society and Hudson Taylor helped him to have some printing done. But John Nevius also helped as an impartial consultant on the New Testament revision. Well into 1865 they worked together, sometimes on the RTS proofs. Thrown together like this, Taylor discovered that John Nevius was in financial difficulties, so he wrote to William Berger about his circumstances and 'Gave Mr. N. 50/- of tythe money. Dear Lord, accept it for Jesus' sake.' The Lord knew how much those fifty shillings cost him personally. Two weeks later another expenditure deserved the journal entry. 'Paid taxes

£1.10.4. Thanks to God for money to do so.' And then he received fifty pounds from Miss Stacey's sister.

Hardly another mention of Mr Russell occurs in Hudson Taylor's journal until he himself was so fully absorbed in the unfolding of his future lifework that his own work on the revision had to take a lower priority.

The furrow and the crop[25] *1864–65*

The words of Samuel Rutherford, 'Why should I start at the plough of my Lord, that maketh deep furrows on my soul? I know He is no idle husbandman, He purposeth a crop' were true of James Meadows through the long months of 1864 and '65. While others came and went, and Charles Gordon tipped the scales against the Taiping rebels, Meadows gave himself to the Bridge Street church and, barely aware of progress, was made into a missionary as mature and effective as it could take others years to become.[26]

When Hudson Taylor sent him off to work and learn with John Jones, he knew how unsparing the example set before James Meadows would be. John Jones would be a hard-working, deeply spiritual companion. Of James Meadows' potential Hudson Taylor had no doubt from the first. Carey, Morrison, Medhurst, Wylie and many others who became outstanding missionaries had no greater advantages when they began. Some were given higher education before they went abroad. Some who were not, like Alexander Wylie, did no less well. But John Jones' rapid deterioration in health was not in the plan. Nor Martha's death and James' loneliness. Yet these were the very factors, the deep furrows which produced the crop of excellence in him. Ill at ease among missionaries with different ways of life, however kind to him, he found the Chinese Christians congenial company and progressed in language and understanding of them far faster than he would have done with his own home and colleagues to keep him isolated.

E C Lord was too busy to give him much time. During Mrs Lord's absence in the States and England he had to keep her orphanage school going, to build the new premises and to pastor the church he had brought into being. To give half of each Sunday to the Bridge Street congregation taxed his time and strength. He could not spend much more with Meadows. John Jones committed the church to his care, but Lord looked to the absent Jones and Hudson Taylor for decisions and was careful not to make changes. James Meadows wrote of him, '[He] is a very patient gentle man, he is very careful lest he should hurt their feelings.'

But Hudson Taylor had learned too well that remote control held too many complications, and kept his hands off Ningbo affairs both while Jones was there and after he left. He considered himself a senior colleague of Meadows, not an employer or even his director, whatever others thought of James as his protégé or 'agent'. But James had learned to respect and defer to Hudson Taylor's judgment and in his letters reported progress and discussed his work with him.[27] In the Chinese too he found an attitude to Hudson Taylor which he frankly stated,

> . . . there is no class of people who will notice anger in you quicker than a Chinaman . . .; they love you, i.e. those who know you, because you are patient with them. [Ni] said, he had never seen your face manifest great anger . . .[28]

It was an ex-Buddhist speaking. To the Chinese that mattered a great deal. In their scale of sins anger ranked with adultery.

Meadows went constantly with the active Christians to preach in Ningbo and the countryside. People in England had no idea of how dense the population of China was, he said, like a forest of trees standing shoulder to shoulder. To make his way through the streets, crowded again since the departure of the Taipings, he had to worm his way with difficulty. The aftermath of the rebellion appalled him.

> In my walks through the city I meet with some horrid sights, some heart-rending scenes. I allude to the poor beggars and refugees . . . When I consider these poor creatures . . . homeless, destitute . . . contending daily with starvation . . . disease and . . . Death, I say to myself, 'Why in the world is Mr Taylor staying there making books, while thousands are perishing to whom he might administer medicine both to their souls and bodies?' Then I begin to think hard things of you *Book-makers*. There seems to be such a mania among the missionaries for making books . . . But I do think my dear brother that your plan, namely in the *Tu-wo* [colloquial] is 'The Plan' – and may God bring it to a successful and speedy termination.

He had not yet related his own rich enjoyment of daily soaking up the Word of God to the need of Chinese Christians for the same.

His concern for Hudson Taylor's and Maria's health is seen in letter after letter. They must not work so hard or they would be unable to care for the Church that needed them. As for bringing others with them, the Ever-Victorious Army was clearing the countryside, Hangzhou had been evacuated by the rebels, the two Chinese evangelists who were urging George Moule to go at once and occupy the city where so much suffering had melted people's hearts, were urging that this was the great moment they had all been waiting for. Moule had gone in October. 'We don't care how soon you come back [Meadows told Hudson Taylor] and bring as many . . . as you wisely can to help push forward the ark of God over this rough road.'

Miss Aldersey's old premises were up for sale, he reported, thinking perhaps that Hudson Taylor would take them for his coming party of missionaries. 'I long for you to come out.' The Valentines arrived in May and the Neviuses left in July to make the voyage up the Yangzi and stay with Griffith John in Hankou before sailing for England. Nanjing fell and the Taiping rebellion was over. Surely the Taylors would be coming soon.

James Meadows' baby was still with Mrs Parker who was 'like a mother to it', and he was on such close terms with the church members that he could say, 'I am a brother of theirs'. But still he was longing for closer friendships with his own people. Dr John Parker and he were going out preaching together and had rented part of a temple in a market town packed three times a week with people from the surrounding countryside, and very responsive to the gospel.

At Yuyao where a year ago only four or five Christians lived, Nevius and a young newcomer, Samuel Dodd, had baptised twenty-four, then fifteen more, and had ten or more preparing for baptism – all the result of those few Christians' witness. In Ningbo Meadows was feeling cheered by four more asking to be baptised, a graduate and a military mandarin among them. The irascible basket-maker Feng Neng-gui had been reinstated and was doing well. And church services were being better attended. Even his own Bible class was looking up. Clearly he himself was improving fast in the language and idiom. One simple countryman named Wang Guo-yao, he reported after one journey, was such a genuine Christian that, 'His reputation for miles around his [home] is good. We scarcely came to a place where they had not more or less heard of Jesus from [his] mouth.'

A very ill eighteen-year-old Buddhist nun who with her Superior had heard the gospel at their convent from another church member, Zhu, was brought to church and gave such clear answers to questions about what she now believed, that tears came to

Meadows' eyes and the evangelist Ni was 'filled with rapture'. Meadows was for caution lest she be baptised too hastily, but E C Lord said, 'You see all the members wish her to be received so I had better receive her.' She died two days later, of 'dropsy'. (More young people succumbed to hookworm and beri-beri than to nephritis, the three common causes of such 'oedema'.) The Superior was believing too, but to leave the convent and let her hair grow again would be interpreted as an admission of immorality and she could not think what to do. James Meadows wrote, 'My heart being full and having none to express freely my ideas to, I thought I would unburden myself in . . . this letter.'

Although by then Mrs Lord had arrived back from the States, Mr Lord was busier than ever. Both Mr Berger and George Müller were supporting the orphanage and the new building was nearly completed. During the American consul's absence Mr Lord was serving as vice-consul.[29] A Chinese merchant greeted Meadows, 'You missionaries are getting on in the world!' 'Do you think so?' he answered, 'As far as I am concerned . . . it is a far greater honour to be a tract distributor for the Lord Jesus Christ than to be a Consul for the British Queen.'

With the departure of the last senior missionary of the American Presbyterian Board, when the Neviuses left in July, their work was in the hands of three young men. The same was true of the CMS work when Russell went and left the Moules in charge. The Lords and Knowltons, American Baptists, were the continuing links with the earlier days.

Following Hudson Taylor's lead, a conference of Ningbo missionaries of all missions decided unanimously to sell all Scripture instead of distributing it gratis, four years before it became official Bible Society policy. And James Meadows wrote of 'a loving, friendly spirit' among the missionaries. But so many of them, he lamented, were so preoccupied with static duties, Church, schools, and desk-work. Hudson Taylor, a field-worker, was so greatly needed, 'I am anxiously awaiting your arrival . . . the apostle Paul bids Timothy after he had become Bishop of Ephesus, to do the work of an evangelist.'

It was evangelism that was being curtailed in Ningbo, at a time when the people were ready to listen. All the same, Mr Lord, scarcely up from his sickbed with what they had thought was 'cholera, that terrible word which strikes terror to some hearts', had baptised fifteen more, four of his own church and eleven Bridge

Street converts. The Buddhist Superior and another novice were among them. The little nun would have been a sixteenth. But what did numbers matter, Meadows commented, so long as their quality was good.

He was making few references to money this year. He had enough. But thanking Hudson Taylor for a note from Scarborough regretting that he could send so little this time, Meadows told him he need not have worried. On the same day a letter came from Mr Berger amply making up the usual amount. But Mrs Lord had heard that the Fullers of the UMFC and Wang Lae-djün were on their way, without Hudson Taylor and Maria, to whom she wrote,

> When do *you* think of coming out. I fear from recent letters that your health is failing and I wish you could see it your duty to bring your work here where your presence is so much needed . . . I feel very much alone here without [Gough] and you and Mrs. Jones.

So changed had the missionary community become. She felt a lack of kindred spirits. But Mrs Lord was working systematically in the villages with Mrs Tsiu 'the man-hunter'.

A small flutter of consternation over the Fullers' impending arrival was troubling them in Ningbo. 'Where will Mr Fuller and family go! You have not mentioned a word about them, which has surprised Mr Lord and myself,' Meadows wrote. But the Fullers were Free Methodists, to be arranged for by them as the Baptists and CMS had done for their men. They arrived with Lae-djün on October 19, but with only two of their three children. As they had feared would happen, the youngest had died, in a typhoon in the China Sea south of Taiwan.

By then people were turning to Christ in 'hundreds [in] the various churches here,' Mrs Lord reported. Everywhere there was a welcome, and Mrs Tsiu was kept busy reading the Bible to people in their homes. But with the New Year, very cold weather and another long drought which left the canals dry or brackish as when Martha died, James Meadows was depressed, heartsick like Mrs Lord from hope deferred, longing to have his close friends Hudson Taylor and Maria with him again. W R Fuller was keeping Wang Lae-djün as his teacher, so the link with home left Meadows feeling all the more solitary. He would have welcomed Lae-djün as his own colleague. 'It is often asked,' Mrs Lord told Maria, 'When are the Taylors coming out, yes, when . . . Mrs. Jones speaks of coming out next year, but I must wait and see.' But news had come of Maria being very ill again at the birth of her third son. 'Only think the happy mother of three sons and one daughter, and it seems like the other day when it was disputed whether you ought to be a wife or not.'

As for James Meadows, she went on tongue in cheek,

> He is growing very wise and can already suggest improvements in translations and in missionary plans which older [missionaries] never thought of! . . . He gives [Mr Lord] much information, talking very knowingly of Chinese customs and habits. Mr. Lord listens as a good little boy should . . . withal I believe he is a good missionary and as such deserves praise.

The truth was, James Meadows lived closer to the Chinese and probably did know better. One of the Christians also wrote to Hudson Taylor, saying of him, 'He is both diligent in the work of God, and speaks the Ningpo dialect very well. He and I are most intimate friends.'

At home in London Hudson Taylor received all this news with relief and satisfaction. By the summer of 1865 he could point to the little Bridge Street church in Ningbo as a demonstration of what one new missionary of James Meadows' type could achieve in three years. After dwindling down from the thirty or more they had been in 1860, and coming perilously close to extinction, the handful of dispirited Christians had recovered and grown to more than forty. Under Meadows' care they were buoyant again and constantly adding to their number. And it had happened while he was learning the language, while he was more aware of his own gnawing distress, overlooking the fact that if a grain of wheat falls into the painfully ploughed furrow and dies it yields 'a crop'.

CHAPTER NINE

NO LESS THAN ALL
1864–65

Recruits for Ningbo[1] *1864*

Whatever happened at home in Beaumont Street, with James Meadows and Mrs Lord writing frequently, Ningbo and the Bridge Street church were never far from the Taylors' minds. Mr Lord had made it clear that while he kept an eye on Meadows and the church members he could not carry responsibility for more than general oversight and certain sums of money – remittances to Wang Lae-djün's wife, support for the evangelist Ni and upkeep of the premises. Most of the Christians were known personally to Hudson Taylor, Maria and Mary Jones, and as James Meadows wrote, sometimes at length, about new believers, they felt they knew them also. Until 1864 Ningbo was in the foreground of Taylor's thinking as he looked and prayed for missionary colleagues to send there. Then, during 1864, as news of the final defeat of the Taipings arrived and a China emerged less hamstrung by war and unrest than he had ever known, wider concepts of what was open to the new missionaries came to him.

The way James Meadows was maturing and winning his spurs as an evangelist and pastor encouraged Hudson Taylor to believe the best of the young men and women he was in touch with in Britain. And Meadows' repeated pleas, laments and rebukes were goading Taylor himself to return to Ningbo as soon as he could. As Russell, Burdon and then John Nevius arrived in London with news at first-hand from the scene, news of 'revival' at Yuyao and Church growth in Ningbo, and of Shanghai missionaries pressing out into the newly pacified areas of Jiangsu and Zhejiang known so intimately to Hudson Taylor, reinforcements for these areas also became his immediate concern. Having a share in sending W R Fuller, E F Kingdon and J D Valentine was a good beginning, and sending back a Chinese like Wang Lae-djün, sound at heart and personally trained for three years, meant that some of Ningbo's needs would be met.

That Fuller and Lae-djün were friends and stayed together after reaching Ningbo, to the Bridge Street church's loss, was immaterial. From the beginning Hudson Taylor had urged the United Methodist Free Church to work there. Denominational differences mattered little where such warm fellowship existed between the churches and missionaries. There was plenty of room for another separate 'station'. But shortly before the Fullers were due to sail, Dr Arthur Tidman, a secretary of the LMS, advised the UMFC leaders not to send them to Ningbo on the ground that it was overstaffed already. Samuel Barton, Foreign Secretary of the UMFC consulted Hudson Taylor and part of the pencilled draft of a letter by Maria, who undertook to reply, explains how they begged to differ.

Miss Aldersey's school, she pointed out, had dwindled to nothing since she handed it over to others, and was 'quite to be looked upon as a thing of the past'. And almost all the experienced Ningbo missionaries had left or died. So the number there was no longer a reason why the UMFC should not work at Ningbo.

> The reasons why they *should*, have I believe been repeatedly brought before you by Mr Taylor – but two of the most important seem to be, – the *encouragement* to labour, and the *facilities* for doing so. When I arrived in Ningpo just 11 years ago, there were not I think more than 20 converts in connection with 3 Missions then established. *Now* . . . there are between 500 and 600. Though we observed, on our return to England, that the Wesleyans seemed much discouraged about China from the fact that their only station was *Canton* a place where the spoken dialect is peculiarly difficult – and where the natives have an intense hatred to foreigners. [Their work was] very unproductive and Wesleyan Christians were naturally coming to the conclusion that *China* was a more discouraging sphere than any other. Hence it seemed that a Society that was *commencing* its labours in that country should choose a part of the field [which] was likely to prove productive, and of the ports longest opened, with one exception [Amoy], Ningpo has been the most so. The facilities and working in Ningpo are perhaps greater than in –

and there the surviving page ended.[2]

As a result the Free Methodists sent the Fullers to Ningbo, and before they sailed in May put another candidate named John Mara in touch with Hudson Taylor for assessment and training.[3] On August 20 he had both Mara and Kingdon's brother at Beaumont

Street and from then on noted frequently 'Mara began Chinese studies', 'Taught Mara', 'Maria taught Mara'. Then in September he reported his satisfaction and advised the UMFC to send Mara out but 'stated that I could not yet fix the time for my own departure', and 'Went over Mara's outfit list with him'. So Mara went to China in 1865.

Richard Truelove, who had joined them in September 1863, was like one of the family, learning Chinese, theology and anatomy alongside Lae-djün, Fuller and the others. When John Stevenson came to London, Truelove gave him his first Chinese lesson. And in spite of certain 'annoyances' about which Hudson Taylor had to speak to Truelove after Mr Berger raised the subject, they all saw him as a Ningbo missionary in training.

Through Hudson Taylor's visits to Portman Square to preach and lecture at Thomas D Marshall's Independent Church at Bryanston Hall, Stephan Paul Barchet had decided in September 1863 that he wanted to go as a missionary to China, and in December began coming to Mile End for Chinese lessons. Then in January 1864 he too moved in to live with them in Beaumont Street.[4] He had a pleasant personality, gentle, affectionate, 'attracting the love of all who know him', yet 'very energetic and industrious . . . resolute and firm'. And the way he had been converted through reading about George Müller's conversion interested Hudson Taylor. In October 1864 Taylor arranged with the London Hospital for him to study medicine gratuitously and he began working for his entrance examination. Eventually he qualified as a doctor, but only the rudiments of medical knowledge were intended in 1864. In January 1865 Thomas Marshall undertook to provide his outfit and passage money to China, hoping he could go with the Taylors, and paid an initial thirty-three pounds to Hudson Taylor for him.

The next recruit to come had been the rugged George Crombie from Aberdeen. They had never before met and his introduction to Hudson Taylor was unusual. Back in 1863 Mary Jones had employed young Annie Skinner as a nurse for her children and Annie had relayed news of China and the Taylors to her fiancé in Aberdeen. George had written to Hudson Taylor in November 1863. More correspondence and a week of getting to know Annie better as a guest at Beaumont Street convinced Hudson Taylor and Maria that these steady Scots countryfolk were good missionary potential. So on May 21, 1864, Hudson Taylor's thirty-second birthday, George Crombie came down for a preliminary visit to the already overcrowded little house. Mr Berger approved of him and offered to help with the expenses of his training and of sending him to China. So when George was free to leave his job, Hudson Taylor sent him thirty shillings for his fare and in November he came again to London, this time to stay.

Long before then No 1 Beaumont Street was far too small for all that was going on. With so much coming and going, and four small children's noises, work on the New Testament revision was difficult. To be ill in bed as one or another so often was must have been intolerable. Together they prayed about moving, gave notice provisionally and started house-hunting. But not until the last week of September when a move was urgently necessary did they find a possible place, 'the only one suitable'. The need to pay a low rental for more accommodation limited them badly. No 30 Coborn Street, Bow, (later No 1), three-quarters of a mile farther east and in a more residential area 'was too large for us, but Mr Gough offered to pay the difference between it and our present rent'. So on September 29 they put down the deposit of two pounds and a month's rent

COBORN STREET HOUSES

and on October 6 moved house, paying eighteen shillings to a man to move all their possessions on his cart. To meet their added expenses they gave up their rented pew at Mr Kennedy's Congregational chapel. The move was quickly finished and in the evening Hudson Taylor lectured on China at Bryanston Hall.

A week later John Stevenson arrived, another Scotsman and of a different type. A Stevenson of his family had been outlawed as a Covenanter in 1684, and John was of the same mettle. But although from a Christian family he himself had only turned to Christ when a serious illness forced him to rethink his life. Then in 1863 he had heard the intrepid missionary to the South Pacific cannibal islands, John G Paton, preach. He resolved to be a missionary himself and started learning a South Sea island vocabulary. But in April 1864, aged twenty and preparing to go up to university, he read in the magazine *Revival* an article about Ningbo and Hudson Taylor, and after a while wrote to him. On June 14 Taylor replied from Scarborough, and John Stevenson never forgot one Garibaldi-like sentence in that letter, 'The needy province of Chekiang might not be as salubrious as the South Sea Islands, but at the worst it could only be a shorter path to heaven.'

Then in the June 23 number of *Revival* Stevenson read Hudson Taylor's Scarborough letter to George Pearse arguing the case for missions to China. It happened that William Berger was in Scotland at the time and Hudson Taylor asked him to visit Stevenson and a friend at Castle Douglas. As a result they offered to go to Ningbo. His friend's family objected and he went no further. Not so Stevenson's parents or Captain John Love, the Laird of Knowes, father of Stevenson's fiancée. So on October 13 John Stevenson arrived at 30 Coborn Street, and was attached as assistant to Henry Lance, the pastor of Berger Hall in Bromley-by-Bow, for training.

At once Hudson Taylor knew he had a man of exceptional promise in his team. For Stevenson also 'believed in work and unwasted days'. During his months in London he transcribed the whole Ningbo romanised dictionary and learned to read and understand the romanised New Testament. He was 'gifted with an accurate and powerful memory' and 'a mastery of facts'. What none could forsee was that John Stevenson was to become for thirty years the Deputy Director of the China Inland Mission, to hold the record for length of service in the Mission and to be in harness until 1918 when he died in Shanghai aged seventy-four, the senior British resident in China.

When Mrs Lord reached Ningbo in July 1864 and found that with the help of Mrs Tsiu 'the man-hunter' she had an unlimited welcome to Chinese homes, she chafed at being so restricted by domestic and administrative duties in her house and orphanage. She wrote to Maria: Was there a young woman who would come and do the day-to-day administration under her supervision? This would free her for evangelism.

On November 3 at a meeting of a new committee formed to support evangelists and missionaries Hudson Taylor mentioned Mrs Lord's request and George Pearse drew from his pocket a letter about a Miss Jean Notman, 'a young woman of good education and gentle birth', apparently just the person needed. Choosing to serve without a promised salary but trusting God to provide for her, she sounded the type they were looking for. And she was prepared to go at once by the 'overland' route via Alexandria and Cairo. The Committee agreed to pay her passage if she proved suitable on further acquaintance.

Hudson Taylor as Mrs Lord's 'agent' went to enquire further about her, introduced her to the congregation at Hackney, asked help to provide her outfit, and took her to meet the Bergers at East Grinstead.[5] He visited Tottenham and at a drawing-room meeting was promised two flannel petticoats and whatever might be needed to complete her outfit, returning with ten pounds from the Howards and fifteen from Miss Stacey to add to the Bergers' fifteen pounds and the waterproof cloak Mrs Berger gave her for the voyage. He saw about her trunk, attended farewell meetings at Portman Square and Hackney, and while she paid a flying visit to Scotland he went to a drawing-room meeting and two others on her behalf, bought her outfit and transacted her business at the P&O steamship office.

On Saturday, December 17, she returned from Scotland exhausted, so he gave her a sedative which kept her asleep most of Sunday, while he laboriously copied a long Chinese vocabulary for her, and at four a m on Monday he swept her off to Waterloo and Southampton, on the way picking up her friend Miss Clara Lowe, the daughter of Napoleon Bonaparte's much-maligned custodian on St Helena, Lieut-General Sir Hudson Lowe.[6] There they reported at the P&O office and went on board ship, chose a cabin, and then visited her relatives. He himself went to a church prayer meeting and when he asked them to pray for her, they asked him to address the meeting. He 'felt too exhausted' but 'was helped'. The next morning he went shopping for her and bought medicines, oranges for seasickness, spare watch glasses and labels. Then they went on board – and found that she would be sharing the same cabin with four Christian women and a Chinese Christian *amah* for the children. So they all sang and prayed together before Hudson Taylor took his leave and travelled home.

A letter from George Müller with thirty pounds was waiting for him. He sat down to enter his J Notman accounts, tackled Russell's Romans with John Nevius the next day, missed his train to Hull, where his favourite aunt Hannah Hardey, the artist, was dying of cancer – he had taken her to the consultants James Paget and Jonathan Hutchinson in October – and set out the next day at six a m instead. Hannah Hardey had never been a strong Christian and Hudson hoped to strengthen her faith as she neared death. Maria was going with him, but during the night their daughter Grace was taken ill. As once before, Maria and he were in a cab together on the way to the station and feeling uneasy about their child, when he remembered that she had been in contact with measles, then a lethal disease. They decided that Maria must return home and quickly divided their luggage.

In the train he worked on proofs for J L Nevius, always intent on saving time and expense. An anxious week followed, with Grace very ill and letters and telegrams passing between them, while Aunt Hannah lingered on over Christmas. His tender letter from Hull to Grace told her how he loved her. If she trusted in Jesus, he would help her while she was sick and take her to be with him if she died. But her father looked forward to being with her again soon. It was Christmas Eve and he felt homesick. Then on December 27 the news of Grace was alarming and he hurried home to be with Maria. The 8.30 p m train reached London at 4.20 a m and he was home by 6.00 – to find her already over the worst. And so the year ended, with his last entry 'J. Faulding at P.M. [prayer meeting]'.

Jennie Faulding had taken to coming Saturday by Saturday to the now inviolably regular afternoon prayer meeting at Beaumont Street and then Coborn Street, and sometimes George Pearse and William Berger as well. Other potential candidates appeared from time to time, or Hudson Taylor met them for an interview. Names drifted in and out of his journal and letters, as on August 16. 'Mr Berger came in the evening. He had been much pleased with Jas. Wilson and John Stevenson . . .' And then, after numerous references to letters and Berger's offer to pay Wilson's fare to China, on September 1, 'Learned that Wilson was in treaty with Presbyt.

Mission Socy., but that Stevenson preferred the path of looking simply to the Lord – [for support].' The vital choice he had himself wrestled with for so long had given Ningbo one and the Presbyterians another. 'Samuel H.', G H Richards, Robert White of Northamptonshire, in ones and twos they got in touch with him. Of James Vigeon, an accountant, and his wife he was hopeful. Vigeon had come to see Jean Notman off at Waterloo, with Angus' *Bible Handbook* and other gifts, and kept in touch with Hudson Taylor afterwards.

But Taylor was also still helping the Societies; E F Kingdon's brother came to discuss going to China; a candidate for service in Africa came for an interview; and his old friend Dr Brown of St Mary Axe invited him to meet his brother, about to leave for India. Together with William Pennefather,[7] Hudson Taylor was strongly supporting a mission for foreigners in London, especially seamen, with both frequent donations and advice as a referee. Henry Lance's Home for Poor and Neglected Girls was another cause he espoused. And he was following the activities of the anti-opium lobby and lecturing more frequently on China.

In August he attended an all-night meeting for prayer at Gloucester Hall in Philpot Street, near the medical college. People of all kinds engaged in Christian work in East London met there, unlimited by time, to pray for the sink of iniquity which was the East End, but letting their prayers range world-wide. Gough and Hudson Taylor were asked to tell about China, and 'China much prayed for' was his journal entry the next day. William Booth was not there that night but within a year he had come at the invitation of the East London Special Services Committee, had been overwhelmed by the spiritual need of Mile End's teeming heathen and had begun to set East London alight with his fiery evangelism and uncompromising stand against evil.

In October the offer made by the Indian government official to the Bishop of Victoria, Hong Kong, of thirty thousand rupees (over thousand pounds) for the cure of opium addicts was referred to Hudson Taylor. He spent a morning considering it, no doubt with Gough who had carried on this work in Ningbo after he had left. But it appears that he decided it would conflict with other claims on his time, for the CMS eventually made use of it in Hangzhou.[8]

He could hardly have been more fully committed to service of many kinds, yet all through this crowded year of 1864, concurrently with the events already described, greater issues were competing for his attention. On into 1865, with increasing intensity, another major involvement was leading him inexorably to the climactic decision of his life.

Widening horizons *1864*

In the autumn and winter of 1863 Hudson Taylor and Maria read Evan Davies' 1845 book, *China, and her Spiritual Claims*. This studious little compilation of facts about China, Confucius, Robert Morrison and missionary enterprise in East Asia to that date, comprised a series of lectures the ex-Malaya missionary Evan Davies had given to his congregation at Richmond, Surrey. His purpose in publishing them was to stir up the Christian conscience on the Church's responsibility to preach the gospel in China. At that time only nine Protestant missionaries were in the five free ports, and he called on the Church and the LMS in particular to treble this number at once.

> Some years ago, it was pleaded that Divine providence directed the Church to other quarters – that China was not open – that her people were inaccessible – that the time had not come . . . But now China is open . . . surely the London Missionary Society is called upon to go forward and treble her exertions on behalf of that land. This is the only Society in all Europe with prepared agency and instrumentality. For all other parts of the mission-field, other Societies are in readiness with men and means, but no one for China. Let the Church arise in generous and legitimate enthusiasm, and the required means, men and spirit, will be provided . . .

In the second lecture Davies emphasised 'the magnitude of this [Chinese] Empire [of] three hundred million human beings'. And on the appointed Jubilee Day of the LMS his lecture was a call for a

> *combined operation* on the part of the universal church, for the salvation of nothing less than the entire family of men . . . The very genius of Christianity . . . shows her to be aggressive. Every disciple should feel that he cannot but declare the things he has seen, heard, and handled, of the word of life . . . *Missionary institutions*, were suggested to the people of God some fifty years ago . . . (and have been blessed by God in practice) . . . What has been accomplished in India, will this same instrumentality achieve for China, and nothing else will . . . let the Church combine her resources, exert her influences, and it is done [if accompanied by 'perseverance' and 'spirituality'].

Twenty years later, in 1864, the LMS and CMS had only about ten missionaries each in China, and all other missions a total of one hundred and eighty-nine.[9] To Hudson Taylor, already stirred to the depths by China's spiritual need, this strong appeal expressed his own thoughts. In those twenty years history had repeated itself. The only passages underscored and annotated in Hudson Taylor's hand refer, in his words, to 'the vanity of hoping to convert China thro' its literati, and by means of books alone' – and in Evan Davies' words, accentuated for Hudson Taylor by the second opium war of 1856–60,

> From *iniquitous war, and a vile traffic*, [Hudson Taylor's emphasis] God, in his providence, has secured greater facilities for the inhabitants of the land of Sinim to come to the Saviour of the world!

An intelligent Chinese, puzzling why Britain did not conquer China by force of arms, had said to Evan Davies, 'the Chinese will make the best Christians in the world – they will thoroughly study the Bible' – as they do their own classics. But apart from these observations, Davies' book made a personal appeal to Hudson Taylor and Maria. As a missionary colleague and the friend and admirer of Samuel Dyer, Maria's father, Evan Davies saluted him as 'one of the most efficient missionaries ever sent forth from this or any other country to the heathen world. . . . He was a man of God.'

Understandably, therefore, the Taylors called their third son, born on June 24, Samuel Dyer Taylor. But the influence of the little book went deep. As they read, the first painful challenge to the Ningbo revision was in progress, with interviews and committee meetings at the CMS and Bible Society. And Truelove and Barchet were beginning their training, while Fuller, Kingdon and Lae-djün were approaching their time to leave. The opposition coincided with and tested Hudson Taylor's response to the challenge of China. If God was calling him to the responsibilities he could scarcely envisage yet, this was the crucial moment when victory or defeat at a spiritual level would spell his acceptance or rejection as the leader of the future.

In their work on the New Testament Gough and Taylor were completing the Acts. For over two years they had worked in a small room dominated by that large map on the wall. It was the Lord's command, that they were putting into good colloquial Chinese, 'Go ye into all the world and preach the gospel to every creature', or one of the great declarations of that gospel, 'God so loved the world that he gave his only begotten son that whosoever believeth in him should not perish but have everlasting life' – but it was less and less Ningbo and more and more the whole of China that filled their minds. In Hudson Taylor's *Retrospect* he recalled, 'In undertaking this work [of revision] in my short-sightedness I saw nothing beyond the use that the Book, and the marginal references, would be to the native Christians,'[10] overlooking its influence on himself.

Slowly he and Gough saw more than a corner of Zhejiang in focus. What was at one stage concern for a single province increasingly became a sense of responsibility for the evangelisation of the whole empire. Zhejiang came to look unfairly favoured by missionaries and by Chinese Christians preaching the good news of the love of God in Jesus Christ while eleven of China's eighteen provinces had no opportunity at all to hear it.

> We often looked from that precious Word, on which we were feasting as well as working, to a large map of the Chinese Empire, and thought of the teeming millions who had never heard the Gospel of God's grace. The thought came over me with ever increasing weight and solemnity, – thirty-three thousand persons will die in China to-day without hope – without God – in the world . . . Our work progressed slowly, yet each month as it passed away was carrying one million souls beyond the reach of the Gospel – twelve millions every year. And this, while to ourselves (as to every individual Christian) was given, without limit, the power to ask in prayer *whatsoever* we will, in the name of our Lord Jesus Christ – power necessarily involving great responsibility. We felt constrained to desire, and to ask God to raise up men to carry the Gospel all over the Empire . . .[11]

Calling Maria and Lae-djün to come and pray with them gave temporary relief, especially when temperamental differences were making co-operation difficult. But as they worked on, hour after hour absorbing the message of Scripture, the Great Commission in the first chapter of Acts – 'you shall be my witnesses . . . to the uttermost part of the earth' – and the outworking of obedience to it in the journeys of Paul and his companions, they recognised inescapably the onus upon themselves.

To Hudson Taylor the apparent unreadiness of the Churches and denominational societies[12] to relate the commission in realistic terms to their own day did not diminish the obligation upon himself to obey. On the contrary, the command 'Pray ye therefore the Lord of the harvest that he will send forth labourers into his harvest' was addressed as personally to him as to anyone. He had been praying, but also relying too much on recruiting new missionaries. As he and his household extended their dependence on God for food and clothes to include the supply of colleagues for China, more young men and women began to approach them.

> I learned that, to obtain successful labourers, not elaborate appeals for help, but, *first* earnest *prayer* to God . . ., and *second*, the deepening of the spiritual life of the Church, so that *men should be unable to stay at home*, were what was needed. I saw that the Apostolic plan was not to raise ways and means, but *to go and do the work*, trusting in His sure Word who has said, 'Seek ye *first* the Kingdom of God and His righteousness, and all these things shall be added unto you.' In the meantime the prayer for workers for Chekiang was being answered.

In the verbatim notes of his reminiscences in old age some expressions relating to this period stand out – his realisation that '[his] heart [was] expanding to the measure of *God*'s thoughts and plans for the future'. And, referring to their rendering of the Greek sense in Ningbo colloquial, 'Just as we found some special feast in the Word, our eye would catch the map! And oh, the thought of the millions for whom nothing was prepared.'

Simultaneously the Word of God and the map of all China were 'growing into me'. A hundred and fifty miles from the coast and treaty ports was still thought of as far inland. Even Griffith John in Hankou was alongside a consul in a treaty port. Wylie and Williamson of the LMS and Bible Societies had the remotest hinterland in mind. A few contemplated really penetrating *inland* in the sense of isolation from other foreigners. And when C R Alford was consecrated Bishop of Victoria, Hong Kong, in George Smith's place, 'so great was his zeal for the evangelization of China, that he even proposed the founding of a new Society for that special purpose'. But the Anglican Church at home rejected it.[13]

While others were waiting 'for God's providence to open China' the few saw that it had already happened. What was needed now was to go in, but there were too few men available to make any impact, and this was largely because the attitude of mission boards and secretaries had changed little since Evan Davies' day.[14] A fresh outlook was needed. Where would European Christianity be if the apostles had waited for safer conditions? The objections raised on political and financial grounds looked more and more unscriptural.

As far as Hudson Taylor was concerned, a series of events began to link up and form a chain, a chain that bound him inescapably to his spiritual destiny. For concurrently the thoughts of other men, in Switzerland, Germany and Britain, were moving in the same direction. The Chinese Evangelization Society and some of its Gutzlavian counterparts on the Continent were defunct, but the seed was germinating.

The great evangelical revival that 'swept across denominational lines' had two effects among many – love of 'the brethren' in other Churches with a new toleration of their differing views, and, going a stage further, soft-pedalling of personal beliefs about interpretative non-essentials in favour of unity and co-operation on all that mattered most. Undenominational congregations calling their own ministers were springing up, as at Bryanston Hall. The Anglican William Pennefather's conference at Barnet and Mildmay was drawing like-minded people of all denominations in growing numbers, leading on to the Keswick Convention with its motto 'All One in Christ Jesus'. St Jude's church in Islington, Pennefather's new charge, was too small to accommodate the crowds, so he enlarged it to hold fifteen hundred, and with twenty thousand pounds contributed by Henry Reed of Tasmania (the evangelist whose 'Give me thine heart' had touched the fourteen-year-old Hudson Taylor) the Conference Centre of Mildmay Park, Newington Green, was built to seat up to three thousand. (Hudson Taylor attended the first Mildmay conference held in July 1864.) As in the Bible Societies, the LMS and the CES, men and women of different persuasions banded together to support and to send missionaries to work at home and overseas. Personal friendships overrode denominational labels and many Christians could worship as happily with one type of congregation as another.

Hudson Taylor had been one of those since his early days in Hull, and with the extension of the trend through the 1859–61 Awakening his own attitude was confirmed. During his five years in London he maintained his formal membership of the Baptist Church in Bayswater while attending Mr Kennedy's Congregational Church in Stepney. He visited churches of other denominations from time to time to hear special preachers, and often 'broke bread' with the Brethren congregations in Hackney, Tottenham, Bristol, Clevedon and East Grinstead. He gladly preached wherever he was invited to do so, and was welcomed to speak at Anglican, Baptist, Methodist, Presbyterian and Brethren meetings, and many more besides, in the same spirit as he worked with or for the various missionary societies. If it was prevailing prayer about urgent matters that he needed, opposition to the Ningbo revision or serious illness in his family, he turned to the saints at Tottenham, Hackney and Clevedon, as he did to his mother and Amelia. This was the measure of their attitude to him as much as of his appreciation of them.

His personal friendships followed the same pattern, as men and women were attracted by his and Maria's selfless friendliness and their devotion to Christ. When he went with Lae-djün and Maria in May 1864 to hear Charles Haddon Spurgeon at the new Metropolitan Tabernacle and made his acquaintance, Spurgeon invited him to address a weekday meeting. A mutual admiration which never faded grew from that beginning. In Hudson Taylor's London office late in life Spurgeon's portrait had an honoured place.

At Barnet and Islington and in connection with the home for foreign seamen in London his friendship with William Pennefather deepened. In Eugene Stock's words, William Pennefather

> was the George Müller of the Church of England . . . a man who walked with God, who simply asked His Heavenly Father for whatever was needed . . . according to that Father's will, and who found these child-like requests granted.[15]

E B Underhill of the BMS was another who opened his home to them and introduced Hudson Taylor to the Royal Geographical Society. And Robert Chapman of Barnstaple, whom Hudson Taylor had first met at George Pearse's, took to him warmly. In 1864 a donation from a Mr Vellacott of Cornwall began another long family connection. These names are like foundation stones in the spiritual edifice about to rise from them.

In 1865 Hudson Taylor was to find new friends in Brethren circles in the West End, while those who befriended him as a medical student in 1852–53, the Howards, Miss Stacey, George Pearse, William Berger and others continued faithful to him as he added to their number. The Brethren who believed in him were at one with his denominational openness, a supra- or trans-denominational largeness of heart, never anti-denominational.

A Presbyterian minister, J M Denniston of Torquay, was another of this open type. Convinced that 'believer's baptism' was right, while actively Presbyterian, he was dubbed 'a Baptist' by the undiscriminating. The chapel in south Hackney where he sometimes preached was near enough to Mile End for Hudson Taylor to attend from time to time, for it had been a sermon by Denniston which had fired William Burns and sent him out as a preacher of revival in 1839.[16] Denniston was to play a key role in Hudson Taylor's life in 1865. Dr William Landels, the minister of Regent's Park Chapel where the Faulding family worshipped, was another, taking Jennie Faulding's part when her parents put the brake on her enthusiasm for China and the Taylors.

Through his visits to Bryanston Hall and dealings with Stephan Barchet, Hudson Taylor made friends with two elders of the church, William Hall and John Challice, who were to become his close personal colleagues a decade later. For the present George Pearse and William Berger meant most to him. The failure of the CES could not diminish Pearse's zeal. His hopes for China and his regard for Hudson Taylor were as great as ever. As 1864 progressed, Hudson Taylor met with these men more often and discussed the implications of the big societies' inability to exploit the open gates of the Chinese empire. They even braved the austerities of Beaumont Street and Coborn Street to spend the night with the family there.

Mr and Mrs Berger became like elder brother and sister to the Taylors and others in their household. From dutiful letters and infrequent meeting, in 1861, their relationship had grown warm until by 1864 weekends at blissful Saint Hill in its many acres near East Grinstead occasionally varied the frugal life in Mile End, and consultation about every aspect of their work was being taken for granted. The timing of their own return to China, the training of Richard Truelove and the others, recurrent threats to the Ningbo vernacular New Testament, and above all the increasingly volcanic turmoil of Hudson Taylor's own thoughts about the future.

So, 'Mr. Berger called' – 'Mr Berger sent £20, half for Richard Truelove' – 'Mr. Berger said he was praying much about the revision' – 'to Bromley, met Jukes, Bergers, Pearse and others' – 'with Maria, Grace, Baby and Sarah [Osborne] went to E. Grinstead. Drove over to Three Bridges for Stephan.' So it went on. And as 1865 dawned, William Berger and Hudson Taylor were inseparably involved in what they thought was the Taylors' imminent departure with that 'goodly number' of new missionaries – Truelove, Barchet, Crombie, Annie Skinner, the Vigeons, and the Stevensons, if not others too. And it was no longer practical business matters they were discussing but the profoundest issues of principle and policy, of leadership and financial solvency. For what they were embarking on together was far and away beyond the Bergers' ability to underwrite.

The Foreign Evangelist Society[17] *1864*

Thanks to George Pearse who kept cuttings of interest from current periodicals, some now among the Hudson Taylor papers, the existence of parallel movements can be traced. Piecing together some of the unconnected evidence throws light on the emergence of the mission Hudson Taylor and William Berger were working towards.

In the correspondence column of the November 2, 1863, issue of the Edinburgh paper *British Herald*, excerpts and editorial comments echoing Evan Davies appeared under the title 'A MILLION OF MISSIONARIES REQUIRED'. Comparing the Godless world to the 'beleaguered prisoners of Lucknow' waiting for a relieving column 'to break through the besieging hosts' to deliver them, the writer claimed that many Christians were ready and waiting for the opportunity to fulfil 'the obligations Christ's redemption has laid upon them. While nations of undying souls are perishing for lack of knowledge, and many of the disciples of Christ are longing to carry to them the word of life, can we sit still?'

'A small party of *pioneers*' was nearly ready to go abroad, the *Herald* stated, to prepare the way for others, starting first in Egypt. The vague idea was that,

> five, ten, twenty of more, of various ranks, professions, trades and callings, should go out . . . [to] work, heal and preach – and look to the Lord alone to support them – using, indeed, whatever the Lord might send from the Church at home (as Paul used gifts sent by Churches – yet also worked with his own hands).

The Moravian and other missions had long demonstrated the practicability of the project. Someone with lands or a large sum of money to devote to the Lord's service could take

> masons, carpenters, blacksmiths and others [with him] as well as educated men who were qualified to learn existing languages, and reduce rude dialects to writing. Or if poor men have a clear call to go, they might go as the Lord opened the way . . .

For military purposes, the article went on, money and men by tens of thousands could be found; and women too. Moreover,

> we don't send out a mere handful of *officers*, but whole *regiments* of rank and file . . . Should we not send out WHOLE REGIMENTS of

> Christian soldiers – not the *driblets* of a few officers . . .? Tens of thousands of Christ-loving men and women – should throw themselves upon heathen shores, to live or die for Christ; and then the enemies of the Lord would become convinced that the Church believed in its Lord, its creed, and its mission. And we believe that if even a few bands of Christians were going out as pioneers, it would arouse the Church from her dream and sloth . . . What we want to see is a universal planting of the standard of the cross on every acre of heathendom . . . Simple faith in God, and an apostolic willingness to endure hardness, and spend and be spent for Christ, are needed for such a mission.[18]

So far it sounded like the *Chinese Missionary Gleaner*'s rhetoric revived. If it were not for the fact that most of this and much more besides was fulfilled in due time, and that Hudson Taylor played a major role in translating theory into practice, the subject could be dropped. Instead the story continued. Hot on the heels of that issue came another with a letter from the notable Dr Johann Ludwig Krapf of Stuttgart and East Africa supporting the appeal,[19] encouraging existing missions but also advocating that

> not only ordained preachers must be sent forth, but as many laymen of decided piety, and gifted with the needful intellectual powers, as may be willing to spend and be spent, beside their secular occupation.

They should not be too young and inexperienced but carefully chosen as 'good soldiers' whose 'joy and ardour' would not change into 'surliness and despondency' when they came up against pagan conditions abroad. But self-support was the practical method he advocated. The 'Chrischona Mission' of Basel was already working on these lines.

In February 1864 the *Herald* reported action. Funds were coming in and the two young men who had begun the correspondence, John Fraser and William Macintosh, were leaving shortly for Cairo. It commented, '. . . there is such a thing as FAITH IN GOD, and being moved, led, guided, sent and prospered by the Holy Ghost.' And a letter followed from a certain M Spittler of Basel, written on January 11, 1864.[20] C F Spittler, the father of the writer, had provided the first impetus to the founding of the Basel Missionary Society, *circa* 1815, but feeling that there was scope for missionaries with less academic training than the prescribed six years' study before ordination, in 1840 he initiated the St Chrischona Pilgrim Mission. Characterised by 'the utmost poverty and simplicity' as the name deliberately implies, the Pilgrim Mission supplied hundreds of missionaries to other societies, including in time the China Inland Mission. In 1859 the younger Spittler's travels in the British Isles had brought him into contact with many young converts of the revival, potential missionaries.

> I repeatedly asked myself, *Where is* the [channel] through which simple-hearted labourers, who . . . wish to devote themselves to missionary work in foreign lands, could reach their purpose? . . . All the colleges existing for that purpose require a preliminary education . . . To raise a missionary agency of a lower kind seems to be a special design of our Lord at this present time, for the carrying out of which He has prepared His instruments in different countries, independently from each other.

He was not referring to manual labourers but using the current term for 'Christian workers'. (See also below.)

The *British Herald*'s comment accepted this thesis and turned to the ways and means.

> For their training and sending out a large sum is needed. Indeed, as the idea takes root in the Christian community, *tens of thousands of pounds* will be required. But the Lord can easily find the necessary funds. 'There is no lack to them that fear Him'; but who will enjoy the privilege of doing this service? . . .

Fourteen years earlier, a letter on the same theme from William Burns, dated November 27, 1850, had been printed in the *English Presbyterian Messenger* and quoted in the CES *Gleaner*.

> What need there is that many labourers of every character and qualification should enter this great Gospel harvest-field – some to teach, some to preach, some to write and translate, etc, etc. I would keep no man back, whatever may be his qualification, if only he has learned to follow Jesus with a single eye, and in all things is ready to put the question of usefulness before that of personal comfort . . .[21]

To the resilient George Pearse these echoes of his own sentiments since the days of the CES would be too welcome not to be discussed with Berger, Hudson Taylor and others. Those weekends and consultations together about China could scarcely disregard articles on the theme. The action they took in the ensuing months supports the assumption.

At the height of the revival in 1859 the new Christian periodical of that name, *The Revival*, appeared in London under the editorship of R C Morgan – of Marshall, Morgan and Scott. Under its later name, *The Christian*, it was to see its centenary and a decade or two to spare. But on March 10, 1864, an editorial by Morgan pointed to 'The instinct of centralization' found even in the early Jerusalem Church as being self-destructive, whereas 'the gospel . . . must have the whole earth for its battle-field'.[22] So the great calamity of A D 70 was necessary to scatter the Church to the four winds as missionaries. The 1859 revival movement was becoming muted, it went on, with the potential in its thousands of converts confined to the British Isles. How good, then, that a movement towards the 'regions beyond' was in evidence. Before John Fraser left the country he suggested that every church in Britain should send and support a missionary, preferably one of its own members. Quoting M Spittler's letter in the *British Herald*, Morgan added,

> it is not unreasonable to suppose that God would put it into the hearts of some to offer themselves, whom men would have deemed little fitted for the work, or unlikely to make such a sacrifice . . . We look with great interest for the development of the Revival in more extensive, more effective, and less cumbrous missionary agency than we have yet seen . . .

The April 7 number of *The Revival* carried a long letter from George Pearse.[23] He took the matter further, succinctly telling the story of 'an independent mission in Ningpo, which has certainly enjoyed the favour and blessing of God', up to the involvement of James Meadows with the church there. This was generalisation focused down to hard facts; Meadows represented the principle already being put into practice,

> . . . but the work needs reinforcing. There is a great opportunity . . . and even labourers of the class similar to our London City Missionaries would find work ready to their hand, as the spoken language is not difficult to acquire, and the written language in Romanized colloquial is easily learned.

It was this letter that had first attracted John Stevenson's attention, aspiring university student though he was. After reading George Pearse's leading article in the May 19 issue, and perhaps J M Denniston's dated May 26, he wrote to Hudson Taylor, who replied from Scarborough.

The May 19 leader entitled *Undenominational Foreign Missions* began with the observation,

> The correspondence . . . in recent numbers of *The Revival* has elicited . . . That many persons in England, without communication with each other, have been maturing plans for the more effectual spread of the gospel in our colonies and in heathen countries, and that these plans are almost identical . . . several friends in Scotland are moving in the same direction . . . A conference was arranged . . . [of] Christian brethren, of different denominations, who were interested in missions to Africa, the West Indies, China, etc, . . . and others who had taken a prominent part in the evangelistic and revival work in our own country; but all deeply interested in the world-wide preaching of the gospel.

Twelve in fact met on May 10 in Mr Pearse's office building at 12 South Street, Finsbury Square, including Hudson Taylor.[24] They began by each in turn explaining how 'he had come to think along these lines and how he thought their common object could be furthered'. At least eight of them had a distinct view to put forward. One proposed a 'Foreign City Mission', another an 'Un-denominational Missionary Society'. Another wanted to help Christian artisans to emigrate. Denniston advocated a training institute for such men. Hudson Taylor 'was interested in China, Ningpo, and missionaries desiring to go (there)'; and others in Africa and India. But they did not stop at that. 'All were agreed that much might be done for the foreign mission field out of the ordinary channel of the missionary societies,' to extend the blessing of the revival throughout the world.

News of Colonel Charles Gordon's new drive against the Taiping rebels appears not to have reached them yet, for Pearse wrote of the Taipings as a missionary objective still – sixty millions of them without one missionary.

> When we know that hundreds of millions in China have never heard the sound of the gospel, and that there is room amongst the many illiterate Chinese for a more humble class of labourers[25] than our educated missionaries, why not ask of the Lord to raise up men and means for this wide field?

And in India too. After all, Jesus chose 'unlearned and ignorant men' as well as educated men like Paul.

> All . . . at the Conference were agreed that . . . the movement must be carried on in *entire harmony* and co-operation with existing missionary societies; and that, in fact, it should supplement them with a more humble class of labourer[26] . . . and . . . enlist as many native

> Evangelists and Bible-readers as possible . . . That the movement should be catholic, i.e. entirely apart from all denominational objects . . . for the sole purpose of preaching Christ.

They urged that self-supporting Christians should be helped to emigrate and witness as they worked. But on this occasion no positive action was taken.

This article in *The Revival* was followed by a letter quoting Dr Krapf and asking why the CMS should find it so hard to send British missionaries that they should 'borrow' Germans, and why three Scottish Presbyterian halls of divinity should have only four or five students prepared to serve in India. Why should there be as many missionaries to the people of Edinburgh as there were missionaries of the three great Presbyterian churches for the whole of India?

> The answer is simply this, instead of going to the workshop, the farm, the merchant's office, and such like sources, as has been done in Germany, we have been looking exclusively to our colleges . . .

When the denominational societies did draw upon such sources, as they did, they sent them to college and turned them into men of another stamp.

Hudson Taylor's journal clarified the intentions of the consulting twelve on one point: they were not founding a new sending society but discovering how best to help those already existing or being formed. His journal for May 10 reads, 'Revision 7 hours. Finished Galatians. Wrote to J. Meadows . . . Attended a meeting . . . where the question of forming a Missions Aids Society was discussed.'

On May 18 he attended the next meeting, which he this time called a 'meeting of Self Supporting Missions'.[27] And a week later it was 'the meeting of the Foreign Evang. Socy.' after which he went on to a meeting of the BMS.

The leading article in *The Revival* of May 26 was in the form of a letter to the editor from the Presbyterian Rev J M Denniston, under the title *Unsectarian Foreign Missions*.[28] As an association bridging denominational lines was likely to be formed he wished to air some thoughts on the subject. Negatively, he suggested that division and divergencies among Christians were regrettable and

> it follows that denominationalism must be an evil in itself, and that denominational missions are not absolutely the best means of spreading the gospel. [But] The denominations do exist . . . Besides, it is a fact that God has used and is using the missionary efforts of his

> people in their denominations far beyond all other agency . . . there is very little . . . being done for foreign lands by any other means. And . . . the wall of separation between the denominations is very much lower . . . on the missionary field than at home . . . they are seeking nothing but to win souls for Christ. [So] I can . . . with all my heart contribute to the support of various denominational missions.

What justification was there then for forming an 'unsectarian', truly ecumenical missionary society like the one proposed? He gave six reasons: it was the true Christian principle; it would supply an object of support for 'Christians who *ought* to be supporting Missions, and are *not*' because of objections to the denominations; for educational and theological reasons there were many potential missionaries who could not serve under any of the denominational agencies; the principle of self-support by missionaries deserved to be promoted; an organisation was needed to find and help the no less needed or efficient missionaries from humbler social levels; and finally, such an association could interfere with no existing Society, but on the contrary help all. 'There is more than enough room for us all in so great a harvest field.'

The Revival of June 16[29] then reported the formation of the FOREIGN EVANGELIST SOCIETY under this title, with the aims agreed on May 10, and another mentioned then but now brought into greater prominence: 'To stimulate Christian men in the army, navy, etc., abroad, and others who leave England for purposes of commerce or travel, to co-operate with the association for the furtherance of the gospel.' George Pearse became the Hon Secretary and J M Denniston, R C Morgan and the 'Rev. J. Hudson Taylor' were on the committee. This appears to be the first use of the style 'Rev.' so far discovered in print, and no indication of his authentic medical status was given.

Minor confusion has resulted from the formation of another, unconnected, organisation in 1871 called the 'Foreign Evangelisation Society', largely to support Christian work on the Continent of Europe.[30] The fact that Donald Matheson who 'would have become a partner in Jardine, Matheson & Co.' was treasurer of this society was an accidental link with China. According to James E Mathieson the evangelist, after Donald Matheson's conversion he could not take part in the opium business and had returned to England.

After the formation of the Foreign Evangelist Society (FES) had been publicised, theorising gave place to specifics and action.

Hudson Taylor's Scarborough letter to George Pearse was published in *The Revival* for June 23.[31] It was 'a matter for devout thankfulness' he began, that there were so many Christian workers in Britain in addition to those in 'the ministry', yet all too few in the circumstances.

> But the field is the world and the gospel is to be preached to every creature. The trophies of the cross are to be gathered from every nation, and people, and kindred, and tongue . . . If . . . in this country God deigns so largely to use [the less educated workers] may we not infer that there is still greater scope for their efforts in the missionary field . . .? Would such [people] be able to acquire the languages necessary . . .? [In China] Malay and Hindoo servants, negro slaves of both sexes, and Europeans unable to read or write a word of [any] language, have acquired with ease a knowledge of the spoken language . . . Some . . . far more correctly than is usual with more educated foreigners . . . [as] every native infant does . . .

He described the circumstances of overwork when he and John Jones were in Ningbo, their health breaking down, the immature Chinese Christians unable yet to do much evangelism or instruction of new believers. The 'city missionary' type of person from Europe would have been competent to help by

> Preaching the gospel, taking charge of out-stations, instructing enquirers, teaching them and others to read, teaching in the [adult] Sunday-schools, visiting the sick, etc. . . . Any one able to take charge of a senior class in a Sunday-school at home, or to preach the gospel to the poor in England, would have been of the utmost service to us in China . . . [For example] James Meadows' progress in the language has exceeded my expectations, and his services to the little flock . . . have been invaluable . . . There are other dear brothers and sisters in the Lord who feel called to serve Him in China, and who, I cannot but feel, are qualified for this service. I trust that He will in His own time, provide the means for their engaging in the study of the language, and for their outfits and expenses to China, as well as their support there. I trust that when our revision of the New Testament is completed, several of them may accompany us to Ningpo.

In Hudson Taylor's thinking, while men would have so much more liberty of movement in China, women were equally needed. So brothers *and sisters* should go. Robert Morrison had advocated this and trained the early women missionaries. Charles Gutzlaff had emphasised the point, and Lobscheid supported him in it. *The*

Gleaner had taken it up and both Hudson and Maria Taylor's personal experience left them in no doubt. China needed women missionaries and they would welcome them as colleagues.

In helping to provide for other people, for Mrs Lord (wife of an American Baptist) and her assistant Jean Notman, Hudson Taylor had no qualms about asking openly for funds, his own faith was not involved in the same way as in provision for his own household or his commitments in Ningbo. And at this stage in his development, where others were concerned as in this instance, he still tended to 'ask the Lord and tell His people'.[32] Before he left Britain again he was giving thanks that God had shown him that he could provide even large capital sums – to charter all the accommodation in a ship – without resort to priming the channels of supply with information. And not only could, but wanted him to confine himself to that way of living, the way he had thought of since his experiments in Hull, and later called 'moving men through God by prayer alone'.[33]

But this was a letter to George Pearse, and reads as if addressed to him as honorary secretary of the Foreign Evangelist Society. If for the eyes of his fellow-members, it said no more on this subject than they probably knew already. Its tone smacks more of a response to a request for the purpose of publication in *The Revival*, a paper which set out to encourage donations to the projects it reported.[34]

So on September 15 Hudson Taylor noted that the FES had received a hundred and three pounds for China; on October 20 he distributed missionary boxes for the FES; on November 3 he spoke to the FES Committee of Jean Notman's need of help; and on the 17th the FES voted to pay for her passage to China, while he informed his friends, the Bergers, Howards, George Müller and others about her. As expected by his colleagues, at the FES meeting on December 29 he 'asked prayer for funds for self and those who go out with us'. This was still months before the CIM was formed or its principles were adopted. Large sums would be needed, more than the FES had any prospect of having at its disposal. If the means were to be supplied, only provision in answer to prayer could be contemplated. These were all people who wanted to help when they could, but were none of them wealthy enough to sponsor a project, either single-handedly or in partnership. So they combined prayer with generosity, multiplying each as the projects they approved of continued to grow. And when Hudson Taylor spoke of others going to China with him he still thought of them as individual companions for whom he was in no way financially responsible, or ever would be. God had called them to go and he was helping them to obey, in the same sense as the Foreign Evangelist Society, a group of twelve men of whom he was one had set themselves to do.

So ended that vibrant, eventful year 1864, in which fidelity and steadfastness had mattered supremely – the springboard of historic 1865.

Preparing to go[35] *January–March 1865*

At some point in the late autumn or early winter of 1864, hopes of returning to China became positive plans. No clear indications of this intention, let alone of a plan, are found in the journal or letters of the period – only hints that preparations for sailing in the spring or summer were under way. Letters of January and February 1865 from James Meadows and E C Lord imply news of such plans. 'I hear through Mrs. Lord's notes from . . . friends that you expect to sail for China the coming Spring,' E C Lord wrote. 'I feel sorry that your dear wife has suffered so much in her health. May God recruit you all and send you out strong and well,' Meadows added.

James Meadows went on to say as if in reply to an enquiry, that none of Hudson Taylor's Chinese clothes were at Mrs Parker's house – the rebels must have taken them. But his books were safely at Bridge Street with him. (Had Hudson Taylor told him to make use of them when James wrote wishing to read natural history?) Meadows continued, 'I have several matters in the church to speak to you about, that I don't like troubling Mr. Lord with.' The letter these remarks were answering must have been written in November 1864 or earlier, but a letter from Jennie Faulding to Maria went further.

340 Euston Road,
Tuesday, Dec. 20th, 1864

My dear Mrs. Taylor,

I got home safely the other evening.

[*Punch* had carried a cartoon of a family 'Going out to tea in the suburbs' all carrying knobkerries and escorted by armed guards, so dangerous were London's streets.]

. . . when you come to see us . . . bring . . . some work for me to do . . . With such a voyage in prospect you must have plenty of needlework . . .

> I am so happy resting in Jesus, and my heart is raised to Him I can't tell you how often for you and China.
>
> I know He will send more labourers, whether He send me or not . . .

New Year's Day was a Sunday but Hudson Taylor stayed at home all day because Grace was still not over her measles. And in his journal he wrote, '"My God shall supply all your need." May this be my motto for the year. He is leading us in a remarkable way. May He make all plain in due time.'

Stephan Barchet's church and minister were well ahead in undertaking to cover the cost of his outfit and passage money, and William Berger contributed fifty pounds towards others' expenses. Hudson Taylor arranged for a ten per cent discount at an outfitter's, and the FES asked him to write a brief history of 'the Ningpo Mission' for them. His journal is peppered with such notes, as though their departure could be sooner rather than later in the spring. But life continued in the established tradition of much coming and going, especially for the Saturday prayer meetings, lessons for the recruits in training, packing and soldering a box of supplies for Jean Notman, lectures on China at one place after another, medical care of friends and neighbours, publication matters to attend to for John Nevius, and always the New Testament proof-sheets, mostly alone. This work was dragging, and his obligations to the Bible Society made his departure dependent on its completion. The end was in sight, if only determined team work could attain it.

On January 13 a sequence of crucial conversations began which in hindsight can be seen to shape the mission-to-be, though Ningbo was all they had in mind at the time. Writing to his mother, Hudson Taylor outlined his busy life and went on,

> We much need your prayers. The responsibility resting upon us is now increasing very much. I must have more grace and wisdom from above, or shall utterly fail . . . We have received more than £100 towards the expenses of outfit etc. Pray for what more may be needed. Perhaps £900 to £1000.[36]

No one had contributed more than fifty pounds in a single donation, so impending commitments were beginning to pass well beyond his experience and reasonable expectations from even his well-to-do friends. Apart from John Mara, the Free Methodist, and the younger Kingdon brother, a BMS candidate, there were six or

'I GOT HOME SAFELY' LONDON IN THE '60s
(by courtesy of *Punch*)

more young men and women in touch with Hudson Taylor who he hoped might go with him. All of them were young. Maria's twenty-eighth birthday on January 16 set her apart, with Hudson Taylor at thirty-two, as the respected seniors. Mrs Lord was corresponding with them about bringing her teenage daughter Mary Bausum. All in all the proposed journey was becoming a major undertaking, with corresponding problems to face on arrival in China, where only the Bridge Street premises and James Meadows' makeshift one-bed garret were in any way at their disposal.

So on January 13 Hudson Taylor had a long talk with his prayerful Clevedon friend Mr Horne 'about our affairs', and 'Mr. Berger called in the evening and raised the question of the young men's going first. May the good Lord guide and direct.'

No longer was the relationship between Berger and Taylor one of benefactor and recipient. The acquaintance begun in 1852 between the manufacturer not yet forty and the medical student of twenty-one had ripened into a partnership of souls growing together. Consultation about everything was assumed. It was no longer Hudson Taylor's work and ideas to which William Berger contributed his comments and funds, so much as their pooled commitment, with Berger playing whatever part he could without experience of China. Both knew full well that they were moving beyond his ability to underwrite the costs. It had become a joint venture of faith. Not to the same extent but more than ever before, both families of Howards at Tottenham were showing their willingness to help. Hudson Taylor or Maria, alone or together, stayed overnight or for weekends with them from time to time.

Barchet and Truelove were ready to go. George Crombie, Annie Skinner and John Stevenson were getting on with Chinese. Stevenson's fiancée was soon to come to London and Jean Notman's friends the Vigeons were hoping to join in before long, if his employers and her parents would release them. Before George Crombie left Aberdeen he had spoken to a schoolmaster friend, George Stott, about China and, undeterred by having lost a leg, Stott was asking about following him. Jennie Faulding's wish to go too was deepening into conviction, but at twenty-one she had little hope of her parents' consent, however highly they regarded the Taylors.

In view of what happened subsequently, Jennie's story must begin to receive detailed attention. She was talking the matter over with a student friend, Emily Blatchley, and before long both were attending the Saturday meetings at Coborn Street together. As vital an association with Hudson Taylor as any other had begun, for these two girls became salient members of the China Inland Mission.

On Sunday, January 15, the seriousness of the whole position was weighing upon him. He was preparing to talk business with the men. That evening he wrote in his journal, 'With Maria humbled ourselves before the Lord with fasting and prayer and confessed our sins and shortcomings, personal, and relative and besought His pardon and favor.' The next day all he entered was, 'Mr. Gough not here all day . . . Had long conversation with the three young men about our mutual relationships.'

Later developments showed that this was about questions of leadership, responsibility, use of funds, no promise of salaries, and so on. He found that the men did not see eye to eye with him. So at the weekend he went to Saint Hill and on a country walk with William Berger on Sunday afternoon covered the whole subject with him. Instead of going to church again in the evening they stayed at home and prayed and talked together 'about Revision and other matters'. Then on Wednesday Berger came to Coborn Road for

> some private conference with Mr. Stevenson and then came in with Mr. Lance and we all had conversation together. They dined here [and] the conversation was renewed, and continued till 4 p.m. Then they left and we engaged in prayer. Mr. Truelove and Mr. Crombie advised me not to attempt to carry out the plan of attempting a partnership arrangement of funds. Then we went to Tottenham to the tea-meeting . . . Asked Miss Stacey, Mr. J.E. Howard, and Mr. R. Howard their opinion of the best arrangement of money matters. They all felt it would never do for me to be a sharer with the brethren: that I must take the responsibility of receiving and using funds . . .

They advised that George Pearse should 'convene a meeting of friends to consider the point' and how funds should be administered in Britain. The Robert Howards put Hudson Taylor up for the night and from there he went to the FES committee meeting and asked their advice on the distribution of funds and the proposals made to him. His own experience of communal living with the Jones family had been so enjoyable and rich in spiritual fellowship; if only that could be repeated. But he was open to the wisdom of others and appears to have yielded without difficulty. What was harder to accept was this role of responsible leadership they were thrusting on him, beyond what he had envisaged. His own concept of companionship in which his knowledge of China made him the natural leader or *primus inter pares* had to be examined.

John Stevenson felt more troubled than the rest about how plans were shaping, and did not turn up for the usual lesson the next day. And on the following Sunday afternoon he was absent when Hudson Taylor

> Spent the afternoon reading and conversing with Crombie and Truelove on the grounds of our confidence, in going forth as we hope to do, looking to the Lord for temporal supplies [Journal].

For years Hudson Taylor had used photographs as reminders to pray for his family and friends. The portraits taken in 1862 of Maria and himself he gave to his friends for this purpose. So now he arranged with a Mile End photographer for fifty copies of a group of five to seven people at six shillings a dozen or five shillings a dozen for a gross. More than one group photograph still brings to life these pioneers who would have been mere names.

On Saturday, February 4, he recorded, Jennie Faulding

> told us she had spoken to her parents seriously about going to China, and that her mother could not give her consent. Prayed with her and advised her to wait on God about it.

But a letter from Jennie after the weekend suggests that she had gained more from it than that. They had positively encouraged her to go on hoping and to discuss it with the minister of her church.

> Yesterday I had a talk with Mr. Landels about my going to China. I prayed much that he might be guided by the Spirit in what he said to me, and you may think how pleased I felt when after some very kind questions he said, 'Well, if you feel it your duty to go, if I were your Mamma I could only say to you "Go and God bless you," and I will tell her so.' . . . it confirmed me in the growing conviction that God is calling me to go. Last week I was feeling very much my own weakness, but on Sunday Jesus 'restored to me the joy of His salvation' . . .
>
> I must thank you again for your great kindness in offering to let me live with you; if I should go with you, I will pray and strive to be to you a sister, a comfort, and a blessing; and I have the fullest confidence that you would fill to me as far as possible the place of the dear ones I should leave behind.[37]

True to his promise Mr Landels took it up with Jennie's parents, and in arranging for Hudson and Maria Taylor to visit them on February 23 she told Maria,

> I am very happy, Jesus is good to me. It has grieved me to trouble Mamma so: but she is very kind. She says now, that she can't give me up at present; but that in two years, if I still wished it and an opportunity offered, she wouldn't hinder me. I think I may yet get her consent to let me go now, but it will be hard work.
>
> Perhaps waiting for two years would do me good, only there is the uncertainty. However I leave it all to Jesus. I am His, and He'll choose the best path for me.
>
> Mr. Landels is very kind indeed. He cheers and sympathizes with Mamma but does not discourage me. Father says little but I fancy he's willing to think about it . . .

In recruiting 'working men' as well as others Hudson Taylor was departing from the practice of established missions. But in encouraging *young* unmarried women to go too he was showing a conspicuous disregard for precedent. From Miss Aldersey and her contemporaries onward single women had served in institutions in East Asia, but very few of them and mostly of a mature age. Maria's own experience of ample scope, even for young girls like Burella and herself, led them to discount the objections raised. If Chinese girls and women were to have an equal chance to hear the gospel, Christian women must go to them, beyond the walls of institutions. And if women in inland China were to hear, missionary women must face the hazards. The younger they were, the better they would learn the language. Quiet work in Chinese homes could be as effective as overt evangelism among men. Nowhere is another consideration mentioned in Hudson Taylor's papers – the need of lonely bachelor missionaries and widowers for women amongst whom to find a partner without taking two years or more away from work to return to Britain – but he had known it and seen it in others, and could not disregard the heartache in James Meadows' letters.

After tea with the Fauldings on the 23rd, Hudson Taylor confirmed Jennie's report in his journal,

> The Lord prospered us and we found that Mrs. F. had agreed to let her go in two years' time, and that in the meantime she might study the language. Mr. Landels thought the Church might send her out and support her there.

He had already asked if he could come to Saint Hill for the weekend, so after attending a confinement from one a m to four a m he did three hours' work on proof-sheets of Galatians, saw some patients and then travelled to East Grinstead. After the Sunday morning service he discussed his problems with Mr and Mrs Berger, a motherly elder sister to him and Maria, and preached at the chapel in the evening. Jennie Faulding, George Stott and John Stevenson – 'as to [his] health, marriage, and fitness for the work', were his agenda for consultation, as well as 'sending home accounts, money acknowledgments, etc.' Their plans for practical co-operation were progressing.

Then on Monday, February 27, he returned to London, placed an order at a shop, called in at Spottiswoode's to look over a proof-sheet, looked in on George Pearse to pay over money for Jean Notman, visited the shipping agents to pay freight on the box he was sending out to her, and the photographers for more of her prayer-photographs, and so home to fit in three hours on New Testament revision, two letters, to James Meadows and Jean Notman, and finally to buy a human head (ten shillings) at the London Hospital. Anatomy still had a place in his training of the men.

The pace of life was too great, and too frequently his journal carried notes like 'Feeling very unwell, unable to take any dinner', without particulars; but he kept going. The problems of working on the New Testament continued. John Nevius helped when he came over from Richmond, but the difficulties appeared insuperable. On February 20 Hudson Taylor noted,

> After our work I spoke to Mr. Gough about our plans and prospects. He agreed to the need for all possible speed, but would not hear of a quick revision. Proposed a visit to the Secy. B.S. [Bible Society] before their next meeting.

Whether that visit took place is uncertain, for dramatic new developments soon threw their ordered lives into confusion. On March 29 Hudson Taylor wrote from Glasgow to the Bible Society saying he expected to leave Britain for China around May 15 and could not therefore give as much time to the revision as previously. The Secretary consulted with Henry Venn about 'the suitableness of some pecuniary allowance being voted to Mr. Taylor', but nothing came of it just then.[38] For, as things turned out, Hudson Taylor continued giving all the time he could until the spring of 1866. Meanwhile he recorded in his journal on March 2,

> Mr. Stevenson called on me, stating that his views as to the nature of the work now coincided with mine, and asking me to take him as a helper in the work. He had determined on marriage.

This was not all good news, for the health of both Stevenson and his fiancée was questionable and first they needed to see a consultant physician. The London Hospital's Dr Andrew Clarke apparently reassured them, and the long, strong partnership between Hudson Taylor and John Stevenson began.

It was a momentous week, for Taylor also wrote inviting the schoolmaster George Stott to London, and Jennie Faulding began Chinese lessons. Years later Hudson Taylor recalled how Stott arrived and was told the difficulties for a man with only one leg in China and how badly it could go with him in a Chinese riot. He replied, 'Oh, that wasn't my expectation at all. I thought that "the lame would take the prey"!' Hudson Taylor's immediate reaction, 'That's the man for China!' led on to George Stott joining the team in training and a long, effective life in China. But the courage was not all Stott's. Hudson Taylor's propensity for taking calculated risks had been exercised again.

So much had already happened, but in comparison with what the months were still to hold, that first week of March was plain sailing. The news John Nevius brought on Monday, March 6, drastically altered their lives.

The book that backfired[39] *March–May 1865*

For the past two or three months Hudson Taylor's mind had been active on preparations for writing a series of articles on China. Back in December W G Lewis, the minister at Westbourne Grove, had shown a new interest in what Taylor was saying in his lectures, and asked him to contribute articles to the *Baptist Missionary Magazine* which he edited. For four weeks Hudson Taylor compiled material and thought over the subject, and on January 13 began to write. All his brooding over the big map in his study and the implications of Christ's command to 'preach the gospel to every creature' came into focus and assumed a clear form as he traced the glory of China's ancient civilisation back through European history and beyond. The content of those articles was later to be carried over and expanded into the small book or 'pamphlet', *China: Its Spiritual Need and Claims*.

> When Jonah threatened the destruction of Nineveh – the Chinese nation was one of the greatest nations of the world. [Chinese astronomical observations recorded two hundred years before Abra-

ham] have been verified by astronomers of our own times. And the oldest record of antiquity, still possessed by the Chinese, graven on the rocks of Hung-shan some half-century antecedent to this early period, was intended to perpetuate the memory of engineering works not less remarkable for extent or difficulty than the pyramids of Egypt.[40]

For forty centuries the growth and extension of settled government in China embraced one-tenth of the total inhabitable area of the world. Giving the statistics continent by continent he showed this statement to be factual. And to help his readers to grasp the immensity of this concept he painted a word picture:

> Could the empire of China be changed from its present form to that of a long strip of land a mile in breadth, a person walking thirty miles a day would require more than 483 years to walk from one end of it to the other.

If that was true of the territory, what of the population, 'scattered as sheep having no shepherd'? Citing various censuses and estimates, from Manchu sources and 'the Marquis de Moges' account of Baron Gros' embassy to China and Japan in 1857–58' he took four hundred million as an acceptable round figure, greatly modifying it a few years later.

> What mind can grasp it? The whole population of Europe is but 270-millions. . . . It has about twenty-two times the population of densely peopled England . . . But were *all* the subjects of the court of Pekin marshalled in single rank and file, allowing one yard between man and man, they would encircle the globe more than ten times at its equator. Were they to march past the spectator at the rate of thirty miles a day, they would move on and on, day after day, week after week, month after month; and more than twenty-three years and a half would elapse before the last individual had passed by.

In contrast, the total of three thousand Protestant Christian Chinese after fifty years of effort would pass by in less than an hour and a half. Four hundred millions 'having no hope, and without God in the world! . . . the view is appalling'. And the daily mortality in so great a nation outnumbered the whole population of Chester and weekly outnumbered the population of Leeds.

> Think of it – a mortality which in less than three months exceeds the whole population of huge, overgrown London; – which in a year and a half exceeds the total number of the inhabitants of our highly

> favoured England . . . And can the Christians of England sit still with folded arms while these multitudes are perishing . . .? . . . Think of the imperative command of [Jesus] 'Go ye into all the world, and preach the Gospel to *every* creature'; . . . and weigh well the fearful words: 'If *thou* forbear to deliver them that are drawn unto death, and those that are ready to be slain; if thou sayest, Behold, we knew it not; doth not He that pondereth the heart consider it? and He that keepeth *thy* soul, doth He not know it? and shall not He render to every man according to his works?'

Then followed a historical review of the response of the Christian Church from Nestorian times in the seventh century to the present day. Paying tribute to the valiant efforts of the Roman Catholic missionaries he went on,

> And never have they given up *their* hold of China. Entering by stealth, living in concealment, . . . ever and anon meeting with imprisonment, sufferings, torture, and death itself, they have presented a remarkable instance of fidelity to their calling . . . [Then] Shall we prove less obedient to the command of *our* Superior . . .? Let us confess our sin, and earnestly seek grace to wipe away the blot from the honour of our Master's cause.

Since 1858 two hundred European priests and nuns were reported to have been sent to China – but only a handful of Protestants.

By his calculation, knowing all Protestant missionaries in China by name, he reckoned that the number left in early 1865 was almost twenty-five fewer than in 1860–61. A great deal had been achieved but 'MUCH, very much remains to be accomplished'. To justify his generalisation he surveyed the eighteen provinces of China one by one in terms of the population and missionaries among them. The first had thirteen missionaries to thirty-one million people – ten times the population of Scotland with its *thousands* of Christian ministers, besides other Church workers. Relentlessly he worked through the whole of China, blending information and anecdote with heart-searching comparisons. As for the eleven unevangelised provinces of the interior, in each case the stark truth was 'NO MISSIONARY' – in all, three hundred and eighty millions out of reach of the few missionaries there were – so 'is it not *your* duty to carry the Gospel to these perishing ones?'

By Sunday, January 15, what he was writing, or dictating to Maria as he walked to and fro in the study, for that was their practice, was striking at his own conscience. He could not challenge others without putting himself in their place. The narrowness of his vision, the short-sighted complacency of concern for Ningbo where so much was encouraging now smote him. This was the underlying cause of that self-humbling with Maria, when they went without food in order to confess their shortcomings and pray for the Lord's 'pardon and favour'.

He sent the articles off to Mr Lewis on Monday, and on that day had the long conversation with the men about their future together. From then on, when asked to preach, his subject as often as not was 'the Great Commission' or 'China's spiritual need'. After publishing one or two instalments, however, Lewis returned Taylor's manuscripts saying that they were too significant to be restricted to his small magazine. Hudson Taylor should amplify them in pamphlet or book form to secure a larger circulation. And this he did during the spring and summer, thinking, calculating, poring over his journals and letters from China and quoting from them to illustrate his points. But the more he prayed and worked the more vulnerable he himself became to the arguments. The responsibility impressed on his readers and audiences for the evangelisation of all China, weighed more and more heavily on him. He had the knowledge and experience. He must go with the companions God had sent him, without more delay – if possible in May.[41]

Glasgow and 'China's need'[42] *March 1865*

The younger Kingdon was facing his decision, talking and praying with Hudson Taylor about applying to the BMS. John Mara of the United Methodist Free Church was working on his outfit. Stott was coming to London. And Stevenson with his mind made up and his medical verdict favourable had his sights on going to China with the others. Nearly five years had flown and apart from Valentine and Fuller, in denominational societies, only two of the prayed-for five reinforcements for Ningbo had reached there, James Meadows and Jean Notman. Stephan Barchet and Richard Truelove had been waiting for the Taylors, until William Berger proposed their going ahead, perhaps with George Crombie too.

Hudson Taylor parted from John Stevenson after the consultation with Dr Clarke and went into the City, to buy more books on China and to attend at Bow Street Police Court on a matter of some money stolen in the post. When he reached home again, John Nevius was waiting. In the sanatorium at Sudbrook Park with Helen, he explained, was a Christian shipbuilder, 'a pious, benevolent man' named Denny. 'He told us of a ship he was about to send to China and offered us a free passage in it.' The Neviuses were soon to return to the United States and could not take advantage of the offer. So they had mentioned that their fellow-missionary Hudson Taylor was ready to send two men to China, and Mr Denney was extending the invitation to them instead.

This was 'the Lord's doing and marvellous in our eyes'. No answer to prayer could be more timely or precise. Stephan Barchet and Richard Truelove could be ready to sail within a few days if they all worked hard. No time could be wasted. Hudson Taylor wrote at once to Mr Berger, Mr Marshall, the minister of Barchet's church and to Stephan himself. Then he went round to the London Hospital, found Stephan at work and gave him the letters. At Coborn Street all was excitement, with Truelove and Barchet like schoolboys dressing up in Chinese clothes.

In the next few days Hudson Taylor went to see William Berger, took the men to meet the FES committee, spent a whole day completing their outfits, and sent Richard off to his home near Barnsley to say goodbye.

On March 13 Mr Denny's letter arrived confirming the free passages, and a farewell meeting for Stephan was held in the West End. When Hudson Taylor addressed the meeting on China, even William Berger 'was greatly affected', rising to say he had resolved to do ten times and, with God's help, a hundred times more for Christ.

Hudson Taylor's next journal entry was made in Glasgow on the 16th, after three more crowded days of packing and listing, sealing and roping, singing and praying all together as their custom was. Leaving London by the nine p m train with 'many of his [Stephan's] friends at the station to bid him goodbye', they travelled through the night. Characteristically Hudson Taylor's note to tell Maria of their safe arrival and to give her their address – 'after a good night [we] shall, with God's blessing be all right' – accompanied two sheets of John Nevius' translation of *Line upon Line*. He had apparently been proof-reading them on the journey.

The steamship *Corea* was not due to sail until after the weekend, but Hudson Taylor had work to do in Glasgow, Dr William Parker's church to visit and interviews to arrange. In the evening of that first day they attended a meeting and afterwards 'had an opportunity of speaking of China's need'. Arising from this he was taken to meet a Mr Forlong, 'interested in China'. Forlong then took him to other meetings where again he was allowed to speak. And the great Andrew Bonar set him to address three meetings at his church on Sunday, on 'China, its claims and needs'. No longer was it China in general. The spiritual claims of China had become the pressing theme which fired his addresses and kindled his hearers. This sequence of events well illustrated what was to be characteristic of Hudson Taylor's public appearances. He spoke from a full heart at one meeting and was in demand at many.

Now the momentum was building up and meetings multiplied. A group of gentlemen met him for breakfast on Monday to hear more. After breakfast three or four young men from Hillhead called, 'desirous of going to China'. And at a tea meeting of sixty he spoke again 'on the need of China' and 'such earnest, powerful, prevailing prayer was put forth for China, as I do not remember to have heard before. The meeting lasted from 6 to 11 p.m.' In a very hasty scribble to Maria that same day, he said,

> I spoke for China on Friday, Saturday, 4 times on Sunday, this morning, this afternoon, and tonight . . . WRESTLE mightily with God for me and for the work. There are six or seven persons saying "Here am I, send me" to God – not to me.

And again the next day, still down-to-earth,

> My Own Darling . . . Are Stephan's Merrino Vests in the Box? I have not got them down in the list of contents . . . I never remember such a meeting as last night's. God was with us of a truth. There will be a great work in China, in answer to such prayers . . .

Tuesday ended without Richard Truelove joining them as expected, and no explanation came in the post. They met each train at the station and did not give up hope until after one a m. A weary Hudson Taylor wrote to Maria on Wednesday with some relief, 'The steamer is run aground – I don't think I can get home *before* Monday night . . . Tell Mr. Gough I am sorry for the delay, but that I am kept here by the Lord . . .'

Four friends came to breakfast, to pray for China, and in the evening Hudson Taylor gave another lecture at Andrew Bonar's church. Before the end of Thursday he was really worried about what could have happened to Truelove. Telegrams to and from his father, James Taylor, supplied the news that Richard had as planned left Barnsley at six-thirty a m on Tuesday.

> Darling, Truelove has not yet turned up. We are anxious about him . . . He should have been here at 6.00 p.m. I met that train . . . If he had come by it he must have run off very quickly. I also met the next train (9.30 p.m.) and Mr. Barchet met the next one (12.15 a.m. – midnight). We met the trains of the next day but in vain. The ship is still on the bank – fortunately for us tho' not for the owners. Poor Truelove must be in sad trouble; of course we are uneasy. We have been to many Hotels and Temperance Coffee Houses but in vain. If he only had gumption (as poor Mr Jones used to say) to telegraph to you or Father for our address he might have got a reply long ago. I hope he is not sick or short of money . . . May the Lord order all for the best . . . I feel weary today. I long to be once more quickly at your side, and to get on with our work.

A telegram from Hudson Taylor's mother brought the information that Truelove intended going to Greenock (having heard, he said, from Crombie that the *Corea* would sail from there). So the search moved to Greenock, again without success. Then as bizarrely as the episode began it sorted itself out – for the present. Trivial as it was in some ways, the light it throws on Hudson Taylor's and Maria's personalities and on subsequent events, justifies its narration. Nothing before had shown how naive this boy from Staincross still was.

Truelove had interpreted his instructions to go to Glasgow as meaning via Glasgow to Greenock, as he explained:

> Once at Greenock, not finding either Mr. Taylor or Mr. Barchet there, and learning that a Steamer (the *Asia*) had left the port that day, . . . and that there was no other Steamer about to leave the port, (not knowing the name of the *Corea*) I concluded that it must have been the one I ought to have sailed in. I therefore followed the Steamer to Cardiff . . . [where it was to put in].

At Cardiff he found the *Asia* but no sign of Hudson Taylor or Barchet, and was told the fare to China would be sixty pounds. So leaving his cabin trunk there he took another train to London, as his money was running low. Late on Friday night he roused Maria out of bed at Coborn Street. She opened the bedroom window to see who was knocking, dressed quickly, prepared food for him and asked if he was ready to set off for Glasgow. By then he had had enough travelling and chose to go to bed, asking Maria to arrange about his trunk. While he slept she found that if she posted a letter at the General Post Office by St Paul's Cathedral before 7.45 a m it would go direct to Cardiff. So she wrote asking the stationmaster to forward the box at once by passenger train, to be collected at Greenock Station, and after praying set out at six a m for the City. Walking to Mile End Gate she was 'so extravagant as to take a cab to the Bank', sent a telegram to tell Hudson Taylor that Truelove had turned up, bought a Bradshaw railway timetable, posted her letter at the GPO and then, 'I had to walk all the way home, [two miles] for I did not want to be extravagant again.'

Richard was still in bed. But studying her Bradshaw Maria found that he must leave Euston Station at ten a m if he was to reach Glasgow before midnight, 'as his catching the steamer or not might just depend upon that'. Snatching a hasty breakfast she 'went with' Richard to Euston. He could not travel third-class by that train so, as she wrote to Hudson in a sixteen-page screed, she

> Saw him into a second class carriage with your address in his purse. We had between us just enough money to pay the fare and two shillings over. I let him take that . . . I felt God had been with us, for we were close run for time. Richard seemed as if he could not realise that we must act immediately . . . What a sad, sad waste of money . . . I am quite used up, having had no rest last night.

As soon as the train had gone she persuaded a telegraphist to accept stamps to send messages to Barnsley and Glasgow – and walked the four miles back to Coborn Street.

> My feet are so swollen and tender I can scarcely hobble about the house . . . May God be with you and bring you through with gain and not with loss. I mean physically, . . . spiritually, and as regards the best interests of His kingdom.

It had been too much. Maria was ill for several days.

Meanwhile in Glasgow on Thursday Hudson Taylor was 'feeling weary after yesterday's work and somewhat depressed'. But he visited Mrs Denny, wife of the ship-owner, was taken to see Loch Lomond from an eminence near Helensburg, and went on to search Greenock again for Truelove. At last on Saturday Maria's telegram solved the riddle and Richard 'arrived at night . . . not seeming to feel at all that his missing the way was his fault.' On Sunday, March 26, Hudson Taylor spoke three times again on 'China's need' and the Great Commission, and in the evening wrote to Maria,

> My dear long-left Treasure,
>
> Days have passed away in the ordering of our Father's providence – happy days, busy days, well filled days too, – and here I am

> detained, till He who sent me here brings me back to you and the more monotonous but not less important work He has for us to do at home . . . I don't know when I shall come home; I don't see my way before me. The Lord is my Shepherd, He will lead me. And He will lead you. . . .

After breakfast with the Parkers' minister and visiting Jean Notman's uncle he begged a sheet of paper from him and wrote asking Maria to send

> a dozen and a half of Miss Notman's portraits, a dozen of Barchet and Truelove, a few of Truelove, and a dozen of self, and a dozen of group in the two postures by tomorrow's book-post . . . Tonight we commend them to the Lord in united prayer. And soon, I hope *they* may be on their way to China . . . Give my Christian love to Crombie and Annie, Stevenson, Mr. Gough and Mrs. Jones. May He draw us nearer to each other, and nearer to Himself. May He make our children His own care and His own by faith in Jesus.
>
> I am troubled to think our rent is not paid. Would it be well to call and say I have been detained in Scotland, but hope to be home in a day or two?

He hired a hall for the meeting 'of Christians of all denominations', noted that a lady donated more than enough to pay for it, and 'gave some account of China's need and the work there', before the travellers were commended to God. In his addresses he was surely saying what part women could play, and 'spoke for Mrs. Lord' and her orphanage school. 'And Grace Ciggie and Anne Stephen spoke to me of going to China.' What began as names among many others, became in time symbols of heroism and faith. Grace Ciggie's was one of these. It was never easy to know what stuff these men and women were made of. What he knew without doubt was that the delays in Glasgow had unburdened his soul about China, only to burden it more strongly than ever.

At last the *Corea* was afloat again and Hudson Taylor himself went in search of Truelove's box, without success, and gave directions for all their other baggage to be taken on board. Then on Wednesday, March 29, they took a boat out to the steamer, 'a magnificent one', arranged their cabins and 'met Capt. Russell, an agreeable man, with whom we came ashore and walked to Helensburgh'. The *Corea* was not sailing immediately, but Hudson Taylor had done all he could and Maria's illness claimed him now. So he left five pounds with Alexander Taylor, a budding recruit who would see the two men again, to recoup Richard for some of his expenses. Then he wound up his own affairs in Glasgow, wrote to the Bible Society (the letter saying he expected to sail himself in mid-May), met friends to take his leave, and caught the nine p m train home – third-class as always. Between the lines of his journal entry lie the unrecorded sympathy and conversation which he summed up in the words, 'Found an old man in the same compartment was a Christian, . . . going to Southampton to bury his daughter.' It would have been unlike him not to remind him of the Scriptures which make death a dawning, not day's end, for the believer – 'every eye shall see Him . . . they shall see His face', '[to] be with Me where I am; that they might behold My glory'.

Last of the five[43] *April 1865*

Every day Hudson Taylor had appointments in town. He addressed a meeting at Welbeck Street, a Brethren venue, on 'China's need'[44] and met Henry W. Soltau, a barrister of Plymouth and Exeter, a man of 'sparkling wit, keen intellect and extensive literary attainment'.[45] That first acquaintance was to lead to two of Soltau's sons, a daughter and three other relatives becoming valued colleagues in the years ahead. On April 6 he called at the CMS to see Henry Venn about the grant for opium addicts and in his absence a telegram arrived from Plymouth – from Stephan Barchet whom they imagined to be half-way to the Cape.

The *Corea* had made good progress after leaving Greenock and was through the Bay of Biscay when she came upon a derelict vessel, abandoned by her crew in a storm but still afloat with thousands of pounds worth of coal as her cargo. Captain Russell took possession of the prize and towed her back to Plymouth. The telegram said, 'Returned to Plymouth with vessel found full of cargo. Send Truelove's box if time from Greenock. Here perhaps till Monday.'

But the time was too short. Then came a second dramatic telegram. Richard had disappeared again. He had not been seen for two days except by some boatmen after dark. A letter was on the way but Hudson Taylor could not wait. Conferring with Gough and Mary Jones he went at once to Paddington, just missed the train, and had to return home.

Stephan's letter arrived and betrayed his anxiety. Uncertain of Richard's intentions, and knowing the hazards of dockland among seamen of no scruples, he had urged on him the need to keep together when they went ashore, and not to take more than a few shillings with him. But Truelove had come up on deck carrying his carpet-bag. 'Wishing to *know* the contents I asked him why . . . and what he had in it. He gave me an evasive answer, and I did not force the question further.' The bag was heavy and after a morning of sight-seeing Truelove tired of carrying it, so they went to the railway station cloakroom to deposit it. Truelove promised not to move from the waiting room while Stephan went to see if a reply telegram had come, about the missing box. But when he got back Richard had gone, leaving no message. Stephan waited and darkness fell.

Thinking he might have returned to the *Corea*, Stephan went back to the harbour. It was foggy and the boatmen said it was too dangerous to cross but he insisted. Richard was not on board either, and did not come. Early in the morning Stephan had gone ashore again and asked for news. Yes, after dark Richard had come to the jetty and chatted with the boatmen for half an hour, but went away saying he would return at seven in the morning. He did not turn up. 'His carpet bag is still in the cloakroom, which may afford some clue . . . as he holds the ticket and I left orders at the cloakroom to detect the person if it were not he.'

When Hudson Taylor reached Plymouth he was met by Stephan and Mr Marshall, the Bryanston Hall minister, whom he had also informed. To his relief they had discovered Truelove. He had gone to another waiting room in a distant part of the station. And when the boatmen told him it was too dangerous to cross to the *Corea* he had asked them to tell Stephan if he came that he was going to a nearby hotel. They failed to do so. Then on Saturday and Sunday he was feeling so unwell that he simply stayed there, sending no message to the ship. His depression deepened and on Monday he bought a ticket to Exeter and returned to the hotel to wait for the train. While he was out Stephan and Marshall, searching high and low, came to the hotel and were told that he had been there but had gone after mentioning Exeter. Following this clue they went on searching and finally came back to the hotel, 'when to their unbounded astonishment they saw Truelove quietly sitting in the coffee-room'. Hudson Taylor's account went on,

> I found Truelove to be in great doubt as to whether to proceed by the *Corea* or not.
>
> *Tuesday 11th.* This morning Mr. Marshall and I fully and strongly put before Truelove the injury to the cause of God, to our little Mission and the personal disgrace that would result if he drew back

> . . . We left him some time to pray about it; after which he decided not to go.

To Hudson Taylor at the time this seemed a disaster. Believing in Truelove's potential as a missionary he saw this irresolute response to seasickness and leaving home as being basically a spiritual failure. With further thought and prayer he could recover, and Hudson Taylor was in no mood to condemn him or write him off as unfit to go. Instead he dealt with him as a pastoral casualty, not pressing him to go but to tell them frankly what he was thinking. No mention was made in the documents of the incident of 'Richard's sweetheart', but that he had an Achilles heel was in no doubt. For the present he kept it to himself. Writing to Maria, Hudson Taylor said, 'Richard has decided, to-day, not to go to China *at present*, but says he is sure that God has called him to go, his only doubt being as to time and way.'

Eventually Truelove wrote Hudson Taylor a note of confession and apology, asking his forgiveness. He had resented his committing the five pounds to Alexander Taylor instead of to himself before the ship sailed from Scotland, and some petty omissions from his outfit! But he had nothing against Stephan or anyone in London or elsewhere, and said he could work happily with Hudson Taylor at Ningbo. If he had not been so seasick and depressed the things that made him give up would not have loomed so large. Finally he met with Berger, Marshall and Hudson Taylor in London and all four signed an agreed statement summarising the episode. And Hudson Taylor and Marshall gave him a memorandum saying they believed his explanations, 'that his not proceeding from Plymouth was not [deliberate] but was the result of a desponding state of mind induced partly by Physical causes, and partly by lack of communion with God.'

But that was some days later. The *Corea* would very soon be sailing again, and a lot was at stake. The free passage to China and considerable expense were in danger of being lost. 'And, above all, we feared the disgrace to the cause of our God, and discouragement to the friends of the mission work,' Hudson Taylor wrote.

Memories of Gutzlaff's bubble and the disintegration of the Chinese Evangelization Society through lack of confidence could not fail to enter Hudson Taylor's mind. But to replace Truelove on the *Corea* could redeem the situation – if there was someone able to go at a moment's notice. Only one possibility existed – George

Crombie. But George and Anne were due to marry before leaving Britain with the Taylors, within the next few weeks. They had been engaged for more than four years.

Having Thomas Marshall with him in Plymouth gave Hudson Taylor the right man to consult and pray with. William Berger was out of reach. For all his frugality Hudson Taylor never hesitated to use money when necessary. This time a gift of thirty pounds from Miss Stacey over and above all foreseen needs was prophetic provision for all this travelling and telegraphing. His course clear, he acted. Time was of the essence. The spiritual nature of his message was paramount. In a sense this was the threshold of the new era in missions, the birth of the Mission that had to be, as yet unformed in his own mind.

> I then after prayer with Mr. M sent the following telegram to Mrs. Taylor. 'Truelove has drawn back. The injury to our cause, the disgrace to our blessed Saviour will be incalculable. If anyone could take Richard's place this would be much lessened. I cannot *ask* Crombie to go, – without seeing his parents, without Annie – on the shortest possible notice. The sacrifice could not easily be overrated. But if he were led to volunteer it would be an odour of a sweet smell to the Lord, whose love is untold, untellable. Just let him see this; and if the Lord leads him to volunteer, reply at once. All can be easily arranged at a slight cost, as if he goes he must leave Paddington by 9.15 Express on Wednesday morning; and one suit of cloth clothes, one tweed, three linen suits must be got at Silver's – other things will get here.

It was already Tuesday afternoon. To Maria he then wrote, counting on the remarkable postal service,

> I do not wish Crombie to be *asked*, much less *pressed* to go. . . . I do not know that in Crombie's place I should be prepared to make such a sacrifice as going out alone would be; or if prepared to make the sacrifice, that I should feel it right to do so – the notice being so short, and Annie having to be left behind. But he is a good man, the dear Lord will teach him, and it seemed right to set it before him, as, if he were to go such glory would accrue to God and such good to His cause.

The telegram reached Maria 'about 3 or 4 p.m.' and she showed it to George and Anne. She then wired to Hudson Taylor,

> George will take an hour or two to consider. Annie is quite prepared to give him up.

It reached Hudson Taylor at six p m. What Anne had said to George was, 'Go. And show that you love the cause of God more than me.'

After two hours spent praying and weighing it up George gave his answer, and Maria sent a second telegram,

> George will go. Annie accompanies him to Plymouth. Will you write to-night to Mr. Skinner, Laurel Cottage, Callington, Cornwall, to come immediately to meet George in Plymouth. Post leaves early morning. Get George cotton socks.

The attention to detail was characteristic of both Hudson Taylor and Maria. An overnight letter was to bring Anne's father to Plymouth by the following afternoon. Whether it succeeded is not mentioned, except that after the ship sailed Anne was apparently cared for and Hudson Taylor was free to look up Mary Jones' adopted son, the Chinese Kying-hae, before returning to London.

After her first telegram reached him, Hudson wrote to Maria,

> How can we give sufficient thanks to God for all His goodness in making Dr. [dear] Crombie willing. If for the best He can make the Captain willing too, and the Owner and give blessing far above our thoughts. Glory be to His Holy Name. May much blessing rest on Crombie and Annie.

Then in a pencilled scribble, 'Yr. telegram to hand. Captain given consent if Owner will. His reply not yet recd.'

Maria at once went with George and Anne into the City and found Silver's already closed. Late as it was, a second shop was open and Freeman the proprietor recognised her. She explained their predicament and asked what other outfitters might be open.

> He took up his hat at once and went with us to see . . . [again] the third was closing, but we were in time. It seemed as tho' God was first showing us our helplessness, and then helping us in our extremity.

So the outfitting was done, Freeman made George Crombie the gift of a waterproof tweed overcoat for the voyage, and they returned home. It was a masterly achievement. The accounts show that their purchases included a frock coat, doe trousers and cloth vest, a tweed suit and three linen suits, all they set out to buy. Late at night Maria sat down to write – probably after chaperoning George and Annie for their last evening together while he packed.

> My precious Treasure,
>
> George has deliberately, prayerfully and I hope rightly come to the

> conclusion to go. He looks forward however to the prospect of Anne's joining him ere long. May our God accept this sacrifice at their hands, rewarding them *in this life* an hundredfold. . . . Annie will go to her own home from Plymouth; it is very near. Poor things! What a trial for them when their marriage seemed so near.
>
> I will say Goodnight; it will soon strike four.

They reached Plymouth by the Express at 4.45 pm. Denny's approval of the change of passenger arrived an hour later. The rest of the outfitting was done there, and with Stephan Barchet they all went on board to pray together in the cabin before the *Corea* sailed. Hudson Taylor assured Crombie that he would do everything possible to send Anne without avoidable delay, but that not a pound was in hand towards the seventy-five or eighty pounds they would need. (Truelove's escapades had cost the equivalent of nine weeks' rent of his room, apart from what Richard himself had spent.) Of the fifteen pounds Hudson Taylor had left he put five into George's hand for incidentals on the voyage, keeping ten for all other purposes. Then they all knelt and prayed that the money for Anne's passage and outfit would be given, and for a suitable escort for her.

Writing from Tenerife, George Crombie enclosed no note for Anne, believing that their prayer would have been answered and she would no longer be in Britain to receive it. In fact she had already sailed on April 26, exactly two weeks after George, with all expenses met and under the escort of a missionary couple in a ship with a Christian captain and chief officer. Her outfit was not skimped, including as it did the usual iron bedstead, bedding, table and chairs and looking-glass for the cabin, a swimming belt, cutlery, crockery – and baby linen. Part of the cost was met by gifts from the Welbeck Street friends, stirred by this tale of exceptional nobility. Five years later Hudson Taylor was to repay his debt of deep gratitude when in a matter of life and death he went far beyond duty to do all he could for them.[46]

When the *Corea* reached the Cape of Good Hope and put into Table Bay for coal, twenty-eight ocean-going vessels and thirty smaller ones were anchored there. Unable to load, Captain Russell steamed on through worsening weather to Simon's Bay. The next day what a local newspaper called 'one of the most destructive gales that has ever visited Table Bay' destroyed all but ten of the ships, with the loss of eighty or ninety lives. But in Simon's Bay no harm was done.

They reached Ningbo in late July and Anne in September. On

October 1 she and George were married and, following the Ningbo custom, on their return from the honeymoon put on a feast for the Bridge Street congregation, now sixty people, at three tables for men and three for women. The same day James Meadows wrote to William Berger in his Marco Polo style,

> I will tell you of a feast we had today . . . Mrs Crombie soon made herself at home among the women, and Mr. C. . . . managed very well, but not so well as his wife. I should think that Mrs. C. will be very useful among the women of China.

Then came the speeches by some of the Christians, such mature Biblical dissertations on 'the marriage-supper of the Lamb' and the union between Christ and his Church that

> the tears came to my eyes, and I felt very much inclined to turn round and embrace brother Crombie saying, 'I would give twenty pounds if you and dear Mrs. C. understood this'. But when . . . I remembered that the [speakers] were converted Chinese . . . I could not but shed tears.[47]

His emotions in any case were very mixed.

Stephan was living alone among the Chinese, under E C Lord's supervision. George and Anne were the last of the five for whom Hudson and Maria had prayed. They saw Meadows, Notman, Barchet and the Crombies as the answer to those prayers they had prayed at Ningbo as they packed up in 1860, wondering if they would ever see China again.[48]

In London the upheaval of losing four of the Coborn Street party, and the spiritual exercise through which he passed, seemed to do something deep for Hudson Taylor. The Ningbo need was met for the present. The other recruits were not ready to go. He could afford to delay his own departure again and try to finish the New Testament. But more, he needed to think through the implications of what he had been writing and preaching, about greater China's need and claims. For no longer was it enough to urge them upon other people. His own thoughts were running ahead. A dry fuse was being laid but he still had little concept of the charge it led to.

CHAPTER TEN

'TO ATTEMPT THE UNPRECEDENTED' 1865

'A special agency was essential'[1] *April–June 1865*

Hudson Taylor's journal ended abruptly on April 11 and was not taken up again until June 12. If in his own hand he had not labelled the next three penny notebooks 'Journal No. 10', 'No. 11' and 'No. 12', beginning his June 12 entry with a summary going back to May 31, the assumption would be that one notebook was missing. He offered no explanation. The claims on his time were enough. But letters supply the lack to some extent. He left no stone unturned to get Anne Skinner away properly equipped for China. His pastoral care for Richard Truelove, to make sure that full understanding and forgiveness were mutual, was time-consuming. And he tried to make up for his long absences by working hard at the New Testament revision with Frederick Gough again. Although they had revised Colossians, only the books up to 2 Corinthians were in print so far. But with the Truelove consultations dragging on into May and his brain mulling constantly over new ideas about China, he was finding it difficult to keep his mind on book-work, he told Maria.

On Sunday, April 16, he happened (if Montagu Beauchamp, one of the 'Cambridge Seven',[2] was right) to attend the morning worship again at Welbeck Street. After the Breaking of Bread various members of the congregation proposed topics for united prayer, and others took them up. When prayer was asked for a sick person in very uninteresting circumstances a long pause followed. As no one else responded Hudson Taylor prayed, in such a way that at the close of the meeting the Dowager Lady Radstock asked one of the leading members, 'Who was that little man who prayed so earnestly? I should like to be introduced to him.' After a short conversation she invited Hudson Taylor to tea at 26 Portland Place where he met her daughter, Lady Beauchamp, and Sir Thomas Beauchamp, Bt. They in turn invited him to Langley Park in Norfolk for a few days when the weather was warmer. And so began a friendship which gave Hudson Taylor the support of young Lord Radstock, the Waldegraves and the Beauchamp family, and brought Beauchamps into the China Inland Mission until the mid-twentieth century.

As well as the revision work in which Maria was still helping with the Ningbo vernacular and preparation of marginal cross-references, Hudson Taylor and she were still compiling material for the articles being pieced together as a book. But a new interest had come into their study of China. Instead of only writing to stir up other people, they themselves had the intention of bringing about the occupation of every province. 'Busy through the week . . . on Sundays we prayed and wrote, and wrote and prayed . . . I walked up and down the little parlour, Maria writing at the table.'

No longer could it be a matter of imprecisely urging others to take the salvation of China seriously – the whole of that great empire must be their objective. And the more they thought and wrote and prayed, the more Hudson Taylor and Maria felt the onus was on themselves. Working on statistics, drawing analogies, planning the presentation, citing his own experiences to arouse others, always the effect was firstly on Hudson Taylor himself. The months and years spent studying the Bible in order to render it correctly in colloquial Chinese had taught him those basic principles now inexorably applied to his present situation,

> not elaborate appeals for help, but, *first*, earnest *prayer to God to thrust forth labourers*, and *second*, the deepening of the spiritual life of the Church, so that *men should be unable to stay at home*, not to raise ways and means, but *to go and do the work* . . .[3]

They would go and he would go, but still he did not see himself as one of them. The concept of a joint venture with himself as leader soon followed.

Financial and political hindrances ought not to be allowed to dictate policy.[4] To wait for the Church to wake up or for China to open up more than it had already opened, was to doubt God and the truth of his Word. The men of faith in God were those who 'subdued kingdoms', 'shut the mouths of lions' and 'in weakness were made strong', disregarding opposition and even destitution. 'And he could not but wonder where European (and English) Christianity would have been, if the apostles had waited . . . readiness to suffer – made the early Christians conquer.'

It all weighed on him obsessively. For if existing societies would not respond to the situation there was 'No hope of getting inland work taken up!' And yet, *if no one else was prepared to act, far from closing the matter did it not open it up, leaving a clear field for someone else*? Why had this not dawned on him sooner?

> At last the thought came: – 'Well if *you* see these things why not go forward yourself and do it? Go yourself to inland China! If power in prayer is given you can get the men and means. Five are already gone. Why not more for inland China?' I had no doubt they *could be obtained* . . .[5]

Now all the telling influences of the past were converging to shape his convictions and drive him to action. The refined gold of Wesleyan Methodism and the faithfulness of his forebears were bearing fruit again: solid teaching by his mother and the immovable faith of his father, 'If we believe not, yet he abideth faithful: he cannot deny himself. He would not be God if he could.' The inspiration of Andrew Jukes in Hull, George Müller's autobiography and the deep godliness of the Tottenham saints, like pillars in his own life structure carried the sound principles of Charles Gutzlaff and *The Gleaner* for him to follow. The gospel must be taken deep into China by foreign missionaries, but 'China can be evangelised only by the Chinese'.[6] So it must be a joint effort, men like James Meadows and Wang Lae-djün working in partnership. The deep devotion and fearless tenacity of William Burns, and the quiet certainty of John Jones that God would provide for him and his family if only he did God's will, had transformed Hudson Taylor's own experimental faith, so that it could embrace far more than his personal needs. And now the strength of the two businessmen Berger and Pearse alongside him gave substance to spiritual confidence.

But two strong objections halted him in his tracks, the danger of undercutting the older societies, and the paralysing fear of launching on a venture that would, like the well-meaning CES, all go wrong – with young men and young women like those around him now, stranded, high and dry, reproaching him for misleading them. How the familiar jibes of Shanghai journalists and missionary critics re-echoed through his mind! If sharing his poverty with the destitute and living like a Chinese in order to be one of them was 'hare-brained', 'visionary' and 'aimless', what would landing a party of novices in trouble far from the treaty ports be called? Yet it was not criticism that troubled him. It was the viability of such a venture.

In a book published conjointly by several missionary societies in Britain, *The Uplift of China*, this statement confirmed the recollections of Hudson Taylor in old age, '[He] tried in vain to persuade existing societies to adopt his plans for a great forward movement.' And when he did arrive in China with his first party of fifteen others, *The Uplift* continued,

> The leading English journal of Shanghai remarked of the enterprise that it could only be the project either of a knave or a fool, and 'we have reason to believe that Mr. Taylor is not a fool'.[7]

Maria, Gough and the Bergers were by his own statement confidants. But George Pearse and the Howard brothers, John Eliot and Robert, with whom he and Maria stayed from time to time with their children, would hardly have been kept in ignorance, though no statement that he consulted them on *this* matter has been found; nor Miss Stacey; nor the praying friends in Clevedon and Bristol. George Müller was sending him donations from time to time and he admired this man of prayer. In the verbatim jottings made as Hudson Taylor reminisced is this note about Müller, 'Many long talks J.H.T. had with him. Felt him to be so wise, and a thorough man of business.'[8] One or two letters asking his parents to pray about specific points may indicate the part these others played at this crucial time. For things were taking shape.

> Months of earnest prayer and not a few abortive efforts had resulted in a deep conviction that *a special agency was essential* for the evangelisation of Inland China.[9]

That had been the first milestone, but in May they were well beyond it. With 'daily conference with my beloved friend and fellow-worker' F F Gough, and 'many days in prayerful deliberation' with both the Bergers and Maria 'whose judgement and piety were of priceless value at this juncture', they began to see light, '. . . and it was concluded that, by simple trust in God', – that is, by not drawing on the ministerial colleges or soliciting funds from the churches which supplied existing societies,

> a suitable agency might be raised up and sustained without interfering injuriously with any existing work. I had also a growing conviction that God would have *me* to seek from Him the needed workers, and to go forth with them. But for a long time unbelief hindered my taking the first step.

'A special agency was essential,' and he was in a position to establish it. If he did, what form should it take? In some ways this was the most straightforward part of the problem. For fifteen years, since 1850, they had been theorising and trying out new approaches. Charles Gutzlaff's principles still appealed to them as correct, if safeguards against his failure were adopted. The CES had failed administratively, not in its principles. Hudson Taylor had learned from Medhurst, Edkins and Wylie of the LMS, and with John Burdon of CMS and William Burns the value of itinerant evangelism, and had contributed to the success of the pioneers by his own innovations. Being a Chinese to the Chinese, in language, clothing and customs, was incontestably desirable, he believed. John Jones and he had lived at close quarters with the Chinese they had won for Christ, and James Meadows was proving again the effectiveness of this conformity.

Educated men were needed for literary and educational work, but inland China would need men like Meadows to be its pioneers. The current trends of thought from which the Foreign Evangelist Society had arisen endorsed the conviction that God was indicating men of the artisan and petty officer type as the pool to draw from without upsetting other missions' practice. Carey, Morrison and other famous missionaries had been working men, but the societies had insisted on educating them – with every justification. In contrast, Robert Moffat had been sent to South Africa with little education. The 'special agency' would require the training that had fitted men to be evangelists or church workers at home, but would add little more than practical training for conditions in China. Educated men would be needed and welcomed by this new society, but it would demonstrate again that the weak and 'foolish' of the world in God's hands could 'confound the mighty'. The head could not say to the feet 'I have no need of you.' Jesus himself had chosen 'unlearned and ignorant men'. In such a large field as China all types would find a place and work together. This was what William Burns had urged in 1851, that missionaries of all kinds were needed, with every type of qualification, and not only ordained ministers and doctors. With such thoughts the concept took shape.

In every mission centre in China so far, the proximity of a great variety of denominations showed that unity is essential and courtesy over differences made co-operation not only possible but enjoyable. Then harmony within an 'unsectarian' or trans-sectarian body should be even more attainable, for it would be supra-sectarian.

Agreement to preach the gospel and establish Churches, and not to propagate particular views of Church government was realistic. True, E C Lord had persuaded Methodist James Meadows to accept 'believer's baptism' in Ningbo, but raised eyebrows need not lead to friction. At 30 Coborn Street Anglican, Brethren, Presbyterian, Methodist, Congregational and Baptist were having no problems on that score. How much more so away from divided Britain. As new believers in China were taught and congregations stood on their own feet they would send some from their own number to work as colporteurs and preachers with the missionaries. In other words, what had been done in Ningbo would be continued in inland China.

The concept they were evolving was of a classless, trans-denominational mission composed of men and women engaged in evangelism, Church-planting and the training of Church leaders. It was to press into the interior 'where Christ had not been named', depending on God alone to guide and provide for them in answer to trustful prayer. To penetrate to every one of the eleven unoccupied provinces would need at least twenty-two missionaries. All that that involved taxed Hudson Taylor's imagination and appalled him. Subsistence in the remote interior would in itself be a major problem of communication and supply. The responsibility was too great, and he shrank from it. On May 18 Hudson Taylor wrote to his parents,

> We much need your prayers for our work and for ourselves . . . more [work] than we have strength for. And in the revision I am very much perplexed as to what to do. We have only got printed off as far as Galatians iv, and May is fast wearing on.

His thirty-third birthday came and went, but the claims of China mattered even more now than progress on the New Testament. And his health was suffering. The Bergers invited him to bring Maria and the children to Saint Hill for a week. He could make it a working holiday, and they could discuss the future at leisure. They went on Wednesday, May 31, and after a week were together so hot on the scent of a solution to so much soul-searching that they stayed until June 12.

On June 1 Hudson Taylor wrote home again, dating the letter 1864 instead of '65 and revealing his tension in the terseness of his style,

> I much need your prayers. I. I desire, if the Lord will, to get 4 Missionaries, 2 married and 2 single, off by the end of the Summer or

> the beginning of the Autumn. The persons are suitable, as far as I can judge; but 3 of them have not fully decided to go. Pray the Lord to make their way plain, if he see it well. II. The expense of sending them and the family of one of them, would exceed £600. Towards this we have [a little] more than £5 in hand. Will you join us in asking the Lord for the rest? III. It is much pressed on me to try to get *20 more* European Missionaries besides these 4, so as to send at least 2 into each province of China proper in which there is NO missionary, and 2 into Chinese Tartary; and to try to send them with an equal number of Chinese Helpers, making in all 48 persons (besides those on the way) requiring support. The expense of these would exceed £5000 a year. Will you earnestly pray God to guide me aright; whether to attempt this or not?
>
> We are preparing a pamphlet on the Spiritual Need of China: we much need God's help in this matter. The weather here is very fine, and the children are famously enjoying themselves.[10]

The lawns and the lake, the rolling Sussex countryside and 'the deep attachment' between the older and younger couples made for peace and happiness. Mrs Berger, 'all love and gentleness', was motherly to Maria with her four children and another on the way, while William Berger and Hudson Taylor walked and talked, 'having much conference about China'. Five or fifty 'persons', five pounds or five thousand per annum, they were in it together.

'Will you join us in praying for £600?' So Bergers and Taylors together were sure enough for that, given the missionaries. And the concept of a missionary team as big as or bigger than any one mission yet had in China, under Hudson Taylor's own leadership if not authority, was more advanced than ever, while the pairing of foreigner and Chinese together extended the influence of Gutzlaff and CES through both men. That was the plan, but while Hudson Taylor asked the weekly prayer meeting at Saint Hill to pray for the twenty-four missionaries for inland China, he had to admit, later, '[I] had not at that time surrendered myself to be their leader.'[11] His thoughts were ahead of his will.

Three days later one of the Glasgow candidates, Alexander Taylor, wrote that for family reasons he must defer going for two years. But not waiting for anything, Hudson Taylor sat down and in a pocket-sized, white leather-bound ledger with a lock, accounted in summary for the monies already received and expended in sending James and Martha Meadows, Jean Notman, George Crombie and Anne Skinner to China. (Stephan Barchet's church had covered his costs.) As major donor for Jean Notman, Miss Stacey audited that statement. But the Bergers had provided £160 for the Meadows and £100 for George and Anne, together with £30 from Miss Stacey and £20 from Jennie Faulding, so William Berger audited those.[12]

But it is the dates and titles of the accounts and audits that capture attention. Quite incidentally, both Hudson Taylor and Berger failed to see (or correct) another instance of Hudson Taylor's tiredness. He gave James Meadows' departure as in 1860 instead of 1862. More significantly, for this and Jean Notman's statement he used the name 'China Mission', no longer the old 'Ningpo Mission'. And (historically), *'J.H.Taylor in account with China Inland Mission'*[13] was the title above Berger's audit on Saturday, June 3, 1865 – the first known use of the name, three weeks before the date, June 25, usually regarded as the date of the Mission's inception.

This special agency was an inland mission, to go where the gospel had never been preached – these raw young men and girls were to do it. Twenty years later Hudson Taylor wrote, 'Before the C.I.M. was founded I told people God was going to open the eighteen provinces.' From that date and the balance of £14.16.0 a trickle of donations followed, day by day through the succeeding weeks, mostly of a few shillings at a time.

Then they were in Coborn Street again, and on June 13 in another letter to his mother Hudson Taylor said,

> We . . . enjoyed the visit, having had all we could wish *but rest*, and that I cannot take when there is an opportunity of labouring for China.
>
> I think I told you of my new project for China, twenty-four European and twenty-four Chinese missionaries . . . Dear Mr Berger has promised to carry on the work at home when we return. We are just now making an effort to get a press and type for China. The expense will not be less than £80. . . . We need your prayers for wisdom, grace, and funds, and for physical strength too to carry all through.

It sounded matter of fact. In reality it was not. He was keeping to himself thoughts so disturbing that he seldom slept more than two hours at a time, or even in a night. In part it was the spectre of Chinese dying by thousands, millions, without Christ, a thought unbearable to him. But it went even deeper than that, and the emotional tension was threatening to break him.[14] He was not willing to do what God was asking of him.

'God's responsibility – not mine'[15] *June 1865*

Immediately on his return to London Hudson Taylor began keeping his journal again. The busy round of seeing about the printing press, candidates, revision, lectures and personal matters continued. 'Got Family Photos. taken. Went to Mr. Faulding's . . . Gave a lecture on China's spiritual need in Mr. Landel's Chapel . . .' But developments in the 'project for China' had pride of place in his entries.

> *Thursday 15th.* Rec[d] Stott's note stating his change of purpose, and intention to leave his situation at once. This was a marked answer to prayer, the more so as I had been unable to write to him about it. . . . Went to F.E.S. and found them willing to help to extent of £200 if 4 persons go out this autumn.

George Stott's prospective father-in-law was adamant in refusing to let his daughter go to China, but Stott could not be deterred.

New moves were being made to bring W A Russell into the New Testament revision and Gough was away to meet him, so the next day Hudson Taylor went out and bought books on the Chinese, Tibetan and Burmese languages. If China, inland, was to be evangelised, they would stop at no half measures. On Saturday the usual prayer meeting was held at Coborn Street. 'Mr. Vigeon came and told us that he and Mrs. V. were decided on going to China. ευλογητος ο θεος' (Blessed be God).

A favourable report on Grace Ciggie of Glasgow arrived; and on June 24 he attended a 'Conference of Evangelists', went on to visit Miss Stacey and stayed there overnight.

Full days and advancing plans, with every indication of more missionaries for China forthcoming, could not resolve his inner conflict. It was intensified. He had no doubt that all the men and women for unevangelised China

> *could be obtained* but there remained the very strongest objection to obtaining them! I saw that in answer to prayer the workers would be given, and their support secured – because the Name of Jesus is worthy. But there unbelief came in!

He was afraid of the consequences – could not bring himself to accept them. His six years in China packed with stress, danger and disappointment, mobs, death and despair left him in no two minds about what lay ahead. Alone they had been as much as he could stand. How could he carry the faults and distresses of so many novice missionaries? So unbelief was the root of his problem. In his *Retrospect*, with the perspective of time, he could comment calmly,

> How inconsistent unbelief always is! . . . I had not then learned to trust God for *keeping power* and grace for myself, so no wonder that I could not trust Him to keep others who might be prepared to go with me. I feared that in the midst of the dangers, difficulties and trials which would necessarily be connected with such a work, some who were comparatively inexperienced Christians might break down, and bitterly reproach me for having encouraged them to undertake an enterprise for which they were unequal.[16]

In such circumstances could he cope? Doubt did not enter into that question. He was sure he could not. To shrink from courting such responsibility and blame was wholly natural and justifiable. Therefore he was personally unwilling to proceed – even while he went ahead with interviews and endless correspondence to help others to do what he also had every intention of doing as an individual. As he put it, '[I] had not at that time included myself among them.' Yet all the time he knew that God was urging him on to accept the responsibilities of leadership of a unified team. And whatever went against God must be from the devil.

> The devil [was] getting me to feel that while prayer and faith would bring me into the fix, one would have to get out of it as best one could. And I did not see that the power that would give me the men (and the means) would be quite sufficient to keep them also! Meanwhile, a million a month in China were dying without God; and this was *burnt into my soul*! If you would pray for preachers, came the conviction, they might have the gospel! And now they perish without it simply because you have not faith . . .[17]

The verbatim notes from which these lines were taken became more terse as he relived the experience and spoke faster.

> For 2 or 3 months, conflict intense. . . . Thought I should lose my reason: yet did not give in! At last became quite ill. [Maria] knew something of it; but to no one could [I] speak fully. Did not want to lay upon her a burden so crushing. These souls! and what Eternity must mean to every one – and what the gospel *might* do for any of them . . .[18]

And again in the *Retrospect*, those marching millions,

> The feeling of blood-guiltiness became more and more intense. Simply because I refused to ask for them, the labourers did not . . . go

> out to China – and every day tens of thousands were passing away to Christless graves. Perishing China so filled my heart and mind that there was no rest by day, and little sleep at night . . .

For weeks he had been pressing China's spiritual need and claims upon the Christian Church – from Glasgow to Plymouth, and Hull to East Grinstead, building in one lecture or sermon upon another in the same churches on the same theme. Quoting from Proverbs 24:11 he repeatedly warned and exhorted his hearers,

> If thou forbear to deliver them . . .; if thou sayest, Behold we knew it not . . . He that keepeth *thy* soul, doth not He know it? and shall not He render to every man according to his works?

And from many other Scriptures,

> Do we really believe that 'this is life eternal, that they might know Thee, the only true God, and Jesus Christ whom Thou hast sent' – that 'the wicked shall be turned into hell, and all nations that forget God'?[19]

Plainly he himself did. Young men and women were offering to go, and older Christians were offering to help in growing numbers. Yet Hudson Taylor himself dared go no further. George Pearse invited him to Brighton for the weekend of June 24–26.[20] J M Denniston was to preach on the Sunday morning, and Hudson Taylor was asked to take the pulpit in the evening. He accepted.

That Saturday morning before he left London, after breakfast with Miss Stacey and the Robert Howards, who were party to the planning, he returned home, to find a note from Gough to say he was not coming in to work on the New Testament. So Hudson Taylor went straight on to Saint Hill, 'and spent some hours in conference with Mr. Berger'. Then on to Brighton to be met by Mr Denniston at the station.

His journal as usual said little, though he had reached the crucial decision of his life. 'Had a long conversation with Mr. Pearse on our work and on co-operation.' And on Saturday, June 25, nothing more dramatic than,

> Heard Mr. Denniston in the morning, preached in the evening on Mt. 28., and met Miss Potter to supper. The latter desires to go to China if the Lord will.
> *Monday 26th.* Retd. by 6.30 train. Called on Mr. and Mrs. Vigeon. Prayed with them that her Father might be made willing to give them

> up. Found Mr. Gough away with his brother. In the evening the Russells took tea with us.

This matter-of-factness continued unbroken through the subsequent days. There was, however, far more to it than that.

After hearing J M Denniston preach, and being stirred by what he said, Hudson Taylor had to get away from other people and think. He could not bear the thought of the thousand or more Christian people in that church enjoying their own security while China's millions were dying without Christ. So he slipped out and went for a walk on the beach until lunch time. There it came home to him that his anxiety about taking responsibility for the young missionaries was because he was misconstruing the facts. If GOD was telling him to do it, as he surely was, and he obeyed, then *all the responsibility was God's, not his own*! 'What a relief!' He could go ahead with the plan to enter every province in China – and prayed at once for the men to do it.

He had with him the Old Testament volume of his pocket-sized Polyglot Bible, with English and Hebrew on facing pages. In keeping with his constant practice of reading four or five chapters daily so as to complete the Bible once each year, he had dates marked in the margins, June 24 beside Job 12, June 25 beside Job 16, and so on. Now he opened his Bible at his marker and entered across the top, '*Prayed for 24 willing, skilful laborers, Brighton, June 25/65.*' So that was that.

> Conflict all ended – peace, joy. Felt as if I could fly up that hill by the station to Mr. Pearse's house . . . And how I did sleep that night! Mrs. Taylor thought that Brighton had done wonders! and so it had.

But first he had that sermon to preach to those hundreds at the evening service. Rid of all inhibitions he could let himself go on the Great Commission, 'Go ye therefore, and teach all nations, baptising . . . teaching . . . and lo, I am with you alway . . .' Matth. 28:19, 20.

The significance of what happened at Brighton seems not to have come fully home to Hudson Taylor until he could look back on it from the distance of decades, but he eventually told the full story (*see* Appendix 4) and over the years it became romanticised, not least in his own thinking. At the time a spiritual transaction took place in which he received the new certainty that carried him confidently through the crises ahead.

With the conflict over and his uncertainties resolved, full days

Prayed for 24 willing skilful labourers at Brighton, June 25/65.

HUDSON TAYLOR'S BIBLE, 25 JUNE 1865
(reduced facsimile)

were a pleasure. One of his first acts was to write and tell E C Lord and the others in Ningbo what that 'goodly number' of reinforcements was turning into. Still hoping to complete the Ningbo Testament before leaving Britain, he had proposals to put to the Bible Society and CMS. On Tuesday, June 27, he

> went to see Mr. Venn, but found him in Committee. Thence to the Bible Socy. Saw Mr. Bergne . . . Arranged for the binding and sending to Ningpo of the Gospels and Acts. Bought 30 vols, 20 in Calf, 10 in Morocco at 3/3 each . . . Then went with Mr Pearse to London and County Bank and opened a/c for 'China Inland Mission'. Paid in £10.[21]

Ten pounds, a symbol of a small beginning with no expectation of rapid growth. William Berger, in whose drawing room the mission's name had been chosen and its nature decided on, weeks before, had used the analogy of a tree. Let it start small and take time to grow, if growth was in its nature. Five thousand pounds a year to keep it going was goal enough for faith to start on. The CES had disintegrated only five years ago, unable to realise an income of far less. George Pearse's summing up of that affair was still fresh in their minds. Before 1860 the Christian public had not become so aroused, he wrote,

> as to warrant our expectation of sufficient help; our faith was weak . . . with some exceptions contributions were on a very small scale and the Committee in their anxiety to enter heartily into the work . . . went beyond their faith and the means which were placed at their disposal.[22]

The Bergers, Taylors and Pearses had progressed since then, but that summary embodied their continuing principles: human planning must be secondary to recognising the will of God; and action must follow provision of the means, lest mistaken zeal lead into debt. The duty of stewardship of personal wealth was dawning very slowly on the minds of even devout Christians. The few were contributing to missions in fair proportion to their wealth, but most in token payments only. Missions could not function on a trickle of small sums. Nor could the liberality of the few like William Berger provide thousands annually. 'The Lord will provide' was in God's wisdom linked to his people's spiritual maturity. For the present the financial needs even for a frugal life-style at Coborn Street were being met from Maria's small income from a trust beyond her control, from a few professional families of substance but not great wealth, from occasional gifts from George Müller, from the collections at church meetings, seldom more than two or three pounds, and for outfits and passages to China from the Foreign Evangelist Society. Ten pounds to open an account for the Mission was representative, and from this point the Taylors' personal accounts would be kept separate. Berger would do all he could. He promised the cost of the printing press and £150, which he increased to £200 when he wrote the cheque on July 4.

Back from the bank Hudson Taylor wrote to S B Bergne at Bible House,

> . . . if you feel it needful to have the work [of revision] completed within some definite time, we *could* finish it in six, four, or even three months, according as we include or otherwise the Epistle to the Hebrews, and the Pastoral Epistles, in the portion we thoroughly study and correct.
>
> You mentioned this morning your intention of consigning the bulk of the Gospels and Acts to the Church Missionary Society . . .

Would it be compatible with this, he asked, for Mrs Lord, whose agent in England Hudson Taylor was, to have a grant of a hundred copies for her work? Then he wrote to George Pearse asking him 'to apply for 150 copies for our Mission'. The grant to Mrs Lord was made the very next day.

Still the work of New Testament revision had to go at his good friend Frederick Gough's pace. Taylor's patience was still tried, if his references to the delays are an indication. But his own preoccupations this summer diverted him as much. That evening he visited the Vigeons and attended the FES Committee.

> There the vote of £50.0.0. each was confirmed for our three Brothers Vigeon, Stott and Stevenson. Then went to Mr. Marshall's and Lectured on 'The present facilities for Evangelization in China'. Spent the night at Mr. Marshall's . . . Returned home for [revision]. Evening saw Mr. Tinling . . . an earnest, devoted young man; truly pious and likely to prove a very valuable Missionary, if not too erratic and wanting in stability and perseverance.[23]

Another great movement, the embryo of the Salvation Army, was conceived within a stone's throw only a week later. On Mile End Waste, at the end of Coborn Street, the teeming thousands of the poor jostled and cried their wares. Striding through them as best he could, young William Booth, three years Hudson Taylor's senior, flamed with compassion for East London's 'irretrievably damned'. At midnight that night he reached home, his eagle eyes shining, and greeted his waiting wife with 'Darling, I've found my destiny!'[24]

Hudson Taylor could have used the same words. The Mission was taking shape.

POSTSCRIPT

K S Latourette of Yale began his Tipple Lecture on Hudson Taylor in 1950 by saying that 'The repercussions of his daring faith were to be felt not only in the vast country to which he gave himself, but also in many other lands.'

Hudson Taylor '. . . a sensitive man of deep affections [whose] most frequent designation of God was Father,' he continued, was challenged by the new liberty to travel *legally* anywhere in the Chinese empire, and both to teach and to accept Christianity. To act on this became an overpowering personal responsibility. He set out to reach the millions not being touched by other Protestant societies, in company with colleagues who, as long as they were 'wise to win souls', could come from any denomination or educational background. Their aim was to preach Christ more than to make disciples, to proclaim the gospel to as many in China as possible. He was content, so Latourette thought, for his Mission to sow the seed and let others reap the harvest; not because other aspects of the great commission were less important but because 'the proclamation of the Gospel was the special task which had been assigned to it . . .'[25]

Such was the view of a historian. If he had seen the Bridge Street church of Ningbo as the embryo of what the China Inland Mission worked to establish everywhere, as Hudson Taylor did, a witnessing nucleus of deeply taught, disciplined, practising Christians, he might have used other words. But his assessments are nonetheless true and his closing words were what would have cheered the innovator had he been able to hear them in advance.

Like Alexander Wylie, Hudson Taylor shunned and feared praise, knowing that God, not he, had done everything. But any review of the work he did and the life he lived must take account of what observers had said. Latourette wrote,

> Tens of thousands in China and elsewhere have heard the Gospel who but for Taylor would have died ignorant of it. Thousands have become Christians who would not have done so . . .[26] It was a daring decision for one man, without financial resources, without the support of an organization, and always in precarious health. More nearly

> than is given to most men, however, Taylor lived to see his vision realized.[27]

And again,

> . . . frail in body and of no unusual intellectual powers, [his] daring, simple faith, utter sincerity, and completely unselfish devotion [contributed, with many favourable factors beyond his control, to the fulfilment of his hopes. He launched out] to attempt the unprecedented [by a] systematic plan which would supplement rather than conflict with existing missions.[28]

For thirty-eight more years he was to be the leader and presiding influence in the largest mission in China. As for the China Inland Mission,

> 'Its beginnings and its development are in some respects the most remarkable chapter in all the history of Christian Missions in China.'[29]

But all of that lay in the future. In June 1865 a thirty-three year-old and his wife of twenty-eight proposed to take a score of inexperienced people younger than themselves beyond the treaty ports of China, where the peculiarities of 'barbarians' were at least familiar, deep into the interior. All the prejudices, hatreds and physical hazards lay before them. But the antagonism of Satan the 'adversary' was most daunting. All of them were agreed on trusting in God alone, not in a remote committee, for the necessities of life. And all faced the high risk of losing their lives or health. In the spirit of David Livingstone (himself a missionary in response to Charles Gutzlaff's appeals), 'Can the love of Christ not carry the missionary where the slave trade carries the trader?', nothing was too much for the just-born China Inland Mission to undertake.

A strong relationship had been developing at Coborn Street. It had impressed James Meadows on his first day in London. A mutual confidence and affection to which everything else was subordinate, it rode above the annoyances and injuries of day-to-day life. It could reach to the farthest corners of China.

Love was the atmosphere, but obedience was the single secret of its existence. If, once Hudson Taylor knew that God's will for him was to call into being this 'special agency' for China and to accept the onus of all it would entail, he had refused, how much he would have lost. God would have used some other instrument. But he did not. Looking back over his youth, from the day of his submission at

Barnsley on December 2, 1849, through his years of testing at Hull and Soho, to the searing crucible of Shanghai, his constancy stands out. Though he flinched, he stood his ground, doing what he believed to be right. This habit of obedience to what he saw as the will of God at any point he gained by cultivating it – from that day at home *when he was seventeen.* Following Jesus he 'learned obedience by the things that he suffered'. Not opting for the easy way out he chose to obey, whatever the cost. More than anything, this fitted him to be given the great assignment that he became willing, on June 25, 1865, to accept.

In the day of small beginnings he had said, 'If I had a thousand lives, China should have them. No! not *China*, but *Christ.*' Within his lifetime he was to see the 'Ningbo five' exceed nine hundred, and within the 'open century' that number was to be multiplied fourfold.[30]

APPENDIX 1

GEORGE MÜLLER
(1805–98)

George Müller was a German, living in Bristol for most of his life. As a boy in Germany he was drunk at fourteen, in jail at sixteen, living 'by lies and deception' at twenty, but converted through seeing for the first time in his life a man on his knees praying. His father's antagonism drove him to plead with God to provide for him when he became a student, and he found employment teaching German to American professors at Halle. Two lessons learned at this time he loved to pass on: prayer and the Word of God lead to guidance; and, continued uncertainty indicates a need for continued waiting. While he was a divinity student he was given free lodging at A H Francke's Orphan Houses at Halle, founded in 1696, which had no source of funds except in answer to the prayers of those in charge. That they should flourish on this supposedly slender footing impressed him deeply.

Rejected by the Berlin Missionary Society as a prospective missionary, Müller offered his services to the London Society for Promoting Christianity amongst the Jews. The society invited him to train in England and he began to evangelise the Jews in London. But he had misgivings about binding himself under its rules. An affluent Exeter dentist named Anthony Norris Groves at this time influenced him by resigning his lucrative practice and going as a missionary to Baghdad 'simply trusting the Lord for all temporal supplies'. Müller then offered to serve in the society without a salary if he might do so with freedom to go where and when the Lord should direct him personally. When they declined, his link with them ended. He was twenty-five.

He took a pastorate at Teignmouth, declaring that the promise of a salary was immaterial to him, but teaching that it was the Biblical duty of the congregation 'to minister in material things to those who ministered to them in spiritual things'.

In 1833 when cholera was raging, he moved to Bristol with his wife, A N Groves' sister, and began to gather orphaned children from the streets and to give them breakfast. Soon they included poor and especially aged people. Then, with only a shilling in hand, they announced their intention of forwarding donations of money to missionaries and to teach and circulate Scripture, and called their organization for this purpose 'The Scriptural Knowledge Institution for Home and Abroad'.[1] A year later, with the motive of wanting to demonstrate that the faithful God still hears and answers prayer, they opened their own orphan house. On November 25, 1835, George Müller wrote,

> Now if I, a poor man, simply by prayer and faith, obtained, *without asking any individual*, the means for establishing and carrying on an Orphan House; there would be something which, with the Lord's blessing, might be instrumental in strengthening the faith of the children of God . . .

Reading from Psalm 81:10, 'Open thy mouth wide and I will fill it', he decided to do so. He asked God for premises, £1,000 and helpers to care for the children. Amounts made no difference to God, he reckoned. Looking to him to provide £250 for twenty children was no different from asking him for £25,000 for two thousand children. God was 'a father of the fatherless'; it was his name. They were his orphans.

In later years Müller said,

> There is *reality* in dealing with God alone. [And again] I have been only once tried in spirit, and that was . . . when for the first time the Lord seemed not to regard our prayer. But when He did send help at that time, and I knew that it was only for the trial of our faith, and not because He had forsaken the work, that we were brought so low, my soul was so strengthened and encouraged that I have not been allowed to distrust the Lord since that time, but I have not even been cast down when in the deepest poverty.

By 1850 big new houses built of stone on Ashley Down, Clifton, housed two hundred and seventy-five children and the staff to care for them. Donations began to increase in amount. In 1857, when Hudson Taylor and the Joneses were back in Ningbo, a second complex was opened for four hundred more children. In 1862 the third for four hundred and fifty, in 1868 the fourth, and in 1870 the fifth brought the total after twenty-five years' work to two thousand children. Those five substantial buildings are still in use, for other purposes. The domestic staff and teachers were an additional responsibility.

> When Müller died in 1898, over ten thousand orphans had passed through his hands in sixty-two years, and about a million pounds had been spent on them. In addition one hundred and fourteen thousand children had attended the day-schools and Sunday schools of the Scriptural Knowledge Institution.[2]

All through these years, George Müller was distributing funds for which he had prayed, to missionaries in many different countries. In 1865 he had one hundred and twenty-two on his list, to whom he sent sums of money. Yet the largest single gift he ever received for any purpose was eleven thousand pounds, in 1884.

Of course Müller was criticised. He caught the public's eye, they said; as a foreigner he was conspicuous and therefore drew donations; his annual reports and accounts attracted money; he had a 'secret treasure' which he drew upon. His replies were characteristic: being a foreigner he was more likely to repel than attract; after even twenty years the novelty of necessary annual reports counted for little in terms of raising the large sums involved; but as for the secret reserves, there was more in that supposition than the critics were aware of – the inexhaustible promises of God were his currency. The only advertising he admitted to was on one occasion when he appealed for – more children to care for. Tuberculosis, the great killer, was coming under control and fewer children were being orphaned.

In January 1857 George Müller, a supporter of the Chinese Evangelization Society, read in *The Gleaner* the story of Hudson Taylor's robbery. His forgiving spirit was the highlight to Müller who immediately sent him forty pounds, the first of many gifts during the rest of his life.

APPENDIX 2

HUDSON TAYLOR AND THE BRETHREN

A sketchy summary, but essential to an understanding of Hudson Taylor and the mission he founded.

Statements that Hudson Taylor was connected with the Plymouth Brethren have sometimes been made, but he himself repudiated them.[3] Misuse of the term 'Plymouth Brethren' and limited knowledge of his relationship with the broader congregations of 'Brethren' described below, account for the confusion. Comparably, his brief membership of the Westbourne Grove Baptist Chapel and link with the Baptist Missionary Society have similarly led to a false label of 'Baptist' being attached to him. He personally held 'believer's baptism' and baptism by immersion (as widely practised outside as well as within the community of Baptists) to be Biblical and preferable to paedobaptism, but not obligatory.

The non-sectarian, trans-denominational principles and practice of the China Inland Mission which he founded owed much to Hudson Taylor's early association with the Chinese Evangelization Society and the (non-Plymouth) Brethren, and especially to his friendship with the ministers and congregation of Brook Street Chapel, Tottenham.

An outline of the origins of the Brethren movement may help to clarify the course Hudson Taylor followed.[4]

About the time of Hudson Taylor's birth, groups of Quakers, other dissenters and 'members of the Establishment' – that is, Anglicans, some of them ordained clergy – began coming together in different parts of England and Ireland for the kind of Christian fellowship they lacked in their own Church circles. Meeting at first on weekdays and then increasingly on Sundays, they studied the Bible together, using the Hebrew and Greek in which many of them were well versed. In time they adopted a New Testament pattern of Church life associated with the 'breaking of bread' as the focal act of worship, while still remaining members of their denominations and 'still officiating in the Church of England'.[5] In growing numbers they followed this practice, without any central organisation or leader or intention to secede, but conferring with each other on their common interests. By the time Hudson Taylor was ten, some assemblies of these brethren in Christ had their own chapels where the new form of worship was observed and their earlier denominational allegiances were discontinued. From being simply brethren in Christ who called each other 'brethren' with Victorian decorum, they gradually and without design became an association of similar yet independent congregations.

In Bristol the two close friends George Müller and Henry Craik, a Presbyterian, were leading members or ministers of the congregation meeting at Bethesda Chapel. Both were intimately associated with the saintly missionary Anthony Norris Groves, whose sister Müller had married, and with Robert Chapman of Barnstaple, barrister of the King's Bench until he became a Strict Baptist pastor, and then a pillar of the Brethren – when Hudson Taylor enjoyed his friendship. The Methodist controversy in Yorkshire led to many finding a spiritual home in such independent gatherings of Christians, of which Andrew Jukes' congregation in Hull, with its peculiarities and individual leadership, was an example. The Brethren at Plymouth were at first led by men like B W Newton and the dynamic and domineering J N Darby. Tragically, the 'Bethesda controversy' that arose in 1848 culminated in the rejection by Darby of Müller and Craik.[6] Those in other assemblies who shared the eirenic George Müller's attitude toward fellow-Christians of differing viewpoints, were alienated by Darby's action, and from then on their paths diverged from his 'Exclusives' known as Plymouth Brethren ('PBs'), a term disowned by both 'Open' and 'Exclusive' Brethren.

Near London, in the residential village of Tottenham, John Eliot Howard, the manufacturing chemist, 'who published two major works on quinology' (the scientific study of quinine) 'and was elected Fellow of the Royal Society in 1874', formerly a Quaker, began holding evangelistic meetings, and with his brother Robert built the chapel in Brook Street. Their father, Luke Howard the meteorologist, joined them later.[7] In Theodore Howard's words, 'My father and uncle were the chief ministers' at Tottenham – distinguishing them from Newton's and Darby's Brethren. At Hackney, a little nearer the City of London, and the home of prosperous businessmen, yet another group of Brethren included George Pearse, William Berger, Philip Henry Gosse the naturalist and father of Sir Edmund Gosse, and a solicitor named James van Sommer, Mrs Berger's brother.[8]

In London itself another congregation met in Orchard Street, St Marylebone, moving later to Welbeck Street, where they were when Hudson Taylor first became acquainted with them. The Howards' kinsman John V Parnell on succeeding to the title of Lord Congleton joined this assembly in London when he moved up from Teignmouth.[9] By the time Hudson Taylor's friendship with the Tottenham, Hackney and Welbeck Street families began, the separation of the so-called Plymouth Brethren who followed Darby, from the independent, 'open' congregations was complete. With twentieth-century hindsight it is too easy to regard these congregations as already forming a new denomination, but this was not the case.

The independent local churches, unconnected apart from oneness of heart and informal consultation between their leaders, taught believers' baptism as the norm and duty of Christians, but did not make it a condition of membership. Whether through the influence of Anthony Norris Groves, a one-time missionary candidate of the CMS and the unwitting initiator of the Brethren movement, or by independent arrival at the same conclusions, they hailed every man and woman 'in Christ' as their brother or sister and welcomed their fellowship at his table. Groves himself wrote,

> We are evidently [ie clearly] called to know nothing among our fellow-Christians, but this one fact – Do they belong to Christ? Has Christ received them? then may we receive them, to the glory of God.[10]

And again,

> As bodies, I know none of the sects and parties that wound and disfigure the body of Christ; as individuals, I desire to love all that love Him. Oh! when will the day come, when the love of Christ will have more power to unite than our foolish regulations have to divide the family of God . . .?[11]

William Collingwood of Liverpool, another leader of the Brethren, wrote in retrospect,

> The chief aim was to exhibit, in a Scriptural way, the common brotherhood of all believers. They recognised no special mem-

bership. That they belonged to Christ was the only term of communion; that they loved one another was the power of their fellowship.[12]

The Howard brothers and their brethren at Brook Street, Tottenham, set out their position in what is now known as *The Tottenham Statement* on admission to communion at the Lord's Table:[13]

> . . . we desire to make known our individual convictions and collective judgment as to the path which we believe to be well-pleasing to the Lord in this matter . . .
> 1. We find our centre of union with each other, and with all saints, in Christ, as *one in Him*, and our power of fellowship by the Holy Ghost.
> 2. We therefore desire to receive to the Lord's Table those whom he has received; time being allowed for confidence to be established in our minds that those whom we receive are indeed the Lord's . . .
> 3. We welcome to the table, on individual grounds, each saint, not because he or she is a member of this or that gathering or denomination of Christians, nor because they are followers of any particular leader, but on such testimony as commends itself to us as being sufficient.
> 4. We distinctly refuse to be parties to any exclusion of those who, we are satisfied, are believers – except on grounds personally applying to their individual faith and conduct.
>
> Adopted by Brethren at Tottenham the 4th of March 1849.

It was with these congregations (and never with Darby's exclusive Plymouth Brethren) that Hudson Taylor was associated, without formal membership. And the foregoing facts in part account for his warmly ecumenical attitude to Christians of all denominations.

APPENDIX 3

'CHINESE GORDON'[14] AND THE FALL OF SUZHOU

Interesting in their own right, these episodes continue the account of the Ever-Victorious Army (pp 292–308) and are relevant to the Hudson Taylor story. They took place in the territory soon to become familiar to him and the first missionaries of the China Inland Mission (Book 4)

From Taicang the route to once beautiful Suzhou, the Taipings' army headquarters, lay through Kunshan, a city on a hill, where the rebels had an arsenal manned by English mercenaries (map, p 292). Strategically placed for access to lakes and waterways crucial to an attack on Suzhou, Kunshan became Gordon's next objective. His ingenuity won the battle before any fighting began. He sent in support of his ground force a paddle-steamer, the *Hyson*, armed with one 32-pounder and a howitzer. By day it belched smoke and shells, with demoniacal yells from its siren. But by night its showers of sparks and bright lights added terror to what had been awe inspiring. Quickly the myth developed that it was amphibious, its huge wheels carrying it across land in pursuit of its foes. By striking at Zhengyi (Chunye) between Kunshan and Suzhou, Gordon threw the Kunshan garrison into a panic and routed twelve to fifteen thousand rebels, killing four thousand and capturing two thousand for the loss of seven of his own men.

The secret of his success lay in his careful personal study of the terrain, the depth as well as the position of the waterways, whether they were open or choked with weeds, and where there was ground firm enough for his fifty-two pieces of artillery. Once an area was made safe, 'boats with mat sails spread, seem[ed] to be moving in every direction over the land' as the populace resumed trading along their canals. His troops carried bridging planks, and pontoons were readily summoned. He formed a flotilla of armed gunboats to cover all movements and, by carrying detachments quickly from place to place, to give the impression of a large force.

Because Kunshan was strategically placed near lakes and major waterways including the Grand Canal, Gordon made it his own headquarters. At this the old-timers of the army who had put down roots at Songjiang became mutinous, until Gordon ordered the execution of the ringleader and threatened the same rough justice for every fifth man among the mutineers. Two thousand deserted, so he trained his two thousand prisoners to replace them! Shanghai now felt so secure that foreign merchants asked permission to build a railway from Shanghai to Suzhou, though the Shanghai-Wusong railway was only projected eighteen months later.

Then followed another melodramatic sequence – humorous in hindsight and sensational in the event. Rewarded for his achievements with promotion to British lieutenant-colonel, Gordon decided to master Suzhou (defended by forty thousand Taipings) by controlling its waterways. On July 27 and 28 he attacked and took Jiapu and Wujiang on the Grand Canal. But a Chinese general executed rebel prisoners after promising Gordon to spare them. And when Gordon had repressed plundering by his men on the ground of their receiving regular pay, he was incensed to learn that their paymasters had defaulted. In Gordon's own words, '. . . We [officers] wear anything we can get, and the men are almost in rags.' So in protest he rode back to Shanghai to resign.

On arrival on August 3 he learned that Burgevine had just seized a steamer and left with three hundred of 'the scum of Shanghai' to enlist under the Taipings. The acute possibility of Burgevine's old comrades in the Ever-Victorious Army defecting to join him immediately spurred Gordon to return at once to Kunshan. After a solitary night ride he rejoined his army in time to meet an attack in great force and beat off the rebels. A false report that Burgevine had taken Gordon prisoner and was moving against Shanghai set the inhabitants by the ears, while Gordon in a letter from only two miles short of Suzhou revealed that Burgevine had secretly visited Shanghai for arms and narrowly escaped capture. He agreed to meet Burgevine on neutral ground and was amazed to hear his proposal that the two of them should combine to seize Suzhou, turn against both Taipings and imperialists, form an army of twenty thousand and march on Peking – which he 'declined'. Gordon successfully negotiated with the Taipings for Burgevine and his men to be handed over to the American consul. And Burgevine admitted in a letter to a Shanghai newspaper that he had planned to trap Gordon while negotiating his own escape from the Taipings. (This colourful character died in 1865 while a prisoner of the imperialists, allegedly through the capsizing of a ferry boat.)

The last chapter of the Suzhou farce was about to be written. Advancing from Kunshan in the east and Jiapu in the south the Ever-Victorious Army and its imperial allies were threatening Suzhou when reports came of forty thousand rebel reinforcements under the Zhong Wang at Wuxi (Wusih), ready to come to Suzhou's relief. Knowing that the Zhong Wang also had Nanjing to defend, Gordon disregarded him and surrounded the city. At that the local Taiping leaders assassinated their most successful military commander and surrendered. And to prevent his own army's old indulgence in looting, Gordon ordered them back to Kunshan while the imperial troops occupied the ancient city.

This narrative continues at p 307.

APPENDIX 4

BRIGHTON, 25 JUNE 1865

A correlation of statements about the Brighton episode – for the record.

By piecing together Hudson Taylor's account in his *Retrospect* and his reminiscences scribbled down by Geraldine Howard Taylor early in the twentieth century, the gaps can be filled in, though many years had passed. The jottings tally with each other.

> Unable to bear the sight of a congregation of a thousand or more Christian people rejoicing in their own security, while millions were perishing for lack of knowledge. [*Retrospect*]
> A thousand souls, in China, will be swept into perdition while they are rejoicing in their Christian privileges . . . Incubus [nightmare] of heathendom on one's soul. Could not bear it. Distress of mind tremendous. Went out, and down the hill, to the beach. Tide was far out. [*Reminiscences*][15]
> I wandered out on the sands alone, in great spiritual agony [*Retrospect*]
> At last the crisis came. Conflict absolutely unbearable! [*Reminiscences*]

Very well, he thought, even if all twenty-four missionaries were to die in the attempt,

> if only *one* heathen soul is saved that would be well worth while . . . if the worst came to the worst, it would still be worth while. All at once came the thought – If you are simply obeying the LORD, all the responsibility will rest on *Him*, not on you! *What a relief*!! Well, I cried to God – *You* shall be responsible, for them, and for me too! Had never before identified [myself] with the band – or yielded to be their leader. Then and there prayed for 24 men for inland China [*Reminiscences*]
> Thou, Lord, shalt have the responsibility. At Thy bidding, as Thy servant, I go forward, leaving all to Thee. [Note by Geraldine Howard Taylor, corrected by Hudson Taylor] . . . there the Lord conquered my unbelief, and I surrendered myself to God for this

service. I told Him that all the responsibility as to issues and consequences must rest with him. [*Retrospect*]
Conflict all ended – peace, joy. Felt as if I could fly up that hill to Mr. Pearse's house. And how I did sleep that night! Mrs. Taylor thought that Brighton had done wonders! and so it had! [*Reminiscences*]

APPENDIX 5

A CHRONOLOGY

*C*1600–1865

(For earlier dates *see* Broomhall, M: *The Chinese Empire*, Index I p. 447)

1516–17	Portuguese traders reach China	1512	Jewish tablet at Kaifeng, Henan
1545	Portuguese massacred at Ningbo	1552	Xavier dies at Shangchuan Is.
1557	Portuguese occupy Macao		
1567	Russian embassy to Peking		
1575	Spanish reach Canton	1579	Valignano at Macao
		1579–1722	Period of RC expansion
		1583–89	Ricci at Zhaozhou
1604	Dutch reach Canton	1600	Ricci heads for Peking
		1610	Ricci dies at Peking
1617	Manchus threaten China	1616, 1622	Persecutions
1624	Dutch occupy Taiwan (expelled 1662 by 'Koxinga')	1625	Nestorian tablet found at Xi'an
1637	British arrive at Canton	1631	Dominicans & Franciscans arrive in China
1644	Manchu Qing (Ch'ing) dynasty begins under Shun Zhi	1642	Kaifeng synagogue (1163) destroyed; rebuilt 1653
1648	First Muslim rising in Gansu		
1650	EIC secures trading rights with China		
1655	Dutch embassy to Peking; also 1664, 1795		
1661	Kang Xi succeeds Shun Zhi	1663	Act of Uniformity in UK
1667	Portuguese embassy to Peking		
1670	British trade at Amoy and Taiwan	1672	Declaration of Indulgence (UK)

1683	Taiwan becomes part of China		
1685	Imperial edict permits trade at all ports		
1689	British open trade at Canton	1696	RC translations of Scripture seen in Peking
		1696	A H Francke starts Orphan Houses at Halle
		1697	Inquisition investigates Rites Controversy
		1698	SPCK founded
		1701	SPG established under royal charter; 117 RC missionaries in China
		1705	Papal legate de Tournon arr. Peking; Francke's Pietists to India
1715	EIC 'factory' opened at Canton		
1720	Canton 'Cohong' initiated; Tibet begins paying taxes to China	1720	Mezzabarba scorned by Kang Xi
1723	Kang Xi succeeded by Yong Zheng	1722–1809	RC decline in China
		1724	Edicts of expulsion and confiscation; Church faces extinction
1728	Wars in Europe; French 'factory' opened at Canton	1725	Syrian MSS of OT and hymns found in NW China
1729	Imperial edict bans opium-smoking	1732	Jesuit training college for Chinese at Naples
1733	Chinese embassy to St Petersburg	1733	Moravians to Greenland and W. Indies
1736	Qian Long succeeds Yong Zheng	1735 Oct	J & C Wesley to N.Am. till 1737
		1737–38	Hodgson, Canton, makes a transcript of RC Scriptures
		1738	Wesleys begin hymn-writing
		1739	Wesleys' spiritual conversion
		1742	Pope places China missionaries on oath
1746	Battle of Culloden, Scotland	1743	David Brainerd to Am. Indians
1755	Cholera epidemic in Britain	1744	Qian Long emperor persecutes Christians
1756	'Black Hole of Calcutta' leads to British domination in India	1756	F Pottier founds W. China mission of Paris Mission

1757	Foreign trade limited to Canton		
1759	Battle of Quebec	1760	Wesley revival begins in UK
1763	Qian Long mosque erected at Peking		
1767	Portuguese import 1000 chests of opium per an. at Canton		
1773	'Boston Tea Party'	1773	Pope Clement XIV suppresses Jesuits
1776	Am. Declaration of Independence	1776	Thos. Coke joins Wesley; to America
1784	First American ship at Canton		
1785	Muslims revolt in Gansu		
1786	F Light founds Penang settlement	1786	Wm. Carey, Bishop Butler appeal for missions; J Wesley stays with J Taylor in Barnsley
		1791 Mar 2	J Wesley dies
		1792	Carey presents his 'Enquiry'
1793	Macartney embassy to Peking; Louis XVI guillotined	1793	BMS founded
		1795	LMS founded
1796	Jia Qing succeeds Qian Long; second edict bans opium-smoking; Napoleon begins campaigns	1798	Chas. Simeon's paper read to Eclectic Soc. (of 1783);
		Mar 7	Wm. Moseley sends circular on Hodgson MSS to bishops, etc.
		1799	CMS founded; Carey and Marshman to Serampore, India

1800–65

1800	Imperial edict bans opium-trading Gt. Britain becomes United Kingdom by union with Ireland		
1802 (&1808)	British occupy Macao	1803	Charles (KFA) Gutzlaff born
		1804	B&FBS founded

1805 Oct	Battle of Trafalgar	1805	RC's map intercepted in China
		1806	Henry Martyn arr. at Calcutta
1809	Napoleon overthrows the Pope	1807	R Morrison arr. at Canton
		1810	Only 31 RC priests left in China
1813	Hong Xiu-quan, Taiping Wang, born	1813 Dec 31	R Morrison completes NT in Chinese; Adoniram Judson enters Burma; July 4 W Milne arr. at Macao; Thos Coke dies on way to Ceylon
1815 June 18	Napoleon defeated at Waterloo	1814	First Chinese baptised by R Morrison; EIC to publish his massive dictionary
1816	Amherst embassy fails at Peking; forces passage of The Bogue, Canton	1816	Marshman's Chinese NT printed; Wm. Milne baptises Liang A-fa
		1817	W H Medhurst arr. at Malacca
1818	First Muslim uprising in Yunnan	1818	First LMS mission to Mongolia; banned RC priest reaches Shanxi from Indo-China
1819	Stamford Raffles founds Singapore	1819 Nov 25	R Morrison completes Chinese Bible
1821	Dao Guang succeeds Jia Qing	1822	Marshman completes Chinese Bible;
1822 Nov 1	Great Fire of Canton		Jesuit order reestablished
		June 2	Wm. Milne dies at Malacca
1824	Dutch cede Malacca to British	1824	RC missionaries enter Tibet
1826	Second Muslim rising in Yunnan; Britain annexes West Burma	1824–26	R Morrison in UK; FRS, etc.
		1826	Chas. Gutzlaff arr. at Batavia, Java; DWC Olyphant arr. at Canton
		1827 Aug	Samuel Dyer arr. at Penang
		1828	Gutzlaff and Tomlin to Bangkok
		1830 Feb 22	Bridgman and Abeel arr. at Macao
1831	Asiatic cholera strikes Britain	1831	Gutzlaff by junk to Tianjin
		1832	Miss Aldersey arr. at Malacca

		1832 Feb	Gutzlaff's voyage on *Lord Amherst*
		May 21	Hudson Taylor born
1833	Wilberforce's Emancipation Bill abolishes slave trade; first steamships across Atlantic	1832–33 Oct–Apr	Gutzlaff's voyage on *Sylph*
		1833	S Wells Williams arr. at Canton; Gutzlaff publishes Chinese monthly paper
1834–40	Serious Muslim rebellion in Yunnan		
1834 Jan 31	EIC leaves Canton	1834	Hong Xiu-quan receives tract from Liang A-fa; Dr Peter Parker arr. at Canton
Apr 22	EIC monopoly ended		
July 15	Lord Napier arr. at Canton		
July 26	Napier rebuffed at Canton	Aug 1	R Morrison dies at Canton
Oct 11	Lord Napier dies at Macao; J Davis becomes Chief Superintendent		
1835	Ci Xi (Yehonala) born; Chas. Darwin's voyage in *Beagle*	1835	Geo. Müller founds Orphan Homes, Bristol; Sept 20 Amelia Hudson Taylor born; Gutzlaff becomes Hong Kong govt. secretary; W H Medhurst voyage in *Huron*; Peter Parker opens first mission hospital; Wm. Dean arr. at Bangkok; Manchurian NT printed; (Sir) Robt. Hart born; (Pastor) Hsi Sheng-mo born; last RC Peking astronomer dies
1836 Dec	Capt. Chas. Elliot becomes Chief Supt. of Br. Trade	1836	CMS sends E B Squire on China enquiry; Perboyre finds 6–8 RC churches in Fujian
1837 June 12	Palmerston demands direct access to Canton viceroy	1837 Jan 16	Maria Jane Dyer born
		June-Aug	DWC Olyphant and Gutzlaff to Japan in *Morrison*; W J Boone to Batavia; Donald Matheson to Hong Kong (resigned 1849 over opium traffic)
1838	Coronation of Queen	1838	J and A Stronach, LMS,

	Victoria; execution at Canton Factory thwarted		arr. at Singapore
1839 Jan 1	Canton trade reopened	1839	Jas. Legge arr. at Malacca; Wm. Lockhart arr. at Macao
Feb 26	Opium dealer executed at Factory		
Mar 10	Commissioner Lin arr. at Canton		
Mar 27–May 21	Capt. Elliot surrenders opium stocks		
July 7	Kowloon affray		
Nov 3	Chuanbi skirmish starts war		
1840 Jan 10	Penny post instituted in UK	1840	Tsar (for Synod) ends LMS mission to Mongols
June 28	Canton R. blockaded		
July 5	Chusan (Zhoushan) Is. occupied		
Aug 15	British ships arr. Beihe (Peiho)		
Sept 15	British ships dep. Beihe		
1841 Jan 20	Chuanbi Convention signed; 'Hong Kong ceded'	1841	Wm. Lockhart opens hospital on Chusan Is.; Mgr Mouly appointed vicar-apostolic of Mongolia, etc
Jan 30	Peking denounces Chuanbi Convention		
Apr 30	Britain denounces Convention		
Feb 26	Bogue forts captured		
May 21–27	Hostilities at Canton		
June 7	Hong Kong declared a free port		
Aug 20	Sir H Pottinger, plenipotentiary, arr. at Hong Kong		
Aug 26	Amoy occupied		
Oct	Chusan occupied again; Zhenhai (Ningbo) occupied		
1842 May 18	Zhapu taken	1842	D Abeel and Wm. Boone to Amoy
June 16	Wusong, 19 Shanghai occupied		
July 21	Zhenjiang (Chinkiang) taken		
Aug 29	Treaty of Nanking opens Canton, Amoy, Fuzhou, Ningbo, Shanghai; cedes Hong Kong to British		

1843 June 26	Cession of Hong Kong proclaimed		
Nov 17	Shanghai opened to foreign trade		
1843–51	C Gutzlaff Chinese Secretary to Hong Kong govt.	1843	Anon. gift, £5000, starts CMS mission to China; Medhurst and Lockhart to Shanghai; J Legge, Anglo–Chinese College and LMS press from Malacca to Hong Kong; missionaries deploy to treaty ports; Lockhart opens hospital at Shanghai; Macgowan hospital at Ningbo
		Aug	LMS and inter-mission conferences at Hong Kong
		Oct 24	Samuel Dyer Sr. dies at Macao
		1844–46	Huc and Gabet through Mongolia and Tibet; 1845 reach Lhasa, deported
1844 July 3	American treaty	1844–50	Gutzlaff's Chinese Union, Hong Kong
Oct 24	French treaty	1844	G Smith, CMS, to China; Am. Baptists and Am. Presby missions in Zhenjiang; Miss Aldersey to Ningbo
		1845	W H Medhurst Sr. travels inland in disguise
1846	Friction at Canton; Palmerston becomes Prime Minister	1846	Wm. Boone to Shanghai; J and A Stronach to Amoy
1847	Coolie trade begins; Chinese emigrants from Amoy	1847	T Hamberg, R Lechler, Basel Mission, begin at Hong Kong; A Wylie, LMS, arr. at Shanghai
Apr 3	British take Canton		
Dec 5	Six British killed near Canton		
1848	Karl Marx's *Manifesto*	1848	J Edkins, LMS, arr. at Shanghai; R H Cobbold, W A Russell arr. at Ningbo
Mar	'Tsingpu Outrage', three missionaries mobbed		
1849	Hong Xiu-quan leads Worshippers of Shangdi; British destroy 81 pirate junks	1849	G Smith, Bishop of Victoria, Hong Kong
		Dec 2	Hudson Taylor dedicates himself to God's service
1850	Dao Guang emperor	1850	Gutzlaff in Europe;

	dies; Telegraph between Britain and France		Chinese Assns. formed; Chinese Union disbanded; F F Gough to Ningbo; CMS to Fujian; Am. Prot. Episc. Church sends first unmarried woman missionary to Shanghai (*see* 1844 Miss Aldersey)
		Aug 17	Hudson Taylor declares China hopes
1851	Xian Feng succeeds Dao Guang; Great Exhibition, London	1851 May–Sept 1852	JHT in Hull
		Aug 9	Chas. Gutzlaff dies at Hong Kong
Aug	Taipings take Yong'an		
1852 Apr	Britain annexes Lower Burma	1852 Aug 18	W Lobscheid arr. in Britain
Apr 7	Taipings break out from Yong'an	Sept	Dyer girls dep. UK with C H Cobbolds
Sept 14	Duke of Wellington dies	Sept–Sept 1853	J H T in London
		Dec 15	J H T, dissection fever
Sept 18	Taipings besiege Changsha		
1853 Jan 12	Taipings take Wuchang	1853–56	Moravian Mission to Tibet (Leh) begins
Mar 19	Taipings capture Nanjing		J S Burdon, CMS, to Shanghai
May	Taipings march north	1853 Jan 12	Dyer girls arr. Shanghai
May 18	Triads take Amoy		
July 5	Yellow R. changes course		
July 14	Commodore Perry arr. at Japan		
Sept 7	Triads seize Shanghai city	Sept 19	Hudson Taylor sails from UK; B&FBS resolves to print 1 million NTs for China, to mark jubilee
Oct 28	Taipings reach Duliu, Tianjin		
Nov 11	Rebels take Fuzhou		
		Sept 20–26	*Dumfries* in storm
1854–56	Crimean War	1854 Mar 1	Hudson Taylor lands at Shanghai
1854 Feb	Taipings withdraw from Duliu	Mar 17	J & H Nevius arr. at Shanghai; R Lechler married at Hong Kong
Apr 4	Battle of Muddy Flat, Shanghai	Mar 23	Mrs Lechler dies
July	Rebels threaten Canton	Apr 11	*Dumfries* wrecked
Oct 15	Envoys rebuffed at Dagu, Tianjin	May 13	Th. Hamberg dies
		Aug 5	Mrs Lobscheid dies
Dec 6	French attack Triads at		

	Shanghai	Aug 30	J H T moves into N. Gate suburb
		Nov 27	Wm. Parker arr. at Shanghai
		Dec 16	J H T's first inland journey
1855–73	Great Muslim Rebellion in Yunnan	1855	Hudson Taylor makes ten journeys inland; Delegates' version of Bible published; A Hanspach, G John, A Williamson arr. in China
1855 Feb	Lord Palmerston Prime Minister		
Feb 17	Triads evacuate Shanghai		
Mar	Taipings retreating from north	Apr 12	Liang A-fa dies
1856 July	Allies evacuate Crimea	1856	J H T makes six more journeys inland and Ningbo (1)
		Mar–July	W C Burns & J H T at Swatow
		Feb	Auguste Chapdelaine's judicial murder in Guangxi
		July 14	J H T to Shanghai for medical equipment
		Aug 19	Wm. Burns arrested
		Aug 18–Sept 30	J H T in Ningbo (2)
Oct 8	*Arrow* incident, Canton, precipitates war 1856–60	Oct 9	Sir J Bowring prohibits Burns' return to Swatow
Oct 23–29	Adm. Seymour attacks Canton	Oct 20	J H T and J Jones arr. Ningbo (3) till Jan 25/27
Nov 20–22	Americans dismantle Bogue forts		
Dec 15	Canton 'factories' destroyed		
1857 Jan 14	Hong Kong poison plot fails	1857 Jan 18	Ningbo massacre plot fails
		Jan 24	W H Medhurst dies in UK
		Feb–Apr	J H T and Jones in Shanghai
Mar	Shanghai currency changed to taels	Mar	J H T proposes to Maria Dyer
May	Indian mutiny breaks out (to Dec 1858)	May 29	J H T resigns from CES
June 26	Ningbo Cantonese massacre Portuguese	June 20	J H T and Jones begin Ningbo Mission
July 2	Lord Elgin arr. at Hong Kong		
Aug 7	British blockade Canton river (French join on Dec 12)		R H Cobbold leaves China

Date	Event	Date	Event
Dec 28–29	British & French bombard and take Canton		
1858	China cedes Amur R. area to Russia; Britain assumes govt. of India from EIC	1858	G E Moule, CMS. arr. at Ningbo
Jan 5	Commissioner Ye captured at Canton	Jan 16	Maria Dyer comes of age
Apr 20	Allied envoys arr. at Dagu	Jan 20	Hudson Taylor and Maria marry
May 20	Dagu forts taken		
June 13	Russian Treaty of Tientsin		
June 18	American Treaty of Tientsin		
June 26	British Treaty of Tientsin		
June 27	French Treaty of Tientsin		
Aug	Atlantic telegraph inaugurated		
Sept	France and Spain at war with Annam		
Oct	Taipings break out of Nanjing		
1859 June 20–25	British, French and American envoys rebuffed at Dagu, Beihe	1859	J L Nevius begins at Hangzhou
		1859–60	J S Burdon at Hangzhou
July 28	Am. envoy at Peking; treaty ratified Aug 16		
Oct	H N Lay opens Canton customs house		
1860 Mar 8	British–French ultimatum to Peking; rejected Apr 5	1860	Orthodox archbishop John (Innokenty) Veniaminov to Manchuria (Amur) and Japan; CES dissolved; Am. Southern Baptists and Methodist New Connexion to Shandong, Yantai; J L Nevius to Japan
Mar 19	Taiping holocaust at Hangzhou		
May 3	Second Taiping breakout from Nanjing		
June 2	Taipings occupy Suzhou; Ever-Victorious Army organised		
June 21	Lord Elgin and Baron Gros arr. Hong Kong		
June	*Great Eastern* crosses Atlantic		
July	Zeng Guo-fan made viceroy and high commissioner		
July 17	F T Ward captures Songjiang; turns tide of rebellion	July 19	Hudson Taylor family leave China in *Jubilee*

Aug 1	Allied force lands at Beitang		
Aug 12	Mongol cavalry defeated at Xinhe		
Aug 18	Allies repulse Taiping attack on Shanghai city		
Aug 21	Taipings withdraw from Shanghai; Allies take Dagu		
Aug 25	Allies occupy Tianjin	Aug	H Blodget preaches in Tianjin; S Wells Williams and W A P Martin interpreter-negotiators with Am. commissioner Ward
Sept 18	Treachery at Zhangjiawan against H Parkes' truce party		
Sept 21	Manchu army defeated; Prince Kong made plenipotentiary		
Sept 22	Court flees to Jehol; plot to kill Yehonala		
Oct 6	French plunder Summer Palace	Oct	Final statement by CES
Oct 13	Peking surrenders		H Blodget preaches in Peking
Oct 18	Lord Elgin orders Summer Palace burnt		
Oct 24–25	Peking Convention signed by British, French; Tientsin Treaty (1858) ratified		
Nov 14	Russian Convention of Peking	Nov 28	J H T and family arr. London
1861	Am. commissioner Ward resigns; Anson Burlingame succeeds, to Peking, till 1867; Adventurer Capt. Blakiston reaches Tibetan border; Hankou and Jiujiang (Chinkiang) open to trade	1861	S I J Schereschewsky to Peking with Burlingame; J L Nevius and two Am. Episcopal missionaries to Shandong; LMS begin at Tianjin; Holmes and Parker murdered at Yantai
Jan 21	H N Lay appointed Inspector-General of Imperial Maritime Customs		
Mar	Adm. Sir Jas. Hope up Yangzi to Yueyang (Yochow), Hunan	Mar	Wm. Muirhead and Schereschewsky up Yangzi to Sichuan
Mar 25	Foreign envoys take up residence in Peking		
Apr	American civil war begins (to Nov 1863)	Apr 3	Herbert Hudson Taylor born
		May 6	J H T begins course at London Hospital

June 30	Robt. Hart and G H FitzRoy *pro tem* in charge of Customs	June	G John and R Wilson to Hankou
		July	BMS invite J H T to lead team to China
Aug 22	Xian Feng dies	July 17	B&FBS appoint J H T to edit revision of Ningbo vernacular romanised NT
Sept 2	German treaty of Tianjin		
Nov 4	Yehonala and Prince Kong usurp government; Yehonala and emperor's mother become regents & dowager empresses (Ci Xi & Ci An)		
Dec 9	Taipings take Ningbo		
1862	By stratagem Tong Zhi succeeds Xian Feng; Tongwen College (interpreters') school of languages opens at Peking		
Jan 11	Taipings threaten Shanghai again, and Songjiang	1862	CMS begins at Hong Kong, Peking; Wesleyans begin at Hankou; J Cox from Canton to Hankou; Wm. Lockhart to Peking with Sir R Alcock; J S Burdon also as chaplain; first converts baptised at Peking; Am. Presby. (North) and BMS (C J Hall and H Z Kloekers) to Shandong, Yantai
		Jan 8	J and M Meadows dep. UK; arr. Shanghai May 24
Jan 15	E T Ward defeats Taipings at Guangfuling		
Feb 25	Taipings defeated at Gaoquiao		
Mar 1	Taipings defeated at Nanqiao; 30-mile zone established		
Mar 14	H N Lay instructed to form a Chinese naval steam fleet		
May 10	Capt. R Dew and French retake Ningbo		
May 13	French declare Settlement at Shanghai		

June 5	French–Spanish treaty of Saigon		
July	Franco–Chinese contingent formed; Li Hong-zhang made governor of Jiangsu	July 29	J H T qualifies MRCS (Eng)
Aug 11	Yuyao (Ningbo) retaken		
Aug 26	Taipings threaten Shanghai again		
Sept 21	F T Ward 'mortally wounded' in taking Cixi (Ningbo front)	Sept 4	Martha Meadows dies at Ningbo
Oct	Li Hong-zhang takes control of Ever-Victorious Army; appoints H A Burgevine		
Oct 24	E-VA takes Jiading		
Nov 19	E-VA routs Taipings at Beihegang	Nov 25	Frederick Howard Taylor born
1862–76	Great Muslim rebellion in NW China		
1863 Jan 1	Abraham Lincoln proclaims abolition of slavery		
Jan 15	Burgevine dismissed		
Jan 17	Franco–Chinese force defeated at Shaoxing (Ningbo front); succeeds Mar 18		
Feb 10	E-VA defeated at Taicang	1863 Feb 2	Dr Wm. Parker dies at Ningbo
Mar 25	Charles Gordon commands E–VA; victories at Changshu, Taicang, Kunshan, Wujiang		
		May 4	John Jones dies at sea
July 20	Shanghai–Suzhou railway proposed		
Aug 2	Burgevine joins Taipings		
Sept	Lay-Osborn fleet arr. at Shanghai		
Oct 15–17	Burgevine and mercenaries surrender to Gordon	Oct 20–21	B&FBS and CMS reaffirm J H T – F F Gough revision of Ningbo vernacular NT
Nov 15	H N Lay dismissed; Robt. Hart appointed Inspector-General		
Dec 4–5	Li Hong-zhang beheads 8 Taiping leaders after fall of Suzhou		

Dec 9	Gordon withdraws E-VA from Li Hong-zhang's control	1864–67	Wm. Burns at Peking; publishes *Pilgrim's Progress* in Chinese
		1864	A Wylie travels in most provinces; J Cox in Hunan; A Williamson in Mongolia; First medical missionary and first baptisms at Hankou; UMFC begins at Ningbo; CMS and Am. Presbys at Hangzhou; Am. Board at Peking
1864	Muslim rebellion begins in Chinese Turkestan		
Jan 30	Gordon and E-VA resume against Taipings		
Mar 31	Hangzhou retaken by Franco–Chinese and imperial forces		
May	E-VA victories at Yixing, Huashi (Huaishu), Changzhou		
June	Burgevine rejoins Taipings	June	Foreign Evangelist Soc. formed
July 19	Zeng Guo-fan takes Nanjing; Taiping princes beheaded	June 24	Samuel Dyer Taylor born
		July	First Mildmay Conference
		Oct 17	J L and H Nevius arr. in London
		Dec 19	Notman dep. UK to Ningbo
1865 Feb 20	Robt. Hart aged 30 takes up headquarters at Peking	1865	Prot. communicants reach 2000; R J Thomas, Nat. B S of Scotland, visits Korea; J L Maxwell starts in Taiwan (Eng. Presby Mission); Am. Board to Kalgan, Mongolian border; David Hill to Hankou
Mar	Pres. Lincoln assassinated	Apr 12	S P Barchet and G Crombie dep. UK
May	Burgevine captured and killed	Apr 26	A Skinner (Mrs Crombie) follows
May 10	American civil war ends	June 3	J H T's account in name of China Inland Mission audited
		June 25	J H T yields himself to be leader of CIM (Brighton)
		July	Wm. Booth discovers his destiny

APPENDIX 6

OUTFITS FOR CHINA
1864–65 examples

For Miss Jean Notman, 1864, costing £33. 16s. 2d.
1 winter dress, 2 skirts, 1 crinoline, 3 print dresses
3 petticoats, 6 nightdresses, 3 vests, 12 pairs drawers, 9 chemises, silk apron
2 doz. handkerchiefs, 9 pairs stockings, 1 ps. diaper, 1 pair gauntlets, 4 pairs gloves, hat, hairnet, scarf
2 pairs boots, 1 pair shoes, galoshes, umbrella
2 combs, hairpins, slide, toothbrush, pomatum, sponge bag, nailbrush, scissors, elastic, sewing-machine needles and oil, bodkins, cotton thread
trimmings, crochet hook and cotton, darning cotton, darning merino, belt ribbon, ribbons, tapes, buttons, pins, hooks, thimble
6½ yards black merino, 10 yards muslin, 1½ yards check muslin, 6¾ yards longcloth, linen, braid, 1 doz. cambric frilling, 9½ yards barege, 26¾ yards flannel, 5 yards red flannel, 6 yards huckaback, 15¾ yards lining, 3 yards ruching
writing desk, pen holders, pens, nibs, quills, cards, 200 envelopes, elastic bands, 1 doz. pencils, slate, slate pencil, India rubber
watch glasses, plates, books etc
trunk, tin-lined box, carpet bags

(Presumably she already had cutlery, crockery, and other omissions)

For George Crombie, 1865, costing £46. 2s. 7½d.
frock coat, doe trousers, waistcoat, tweed trousers, coat, vest, 3 linen coats and vests, 2 pairs drill trousers
4 flannel shirts, 4 calico shirts, 6½ doz. collars
waterproof coat, felt hat, cloth cap
3 pairs boots, 2 pairs braces, 1 doz. pairs socks, pants
1 feather pillow, 1 counterpane, 1 pair blankets, 3 pairs linen sheets, 4 pillowcases
1 rug, mosquito curtains, lining for same, 1 Toralium,[16] ½ doz. towels, 1 bag haberdashery

iron chair, bedstead and beds (?mattresses), 1 looking glass, walking-stick, camp stool, life-belt, 8-day alarm clock, fishing tackle, string, penknife, strop, medicines, scales
writing paper, notebooks, 500 envelopes, 3 doz. pencils, 1 doz. penholders, 1 gross pens, India rubber, 1 qt ink, writing case
coffee mill and pot, teaspoons, dessertspoons and forks, tablespoons and forks, dessert and table knives, all 3 each, groceries, shoe blacking
carpet bag, packing case, cooking stove, pipes and utensils, carpenter's tools

OMFA 13/4A

NOTES

Abbreviations: (*see also p 11*)

E-VA	=	Ever-Victorious Army
HTCOC	=	Hudson Taylor and China's Open Century
FHT	=	Frederick Howard Taylor
JHT	=	J Hudson Taylor
MGT	=	Mrs Howard Taylor, née Geraldine Guinness
OMFA	=	Overseas Missionary Fellowship Archives

Page Note

Preface

7	1	Stock, E: *The History of the Church Missionary Society*, Vol II p 300; HTCOC Book 2, pp 491, 540–1, Index

Prologue

21	1	Jones: Personalia; HTCOC Book 2, pp 522, 535, Index
21	2	HTCOC Book 2, pp 530–5
21	3	Gough: Personalia; Stock, E: op. cit. I, pp 473–4
21	4	Parker, Wm.: Personalia; HTCOC Book 2, Index
21	5	Aldersey: Personalia, Index; her school was independent, linked with the CMS through the marriage of her protégée Mary Ann Leisk to W A Russell of Tipperary; Stock, E: op. cit. II, pp 67, 293–5
21	6	Ningbo: Personalia; Book 2, Index
23	7	*ibid*
23	8	JHT: HTCOC Book 1, Appendix 6, Index; Book 2, pp 524–6
23	9	Burns: Personalia; HTCOC Book 1, Index; Book 2, pp 524–9, Index
23	10	Canton: HTCOC Book 2, p 540, Index
24	11	Russell: CMS *Intelligencer*, Nov 1856, cited CES *Gleaner*, Dec 1856
24	12	Smith: Personalia; HTCOC Book 1, Index; Book 2, Index
24	13	German: Personalia; HTCOC Book 1, Appendix 6, Index; Book 2, pp 553–9, Index
24	14	Smith: CES *Gleaner*, July 1857, letter of April
25	15	Tiejiu: HTCOC Book 2, p 447, Index
25	16	Burns: HTCOC Book 2, pp 524–9

Chapter 1

27	17	Gutzlaff: Personalia; HTCOC Book 1, Index; Book 2, Appendix, Index
27	18	*Arrow*; *lorcha*; Bombardment: HTCOC Book 2, Index; Parliamentary Papers: *A Century of Diplomatic Blue Books*, 152/506c, (2163) p 51; Morse, Hosea Ballou: *The International Relations of the Chinese Empire*, Vol 1 Chronology; etc
28	19	Hair: usually evidence of vitamin deficiency. Two watch-chains exist, made from JHT's undyed *bianzi*!
30	20	Bridge Street: Wugyiaodeo in MSS

30 21 Shanghai: HTCOC Book 2, pp 267, 293

32 22 OMFA: 2314, 26 Dec 1856

33 23 JHT letter: 12 Jan 1857; OMFA: 2411

33 24 The first instance of John Jones teaching JHT to live by faith.

34 25 Debt: Taylor, J H: *A Retrospect* (18th edn.), p 96

36 26 Martin, W A P: *A Cycle of Cathay*, p 214

36 27 Op. cit. *c*. p 210

37 28 *ibid*

37 29 Dyer: HTCOC Book 1, p 280

38 30 Buckland: Davies, Evan: *Memoir of the Reverend Samuel Dyer*, 1846; gave Miss Buckland as 'governess'; corrected by her in OMFA: 4325e

40 31 Davies, Evan: op. cit.; Personalia; HTCOC Book 1, Index

40 32 Agnes Gutzlaff: HTCOC Book 2, p 497, Note

40 33 Maria: OMFA: 4328a, contains a lock of her hair with a note in JHT's handwriting. Photographic materials in the mid-nineteenth century lacked gradation between black and white, so giving false impressions of tone; Maria was blonde-brunette, not dark.

41 34 Diary: OMFA: 2421

41 35 Bausum: Personalia

43 36 Hart: Personalia; HTCOC Book 1, Index; Brendon, Juliet: *Sir Robert Hart*, 1909; Martin, W A P: op. cit.: 'His career, to which there is no parallel in the East or West . . .'; Woodcock, George: *The British in the Far East*, p. 69: 'a mandarin many times honoured . . . was often abused by the British merchants for his thoroughness and incorruptibility'; Morse, W B, op. cit. 2.34f

43 37 Plot: OMFA: 1/3–68/262; 2411; 2421; Taylor, J H: *China: Its Spiritual Need and Claims*, p 51; CES *Gleaner*, May 1857, p 67

43 38 Hong Kong: Parl. Papers: op. cit. 533e, p 169; Legge, H F: *James Legge*; Martin, W A P: op. cit. p 143 ff; CES *Gleaner*, April 1857, pp 55–6, W Lobscheid, 30 Jan letter

44 39 Burns, Fishbourne: CES *Gleaner*, June 1858, p 79; Personalia; HTCOC Book 2, Index

50 40 Eloped: HTCOC Book 2, p 54; third daughter of John Taylor's fourth daughter, married de Mirimonde

51 41 Bowring: Woodcock, G: op. cit., p 66

52 42 Bund: Pott, Hawks: *A Short History of Shanghai*, p 41

52 43 Williamson: CES *Gleaner*, August 1857

53 44 Aitchison: *ibid*

57 45 Most quotations on this subject are from letters to Maria's uncle, William Tarn, and brother, Samuel Dyer; OMFA: 2411–4; 2421–4; 2431–3; (*see on*, p 79)

58 46 PB: *see on*, p 81 and Appendix 2

59 47 Maria: OMFA: 2422A

64 48 JHT letter: 1/3–49/236, 24 Sept 1856

65 49 'odd sparrow': Pierson, A T: *George Müller of Bristol*, p 73

66 50 Müller, George: *Autobiography*, 1905 G F Bergin edn., p 693, summary: Coad, F R: *A History of the Brethren Movement*, p 53

68 51 Resignation: OMFA: 1/3–77/288, 29 May 1857

69 52 Taylor, J H: *Retrospect*, pp 96–7

71 53 Elgin: CES *Gleaner*, Aug 1857, p 117

71 54 Coolie traffic: CES *Gleaner*, July 1857, p 111 ff; *Overland China Mail*, 15 Jan 1857; 15 Feb 1857; 30 Mar 1857; 15 Apr 1857; Capt Fishbourne at CES Annual Meeting, May 1858; CES *Gleaner*, May 1858, pp 77, 117

Chapter 2

75 1 Rebellions: HTCOC Book 1, Index: The Hakka people chiefly occupied Guangdong and Guangxi provinces; the aboriginal races pervade the SW, Guangxi, Guizhou, Yunnan and Sichuan; Muslims were scattered throughout China, but most numerous in Yunnan and to the NW; the Nian-fei in the NE, mainly Shandong and Henan.

79 2 OMFA: 2411–4; 2421–4; 2431–3; 2441. For reasons which will emerge in this and the next book, the very full letters are quoted freely.

82 3 Diary: OMFA: 2421

86 4 Hobson: Personalia; HTCOC Book 2, Index; distinguish John H from Dr Benjamin H, Robt Morrison's son-in-law, of Canton and Shanghai.

87 5 Berger: typhoid fever had not yet been distinguished from typhus (*see* p 268)

90 6 Letter: property of Taylor family

91 7 *See* Note 2 above; considerable abridgement is inevitable.

102 8 Dream: OMFA: 2411, 20 Oct 1856, JHT to Amelia

103 9 Meet: OMFA: 2411; 2421; 2441

105 10 Elgin: Pott, Hawks: *A Short History of Shanghai*, p 44; Morse, H B: *The International Relations of the Chinese Empire*, Vol 1; Michie, A: *The Englishman in China* (J Rutherford Alcock); Legge, H E: *James Legge*; Martin, W A P: *A Cycle of Cathay*; Stock, E: *History of the CMS*; Haldane, Charlotte: *The Last Great Empress of China*; Forbes, A: *Chinese Gordon*; Hong Kong *China Mail*, 6 August 1857; CES *Gleaner*, Nov 1857, p 164; Mar 1858, pp 33–4, 40; Personalia, Bibliography; HTCOC Book 2, pp 547, 568

106 11 Ci Xi: Personalia; Morse, H B: op. cit. *passim*; Haldane, C: op. cit. *passim*

106 12 Yehonala (Ci Xi): born 3 Nov 1835

108 13 The last day of Maria's minority; born 16 Jan 1837

108 14 Chapdelaine: Personalia; HTCOC Book 2, pp 528, 542; Morse, H B: op. cit.; Latourette, K S: *A History of Christian Missions in China*, pp 244, 275, 325

108 15 Credentials: Stock, E: op. cit. II, 306

110 16 Martin, W A P: op. cit. *c.* p 145; Covell, R: *W. A. P. Martin, Pioneer of Progress in China*, pp. 89f; Personalia, HTCOC Book 1, Index

110 17 Personalia; HTCOC Book 1, Index

115 18 Russell: OMFA: 2441; Russell's sense of fair play, and concern to protect Maria from one whom he judged unworthy of her, were commendable; a frank presentation of the facts is given with the generous approval of the CMS; no living relatives have been traced, but apologies are tendered to any there may be.

120 19 Müller: OMFA: 2424

121 20 OMFA: 311–2; Taylor, J H: *China: Its Spiritual Need and Claims*, pp 54–6

123 21 Arbitration: OMFA: 2441

126 22 Dyer-Tarn correspondence: property of the Taylor family.

Chapter 3

127 1 OMFA: 311
129 2 Probably scabies, from contact with many poor.
129 3 George Piercy: Personalia
131 4 George Moule: Personalia
132 5 CES *Gleaner*, May 1858, p 60
134 6 Parker: Lockhart, Wm: *The Medical Missionary in China*; CES *Gleaner*, May 1858, p 80; Sept 1858, p 156; OMFA: 1/3–88/5, 8 Dec 1857; 1/3–92/1, 14 Oct 1858; 1/3–98/2
138 7 Qi Ying: Personalia; HTCOC 1, pp 268, 270, 296, Index; CES *Gleaner*, July 1851, p 11, F Genähr to G Pearse: '. . . the Chinese Cabinet minister, Kiying . . . has written seven volumes . . . He says, "The books translated by Western men narrate the actions He [Jesus] wrought, with great perspicuity . . . He gave up His body to save the world; He died and rose up again . . . I came to know that what they teach had really nothing in it that was not good. I felt that I ought therefore to memorialize the emperor, and request that . . . he would not persecute or prohibit it . . . How great are the works of God, shedding lustre through all time! . . . Oh, that you, men of the world, would change your hearts, and reform your lives!" . . . We regret to hear that his sympathies towards foreigners have been the reason of his recent degradation.'
138 8 Burns: OMFA: 2315, 2321
138 9 Elgin: Stock, E: *History of the CMS*, II.302; CMS *Intelligencer*, 1858, p 149
139 10 Opium: Stock, E: op. cit. II.303 paraphrased
139 11 Tael: HTCOC Book 1, Appendix 7
139 12 Society: CES *Gleaner*, Dec 1856, p 150; later 'The Society for the Suppression of the Opium Trade'; *see* Personalia; Broomhall, B: *The Evangelization of the World*, 1889 (adv.)
139 13 Venn, H: Personalia; HTCOC Book 1, p 275 Note 28, Index; Book 2, p 549 Note 19
140 14 Martin, W A P: *A Cycle of Cathay*, pp 187f
141 15 *ibid*; *Chinese Recorder*, Vol 10, pp 223f
142 16 Qi Ying: Fairbank, J K: *Trade and Diplomacy on the China Coast*, p 112
142 17 *Chinese Recorder*, Vol 10, pp 223f; Morse, H B: *The International Relations of the Chinese Empire*, Vol 1
142 18 Martin, W A P: *ibid*; Michie, A: *The Englishman in China*
143 19 *Chinese Recorder*, *ibid*
144 20 *ibid*
144 21 Latourette, K S: *A History of the Expansion of Christianity*, Vol VI, pp 258–9; *A History of Christian Missions in China*, pp 273–5; Smith, A H: *The Uplift of China*, pp 77–8; Taylor, J H: *China: Its Spiritual Need and Claims*, p 42
144 22 CES *Gleaner*, Oct 1858, pp 122f; *Times*, 16 Sept 1858
144 23 CES *Gleaner*, *ibid*
145 24 *Chinese Recorder*, Vol 10, p 226
145 25 CES *Gleaner*, Feb 1859, pp 17–18
146 26 *Chinese Recorder*, 1879, Vol 10, p 202; Mouly's report, Paris, July 1861
146 27 Michie, A: op. cit.
146 28 Haldane, C: *The Last Great Empress of China*, cited p 36

147 29 Seals: Thompson, R Wardlaw: *Griffith John*, p 84
147 30 Rock: HTCOC Book 1, p 62; *London Missionary Chronicle*, cited in CES *Gleaner*, Mar 1859, p 34
147 31 Appeals: CES *Gleaner*, Feb 1859, p 20
147 32 CMS: Stock E: op. cit. I.474
147 33 Wentworth: 28 Sept 1858; CES *Gleaner*, Feb 1859, p 21
148 34 Douglas: 20 Oct 1858; CES *Gleaner*, *ibid*; Latourette, K S: *Christian Missions*, p 376
148 35 JHT: CES *Gleaner*, op. cit. pp 26–7
148 36 Cox: 25 Oct 1858; *Wesleyan Missionary Notices*, CES *Gleaner*, Mar 1859, p 25
149 37 Preston: 26 Oct 1858, CES *Gleaner*, op. cit. p 36
149 38 Latourette, K S: op. cit. p 405; CES *Gleaner*, Feb 1859, pp 15–16
150 39 Wylie: Cordier, H: *The Life and Labours of Alexander Wylie*; BFBS Annual Report, 1858–59
150 40 op. cit. 1859
151 41 CES *Gleaner*, 1859, pp 11, 33–5, 46–50, citing CMS *Intelligencer*; *London Missionary Chronicle*
151 42 MacGillivray, D: *A Century of Protestant Missions in China*, p 5; CES *Gleaner*, Apr 1859, pp 46–50; Thompson, R W: op. cit. pp 84f
152 43 Burdon: CES *Gleaner*, op. cit. p 49
153 44 G John: Martin, W A P: op. cit. p 69
153 45 OMFA: 311; 312; E214b; CES *Gleaner*, Dec 1858, pp 154–5
157 46 OMFA: *ibid*; 1/3 *passim*
158 47 Parker: OMFA: 311; 1/3–88/5, 8 Dec 1857; 92/1 14 Oct 1858; CES *Gleaner*, May 1859, p 63
158 48 Medical: CES *Gleaner*, 1858, p 156; 1859, p 40
159 49 Gamble: *Chinese Recorder*, Vol 10, pp 208f
159 50 Feng, Ni, etc: their significance becomes apparent in Book 4.
162 51 Shandong: CES *Gleaner*, Mar 1859, pp 37–8
164 52 Holmes: *Chinese Recorder*, Vol 12, pp 87, 131
165–6 53–5 JHT: OMFA: 311, 15 Nov 1858; 1 Dec 1858

Chapter 4

170 1 Hangzhou: Nevius, H: *John Livingston Nevius*, pp 165–86; *Chinese Recorder*, Vol 7, pp 344f; Vol 9, p 287; Broomhall, M: *The Chinese Empire*, pp 78, 441
170 2 Nevius: Nevius, H: op. cit. Foreword by W A P Martin; Martin, W A P: *A Cycle of Cathay*, pp 112f, 213f
170 3 The Bridge Street church became the seed-bed of the early work of the China Inland Mission and its members the first colporteurs and evangelists; the church-planting at Ningbo was typical of what followed all over China – hence these names and details; OMFA 1/3–96/2, 15 Feb 1859; 311; 312
172 4 OMFA: 1/3–96/2
172 5 OMFA: op. cit.; 312
173 6 OMFA: 1/3–102/1, 2
175 7 Taylor, J H: *China: Its Spiritual Need and Claims*, p 58; OMFA: 1/3–96/2; 312

176 8 Neill, Stephen C: *A History of Christian Missions* (The Pelican History of the Church), p 289
177 9 Pastor Xi (Hsi): Taylor, Mrs Howard: *The Fulfilment of a Dream*; Latourette, K S: *A History of the Expansion of Christianity*, Vol VI, pp 357–8; *see* HTCOC Book 5
178 10 Wang: *see* Index; and HTCOC Book 4
178 11 Training: OMFA: 1/3–103/1
180 12 Legge: CES *Gleaner*, July 1859, pp 84–5 (79–89)
181 13 Morse, H B: *The International Relations of the Chinese Empire*, Vol 1, Chronology; Broomhall, M: op. cit. pp 19–20; Michie, A: *The Englishman in China*; Forbes, A: *Chinese Gordon*; Latourette, K S: *A History of Christian Missions in China*, p 272; Martin, W A P: op. cit.
183 14 Edict: Latourette, K S: op. cit. p 306
183 15 Nevius, H: op. cit. pp 152f, 172f
187 16 OMFA: 1/3–103, 2, 3; 3121
188 17 Taylor, J H: op. cit. p 59
192 18 'Awakening': Stock, E: *History of the CMS*, II. 28–32; Orr, J E: *The Second Evangelical Awakening in Britain*, pp 37, 47, 52, 131, 176–7, 232, 234
193 19 Taylor, M Geraldine: Orr, J E: op. cit. p 263
193 20 Soothill, W E: *Timothy Richard of China*, p 27
193 21 OMFA: 1/3–103/3ff; 312
193 22 Deaths: Smith, A H: *The Uplift of China*, p 151
194 23 Stock, E: op. cit. II.34
196 24 op. cit. II.307
196 25 OMFA: 3125, 16 Jan 1860; *see* p 384 note 8
197 26 OMFA: 1/3–104/1
198 27 OMFA: 3125, 14 Feb 1860

Chapter 5

201 1 Broomhall, M: *The Chinese Empire*; Forbes, A: *Chinese Gordon*; CES *Gleaner*, 1859; Haldane, C: *The Last Great Empress of China*; Hook, B: *China's Three Thousand Years*, Part 4; Latourette, K S: *A History of the Expansion of Christianity*, Vol VI; *A History of Christian Missions in China*; Martin, W A P: *A Cycle of Cathay*; Michie, A: *An Englishman in China*; Morse, H B: *The International Relations of the Chinese Empire*, Vol 1, pp 588f; Vol 2; Chronology; Moule, A E: *Recollections of the Taiping Rebellion* (Lecture); Pott, Hawks: *A Short History of Shanghai*; Thompson, R W: *Griffith John*
203 2 Zeng: Imperial victor in the north; Personalia; HTCOC Book 2, p 176; Hook, B: op. cit. pp 156f; Morse, H B: *ibid*; Vol 1, pp 592f
205 3 OMFA: 3123–5; Taylor, J H: *China: Its Spiritual Needs and Claims*
209 4 Martin, W A P: op. cit. p 214
209 5 Latourette, K S: *Expansion of Christianity* , VI.328; cf also *Christian Missions*; Tipple Lecture
209 6 Hong Ren: Latourette, K S: *Christian Missions*, p 293; McNeur, G H: *Liang A-fa*, p 78; Pott, Hawks: op. cit. pp 43–50
211 7 Moule, A E: op. cit.; Thompson, R W: op. cit. pp 125ff

213 8 Moule, A E: op. cit.
214 9 Griffith John: cited, Latourette, K S: op. cit. p 291 footnote
214 10 Michie, A: op. cit.; Forbes, A: op. cit.; Haldane, C: op. cit. pp 35–9, 56–8 – a lively, colourful account; Morse, H B: op. cit. I.588f, 595f
215 11 Dagu: strictly, Dagu is on the south bank of the Beihe and Tanggu on the north bank, but both together were called Dagu (cf 'Hankow').
215 12 The 67th (South Hampshire) Regiment won five of the seven Victoria Crosses awarded for conspicuous gallantry, when they swam across two wide moats under heavy fire, and Lieutenant Henry Edmund Lenon, thrusting his sword-point into crevices in the masonry for a foothold, with fellow-officers and men scaled the stoutly defended wall and took the fort. Wolseley, Field-Marshal, Viscount: *The Story of a Soldier's Life*; Dempsey, J in *The Royal Magazine*, Vol XXIV; Lenon family records.
215 13 Xian Feng edict, 6 Sept 1860; Haldane, C: op. cit.; Morse, H B: op. cit. I.608f
217 14 Martin, W A P: op. cit. p 218
218 15 Emperor: quoted, Haldane C: op. cit. p 39; Morse, H B: op. cit. I.595f
219 16 Forbes, A: op. cit. p 25; Haldane, C: op. cit.; Martin, W A P: op. cit. p 218; Morse, H B: *ibid*, says the exiled emperor's orders reached Peking after Heng Qi had ordered their release.
220 17 'Slender thread': Martin, W A P: op. cit. p 344
221 18 Convention: Parliamentary Blue Books, etc; Morse, H B: op. cit. I.613f; Latourette, K S: *Christian Missions*, pp 273–7; Stock, E: *A History of the CMS*, II.303–4; Hook, B: op. cit.
221 19 Opium: approx. 1 kilogramme per 60 kilogrammes weight.
223 20 Mouly: *Chinese Recorder* Vol 10, 1879, p 202; Latourette, K S: op. cit. p 308; HTCOC Book 2, Index
224 21 Russell: Stock, E: op. cit. II. 303–5; CMS *Intelligencer*, 1860, p 98
224 22 Treaties: Latourette, K S: op. cit. pp 277–81, 305–7; Smith, A H: op. cit. p 228; Morse, H B: *ibid*
224 23 Passports: Neill, S C: *A History of Christian Missions*, p 409

Chapter 6
229 1 *Jubilee:* JHT's log of voyage, OMFA: 3211; 3219a, letters
233 2 OMFA: 3212b–d
235 3 OMFA: 3212e, f; 3219a
237 4 Personalia; HTCOC Book 1, Appendix 6, Index; Book 2, Index
237 5 Personalia; HTCOC Book 1, Index
238 6 OMFA: 1/4; A122c = CES/GP Notes
238 7 CES a/cs: none in CES *Gleaner*, 1850–53; first published May 1854; receipts of 1853–54 = £1773; May 1855–56 = £2440; 1856–57 = £2441; 1857–58 = £1606; 1858–59 = £2542; 1859–60 = £336; total = £11,138
239 8 CES *Gleaner*, Sept 1860, p 3
240 9 *See* p 70f
242 10 Opium: Latourette, K S: *A History of Christian Missions in China*, p 359
242 11 Delamarre: *Chinese Recorder*, Vol 12, 1881, p 10
243 12 OMFA: 3212 f–h
243 13 Orphans: Tianxi and five of p 207

245 14 Meadows: OMFA: 3213
246 15 Latourette, K S: Tipple Lectures, *These Sought a Country*
246 16 Societies: OMFA: F H Taylor *Reconstruction*, p 243; E 423
248 17 Reinforcements: to be considered in greater detail in Book 4; cf. Stock, E: *History of the CMS*, I. 376; 468–9; 474; II.306
248 18 OMFA: E423; Stock, E: op. cit. I.474; II.9, 299, 306, 337, 474, 579
251 19 *Minutes of BMS China Sub-Committee*, 1853–68, 14 March 1861. This Sub-Committee had been set up on 19 Feb 1861 (Minute No 327) following a resolution on 22 Jan (Minute No 304) on the subject of the China Mission (*see* Book Three *passim*).
251 20 E413. The BMS Committee had resolved to locate six of its present missionaries in Nanjing or its vicinity. A resolution of the 17 April meeting, at which the chair was taken by J C Marshman (author of the *Life and Times of Carey, Marshman and Ward*, 1859) and W G Lewis and Wm Landels of Regents Park Chapel also spoke, approved the Committee's decision and looked to the Churches to support the venture.
251 21 *Minutes of BMS General Committee*, Vol 0 p 82, Minute 44, 10 July 1861
251 22 Liverpool Conference on Missions, 1860, Report p 321; forerunner of united missionary conferences, London, 1878, 1888; Stock, E: op. cit. II.32, 34
252 23 Bible Society: *Minutes of General Committee*, 1 April 1861, Minute 54; Editorial Correspondence, No 2 pp 64–72
253 24 Bible Society: *Minutes of Editorial Sub-Committee*, 17 July 1861, Minute 35
253 25 Rev John Mee, Anglican Secretary, 1858–61, with S B Bergne (1854–79)
254 26 Bible Society: *Minutes of Editorial Sub-Committee*, 17 July 1861, Minute 30
255 27 CMS: Stock, E: op. cit. I.474; 'the C.M.S. China Mission has never been in the front rank of agencies in [China]. India and Africa have generally claimed the largest places in the Society's thoughts.'
255 28 CMS: note also Stock, E: op. cit. I.376: in the first forty years of the CMS's existence, only sixteen university men went overseas under its auspices. Between 1841 and 1848 under Henry Venn the same number were sent, including George Smith, Thomas McClatchie, R H Cobbold, F F Gough and W A Russell.
256 29 OMFA: 3214h
257 30 Jehol: *pinyin* = Rehe, Warm Stream (it never froze), now Changde, part of Hebei province; Haldane, C: *The Last Great Empress of China*, pp 38–58; Morse, H B: *The International Relations of the Chinese Empire*, Vol 2, pp 52f
261 31 Moule, A E: *Recollections of the Taiping Rebellion* (lecture); Morse, H B: 2.64f
262 32 Yangzi: Parliamentary Papers: *A Century of Diplomatic Blue Books*, 176/596b (2777) p 311
Truce: *London Gazette*; E 4/12
262 33 Michie, A: *The Englishman in China* (J Rutherford Alcock) Vol I, p 200
262 34 Schereschewsky: Boone, M: *The Seed of the Church in China*, pp 228–31; Latourette, K S: *Christian Missions*, pp 368ff
264 35 Thompson, R W: *Griffith John*, pp 159–60

265 36 Burdon: *Chinese Recorder*, 7.344; Moule, A E: *The Story of the Cheh-Kiang Mission*, p 24; HTCOC Book 4, Index: *see* Moule, Valentine, Stevenson, Hangzhou, Shaoxing.
267 37 East End: Collier, Richard: *The General Next to God* (Wm Booth and SA) pp 22–5 (a Book Society Choice)
267 38 Whitechapel: Linton, E Lynn: *A Night in a Hospital, Belgravia Magazine*, July 1879
268 39 Louis Pasteur was formulating his 'germ' theory. Not until young Joseph Lister learned in 1865 of Pasteur's work and tried to kill germs in open wounds with carbolic acid sprays, did antiseptic surgery come in. In Asinov's phrase, together they 'converted hospitals into something more than elaborate pauses on the way to the grave'.
268 40 John Adams and Thomas Blizard Curling, the surgeons, and Andrew Clarke, the physician, showed JHT many a kindness; but also a new Assistant Surgeon, Jonathan Hutchinson, knighted later.
269 41 OMFA: 3213–4; 3219a; E4 *passim*; FHT *Reconstruction*.
270 42 OMFA: 3213
273 43 Ningbo: OMFA: 3216a; E424b; Moule, A E: *Recollections*; Stock, E.: op. cit. II.311; Latourette, K S: op. cit. p 294; Pott, Hawks: *A Short History of Shanghai*, pp 57f
276 44 Expansion: this subject needs a big canvas, impossible here: Books 4–6 return to it; cf. *Chinese Recorder* Vol 8, 129, 208, 302, 308, 313, 380, 455; Latourette, K S: op. cit. pp 256–9, 357–77, 438; *Expansion of Christianity*, p 253, passim; Stock, E: op. cit. II. 579–87; Smith, A H: *The Uplift of China*, passim; MacGillivray, D: *A Century of Protestant Missions in China*, *passim*; Thompson, R W: *Griffith John*, pp 165f
276 45 Batak: Neill, Stephen C: *A History of Christian Missions*, p 348
277 46 Lockhart: Latourette, K S: *Christian Missions*, p 364; Blodget: Latourette, K S: op. cit. pp 366, 430–1; Broomhall, M: *The Chinese Empire*, p 105; Dr Henry Blodget of the American Board (ABCFM) had preached in the streets of Peking in 1860 after the capitulation.
277 47 CMS: Stock, E: op. cit. II.582
278 48 Veniaminov: Neill, S C: op. cit. p 443
279 49 Methodist: *Chinese Recorder*, 1877, 8.460–1
279 50 Mobs: Roman Catholic, reflecting the state of RC–Protestant relations everywhere at this time.
279 51 BFBS *Annual Report*, 1862

Chapter 7
281 1 OMFA: 3219a; E421
282 2 Russell: *see* p 115, note 18
282 3 OMFA: 3216a; probably Alford's *Commentary on the Greek Testament*; re C R Alford; Stock, E: *A History of the CMS*, II.584–9
282 4 OMFA: 3216b
284 5 OMFA: 3219a
284 6 *Minutes of Council*, Royal College of Surgeons, 10 July 1862
285 7 OMFA: 3219a, 19–20 July 1862: on 8 July 1857, Hudson Taylor in Shanghai had received a letter from Mrs E R Tozer of Tottenham, quoting Acts 12:11, 'the iron gate opened to them of its own accord' and

saying, 'He can and I believe will . . . cause that the Iron Gate should open of its *own accord* [to you]'.

286 8 MRCS: *see* also pp 382–3: in contemporary terms this was full medical qualification.

288 9 OMFA: 3215; 3217; 3219. Frederick Howard Taylor's birth on 25 Nov 1862 was registered in 'Mile End Old Town in the County of Middlesex' and his father's profession was given as 'Baptist Missionary', although Hudson Taylor was by then a 'Surgeon' (MRCS).

290 10 *See* Index; Forbes, A: *Chinese Gordon*, pp 39f; Latourette, K S: *A History of Christian Missions in China*, pp 294–5; Little, Mrs A: *Li Hung-chang, His Life and Times*, *passim*; Morse, H B: *The International Relations of the Chinese Empire*, Vol 2; Moule, A E: *Recollections of the Taiping Rebellion*; *The Story of the Cheh-Kiang Mission*; Pott, Hawks: *A Short History of Shanghai*, pp 52f; Woodcock, G: *The British in the Far East*, *passim*; Parliamentary Papers, *A Century of Diplomatic Blue Books*, 181/605a *et seq* (2976) p 15; 188/632(3104) p 375

291 11 Little, Mrs A: op. cit. pp 1–5, 15–27; Personalia; HTCOC 4–6 are to show Li Hong-zhang's importance to the whole century and to the CIM in particular.

291 12 Shanghai: Pott, Hawks: op. cit. pp 53–5

293 13 30 miles: op. cit. p 58; Forbes, A: op. cit. p 40

293 14 Ningbo: Forbes, A: op. cit. p 42; Moule, A E: op. cit.; OMFA: 3219, 13/2; Morse, H B: 2.78f

294 15 Ningbo: OMFA: 3216a, b

294 16 Dew: Moule, A E: *Recollections*; Stock, E: op. cit. II.311f; OMFA: 424b

294 17 Moule, A E: *Story of the Cheh-Kiang Mission*, (2nd edn) pp 61–70; *London Gazette*, 14 July 1862 OMFA: E424b, detail

297 18 Refugees: Moule, A E: *Recollections*; Morse, H B: op. cit.

298 19 Homely: friendly, warm-hearted; cf N American 'homey'.

299 20 Morse, H B: *ibid*; Forbes, A: op. cit. p. 42; OMFA: 3216c

300 21 Dew: OMFA: E426, 22 Sept 1862

302 22 Fear: OMFA: 13/2, 24 Sept 1862

303 23 Ward: Morse, H B: op. cit. *ibid*; Forbes, A: op. cit. p 42

304 24 Hart: Morse, H B: op. cit. 2.81, citing *Records of the Tsungli Yamen.*

304 25 Taipings: *Chinese Recorder*, Vol 7, 1876, pp 344f

304 26 Forbes, A: op. cit. pp 41–115; Pott, Hawks: op. cit. pp 58–60; Woodcock, G: op. cit. *passim*; Morse, H B: op. cit. pp 83f; *Memoirs of Li Hung-chang*, pp 66, 68 in Allen, B M: *Gordon in China* (1933), p 69, quoted in Neill, S: *Colonialism and Christian Missions*

304 27 Settlement: Woodcock, G: op. cit. p 128

304 28 Little, Mrs A: op. cit. p 17

307 29 Forbes, A: op. cit. pp 87–95; Little, Mrs A: op. cit. pp 28–38; Martin, W A P: *A Cycle of Cathay*, pp 347f; Morse, H B: op. cit. 2.101–2 (92–107)

307 30 Imperial (Double) Dragon (1881): Morse, H B: 2.107; Werlich, R: *Orders and Decorations of All Nations*; Brunnert, H S and Hagelstrom, V V: *Present Day Political Organisation of China* (1912); awarded in first division, third class, to JHT's surgeon nephew, son of Amelia, in the closing years of the dynasty

308 31 Morse, H B: op. cit. 2.25, 34, 138f; chronology, p xxv

308 32 Parker: OMFA: 4242a, 5 Nov 1862; 20 Jan 1863; *United Presbyterian Missionary Record*, 2 Feb 1863

309 33 Meadows letters: OMFA: 13/2, 19 Nov 1862 *et seq*

309 34 Jaundice: *see* pp 199, 206; OMFA: 13/2, 21 Jan 1863

309 35 Parker: OMFA: E424a, G E Moule, 4 Feb 1863; 3219b, 16 Feb 1863; 13/2, 19 Feb 1863

316 36 Martha: OMFA: 13/2; 3210; E426, 7 Sept 1863

317 37 Meadows: OMFA: E426, 7 Sept 1863

317 38 OMFA: E426; 13/2; 3219

319 39 Income: OMFA: 3219, 13 Feb 1863; to this day, twelve decades later, the same system is observed in Hudson Taylor's mission. Every three months, all funds received are shared equitably between all members, after the primary operating expenses have been met.

319 40 CIM: Hudson Taylor always regarded the start of the Ningpo Mission as the conception of the CIM, although, after John Jones' death and Mary's settling in London, he did not list them as members of the mature mission.

321 41 OMFA: 3215; 3217; 3219; E432 (typed extracts); 3 Book 4, JHT's notebook journal.

322 42 Stock, E: op. cit. II.26–9; Shaftesbury's Religious Worship Act (1855) made legal any religious meetings in unlicensed places. The SPG led the way by opening its public meetings with prayer, and a few ministers began preaching in the open air. Services were begun in Exeter Hall, Strand, at which Charles Haddon Spurgeon, and the Hon Samuel Waldegrave, Bishop of Carlisle, and Robert Bickersteth, Bishop of Ripon (previously on the CES Committee) preached. Encouraged by the success of the Exeter Hall meetings, the Bishop of London, Tait, introduced the 'absolute novelty' of evening services in St Paul's Cathedral and Westminster Abbey. When Bishop Tait exhorted 1000 clergy and laity for five hours in St Paul's, 'to be up and doing for the evangelisation of London', *Punch* carried a cartoon of the event. Reginald Radcliffe's theatre services for shirt-sleeved audiences began in 1860. Compare conditions and practices in China!

323 43 Tablet: *see* HTCOC 1. 44–6 and Index; presumably defending the view that the Nestorians in China were positive Christians.

325 44 Douglas: Stock, E: op. cit. II.293; Broomhall, M: *The Chinese Empire*, p 440; Personalia; HTCOC Book 2, p 449

326 45 Francke: Neill, S C: *A History of Christian Missions*, pp 228–9; Personalia

328 46 OMFA: 3217a–k; 13/4

329 47 BFBS: OMFA: 3 Book 4, 29 June 1863; Samuel Brodribb Bergne, Independent Minister, Secretary of BFBS, 1854–79; Anglican secretaries = John Mee, 1858–61; Charles Jackson, 1862–79 (cf John Jackson, Asst. Foreign Secretary, 1823–49).

331 48 BFBS: Minutes of Editorial Sub-Committee, No 7, 15 July 1863, Minutes 8–10

331 49 Robert Cleaver Chapman: (1803–1902) solicitor; a leading member of the Brethren; Personalia; Coad, F Roy: *A History of the Brethren Movement*, pp 69f

331 50 OMFA: 3217d, Sat. evg. 19 Sept 1863

332 51 Pearse: not an elected member of BFBS committee, but entitled to attend and vote if a Governor by a life-subscription of £50, or £5 annually. John Eliot Howard was a member.
333 52 OMFA: 3217e, 7 Oct 1863
334 53 Cainan: OMFA: 3217h, to Mrs Ranyard as editor – an indication of the standard of revision: Luke 3:36, Cainan omitted from Hebrew texts of Gen. 11:12 on moral grounds, but not from Septuagint. 'Unless you allow his presence in the list, you meet with very serious difficulties in reconciling the chronology of the older commentaries; with it there is little difficulty in doing so.'
334–5 54, 56 *Minutes of CMS Committee*, Vol 35, 20 Oct 1863
334 55 *Minutes of BFBS Editorial Sub-Committee*, No 7, 21 Oct 1863, Minutes 41–3
336 57 Russell: Stock, E: op. cit. II.579
336 58 OMFA: 3215; 3219b; 13/2; 3 Book 4
337 59 Soothill: Latourette, K S: *History of Christian Missions in China*, pp 382, 431, 626, 632, 651; Broomhall, M: *The Chinese Empire*, pp 403–4
337 60 Maxwell: Personalia; Broomhall, M: op. cit. pp 65–6, 401, 442; *Chinese Recorder*, Vol 5, p 143
338 61 Gough: appropriately, after five years they married, and in 1869 returned to Ningbo in CMS, after consulting JHT about joining the CIM.
338 62 Groves: HTCOC Book 3.80; OMFA: E427, *Revival* cuttings, p 388
339 63 OMFA: D322
339 64 OMFA: *Occasional Papers*, No 2, p 4
341 65, 66 OMFA: 3 Book 4, No 3

Chapter 8
347 1 Taipings: Broomhall, M: *The Chinese Empire*; Forbes, A: *Chinese Gordon*; Hook, B: *China's Three Thousand Years*, Part 4; Latourette, K S: *The History of Christian Missions in China*, pp 294–5; *A History of the Expansion of Christianity*, Vol VI, pp 361–3; Little, Mrs A: *Li Hung-chang*; Morse, H B: *The International Relations of the Chinese Empire*, Vol 2; Moule, A E: *Recollections of the Taiping Rebellion* [lecture, Shanghai, Dec 1883, *Chinese Recorder* (?) 1884]; Thompson, R W: *Griffith John*
347 2 Hart: Morse, H B: op. cit. 2.106f; Forbes, A: op. cit. pp 97–8; Haldane, C: *The Last Great Empress of China*, pp 60–1
348 3 E-VA: Morse, H B: op. cit. 2.110
349 4 Gordon: Forbes, A: op. cit. pp 94–5, 113–4; Morse, H B: op. cit. 2.109; Little, Mrs A: op. cit. p. 49; 'He seemed to control his followers by an intuitive influence, and the buoyancy of his temperament sustained him in every situation.' 'No matter how sombre the situation, if there be a comic side to any incident, Gordon sees it and enjoys it.' Forbes, A: op. cit. pp. 45, 2
350 5 Burgevine: Morse, H B: op. cit. 2.110
350 6 Rebellions: *see* p 75 Note 1; p 356; Muslim, Yunnan-Guizhou, 1862–73; Miao, Guizhou, 1854–73; Morse, H B: op. cit. 2.113–4; Broomhall, M: *The Jubilee Story of the China Inland Mission*, Index; Latourette, K S: *Christian Missions*, Index; Hook, B: op. cit. pp 156f

351 7 Bao-jia: observed by present writer; Hook, B: op. cit.

352 8 Zeng: *Peking Gazette*, 19 June 1864; Morse, H B: op. cit. 2.110; Little, Mrs A: op. cit. p 50; Haldane, C: op. cit. pp 66–7

352 9 Arsenals: Morse, H B: op. cit.; Hook, B: op. cit.; Little, Mrs A: op. cit.

353 10 Hart: Morse, H B: op. cit. 2.138f; Little, Mrs A: op. cit. pp 63–4

353 11 'IF': Moule, A E: op. cit.; Latourette, K S: op. cit. pp 291–9; Stock, E: *The History of the CMS*, II.312: 'Did ever Christendom have so golden an opportunity of winning a great Heathen nation for Christ?'

357 12 Tian Wang: Latourette, K S: op. cit. p 293

358 13 Martin, W A P: *A Cycle of Cathay*, pp 138–42

358 14 Latourette, K S: *Expansion of Christianity*, p 362

361 15 Hangzhou: Stock, E: op. cit. II.582–3 paraphrased

361 16 Wylie: *Chinese Recorder*, Vol 1 p 149; Latourette, K S: *Christian Missions*, pp 265, 436–8; Broomhall, M: *The Chinese Empire*, p 439 and *passim*
Williamson: Latourette, K S: op. cit. pp 381, 438, 440; Broomhall, M: op. cit. p 437 and *passim*

362 17 Burns: Broomhall, M: op. cit. *passim*; Latourette, K S: op. cit. pp 257–9, 264, 396; HTCOC Book 1, Index; Book 2, Index; Book 3, Personalia, Index

362 18 Chinese: *Chinese Recorder*, June 1925, p 379; HTCOC Book 3, 577

363 19 Christians: Latourette, K S: *Expansion*, p 337; *Christian Missions*, p 479

363 20 Apathy: to be examined in Book 4

364 21 Agency: Taylor, J H: *A Retrospect* (1954 edn) p 113

365 22 OMFA: 3 Book 4 (JHT's notebook journals), Nos 1–12

369 23 *ibid*

370 24 Nevius, Helen: *John Livingston Nevius*, p 258; OMFA: 3219c, 3 Book 4

371 25 OMFA: 13/2 *passim*; *The Letters of Samuel Rutherford* (1600–61); *The Loveliness of Christ*, selections by E S Lister (Bagster & Sons, Ltd.)

371 26 Meadows, Bridge St church: again, detail which might otherwise be omitted is retained to illustrate the kind of experiences to be shared by hundreds of young men and women after him, and by other rudimentary churches.

372 27 To the present day this has continued to be the relationship between leaders and led in the mission.

372 28 OMFA: 13/2, 22 Dec 1863

374 29 Consul: R Q Way, J Quarterman and E C Lord, at various times.

Chapter 9

377 1 Recruits: OMFA: 3217; 3219 (letters): 3 Book 4 (journal); E427 (Pearse scrapbook); Taylor, J H: *China: Its Spiritual Need and Claims*, pp 63–71, *passim*

378 2 UMFC: OMFA: 3217k

378 3 UMFC: OMFA: 3 Book 4, No 5

379 4 Barchet: Taylor, J H: *ibid*; OMFA: 3 Book 4, Nos 4, 5

382 5 Notman: OMFA: 3219b; E427; 13/2; 3 Book 4; FHT Reconstruction p 386; Appendix 6. Her outfit for several years involved 6½ yards of black merino, 20 yards muslin, 21 yards flannel, 5 yards red flannel, 1 crinoline, 12 pairs drawers, 6 nightdresses: OMFA 13/4A

382 6 Lowe: OMFA: E432.26. She had taught English to the Tsar's family and lived in the palace at St Petersburg (Leningrad). Sir Robert Peel had recommended Miss Lowe to the Queen for a pension in recognition of her father's services.
384 7 Pennefather: HTCOC 1; Personalia; Stock, E: *The History of the Church Missionary Society*, Vol II p 30
384 8 Opium: Stock, E: op. cit. II.207. The first instalment had come to F F Gough in Ningpo through George Smith, Bishop of Victoria, Hong Kong, in June 1860, but when JHT could take no more addicts, Gough had himself treated 113 under JHT's guidance – the forerunner of the opium refuge which developed into Dr Duncan Main's hospital at Hangzhou.
386 9 Statistics: Latourette, K S: *A History of Christian Missions in China*, pp 405–8; *Chinese Recorder*, Vol. 9.5
387 10 Taylor, J H: *A Retrospect* (18th impression) p 112
387 11 OMFA: *China's Millions*, April 1878
387 12 Societies: Stock, E: op. cit. II.337; III.21; 'Henry Venn told the Islington Clerical Meeting that while "the extent and influence of Evangelical Truth in the Church had very largely increased", missionary zeal had distinctly "retrograded" [as seen in] "a failing treasury and a scanty supply of candidates".'
388 13 Alford: appointed bishop 1864; Stock, E: op. cit. II.584–9; Broomhall, M: *The Chinese Empire*, p 23; (HTCOC Book 4)
388 14 OMFA: E431, M G Taylor's verbatim notes of JHT's recollections.
390 15 Pennefather: Stock, E: op. cit. III.21
391 16 Denniston: OMFA: 3221m, wife's letter; E427; FHT Reconstruction p 441
392 17 FES: OMFA: E427, from G Pearse's scrapbook
393 18 *British Herald*, 2 Nov 1863
393 19 Johann Ludwig Krapf, 'discoverer' of Mt Kenya and Mt Kilimanjaro; *ibid*, Nov 1863, letter dated 10 Nov; Neill, S C: *A History of the Expansion of Christianity*, Vol VI, pp 33–4: sent by CMS; Krapf in East Africa from Ethiopia to Zanzibar.
393 20 Spittler: OMFA: E427; *The Revival*, Vol X, No 242, March 1864
394 21 Burns: CES *Gleaner*, March 1851, p 22; letter, Canton, 27 Nov 1850
395 22 OMFA: E427: *The Revival*, *ibid*
395 23 OMFA: E427; op. cit. No 246
396 24 OMFA: E427; op. cit. No 268, 8 Sept 1864
396 25, 26 Labourers: *see* p 394, meaning 'Christian workers' in the sense of King James AV; not 'manual labourers' but artisans and later specifically of better education, clerks, governesses, instead of university graduates.
397 27 OMFA: 3 Book 4, journal; E427, *The Revival*, X No 252, 19 May 1864
397 28 op. cit. X No 253
398 29 op. cit. X No 256
398 30 Foreign Evangelisation Society: OMFA: E439
399 31 E427; *The Revival*, X No 257
400 32 'Ask . . . tell': Stock, E: op. cit. III. 679, title of CMS President's letter.
400 33 'God alone': Taylor, J. H: *A Retrospect*, p 21
400 34 *The Revival*, note of 23 June
401 35 OMFA: 3 Book 4 (journal); 3219c, (letters)

402 36 OMFA: 3219c, 27 Jan 1865
406 37 OMFA: 3219c
408 38 BFBS: *Minutes of Editorial Sub-Committee*, 18 April 1865, Minute 23
409 39 Taylor, J H: *China: Its Spiritual Need and Claims*; so, for the first six editions, then *China's Spiritual Need and Claims.*
410 40 op. cit. p 8; the Great Wall and Grand Canal.
412 41 BFBS: *Minute of Editorial Sub-Committee*, 18 April 1865, Minute 23
412 42 OMFA: 3219c (FHT abstracts): 3221 Truelove episode; 3 Book 4 No 8 (journal)
418 43 OMFA: 3221; 3 Book 4 No 9; 13/3–5 (surviving cash accounts)
418 44 Welbeck St: ie before the occasion of Montagu Beauchamp's account, OMFA: 10.331 (HTCOC 3.575), not JHT's first attendance there, throwing doubt on the accuracy of Beauchamp's hearsay account of the occasion in his childhood.
418 45 Soltau: Rowdon, H H: *The Origins of the Brethren*, p 161
423 46 Crombie: Taylor, J H: op. cit. pp 74–8; OMFA: 13/5; HTCOC Book 4
424 47 OMFA: *Occasional Papers*, No 1 pp 13–14
424 48 op. cit. 1.10

Chapter 10

425 1 Agency: Taylor, J H: *A Retrospect* (18th impression) pp 111–15; OMFA: 3219c:3 Book 4, No 10
425 2 Beauchamp: OMFA: 10.331
426 3 Taylor, J H: op. cit. p 112
426 4 Policy: OMFA: E431 p 10, verbatim notes
427 5 *ibid*
427 6 Chinese: *Chinese Recorder*, 1925, p 379; Weise, J: *The Early History and Development of the Berlin Missionary Work in South China*; a paper read before the Canton Missionary Conference, 29 Mar 1924
428 7 Knave: Smith, A H: *The Uplift of China*, 1909, p 172
428 8 Müller: OMFA: E431, verbatim notes
428 9 Inland: Taylor, J H: op. cit. p 113
431 10 OMFA: 3222
431 11 Leader: Taylor, J H: op. cit. p 114
432 12, 13 Audit: OMFA: 13/3
432 14 JHT: An undated photograph of a gaunt, hollow-eyed Hudson Taylor has been attributed to this period, but others show him in good physical condition. The photograph therefore belongs either to 1860 or, more likely, a decade later, 1871, ie five years before or after 1865.
433 15 Taylor, J H: op. cit.; *China: Its Spiritual Need and Claims*; OMFA: 3219c (letters); 3221; 13/3 (a/cs); 13/6; E431 (verbatim notes); 3 Book 4, No 10 (journal)
434 16 Taylor, J H: *A Retrospect*, pp 113–4
434 17, 18 OMFA: E431 p 12
435 19 Taylor, J H: *China*: op. cit. p 22
435 20 Pearse had moved in March to 3 Buckingham Road, Brighton, expressly to support evangelists working in the towns and villages of Sussex. Denniston was spending a few weeks at Brighton.
438 21 OMFA: 3 Book 4, No 10; Why no reference to William Berger, his

co-founder and co-signatory at the bank? Perhaps communication with him was too obvious to be mentioned. To call in at East Grinstead on the way to London or to meet at Coborn Street or the factory in Bromley-by-Bow could be taken for granted. Or had the spiritual exercise at Brighton on 25 June been so personal, with Hudson Taylor simply facing up to measures decided upon in prior consultations, that there was no need to say more? Was Pearse, the City stockbroker, more handy to go with him to the bank, or did Hudson Taylor absent-mindedly write 'Pearse' instead of 'Berger'? – for, three lines below, he went on, 'wrote also to Mr. Pearse'.

438 22 OMFA: A122c: M G Taylor's verbatim notes from G Pearse.

439 23 Tinling: nothing more than the name links him with the Lieutenant Tinling killed fighting the Taipings (qv).

440 24 Booth: Collier, R: *The General Next to God*, p 26

Postscript

441 25 Latourette, K S: *A History of the Expansion of Christianity*, Vol VI, p 329

441 26 Latourette, K S: Tipple Lectures: *These Sought a Country*

442 27, 28, 29 Latourette, K S: *A History of Christian Missions in China*, pp 382–4

443 30 'A thousand lives': In 1906, 849 were still on active service; by 1912 there were 1009; in 1915, 1063 with 2765 Chinese colleagues, in 1327 centres, recording over 5017 baptisms; in 1934 the current membership of the CIM (including associates) reached its peak at 1368 on the active list. In the first forty years of the mission's existence, £1-million were received; £4-million more in the next thirty years, and £7-million between 1935 and 1965. (Lyall, L T: *A Passion for the Impossible*, pp 80, 112, 212; Broomhall, M: *The Jubilee Story of the China Inland Mission*, Appendix III, pp 372–3)

Appendix 1

445 1 *Autobiography*, p 64; source of donations to Hudson Taylor and CIM

446 2 Coad, F R: *A History of the Brethren Movement*, p 53; *Autobiography*, p 693 summary

Appendix 2

447 3 'PB': originating with M A Aldersey, Ningbo; denied by Hudson Taylor to Tarn, OMFA-2542

447 4 Brethren: Groves, Mrs: *Memoir of the late Anthony Norris Groves*, 1st edn 1856, 2nd edn 1857; Rowdon, H H: *The Origins of the Brethren, 1825–1850*, publ. 1967; Coad, F R: *A History of the Brethren Movement*, publ. 1968

448 5 Still C of E: Groves, *Memoir*, p 30; Rowdon, H H: op. cit. p 172

448 6 Bethesda: Coad, F R: op. cit.; OMFA-2211, pamphlet

448 7 Howards: Rowdon, H H: op. cit. pp 162–3; Luke Howard: Coad, F R: op. cit. p 76

449 8 Gosse: Coad, F R: op. cit. p 222; van Sommer: *ibid*, p 166

449 9 Parnell: *ibid*, p 75

449 10 Groves: op. cit.
449 11 Groves: op. cit. p 31, quoted on Coad, F R: op. cit. jacket
450 12 Collingwood: Coad, F R: op. cit. p 253
450 13 *The Tottenham Statement*: Coad, F R: op. cit. p 301

Appendix 3
451 14 Gordon: Morse, H B: *International Relations of the Chinese Empire*, Vol 2, pp 96f; Forbes, A: *Chinese Gordon*, pp 44–115

Appendix 4
454 15 OMFA: E431

Appendix 6
471 16 Toralium: probably the trade name for 'a coverlet draped over a bed or couch'. (R W Burchfield, Oxford Dictionaries, personal communiction)

PERSONALIA

ABEEL, David, American Seamen's Friend Society, chaplain; 1830–33 Canton (Guangzhou), Bangkok; 1839–45 Am. Board (ABCFM); 1842 Gulangsu Is., Amoy; initiated women's missionary socs. in UK, USA

ADAMS, J, surgeon, London Hospital; member of Council of Royal College of Surgeons

AITCHISON, William, Am. Board; 1854 Shanghai, Pinghu

ALCOCK, Sir John Rutherford (1809–97); MRCS at 21; 1832–37 Peninsular Wars, Dep.-Director of Hospitals; 1835 partially paralysed; 1843 Diplomatic Service; 1846 HBM consul Fuzhou (Foochow), Amoy, Shanghai; 20 June 1862 knighted, KCB; HBM minister, Peking

ALDERSEY, Miss Mary Ann (*c* 1800–64); 1824–5 learned Chinese from R Morrison; 1832 Malacca (Melaka); Batavia (Jakarta); 1842 Hong Kong; 1843–59 Ningbo

ALFORD, C R, 1864 Bishop of Victoria, Hong Kong; proposed a new C of E society for East Asia; 1874 resigned

AMHERST, William Pitt, Lord Amherst, 1816 Peking embassy; 1823 Gov.-Gen. of India; first Burma war; 1826 earldom; d. 1857

BALFOUR, Capt. George, officer 1840 opium war; 1843–46 first consul Shanghai; Major-Gen., CB, nominated JHT for FRGS

BALL, Richard, businessman, Taunton, Somerset; moving spirit in Chinese Association and Chinese Evangelization Society (CES); editor, *Chinese Missionary Gleaner*; author, *Handbook of China*, 1854.

BARCHET, Stephan Paul, German; 1865 Ningbo, sent by JHT; later doctor of medicine

BARNARDO, Thomas John (4 July 1845–19 Sept. 1905); 1862 converted; 1866 met JHT in Dublin; April 1866 to London

BARTON, Samuel, 1862 Missionary Secretary, United Meth. Free Church

BAUSUM, J G, independent, Penang; 1845–46 m. Maria Tarn Dyer, mother of Maria Jane

BAUSUM, Mrs, 2nd wife of J G Bausum; mother of Mary; 1856 Ningbo; 1861 m. E C Lord (qv)

BAUSUM, Mary, daughter, m. Dr S P Barchet (qv)

BEAUCHAMP, (Sir) Montagu (Bart.) (1860–1939); son of Sir Thomas (qv); nephew of Lord Radstock (qv); Cambridge Univ. oar; one of the 'Cambridge Seven'; 1885 to China; made several journeys with JHT

BEAUCHAMP, Sir Thomas Proctor-, 4th Bt of Langley Park, Norfolk; m. Hon. Caroline Waldegrave, daughter of second Lord Radstock (qv); supporter of JHT, CIM

BELL, Henry, UMFC, Barnsley; close friend of James Taylor (qv); confidant of James Meadows (qv)

BERGER, William Thomas (*c* 1812–99); London starch manufacturer; JHT's friend, supporter, co-founder of China Inland Mission; first Home Sec., benefactor

BERGNE, Samuel Brodribb, Independent minister, co-Sec. British & Foreign Bible Society, 1854–79

BETTELHEIM, Dr B J, converted Jewish physician; Loochoo Naval Mission to Ryukyu Is. 1845–53; strongly opposed

BICKERSTETH, Robert, member of CES committee; Bishop of Ripon

BIRD, Charles, Gen. Sec. Chinese Evangelization Society

BLAKISTON, Capt., adventurer; 1861 reached Tibetan border

BLODGET, Henry, DD (1825–1903) Am. Board; 1854 Shanghai; 1860 first Prot. to preach at Tianjin, Peking; 1864 translator, Peking 30 years

BOGUE, Dr, principal Missionary Academy, Gosport, *c* 1805–20; friend of Dr Wm Moseley (qv); nominated R Morrison, S Dyer to LMS for China

BONAR, Andrew, Scottish divine

BONAR, Horatius (1808–89); Scottish divine, hymn-writer

BONHAM, Sir George, *c* 1856 HBM plenipotentiary, Hong Kong, after Bowring (qv)

BOONE, William Jones, Sr, MD, DD; Am. Prot. Episcopal Church; 1837 Batavia; 1840 Macao; 1842 Gulangsu Is., Amoy, with Abeel; 1844 Bishop, Shanghai; d. 1864

BOOTH, William (1829–1912); Methodist evangelist; then Methodist New Connexion; 1865 'found his destiny' in London's East End and formed The Christian Mission; 7 Aug 1878 changed its name and form to Salvation Army

BOWRING, Sir John (1792–1872); HBM consul, Siam, Canton; 1854 plenipotentiary, last Supt. of Trade; Sinologue

BRADLEY, Daniel Beach, MD, Am. Board (ABCFM); 1840–49 Bangkok, physician to Thai royal family

BRIDGMAN, Elijah Coleman, DD (1801–61); Am. Board (ABCFM); 1830 Canton; 1832 first editor *Chinese Repository* with R Morrison; 1843–44 US interpreter-negotiator; 1845–52 translator, Chinese Bible, Delegates' Committee, Shanghai

BRIDGMAN, Mrs, 1845 Canton; 1847 Shanghai; 1864 Peking

BROOMHALL, Benjamin (1829–1911); m. Amelia Hudson Taylor; 1879–95 Gen. Sec. China Inland Mission; editor, *National Righteousness*, organ of anti-opium trade campaign, to 1911 (*see* Maxwell)

BRUCE, Sir Frederick, brother of Lord Elgin (qv); 1858 envoy, rebuffed by emperor; 1859 repulsed at Dagu, Tianjin; 1860 first Br. Minister, Peking

BURDON, John Shaw (1829–1907); CMS; 1853 arr. Shanghai; pioneer evangelist; m. Burella Dyer (qv); 1862 Peking; 1874 3rd Bishop, Hong Kong; Bible translator

BURGEVINE, H A, Am. soldier of fortune; after F T Ward, commanded Ever-Victorious Army; later joined Taipings

BURLINGAME, Anson (1820–70); barrister, Congressman, Methodist; 1861–67 US minister, Peking, appointed by Abraham Lincoln; ambassador-at-large for China.

BURNS, William Chalmers (1815–68); first English Presby. to China; 1847 Hong Kong; Amoy; 1855 Shanghai; 1856 Swatow; 1863 Peking; d. Niuchuang; translator of *Pilgrim's Progress*; close friend of JHT (qv)

CAI YUAN (Ts'ai Yuan), a prince of Yi, conspirator with Prince Cheng (qv) and Su Shun (qv) to kill the heir presumptive's mother Yehonala (qv) and seize government as regents

CANNING, 1st earl (1812–62); 1855 Gov.-Gen. of India during mutiny; 1858 first viceroy; 1859 earldom

CAREY, William (1761–1834); founder of Baptist Miss. Soc.; 1793 India; 1800–30 Prof. of Oriental Languages, Calcutta

CAVAN, Earl of; Welbeck St Brethren; member of CES committee; supported JHT and CIM

CHALLICE, John, director of six companies; deacon, Bryanston Hall, Portman Square; member, first CIM council; treasurer UK; d. 1887

CHAPDELAINE, Auguste, Paris Mission (Société des Missions Étrangères de Paris); 1856 executed

CHAPMAN, Robert Cleaver (1802–1902); High Court attorney; C of E; 1832 Strict Baptist minister; Brethren; 2nd Evang. Awakening evangelist; JHT's friend

CHEETHAM, Charles, Foreign Missionary Sec., UMFC after R Eckett

CHENG, General, most successful of imperial army commanders against Taipings; 1864 killed in action

CHENG, Prince, conspirator in Jehol plot with Cai Yuan (qv) and Su Shun (qv)

CHIANG Kai-shek (b. 1887); friend and brother-in-law of Sun Yat-sen; statesman, Kuomintang, President of Republic of China; 1937–44 generalissimo in war with Japan; 1927 m. Soong Mei-ling; made Taiwan an industrial success

CH'I SHAN, *see* Qi Shan; CH'I YING, *see* Qi Ying; CHIA CH'ING, *see* Jia Qing; CH'IEN LUNG, *see* Qian Long; CHU CHIU-TAO, *see* Zhu Jiu-Dao; CHUNG WANG, *see* Zhung Wang

CI AN (Tz'u An) empress consort of Xian Feng; with Ci Xi (qv) co-regent of Tong Zhi (T'ung Chih) emperor

CIGGIE, Grace; 1865 Glasgow recruit for Ningbo; 1870 m. George Stott

CI XI (Ts'u Hsi) (1835–1908); Empress Dowager; Yehonala, the Concubine Yi; empress regent to Tong Zhi (Chih); 1860–1908 supreme power in China

CLARENDON, Earl of (1800–70); Foreign Sec. to Lord Aberdeen 1853, Lord Palmerston 1855, Lord Russell 1865, Gladstone 1868

CLARKE, Dr Andrew, renowned physician, London Hospital

CLELAND, J F, LMS, 1850 Hong Kong

COBBOLD, R H, CMS, 1848–62, Ningbo; translator, Ningbo romanised vernacular NT

COKE, Thomas, Oxford Univ.; Anglican clergyman; 1776–1813, Wesley's colleague; 1786 appealed for missions to New World; first bishop, Am. Methodist Episc. Church; d. 1813 on way to India

COLLINGWOOD, William (1819–1903); Fellow of Royal Water-colour Society; Oxford; 1839 Liverpool; C of E until Brethren; 1850 responded to C Gutzlaff, supported CES; met JHT Sept 1853 and supported JHT/CIM

COLLINS, W H, CMS Shanghai

CONGLETON, John Vesey Parnell, 2nd Baron (1805–83); Brethren, Teignmouth, London, Orchard St., Welbeck St.; travelled widely; donor to JHT/CIM

COX, Josiah, Wesleyan Meth. Miss Soc.; 1852 Canton; 1862 Hankou; 1865 Jiujiang (Kiukiang); d. 1906

CRAIK, Henry, Presbyterian then Brethren; close colleague of Geo. Müller, Bethesda chapel, Bristol; 1863 author, *New Testament Church Order*

CRANAGE, Dr J Edward, Anglican; 1859 witnessed Welsh revival, conducted meetings at Wellington, Salop, to pray for revival, mass attendance

CROMBIE, George, Aberdeen farmer; 1865 JHT's second recruit, to Ningbo

CULBERTSON, Dr M S; Am. Presbyterian; 1850 Shanghai, co-translator of Delegates' Version, Chinese Bible (NT); with E C Bridgman (qv) of OT, 1852; d. 1862, cholera

DAO GUANG (Tao Kuang); 6th Qing (Ch'ing) emperor, 1820–51; China torn by rebellions

DARBY, J N (1800–82); barrister, ordained Anglican, resigned 1827; trilingual preacher; leader of Exclusive Brethren

DARWIN, Charles Robert (1809–82); 1835 voyage in *Beagle*; author 1859 *Origin of Species*; 1871 *Descent of Man*; FRS; buried in Westminster Abbey

DAVIES, Evan, LMS Malaya; author, 1845, *China and her Spiritual Claims*; 1846 *Memoir of the Reverend Samuel Dyer*

DAVIS, Sir John Francis, Bart, Chief, Hon. East India Co., Canton; friend of R Morrison; 1844 HBM plenipotentiary, after Pottinger (qv); Supt. of Trade, Hong Kong

DEAN, William (1806–77); Am. Baptist; 1834 and 1864 Bangkok; 1842 Hong Kong

DELAMARRE, Abbé, Paris Mission; 1858–60 interpreter, French treaty; falsified Chinese version

DE LA PORTE, Dr, French Prot. medical; 1847–57 Swatow, Double Island

DE MÉRITENS, 1860 with Abbé Delamarre, interpreter for Baron Gros, Peking

DE MOGES, Marquis; 1857–58 member of Gros embassy to Tianjin and Japan

DE MONTAUBAN, 1860 French general with Baron Gros, Peking; plundered Summer Palace

DENNEY, Mr, Scottish ship-owner; 1865 gave free passages to China to Barchet and Crombie (qv)

DENNISTON, J M, Presby. minister, London, Torquay; associated with W C Burns revivals and JHT founding CIM; co-founder Foreign Evangelist Soc.

DENT, Thomas and Launcelot, high-living merchant ship-owners; chief rivals of Jardine, Matheson

DERBY, Lord; 14th earl (1799–1869); Prime Minister in govts of 1852, 1858, 1866

DE TOURNON, Charles Maillard (1668–1710); papal legate to China 1705; antagonised Kang Xi (K'ang Hsi) over Confucian rites

DEW, Capt. Roderick, RN, 1862 commander, Ningbo front, against Taipings

DODD, Samuel, Am. Presbyterian; 1861 Ningbo; 1865 married Crombie–Skinner (qv)

DOUGLAS, Carstairs, LL D (1830–77); English Presby. Mission; 1855 Amoy; introduced J L Maxwell (qv) to Formosa (Taiwan); knew JHT Shanghai, London

DYER, Burella Hunter, b. 31 May 1835; elder daughter of Samuel Dyer Sr; 1857 m. J S Burdon; d. 1858

DYER, John, Sec., Royal Hosp. for Seamen, Greenwich; 1820 Chief Clerk to Admiralty

DYER, Maria Jane; b. 16 Jan 1837; younger daughter of S Dyer Sr; 20 Jan 1858 m. JHT; d. 23 July 1870

DYER, Maria Tarn; daughter of Wm Tarn Sr, director of LMS; 1827 m. Samuel Dyer Sr; 1845/6 m. J G Bausum; d. 21 Oct 1846

DYER, Samuel, (1804–43); son of John Dyer (qv); Cambridge law student; LMS; m. Maria Tarn, daughter of LMS director; 1827 Penang; 1829–35 Malacca; 1835–43 Singapore; d. Macao

DYER, Samuel Jr; b. 18 Jan 1833, son of Samuel and Maria Tarn Dyer (qv); 1877 agent of B&FBS, Shanghai, after Alex. Wylie

ECKETT, Robert, Foreign Missionary Sec., UMFC; d. 1862

EDKINS, Joseph (1823–1905); LMS evangelist, translator, philologist, expert in Chinese religions, author, well-known to Taiping rulers; 1848–60 Shanghai; 1860–61 Shandong, Yantai, and Tianjin; 1861 Peking

EITEL, E J, PhD; Basel Mission, S. China, 1862–65; 1865–78 LMS Peking; Sinologue; Dec 1862 baptised first Peking Prot. Christian; 1878 *et seq* adviser to Hong Kong govt

ELGIN, Earl of, son of Thomas Bruce, 7th earl (Elgin marbles); 1857 Indian mutiny; 1858 envoy, Treaty of Tientsin; treaty with Japan; 1860 second opium war, captured Peking, burned Summer Palace, negotiated Peking Convention

ELLIOT, Capt. Charles, RN, 1835 third Supt. of Trade, Canton; 1836 Chief Supt.; confronted Commissioner Lin (qv); 1840–41 political chief in first phase of first opium war; HBM plenipotentiary, negotiated Convention of Chuanbi

FAULDING, Jane E (1843–1904); m. JHT 28 Nov. 1871; 1877–78 led CIM team, Shanxi famine relief, first Western woman inland

FAULDING, William F, father of Jane E Faulding (qv)

FENG Neng-gui, Ningbo basket-maker, member of non-idolatrous Buddhist sect; became evangelist, pastor

FISHBOURNE, Capt., RN, rescued Amoy victims; strong supporter of missions and anti-opium soc.; later, evangelist

FLEMING, T, 1860 CMS recruit taught by JHT; Ningbo, Hangzhou; 1863 invalided home

FORREST, R J, 1860 HBM consular interpreter, later consul, Ningbo and other places

FORRESTER, Col, 1861 second-in-command to F T Ward, Ever-Victorious Army; captured by Taipings at Qingpu; refused to succeed F T Ward

FORTUNE, Robert, Royal Hort. Soc. botanist; 1843 arr. China; explorations 1843–46, 1848–51, 1853–56, 1861–62, disguised as a Tartar; supplied India with tea plants

FOWLER, Robert, treasurer of CES, 1859–60

FRANCKE, August Hermann, pietist, 1696 founded Orphan Houses, extensive by 19th century; prof. divinity, Halle Univ. Germany; d. 1727

FRASER, John, Scottish missionary to Egypt; initiated movement resulting in Foreign Evangelist Society

FULLER, W R, first United Meth. Free Ch. missionary to China; trained by JHT; 1864 Ningbo

GAMBLE, William, Am. Presby. Mission Press; 1858 Ningbo; 1860 Shanghai; friend of JHT, CIM, received Lammermuir party

GENÄHR, Ferdinand, Rhenish (Barmen) Mission; 1847 Hong Kong, Guangdong (Kwangtung) under C Gutzlaff; m. R Lechler's sister; one of the first Prot. missionaries to reside outside treaty ports; d. 1864

GENGHIS KHAN (1162–1227); Mongol conqueror of N. China, W. Russia, Central Asia, NW India to Adriatic; military genius

GLADSTONE, William Ewart (1809–98); three times prime minister, 1868–97

GOBLE, Jonathan, Am. marine under Commodore Perry, to Japan as missionary; 1870 invented rickshaw

GODDARD, Josiah, Am. Baptist, Bangkok; 1848 Ningbo

GORDON, Lt. Col. Charles George (1833–85); 1860 Tianjin, Peking campaign; 1862 Shanghai, commanding Ever-Victorious Army; 1864 Taiping Rebellion ended; honoured by emperor and Queen Victoria (CB); 1865–71 London; donor to JHT; 1880 adviser to Chinese govt.; 1883–85 Major-Gen., Sudan

GOSSE, Philip Henry (1810–88); naturalist, author; 1855–66 *Manual of Marine Zoology*; 1860–62 *Romance of Natural History*; through W T Berger joined Hackney Brethren; early donor to CIM

GOSSE, Sir Edmund Wm (1845–1928) (aged 15–20 while JHT at Mile End); 1867–75 asst. librarian British Museum; poet and critic; 1904–10 librarian, House of Lords; author, histories of literature, and *Father and Son*, biographical

GOUGH, Frederick Foster (DD), CMS 1849–62 Ningbo; 1862–69 London, Ningbo vernacular romanised NT revision with JHT; 1866 m. Mary Jones (qv); 1869 Ningbo

GOUGH, Mary (Ellen) daughter of FFG and first wife

GOUGH, Mrs Mary, first wife of FFG, d. 1861

GRANT, General Sir Hope, 1860 commander, land forces, under Lord Elgin

GROS, Baron, 1860 French plenipotentiary, second opium war, Peking treaty, plundered Summer Palace

GROVES, Anthony Norris, (1795–1853); early exponent of 'faith principle'; brother-in-law of G Müller; missionary to Baghdad; initiator of Brethren movement

GUINNESS, H Grattan, DD, FRAS; gentleman-evangelist, 1859 Ulster revival, drew thousands; JHT's friend from 1865; founded East London Institute (Harley College), trained 1,330 for 40 societies of 30 denominations; initiated RBMU; greatly influenced Barnardo; author, astronomy, eschatology

GUINNESS, M Geraldine (1862–1949); daughter of H. Grattan Guinness (qv); m. F Howard Taylor (qv); author, biography of JHT

GUTZLAFF, Agnes, blind Chinese adopted by Mrs Gutzlaff; educated in UK; teacher in Ningbo under Miss Aldersey (qv)

GUTZLAFF, Charles (Karl Frederich August) (1803–51); 1826–28 Netherlands Miss. Soc., Batavia (Jakarta), Java; 1828 independent, Bangkok; 1829 m. Miss Newell, Malacca, first single Prot. woman missionary to E. Asia who d. 1831; 1831–35 voyages up China coast; 1834 m. Miss Warnstall d. 1849; 1839 interpreter to British; 1840 and 1842 governor of Chusan Is.; 1842 interpreter-negotiator, Nanking Treaty; 1843–51 Chinese Sec. to British govt Hong Kong; initiated Chinese Union, Chinese Associations and missions; 1850 m. Miss Gabriel

HALL, Charles J, 1857 CES missionary Ningbo; 1860 Shandong; d. 1861

HALL, William, businessman; deacon, Bryanston Hall, Portman Square; member of first CIM council

HALL, William Nelthorpe, Methodist New Connexion; 1860 Tianjin; d. 1878

HAMBERG, Theodore, Basel Mission; 1847 Hong Kong, under Gutzlaff (qv); with R Lechler (qv) to Guangdong (Kwangtung) Hakkas; first Prot. missionaries to reside outside treaty ports; d. 1854

HANSPACH, August, Chinese Evangelization Soc. of Berlin (Berlin Missionary Soc. for China); 1855 Hong Kong; 11 years extensive inland travel

HAPPER, Andrew P, DD; Am. Presby. 1844 Macao; 1847 Canton

HARDEY, Richard, early photographer, Hull; m. Hannah Hudson, portraitist

HARDEY, Robert, surgeon, Hull Infirmary and medical college; JHT his assistant

HART, Sir Robert, b. 1835; 1854 Ningbo, consular interpreter; 1857 Canton; Nov 1862 Inspector-General, Chinese Imperial Maritime Customs; 1865 Peking

HAVELOCK, Major-General Sir Henry, KCB (1795–1857); hero of Indian mutiny, Cawnpore, Lucknow

HENG QI, Canton customs official; 1860 Chinese government minister, Peking, ordered release of Parkes (qv) Lock (qv) survivors; opened Anding Gate of Peking to Elgin

HILL, David (1840–96); 1864 Wesleyan Meth. Miss. Soc., Hankou with J Cox; 1877–78 famine relief in Shanxi; led Pastor Hsi (qv) to Christ; 1896 d. of typhus while doing famine relief

HOBSON, Dr Benjamin, LMS; 1841 Macao; 1843 Hong Kong: 1846 Canton; 1856 Shanghai

HOBSON, J, CMS, chaplain to Br. community, Shanghai; JHT's friend

HOLLAND, Capt., 1863 Gen. Staveley's chief-of-staff; commanded E-V Army after F T Ward's death (qv); defeated at Taicang

HOLMES, J L, Am. Southern Baptist; 1860 pioneer of Shandong, Yantai (Chefoo); killed

HONG REN, cousin of Hong Xiu-quan; known as Gan Wang, Shield King; ex-evangelist

HONG XIU-QUAN (Hung Hsiu-ch'üan) (1813–64) Taiping Wang, leader of Taiping rebellion; 1837 visions and fantasies; 1844 began preaching; 1846 with Hong Ren (Hung Jen) (qv) taught by I J Roberts (qv); 1849 led Worshippers of Shangdi; 1851 began hostilities; 1852 assumed imperial title; 1853–64 Nanking; 1853 advance to Tianjin halted; 1864 suicide

HOPE, Vice-Admiral Sir James; 1860–62, naval commander-in-chief, China; 1861 negotiated 'year of truce' with Taipings; opened Yangzi River to foreign shipping

HORNE, Mr, leading member of Brethren, Clevedon, Bristol; confidant of JHT

HOWARD, John Eliot (1807–83); quinologist, FRS, Fellow of Linnaean Soc.; manufacturing chemist; early leader of Brethren, Tottenham; member of B&FBS committee and CES Board; JHT's close friend and supporter

HOWARD, Luke, meteorologist, father of John Eliot and Robert

HOWARD, Robert, brother of John Eliot; also chemist, leader of Brethren, on Board of CES; supporter of JHT and CIM

HOWARD, Theodore, b. *c* 1840, son of Robert Howard (qv); Oct 1872 member of first Home Council of CIM; Oct 1875, Chairman; Feb 1879 Home Director; d. 1915

HSI SHENG-MO, *see* Xi; HSÜ KUANG-CH'I *see* Xu; HSIEN FENG *see* Xian.

HUC, Abbé Everiste Régis, travelled with Gabet 1844–46, Mongolia, Tibet; 1846 in Lhasa, deported; 1857 author, *Christianity in China, Tartary and Thibet*; d. 1860

HUDSON, Amelia (1808–81); m. James Taylor; mother of JHT

HUDSON, Benjamin Brook (*c* 1785–1865); Wesleyan Methodist minister; portraitist; grandfather of JHT

HUDSON, T H, General Baptist Mission; 1845 Ningbo; 1850–66 translated NT into *wenli* (literary Chinese)

HUNG HSIU CH'ÜAN, *see* Hong Xiu-quan; HUNG JEN, *see* Hong Ren

HUTCHINSON, Sir Jonathan (1828–1913); 1859 general and ophthalmic surgeon, London Hospital; 1882 FRS; 1889 President RCS; Nov 1908 Knight Bachelor; benefactor of JHT

INNOCENT, John, (1829–1904), Methodist New Connexion evangelist; 1860 Shanghai; 1861 Tianjin with W N Hall (qv); 1864 visited Mongolia

JACKSON, Charles; 1862–79 Anglican Sec. of B&FBS with J Mee (qv); cf John Jackson B&FBS 1823–49

JOHN, Griffith (1831–1912); LMS; 1855 Shanghai; pioneer evangelist; 1861 Hankou; 1863 Wuchang; 1867 Hanyang

JOHNSON, Stevens, Am. Board, Bangkok; 1847 Fuzhou (Foochow)

JONES, John, CES; 1856–57 Ningbo; independent, 1857–63; early exponent of 'faith principle', influenced JHT; d. 1863

JONES, Mary, wife of John; 1863–66 with Hudson Taylors, London; 1866 m. F F Gough

JUDSON, Adoniram (1788–1850); Am. Board, became Baptist; 1813 pioneer with wife in Burma

JUKES, Andrew, East India Co. officer; deacon, Anglican Church; *c* 1842 independent minister, Brethren congregation; 1866 built Church of St John the Evangelist, Hull

JUNG LU, *see* Yong Lu

KANG XI (K'ang Hsi); (1662–1722); 2nd Qing (Ch'ing) dynasty emperor, for 60 years; aged 7 dismissed his regents; one of China's strongest rulers; pro-Christian; 1692 Edict of Toleration; 1700 pro-Jesuit, anti-Rome

KENNEDY, Rev., Congregational minister, Stepney

KEESON, Dr; 1863 Secy. Wesleyan Meth. Miss. Soc.

KINGDON, Edwin Frank, BMS recruit trained by JHT; 1864 Shandong, Yantai

KLOEKERS, Hendrick Z, Netherlands Chinese Evangelization Soc.; 1855–58 Shanghai; 1862 BMS; 1862–65 Shandong, Yantai

KNOWLTON, Miles Justice, ABMU; 1854 Ningbo; friend of JHT

KONG, Prince (Prince Kung); (1833–98); brother of Xian Feng (Hsien Feng) emperor; 1860 *et seq*, leading statesman

KRAPF, Johann Ludwig (1810–81); missionary linguist; 1836 sent by CMS to Ethiopia; 1844 Mombasa; 1853 to Europe

KREYER, Carl T, ABMU; 1866 Hangzhou (Hangchow); lent his home to Lammermuir party

LAGRENÉ, M, French envoy, 1843 treaty; negotiated edicts of toleration by Qi Ying (Ch'i Ying), for Prots. as well as RCs

LANCE, Henry; 1864 minister in Devonshire twenty years; Berger Hall, Bromley-by-Bow

LANDELS, Dr William (1823–99); minister Regent's Park Baptist Chapel

LATOURETTE, Kenneth Scott, late Willis James and Sterling Prof. of Missions and Oriental History, Yale Univ.; author, *see* bibliography

LAUGHTON, Richard Fredk, BMS; 1863 Shandong, Yantai

LAY, George Tradescant, naturalist; 1836–39 agent for Bible Soc. (B&FBS); 1840–42 interpreter, opium war; HBM consul, Canton, Fuzhou (Foochow), Amoy; co-founder of 'Medical Missionary Soc. in China'; d. 1845, Amoy

LAY, Horatio, HBM consul, Fuzhou, Canton; 1866 first Inspector-General, Chinese Maritime Customs; negotiated 'Lay-Osborne fleet'; 1862 dismissed; succeeded by Robert Hart (qv)

LECHLER, Rudolf (1824–1908); Basel Mission pioneer; 1847 Hong Kong Guangdong (Kwangtung) Hakkas, under Gutzlaff, with Hamberg (qv); 52 years in China, to 1899

LEGGE, James, DD, LL D (1815–97); LMS; 1839–43 Anglo-Chinese College, Malacca; 1843–70 Anglo-Chinese College, Hong Kong; translator, Chinese classics; 1877–97, Prof. of Chinese, Oxford Univ.

LEISK, Mary Ann, aged 14 to Ningbo as protégé of M A Aldersey (qv); m. W A Russell; d. 1887

LEWIS, William Garrett, Baptist minister, Westbourne Grove Ch., London; urged JHT to publish *China: Its Spiritual Need and Claims*

LI HONG-ZHANG (Li Hung-chang) (1823–1901); holder of the highest academic degrees, highest honours after defeat of Taiping rebels; the Grand Old Man of China, leading statesman until death

LIANG A-DE (Liang A-teh); son of A-fa; translator to Lin Ze-xu (qv); interpreter for British, Nanking Treaty; Chinese Imperial Maritime Customs

LIANG A-FA (1789–1855); Canton engraver-printer; 1815 to Malacca with W Milne; 1819 Canton, colporteur; arrested, flogged; 1821 Malacca; 1828 Canton; 1834 arrested, escaped, betrayed, escaped; 1839 returned, tolerated by Lin Ze-xu (qv); first Prot. pastor; 1845 mobbed; d. 1855

LIGHT, Francis, captain of merchantman; 1786 occupied Penang Is., founded Georgetown

LIN ZE-XU (Lin Tze-hsü), gov.-gen. of Hubei-Hunan; viceroy-commissioner, Canton, to control opium traffic; 1839 strong-arm methods contributed to war, 1840–41; disgraced, exiled

LISTER, Joseph, Lord, PC, OM, FRS; (1827–1912); father of asepsis and antisepsis, 1895–1900 Pres. Royal Soc.

LIVINGSTONE, David (1813–73); 2 years at Charing Cross hospital; in response to Charles Gutzlaff, 1840 offered to LMS for China; owing to opium war, sent to S. Africa; 1841–52 southern travels, Lake Ngami, Zambesi; 1852–56 trans-African exploration; 1858–63 leading expeditions; 1866–71 liberator of slaves; d. 1 May 1873

LOBSCHEID, Wilhelm, Rhenish (Barmen) Mission to China; Guangdong (Kwangtung); 1852 CES, resigned 1856; 1855 interpreter, *Powhattan* voyage to Japan

LOCK, Sir Henry, 1860 private secretary to Lord Elgin (qv); with Parkes (qv) prisoner; historian of second opium war; 1889–95 Governor of the Cape, S. Africa

LOCKHART, William (1811–96); surgeon, FRCS; LMS; 1839 Macao; 1840 and 1843 Shanghai; 1840–41 Chusan with Gutzlaff, first British missionary Hong Kong; 1848 mobbed in 'Qingpu (Tsingpu) Outrage', Shanghai; 1861 first Prot. missionary in Peking

LORD, Edward C, ABMU; 1847 first Am. Baptist, Ningbo; 1863 independent Am. Bapt Mission, Ningbo; 1877 still there; US consul; JHT's friend

LORD, Mrs (1) d. Jan 1860; (2) Jemima (Bausum) m. 1861

LOVE, Capt. John, laird of Knowes, father of Mrs J L Stevenson

LOWE, Lieut-Gen. Sir Hudson (1769–1844); 1814 knighted; 1815 Governor of St Helena, custodian of Napoleon; daughter, Clara M S Lowe

LOWRIE, Reuben, (Robert, in some sources) took brother's place; 1854 Shanghai

LOWRIE, Walter, US senator, resigned to become Sec. of Am. Presby. Mission

LOWRIE, Walter M. (William in some sources), son of senator; 1845 Am. Presby. Mission, Ningbo; 1847 drowned by pirates

MACARTNEY, Lord, 1793 embassy to Peking, failed

MACGOWAN, Dr D J, Am. Baptist physician; 1843 Ningbo

MACKAY, George Leslie (1844–1901); first Canadian Presby. missionary to China; 1872 N. Taiwan; 60 churches at his death; founded Taiwan Theol. College; 1894 Moderator of Can. Presby. Church

MACKINTOSH, William, with J Fraser (qv) initiator of FES; missionary to Cairo

MAGRATH, Miss, CES missionary; 1857 arrived in Shanghai, Ningbo; soon independent, Hong Kong

MAIN, Dr Duncan; 1881 CMS Hangzhou; developed a large hospital and medical school; 1892 leprosarium

MARA, John, United Meth. Free Ch.; trained by JHT; 1865 Ningbo

MARSHALL, Thomas D, minister, Bryanston Hall, Portman Square

MARSHMAN, Joshua (1768–1837); 1799 with Carey, Serampore; 1811 completed Chinese NT; 1822–23 OT

MARTIN, William Alexander Parsons, DD, LL D; (1827–1916); Am. Presby. Mission; educationalist; 1850–60 Ningbo; 1862 Peking; 1869 president, Tongwen Imperial College; 57 years in China; book on Christian evidences had huge circulation, China, Japan

MARTYN, Henry (1781–1812); 1801 Senior Wrangler, Fellow of St John's, Camb.; 1806 Calcutta; 1810 completed Hindustani (Urdu) NT; 1811 Shiraz, Persia; 1815–16 Martyn's Persian NT published

MATEER, Calvin Wilson (1836–1908); Am. Presby., educationalist; 1864 Dengzhou, Shandong; founded Shandong Christian Univ.; opponent of J L Nevius' methods

MATHESON, Donald, merchant partner, Jardine, Matheson; 1837 Hong Kong; converted, resigned 1849 over opium traffic; active in Presby. Missions; 1892 chairman, Soc. for the Suppression of the Opium Trade

MATHIESON, James E, gentleman-evangelist in 19th-century revivals; active in anti-opium campaign (*see* Maxwell)

MAXWELL, James L, MD; b. 1836; English Presby. Mission; 1863 Amoy; 1865 pioneer, Takao, Taiwan; 1885 founder, Medical Missionary Association (London); 1888 co-founder with B Broomhall (qv), 'Christian Union for the Severance of the Connection of the British Empire with the Opium Traffic'

McCARTEE, Dr D B, MD; Am. Presby.; 1844 Ningbo; adopted orphan who became first Chinese woman doctor educated in US

McCLATCHIE, Thomas; CMS; 1845 Shanghai with George Smith (qv)

MEADOWS, James J (1835–1914); JHT's first recruit to Ningbo Mission, 1862, and CIM; wife Martha d. 1863

MEADOWS, Thomas Taylor, heroic interpreter; HBM vice-consul, Ningbo; certified JHT's marriage

MEDHURST, Sir Walter Henry, son of W H Medhurst DD; HBM consul, and ambassador, Peking

MEDHURST, Walter Henry, DD (1796–1857); LMS printer; 1817–20 Malacca; 1820–21 Penang; 1822–43 Batavia, Java; 1826 toured Chinese settlements on Java coast; 1835 voyage of *Huron* up China coast; 1843 Shanghai, interpreter-adviser to Br. consul G Balfour (qv); 1845 inland journey in disguise; 1848 victim of 'Qingpu (Tsingpu) Outrage', Shanghai; translator, Delegates' Committee, 1852 Chinese Bible; doyen of Br. community

MEE, John, 1858–61 Anglican Secretary of B&FBS, with S B Bergne

MÉRITENS, Baron de, with Abbé Delamarre (qv) interpreter to Baron Gros (qv) 1860

MEZZABARBA, 1720 papal legate after Mgr de Tournon; concessions on Chinese rites repudiated by Rome

MILNE, William, DD (1785–1822); 1813 Macao; 1815–22 Malacca; 1818 Anglo-Chinese College, Malacca; Hon. DD Glasgow; baptised Liang A-fa (qv); 1822 completed OT translation with R Morrison

MILNE, William C, son of William and Rachel Milne; 1842 Chusan Is.; 1842–43 Ningbo; 1846 Shanghai; 1857 travelling sec., Chinese Evang. Soc.

MOFFAT, Robert (1795–1883); LMS; 1817 S. Africa, 50 years; close friend of Matabele chief; 'apostle of Bechuanaland'; initiated Botswana Church; daughter married D Livingstone

MORGAN, Richard Cope (1827–1908); editor, *The Revival* (*The Christian*); chairman, Marshall, Morgan & Scott; co-founder, Foreign Evangelist Soc.

MORRISON, John Robert (1814–43); son of R Morrison; aged 16 official translator, East India Co.; Canton; 1842 interpreter-negotiator to Sir H Pottinger, Treaty of Nanking; 1843 Chinese Sec. to Gov. of Hong Kong; chairman, first LMS and General Missions Conferences, Hong Kong

MORRISON, Robert, DD, FRS (1782–1834); LMS; 1807 Macao, Canton; 1813 completed Chinese NT; 1814 first convert; 1816 interpreter-negotiator to Lord Amherst embassy; 1817 Hon. DD Glas.; 1819 completed OT with Milne (qv); 1822 completed Chinese dictionary; 1824 FRS etc.; 1834 interpreter to Lord Napier; d. Aug 1

MOSELEY, William, LL D; Congregational Minister; 1798 found in British Museum MS of RC Chinese translation of NT books; urged translation of whole NT; introduced R Morrison to LMS and to Dr Bogue (qv)

MOULE, Arthur Evans, CMS; 1861 Ningbo; 1876 Hangzhou (Hangchow); archdeacon

MOULE, George Evans, CMS; 1858 Ningbo; 1864 Hangzhou (Hangchow); 1880 Bishop in Mid-China

MOULE, Henry, Anglican minister; father of Handley, Bishop of Durham; George (qv) Bishop in Mid-China; and Arthur (qv) archdeacon, Ningbo

MOULY, Mgr Joseph Martial, Lazarist; 1841 vicar-apostolic, Mongolia &c; sent Abbé Huc and Gabet on Tibet journey; 1853 deported; 1856 vicar-apostolic N. Zhili (Chihli) (Peking); 1861 obtained territorial concessions for RC Church

MUIRHEAD, William, DD (1822–1900); LMS; evangelist, renowned preacher, translator; 1846–90 (53 years) at Shanghai; 1848 victim of 'Qingpu (Tsingpu) Outrage', Shanghai

MÜLLER, George (1805–98); German-born; married sister of A N Groves (qv); 1832 read biography of A H Francke; 1835 founded Orphan Homes, Bristol, 2,000 children, financed 'by faith in God'

NAPIER, Lord, 1834, William IV's envoy to China; Chief Supt of Br. Trade; d. 1834

NAPOLEON I, Bonaparte (1769–1821); 1799 proclaimed himself First Consul of France; 1804 Emperor; 1805 virtually dictator of Europe; 1814 abdicated, sent to Elba; 1815 escaped; 18 June 1815 Waterloo; exiled to St Helena

NAPOLEON III, Louis (1808–73); 1848 made Pres. of French Republic; 1852 *coup d'état*, made Emperor; 1870 Franco-Prussian war wrecked second empire; died at Chislehurst, England

NEILL, Stephen C, b. 31 Dec. 1899; Fellow of Trinity College, Cambridge; CMS missionary in S. India; Anglican Bishop of Tinnevelly (120,000 members); co-negotiator of Church of South India; professor of missions

NESTORIUS, bishop of Constantinople until Council of Ephesus, AD 431; d. 451; Nestorianism extended to Syria, Persia, India; AD 635 to China (*see* Alopen); Nestorian monument erected 781, discovered 1625 near Xi'an (Sian)

NEVIUS, John Livingston (1832–93); Am. Presby. Mission; 1854 Ningbo; 1859 Hangzhou (Hangchow); 1860 Japan; 1861 Shandong (Shantung); Bible translator, author; 1890 Korea, exponent of 'indigenous church' policy

NEWTON, B W, dominant leader of Plymouth Brethren, at first with Darby (qv);

'Bethesda controversy' was over views propounded by Newton

NI YONG-FA; 1857, leader of reformed Buddhist sect shunning idolatry; JHT's convert and first baptised at Ningbo; became preacher

NOEL, Rev. and Hon. Baptist; Anglican clergyman; 1848 became Baptist; revivalist, 21 Sept 1859 drew 20,000 at Armagh

NOMMENSON, Ludwig Ingwer, Rhenish (Barmen) Mission; 1862 pioneer of Bataks, Sumatra, after Lyman and Munson were martyred

NORRIS, Sir William, Chief Justice, High Court, Straits Settlements; friend of Dyers (qv)

NORTH, Brownlow, b. 1809, grandson of bishop successively of Lichfield, Worcester, Winchester, whose brother, Lord North, was Prime Minister to George III; roué, converted aged 45, studied Bible and prayed for two months, then began as evangelist; Free Church of Scotland; drew thousands

NOTMAN, Jean, recruit sent by JHT to Ningbo, 1864; assistant to Mrs Bausum (qv)

OLYPHANT, D W C, Am. Presby. merchant ship-owner, partner of C W King; 1826 Canton, donated press and office for *Chinese Repository*; donated 51 trans-Pacific passages for missionaries; d. 1851

PALMERSTON, Viscount (1784–1865); Tory Whig statesman, 1808–65; 1830–51 periodically Foreign Sec.; 1855, 1859–65 Prime Minister

PARKER, Dr John, brother of Dr Wm Parker; 1863 Ningbo, independent; 1865 United Presby. Ch of Scotland, Ningbo

PARKER, Dr Peter, MD; (1804–88); Am. Board (ABCFM); 1834 Canton; first medical missionary in China (not first western physician); 1835 Ophthalmic Hospital; 1838 formed 'Medical Missionary Soc. in China'; 1843–44, semi-skilled interpreter-negotiator for US treaty; 1850 General Hosp, Canton; several times US chargé d'affaires and minister

PARKER, Dr William, CES 1854–61; Shanghai, Ningbo; d. 1863

PARKER, H M Am. Episc.; Shangdong (Shantung); 1861 martyred, Yantai (Chefoo)

PARKER, Mrs Wm (1) d. 26 Aug. 1859 of cholera; (2) m. 1861; 1862 with Dr Parker (qv) to Ningbo; widowed 1 Feb 1863

PARKES, Sir Harry S.; *c* 1850 HBM interpreter; 1860 hero of Tianjin-Peking campaign; 1856 vice-consul Canton; 20 May 1862 knighted KCB; HBM minister, Peking; 30 Nov 1881 GCMG

PARNELL, J V (*see* CONGLETON)

PASTEUR, Louis (1822–95); French scientist; identified and designed measures against bacteria, applied by Lister (qv); developed immunisation against rabies, &c

PATON, John Gibson (1824–1907); 1847–56 Glasgow city missionary; 1858 Tanna, New Hebrides; 1864 Moderator of Reformed Presby. Church; 1866–81 Aniwa, New Hebrides, S. Pacific

PEARCY, George, Am. Southern Bapt, Shanghai; cholera at Shanghai, nursed by JHT

PEARSE, George, London stockbroker; CES foreign sec.; co-founder Foreign Evangelist Soc.; friend and adviser of JHT's; later missionary to N. Africa, initiated N. Africa Mission

PENNEFATHER, William (1816–73), vicar, Christ Church, Barnet; 1864 St Jude's Mildmay, N. London; convener, Barnet and Mildmay conferences; deaconess school; hymn-writer, friend of JHT

PERRY, Commodore, 1853–54 Am. treaty with Japan

PIERCY, George, 1850 to China at own expense; 1851 Canton; 1853 adopted by Wesleyan Meth. Miss. Soc.; joined by Josiah Cox (qv)

PIERSON, A T, American church and missions leader; biographer of G Müller; friend of JHT and CIM

POTT, F L Hawks, DD; Am. Prot. Episc.; president, St John's Univ., Shanghai; historian of Shanghai

POTTER, Miss, CIM recruit, met JHT at Brighton, 25 June 1865

POTTIER, François, founder 1756, West China mission of Soc. des Missions Étrangères de Paris

POTTINGER, Sir Henry, 1841 HBM plenipotentiary, Supt of Trade, succeeded Capt. Charles Elliot; concluded first opium war; 1842 'diplomatic honeymoon' with Qi Ying (qv), negotiated Nanking Treaty

PRESTON, John, Wesleyan Meth. Miss. Soc.; 1855 Canton

QIAN LONG (Ch'ien Lung) (1736–96); 4th emperor, Qing (Ch'ing) dynasty

QI SHAN (Ch'i Shan), 1840 gov. of Zhili (Chihli); viceroy of Canton after Lin Ze-xu (qv); cashiered, exiled, after Convention of Quanbi (Ch'üanpi)

QI YING, 1842 succeeded Qi Shan; initiated 'diplomatic honeymoon', negotiated Nanking Treaty; gov. of Canton; issued edict of toleration

QUARTERMAN, J W, Am. Presby.; 1847–57 Ningbo; smallpox, nursed by JHT; d. 1857

RADCLIFFE, Reginald, b. 1825, solicitor, gentleman-evangelist of second evangelical awakening; imprisoned for preaching in open air; 1860–61 London, inspired Wm Booth and Barnardo; friend of JHT

RADSTOCK, Dowager Lady; mother of Lord Radstock (qv), Lady Beauchamp (qv), Hon. Miss Waldegrave (qv); Welbeck St Brethren; friend and supporter of JHT

RADSTOCK, Lord; Hon. Granville A Wm Waldegrave (1833–1913); 3rd Baron; Anglican evangelist in aristocratic Russian, E. European society; closely associated with Brethren; friend of JHT and CIM

RAFFLES, Sir Thomas Stamford (1781–1826); 1805 Penang; 1811–16 lieut-gov., Java; 1817 knighted; 1817 *et seq* gov. of Sumatra; 1819 founded Singapore; 1820–24 gov. Singapore and Bencoolen, Sumatra

RANKIN, Henry V, Am. Presby.; 1847 Ningbo; co-translator of Ningbo vernacular NT

REED, Henry; Tasmanian gentleman-evangelist, influenced JHT *aet* 14; donated £20,000 to build Mildmay Conference hall; £5,000 to Wm Booth personal endowment

REED, Hon. W B, US ambassador, Peking, 1858–60

RICCI, Matteo/Matthew (1552–1610); Soc. of Jesus; 1582 Macao; 1585–89 Zhaoqing, Zhaozhou (Chaoch'ing, Chaochow); 1601 Peking; by 1605 had converts at Court and Hanlin Academy, 200 neophytes; enjoyed confidence of Kang Xi (K'ang Hsi); policies repudiated by papacy

RICHARD, Timothy (1845–1919); missionary educationalist; 1859 convert of Welsh revival; offered services to JHT, referred to BMS; 1870 Shandong; 1876–79 famine relief, founded Univ. of Shanxi, Taiyuan and Christian Literature Soc.; his policies akin to the techniques of Ricci (qv); adviser to emperor and Chinese govt; received two of the highest honours of the empire

RIPON, Bishop of (*see* Bickersteth)

ROBERTS, Issacher Jacocks, (not RJR as in some sources); Am. Bapt; 1833–67

Canton, Shanghai, 1837 Canton, taught Hong Xiu-quan (qv), Taiping leader; 1842 first missionary in Hong Kong, with J L Shuck

RUSSELL, Lord John (1792–1878); 1st earl; 1832 Reform Bill; 1846, 1865–66 Prime Minister

RUSSELL, William Armstrong, CMS; 1847 Ningbo; 1872–79 first bishop in N. China; d. 1879

RUTHERFORD, Samuel (1600–61); Scottish divine; prof. of divinity, St Andrews Univ.

SCHALL von BELL, Johann Adam (1591–1666); Soc. of Jesus; astronomer; 1622 Peking; 1645 president, Imperial Board of Astronomers; 'chaplain' to imperial palace

SCHERESCHEWSKY, Samuel Isaac Joseph (1831–1906); converted rabbi; Am. Prot Episc.; 1859 Shanghai; 1862 Peking; 1877 bishop; 1881 paralysed; for next 25 years China's greatest Bible translator

SCHMIDT, Charles, 1864 officer of Ever-Victorious Army, converted through James Meadows (qv); became missionary in Suzhou; friend of JHT

SEYMOUR, Admiral Sir Michael, commander-in-chief, East Asia; 1856 blockaded, bombarded, occupied Canton; deported viceroy, Ye Ming-sheng (qv)

SHAFTESBURY, Lord; Anthony Ashley-Cooper, 7th earl (1801–85); evangelical philanthropist

SHUN ZHI (Shun Chih), first Qing (Ch'ing) dynasty emperor, 1644–61

SIMPSON, Sir James Young, Bart FRS (1811–70); Scottish surgeon, established chloroform anaesthesia; evangelical Christian

SISSONS, Elizabeth, rejected JHT's proposals

SKINNER, Anne, fiancée of George Crombie (qv); 1865 Ningbo

SMITH, George, CMS; China survey, 1844; 1846 returned with T McClatchie (qv); 1849–64 first Bishop of Victoria, Hong Kong

SOLTAU, Henry W, barrister, Plymouth and Exeter Brethren; sons George, Henry, daughter Henrietta, son-in-law Richard Hill all served in CIM

SOOTHILL, W E; United Methodist Free Church, Ningbo, Wenzhou; educationalist, author, translator; 1920–35 Prof. of Chinese, Oxford Univ.

SPITTLER, C F (and son) founded St Chrischona Pilgrim Mission; influenced formation of Foreign Evangelist Soc.; many St Chrischona missionaries in CIM during 19th and 20th centuries

SPURGEON, Charles Haddon (1834–92); renowned Baptist preacher, Metropolitan Tabernacle; lifelong friend of JHT

STACEY, Miss, one-time Quaker, member of Brook Street chapel, Tottenham; long a friend of JHT

STAVELEY, Sir Charles, 1862 commander, British land forces, China

STEVENSON, John Whiteford (1844–1918); son of laird of Thriepwood, Renfrewshire; with G Stott (qv) first of CIM after Crombie (qv); Oct 1865 dep. UK; 1866–74 Ningbo, Shaoxing (Shaohsing); 1875–80 Burma; 1880 crossed China W. to E. 1,900 miles; 1885–1916 deputy director, CIM

STOCK, Eugene (1836–1928); CMS Editor 1875–1906; historian

STOTT, George, Aberdeenshire schoolmaster, one-leg; 3 Oct. 1865 dep. UK; 1866 Ningbo; 1869–89 Wenzhou (Wenchow); d. 1889

STRONACH, Alexander, LMS; 1838–39 Singapore; 1839–44 Penang; 1844–46 Singapore; 1846 Amoy

STRONACH, John, LMS, 1838–76, 30 years without furlough; 1838–44 Singapore; 1846 Amoy; Bible translator, Delegates' Committee, 1852; S Dyer's friend

SUN YAT-SEN (1867–1925); 1891 first medical graduate, Hong Kong; 1905 founded China Revolutionary League, in Europe, Japan; 1911–12 founder and first president Republic of China; m. descendant of Paul Xu (*see* Soong).

SU SHUN, Grand Secretary, extortionist, conspirator with Cai Yuan (qv) and Prince Cheng (qv) in Jehol plot

TAIT, Archibald Campbell (1811–82); headmaster of Rugby; 1856 Bishop of London; 1869 Archbishop of Canterbury

TAO KUANG (*see* Dao Guang)

TARN, Joseph, son of William Tarn Sr (qv), cousin of Maria Taylor

TARN, William Jr, son of William Sr (qv); cousin of Maria Taylor; Secretary, RTS

TARN, William Sr, brother of Samuel Dyer Sr's wife; director, LMS; guardian of Burella and Maria Dyer (qv)

TAYLOR, Amelia (1808–81); first daughter of Benjamin Brook Hudson; JHT's mother

TAYLOR, Amelia Hudson (1835–1918); JHT's sister

TAYLOR, Arthur, CES missionary, Hong Kong, 1853–55

TAYLOR, Frederick Howard (1862–1946); second son of JHT and Maria Jane Dyer; 1888 MD (Lond.); 1889 MRCP; FRCS (Eng.); m. M Geraldine Guinness; CIM missionary, biographer of JHT

TAYLOR, James Hudson (21 May 1832–3 June 1905); 1853 dep. UK; 1 Mar 1854 arr. Shanghai; 20 Jan 1858 m. Maria Jane Dyer; 1857 with J Jones (qv) began Ningbo Mission; June 1865 founded China Inland Mission; 28 Nov 1871 m. Jane E Faulding; 3 June 1905 d. Changsha, Hunan

TAYLOR, James Jr (1807–81); JHT's father

TAYLOR, James Sr (1749–95); host to J Wesley

TAYLOR, John (1778–1834); 1799 m. Mary Shepherd (*see* Wm. Shepherd)

TAYLOR, Louisa Shepherd, b. 1840, second daughter of James Taylor (qv) and Amelia Hudson

TAYLOR, Maria Jane, née Dyer (1837–70); daughter of Samuel Dyer (qv); wife of JHT; mother of Grace, Herbert Hudson, Frederick Howard, Samuel, Jane, Maria, Charles, Noel

TAYLOR, M Geraldine (*see* Guinness)

THOMAS, R J, LMS, 1865 distributed scripture for Nat. Bible Soc. of Scotland for 2½ months on Korean coast; 1866 again, killed

TIDMAN, Dr Arthur; Foreign Sec., LMS; member CES General Committee

TONG ZHI (T'ung Chih) (1856–75); 1862 succeeded Xian Feng emperor

TRESTRAIL, Frederick, BMS Secretary with E B Underhill (qv)

TRUELOVE, Richard, 1865 recruit for Ningbo, failed to go

TSENG KUO-FAN (*see* Zeng); TZ'U HSI (*see* Ci Xi)

TSO TSUNG-T'ANG (*see* Zuo)

UNDERHILL, C B, Sec. BMS; friend of JHT, nominated him for FRGS

VALENTINE, Jarvis Downman, CMS recruit taught by JHT; 1864 Ningbo; 1870 Shaoxing; d. 1889

VALIGNANO, Allesandri (1537–1606); 1579 Jesuit Visitor to Japan

van SOMMER, J, member, Hackney Brethren circle with W T Berger (qv) (brother-in-law) and Philip H Gosse (qv); editor, *The Missionary Reporter*

VAUGHAN, Marianne, first fiancée of JHT

VENIAMINOV, John (Innokenty) (1797–1879); Russian Orthodox pioneer, Aleutians, Kuriles, N. Siberia, Manchuria, Japan; Metropolitan of Moscow; founded Orthodox Missionary Soc.

VENN, Henry, Sr and Jr, secretaries of CMS (*see* HTCOC Book 1 p 386)
VENN, John, member of Eclectic Society (Clapham Sect); father of Henry, Sr
VERBIEST, Ferdinand (1617–88), Jesuit astronomer, Peking
VIGEON, James and Mrs, 1865 recruits for Ningbo, prevented from going
VOGEL, Karl, Kassel Miss. Assoc.; 1847 Hong Kong, Guangdong (Kwangtung); Gutzlaff's recruit
WADE, Lieut Thomas Francis, British forces, Ningbo, 1841; vice-consul Shanghai under Alcock; Battle of Muddy Flat; became Sinologue, HBM minister, Peking, knighted
WALDEGRAVE, Hon. Miss, daughter of Dowager Lady Radstock (qv); supported CIM
WANG GUO-YAO, 1864 peasant convert, irrepressible evangelist, village pastor
WANG LAE-DJÜN (Wang Li-jun), Ningbo Mission convert; with JHT London, 1860–64; pastor, Hangzhou (Hangchow)
WARD, Col Frederick Townsend, Am. commander, Ever-Victorious Army; 1862 mortally wounded at Cixi (Tzeki), Ningbo
WARD, Hon. John E, 1859 US plenipotentiary; 1860 at capture and Convention of Peking
WAY, R Q, Am. Presby.; 1844 Ningbo; brother-in-law of J W Quarterman (qv)
WELLS WILLIAMS, Samuel, DD (1812–84); Am. Board, printer, scholar; 1833 Canton; 1847 author *The Middle Kingdom*; 1851 succeeded E C Bridgman (qv) editor, *Chinese Repository*; interpreter to US legation, Peking; chargé d'affaires to 1876; Prof. of Chinese, Yale Univ.
WELTON, Dr W, CMS; first medical, Fuzhou (Foochow)
WENTWORTH, Dr E; Fuzhou missionary; 1858 appealed for missionaries and for comity partition of China between missions
WHITWORTH, John, architect friend of JHT from youth
WILLIAMS, Sir George (1821–1905) of Hitchcock, Williams & Co., St Paul's; 1844 founded Young Men's Christian Assn
WILLIAMSON, Alexander, LL D (1829–90); 1855 LMS Shanghai; 1863 National Bible Soc. of Scotland, Shandong, Yantai; 1865 Peking, Mongolia, Manchuria; 1887 founded Christian Literature Soc.
WILSON, James; 1864 recruited by JHT; joined Presby. Mission Soc.
WILSON, Robert, MD: 1861 LMS, Hankou with Griffith John
WINNES, Ph., Basel Mission; 1852 joined Theodore Hamberg (qv), Guangdong (Kwangtung) after R Lechler died
WYLIE, Alexander (1815–87); LMS; 1847 Shanghai, printer, Delegates' version of Bible; 1863 Bible Soc. (B&FBS); one of the greatest Sinologues
XAVIER, Francis (1506–52); Basque co-founder with Ignatius Loyola of Jesuit order; 1542 India; 1549 Japan; 1552 d. Shangquan (Shangch'üan) Is., near Macao
XI LIAO-ZHU (Hsi Liao-chu, Hsi Sheng-mo) (1835–96); graduate (Xiu-cai) of Shanxi (Shansi); 1879 converted through David Hill; hymnwriter, well-known as 'Pastor Hsi'
XIAN FENG (Hsien Feng) 7th Qing (Ch'ing) dynasty emperor (1851–61)
XU GUANG-QI (Hsü Kuang-ch'i); Ming dynasty official; convert of Matthew Ricci before 1610; 1850 his family home Xu Jia Hui (Siccawei) became Jesuit headquarters, near Shanghai
YE MING-SHENG (Yeh Ming-shen), imperial commissioner and viceroy, Canton; 1856–57 *Arrow* incident and Br. attack on Canton, captured, d. Calcutta

YEHONALA, *see* Ci Xi

YI, Concubine (*see* Ci Xi)

YONG LU (Jung Lu), imperial bannerman (equiv. Brigade of Guards); perhaps father of Yehonala's son Tong Zhi (T'ung Chih), emperor; long-time adviser to Ci Xi, Empress Dowager

YOUNG, Miss, sister of Mrs John Jones (qv)

ZENG GUO-FAN (Tseng Kuo-fan) (1811–72); scholar, provincial governor; 1854 defeated Taipings; viceroy of the 'Two Jiangs' (Jiangxi, Jiangsu), then of Zhili (Chihli)

ZHU JIU-DAO (Chu Chiu-tao), Taiping rebel leader; planned anti-Manchu, pro-Ming revolt; joined Hong Xiu-quan (qv) to wage Taiping rebellion

ZHONG WANG (Chung Wang), Taiping 'Loyal Prince'; military strategist, commander in final successes, 1863–64, before defeat ending rebellion

ZUO ZONG-TANG (Tso Tsung-t'ang), native of Hunan; successful imperial general vs Taipings in S. China; 1860s built naval dockyard at Fuzhou; 1870 appointed to suppress Muslim rebellion in NW, completed 17 Dec 1877 at fall of Kashgar

BIBLIOGRAPHY

	British Library ref.
B&F Bible Society, *Monthly Reporter*, Vols 1, 2;	P.P.926f
History of the B&FBS, Vols 1, 2	3129.e.76
BENTLEY-TAYLOR, David, *Java Saga: Christian Progress in Muslim Java* (*The Weathercock's Reward*), CIM/OMF Books 1967/75; *My Love must Wait*, Hodder & Stoughton	
BERESFORD, C W D, *The Break-up of China*, 1899	8022.dd.32
BOONE, M Muriel, *The Seed of the Church in China*, St Andrew Press, Edinburgh	
BREDON, Juliet, *Sir Robert Hart*, Hutchinson & Co, 1909	010817.de.10
BRIDGMAN, Mrs E J G, *The Life and Labors of Elijah Coleman Bridgman*, 1864	
BRIDGMAN, Elijah C and Eliza J G, *The Pioneer of American Missions in China*, 1864	4985.aaa.27
BRINE, Lindesay, *The Taeping Rebellion*, 1862	9056.b.10
BROOMHALL, Benjamin, *The Evangelization of the World*, CIM 1889	
BROOMHALL, Marshall, *Heirs Together: A Memoir of Benjamin & Amelia Broomhall* Morgan & Scott/ CIM 1918	4908.e.6
John W. Stevenson: One of Christ's Stalwarts Morgan & Scott/CIM 1919	4956.aa.33
Hudson Taylor: The Man who Dared, Religious Tract Society/CIM	4907.aa.34
Hudson Taylor: The Man who Believed God, Hodder & Stoughton, 1929	4907.dd.21
Robert Morrison: A Master-builder, CIM 1924	4908.ee.24
The Jubilee Story of the China Inland Mission, Morgan & Scott/CIM, 1915	4763.g.4
Hudson Taylor's Legacy, Hodder & Stoughton, 1931	10823.a.16
By Love Compelled: The Call of the China Inland Mission, CIM 1947, (H&S 1936)	4768.a.34
The Chinese Empire: A General & Missionary Survey, Morgan & Scott/CIM 1907	4767.eeee.4
BRYANT, Sir Arthur, *A Thousand Years of the British Monarchy*, Collins	
BURNS, Islay, *Memoir of the Rev. William Chalmers Burns*, London, 1885	
CARY-ELWES, Columba, *China and the Cross*, Longman, Green & Co, 1957	4768.ccc.21

CHINA MAIL, (Hong Kong) British Library, Colindale

CHINA'S MILLIONS, Magazine of the China Inland Mission, 1875–1951

Chinese Evangelization Society, *REPORT*, 1853

CHINESE RECORDER AND MISSIONARY JOURNAL: Vol 1, 1868 et seq

CLARK-KENNEDY, A E, '*The London' (Hospital)*, 2 vols

CMS, *CM Gleaner, Intelligencer, Register, Reports*, Church Missionary Society

COAD, F Roy, *A History of the Brethren Movement*, The Paternoster Press, 1968

COLLIER, Richard, *William Booth: The General Next to God*, Collins, 1965 X.100.1629

COLLIS, Maurice Stewart, *Foreign Mud*, 1946 9059.df.15

CORDIER, Henri, *The Life of Alexander Wylie*, 1887 10803.cc.4/6

COVELL, Ralph, *W.A.P. Martin, Pioneer of Progress in China*, Wm B Eerdmans Publishing Company, 1978

DAVIES, Evan, *China and her Spiritual Claims*, John Snow, 1845 1369.b.24

Memoir of the Reverend Samuel Dyer, John Snow, 1846 1372:c:20

DYSON, Verne, *A Hong Kong Governor: Sir John Bowring*, Macao, 1930 010822.df.39

EAMES, James Bromby, *The English in China*, 1909 09008.f.19

FAIRBANK, John King, *Trade and Diplomacy on the China Coast*, 2 vols, 1953 edn, Cambridge, Massachusetts Ac.2692.10

FORBES, Archibald, *Chinese Gordon*, George Routledge & Sons, 1884

FOREIGN OFFICE LIBRARY, Public Records Office, *A Century of Diplomatic Blue Books*, China FO/17

GLEANER, CES, *The Gleaner in the Missionary Field*, *The Chinese & General Missionary Gleaner*, *The Chinese Missionary Gleaner*, Chinese Evangelization Society, 1850–60

GROVES, Mrs, *Memoir of the late Anthony Norris Groves*, 2nd edn, 1857

GUTZLAFF, Charles, *A Journal of Three Voyages along the Coast of China in 1831, 1832 & 1833 with notices of Siam, Corea and the Loochoo Islands*, 1833 1046.c.16

Report of Proceedings on a Voyage to the Northern Ports of China (*see* LINDSAY, H H), 1833 1046.c.15

HACKNEY GAZETTE, *North London: Historical Associations*, 1928

HALDANE, Charlotte, *The Last Great Empress of China*, Constable, 1965

HART, Sir Robert, *These from the Land of Sinim* 8022.cc.48/01 and 0817.d.10

HOLT, Edgar C, *The Opium Wars in China*, 1964 edn. X.709–581

HOOK, Brian, *China's Three Thousand Years*: Part 4, The Modern History of China, *The Times* Newspaper (publishers)

HUC, Evariste Régis, *Christianity in China, Tartary and Thibet*, 1857 — 2208.bb.8

Life and Travel in Tartary, Thibet and China, 1867 — 10057.aa.39

HUGGETT, Frank E, *Victorian England as seen by PUNCH*, Sidgwick & Jackson, 1978

INGLIS, Brian, *The Opium War*, Hodder & Stoughton, 1976 — 09059.pp.30

KNOLLYS, Sir Henry, *Incidents in the China War, 1860*, 1875 — 9056.bb.19

English Life in China, 1885 — 10058.e.31

LATOURETTE, Kenneth Scott, *A History of Christian Missions in China*, SPCK, 1929 — 4763.g.4

A History of the Expansion of Christianity 1800–1914, Eyre and Spottiswoode — 4533.ff.22

These Sought a Country: Tipple Lectures, 1950 edn, Harper & Brothers — 4807.e.25

LEGGE, Helen E., *James Legge (1815–97)*, Religious Tract Society, 1905 — 04429.1.37

LINTON, E Lynn, *A Night in a Hospital*, (from magazine *Belgravia*), 1879

LITTLE, Mrs Archibald, *Li Hung-chang, His Life and Times*, Cassell & Co Ltd, 1903

LOCKHART, William, *The Medical Missionary in China*, 1861 edn — 10058.d.16

LYALL, L T, *A Passion for the Impossible*, Hodder & Stoughton, 1965; OMF Books, 1976

MacGILLIVRAY, Donald, *A Century of Protestant Missions in China*, (Centennial Conference Historical Volume), Shanghai 1907 — 4764.ff.11

MARTIN, W A P, *A Cycle of Cathay*, 1896 — 010056.g.7

McNEUR, George Hunter, *Liang A-fa*, Oxford University Press China Agency, 1934

MEDHURST, W H, Sr, *China: Its State and Prospects*, John Snow, 1838 — 571.g.10

A Glance at the Interior of China in 1845, Shanghai Mission Press, 1949 — 10055.c.25

MEDHURST, Sir Walter H, *Curiosities of Street Literature in China*, 1871 — 10057.aaa.16

The Foreigner in Far Cathay, Edward Stanton, 1872 — 010058.ee.35

MICHIE, Alexander, *Missionaries in China*, Edward Stanford, 1891 — 4767.ccc.10

The Englishman in China: as illustrated in the Career of Sir Rutherford Alcock, Wm Blackwood & Sons, Edin, 1900, 2 vols — 09057.d.3

MORRIS, E W, *The London Hospital*, Edward Arnold, 1910

MORSE, Hosea Ballou, *The International Relations of the Chinese Empire* (9 vols), vols 1–3, 1910 2386.c.17

MOULE, Arthur E, *The Story of the Cheh-Kiang Mission*, CMS, 1879

MÜLLER, George, (ed G F Bergin), *Autobiography: Narrative*, J Nisbet & Co Ltd, 1905

NEILL, Stephen, *A History of Christian Missions*, (Pelican History of the Church) Penguin Books, 1964; *Colonialism and Christian Missions*, Lutterworth Press: Foundations of Christian Mission, 1966

NEVIUS, Helen S C, *The Life of John Livingston Nevius*, Revell, 1895 4985.eee.5

NORTH CHINA HERALD (Newspaper) British Library, Colindale

ORR, J Edwin, *The Second Evangelical Awakening in Britain*, Marshall, Morgan & Scott, 1949

PARLIAMENTARY PAPERS 1831–32, Vols VII, X, XI, XXXVI, XLI (*see* Foreign Office, 1840–60 opium wars) 1857 XLIII relating to the opium trade with China Official Publications Office

PIERSON, A T, *George Müller of Bristol*, Jas Nisbet & Co Ltd, 1905

POLO, Marco, *The Book of Ser Marco Polo, The Venetian*, 1298, First printed edition 1477 (*see* YULE)

POTT, F L Hawks, *A Short History of Shanghai*, Kelly & Walsh, 1928 010056.aaa.46

PUNCH Panorama 1845–65 (*see also* HUGGETT, F E)

ROWDON, H H, *The Origins of the Brethren*, Pickering & Inglis, 1967

SELLMAN, R R, *An Outline Atlas of Eastern History*, Edward Arnold Ltd

SMITH, Arthur H, *The Uplift of China*, The Young People's Missionary Movement of America, 1909

SOOTHILL, Wm E, *Timothy Richard of China*, Seeley, Service & Co Ltd, 1924

STOCK, Eugene, *A History of the Church Missionary Society*, Vols I–III, 1899–1916 4765.cc.28

TAYLOR, Dr and Mrs Howard, *Hudson Taylor in Early Years: The Growth of a Soul*, CIM and RTS, 1911
Hudson Taylor and the China Inland Mission: The Growth of a Work of God, CIM and RTS, 1918
Hudson Taylor's Spiritual Secret, CIM, 1932

TAYLOR, Mrs Howard (M Geraldine Guinness), *The Story of the China Inland Mission*, 2 vols, Morgan & Scott, 1892
Behind the Ranges: A Biography of J.O. Fraser, CIM
Pastor Hsi: One of China's Scholars, (2 vols), CIM

TAYLOR, J Hudson, *China: Its Spiritual Need and Claims*, 1st–6th edns, 1865 et seq, CIM
China's Spiritual Need and Claims, 7th edn, 1887, CIM

8th edn, 1890, CIM
A Retrospect, 1875 CIM
After Thirty Years, Morgan & Scott and CIM, 1895
Occasional Paper, Vols 1–6, Jas Nisbet & Co
THOMPSON, R Wardlaw, *Griffith John: The Story of Fifty Years in China*, The Religious Tract Society, 1907
WALEY, Arthur David, *The Opium War through Chinese Eyes*, London, 1958 09059.pp.30
WANG, Mary, *The Chinese Church that will not Die*, Hodder & Stoughton
WOLSELEY, Field Marshal, Viscount, *The Story of a Soldier's Life*
WOODCOCK, George, *The British in the Far East*, Weidenfeld & Nicolson, 1969, (A Social History of the British Overseas)
YULE, Sir Henry, *The Book of Ser Marco Polo the Venetian*, 2 vols 1878

Index